I0660871

Samuel Roth, Infamous Modernist

University Press of Florida

Florida A&M University, Tallahassee
Florida Atlantic University, Boca Raton
Florida Gulf Coast University, Ft. Myers
Florida International University, Miami
Florida State University, Tallahassee
New College of Florida, Sarasota
University of Central Florida, Orlando
University of Florida, Gainesville
University of North Florida, Jacksonville
University of South Florida, Tampa
University of West Florida, Pensacola

UNIVERSITY PRESS OF FLORIDA

Gainesville

Tallahassee

Tampa

Boca Raton

Pensacola

Orlando

Miami

Jacksonville

Ft. Myers

Sarasota

SAMUEL ROTH

INFAMOUS

MODERNIST

Jay A. Gertzman

This book may be available in an electronic edition.

First cloth printing, 2013
First paperback printing, 2015

Library of Congress Cataloging-in-Publication Data
Gertzman, Jay A.
Samuel Roth : infamous modernist / Jay A. Gertzman.
p. cm.
Includes bibliographical references and index.
ISBN 978-0-8130-4417-0 (cloth: alk. paper)
ISBN 978-0-8130-6132-0 (pbk.)
1. Roth, Samuel, 1893–1974—Biography. 2. Publishers and publishing
—United States—Biography. 3. Modernism (Literature)—United States.
4. Literature, Modern—20th century—Biography. I. Title.
Z473.R78G47 2013
070.5092—dc23
[B]
2012039460

University Press of Florida
15 Northwest 15th Street
Gainesville, FL 32611-2079
http://www.upf.com

For Karin

... intellectual curiosity, egocentricity, feverish anxiety about life, cynical wit, sarcastic irony, social discontent, arrogance, extreme cleverness, pungent and often redundant words, sexual frankness on one side and sexual mysticism on the other.

Burton Rascoe, "The Judaic Strain in Modern Letters," *The Menorah Journal*, August 1923.

Life *is* and.

Philip Roth, *The Counterlife*

CONTENTS

One windy night in 1893 or 1894 in a shtetl in eastern Galicia, while a fire destroyed his father's inn, Samuel Roth was born. According to him, a rival innkeeper had perpetrated this piece of treachery. Possibly it was a cousin, not Sam, who was born that night; possibly his father never owned an inn. "According to him" will be an often-used phrase in this biography, not because Roth had a poor memory (he didn't), or because he was melodramatic (he was). It's because of his compulsive self-invention, and the divinely pre-ordained destiny he envisioned for himself. The consequent crazily woven tapestry of his career was fueled by Roth's seeing events according to needs that were often at odds with reality itself.

Sam Roth's daughter, Adelaide, knew her father was unusual. What does a preteen son or daughter do when a classmate taunts her or him with "Your father's in jail"? How many teenagers are told how to respond when an FBI agent or a process server comes to the door? How do a fourteen- and a sixteen-year-old not worry that they have betrayed their father when they are forced to testify that they worked with him, handling packages in his office? Family life revolved around defending him, legally and to people they encountered. Roth spent about one-ninth of his adult life behind bars. His reputation was that of a bold literary "pirate," issuing unauthorized editions of modernist sensations such as *Ulysses* and *Lady Chatterley's Lover*. He had been vilified by the literary community of two continents in the 1920s for the Joyce and Lawrence publications. But in the absence of an international copyright agreement and because Joyce did not establish a U.S. copyright by having the work printed in this country, what Roth did was not illegal. Rather, it violated the protocols of mutual fair dealing between publishers and authors.

Even more infamous was a book he wrote in a fit of spite at booksellers and lawyers after his bankruptcy in 1933. It was titled *Jews Must Live: An Account of the Persecution of the World by Israel on All the Frontiers of Civilization* (1933) and offered the Nazis a serendipity when they most needed it. They advertised it in skywriting and in print media as the testimony of a Jew himself. A generation later, Roth was again held up to widespread public ridicule, by a Senate investigating committee, Walter Winchell, the FBI, the Post Office, and the legendary New York district attorney Frank Hogan, for supposedly inciting juvenile delinquency by targeting teenagers as purchasers of his books and magazines.

It's common for people to be unable to see themselves as others see them, and never more so than when pride, reputation, money, and power are at stake. When individuals are thrown into the spotlight, they struggle either to hold onto what progress they have made or to rewrite history. They often trap themselves in myths of their own making. Sam Roth was an all-time master of self-justification. Being irrepressible, he was judged to be shrill; being belligerent, he was seen as fanatical. When he refused to admit that he made money from taking advantage of customers' interest in "crude" sex and violence, he was labeled a renegade publisher hiding behind modernist classics, albeit sometimes expurgated for easier distribution. Publicizing himself as a Johnny Appleseed, bringing to ordinary Americans the classic literature, four-letter words and all, of two continents, he expected his fellow citizens to see him as a martyr to the cause of freedom of expression. They didn't. But in some weird way, he was right. His prison terms were for distributing obscenity. The laws that interdicted the subversive, sexually explicit modernist texts he published, however, were judged unconstitutional while he was serving his second term in federal prison.

Roth was also a master of prurient advertising, and no amount of warning deterred him. He insisted on putting himself directly in the line of fire in this regard—right in the spot that municipal, state, and federal law enforcement officials reserved for pariah businessmen in that part of the "forbidden fruit business," or the underground urban economy, that sold printed work deemed titillating or obscene. His motives included both self-aggrandizement and monetary gain. And once the veils of literary, academic, and class status are considered and lifted, the motives of opponents such as James Joyce, Frieda Lawrence, Herbert Hoover, various federal judges and district attorneys, and officials of anti-vice societies reveal themselves as similarly mixed. Shrillness, belligerence, and/or the use of what might be called "spin" are equally accurate when applied to erotica distributors, 1950s garment center executives, politicians, investment bankers, and real estate speculators who attended what were called "Sex Circuses" in east Midtown apartments—and their modern-day counterparts.

His struggles in the marketplace of ideas that was the twentieth century guaranteed Samuel Roth a frenzied life. But there was another string to his bow. He took arms (like American businessmen and politicians, he used such military metaphors often) in the most frenzied skirmish of all for a Jewish American immigrant, the conflict between his faith and Christianity. At various low points of his career, he experienced and wrote up visions of a Jesus-ordained mission to reconcile the two faiths. "If not I, who?" was his mantra, used conspicuously when he published an attack on Herbert Hoover during the 1931 presidential campaign. The question was a kind of trademark of Roth's attempt to circulate abrasive ideas loudly and memorably, so people would hear him. His six-hundred-page novel, *My Friend Yeshea* (1961), in which he accompanied Yeshea (Jesus) on the journey to Jerusalem and crucifixion, can be seen as part of this attempt. Roth writes that Yeshea transported him to heaven for an audience with Yahweh, who appointed the publisher as one of the thirty-six *tzaddikim* ("just men") in his generation. Charged with bringing peace to a world at (cold) war, Roth tried to publicize this mission, advertising as best he knew how, in subway posters and by circulars, the book as a "last hope" for spiritual renewal. He also proposed a talk in Times Square. The mission did not withstand public indifference. Toward the end of his life, Roth wrote a set of poems, his own version of the Psalms of David.

After her father died, Adelaide Kugel ("Chig" to her family and friends) gathered information for an intended biography. Although Roth's legal troubles and imprisonment had made it financially impossible for her to go to college, she was her father's daughter and thus a natural scholar, with her training a result of research assignments Sam had given her from prison in 1937 and 1938. After her mother's death in 1976, Adelaide began the task of rummaging through "the accumulation of their lives." She located and gathered Sam's amazingly varied unpublished writings, his correspondence, and his legal documents. Her biography was her way of coming to terms with the part poet, part prophet, part businessman who had been her father, providing renewed contact as well. "I loved and respected him." She must have missed him. Whatever the rewards of suburban motherhood, she often contrasted the vivacity and drama of life with her parents to the predictable equanimity of her Connecticut life.

Adelaide Kugel's files include letters, detailed timelines, FBI files, court transcripts, financial information, books her father published and/or wrote (including his annotations), and newspaper clippings. Her analysis of Joyce's allusions to her father in *Finnegans Wake* would impress any scholar or Joyce aficionado. Beginning in 1982, she wrote and revised most of a well-researched and clearly written biography, to be called "In a Plain Brown Wrapper." She would have finished and published the work but for a stroke she suffered in 1994, which left her with aphasia, a condition that makes it difficult to express oneself in words.

Her father's brilliant assistant, the iconoclastic polymath Gershon Legman, had offered his help with her biography. Legman described what he thought were the two cruxes in Roth's career: his exile from the literary community for pirating Joyce's *Ulysses,* and "the conspewing [*sic*] of him by the literary community after *Jews Must Live.*" The parallels between Roth and Joyce stunned Legman; he alluded to Sam as Shem to Joyce's Shaun. Roth's daughter's understanding of these secret sharers is astute, the one yearning for the other's poetic genius and the Irishman envying the Jewish outsider's dispassionate perceptions about the desires of the people among whom he lives, and in many cases, whom he must make his customers.

As someone to whom fell the risky job of transferring from sexually explicit artists to wary customers what the latter would not risk acquiring on their own, Samuel Roth was doing what middlemen had done in Europe for centuries. The transportation network for moving capital, goods, and services had been maintained for Christian landowners and politicians by Jewish financiers, agents, exporters, innkeepers, and itinerant book and art dealers. Some of these middlemen dealt in illicit materials, which meant they not only knew how an underground economy worked but had a precise awareness of what appealed to their often-furtive customers. They also had a disdain for the moral indignation and the ostracism that attached themselves to these activities and were used to describe the erotica dealer as a pariah businessman (this is no longer true since pay-for-view Internet companies largely replaced organized crime as distributors; the former have much more capital with which to produce respect). Thus the erotica dealer was a social outcast, thought unclean and shameless, and suspected of the worst kind of subversion, that of the minds of the young. To do the work, one had to be the kind of outsider who kept his uneasiness and shame from almost everyone, including loved ones. That, I think, is what Legman meant when he said that Joyce was in many ways fascinated by Roth, and it is one affinity the great writer has for *Ulysses'* young and intellectually princely Stephen. Another comparison is that, as self-conscious as Stephen and James Joyce, Roth could not live without writing. The Roth Archive deposited in 2005 at Columbia University contains typed and handwritten book manuscripts, letters, poems, aphorisms, and marginalia, some scribbled in notebooks, some on scrap paper, envelopes, and other species of ephemera.

To see a person like Sam Roth dispassionately is not easy. If we can't accept his own pronouncements about himself, or the stated opinion of James Joyce, D. H. Lawrence, Ezra Pound, some state and Supreme Court justices, J. Edgar Hoover, the *New Yorker* and *Vanity Fair,* Walter Winchell, showbiz figures, upscale New York booksellers, and pornographers from Jack Brussel to Larry Flynt, we can hardly accept the perspective of a loving daughter. As one of Saul Bellow's narrators observed, "It's usually selfish people who are loved the most. They do what you deny yourself, and you love them for it."

What is the necessity of a book-length study built on the good fortune of the archive now, some forty years after Samuel Roth's death? There are various answers. Contemporary admirers of Joyce considered Roth a pirate and a swindler; some still do. When I spoke on Roth at New York's James Joyce Society in 2009, I made the point that *Ulysses* had not been copyrighted in the United States and was thus in the public domain in the 1920s. I added that Roth did pay for the "Work in Progress" excerpts and offered a fair price for the *Ulysses* segments, although only after he began publishing them. A member of the audience told me that all my excavations of Roth's motives, and the motives of Joyce and his friends, would not change the fact that Samuel Roth was the (Ponzi-scheme artist) Bernie Madoff of his day. It's a bum rap. Research into Joyce's behavior toward supporters like Sylvia Beach, Ezra Pound, and Robert McAlmon has made later scholars aware that Joyce protected his own interests very shrewdly. The ways in which the International Protest revealed Joyce's rather callous shrewdness and exaggerated Roth's criminality are my contribution to the "great *Ulysses* hullabaloo." Joyce gave writers and journalists of the time just the right amount of information so that he would seem an undeserving victim, and Roth an unprecedented despoiler of contemporary literature. As a businessman, Joyce habitually did what he had to do. (This was the case, for example, when he took back the rights to *Ulysses* from Sylvia Beach once a legal American edition was in the offing.) The Roth Archive shows just what the ostracism from his profession resulting from the Joyce affair meant to Roth. It reveals as well his moxie in responding to it, and how it conditioned the rest of his career. It includes also material regarding Roth's dramatic appearance in 1950 before the Joyce Society at the Gotham Book Mart.

Roth's correspondence is essential to showing the threat to the marketing of modernism that Roth's magazine publications of 1925–27 represented. The letterheads themselves for his *Two Worlds* magazines contain prospectuses that, revised from letter to letter, describe just what he intended. He succeeded with *Two Worlds,* an innovative quarterly available only by subscription. His ambition led him to contact, and follow the advice of, his friend Morris Eisenman, then one of New York's leading distributors of mass-market periodicals. The result was Roth's newsstand-distributed *Two Worlds Monthly,* which required more capital than Roth had. It failed, but not before its editor presented to a very different readership than that of European literary periodicals and privately published books, and in a very different format, twelve episodes from *Ulysses.* The *Monthly* presented a new problem for Joyce and his friends, for they needed to control the modes of production.

Not only the correspondence but also the advertising circulars and ledgers in the Roth Archive show Roth's efforts to not only make money from prurient titillation but also to broaden the horizons of middle- and working-class readers from the heartland of America, as well as city dwellers who worked in offices and stores and in the professions. In his 1920s magazines, in his under-the-counter pornography of the interwar period, and in the largest mail-order book business of the 1940s and 1950s, he introduced to a broad audience writers such as Joyce, Lawrence, Paul Morand, Céline, Genet, and the objectivist poets, including Charles Reznikoff and Louis Zukofsky. He also published writers of the Southern Gothic genre, and published as well one of the best send-ups of it. *A Scarlet Pansy* (1933) was an early novel about transvestites; another pseudonymous work presented an African American protagonist's attempts to marry a white woman and join a Madison Avenue social and artistic set. Roth gave wide circulation to important novels about the predatory racket of clairvoyance at both upper- and under-class levels (*Nightmare Alley*) and about child abuse (*Forlorn Sunset*). All of these works were modernist projects. His advertising methods—extensively documented by the listings he kept of targeted media, text, illustrations, expenses, and sales figures for the books themselves—offer an understanding of the uniquely American nexus of mass popular entertainment and avant-garde poetry and prose.

That nexus is the most significant aspect of Roth's long struggles with censorship, whether the adversary be Customs, the New York police, district attorneys, or the Society for the Suppression of Vice. His correspondence with lawyers, their briefs, the trial transcripts, and the details of the numerous Post Office hearings Roth requested all reveal the standards on which were based the laws that the police, politicians, lawyers, and judges used to interdict his books, magazines, and circulars. This information is a compendium of First Amendment history. Roth's archive does not lose significance today, when censorship focuses on electronic media rather than print. It shows how tightly the censorship was connected to protecting social and professional elites from the challenge to their ascendancy that developed when less-privileged people became aware of the choices they had regarding their sexual nature. Protecting the status quo is a significant motive for management of what is called "the social media" today, so important for entertainment, job advancement, social demeanor, and what is believed to be personal fulfillment. Concern about sexual freedom (much more than violence) results in a policing that in Roth's time was termed "informal" monitoring (i.e., without court action). Today it is termed "surveillance" of "offensive" postings, some of which are forbidden because they might be accessed by children. It was not only the child's innocence that the designated monitors in Roth's time wanted to protect; it was even more so established notions of "decent" speech. Throughout Roth's career, this reasoning was used by what he called "Dame Post Office." It was "The Roth Case" (1957) and Roth's Supreme Court appeal that finally provided the rationale that made the "Hicklin Rule" (established in 1868 in British law) constitutionally obsolete. Hicklin had stated that adults must sacrifice their own access to information that might debauch the most immature member of a community. After 1959 the criteria became literary, artistic, political, or scientific (LAPS) value, as well as the target readership of a work and the publisher's marketing tactics. The "LAPS test" replaced Hicklin with criteria recognizing adults' right to information and art, even if erotically compelling.

Roth's Supreme Court appeal was rejected in 1957, but the minority opinion was used two years later to allow Grove Press to distribute *Lady Chatterley's Lover* through the mail, because it passed the LAPS test, which established its value as a classic, and it was presented to the public as such rather than with prurient enticement. The decision meant that sexually explicit work was not censorable if it was redeemed by the criteria defining a literary classic. It would draw a caustic nod from Gershon Legman, who once remarked that "people carry censorship around with them in their heads." Certainly Roth helped exploit the kind of shame regarding eroticism to which Legman referred. However, by stubbornly raising the question of whether prurient interest precluded the ability to think and learn about what one read, Roth helped set the stage for a law permitting erotic material to be read by a general, non-credentialed population who had real need of it to determine essential personal choices.

The persistence of the taboos regarding sexual explicitness, particularly when children were exposed to it, was once again recently exemplified. In a June 2011 Supreme Court discussion about a California statute that banned the sale of violent video games to children, there was an interesting discussion by some justices regarding what laws might legally restrict minors from accessing "obscene" content, as opposed to violence. The former laws, several justices felt, were still viable, while children may choose to view interactive violent displays. Sex is a more problematic subject than violence, and possibly more subject to regulations than persistent, militaristic violence. Taboos have a magical persistence.

In January 2012 the Court heard an appeal from a network broadcasting company which the FCC had fined for a program showing nudity and including "indecent" expletives. Despite the ubiquity of swearing and nudity on cable TV and the Internet, some justices felt that indecent speech should be banned from broadcast TV except during the late-night "safe harbor" period. Chief Justice Roberts said there should be some medium where nudity and curse words should be forbidden. Justice Scalia likened the "symbolic value" of decency to conventions of sober dress for visitors to courtrooms. An FCC lawyer stated that while nudity in *Schindler's List* and curse words in *Saving Private Ryan* are appropriate, when "your 13-year-old brother" or a "bully in the schoolyard" is cursing, those children are doing something harmful. That such situations are inevitable was not at issue, any more than, in Roth's day, the inevitable saturation of respectable movies, advertisements, and magazine articles with titillation was considered comparable to what his own products were supplying. Only the latter were disreputable.

Alfred Kinsey collected many of the advertising materials of "erotica producers." Together with those available in the Roth Archive, they reveal how such circulars reinforce gender and sexual stereotypes about "pansies," "flagellants," "showgirls," or "fetishists." Roth exploited guilty curiosity about incest, hermaphroditism, lesbianism, and child abuse with a sensationalism that demeaned the edifying content in some of the works themselves. Paradoxically, his own unpublished fiction in the archive tells a different, self-hating story. In these writings he showed the harm done by passive, indiscriminate prurience, rooted in contempt for its subjects. His stories describe the psychic paralysis that women suffer by being displayed on stage and screen and in pictures and text.

Finally, it is a good time to be reminded of the materialistic and spiritual resources of Jewish immigrants in the early twentieth century. Jewish people are now integrated into post-Holocaust, post-industrial American society so completely that the character and passions of their grandparents is often lost to them, as are the distresses of a Lower East Side life: the fourteen-hour work-days, the anxieties of the *luftmensch* (literally "air-man," working on schemes to get his feet on the ground and money in his wallet), the patronizing censure of uptown well-established Jews, and the anti-Semitic threats unleashed by the Depression. The history of one's people should be as ever-present as the eternal light in the front of the synagogue ark. The career of Samuel Roth embodies painful contradictions: poet, publisher, social critic, reputed "King of the Jews," self-hating writer of a notoriously anti-Semitic book, and later, author of *My Friend Yeshea,* a visionary novel about his own journey with Jesus to Jerusalem. It is a fascinating kaleidoscope of elements that compose the social and spiritual Jewish American story.

I am struck by the congruence of Samuel Roth's life to the fiction of great twentieth-century Jewish writers such as I. B. Singer, Malamud, Bellow, Delmore Schwartz, and Philip Roth. Like their work, it has much to say of desire for security, urban life and its tension and exhilaration, wounded self-awareness, paranoiac self-deception, the intimate awareness of the need of the Jew to struggle with God's power, and the American dream. The family dynamics of responsibility and affection are central in these fictions. Specifically, the following resonances are most evocative: Charles Reznikoff's *By the Waters of Manhattan* (the young bookseller protagonist is based on Roth), Edwin Arlington Robinson's "The Wandering Jew" (in which poem his daughter saw Samuel Roth strongly reflected), Sholem Asch's *The Nazarene* (the model for *My Friend Yeshea*), Heine's "Hebrew Melodies," the Old Testament's Psalms of David (from both of which Roth "redacted" his own version), and Abraham Cahan's *The Rise of David Levinsky* (which depicts a journey much like Roth's from talented student in an Old World shtetl to successful American businessman). Roth's story reminds us as well of Joyce's *Ulysses.* Leopold Bloom and Sam Roth were both advertising men, urban explorers, defenders of their people, prodigal sons, and tender devotees of femininity (one of Roth's last poems describes his getting into a cab for a trip to the doctor and hopping out again to follow a hip-swishing young woman, much like Leopold Bloom ogling women all bloomsday long). Both Roth and Bloom were partly assimilated Jews in Christian cultures who were proud to remain outsiders as much as, if not more than, they wanted respect from their fellow citizens. And yet, Bloom identifies his nation as Ireland, Roth his as America. Roth's story is equally relevant to Dostoyevsky's *The Double:* an intensely self-conscious individual believes that he lives with a conflicting nemesis or alter ego, a powerful and envied shadow self (sometimes "Mishillim," sometimes "David Zorn" or "Norman Lockridge") who is inexorably replacing him.

Apropos of *The Double,* Roth once described himself as "an Austrian Jew, at war with himself and his race." These are the words of a man desperate to mollify his conscience. Samuel Roth could only express himself, and hide a confusion of purpose and identity, by presenting himself to the world in a panoply of disorienting mirrors like those offered in circus fun houses. He knew this, and it mattered deeply to him. He titled his autobiography, composed over four decades, "Count Me among the Missing." Its epigraph, with a touch of self-pity, quoted Yeats regarding "the growing murderousness of the world."

Roth's writings and career are those of one who knew he lived in two worlds, and they were not the two worlds of the European and American avant-garde writers he introduced to readers in his mid-1920s magazines. Two worlds: the center of one is the spiritual light that for the Jewish mind is Shekinah, the universal force of God's glory. It brings peace and fulfillment as rewards for passive self-denial. The other world is secular: money. Neither bears up under the weight of skepticism, but the doubt of those who live only in one is immaterial to those who live in the other. Roth lived in both, just as did not only Cahan's David but many of the protagonists of Malamud, Bellow, Singer, and Philip Roth. The result was self-division, a sense of betrayal, and the desire to atone for his secular, sensual, sometimes venal successes.

There's a remarkable amount of self-aggrandizement, self-deception, spite, insecurity, shame, and illusions of atonement in Samuel Roth's story. There's also an understandably intense grasping for recognition as a writer, businessman, freedom-of-expression advocate, and pious Jew. Roth had four visits from Yeshea, from the time he was ten and continuing for the next thirty years. After that, during his two five-year federal prison stretches, he wrote two lengthy narratives of atonement and reconciliation with his faith and his late parents. Yeshea did not appear to him at those times. But he was a presence in the narratives. In *My Friend Yeshea* he took Roth-called-Mishillim-the-peacemaker to the throne of the Almighty himself, to be proclaimed a just man in his generation and given a specific mission to reconcile Judaism and Christianity. There was no difference between Yeshea appearing to him and being a character in a narrative. Both manifestations were illusions needed to sustain the man's spiritual faith. In each juncture in Roth's life, he (as D. H. Lawrence said) healed his psychic emptiness by writing, in Roth's case, about God's saving grace. That the Messiah's earlier appearances were written down in an autobiography, and the latter ones in a novel, is of no significance. In both, Roth wrote his salvation. In doing so, he found relief for his deepest anxieties. This is not self-deception: it is creating, or resorting to Hasidic

Judaism to uncover, a metaphysical reality with which one can live. How many twentieth-century poets or businessmen (let alone pornographers) have the imagination, energy, ambition, and willingness to persevere in this way?

In one of Roth's finest lyrics, the speaker faces the "wrath of midnight storms" and prays that God "hurl me, / If so you will, down the ravines of death." But the poem has a heroic resolution, as the speaker finds in the midnight heavens his, and only his, destiny "in stern creation": "There is my star." The poem, the intensity of which won it a place in the prestigious *Poetry* magazine in 1920, is titled "Kol Nidre."

This is an American success tragedy, or tragicomedy, if you prefer. But not just one of religious and secular failure or success. Sam Roth experienced plenty of both. "The burden isn't either/or," as Nathan Zuckerman stated in Philip Roth's *The Counterlife*, "Life *is* and."

In 2005, Samuel Roth's grandchildren donated an extensive collection of their grandfather's papers and books to the Department of Rare Books and Manuscripts at Columbia University. In addition to Roth's own publications and published and unpublished writings, there is correspondence to and in some cases from Pound, Sylvia Beach, Harriet Weaver, T. S. Eliot, Arthur Garfield Hays, John Slocum, Ben Abramson, and John Rodker. There are also drafts of Roth's autobiography, "Count Me among the Missing," and his daughter's memoir of her father, "In a Plain Brown Wrapper." Both are unpublished. I want to thank the grandchildren for their generous sharing of information with me, for allowing me access to the archive, and for permission to use the following images for illustrations: figures 1, 2, 6, 11, 13, 14, 15, 16, 17, 22, 23, 24, 25.

I want to sincerely thank the following persons and institutions for their help:

Fred Dennis, Greenwich, Connecticut, for permission to use a letter of May 10, 1922, from the Sylvia Beach Papers, Manuscript Division, Department of Rare Books and Special Collections, Princeton University Library, and for permission to reproduce that letter (my figure 9) and an advertisement in *The Saturday Review* for four of Roth's magazines.

Krzysztof Willmann, a Polish scholar who sent me late-nineteenth-century and present-day maps of the shtetl where Roth was born, and of the surrounding territory. He also directed me to Internet sites with information about the history of these locations. I am indebted to him for most of the details regarding Nuszcze (including the correct spelling).

Judith Legman, La Clè Des Champs, Valbonne, France, for permission to use information from Gershon Legman's unpublished "Peregrine Penis: An Autobiography of Innocence," and for permission to use the image of Gershon Legman she kindly sent me.

Maryjane Treloar, Saratoga Springs, New York, for permission to quote from an unpublished essay by Arthur Sainer titled "He Was Dreaming His Better Self," and for permission to reproduce photos of the Yussef Roth family (1907) and Samuel Roth (1915). She has also permitted me to reproduce the photo of The Poetry Book Shop.

Myra Hindus, Jamaica Plain, Massachusetts, and Linda Simon, Skidmore College, for permission to use Milton Hindus's unpublished 1983 essay "Samuel Roth."

The Arents Library, Syracuse University, Syracuse, New York, for access to its Grove Press Archive.

The Carl A. Kroch Library, Cornell University, Ithaca, New York, for access to the Lynn Womach Papers.

The Elihu Burritt Library, Central Connecticut State University, New Britain, Connecticut, for access to the Canon Clinton Jones Archives.

The Dorot Jewish Division of the New York Public Library, Stephen Schwartzman Building, for various reference materials, including copies of early editions of *The American Hebrew* and *The Menorah Journal*.

The Herbert Hoover Presidential Library, West Branch, Iowa, for the "Misrepresentation Files" of papers about the anti-Hoover scandal books of 1931.

The Humanities Research Center, University of Texas at Austin, for the Morris L. Ernst Papers.

The Jacob Rader Marcus Center of the American Jewish Archives, Cincinnati, Ohio, for a photograph of Maurice Samuel.

The Kinsey Institute for Research in Sex, Gender, and Reproduction, Bloomington, Indiana, for permission to reproduce the circular "Violence in the Handling of Women" (Vertical File, Erotica Producers, 20th Century, Samuel Roth).

The Library of Congress, for the Names and Records of Persons Arrested Under the Auspices of the New York Society for the Suppression of Vice (the Ledgers of John S. Sumner), Manuscript Division of the Library of Congress.

The National Archives and Records Administration, Bureau of Prisons Records, for the photograph of Frederick "Fritz" Joubert Duquesne.

The New York City Municipal Archives, for permission to reproduce the Tax Department 1940 photo of 96 Willett Street, Manhattan.

New York Public Library, Manuscript Division, research libraries,

Schwartzman Building, for access to the John Quinn Papers and the Berg Collection.

The Princeton University Library, Manuscript Division, Rare Books Library, for access to the Sylvia Beach Papers.

The Robert D. Farber University Archives and Special Collections Department, Brandeis University Libraries, for the letters Samuel Roth wrote to Milton Hindus in the Milton Hindus Papers.

The U.S. Department of Justice, Record Information/Dissemination Service, for part of the FBI files on Fritz Duquesne.

Michael Ryan, curator of the Rare Book and Manuscript Library, Columbia University, and his staff were extremely helpful and I am grateful for their assistance. I made requests of all kinds to them, especially of Jane Seigel and Susan Hamson, for five years. All responses were considerate and resourceful, the apex of professionalism.

Amy Gorelick, acquisitions associate director and editor in chief at the University Press of Florida, for guiding me through the process for revising and presenting my drafts to the proper agencies, and for very important suggestions and critiques.

Mary Dearborn and Jonathan Lawrence, for skilfull copyediting.

The State Historical Society of Wisconsin, for the John S. Sumner Papers.

Robert Spoo, Chapman Distinguished Professor of Law, University of Tulsa, for his astute and inclusive understanding of nineteenth- and twentieth-century copyright and intellectual property law.

J. C. Cloutier, Ph.D. student at Columbia, did a splendid job of preparing a checklist of the Roth Archive.

I am grateful to Karin Thieme, a graphic designer in Edgewater, New Jersey, for her splendid work in formatting the illustrations.

I want to thank the editors of the following journals for permission to reprint essays of mine containing material that appears in this book:

Fordham University Press, for "Not Quite Honest: Samuel Roth's 'Unauthorized' *Ulysses* and the 1927 International Protest." *Joyce Studies Annual* (2009): 34–66.

John Wiley and Sons, for "A Scarlet Pansy Goes to War: Subversion, Schlock, and an Early Gay Classic." *Journal of American Culture* 33, no. 3 (2010): 230–39.

Penn State University Press, for "The Early Poetry of a Pariah: Samuel Roth." *Studies in American Jewish Literature* 28 (2009): 55–73.

Without the advice and generosity in providing information of the following people, I could not have completed this biography:

Jack Alter; Laura Bailey; Lucia Begg; Minnie Brussel; Sonia Coleman; Mary

Dearborn; Chris Eckhoff; Sara Fishkin; Harry Friedberg; Betty Florentine; Steven Gertz; Gloria and Arthur Goldstein; Rudolph Grey; Hugh Hagius; Earl Kemp; Madeline Kripke; Judith Legman; Arnold Levy; Carole Livingstone; Maggie McNeely; David Moody; Benjamin Nathans; Neil Pearson; Christopher Pollnitz; Paul Poplawski; Barney Rosset; J. B. Rund; Michael Ryan; Arthur Sainer; Bill Satin; Leila Sauerbach; C. J. Scheiner; Jane Siegel; Robert Spoo; Bill Stevens; Dave Stewart; Michael Sweeney; Carole Stuart; Lyle Stuart; Gay Talese; G. Thomas Tanselle; Alison Tartt; Krzysztof Willmann; Alan Wilson; Eva Wolynska; Lorraine Zywotow.

Acknowledgments

CHAPTER 1

1893–1916

From a Galician Shtetl to Columbia University

The air in late September is mild in the western Ukraine, and the sunset is unhurried. "The earth darkens slowly," recalls the writer who would assume the name Samuel Roth in America; his Hebrew name was Mishillim (the name may refer to one of the builders of the Second Temple, or may connote "peace-bringer").[1] The manuscript in which the phrase appears is Roth's unpublished autobiography, "Count Me among the Missing" ("CMAM"), which is a source of vivid details about Jewish life in eastern Europe.[2]

Before World War I's ravages and realignments, which destroyed 50 percent of Roth's shtetl, the area was part of the province of Galicia, an economically backward place under the control of the Austrian empire. Mishillim's hometown was called Nuszcze. Jews had inhabited this small crossroads community on the banks of the River Seret for centuries, together with Polish Roman Catholics and Ukrainian Greek Catholics.[3] In Polish or Ukrainian shtetls, a visitor might experience what was less ubiquitous in reality than in Yiddish fiction: muddy streets and floors, rubble, leaky roofs, ill-lit and twisting streets, slop pails, rickety furniture, ramshackle prayer houses, and people on the verge of starvation. These features did not apply in all shtetls, at least not in all sections of the Jewish quarters, despite rampant Jewish poverty in the late decades of the nineteenth century.[4] Many Polish small towns were carefully laid out, and administered by a Polish lord and Catholic bishop. Jews and Christians lived in proximity to each other, their places of worship not far apart. Jews wished to live near the market square, whether or not Christians

Figure 1. Drawing of Ustcha, Galician shtetl where Samuel Roth was born. Roth Archive, Rare Book and Manuscript Library, Columbia University. By permission of the Roth estate.

lived there too.[5] In Nuszcze the ruins of a Catholic monastery towered on a hill, and the town house of the Polish lord, or *puretz,* was another landmark.

Dark roads wound though forests beyond which stood the brick, mortar, and stone of golden cities. About fifteen years after he left what in his poems he called "Nustscha," with Galician earth the scene of battles and ethnic violence, Roth wrote a tender, elegiac sonnet sequence to his birthplace. It marked the apex of his career as a young poet.

> To dream away a Sabbath afternoon
> Upon the hillside shadowing the lake
> Wherein dim palaces of crystal wake
> To view and stay and do not vanish soon[6]

These poems depict, as do the stories of Sholem Aleichem, S. Y. Agnon, I. L. Peretz, and other writers, a place of collective Jewish myth. From archetypical narrow lanes where people share not only space but a communal togetherness, immigration takes shtetl dwellers not to Jerusalem but to where their souls, as Roth puts it, "cry lonely through the lofty towers." They left, as Roth shows in

Samuel Roth, Infamous Modernist

the early chapters of "Count Me among the Missing," not only because of the heavy hands of the Polish lords, but also because their own rabbis, teachers, and wealthy merchants were compliant with the lords of the manor and the status quo.[7]

"The Strangest Things Happen on Yom Kippur"

One Day of Atonement eve at the turn of the twentieth century, Mishillim watched "black, mournful groups of men, women, and children, on foot and on horseback, in buggies, and in wagons" gather at the synagogue steps. Jews had come to Nuszcze for the Day of Dread: sorrow, humility, and submission. Mishillim witnessed the adult men prostrating themselves in humiliation at the synagogue steps, allowing other male congregants to flagellate and walk on them. Whatever else it signified, this acquiescence was a gesture of trust in the willing victim's fellow Jews.[8] Inside, the voice of Yussef Leib (the word connotes "Lion" in Yiddish and German), Mishillim's father, personified holiness to the congregation he led in the rising and falling Jewish "soul-breath," Kol Nidre. Mishillim, his mother, Hudl, and his sister, Soori, told their father that it was as if they had never seen him before, so awesome did he appear in the glow of the candles with the congregation spread before him. This was an evening on which sincerely observant Jews thought gravely of their broken vows to the Almighty, not about their pleas and deals with other Jews, tax officials, peasant farmers, and the magnates and aristocrats at the manor house. "With Yussef Leib chanting [Kol Nidre], it became a song of triumph over the obstacles of creation which forever keep the soul of man on the threshold of sanctity, though unable to pass into the citadel" ("CMAM," 4). Sadness (also present in Yussef's voice) and contrition brought with them the sanction to approach God. That solemn dignity was the ultimate blessing.

Yussef Leib had needed to hurry to get to synagogue on time. His boss, Reb (i.e., Mr.) Shoolem, a wealthy lumber contractor, had sent him to Lemberg to speak with some merchants there. Upon arriving, Yussef learned that there was no one to see. Reb Shoolem had competed with Yussef to lead the congregation, and the only way he could do so was if the much better singer was otherwise engaged. In a culture where a hierarchy of social standing was deeply rooted, Reb Shoolem was a *sheyneh*, a Jew of distinction. The *prosteh*, unschooled common laborers, sat in the corners of the synagogue, far from the sheyneh.[9] A dark mood enveloped Shoolem as Yussef sang. Someone would pay for his not singing Kol Nidre, Day of Atonement or no. It was Lippe Goy, a vulgar swineherd turned innkeeper, who paid. He was nicknamed "Goy" because of his ignorance of Jewish ritual. Because he recently struck his wife—and because his son Asher was almost as good a Hebrew school student as Mishillim—Lippe stayed to pray all night with the most devout, including Asher. But he fell asleep.

"The strangest things happen on Yom Kippur," one of the sheyneh commented. The tittering continued as Lippe's head nodded ever lower over the prayer book. His son's voice "probed the depths of human anguish" as he tried to wake his father. At some predawn hour, Asher left the synagogue. Perhaps he had recognized Lippe's condition as his own inheritance. He had confided in Mishillim that the rabbi never visited the house of his father. At dawn, as women and children reappeared, Lippe awoke and stormed out in humiliation. A short time later, Reb Shoolem saw Lippe enter and approach him, a hand on his own throat. "Here's something else to laugh at. My son—they've just picked him out of the millstream." Two peasants carried the body to the prayer table; a prayer was offered as the women started to lament.

The class inequality of Nuszcze was part of the changing, and increasingly secular and class-conscious, nature of shtetls in young Roth's time.[10] That aside, how much of his Yom Kippur story is true is anyone's guess. When Roth published his prison memoir, *Stone Walls Do Not,* in 1930, he refers to Asher being in his thoughts during World War I.[11] Roth was always reshaping and reinventing his story, sometimes because he wished it to be recognized as part of the achievement of the Hasidic masters, and the eastern European Yiddish fiction writers, from Mendele Moykher Sforim to the Singer brothers. Their pages revealed the mundane and spiritual conditions that physically and morally challenged the shtetl communities. Many of Roth's stories use techniques of Yiddish narrative; he must have read these writers extensively. He introduced the scholar Milton Hindus to Isaac Linetzki's autobiographical *The Polish Lad;* the author, little known in America at the time, had grown up in a Polish shtetl a generation before Roth.[12]

The First Roth in Nuszcze: A Fable of a Bold Risk-Taker

"Count Me among the Missing" begins by describing how the Roth family patriarch, Jerosh, gained the respect and patronage of Nuszcze's "Squire," Stephan Weyzmann. It is difficult to believe that a lone man—however forceful, shrewd, muscular, and irresistible to women, and however fiery his disposition—could have committed the mischiefs, assaults, and crimes this Jerosh did and survived. Perhaps some of the story's details were elaborated by the relatives from whom Roth heard it, or by Roth himself. If there is any historical precedent, however slight (Roth's unruly fantasies often grow from what he has seen, heard, or read), it might be one Abraham Maendel or Mandel, later called Kriegshaber (the name means "warmonger" in German). He was a daring and resourceful eighteenth-century Jew, a supplier of horses to the Austrian Army, who, without permission from the authorities, created the Krasna Glass Works in Bukovina.[13]

Jerosh's story as the Roth family nurtured it symbolized many of the simmering resentments eastern European Jews harbored against the autocratic lords, their deputies, and Christian peasants. With all its sinister convolutions, it serves as a keystone of Roth's autobiography. The reason is that Jerosh's behavior was both audacious and had at least something in common with the character of his descendants. They were not violent, but the occasional grim frankness of Sam's father in dealing with his puretz shows him to have had something of Jerosh's blood in his veins. Furthermore, it was necessary at times for the Roths of Nuszcze, and those in Lemberg, to ignore protocols and conventions. Survival often required being opportunistic, cold-hearted, venal, and devious: in a word, foxy. Such behavior is that described by Yiddish writers such as Franzos, Aleichem, and Sforim. The latter described his work as depicting "my people, my poor unfortunate people."[14] He was being neither sentimental nor judgmental.

Around the third decade of the eighteenth century, a small, pale-faced man with flaming red hair appeared on the outskirts of what was then a tiny village ("CMAM," 1–7). Leading a heavily laden donkey, and without asking the squire's permission for using his property, he entered an abandoned hut. That was as insolent as his strange muttering and bowing before an old book was outlandish. Jerosh grabbed three women as they came for water at a town spring, choosing fully mature ones and seizing them from behind so they could not identify him. When Pon (Lord) Weyzmann accused him of this, Jerosh responded, "You might find it harder to evict than to trap me, your Excellency." Jerosh told Weyzmann that he and his network of Jewish contacts could make a lot of money for Weyzmann, and intimated that he would be honest, for Jews knew their limits.

Sam Roth was as proud as Jerosh of Jewish resourcefulness. In an unpublished play, "Prince Hal and the Jewish Proposal" (c. 1955–60),[15] he has a Jewish ambassador anticipate the return of Jews to England by 250 years. He tells Hal (and Chaucer) that the European Jewish financiers always get their money back from kings who appropriate it by requesting the sum as security for loans to other kings. "We have the money" that Henry IV needs.

The squire, knowing from his fellow landowners the value of having a circumspect and hardheaded Jew handle his affairs, decided to "give it a try." After that meeting, all Nuszcze referred to Jerosh as "The Fox." Generations of his descendants worked as contractors and advisers. It was something Polish lords in general encouraged, for they knew Jews had built over centuries the network necessary to trade extensively and cleverly throughout Europe.

Sometime after Jerosh settled into his hut, a woman came to live with him, apparently out of wedlock. The puretz's deputy, or *voyt,* and two of his men were sent to inquire. Before a fortnight had passed, one of the men had to leave the region because a fire had destroyed his family home. Another was found under a tree with a broken neck. And the body of the voyt himself was found under a "manure pile, the fleshy parts of his head, chest and thighs eaten away by swine." Roth tells us only that some time later Jerosh himself died suddenly, not specifying when or how. And so, after showing us that the founder of his family line was fearless and cunning, quick-tempered and arrogant, a rapist and an arsonist, Roth leaves us with the near certainty that this ancestor murdered three people.

About 250 years after Jerosh's days on earth ended, Samuel Roth told the literary establishment of England and America that they "lied in their teeth" when they accused him of pirating and bowdlerizing Joyce's *Ulysses.* A few years later, he published a book so powerfully critical of sitting president Herbert Hoover that the president's men launched a secret investigation. Like Jerosh, Samuel Roth was resourceful and irrepressible. The first sentence in "Count Me among the Missing" is, "The most important events in our life break before we are born." It suggests, among many other convictions, that Sam and Jerosh shared a destiny their Creator had foreordained. An astute (but radically pessimistic) Jewish historian of the late nineteenth century wrote that his people revered forebears "as a well from which [they] suck new dreams of hope. The past of the Jew is not really his past, it is always only his future."[16] The title itself, "Count Me among the Missing," suggests one whose fate is unknown, someone lost in war and accident, and also something perpetually elusive, the meaning of which, when considered in its relation to human destiny itself, can only be known at the end of days.

Shtetl Jews: Economic Survival and Personal Integrity

According to Samuel Roth, his birth was auspicious. It occurred only a week after his father's tavern, or *kretchma,* burned down, the fire having been set by the godless Lippe Goy, then a treacherous competitor.[17] Yussef had to ask the puretz, Pan Yanik, for help.[18] But His Excellency was angry with Yussef, because the latter had not followed his father as one of Yanik's go-betweens, conveying from the manor house to the district the puretz's decisions regarding taxes, the hiring of peasant workers, and the repair of infrastructure.[19] Yussef's refusal to follow in his father's footsteps was a sign of disrespect and independence. His post-fire visit to the manor house reinforced this impression. He asked His Excellency to allow him to collect money due him from Vassily, a shepherd, indirectly accusing the puretz of ordering the peasants not to repay him. Yussef did offer his services, but he did so only after tricking the illiterate Vassily into signing a paper that gave Yussef and his family, in lieu of money owed, the right to live in the shepherd's house.

Ordinarily, this would have been considered Jewish effrontery, and would have outraged Yanik. But Roth, most likely fabricating a coherent plot, tells us Yussef had a potent bargaining chip. The Roth extended family, as Sam describes it, included distant relatives of great wealth, Frankfurt bankers with an office in Lemberg. It seems that a great-uncle left Nuszcze early in life, became rich, and settled in Frankfurt, adding "-child" to his family name (10). If Pon Yanik thought Yussef Leib able to access such wealth, it would have pleased him even more than Yussef's offer to work for him. Weighed against at least this latter prospect, Vassily's signing a paper he could not read was as a feather measured against a golden carriage. On the puretz's orders, the ancient Vassily hobbled to the attic in retreat.

The connection with the puretz and rumors of wealthy relatives conferred status on the family. On one occasion, his *melamed* (Hebrew teacher) encouraged Mishillim to study hard to please "your great relation" ("CMAM," 58). He had begun early, reading his father's three favorite books of the Old Testament, Genesis, Ecclesiastes, and Job, in Hebrew before he was five years old.[20] Reb Zorakh would not have paid that kind of attention to the equally bright Asher, whose crude father was incapable of reading the Bible. In "Count Me among the Missing," Asher has the role of a shadow of what Mishillim himself might have been but for the accident of birth. Status is a kind of king, even in a small town in poverty-wracked Galicia.

The Jewish Haskala (Enlightenment) and socialist movements were well under way at this time, and the process of modernization was inexorable. But Nuszcze, despite its location on a river, its crossroads, and its nearby railroad, continued to function in traditional ways, in contrast to Brody, a large town that was a Haskala stronghold from the beginning of the century.[21] Roth tells us that his father was supportive of the institutional status quo, despite his attempt to stay independent of the puretz. Galician shtetl Jews, of which there were more than six hundred thousand at the time, were largely unassimilated.

Yussef did not send Mishillim to the state public school. There, he would have learned German, been exposed to modern ideas, and therefore may not have concentrated on the training necessary to become a rabbi. The Roth family was Hasid, which explains why, when Mishillim was eight or nine years old, the rabbi insisted on performing an exorcism on him to drive out an evil spirit. In towns with rabbis who took a more rational approach, and where Hasidic mysticism was considered retrograde, citizens were embarrassed to speak of any exorcism that had taken place.[22] This was not the case in Nuszcze. The contemporary poet and Haskala advocate Y. L. Gordon thought such rural Jews were "historically asleep."[23]

In the synagogue and prayer houses, ascetic scholars who daily parsed the Law and depended on the charity of their neighbors for food preached patience and thankfulness that God had allowed only the Jews to someday see his face.[24] Hasidic shtetl-dwellers' passion for Judaism, spiritual love of the Sabbath, and submission to their rabbi's ultimate judgment was non-negotiable. Their belief that the devil walked among them was widespread. As Sholem Aleichem, Karl Emil Franzos, and Bashevis Singer document in their stories, they believed their souls might be fatally infected by visits from demons, and had to be protected by holy men who could vanquish them.

Sam Roth's father was a good supervisor of workers on the manor lands, but he lacked the shrewdness and flexibility of the entrepreneurial Jew who got rich cooperating with a puretz. Y. L. Peretz used the term *schutz-Jude* (sheltered Jew) to stigmatize those who made such practical concessions to the powerful.[25] The Roth family patriarch Jerosh, as Roth presented him in "Count Me among the Missing," was a man of very different convictions. So was the American Samuel Roth, who had more than his father had of the spirit of Jerosh. Yussef was pious, and he well understood that he lacked the entrepreneurial genius of Reb Shoolem. If Yussef fell from grace with the puretz— which would also have meant being cast out by Shoolem—how far was he from becoming a homeless pariah? There was another complicating factor, relating to a recent increase in Polish anti-Semitism. This was the movement to stop non-Jews from hiring Jews as middlemen or buying goods from them.[26] Yussef thus endured Pan Yanek in return for his shelter. But it galled his soul.

White Streams, and the Monster Thereof

It was as hot and still an afternoon as the one in which Romeo and Juliet's plans were ruined by a malevolent fate. "By noon [the sun] had swallowed every cloud in sight and was burning fiercely in an empty sky."[27] Mishillim was drawing water at the town spring when he saw Feige, his first love and the daughter of Lippe Goy, sleeping by the pool. Perhaps there is an allusion to Jacob and Rachel at the well (Genesis 29), which also was an unacceptable pairing (since her father had planned for Jacob to marry Rachel's older sister). In any event, the thunderbolt. In Nuszcze, it was of course frowned upon for a respectable family to allow its son to show interest in the daughter of a swineherd, quite apart from the suspicion that Lippe had burned down Yussef's inn. When Feige visited Mishillim a bit later, she told him she would never go to his house again, because "Your mama thinks our family's too common to associate with."[28] Her status might have increased his desire, if folklore is a motive for as well as a reflection of human conduct, especially for those who would not have heard of Romeo.

Trembling uncontrollably, and moved from deep within him, Mishillim crept ever nearer, almost close enough to grab hold of one delicate foot. At that moment the universe changed. As if the sun had been eclipsed, a strange half-light suffused the air around the spring, and what seemed to be large, "darkly palmed" hands "caressed" his eyelids. Mishillim experienced the waters parting, and then, "quite suddenly,"

> a beast, large and rectangular, head like an ox and belly livid as a storm cloud, surfaced from the spring and began to swim toward him. Mishillim's trembling grew more violent, his subconscious purpose weakened, and he withdrew the [i.e., his] threatening hand. He struggled to his feet, hastily picking up the pitcher, and hurried up the darkening slope. . . . Among the grass and rocks on his way, and in the upper fields too, as he ran, Mishillim thought he saw a shapeless black creature so thin that it might have been no more than a shadow writhing close to the ground, and in its pursuit of him extending now an arm and now a leg piteously in the air, until it finally fell out of his vision. For one moment before the end he thought he caught a glimpse of an animal face: red, fleshy, overgrown with hair that cleared over two clean, bright, widely parted lips. Mishillim saw it turn back until it reached the edge of the slope and rolled soundlessly down the decline. ("CMAM," 49)

Looking back at this key moment in his life as a boy, Roth depicts the way shtetl authorities—family, physicians, and rabbis—managed prepubescent lust. Some of their attitudes had already taken root in Mishillim's soul or else he would not have seen, or written that he had seen, at the point of reaching

Feige's dormant body, a "beast." That it was horned, bullish, hairy, and subhuman, with weirdly sensuous lips and an underside red and stormy, suggests what rabbis and parents defined as the infectious virulence of sex. Its body suggested a kind of death-like negative shape, waving (why "piteously"?) at Mishillim's retreating form. Its thinness connotes the belief in masturbation as weakening the body, making procreation impossible and unhinging the mind. The result: the offender was isolated from the community as a degenerate.

Hasidism taught a prodigious need to keep the young free from disease, to which an immoral use of the body—sexual activity—would, it was believed, inevitably lead. Parents must supervise their children closely. After Mishillim arrived home in a state of collapse, Yussef and Hudl put him in bed and attended him unceasingly. Following Hasidic convention, Yussef reported the circumstances to his rabbi, to whom was delegated awesome power to bring the affected child back to a "normal" state. Unlike a secular authority, the "wonder rabbi's" gifts of healing were those of a premodern physician of the soul. Certainly it is improbable that Yussef would have turned first, as "Count Me among the Missing" reports, to Herr Sustock, a retired doctor, to examine his son. Roth tells us the doctor is living in a house provided by the puretz (why?).[29] The physician recognizes the element of hysteria in Mishillim's vision and his temporary loss of speech. When Mishillim tells him it was Feige who was sleeping by the spring, the doctor discounts the reality of the beast, opting instead for an explanation in keeping with a "great doctor" who "is curing people in Vienna." After several interviews, Sustock notices semen on Mishillim's bedclothes. That morning, when his mother came to wake him, he was so completely under the covers that she told him she would have thought, if he had not obviously been thrashing around, that he had died.[30] Herr Sustock tells the boy that an erection is nothing to be ashamed of.[31] (It is a bit unusual, but not aberrant, for a boy of nine to masturbate.)

If the doctor is an invention, the reason for his presence is to contrast an Enlightenment diagnosis with an age-old Hasidic one. Yussef's next move—the expected one—was to rely on venerable spiritual authority. Rabbi Zorakh, citing the Zohar, identifies what Mishillim saw as a *khayi rui [ruach]*, a demonic spirit that must be exorcized immediately. It enters a victim through his eyes, fills his soul with a secret "distillation," and spreads its poison to the victim's loved ones. The urgency was increased because the victim was a "man-child." This demon's power, as well as its appearance, suggests that its hold over the human body is sexual. That love enters through the eyes is a medieval amorous conceit, and the poisonous distillation suggests semen. The spread

Samuel Roth, Infamous Modernist

of infection to other family members implies incest, showing how restraint of sexual impulse ("subconscious purpose") is essential to the coherence of the nuclear family. Hasidic belief in demons is one way not only of frightening devout Jews but also of making them aware of a personal God. "Why does He put him [a dybbuk, or evil spirit installed in a human form] in and take him out? That gives people fear of God and love of God and belief in God—that it should be easier for a person to believe in God."[32] For the bedridden Mishillim to watch the rabbi, his father, and enough adult males to make up a *minyin* entering his room on a rainy night with a Torah must have been frightening. But it was also an act of communal as well as filial love. As Reb Zorakh swung the sacred scrolls over the boy, he supplicated the "help" of the Holy Torah in driving the demon "out of his hiding in the boy Mishillim ben Yussef Leib, so that the boy's heart may not remain eternally closed to our Father, to you, and to his obligations in the world" (55).

The boy kissed the Torah. Thunder deafened, and lightning blinded, those gathered, as Mishillim sensed a "tremendous resentment . . . in the world outside the rained-on window." It was as if the clouds themselves were foot soldiers and warrior cavalry waging battle.[33] Could this "resentment," Roth's text suggests, be an earth-spirit's grief at the human animal's rejection of its own bodily impulses? Could it even be a kind of Frankenstein's monster (who was only ugly in appearance, and in defending himself against mobs), some part of Mishillim's own nature, resenting the rabbi and the father for shaming and confining him? This *khayi rui* was brought into existence because of a young male's attempt to access life and vigor, and was immediately rejected as repulsive and an intolerable danger to everyone. Yet the resentment, whether from a demon or the natural world, silently found its way into Mishillim's heart, soon to make itself known to his parents and rabbi.

The minyin held its breath. Perhaps the storm was an omen that the demon had won. But the rabbi smiled at the thunder. The exorcism, and the rabbi's statement that Mishillim was "clean" and would stay so if he obeyed the Law, made Hudl and Yussef, if not Mishillim, feel very much better than Dr. Sustock's advice had. A charismatic healer's way of molding private lives into conformity with a healthy social unit easily displaced a scientific one's. Through the former, Mishillim was restored to the community. The next morning he left his sickbed. His mother told him, "The whole world is waiting for you."

As an adult, Roth never lost his sense of divinely ordained mission. The rabbi's blessing and restoring him was a key moment for him. However, integral with restoration to health and community was an awareness that he must keep intense, unshakable desires to himself—something Herr Sustock, if he were the chief authority, would have prevented. When his mother told him that Yussef Leib informed the rabbi about the monster, Mishillim's "heart cried out in wrath. Yesterday he would have told the story of the beast to anyone without a quaver of shame. Suddenly the matter had become personal to him—how he did not yet understand. He grated his teeth. There was a choking in his throat."[34] Soon after his exorcism, his parents required the boy to sleep in the same bed as his father ("CMAM," 59). This also the boy resented. And worse was to come. Resentment, as Roth would eventually learn from one of his favorite writers, Nietzsche, flows from fear and hatred of difference, and especially from the bitter heart of an outsider impotent to fight an oppressor. Roth's *khayi rui* felt it at having been exorcized. Young Roth, and David Zorn, felt it at having their sex instinct shamed and repressed.

Almost immediately after Mishillim returned to school, he began occasionally playing hooky, dreaming of Feige. One afternoon, the rabbi upbraided the boy for not knowing his lessons. Mishillim's injured pride—unlike most boys, he had never been beaten—triumphed over all sense of decorum. He threw a heavy prayer book at Rabbi Zorakh, breaking his glasses, and bolted. When he heard that he had injured his melamed, Mishillim felt that he had fallen back into the clutches of the demon Zorakh had exorcized. He left his house in the evening ("the moon stared like a woman half seen through a grey veil"), thinking not of inflicting harm on himself but of escaping Nuszcze forever. He went straight to see Feige; they embraced, only to be yanked apart, not by a demon, but by a livid Lippe Goy. The incident ended with Mishillim being picked up on the road to Zlocsow by a kindly peasant, Punki, and discovering that his rabbi had not been seriously harmed.

One version of Roth's autobiography was in the form of a novel, some chapters of which he published in *Two Worlds* in 1926. It bears the titles "White Streams" and "The Natural History of David Zorn." Figure 2, a proposed title page for the novel, shows outstanding similarity, especially in the fleshy mouth, straight nose, and hooded eyes, to a 1938 photo of the poet Delmore Schwartz glaring at his reflection in a mirror.[35] "David Zorn" (the last name means "anger" in German) is an invention of Roth when he was in his late twenties. Of the biblical King David, Roth writes, "As he was the most faithful of people, David was also the most rebellious; the gentlest of all souls, as [*sic*] also the most violent" ("CMAM," 75). Mishillim (and Samuel Roth) had these traits, but in important ways, "David Zorn" is only one facet of Mishillim (and Samuel Roth). David is more like Jerosh in "Count Me among the Missing" than Mishillim.

Figure 2. Trial title-page design for one version of Roth's unpublished autobiography. "David Zorn" is one of Roth's aliases. Roth Archive, Rare Book and Manuscript Library, Columbia University. By permission of the Roth estate.

Roth wrote about David Zorn as a young man, taken by the power of modernist, sexually explicit writers, two of whom, D. H. Lawrence and James Joyce, he was publishing (without the authors' permission) in one of his literary reviews. In "White Streams" he was transmuting into autobiographical fiction both the community's love and its repressive qualities that had made him the conflicted adult he became: part iconoclast, part Jewish idealist; part idolater of beautiful actresses, part loving family man; part feckless self-promoter and part self-hating apostate; part artist and part businessman. That slippage in identity is a modernist touchstone. So is the dream of redeeming the mind and heart from contradictory identities.

"White Streams" describes "David's" relishing in his imagination his stealthy approach to the sleeping Feige, as he lies in bed, awaiting the rabbi's exorcism. "I saw as well as felt the sweetening of my secret flesh, followed slowly, overwhelmingly by a delicious languor, in which it became an inert body drifting lazily on a warm sea."[36] "White Streams" alludes to Aleister Crowley's first book of poetry, *White Stains,* many copies of which were destroyed (long after its appearance, although it was censored upon publication in 1898) by British customs in 1924. Roth was impressed by the magician, occultist, and self-styled sexual athlete Crowley when he visited Sam's Poetry Book Shop in 1920.[37] Had Rabbi Zorakh been able to intuit the kind of father Mishillim would be to the man Samuel Roth, his post-exorcism smile would have been replaced by tight-lipped sadness. Throughout his adult life, Roth was extremely active sexually, sometimes adulterously. Writers he admired, and many friends, were extraordinarily interested in sex.

Yussef Leib to the Golden Land

One night in December 1899, His Excellency made explicit what before he had kept to himself and his circle of friends. He asked Yussef if he was withholding some money for his own use. For Yussef, it was the last straw. Knowing that Yanik's word was literally law, and fearing arrest or the shame of being removed from Nuszcze by the puretz's men, he left for America that same night, probably traveling by railroad to Belgium and taking steamship passage in steerage. The Ellis Island immigration papers indicate he arrived on May 1, 1900, from Antwerp, his point of departure being the town of Kasimirowka.[38] He would have had a support system and a *landsmanshaftn,* or regional mutual aid society, to help him when he arrived in New York.[39]

Now Mishillim learned a lesson very different from any that his father or his rabbi could teach him, one similar to what Asher, Lippe Goy's son, could have spoken of. Hudl, Mishillim, Soori (Sadie [Ruth refers to her as Sarah]), and Moishe (Max) suffered just as did many of the most ill-fed, ill-clothed, and ill-housed in the isolated shtetls. Hudl had to carry wheat, flax, and eggs on her back, selling them door to door. It took Yussef three years to save enough money for steamship fare for his family. Until his father's departure, Mishillim's time in Nuszcze was more fortunate than that of most of the other shtetl children (of whom there were many much poorer than he). Designated as a promising student of good appearance with viable social skills, he was not relegated to a set role such as artisan or laborer.[40]

The Passage Out

In 1903, following a circuitous route from Lemberg to Vienna to Cracow to Hamburg, Hudl and her children sailed (according to Ellis Island records, on May 29, 1903) in the steerage section of the steamship *Praetoria* ("CMAM," 89). There, Mishillim, in his bed (one of a hundred ranged in tiers of six), read an evangelical pamphlet given him upon boarding. Its story, about Yeshea, the Messiah, enthralled him, perhaps because it described another brilliant boy who stunned the wisest holy men of his time by answering all their questions and posing some the rabbis themselves could not answer. Crucified, Yeshea waited "by God's side for the return of his people." For three days, Mishillim read the pamphlet aloud to fellow steerage passengers, who, he opined, did not know he was talking about Jesus. On the fourth day a "red-bearded Rabbi from Pinsk" descended to the ship's hold and ripped the work from Mishillim's hands, warning him "at the risk of his immortal soul" never to read it again ("CMAM," 89–90). This, as his daughter points out, was Roth's first experience with literary censorship.[41] It was also a continuation of the need to disentangle himself from the strictures that his father and his rabbi had recently enforced. Both would have been as apoplectic as the red-beard at finding Mishillim with evangelical material.

His avowed response was a lifelong obsession not only with fighting conventions but with accomplishing what no other Jew has done since. Many years, and two five-year federal obscenity convictions later, Roth wrote *My Friend Yeshea* (1961), published after his release from the last of those jail terms. He advertised the book in a way that showed, if nothing else, that the fire of his belief had in no way been smothered: "That night (on the Praetoria), while Mishillim was asleep, Yeshea made his first earthly appearance to him, in the form of an image before which Polish peasants knelt at the roadside. All differences between Jews and their persecutors must be abolished, Yeshea informed Mishillim. Only then would the world know peace."[42]

The final story Roth tells about the passage to America is as revealing as it is dramatic. Briefly, it tells of Mishillim being called to the bedside of a dying child. Her mother's death had taken with it the girl's will to live. Her father had heard of the boy's impassioned recitations from the pamphlet and hoped to make his daughter take notice of him and his message. Mishillim chants psalms and kisses the child, but she dies. He is just a well-meaning kid out of his depth and trying his best. Meanwhile, the father, ironically a doctor, stands by helplessly and stoically. When his daughter passes, he silently closes her eyes and gives Mishillim some money. He, like the tragic burden he carries, remains a mystery. Certainly, Mishillim does not try to fathom it. But the next day, understandable curiosity gives implacable chaos a chance to drown him. On his way to observe the burial at sea, he is almost swept overboard: "out of nowhere, he found himself in a wild darkness of sound such as he had never before encountered, a combination of wind and water the first of which felled him to the deck while the second hurled him with incredible speed in the direction of the slender railing" ("CMAM," 90–92). Not biblical verses but an able seaman saves the terrified child, once again beyond his depth. And this, as much as the story of his first brush with censorship, may be the really significant episode in Mishillim's voyage to America and Roth's reason for relating the two incidents. Samuel Roth was often accused of losing touch with reality. But not here—or did he?

Roth states that almost drowning was his second brush with death (the first being the fire that destroyed his father's kretchma). He seems to be suggesting that God had saved him for the mission Yeshea had in mind for him. If that is his real reason for telling the story—and the paragraphs about Mishillim and the dying child stand by themselves as good writing—it shows that as an adult, he still has to recognize that pride and self-importance can infect piety. The fabric of Roth's adult life might have unfurled as a gentler tapestry of cause and effect if he had considered the universal pathos of the events in the stateroom and on deck to constitute something at least as important as the revelation of his sense of personal mission. But then, he would not have been Mishillim, David Zorn, or Samuel Roth.

Mishillim's father's American life was to begin on the Lower East Side, where Yussef met Hudl, his two sons, and his daughter at Castle Garden and bundled them onto a horse-drawn streetcar.

Samuel Roth, Infamous Modernist

Tenement Apartments, Gloomy Intensity, Creative Energy

Yussef had rented a furnished apartment at the southwestern edge of the Lower East Side, where Galician immigrants usually settled. The rooms seemed immense to a shtetl boy. Here Mishillim, soon to be known simply as Sam or Sammy, encountered his first mirror, a not insignificant discovery for one so self-absorbed. But due to his father's impending failure in the clothing business (he was in partnership "cutt[ing], sew[ing], and press[ing] pants"), the Roths moved to less expensive locations, where they encountered rats, bedbugs, and filthy outhouses. These disasters brought the Roths to 17–19 Lewis Street. Frequent change of residence was common in the Lower East Side; there was one tenement on Lewis Street that had housed 119 separate families from 1895 to 1899.[43] The Lower East Side was the most crowded part of the city, with the great majority of residents being immigrants or first-generation Americans.

In their own rooms, the Roths somehow found room for four boarders ("CMAM," 98, 101). Yussef, after his needle trade business failed, became a butcher.[44] People had to eat. In the Tenth Ward at the turn of the century, there were 140 groceries and 131 butcher shops.[45] In America one could not live on the edge of poverty and simply pray for what in the shtetl was called *parnassah* (sustenance). A secure American future had to contain not only adequate income but also, as Roth remarked, insurance, savings accounts, and other secular essentials ("CMAM," 97). No wonder his father spoke so much about money, rather than scriptures.[46] By 1907—a terrible year of financial panic and food shortages for the poor—the Roths were living behind Yussef's kosher shop at 96 Willett Street, near where Grand Street intersects with East Broadway. Yussef might have noticed that a grocery store was conveniently located on the other side of the stoop. It was owned by Joseph Alter. The Alters and the Roths climbed toward bourgeois security together, under the approach to the Williamsburg Bridge. The rooms were dark and cramped, and the first-floor toilet, Adelaide Kugel states, "was as filthy as the East Side itself." Both men may have shaken their heads in sympathy with immigrants more unfortunate than they. Neither had had to peddle from pushcarts summer and winter, or worse, go door-to-door with heavy sacks, hoping to find housewives willing to buy a nickel's worth of goods.

The ground constantly shook, from Lewis to Willett, from the machinery at the enormous Hoe printing factory at East Broadway and Grand. Young Sammy accepted his father's dismal explanation for this phenomenon. "It was

Figure 3. 96 Willett Street, c. 1940, where Yussef Roth opened a butcher shop in 1907. By permission of New York City Department of Records, Municipal Archives, Tax Department Photo.

the fish Leviathan—on which the world rests—so displeased with how things went with God's favorite people that it had indigestion which caused it to tremble and the whole earth with it" ("CMAM," 99). The most immediate manifestation of how things had been going was the Hoe factory riot in 1902. When the funeral procession of a chief rabbi passed the massive building, Irish workers threw water and various objects at the mourners, which occasioned an attack on the factory by the usually passive Galician Jews, enraged at this intolerable insult to their rabbi.[47]

Yussef Roth's gloominess was part of the price he paid for an intense drive to succeed that, for many Jewish American immigrants, was a survival strategy. Irving Howe and Milton Hindus have both noted that hard work and creativity—"a kind of cultural fever, a turbulence of excitement," in Howe's words—were hallmarks of Lower East Side Jewish life.[48] This expense of energy meant gloomy apprehension as one confronted insecurity, betrayal, and consequent self-betrayal. It conditioned Yussef Roth as much as it did the writers of Call It Sleep and The Rise of David Levinsky, the actors and playwrights of the Yiddish Theater, or the sculptor of Jacob and the Angel. The quality of apprehension had an ironclad component: seriousness, what Howe characterized as "that special tone of moral intensity and intellectual feverishness."[49] In his Leviathan analogy, Yussef might well have had in mind not only the Hoe factory but also the Jews in the Golden Land whose struggles forced them to substitute the bitch-goddess of success for piety even on the Sabbath. Moral intensity could only exist if there was money for food and four walls. Sholem Asch writes of a typical garment trade factory where operators tended rows of tightly packed sewing machines in a fetid atmosphere, competing to please the foreman, who could hire or fire. In this kind of shop, "Jewish Asthma" lurked. It was called that by family doctors who knew that their patients, terminally ill with TB, wanted an official diagnosis that would allow them to work until their final days to provide for their loved ones. Samuel Ornitz delineates Jewish children ashamed of their parents' postures, accents, clothing, and demeaning "greaser" occupations. He traces the evolution of the term "Jewish head" ("Yiddishe Kop") from the connotation of piety and learning to an epithet synonymous with the verb "to jew down," used sardonically by Jews themselves.[50] Survival required a scramble up from the depths, even in a battle against the titan Leviathan, not to mention loss of ethnic identity. So be it. As one of Sam Roth's favorite poets, Yeats, said, and later Delmore Schwartz brilliantly reiterated, "In dreams begin responsibilities." That was as true concerning a mission from Yeshea as it was of a successful Willett Street grocery and butcher shop.

Figure 4. Photo of Yussef and Hudl Roth and their family taken 1907. *Left to right*: Moe, Hudl, Yussef, Sadie, Yetta (Teddie), and Sam. By permission of Maryjane Treloar, and Roth estate.

Happily for Sam and Pauline's own offspring, dismal introspection did not pass from father and son to the Roths' neighbor, the grocer Joseph Leib Alter. Later, as a preteen in the late 1920s, Adelaide Roth enjoyed the family visits to the Alters immensely. Well spoken, charming Pauline Alter was a center of attraction. Sam Roth first saw her when she was twelve; they married in 1918. With a performer's verve, she could mimic all the parts of a play she had just seen, including Yiddish dialect. But when the boy next door, the "poet with the patched pants," came courting, she was demure, a nice Jewish girl. The family doctor, not an admirer of that boy, remembered him maneuvering her into a corner of the room and reciting poems at her "by the hour."[51]

Mishillim on the Streets, Age Ten to Fourteen

Sam Roth took pride in asserting that as a boy he got to know the area's pimps and thieves as well as its doctors and lawyers ("CMAM," 127). With kid brother Moe, Sam provided their father with empty storage boxes from the Fulton

Samuel Roth, Infamous Modernist

Fish Market and with ice from the docks. Another unpleasant trip must have been from his father's butcher shop to a wurst factory carrying a pail of trimmings and rancid fat.[52] Passing through what the Jewish youngsters called "Mick country," Sam and Moe sometimes were stopped by young toughs who tried to extort money or goods to let them pass. "Micks didn't stop at tossing empty bottles to make a point," Roth later said.[53] His wariness about street attacks, bred in the bone of many an American city dweller, extended well into his adulthood. In London in 1921 he saw two men approach him while walking alone deep in the night with a lot of money in his wallet. Instead of waiting for them to speak, he "lashed savagely out at them, aiming at their faces" (207–8). The story tells us as much about Sam's Lower East Side background as it does about his personal pugnaciousness.

When Roth was a boy, the surging energy of life on Rivington or Grand Streets or East Broadway was undergirded by an aggressive nastiness—from homeless transients, pimps, street gangs, and petty thieves—that left a stamp on many an ordinary boy's behavior patterns. Roth gives a few choice examples. Sneaking on board an iceboat, they tease a drunken guard. Seeing a neighborhood girl walking with a pimp, his gang shouted "Mary the whore!" ("CMAM," 102). More than once the boys stumbled over the feet of an unconscious, bloody female protruding from an alley. They covered their eyes in mock shame. The neighborhood epithet for this kind of homeless female derelict, believed to be Irish, was helpful in inhibiting sympathy for a Mick: "Mary Sugar Bum." It referred to the Irish custom of adding sugar to gin.[54] Sammy encountered one of these outcasts while working at a neighborhood drugstore when he was thirteen. A woman wearing "everything she owned" stepped into the store's telephone booth. When she left, he had to clean up the defecation (114).

Roth's circle of friends on Lewis Street could hardly be described as a gang, like "The Cherry Street Boys," remembered a member, later the world-traveling journalist and poet Harry Roskolenko: "Our slum poverty was alive and deadly in our bones."[55] This observation was epitomized by Sam's friend Bones. After his mother's death, his father had turned their apartment into a house of prostitution. Bones became increasingly withdrawn. Eventually, his father and two of his whores were arrested, and Bones stayed on in the apartment alone, eating the meals residents of the building had left for him at his door. (At the time, there were no institutions on the Lower East Side to help Jewish children under twelve who were not being cared for properly.)[56] One particular night, Bones did not join Sammy and his friends in the preparations for the traditional bonfire. He had his own plan. That night the lumberyard near Lewis Street's old flour mill went up in flames three stories high. Roth recalls, "What caused the whole city to gasp was that—until it vanished in smoke—the figure of a little boy was seen waving to the world from the lumber yard's roof platform, waving frantically, whether for rescue or in mockery no one will ever be able to say" (125). It's hard not to see Sammy Roth as another promising shtetl youth transformed into a drifting, hooky-playing, Lower East Side street kid with drastically less supervision paid him than in Nuszcze. He had been forced to repeat the fifth grade in 1906. After that, he acquired working papers (his father had for this reason given his birth date as 1893) and left school until 1907. He made up his lost time and graduated Public School 188 when he was fifteen,[57] then entered Townsend Harris Hall High School, but left without graduating in 1910.[58] Only his sympathy for girls whose sole escape from drudgery was contracting with pimps (he would not join in the shouts of "Mary the whore") and his tearful farewell to Bones revealed the moral sensitivity of Mishillim in Galicia. The latter was muttered into his bedclothes on the night of his friend's death: "Some fire, Bones."

The complexity of victimhood, and responsibility for it, concerned Roth from start to finish of his career. Approaching sixty, he wrote an essay on his conversations with a "street walker" at the Theodore Roosevelt Park behind the planetarium at Eighty-first Street, near his apartment.[59] Observing the woman sitting on a bench in the late afternoons opposite his window, and seeing her shivering in the early winter cold, he would cross the street and sit next to her, or walk with her. Once, they passed under a movie marquee; a lobby poster featured Betty Grable high-kicking, in tights. Grable's life had been filled with the "wonderful nothings which crown the life of the Hollywood celebrity . . . applauded by the amoral millions who badly need the lie ["happily ever after"?] upon which even the great dramatic roles are built." The poster, appropriately, was probably for *How to Marry a Millionaire* (1953). The contrasts Roth makes with the ill-clad, sick streetwalker favor the victim rather than the fantasy object, the film star.

His curiosity about and empathy for the victimized—and the nebulous complexity of victimhood, what it saves one from, and martyrdom—is what makes his first published story so promising. "The Hunt" (1914) is an understated reporting of the despair in the hut of a forest warden and his wife after their daughter had left it to become part of the household of her Polish lord. One day, he drops her off for a heartbreaking visit while hunting nearby. To her father, she is dead, having been hunted down by the puretz. "The hunted are us Jews," the warden says. Roth leaves it to the reader, as her understanding

Samuel Roth, Infamous Modernist

mother pours tea for her daughter, to decide whether father, mother, or daughter is most enslaved by the status quo, and which of the three has let it destroy his or her emotional equilibrium.[60]

Girlie Pictures, Nickelodeons, and Sam's First Job

In a time and place of increasingly accessible technological innovations, nothing reshaped a young immigrant's self-awareness more than prurient spectatorship. Moving pictures offered him "old sensations in new forms, whose images were new, though their effects on him were as deadly as the old" ("CMAM," 119). By "old" he may have meant the "girlie" and detective magazine covers and calendar pinups. Young Roth's visits to the Clinton Street nickelodeons coincided with his job hunting after the closing of the drugstore in which he had been clerking when he was fourteen or fifteen. These establishments, which burgeoned in the first decade of the century, were in their last years of operation, being replaced after 1910 by movie "palaces." They were working-class places, often uncomfortable and bad smelling. Their darkness made them slightly risky for women to patronize, although lots of women came. Young Roth paid admission out of money his father had given him for job-seeking transportation. He writes of auditoriums, not peep machines, and their daytime audiences. He observed men sitting far apart from each other, guarding their privacy, hats in hands and hands on laps. Many of them left when women arrived, some without escort. "Why were they so restless under the grimaces of the faces of the beautiful women shown on the screen?" Roth asked himself. "Why are they so proud, so touchy, so lonely—these day patrons? Why do they behave like worshipers in a temple where deities demand the most fleshly obeisance?"[61]

By 1914, when Roth was patronizing Third Avenue movie theaters, he had a crush on a starlet, a woman he remembers as Lucille Swilson but whose last name was probably Wilson.[62] The twenty-year-old Roth had seen a newspaper photo of Wilson, sitting with legs crossed, accompanying a story about her being arrested and charged with "improper conduct." It made his "mind reel" with what she might have been doing. His moviegoing became compulsive; like many other young men, he tried to seclude himself from other patrons, for the same reason that the men scattered among empty seats at the Nickelodeons placed their hats over their laps. He was looking for well-dressed, long-legged actresses in that cross-legged posture: it was a fetish connoting "complete abandonment and the promise of infinite delight."[63] Sam was hooked on a concoction that combined a Venus with a sex object, the refined and the everyday.

By 1926, when he would found *Beau,* one of the earliest pre-*Esquire* American men's magazines, Roth would show that he had absorbed the genius of impresario Flo Ziegfeld for presenting artfully adorned and posed femininity to his readers. Ziegfeld's great discovery, according to Roth, was like a brilliantly styled two-pronged fork that held separate delicacies. One was the theater itself, a place of magic the origin of which was worship of the ineffable. Chants of religious awe in communal gatherings were replaced in modern times with awestruck scrutiny in playhouses of the artfully decorated woman. The other, interrelated delicacy was a woman who projected for the customer the middleman publisher's or impresario's own desire. Ziegfeld's girls "remodeled for the world the burning image in his own heart." Every issue of *Beau* presented an artful frontispiece image of a showgirl "not because it would sell but because of my own organic need" ("CMAM," 174).

At thirteen, Sammy had an early tutor in contemporary methods of relieving sexual tension: his first boss. This was a Dr. Blitz, who owned a drugstore at the corner of Broome and Cannon Streets, three blocks south of Willett. Roth got the job, soon after having received his working papers in the mail in 1907, by addressing a postcard to the druggist. His sales pitch was that the druggist's patrons would be even better served by the man's good work if he had an assistant to do the menial and time-consuming labor of the business. "And that is how—without consciously meaning to—Mishillim discovered his one earthly talent, the writing of selling [*sic*] advertising copy" (110).

Blitz had mounted images of nude women on the wall behind which he filled prescriptions, and in his storage space, to make his workplace more agreeable. He was interested in the contrast between the icon and its embodiment in his mistresses. "Some differences between her and the fat peroxide bitch upstairs, eh?" He had found his assistant looking hard and long at the images. "Stop looking so hard at her or you'll wear her out." That sentence haunted Roth when he became a publisher of erotica, as several of his stories and advertisements show. The ambience of Blitz's place was more fit for a cigar store or pool hall. That made Sammy feel he could confide to Blitz that he had a new dream girl, a blonde he had only glimpsed as she entered Public School 110 across the street. "You violate her every night in your dreams, don't you," sneered the druggist. "And plan to make an honest woman of her when you grow up." Blitz had just about said that Mishillim, like himself, was bound by the image or idol of female perfection, and would substitute it, as Blitz had

Samuel Roth, Infamous Modernist

done, for a flesh-and-blood relationship. Or would learn to. That would be a trap, but the scrutiny of friends, family, and rabbi was also a trap, as Mishillim had experienced in Nuszcze. "Remember this: before you marry a fleshly female you'll have to get a rabbi's divorce decree from yourself" (114).

In Galicia, Mishillim's preadolescent erotic instinct meant an attempt in which the entire community participated to drive out the Evil Inclination, or the serpent's blandishments. In the case of a boy chased by a demon while tentatively touching a girl's leg, the rabbi recognized that the youth's inclination was to sexual desire. In America, Mishillim, quickly morphing into Sammy, found himself the assistant, for three dollars a week, to a randy druggist. What Mishillim learned from Blitz he later used, once his metamorphosis to Sam Roth was complete, to make good money. This kind of progression from youthful submission to providing services in order to become self-sufficient is typical of the experience of immigrants from tight-knit shtetl communities where rabbis served as judges of secular disputes and legislators for the health of the soul. The Golden Land changed that, which is why rabbis sometimes referred to America as "the thief."

Roth's Estrangement from His Father

The drugstore closed down after Dr. Blitz was arrested for assaulting a woman. Due to the good advice of one of the family's female boarders, Yussef allowed his son to return to school. Although no bar mitzvah is mentioned in "Count Me among the Missing," "David Zorn's" novella "Open Plumbing" describes the protagonist studying for one, again due to the same boarder's recognition of the boy's high intelligence.[64] His job hunting after Dr. Blitz did not go well; near-compulsive movie theater visits must have had something to do with that. For periods of time while he was thirteen and fourteen he lived with friends, after his father's edict to the effect that without a job, he should leave the house. It was about this time that he decided he wanted to become a poet. It was not good timing, as he had flunked out of Townsend Harris. His father was bitter. "King Solomon wrote, and you'll write. You're going to get a job or get out of the house!" ("CMAM," 129–30).

A neighbor described the Roths as a "typical Jewish East Side family—pious, sincere, self-supporting," with "a hard working, pious gent" at its head.[65] From the inside, a father-son dynamic was working itself out, one not unusual in Lower East Side life. Yussef was an observant Jew and spent much of his non-working hours in synagogue, but Sam had already decided that his father had been diminished in America before the rest of the family even arrived. Roth's daughter tells the following story, which shows that Sam's sister, Soori, thought so too. Soori had left home a few months before Yussef had sneered at Sam's ambition to be a poet. She took a job as a domestic, a kind of work considered so demeaning for a Jewess as to bring shame upon her parents. It was Hudl, not Yussef, who wanted Soori back (similarly to the mother in "The Hunt," who welcomed her daughter back although her father turned his back on her).[66] What she and her brother had in common—his daughter intimates that this is why they were close at the time—was how they had come to regard their father. In America, it seemed to them, their father's chief concern regarding his children had become the money they could bring into the household. Accepting money from a daughter who earned it by sweeping floors would have been considered disgraceful by Jewish acquaintances. Many first-generation offspring disrespected their immigrant fathers for their "greaser" jobs, "mocki" accents, Jewish gestures and clothing, and disdain for American culture. But Yussef angered Soori and Sam Roth by his insistence that they bring in money while dismissing what they saw as opportunities to participate in the range of opportunities America offered.

The profound bond between orthodox Jewish father and son is codified in Talmudic teaching. The Talmud suggests that the best age for the father to "guide [his son] with ethical reproof" is from the ages sixteen to twenty-two. Had Yussef stayed in Galicia that most probably would have been the case, despite father and son sleeping in the same bed to stop Mishillim's masturbating. He would have likely suppressed his inchoate resentment and continued to revere and obey his father. What once would have been seen as fatherly discipline seemed to Yussef's eldest, Americanized son and daughter to be imperious and at the same time abject. Working from 5 A.M. to 9 P.M. in a failing business trapped Yussef (and many other immigrant Jewish men) in distinctly non-patriarchal behavior. Roth's father no longer looked directly into the eyes of his children, observed Sam. His eldest son thought he was afraid of them.[67]

When Sam did errands to the Catherine Street shop, he found his father "bowing over those machines even more earnestly than men bow at prayer" ("CMAM," 107). One Sabbath afternoon, after his father told him about his having declared at Ellis Island that his son was not twelve, but thirteen, the boy refused to follow Yussef to the evening service, despite his mother's fury (104). This estrangement grew routine once Roth's announcement that he wanted to be a poet was greeted by his father's "Let the rich sing. . . . We are poor; we must work" (132). By 1915, Samuel chose times to visit his dying mother when Yussef was not at home.[68]

Clearly, Yussef felt the same disappointment in his son that Sam found in him. The son blamed his father for a lot. He would explain his indifferent schoolwork as due to dislike of routine instruction and disillusion at not only being just another boy but a much older one than his fifth-grade classmates. Fair enough. But the division between father and firstborn son also grew out of the latter's need to be considered as special by others as he believed himself to be. It went far beyond self-confidence. It was a callow egotism. The belief set him apart in a way that hurt his father, and later his own wife and children.[69] But it also gave him a sustaining sense of mission. His father would not now make a rabbi of him. So, however Yussef sneered about Solomon, his son would make a poet of himself. Adelaide recognized in that one of her father's most heroic resolutions. Unlike some others, it was not self-delusional. By 1918, he had done it.

After his 1918 marriage celebration in the in-laws' Newark home, his eldest son saw Yussef only twice before his father's death in 1933. In that year, as Yussef was dying of cancer, "truly overcome with remorse, [he] rushed to his bedside," Adelaide wrote. It was a rainy Sunday afternoon. She and Richard waited downstairs while their parents spent "what seemed like hours" in the bedroom. Only then, looking back at the long family journey and understanding it in his heart as he had not previously, Sam Roth wept ("sad and frightening to see"). A similar late-blooming humility had possessed him at Hudl's death. At the funeral, he was so distraught that he almost stumbled into her grave.[70] He had long thought her to be indifferent and unsupportive, but a week after her funeral she haunted his dreams. "My mother, my white one, my princess. . . . Sometimes I lose sight of her . . . and I remember her warning that if I am not careful these books of mine will spoil my eyes," he later wrote.[71]

What must Roth have felt when he became aware of a typed will signed by Yussef shortly before his death? For perhaps the first time in America, the father referred to his firstborn son as Mishillim. Adelaide explains that her grandfather used the American names of his other children but addressed his eldest son as he did in Galicia because Sam had hardly spoken to him since Hudl's death. The dying father may have been reminding his son of the promise and obligation a Hebrew name connoted. Dividing his assets among his other children, he left "Mishillim" no more than a pittance. Adelaide recognized the ultimate reality of this eastern European–Lower East Side father-son dynamic: Samuel Roth regretted the self-inflicted wound of his break with his father. "The fact that he used Mishillim as his persona [in one version of "Count Me among the Missing"] is proof of the late-formed love" allowed birth only at the father's deathbed.[72]

Frank Tannenbaum

Frank Tannenbaum, whom Roth met in 1911 at a meeting of young people interested in prepping for college entrance ("CMAM," 135), was the most influential friend of his youth. Three inches shorter, a year older, and built like a fireplug, Tannenbaum had the same somber good looks and restless intensity as Roth. He was equally aggressive. Frank had found an outlet for his ambition that gave his life direction and that had won him the respect of downtown Bohemia's well-known advocates of social reform, most notably Emma Goldman. Having left his immigrant parents' upstate farm, when the two first met Tannenbaum was organizing longshoremen on the docks while living with relatives and doing odd jobs.

Frank needed an editor, and he saw in Samuel Roth's intensity a potential hard worker. In Sam's brooding restlessness, Frank hoped he had found a blood brother. Roth's writing abilities could be a complement to his own genius for practical leadership. Soon, Frank was visiting Yussef and Hudl to introduce himself and to inform them that he and their son wanted to room together in an apartment Frank had rented on Broome Street. When Frank went to jail for his IWW-inspired "direct action" to help homeless men in the killing winter of 1914, Frank and Sam had to give up their apartment. Roth tells us he spent his days reading in a public library, raiding restaurant discards for food, and sleeping in hallways and under bridges. But when the weather got cold, he returned to 96 Willett Street. By then, he had a job as a cashier in a restaurant. No more raiding of garbage pails.[73] Yeshea entered his dreams one sleet-slick winter night, telling him he was "still running" and "must make a stand." He probably did not mean that the young man should answer Yiddish newspaper advertisements for prospective husbands. The resultant free meals prevented Roth from having to cost his family the money to feed him.

Sam's major "stand" was the act of becoming a professional author. He had written a pamphlet issued by the Students' Aid League in 1911 or early 1912, a set of cliché-ridden, awkwardly stentorian verses titled "The Poet's Sufferings."[74] For the next six years, more short stories, children's stories, reviews, poems, and an excellent translation of an Abraham Reisen story appeared in the *Hebrew Standard, The Menorah Journal, The Bookman, The Maccabean,* and *The Jewish Exponent*.[75] Many of Roth's early stories, written from 1915 to 1917, were published in *The Jewish Child*.[76] They revolved around a circle of street kids of which Sam and Moe were a part before the Roths moved to Willett Street. Written for a young Jewish audience (and their parents), the stories were suitably moralistic and most had happy endings.[77]

Roth's first editing job was an anthology *New Songs of Zion* (The Judean Press's "Little Zionist Classics, no. 1") in 1914.[78] Some of the volume's contributors were Israel Zangwill, C. N. Byalik, Emma Lazarus, and Yehoash (Solomon Blumgarten); later, he took advantage of the opportunity for networking. Roth contributed his translation of Byalik's celebrated "The City of Slaughter," and his lyric "Sand and Stars," which addresses God with an anxiety similar to Byalik's: "The stars—the stars! Where are they, O Lord?" In 1914 the Bloch Publishing Company issued Roth's play for children, *The Broomstick Brigade: A Play of Palestine*.[79] "Writing for the Anglo-Jewish press yielded little in money but much in the admiration of its readers. I received at least four or five complimentary letters a week" ("CMAM," 145). He also got himself his first office, a room in a house across Willett Street from number 96.[80]

His pamphlet titled *Louis Lingg, Anarchist* (signed "Yours for the Revolution, Samuel Roth") appeared possibly as early as the year he met Frank, for it is alluded to in "The Poet's Sufferings." Lingg was arrested for his alleged part in inciting Chicago's Haymarket Riot (1886).[81] He became a tragic hero to his supporters, committing suicide in prison after writing "Long Live Anarchy" in his own blood on the walls of his prison cell. It was Tannenbaum who must have assigned Roth the task of publicizing Lingg to members of the Students' Aid League, an anarchist-supported organization that, as a recruiting technique, prepped working-class youth for the Regents Exams. Probably Sam had learned about Lingg from listening to Goldman and Berkman at the offices of *Mother Earth,* which Goldman edited. Frank had introduced his roommate to them, probably at the apartment. As kind and as widely read as she was committed to destroying capitalism, Goldman took the time to make Roth aware (according to him) of the works of Dostoyevsky, Strindberg, Pushkin, and Tolstoy.

Roth had no intention of emulating Frank's social idealism and self-sacrifice, which led to the very successful direct action in 1914 and his joining the strike against Standard Oil in Bayonne the following year.[82] Roth, in fact, despite his convenient "Yours for the Revolution" salutation in the Lingg pamphlet, was an avowed social and political conservative from his formative years, despite Frank, and despite his eventual fame as a First Amendment martyr. Contrast the two boys' reasons for estrangement from their fathers. Tannenbaum left home after an argument with his father about wages.[83] It was a political awakening rather than a personal resentment, one based only secondarily on financial expectations and primarily on his social conscience. Tony Michels's work on Yiddish socialism uncovered incidents of contemporary Jewish sons' socialist activism motivated by their fathers' "petit bourgeois" focus on security, respectability, and the conventions they brought with them from the shtetl.[84] Roth's rebellion had little to do with reforming social conditions caused by poverty and neglect. This was despite what had diminished his father in his and Soori's eyes, or what he had seen on the streets: the prostitutes and the female derelicts; the Mary Sugar Bums; the abuse of his own friends, especially the suicidal Bones, at the hands of parents or stepparents who used poverty to sanction cruelty; the sweatshop laborers with fifteen-hour days; the teenage prostitutes and their pimps; the pathetic alcoholics; the predatory gang activity based on ethnic hatreds.

This is what Roth remembered about how the endless discussions with Frank resolved themselves: "For Mishillim, the world was an arena, in which men and women were gladiators struggling for mastery under defined rules of fair play. . . . Frank's passion was for equality of opportunity for all, always. No man was better than another. No man deserved more of the good things of life than another" ("CMAM," 137). When he wrote this, Roth may have recalled Teddy Roosevelt's 1910 "square deal" speech, where he committed himself to "fair play under the present rules of the game." Partly a victim of, and partly a clever accomplice in, those rules, Sam Roth cleared a path to success, despite the smuthounds of the anti-vice societies and of the Post Office, in the business of popular publishing.

Tannenbaum was made of different stuff. He stood for what Roosevelt articulated in the second part of the sentence just quoted: " . . . having those rules changed so as to work for a more substantial equality of opportunity." A quarter century later, Roth wrote to Frank (the two had met at one of the latter's lectures), "When you reminded me that we had never agreed on anything, I realized that our differences were never really important. Neither of us belong [sic] to the multitude of mankind whose whole business of life is advancing personal interests, and that makes a fellowship which supersedes all other considerations."[85] The self-justification in that statement may have made Tannenbaum wince. However, with Roth, idealism was tightly bound up with good business.

Samuel Roth, Infamous Modernist

Frank in Bayonne, a Season in the Country, Columbia University

After his friend's release from the workhouse, Roth found an apartment on West Eighth Street whose owner would take an ex-convict. There, Frank introduced Sam to notables from many fields: publishers such as Beatrice Kay (Alfred Knopf's sister); the Boni brothers; Thomas Seltzer; editor Max Eastman; writers like Floyd Dell and Arturo Giovannitti; public figures like Aimee Semple MacPherson and John Barrymore; and Sam's favorite, *The Masses'* cartoonist, Art Young. He probably met Louise Bryant and John Reed there also.[86]

In July 1915 the sheriff of Bayonne, New Jersey, arrested Frank for speaking before striking mill workers at the Standard Oil Plant in Bayonne. He had been warned to stay away. After three days, and with a settlement in the offing, the sheriff released Frank, sincerely congratulating him on "sticking [up] for your beliefs. You're a fighter and I like a fighter."[87] The activist, heavily battered by the cops while in custody, spent the next week in bed. Later that summer he invited Sam to spend the rest of the year with him while he recuperated on his parents' farm. Those months comprised, Roth remembers, one of the happiest periods in his life ("CMAM," 141).

While at the workhouse on Blackwell's Island in 1914 (in 1921 the name was changed to Welfare Island), Frank had received a letter from Grace Hatch Childs, a prominent social worker whose husband, Richard, was one of the Progressive Era's leading fighters for reform of voting procedures and urban administration. After his release they met, and Mrs. Childs, seeing in the intrepid Frank a future progressive leader, agreed to pay for his four years in college.[88] He worked to get Roth (another high school non-graduate) a faculty scholarship by contacting the poet and Columbia professor John Erskine.[89] Roth entered the university with Tannenbaum in the fall of 1916, spending 1917 at Columbia also.[90]

Taking the liberty of showing Erskine some of Roth's sonnets, Tannenbaum soon after initiated the concept of the Little Magazine, to be called *The Lyric*.[91] With it, Roth gained a reputation as a hard-driving and discriminating editor, capable of bringing to people's attention some of the best poets in America and England. The first number was published in May 1917, with five more issues through October. Erskine acted as literary adviser. Among the contributors to the first eight-page issue were Louis Untermeyer (founder of *The Seven Arts* and at the time a contributor to *The Masses*), Margaret Widdemer, Laura Benet (William Rose's sister), and Herbert Brucken (editor of

the literary journal *The Minaret*). Poets in the four subsequent 1917 issues included Sara Teasdale, Amy Lowell, James Oppenheim, Leslie N. Jennings, John Gould Fletcher, Babette Deutsch, Clinton Scollard, William Rose Benet, and D. H. Lawrence.[92] There were two supplements and, also in 1917, four separate volumes, carrying the imprint "The Lyric Publishing Company." The first was Erskine's *The Shadowed Hour,* which he subsidized himself.[93] Roth's own book of poems, *First Offering,* was published in October 1917.[94] There was no impropriety, by the way, on Roth's part regarding reprinting three poems from Lawrence's *Look! We Have Come Through!,* in versions recently revised for their appearance in the book of that name, in *The Lyric.* In fact, according to Lawrence scholar Christopher Pollnitz, if Roth's request had reached the poet, he would have been glad to oblige.[95] This contrasts starkly with the editor's objectionable, because unauthorized, printings of a story and two poems of Lawrence's in *Two Worlds Monthly* in 1926–27.

Even apart from the free and flattering advertisements they provided for writers and their publishers, there is every indication that Roth and his coeditor, Frank Tannenbaum (chiefly the former; this was his chosen profession), had done exceptionally well with their magazine. A *New York Times Book Review* essay on recent poetry found that the bound volume of the first six numbers of *The Lyric* "essays a higher and more ambitious flight than most [college magazines], and with considerable success."[96] Those who wrote directly to Roth congratulating him on the magazine were just as impressed. Giving constructive evaluations of *The Lyric*'s contents and grateful for how their poems looked in print, contributors were universally enthusiastic.

Amy Lowell, who sent Roth a poem only because of previous gratifying experiences with Columbia staff and students, told him she did not hold out much success for little magazines like *The Lyric.* Their subscription lists were too small and distribution to bookstores was difficult. The war made it even more chancy. Roth demurred, but Lowell was right. The magazine did not survive 1917 as a university-sponsored publication. Part of the reason was that Roth had decided, after the first volume was complete, to change its focus, making it a literary journal rather than simply a poetry magazine. Hearing of this, Tannenbaum resigned as coeditor.[97] He did not see how such a review could compete with nationally distributed ones like *The Dial.*

Figure 5. Sam Roth, seated with dog, and Frank Tannenbaum, standing above Sam, on the Tannenbaum farm, fall 1915. By permission of Maryjane Treloar and the Roth estate.

Nothing came of Roth's plan. That, and other incidents, made his daughter conclude that eventually her father "made a mess of *The Lyric*."[98] One reason is his incompetence at handling the details of business affairs. Erskine was critical of his bookkeeping on the professor's own supplement.[99] Adelaide was also thinking of an overly ambitious poetry contest her father organized after the war, when Roth resumed *The Lyric* independently. Another problem was his over-aggressive demeanor. Frank wrote a critical letter warning him that he was getting a reputation for arrogance and short temper, specifically because he made people feel that since they were not as brilliant as himself, they were wasting his time.[100]

On the eve of America's entry into the war, the two friends each got married. With a world war in progress, they thought it their "first duty" ("CMAM," 159). Frank had fallen in love; Sam responded to Pauline's love for him. Tannenbaum and Roth were eventually drafted, but Roth, not called to serve, went to work for the Jewish Welfare Board. With the Armistice, Frank returned to Columbia to work toward his Ph.D. Sam did not. He began his family life, continuing *The Lyric* on his own, getting essays, reviews, and poems published and making a name for himself as a rising man of letters in New York.

CHAPTER 2

1917–1925

Prelude to an International Protest:
A Rising, Pugnacious Man of Letters

The decade between Samuel Roth's twenty-fifth and thirty-fifth years of age, the middle of his journey, included accolades and humiliation, recovery and betrayal, profits and bankruptcy. It was a disorienting seesaw on which iron will fueled perseverance.

A Tortured Wedding Night

"But who could show Mishillim so much love that he would notice it?" A strange thought for a bridegroom. This is what Roth recalls he asked himself as he accepted congratulations at the party following his marriage on May 18, 1917 ("CMAM," 159). Yet Pauline's commitment to her "poet with the patched pants" was so ironclad that it survived a serious flirtation her intended initiated with the poet Marie Syrkin, a fellow member of the small group of writers called the Ugerki, in 1916.

Marie and Maurice Samuel (later novelist and biographer of Sholem Aleichem, Y. L. Peretz, and Theodor Herzl) were in love. Roth admired Maurice, but he took advantage of Maurice's absence from New York to kiss Marie one summer night as they were talking outside the seaside hotel where Marie and her family were passing the summer. In the case of an aspiring ghetto boy with as yet inchoate dreams and desires, it is impossible to tell just what mixture of sexual libido and ambition overpowered his responsibility to Pauline, Maurice, and Marie. She was a beautiful, brilliant young woman and the daughter of a famous Socialist Zionist, Nahum Syrkin. Marie saw Sam as "an ascetic looking young man, rather handsome, tall, thin, dark, always filled with prophetic fulminations."[1] In those days, the kiss was a declaration of serious commitment between a young man and woman. Roth recalled in "Count Me among the Missing" that Marie had "shook to its foundations the citadel of his life with Pauline."[2] Maurice's response was understandably indignant, if gentlemanly. He pointed out to Sam that he was not ready for marriage, having been seeing prostitutes and flirting with many women. The rift between Marie and Maurice was resolved, although Roth's close friendship with both had been sorely wounded.[3]

Roth's wedding-night question might be rephrased as follows: Could he return other people's love? How much love did his father, mother, and wife need to offer him so he would be sure to accept it, and take the responsibility of returning it? That question might have been what he meant by calling his love for Pauline an insecure "citadel." A loving commitment would mean prioritizing, on some occasions, his loved one's desires and plans over his own. Only that way would his love be a mighty fortress. If he did not have the strength to erect such a fortress, and went his own way, he would take that path staggering under guilt. His awareness of this universal challenge shows moral acuity. His choices often pointed in another direction. When Charles Reznikoff used Samuel Roth as the model for his protagonist in *By the Waters of Manhattan* (1930), his dispassionate understanding of his friend's ambitions and his dilemma is one of the book's strongest features.

On that same far-from-carefree wedding night, Roth had an equally idiosyncratic thought, which he records in "Count Me among the Missing" with seeming objectivity. He writes of himself in the third person. The couple stayed at the apartment Sam had shared with Frank "in his golden days" before entering Columbia. It was all he could afford. At least the newlyweds were alone. Pauline undressed in front of the bed "he and Frank had occupied."

> And he [Roth] thought: "The river which divides the two worlds
> we live in will need more enchantments even known to Caballah to
> modify and rearrange these profound, contradictory appearances into
> any semblance of unity.
> God. God. God." (161)

His daughter thinks this passage may indicate Sam and Frank shared a physical passion for each other. If Roth was bisexual, he hid it deeply. In 1942 he wrote cryptically that Frank "befriended me, and that leads to something for which we haven't yet an appropriate name, though I know it is not friendship."[4] The last line of helpless silent invocation in the wedding-night bedroom

Samuel Roth, Infamous Modernist

("God. God. God")—which may be both a nervous bridegroom's thought and the middle-aged writer's own perspective on this key moment—is more than a deep sigh of resignation. It suggests not only replacement of a loved one with a very different person but an intimation of abandonment at least as old as what Mishillim felt when his father told the rabbi about his son's masturbating. In both cases, a deep mutual need bows to the consoling promise of maturity, community trust, and God's blessing. It seemed, although Mishillim could not articulate it at the time, that his father had chosen patriarchal duty over his son's individuality. Although Roth does not tell us that his father's act was a version of Abraham's binding of Isaac, it might have produced a powerful emotional shock (whether or not Isaac suffered one has been debated). It quite possibly replaced innocent trust with wary, fear-soaked responsibility. Calling desperately on God for relief on one's wedding night would bring solace to a man doubting the affection of loved ones. Roth's daughter remarks that his earlier question at the wedding celebration about whether he could acknowledge love "is surprisingly perceptive from my egocentric dad."[5] The same awareness seems to be a feature of watching his bride undress and feeling his heart pound, an anticipation of something very different from desire for her. Was whatever now-shattered mutuality he shared with Frank transferable to a woman?

The critic Burton Rascoe (see epigraph) stated that integral to the "Judaic strain in modern letters" is a wavering between extremes of idealism and fervid anxiety. Writers, and their protagonists, know that trust of others and in an inscrutable divine strategy for mankind replaces one's demons with mutuality and its duties. However, they "never take things easy or let well enough alone."[6] "Egocentricity" and "sarcastic irony" are other Judaic traits Rasco points to. Writers remain conscious that love and duty throw a net of restraint over self-fulfilling cravings and ambitions. Their demons have rooted so deeply in their flesh and psyche (as Mishillim's own *khayi rui* had done) that exorcizing them is to wrestle with one's own double (as in Cahan's *The Rise of David Levinsky*, Ornitz's *Haunch Paunch and Jowl*, or I. B. Singer's "Taibele and Her Demon"). "Jewish ambivalence" is at work. As Rascoe writes, citing Heine, the modern "Judaic" writer must describe these splits or contradictions. Ironically, perhaps the best example may be not a Jew but the anti anti-Semitic modernist, James Joyce, writing about his own Ulysses, cuckolded Leopold Bloom, whose humiliations, isolation, masochistic erotic self-reflections, facing up to persecutors, and visions of "the opposite of hatred" he shared. As Philip Roth asserted, "Life *is* and."

Existing within this strain are Samuel Roth's confinement in responsibilities to his country at war, his love for and resentment of his father, and his doubts and yearnings regarding Marie, Frank, and Pauline.

By the Waters of Manhattan

Charles Reznikoff's *By the Waters of Manhattan* is a gentle, almost elegiac picture of Jewish Lower East Side life, shadowed by the suffering of the protagonist's mother, and her dogged resourcefulness in coming to America and managing a home for her husband and their two children. The son, Ezekiel, was based on Samuel Roth, who did not like the novel, although he admired Reznikoff's poetry and had published a forty-eight-page selection in 1920. The sunlight and the shadows Reznikoff depicts are in Lower East Side souls as well as streets. They symbolize the pleasures and the painful metamorphoses of the immigrants struggling to become Americans. Another achievement is showing the intensity of his protagonist's American dreams: his needs are for reputation, sex, capital, and getting published. No writers, artists, or radicals frequent Ezekiel's bookstore, which was modeled on Roth's Poetry Book Shop, but on a much more modest scale. However, Ezekiel, like Roth, did sell many books on consignment.[7] Both had homemade placards with comments on various books, and both had their own name on every sign. And Ezekiel does read aloud, although without Roth's insistence, poems by his favorite author, "J. P. Irvine" (E. A. Robinson).

Why did the proprietor of the Poetry Book Shop, without mentioning the intimate familiarity of its setting and protagonist, dislike *By the Waters of Manhattan* enough to write (probably many years later) that Reznikoff had "broken" his promise of being a leading and little-appreciated poet? An answer lies in the final pages, when Ezekiel, looking into a mirror, sees a "swindler." That would have probed a wound in Sam's psyche, one related to his ambivalence about his marriage as an insecure "citadel" and his sharp awareness of betrayal, his own and other people's. Ezekiel finally makes a success of his bookstore and is deeply involved in an affair with a beautiful woman, half Jewish. He may love her, and is sensually aroused, but regrets the loss of freedom. While Reznikoff would most likely have known nothing of Roth's ambivalence on his wedding night, the panicky questions the latter asked himself (and God) are similar to Ezekiel's problem, which involves the question of to what degree responsibility for his loved one blocks strictly personal needs. Also, Ezekiel's bookstore business anchors him to a set of routines regarding assets and debits. That being so, he has swindled himself, and his loving mistress.

The word *swindle*, from the hard-nosed, all-consuming business world, is well chosen. Ezekiel feels that his newfound responsibility as shop owner and lover takes the form of a double door, one marked "love" and the other "money," perhaps closing off a life-giving destiny.

"My work is with the spirit of man," says Ezekiel, striving to sing as his parents could not in a strange land. Roth, reading Reznikoff's novel, would not believe that its author, in his protagonist Ezekiel, had uncovered his own heart and soul, he who was also David Zorn, disdainer of schlemiels and swindlers, and Mishillim, acolyte of Yeshea. Milton Hindus (in 1950 Roth published his groundbreaking study of Céline) wrote that Reznikoff's protagonist was modeled on Stephen Dedalus, another withdrawn young man struggling to sing hymns composed in suffering. Ezekiel, like Dedalus, was destined to escape from the nightmare of history, not make money, argues Hindus.[8] The implication, a just one, is that Ezekiel is unlike Roth, who became a publisher of borderline erotica and gossip books. Further, Reznikoff was not commenting on his friend specifically but on young Jewish writers generally, struggling for a stable personal identity. Still, the consonance between Ezekiel and Samuel is clear, and was unlikely to have escaped Roth. It may have alienated and shamed him. He would have first read the novel either when he was in prison or when he had just been released, due to his selling contemporary classics like *Ulysses, My Life and Loves,* and *Lady Chatterley,* but without the permission of the Vice Society smuthounds, the police, or the authors. Perhaps he did not want to be reminded how remote he was from delineating "the spirit of man."

The Poetry Book Shop

The bookshop owner spends idle hours watching the legs of female passersby; his store being three steps down from the street, their legs were irresistible. Aleister Crowley enters the shop while Djuna Barnes is browsing; she screams and runs out (he had run after her with his fly open when she answered his advertisement for a secretary). The owner introduces Mark and Carl Van Doren to Edwin Arlington Robinson at one of his weekly dinners with the poet; it is due to this meeting that *The Nation* publishes Robinson's poetry.[9] A woman from Louisville, with whom the owner is in love, is present when a city marshal attempts to padlock the place for non-payment of rent. She writes a check for the necessary funds. In the back room is, not a set of pornographic books (they are in a corner cabinet), but a still. In this room Remo Buffano stages marionette performances, Man Ray takes photographs, and the proprietor himself gives a course of lectures on American poetry (six talks for five dollars). In the office, writers, including poet Charles Reznikoff, borrow the owner's typewriter to prepare submissions.[10]

The last of these stories about Sam's Poetry Book Shop ("will reconcile mankind to Greenwich Village," stated its newsletter) may be the only one he has not embellished. He opened it at 49 West Eighth Street in the West Village in the fall of 1919, naming it after Harold Monro's renowned London bookstore. Roth soon moved to larger quarters at number 61.[11] It was not financial success that caused the move, and the shop failed late in 1920. Meanwhile, it was clearly a lot of fun. Roth met writers, political radicals, actors, and editors such as Sholem Asch, Edna St. Vincent Millay, Floyd Dell, Mina Loy, Louis Grudin, John Reed, Louise Bryant, Ben Reitman, Rose Pastor Stokes, Ludwig Lewisohn, and Maxwell Bodenheim.[12]

He published a catalogue in early 1920 that indicates he kept a fine selection of American and English poetry.[13] The former, Roth said, was his major concern, for the country was underrepresented in published poetry books. His catalogue excerpts poetry from *The Lyric*: Robinson, Erskine, David Morton—and Samuel Roth. Among the more expensive works catalogued were the kind of gallantiana, or books with esoteric or erotic subject matter, that censors would probably overlook. Examples are George Moore's *Story Teller's Holiday* ($35) and Pierre Louys's *Aphrodite* ($25). Roth also printed up occasional newsletters and his summaries of books published. His bookshop did not fail for lack of effort on his part, but for the thinness of his resources.

Another signal feature, adopted by Reznikoff for his novel, and typical of the pugnacious owner, was a set of placards containing Roth's comments on some of the books. He placed these on a counter displaying the books on which he had strong opinions. "You will find a complete alphabet in some of these pages. In cutting out the letters for your collection be careful not to spoil them as they are the only pages of this book which maintain their integrity." "He stands erect in these pages who cannot do so anywhere else."[14] Roth describes these "as causes which underlay the unpopularity of my business." Each placard was signed "Samuel Roth." Adelaide says her father loved to see his name in print. As the owner of the New York Poetry Book Shop, he was, after all, a center of attention for noted artists and writers.[15] But that was because they were patronizing his shop, and in some cases taking advantage of his willingness to store their property, kibitz with them and their friends, take them to dinner, lend them money, and let them use his typewriter and back room. Of course it was true that Roth had been an editor, and was a writer

CATALOGUE OF SAMUEL ROTH *at the* NEW YORK POETRY BOOKSHOP 49 West 8th Street, NEW YORK

January 1st, 1920

Figure 6. Catalogue of books for sale at Sam Roth's Poetry Book Shop. Note the entrance is three steps down from the street. By permission of the Roth estate.

himself, his latest book-length poem having been published in 1919 by Boni and Liveright (*Europe: A Book for America*).

There were precedents in Greenwich Village for Sam Roth and his eccentric bookselling style. The most notable was the saturnine Joseph Kling,[16] known for throwing people out of his shop, as Roth bragged that he did in the case of Herbert Gorman, whose first book of poetry *The Lyric* had issued ("CMAM," 247). Kling, like Roth, was a Little Magazine publisher. His *The Pagan* (1916–22) took its place among Village institutions. Like Roth a poet and editor, he often self-published. Bernard Guilbert Guerney, at the Blue Faun Book Shop on Twenty-third Street, published his own satiric avant-garde tabloid-style newspaper titled *Jack Ketch the Hangman* (subtitle: "What America Needs Is a Good Swift Kick in the Pants").

A photograph of the Poetry Book Shop shows a handsome layout. Bookshelves ran along the length of the east and west walls. Entering, one's eye fell on a long center table with the most salable works; a rolltop desk, with typewriter; and, as far from the entrance to the shop as possible, a smallish, narrow bookcase with glass-enclosed shelves. Beyond the glass were books considered pornographic, having been declared illegal due to contemporary court action by reason of their explicit sexual slang or because of their descriptions of sexual acts.

Sam's assistant at the shop was Herbert Diamant. When the shop opened, Herbert was a constant browser from open time to closing, never buying a book but resuming the next morning at the page where he had left off the previous day. One morning he collapsed in the street due to near starvation. Roth, sympathizing with a ragged, friendless scholar such as he had himself been five years earlier, gave him a job ("CMAM," 167–68). Pauline called Herbert "the ghost." He often did not look up from a book he was studying if a customer asked a question. As Adelaide Kugel noticed, Herbert's real function was as a "paid confidant for Sam." When Roth sought Herbert's advice about whether he should go to Europe, the answer was that he should; "Pauline would be all right." Which is why he asked.[17] The prologue to Roth's own self-destructive, anti-Semitic *Jews Must Live* begins, "Dear Herbert." Herbert was the one person who would not be reproachful toward the *meshuganah* writer.

Sam writes in detail about how he acquired the pornography in the glass case. Fourth Avenue's Book Row was the country's premier location for learning about books by kibitzing with the bookshop owners and clerks. Alexander Deutschberger's book and magazine shop occupied the basement at 117 Fourth Avenue.[18] Upon one of many visits, Roth learned that Deutschberger

Figure 7. Sam Roth (*right*) and his cousin and close friend, Joseph Roth, at the Poetry Book Shop in 1920. Note roll top desk with typewriter at back left (used by various Village writers as well as Roth), the books with upper covers visible (some with placards by Sam Roth commenting on the work), and the small glass-covered cabinet at Sam Roth's left where erotica was kept. By permission of Maryjane Treloar and the Roth estate.

was on a ninety-day "business trip": on Blackwell's Island for selling a copy of *Fanny Hill.* Roth sent him two dollars a week for the period when he was in jail, and after the bookseller's release he retired to Paris, from whence he shipped a package to the Roth apartment on the Grand Concourse. He wrote that it was in return for his young friend's generosity, so Sam expected it to be pornography. Eventually, bookseller Frank Shay bought the lot (or that part of it Roth was willing to part with), and thus Sam found his generosity to the bearded basement bookseller well rewarded. He realized $130, which may have helped him finance the prizes for his poetry contest ("CMAM," 176–79).

The Lyric after the War

After the Armistice, Roth resumed publishing *The Lyric,* with the first number of volume 3, dated January 1919. The final postwar issue had been January/February 1918, the third number of volume 2.[19] His major goal being solvency, and knowing that a lofty purpose would attract subscribers, he founded the Lyric Society. Drawing on his experiences as editor, he stated, "Writing verse is the most universal occupation in this country," for he had read contributions from people as diverse as street sweepers and railroad moguls. He rehearsed his achievement of getting many good poems in print, listing once again the poets whom *The Lyric* had published. Such enthusiasm was sure, he believed, to make practicing poets want to contribute. So would the plan to hold a contest, endowed by "a generous American" (possibly in-law Samuel Alter), to choose three books to be published in 1919. The winning authors would each receive $500. Two "representatives" would travel throughout the country to arrange for booksellers and libraries to carry *The Lyric*. Assuring readers of the March 1919 number that "the seeds of the idea have been sown broadcast throughout the land," he called for $5,000 to continue the good work the representatives were about to begin.[20]

While there were no more issues of *The Lyric* after 1919, Roth did manage partial success, for he was able that year to put out five numbers of volume 3 and the double issue (numbers 1 and 2) of volume 4. He may have gotten a few generous donations, in addition to the unnamed patron—if he existed—who gave at least $1,500 for the contest to choose three books. Roth admitted he took out a loan to keep the Lyric Society and its contest solvent.[21] If the $1,500 came from a bank loan, it is a further indication of Sam Roth's daring, and financially unwise, risk-taking to further his career. Five years later he would overextend himself by publishing four magazines, one of which contained the infamous *Ulysses* excerpts.

Volumes 3 and 4 of *The Lyric* featured poems by E. A. Robinson, Clinton Scollard, Babette Deutsch, Louis Grudin, and Clement Wood. The poetry prizes were awarded, although the process just about sent the editor around the bend.[22] The volume of submissions made it difficult for Roth to plow through them, as he had to find time for his child's and wife's needs. He was also in the process of renting space for his next project, the Poetry Book Shop. After an explanatory letter to W. S. Braithwaite, the only remaining judge in addition to himself, Roth declared Edwin Arlington Robinson the first-prize winner for *Lancelot* and mailed him the $500 check. It seemed this was the only prize awarded. Roth arranged for Thomas Seltzer to publish *Lancelot* in 1920, with 450 copies specially bound for the Lyric Society in 1921.[23] Despite his labors at his failing magazine and at his bookshop, Roth published a long appreciation of Robinson in *The Bookman* early in 1920.[24] Robinson responded gratefully, assuring Roth he read the piece "with a very real sense of obligation. . . . Your generally positive note is something very rare."[25]

Edwin Arlington Robinson

Roth first read Robinson's work while at Columbia. He became such an enthusiast that, on a visit to London in 1921, he convinced Thomas Moult, editor of the literary magazine *Voices,* to dedicate a number to Robinson.[26] He also spoke at that time to a leading British literary journalist, J. C. Squire, who later wrote a long article about Robinson in the *London Mercury.* Squire welcomed Robinson to London in 1923; his 1921 letters to Roth indicate that the latter had sent him some of the poet's work. Roth may well deserve more credit than he has been given for preparing the way for Robinson's warm reception two years later, in which Squire was a key figure.[27] One night a tipsy Frank Harris, seeking shelter from the rain, opined that there was little use for a poetry shop in a country where no one wrote good poetry. This was equivalent to asking Rudyard Kipling if there were any real men left in England. "No one?" A copy of *The Man against the Sky* was brandished, and recited from ("CMAM," 173–75).

Roth's best appreciation of "E.A.R." is not in his interesting essay in *The Bookman* but in a more idiosyncratic piece, also in that journal, about a bookseller who introduces a female British browser to the poet's work.[28] From this we learn the poems Roth liked most: "The Man against the Sky," "Eros Turannos," "Flammode," "Calverly's," as well as "Children of the Night," known for its character sketches. He also states that he thinks Robinson a prophet of an ongoing degeneration in American moral resolve and intellectual rigor. Writing about people "on the edge of the abyss, . . . the kindliness of [Robinson's] bearing forebodes evil. Knowing our doom, he loves us." In his essay in *The Bookman,* Roth asserted, "Robinson insists on individual and national righteousness, on mercy and gentleness to the old and bereaved—indeed his insistence on the ancient virtues is, under the circumstances, nothing less than iconoclastic."[29] Regarding the issue of *Voices* devoted to him, Robinson wrote Roth, "I hope you understand how much indebted to you I am for your loyalty to me and to my work."[30]

When Samuel Roth knew him, Robinson was pursuing what this austere and single-minded craftsman had described as "the Gleam, the Vision, and the Word" that people who recognize their inner force must struggle toward. To consider Roth's appreciation of Robinson is a way of seeing what he learned from this major poet and of understanding as well that he could not follow him in his dedication to art. "John Everdown," whose compulsion to "follow the women wherever they call" was especially strong when he could hide it by arduous journeys under cover of darkness, must have given Roth a start, especially if he read it in 1916, when he made advances to Marie Syrkin despite his understanding with Pauline, or in 1921, when he had the aforementioned affair with a young woman on the boat to London. The extent to which Roth ultimately lost his focus as poet, man of letters, and literary publisher—due to the international protest regarding his reprinting of *Ulysses*—is an echo of the fate of some of Robinson's subjects in *Children of the Night, The Man against the Sky,* or *The Town Down the River,* all books his friend and admirer read and advocated for his readers, customers, interviewees, and fellow poets. Adelaide Kugel thought "The Wandering Jew" (in *The Three Taverns,* 1920) was modeled on Robinson's observations about her father. She also argued that Robinson knew about Sam's interest in prophecy, as he well might have done; the prophetic *Europe: A Book for America* appeared in 1919.[31]

Roth's Poetry and Prose, 1917–1925

That Samuel Roth was a poet of promise in his twenties is confirmed by a score of talented writers who were contributors to *The Lyric,* fellow editors, and friends. He contributed to a large number of periodicals: *Poetry, The Menorah Journal,* the *Boston Evening Transcript, Contemporary Verse* (the most successful poetry magazine after Harriet Monroe's *Poetry*), *Minaret,* and *Midland.* Louis Untermeyer, in a lengthy 1921 essay in *The Menorah Journal* on "The Jewish Spirit in Modern American Poetry," listed Roth among "younger poets" such as Louis Gruden, Elias Lieberman, Arthur Guiterman, and Franklin P. Adams, praising his "sonnets and unrhymed philippics." Marguerite Wilkerson printed one of his excellent "Nustscha" sonnets in her anthology *New Voices* (1919); Stanley Coblentz anthologized eight of these in *Modern American Lyrics: An Anthology* (1924); and Israel Zangwill recommended him as one of the "young poets of the Diaspora" in a major speech on American Zionism.[32]

Marie Syrkin was moved by a few of his solemnly meditative poems, especially "Yahrzeit," in *The Nation* in 1920. She did take the occasion to remind "the King [who] can do no wrong" of the "horrible lapses of taste and rhythm" in other poems. "Of course, by now you are mortally offended and have consigned me to the ignorant rabble that dares dictate to genius."[33] She was back again when Sam published a cleverly phrased bit of light verse poking fun at a poem by Arturo Giovannitti in *The Liberator* (a successor to *The Masses*) in 1919. "Why oh why do you do it? ... You could produce *big* stuff but thru sheer perversity and laziness you write verse in which flashes of real beauty and blatant amateurishness play hide and seek." "Don't be angry," she concludes, "I write this for your soul's sake."[34] She thus anticipated Siegfried Sassoon's more dispassionate opinion when Roth showed him some of his verses two years later.[35]

Roth's most impressive lyrics not in sonnet form were published in *The Nation* and *Poetry*.[36] Dramatic monologues, they show more Robinsonian influence than does his other work, being intensely revealing depictions of inner tension and troubled self-awareness. They embody the eastern European Jewish awareness of the saving grace of faith in extremis. "Yahrzeit" is a dialogue between a man who appears on a rainy night to light mourning lamps, and a young man whose beloved has abandoned him. He decries the lamplighter "as merciless as God." The experience of spiritual numbness, paralysis of will, and isolation is a universal Jewish leitmotif, as is the Diaspora setting: a stormy night, a hovel, an ominous flickering of the yellow candlelight. The lamplighter spends the night in the young man's shack. Dawn nears; the guest rises to pray and leave, telling his host with merciless bluntness that he has to deal with his loss by expressing a universally shared love that is not subject to betrayal:

> Do roadways lift themselves toward the sky?
> Do stones roll passionately into brooks?
> And have you ever seen a hillside lift up arms
> And reach out to the passing clouds for love?
> You are a road, a stone, a hillside, brother.

The simplicity of the diction, imagery, and rhythm, and the free-verse medium, give a dignity that show the poet learned from his critics, and Robinson. So does the guest's unstated respect for his "brother"; he chooses to let him see for himself how three seemingly paradoxical events—roads lifting themselves to the sky, stones rolling themselves into water, and hillsides lifting themselves high enough to envelop clouds—can have a spiritual reality, instead of being tropes in a love song.

The poem "Kol Nidre" was honored by an appearance (after revisions) in *Poetry*. It's about history as nightmare: being caught up in a mystery one is not able to renounce or find one's way out of. God's command to Abraham regarding the sacrifice of Isaac was the first such event, taking place not in myth but in Jewish history.[37] It did not end in nightmare, although it might have the source of many in Isaac, including those about the "end of days" he tried to reveal on his death bed (Genesis 49:1-3). Roth's "Kol Nidre" gives his readers a reality check that enforces grim attention. Hearing the chant on the eve of the Day of Atonement brings to the speaker's mind armies "without a battle cry" retreating, "wrath of midnight storms," shofars sounding days of reckoning for heedless dead, ancient Israel losing its faith, lifelong anxiety and, still, the need to question. "God! Will this never have end?" With that, "a knock upon my window pane, fumbling / Black flapping wings, a voice wild with despair; / "Traitor! What have you mused in Ascalon?" Ascalon is a city in the Negev, site of both Philistine and Jewish atrocities during ancient wars. Guilt is as vivid as humiliation and confusion in Roth's poem; despair becomes a death wish.

> Hurl me,
> If so you will, down the ravines of death,
> Where every sunbeam is a thorn to prick,
> And every flower is a wound to bear,
> All loveliness a memory of wrath
> And spirit madness!

A convincing sense of spiritual agony is difficult to sustain—and any decline into bathos would have been evident to the editors of *Poetry*. Roth presents too strong a statement of endurance to let that happen. The last stanza finds the singer moving on, and the speaker exclaims, "*There* is my star!" God is stern, but also a star creator, each are someone's guardian angel. There's an integrity, intensity, and natural human voice in both poems that would make Robinson proud. Among Roth's contemporaries, Emma Lazarus, James Oppenheim, and H. N. Bialik achieved similar effects with similar subjects.

The predominant form Roth mastered was the sonnet. They appeared in *Contemporary Verse, Minaret*, the *Boston Evening Transcript*, and *Poetry* before he left for England. The elegiac sonnet sequence "Nustscha" is a triumph, although some archaic phrasing and forced rhyming is, despite Marie's playful scolding, still present. Marguerite Wilkerson wrote him that he had made his "words and phrases and sentences sound natural—as if they belonged to human mouths and voices."[38] Jessie B. Rittenhouse, poet, anthologist, and influential critic for the *New York Times* and several periodicals, loved particularly numbers 11, 12, and 13, about Roth's uncles:[39] the hunter, Raphael; Mendel, the shepherd; and Aaron, the scholar, at the shivah (weeklong mourning period) for his father's death, opening "the yellow book":

> And slowly read into the trembling air
> And they leaned forward at the mellow sound,
> And glory lingered in their very look,
> And in their hearts they thought that God was there.

"Filled with the beauty of strange places and strange life," Rittenhouse said of these sonnets, and added that the characters provided both concreteness and empathy to the poems. So did the portrait of the father, stern, meditative, aloof, and the one chosen to chant blessings. The speaker assimilates his own innocence as a child with the natural progression of time in his birthplace:

> He who on a wall
> Watched the boughs darken under drifting snow;
> In every opening blossom saw an elf,
> In each closed flower felt the darkness swell;
> And from each autumn leaf saw the light fall
> Over the earth—a sad, strange lad—myself.

The overwhelming presence in the sonnets is the eponymous town itself, called forth in the first word and addressed directly in almost every poem. In the last line in the sequence, the narrator is in tears. But they are not tears of sentimentality. The sadness is a universal adult response to the experience of loss and fallibility. It has also something of a traditional Jewish consciousness in the hints at self-reproach and patient humility: "One may come and beat / Loud at my door and clamor, and I shrink / To open lest he see how poor I am." The publisher Samuel Roth could not afford to respond this way when the knock, on various occasions from 1928 to 1954, was by the police.

The five "Sonnets on Sinai" that *The Menorah Journal*[40] published show almost complete restraint of the lapses Marie Syrkin pointed out: posturing, clichéd phrasing, archaisms, inverted adjective-noun combinations, and consequent awkward verses. However, the epic force of the story Roth tells is well sustained, the imagery effectively graphic and mysterious, and Moses' voice forebodingly scintillating. Moses returns the Ten Commandments to God due to the failure of men to obey the Covenant:

> Know: I shall stand once more at Sinai's foot,
> Torah in hand, world white to Heaven's rim,
> Thunder shaking the highland to the root;
> At God's descent shall the heavens dim
> And as His voice will bid all earth be mute
> I'll rise and give the Torah back to Him.

The finality of such an act would be devastating. Roth's invitation to the reader to consider it gives an arresting intensity to his poem.

As a poet, Roth once more attempted this kind of mystic eloquence. This was *Europe: A Book for America* (1919), the most ambitious work of his youth, in which he attempted "the warning voice" he had used—with more success— in the "Sonnets on Sinai." It's clear from the dedicatory verses to C. N. Bialik ("Look West / And call for me!") that the prophetic voice in the 107-page poem is that of Roth himself. His voice in the first half of the book is callous, contemptuous, and sadistic. Europe should be fed a diet of dung; its people are degenerating into beasts who will soon throw children from the Eiffel Tower for amusement; they will sneer at women's suffrage and shorter work hours. Europe's leaders are worth only contempt. "Europe, let me be your doctor. / With a hammer let me break open those iron jaws / And pour a pail of your bitterest spleen down / Your throat."

All this in philippics of no more than twelve lines each. Roth was definitely capable of subtlety, but he does not invite multiple interpretations or show an ironic voice in *Europe*. The *Hebrew Standard* heard "a bruised soul, that has suffered variously and vicariously through all the ages, that speaks now pitifully, now boldly, now almost blasphemously, but at its best, reaches the nobility and optimism of the ancient sages and most reverently declares its faith in the everlasting God." This reviewer, like the *New York Evening Post*'s, seems to have been especially impressed by the second part of the book, where Roth appeals to the Zionist impulse of his own people. "The face of Israel will shine with power when Europe / Will be a name difficult to remember." The speaker also contrasts America with Europe, praising it as replacing the high culture of Europe with its own creativity. It's puzzling that Roth sees his own country's genius in the "terrible wisdom / Of Baseball, Football / And Boxing." He may be referring to the ideal of competition under rules ensuring fairness for all, regardless of race or class. Solely in America and Israel will the Jewish people be happy, according to Roth.

Only Herbert Gorman, in the *New York Sun,* and Nelson Crawford, in *Poetry,* felt that Roth's disquisitions on history and politics were without coherent purpose.[41] The *New York Post* review, though mixed, was probably the one most likely to entice readers. Roth thought so, for he quoted from it in full-page advertisements for *Europe* in several issues of his *Two Worlds Monthly:* "From his observation tower in that section of New York in which East and West meet, in which commerce and art and wild pleasure mix elbows . . . Samuel Roth has looked up and down the world and seen many things and prophesied." The book was also praised by reviewers in *The Nation,* the *Hebrew Standard,* and the *New York Sun* as "visionary" and "reverent."

Europe would appeal principally to a Jewish American audience. Judging from the reviews, it found its target. The *Menorah Journal*'s "Lithmus" reviewed *Europe* with Waldo Frank's *America* as "Two Arraignments of Present

Day Europe"; he praised Roth's poem for being more subtle than its speaker's pronouncements would indicate. The poem had "the passionate restraint of genuine inspiration." Elias Lieberman, in *The American Hebrew,* concluded his lengthy appreciation by declaring that in *Europe* Roth had realized the "promise" indicated by *First Offering.*[42]

The volume's final poem, "Thus Saith the Lord," is the longest and most audacious. God speaks to the Hebrew poets through the ages, who seem to morph with Roth himself. When God speaks to this paragon, he becomes a humble admirer. "I, your God, whose earnest / Is only of darkness and desolation, dared not look out often for fear of meeting your eyes." But the Almighty must now do so, after Jews for centuries settled for selling goods in the shtetl market squares, meanwhile in the streets absorbing beatings from the "gentiles" that "I, your God, was powerless to stop." The experiences of America, and Zionism, now present themselves as events that will put a stop to the nightmare of history. God actually prostrates himself in requesting forgiveness for tolerating the contempt "your own people" directed to this poet and, marching with him, the exiled prophets of the ages. That the Messiah would be despised as an (apparent) apostate by fellow Jews is a core Hasidic belief.[43] The Almighty confesses: "wearied of watching from the skies / the creeping ways of lice and men, and [*sic*] in one ter- / rible moment the keys of creation slipped from / my fingers down into the fathomless depths of chaos. / . . . But I dreaded only your coming." Now, in redress, God will muster out of the clouds and lightning the force to destroy the small minded who "sneered at your youth / And mocked your manhood." None of the critics comment on this bizarre final section. Its unmistakable criticism and even humbling of God himself in Jewish tradition is older than Spinoza, or Jesus, allusions to whom in Roth's poem are not unexpected, given the appearances of Yeshea to him. That God's weakness or even madness must be confronted is Hasidic as well.[44]

Although Charles Reznikoff and Louis Zukofsky were friends as well as employees in Roth's English Institute, and although he corresponded with Ezra Pound, Amy Lowell, and H.D., Roth never experimented with objectivist, symbolist, or imagist verse. He disciplined himself to stay within traditional stanza forms. His themes—anxiety and loneliness, the experience of spiritual sloth, atonement, the responsibilities of the future, the ability to face God—are those of the Enlightenment, the Diaspora, and the Jewish American experience. The poets he published in *Two Worlds* were modernist in their sexual explicitness, terse diction, and suggestive images but were conventional in diction and style: Arthur Symons, E. Powys Mathers, D. H. Lawrence, Thomas Hardy, Carl Rakowsi. In an open letter to *The Nation* in 1920, Roth identified his favorite English and American poets: Thomas Hardy, G. K. Chesterton, Ralph Hodgson, Masefield, Vachel Lindsay, Sandburg, Frost, and of course Robinson, Yeats, Pound and Eliot as well as the high modernists.[45]

Roth's most ambitious prose writing was his *Now and Forever: A Conversation with Mr. Israel Zangwill on the Jew and the Future With a Preface by Mr. Zangwill, the text by Samuel Roth* (1925). The dedication is to Rabbi Judah L. Magnus, the first chancellor of Hebrew University and founder of the American Jewish Committee. Magnus believed that the Diaspora experience and Palestine were both good choices for Jews. However, he felt that if a Jewish state in Palestine could not be an entity in which cooperation between Jews and Arabs was a first principle, Jews should not support it. Nor, he also believed, could a Jewish state be founded "upon the bayonets of some Empire," and thus be dependent on the political will of the great powers.[46] These beliefs are echoed in the passages Roth attributed to himself in his "conversation" with Zangwill. He is honest enough to have Zangwill respond that "You now sound like a reformed rabbi talking about the Jewish mission."[47] That of course would be Magnus himself.

Roth wants to stress that a nation-state is not the remedy for anti-Semitism. That challenge must be met locally. He criticizes Zionists for courting England, France, and Turkey while making no contact with Palestinian Arabs. Zionists, he wrote, paid no mind to the 600,000 Arabs or to the way peoples of the Middle East thought and worshiped. Giving Zangwill the objection that political realities forced the Zionists to this approach, Roth is able to reply that the progress of Zionism is an illusion and in that in future, if actualized, it may cause a tragedy: militant Zionists may forget to be Jews.[48]

Roth's arguments in *Now and Forever* are in the high tradition of Jewish morality and social justice. Roth might have been more specific about naming some of his contemporaries who made these arguments, but that would have had the effect of making a prospective publisher doubt that his contribution was worth the effort. Early in 1918, for example, Louis Brandeis wrote to Chaim Weizman that in a Jewish state none of the natural resources of Palestine should be given to private developers, that cooperation with Arabs was essential, and that business interests should be subordinated to joint development of the land.[49] The problem with the central argument in *Now and Forever* is that not only Felix Frankfurter, Louis Marshall, and Jacob Schiff, but Magnus, and Zangwill himself, expressed reservations about Zionism, and especially Palestine, much more forcefully and in more detail than Roth did. Further, Zangwill is slighted at key points. He was suspicious of the plans for a Jewish homeland in Palestine for reasons Roth attributed to himself. Zangwill, unlike Roth, made many efforts over two decades to convince Jews to settle in various locations, but not Palestine, because of the political allegiances they would have to develop. Those locations included Africa and America. He stated, in fact, that the essential value of Zionism was that it gave Jews a spiritual identity, albeit one that he hoped would flourish in a national home.[50]

Roth's conclusion, morose and neurotic, is deeply at odds with Zangwill's respect for human potential, which extended to appealing to the better side of spokespeople for imperialist powers (he was a patriotic Englishman). Roth predicts that after about a century, America will persecute and banish its Jews. It will by that time have become "a sort of glorified KKK. . . . I expect to be living when they will be roasting Jews alive on Fifth Avenue."[51] He further predicts a kind of dark leader who will spread destruction through Europe.

It is passages like this, containing the "hysteria of petulant prophecy" Roth himself attributed to Zangwill's plays,[52] that some reviewers hooted at, and that Roth sought to excuse by having (a bit inaccurately) quoted Whitman on his title page: "Do I really contradict myself? / Well, then, I contradict myself." The *New York Times Book Review* devoted three columns to the book, which, as Adelaide Kugel notes, may have been due to McBride and Company's publicity agents. The anonymous reviewer thought the work exploited Zangwill's reputation and provided mere talk, not intelligent conversation, about a Jewish national home. He also thought the author seemed to have an inflated sense of his abilities, and thus interpolated too much autobiographical material.[53] The *Boston Evening Transcript* review focused on Roth's predictions of the hopelessness of having a Jewish state in the twentieth century, and the destruction of Europe because of its treatment of its Jews. This review cast Roth as an angry ingrate and a Cassandra.[54]

The *Transcript* implied that *Now and Forever* might incite anti-Semitism. An appreciative review by Franklin Gordon in *The American Hebrew* also raised that possibility. Gordon probably had in mind statements such as those the *Transcript* mentioned, and especially two others: Roth's declaration that Jesus was a malcontent who spoke exclusively to Jews, not pagans, and the prophecy of the eventual massing of the Jews in the Middle and Far East. Adelaide Kugel points out that Gordon proved to be right. In 1937, Alfred Rosenberg "quoted and misquoted" parts of Roth's predictions on "The Future" in a speech and an essay.[55] Roth's *Jews Must Live* had by then made him an unwilling tool for the Nazis. Although Gordon warns readers that Roth makes sweeping statements about the Jews in Europe and their dire fate in America, he clearly enjoyed and recommended *Now and Forever*.[56] He liked the way Roth, a "Jeremiah" indeed, forces his readers to think about so many contemporary problems facing his people. *The Independent* reviewer was also admiring, declaring the book "stimulating" and "animated," if "somewhat incoherent."[57]

Roth's daughter believed that *Now and Forever* improved Roth's reputation significantly. *The American Hebrew* listed Gordon's essay among the other major articles in that week's issue. Its title was "A Playboy Prophet in Israel," and its subtitle puts Roth on a par with one of the most esteemed Jewish writers: "Samuel Roth Takes Issue with Zangwill on the Jews and Their Future." While the "playboy prophet" epithet takes away as much as it gives, the headline certainly did attract readers of the weekly, which at that time appealed to a literate and upscale audience. He seems to have meant by "playboy" Roth's high-spirited willingness to be controversial. This was four months prior to the appearance of *Two Worlds* and its stated objective of "Increas[ing] the Gaiety of Nations."

Considering what was about to happen to Roth's reputation—due to the contumely the literary establishment was to spew his way after his unauthorized reprinting of Joyce's work—the *Now and Forever* reviews are an ironic high mark. Adelaide Kugel cites one other indication that the book was indeed taken seriously. Mendel Beilis was a Russian Jew jailed in 1913 for, but finally acquitted of, ritual murder and well poisoning (as in Malamud's *The Fixer*). In 1925 the Beilis Publishing Company asked Roth, on the basis of reading *Now and Forever*, to translate his story from Yiddish.[58]

When McBride and Company finally published *Now and Forever* in 1925, it was not the book for which Zangwill had provided an introduction five years earlier. Roth had been shopping the manuscript around in England and America for several years before revising it as a dialogue, so that the name of the great writer could appear on the title page. In London, Roth had shown Zangwill a draft called "The Jew and the Future," which was not a dialogue between Roth and Zangwill. "I must protest at once," Zangwill wrote Roth upon reading the final version, *Now and Forever*, "against my preface being put to a book for which it was not written, and for which it would have been superfluous, since I am having my supposed say throughout."[59] He did say that there was much that was "stimulating" in *Now and Forever*. Zangwill was the consummate gentleman and scholar.[60]

"An Impetuous Quick-Headed Fly-Off-the-Handle"

As Roth had gotten more assured of his abilities as editor and writer, he had become avid for recognition. He had, after all, suggested to his father that writing poetry was his destiny, his *taklis*. A Jewish son takes such a declaration very

Samuel Roth, Infamous Modernist

seriously. *Taklis* implies a sense of one's fate in God's orderly design, hidden from people whose eyes and heart are on the practicalities of survival. Frank Tannenbaum was hard-driving and abrasive also, but he saw Sam's immodest behavior as presumptuous, given its context. "You must learn to be more modest about the *Lyric* and more considerate of other people's vanity if you do not want to alienate the *Lyric*'s friends."[61] There's certainly an element of cunning in Roth's drawing attention to himself by critiquing fellow writers such as Untermeyer (who dared criticize some of the poems in *First Offering*),[62] Bercovicci, and later, Maurice Samuel, Pound, Eliot, the Hebrew scholar Horace Kallen, and even Carl Sandburg. But other factors were involved. His bluster suggests a neurotic insecurity, a panic that surfaces in times of stress. Roth thought Frank had "undoubtedly" accepted the accusations about his pirating parts of *Finnegans Wake* and *Ulysses* in 1926. "So was the first big lie imbedded in Mishillim's life—with the tender nursing of the only man he ever knew of whom he could say that he was his friend" ("CMAM," 184). The only truth of this statement is in its final phrase: outside of Frank, Roth had no male friends he would not rather compete with than open himself to.

Not only Frank Tannenbaum but also Clement Wood (who warned "Don't be such an impetuous quick-headed fly-off-the-handle") told him his irascibility was making him enemies.[63] Marie Syrkin, despite her respect for his promise as a poet, wrote about "the evil doings of which you darkly hinted in your note to me [that] had been responsible for my failure to see you. What were they, Sammy? How did you antagonize various 'gentle people'?" Thomas Moulton of *Voices* replied to a testy letter by reminding him, "You get frightfully indignant and sarcastic whenever you don't find me coming up to expectations . . . [but] you come along and behave so rudely to Bessie [his wife] that she is ill for several days after it."[64]

The quarrel Roth picked with *The Menorah Journal* in December 1921 is an example of the self-importance that first surfaced while he was editing *The Lyric*. The *Journal* was the ideal medium for a young Jewish writer, and it had published one of his early triumphs, the "Sonnets on Sinai," in December 1917. Founded by Henry Hurwitz in 1915, it was the most prestigious periodical displaying the variety of literature of the American Diaspora. The journal published widely on Zionism.[65] Where better for the author of *Europe: A Book for America* to find an audience? Where better to explain why Roth hoped (as he expressed in *Europe*) his country would be able to shape a "national culture" that in modern Europe had degenerated, he believed, into an excuse for engaging in a world war?[66]

Roth was irritated by the way Hurwitz introduced, in the December 1921 issue, the preface that Israel Zangwill wrote to Roth's then-unpublished "The Jew and the Future." Zangwill had given Roth permission to publish his preface in an American periodical.[67] *The Menorah Journal* had accepted the essay and paid Roth well. Roth objected, first, to the *Journal's* statement of copyright for it without having asked him, and then to Hurwitz's short introduction, which naturally was chiefly about Zangwill. Adelaide Kugel explains that her father was a bit panicky about not bringing in enough money to support his family.[68] Even so, what kind of responsible adult lets brooding resentment block a promising way to advancement? Roth's querulous letters to the *Journal* are perfect specimens of the kind of petulance, as when the boy Mishillim threw a heavy prayer book at his rabbi, that rebounds upon its author.[69] One could only speculate what Hurwitz might think of a man who wrote him, "I'm not a bit grateful to you for making another Jewish connection of mine an unpleasant one"?[70]

Fast One: Closing Shop and Sailing to London

In a partially crossed out passage Roth wrote in England as preface to an account of his meetings there with British literary figures, he stated, "About a year ago it became necessary for me to leave the United States, and . . . I chose England for a refuge [some material crossed out], from relatives who were creditors and creditors whose insolence exceeded even the natural insolence of relatives."[71] These generous relatives included his in-laws. Stating a decade later that he owed creditors less than $3,000 when he closed his doors at 49 West Eighth in 1921, he claimed it was "a very trifling price for America to pay for my Poetry Shop."[72]

Joseph Freeman, a journalist (later a social activist) who knew Roth from patronizing the bookshop, wrote him in 1921 that in the two weeks since his own return from England, "I have already had a dozen occasions to defend you against your enemies and to spread your fame amongst my friends."[73] Some of those enemies would have been creditors.[74] His daughter thinks his debts exceeded the $3,000 figure. "There was a good deal of ill will toward him in the trade."[75] (He did plan to repay what he owed, sooner or later.)[76]

Another reason for his prompt departure may have been that Pauline did not like the idea of Sam's leaving her so soon after the shock of her mother's death. She had two preschool children and little capital. She later told Adelaide that she feared her husband might not return, and did not see him off at the dock when he sailed on January 17, 1921. She knew he was philandering, and that one of his conquests was a copper-haired woman named Jacqueline

Embry, who had given him a check to stave off the bookshop's foreclosure. Their affair began with correspondence and continued with tender letters during the spring of 1920 and during Roth's tenure in London. They may have slept together before his bookshop closed. "A few of these nights belong to you."[77] What would happen, his wife asked herself, when he was alone in a European capital?[78]

In fact, something surely did. Perhaps many things. Roth never lost an opportunity, in public, of referring to his wife as "Gorgeous" or "Beautiful," forcing people, even those who did not know of his proclivities, to believe he was protesting too much.[79] When he was publishing *Beau: The Man's Magazine*, a revue of entertainment, fashion, and the high life, in 1926–27, he reviewed Broadway shows and nightclub acts, meeting entertainers such as "Bee" Jackson, Myrna Darby, and Louise Brown, with whom he had relationships. Gershon Legman informed Adelaide Kugel, when she was planning her memoir of her father, that Roth planned to use a "private subscription theater" as a "feeder of actresses to him, in the Nassau Hotel in Long Branch, L.I., where he took them."[80] He told Adelaide that her father met Mae West and, in an ecstasy of *chutzpah*, proposed her starring in a production of *Troilus and Cressida*.[81] The great actress Helen Gahagan, for whom Roth wrote a play, *Golden Hair*, about Helen of Troy, enjoyed his attentions enough to write, "Have you ever . . . found yourself running with your arms stretched wide faster and faster until something seemed to have carried you along—until you became as light as one of those tiny leaves on one of the great black trees that you've left behind and find your breath leaving you and you are flying through the night—its like that."[82] Frances Fletcher, a poet and translator, said that their meeting gave her "profound satisfaction (pleasure is too superficial a word). . . . You are an amazing person of meteorlike qualities. You quite took my breath away."[83]

Samuel Roth's major London affair was with Joan, a beautiful young woman ten years younger than he.

A Rescue in Markham Square: Mishillim "Knelt Down . . . and Meticulously Kissed Each of Her Toes"

With his funds for a London stay almost evaporated, Roth struck up a conversation with a tall, slender brunette (his favorite attributes in a woman) of about seventeen, to whom he refers as Joan (no family name is given). He offered to find her a job, which he explained was "to live in my house and help me with typing manuscripts." Roth had learned she was desperate to move out of the flat of the man who had brought her to London. The latter had been

Figure 8. Helen Gahagan (*left*), classical actress, and Myrna Darby (*right*), dancer, in Roth's magazine *Beau*, November 1926 and March 1927 issues, respectively. From the collection of the author.

suggesting that she become a streetwalker, contracting with him in return for protection and advice. For two weeks after Joan joined Roth in a Markham Square flat, he waited impatiently for an advance from *The Bookman* for an article the magazine had agreed to publish. Joan brought home some money, deceiving him for two weeks with stories of a showgirl friend who was willing to lend the couple a few pounds a month. She had been prostituting herself. Roth was overcome, he tells us with painful truthfulness, by shame and self-reproach. The reason was that instead of pity for her, he was thinking, despite himself, that "she were something reprehensible, an animal and unclean."

Humbling himself, Roth wandered around London, taking shelter for the night with homeless people in the church of St. Martin's in the Fields. There he had a visit from Yeshea, who criticized his taking up space that penniless people needed more than he. The Messiah reminded Roth of his responsibility to Joan after his return to the United States ("CMAM," 223–29). "It was a dank, cold, grey dawn to which Mishillim awoke, a purged man, and his energies renewed, returned to Markham Square." There, "He knelt down before [Joan] and meticulously kissed each of her toes."[84] Kissing of feet is an act of loving humility, of course, and important in the story of Jesus. But kissing toes, which

Samuel Roth, Infamous Modernist

Roth uses in his novel *Bumarap* (1947) to denote a humble man's gratitude for intercourse, is sensual, perhaps fetishistic.

Roth tells us that when he was about to leave London, he sent Joan to a male friend who would give her money to go back to her parents. Later he discovered she did not take the money; he conjectures that the friend had made the offer contingent on her sleeping with him. That says something about Roth's distrust even of friends, or more likely his keen desire to make himself feel better. Perhaps the root of the guilt lay in what he could have chosen to do, but did not, when his father sent him money for return fare to America. He could have stayed (which Pauline had been afraid he might do), or taken Joan with him. Of course that would be a betrayal of family and friends, but he had already done that in becoming involved. Joan had acted with the humblest and most self-demeaning compassion when the couple had to have money to carry on. He knew his lack of money had made the invitation to live with him irresponsible in the first place. He knew how low it had been of him to think of her as "unclean." It was a dilemma. He took the easy way out: he left Joan behind.[85] That is a betrayal. He does not tell us that, or that he believed it was. What he does tell us, without attributing the decision to Yeshea or destiny, means he had stood on a precipice, turned around, and headed home.

London Business

Of course, the motives for Roth's trip were professional. He had been told, by Frank Harris and others, that London was a much better place to write and meet writers than America. Acquiring press credentials, but no salary, from the *New York Herald,* he planned to send the paper columns about British writers. He contacted British publisher J. M. Dent about a book, or perhaps two, introducing Britons to contemporary American poetry.[86] The outline specifies a chronological arrangement in seven sections. He successfully solicited Ezra Pound, for whom teaching Europeans about American creative genius was of paramount importance, to write marginal commentary.[87]

Dent, however, was displeased with Pound (possibly because of his experience while publishing *The Spirit of Romance* in 1910).[88] He would publish the book, if Roth could find an American publisher who would allow the British firm to use their plates. Roth later said that on his way back to America he threw the manuscript into the ocean, doubting the value of what he had written and also believing, with no evidence, that Dent was antagonistic to the project.[89]

One of Roth's major efforts in England was shopping around his novel about his Galician boyhood, "White Streams." He sent a copy to H.D. (the imagist poet Hilda Doolittle, wife of Richard Aldington and friend of Lawrence, Amy Lowell, and Pound); she wrote that it was "full of a strange power of which I am not a little afraid."[90] Another plan was to discuss with Israel Zangwill the *Now and Forever* project. No less important was Roth's goal of publishing James Joyce. With his excellent instincts for innovative writing, he admired Joyce and wanted to tell him so. Having witnessed the fate of *The Little Review*'s editors when they published excerpts from *Ulysses,* he had in mind taking up the cause himself. He queried the novelist by letter, "Why is *Ulysses* not yet in book form?"[91] Near the end of his life, Roth wrote an unpublished essay on *Ulysses* in which he said that the censorship of excerpts from the novel in *The Little Review* by the New York Society for the Suppression of Vice, "More than anything else . . . made me determine to close the shop and migrate to England."[92] Beneath the layers of rationalization and self-justification in this statement is the one that Roth cultivated most strongly in his mid-twenties: showmanship. In London this quality did him some good—and considerable harm.

Joseph Freeman encountered Roth often during his stay in London. In his *An American Testament,* he uses the name "Knox," not Roth. The details about Knox include his attending Columbia University, running a bookshop, editing a poetry magazine, and being commissioned to write articles for a newspaper. This Knox cut "a tall, bizarre and impressive figure with his cloth cap, thick eyeglasses, J. M. Barrie moustache, fur-collared coat and heavy Malacca cane." He brought the cane, coat, and also a faux-British accent and colloquialisms back to the States with him.[93] In the booming voice of a Yiddish actor, he deprecated such contemporaries as Dreiser ("a *potz!*") and Sherwood Anderson ("a *shmok*"). The Zionist Jews in Palestine, Knox opined, will chose a king for themselves. Jewish leaders have always been men of letters; peering ten years into the future, Knox predicted that he would be that poet-leader. The Knox-Roth congruencies are unmistakable, although exaggerated.[94]

Roth was not a success as a literary journalist, but he accomplished most of the networking goals he set for himself before he returned. He seems to have written to every major author living in England, and spoke with an impressive number of them. He had to move out of the plush Savoy Hotel after a few weeks, but cannily used the hotel stationery. That might impress writers to whom he introduced himself as not just a journalist but also a publisher (as he did with Joyce). He met George Moore (Roth was especially interested in his plan to publish his erotic stories in private editions ["CMAM," 208,

221–22]), Arthur Symons, Sir John Squire, Thomas Moult, Edmond Gosse, Aldous Huxley, H.D. and her companion Bryher (with whom Roth enjoyed tea on several occasions ["CMAM," 221]), and T. S. Eliot (who had cordially agreed to a meeting but whom Roth thought aloof).[95]

Roth was unsuccessful with his proposed book of essays on the writers he met on his trip. The partial draft he completed contains judgmental statements with either no evidence given or comments padded in abstract and hazy phrasing. Eliot he respects for his criticism but not for his poetry. Pound he acknowledges (this was 1921) for his rectitude and fair dealing, not for his imagistic poems. Even John Gould Fletcher is praised only for letting Roth use his library and not for his writings.[96] Roth often showed this kind of churlishness toward people who had helped him. It was one way of proving his exceptionality to the one person who was already convinced of it—himself.

The English Institute

In relying on Yussef's stern advice to return to the States, and accepting his money to do so, Roth was admitting that he had failed to make a living either as a journalist for the *New York Herald* or as a self-sustaining writer. When Pauline met him at the dock, she remarked how thin he was; so many meals had he missed that he had lost twenty-one pounds.[97] There is an interesting congruence here between father and son. Yussef had been forced to turn to working for the puretz after failing with his inn, just as Sam now found he could not make a living as a writer. But the son had entrepreneurial abilities and the freedom to use fruitful resources, which his father lacked. He found a way to recoup his finances and approach his goal from a different direction, as a teacher and editor of literary magazines.

Taking advantage of the legal requirement that immigrants learn English in order to become citizens, and drawing on his experience with teaching the language to soldiers while working for the Jewish Welfare Board during the war, Roth founded the English Institute (later and more grandly called the American Academy of English) at 253 East Houston Street. He conceived a clever circular in Yiddish, in which a phrase that in translation meant "learn under four eyes" not only suggested ethnic solidarity but also intimated that students would learn by one-on-one teaching. He hired fellow poets Louis Zukofsky, Louis Grudin, and Charles Reznikoff, as well as others "loosely chosen," including one of his brothers-in-law. All worked part time, for low wages.[98]

The school put Roth back on his feet financially. Pauline's success as a milliner was another source of funds. It was time to enter the magazine-publishing business. The free publicity the anti-vice societies' confiscations provided for erotic texts, coupled with increasing urban readership for them, created opportunities for publishers who knew the available material, their printers, and writers. It was a golden opportunity, both to make himself sought after by other writers and to make his own work visible. *Two Worlds*, "Devoted to the Increase of the Gaiety of Nations," began publication in September 1925.

Samuel Roth, Infamous Modernist

CHAPTER 3

1925–1927

"Damn His Impertinence. Bloody Crook": Roth Publishes Joyce

The infamous *Ulysses* excerpts of 1926 and 1927 established for Samuel Roth a uniquely degraded status within the literary profession. His business tactics were rash and full of chutzpah. They set off a cascade of events immersing Joyce's publishers, lawyers, newspaper editors, and journalists writing in the *New York Post, The Nation, transition,* and *The New Statesman.* Hard facts flowed headlong together on both sides with panic at lost revenue and self-serving notions of High Art versus mercenary motives for exploiting prurience. One of the most discordant noises in the maelstrom was Roth's own outrage. "Hardy" was Herbert Gorman's way of putting it; his "hide was apparently that of a rhinoceros."[1] Gorman was Joyce's first biographer, another Roth friend turned enemy. Only two years after he had launched his *Two Worlds* quarterly Little Magazine, Roth found himself a pariah to whom both sexually explicit avant-garde writers and conservative moral authorities directed terms such as "scoundrel," "rat," "smut monger," "pirate," and "pornographer."

Roth's *Two Worlds* Enterprise Begins; Joyce's "Work in Progress" (1921–1925)

Roth wanted to launch what he hoped would become the first magazine in his publishing "empire" with a sensation. He thought somehow he could publish entire novels, starting with *Ulysses,* in a single issue (Roth's daughter makes the point that when he first considered printing *Ulysses* in one issue, he probably had not seen Sylvia Beach's 732-page edition).[2] Advertising a complete novel,

TWO WORLDS

A LITERARY QUARTERLY
EDITED BY SAMUEL ROTH

New York May
10th 1922

Dear James Joyce—

If you will read the prospectus at the right
of this note you'll get something of an idea
of the sort of magazine T w o   W o r l d s
is to be. Among other things we shall try to
publish a novel complete in every issue – I
already have one very fine one in view. But
if possible I would like to begin the series
with a novel by you. On its appearance in my
first issue I shall send you an advance royalty of one hundred dollars and later fifteen
■cent on the sales of the issue.

■■you have not a novel on hand let us see
■■thing you do have – a play, a story or an
essay.

Also, I would like a copy of Ulysses for review – even if I have to pay for it, as I
shall be glad to if there are no more review
copies left. I would like to devote a special
article to it in the first number, so please
turn this request over to whoever has charge
of such matters. I wish you would sign the
copy you send to me.

And let me hear from you very soon.

Faithfully,

Samuel Roth

Several years ago Mr. George Moore prefaced
a new book with the announcement that, due
to the difficulties his work was continually en-
countering in the moral business of publication,
he would henceforth issue all his books privately. He felt certain, he wrote, that his readers would eventually come to the conclusion
already reached by himself that his only alternative was not to publish at all.

The reception accorded by his readers to Mr.
Moore's subsequent books, published privately
and at a substantial price, encourages the hope
that there is among readers of English an understanding of the choice that at least once in
a lifetime confronts the conscientious writer in
these English countries. In the wake of Mr.
Moore in his new venture have followed other
contemporary writers, notably Mr. James Joyce.

The privately printed book has never been
adequately appraised. Like Anonymous, it is
without a biographer. It is not always bad and
it has been very good. At its dullest it is not
as distasteful to me as the hard boiled, carefully controversial product which basks in the
assurance of a publisher's trade mark. So it
came about that in the midst of a discussion of
the programme of the new quarterly I made
the suggestion afterwards adopted that *Two
Worlds* be limited to a certain number of copies
and issued only to subscribers.

The advantages of private publication to honest writing having been made apparent it was
asked: but why make it a *magazine?* It is very
important, I explained, that *Two Worlds* be a
magazine. A magazine differs from a book in
several important ways. It is, among other
things, closer to the original manuscript. A
book appears fully armed out of the advertising columns of a publisher. A magazine is
written. Be it good or bad, a book is accepted
as something accomplished, beyond revision.
The tradition of the magazine is alive with the
hazard that underlies the firmness of the
printed word. It is fitting that a living
writer, especially a young writer, should publish in a magazine. The only excuse for his
not doing so is that there is no magazine to
take his work. That sometimes happens.

Latterly, the only magazine ready to print
the best being written in English by contemporary writers has been The Little Review
which Mr. Ezra Pound helped to make illus-
trious. But The Little Review, always under
the surveillance of the censors of the living
word, has often had to disappear from view.
So that the grand enterprise of its career, the
printing of *Ulysses* (which *Two Worlds* had
it been in the field, would simply have included in one issue) stumbled through several
years only half way towards completion. However, *Two Worlds* is not designed to take the
place of any periodical. Besides doing its
share in the work of sifting out the grain from
the chaff where the chaff is plentiful it will
serve established writers as the organ of their
opinion and as a refuge from their persecutor.

Two Worlds will appear quarterly—on the
fifteenth of every *September, December, March*
and *June.* It will be attractively printed and
bound, and will have about two hundred
pages. Every issue will contain a complete
novel, a play, a short story, verse, and reviews of the books and plays of the period.
Seven hundred and fifty copies will be printed
and numbered, seven hundred to sell at one
dollar and a half a copy, and the first fifty,
to be signed by the leading contributors, at
three dollars each.

Figure 9. Roth's letter to Joyce, May 10, 1922. Sylvia Beach Papers, Manuscripts Division, Department of Rare Books and Special Collections, Princeton University Library. By permission of Fred Dennis.

not to mention one by Joyce, would be a good way of increasing circulation. The single-issue gambit would also be enticing to a writer, even if the logistics, necessarily, were unclear. Roth's first contact with Joyce, a February 12, 1921, letter, contained the tentative query, "Why is *Ulysses* not yet in book form?"[3] The publisher of *The Egoist*, Harriet Weaver, wrote lawyer and Joyce's friend John Quinn in September 1921 that she had twice refused Roth's request to

Samuel Roth, Infamous Modernist

publish it.[4] As bizarre as his plan to publish a new novel in each issue seemed, he did have one "in view," according to a prospectus printed in column form in the right quarter of his *Two Worlds* letterhead. The work was the eighth volume in Dorothy Richardson's "Pilgrimage" series.[5] By 1926, another six were certain, according to him, composing "the tremendous cycle of David Zorn [Samuel Roth]."[6] Possibly, Roth floated this offer to many writers, Joyce being only one. He may have been planning to ask a writer, as the magazine went to press, if, in the interest of space, he or she would consider abridging.[7]

Roth's May 10, 1922, letter, asking Joyce for "a novel [*Ulysses*] by you," was typed on his ingenious *Two Worlds* letterhead. (The *Revue des Deux Mondes*, [1829 to date] was a very influential Paris journal.) At this time he had no money to publish this subscription magazine. He hoped to get sufficient funds more quickly than he was able to. There is no trace of a permission letter from Pound, which Roth asserted was dated July 3, 1922. That missing letter may have suggested *Ulysses* as the featured work in the first issue of *Two Worlds*. We do have one dated the next day. In it, Pound stated, "I wrote yesterday, this is epistle II."[8] It may be that Pound did suggest Roth begin his quarterly with excerpts from *Ulysses* and "Work in Progress" as well.[9] But even if that missing July 3 letter were found, three years is a long time to assume that an agent will not have changed his mind about permission. In not informing Pound and Joyce in 1925 that the first issue of *Two Worlds* would come out presently, Roth was churlishly inconsiderate.

The 1921 conviction of Jane Heap and Margaret Anderson, the editors of *The Little Review,* for publishing excerpts from *Ulysses*[10] factored into Roth's decision not to begin *Two Worlds* in 1922. Further contributing to the delay were Roth's lack of money and a letter from Henry Seidel Canby, the *New York Post*'s literary editor, warning him off. "To publish your advertisement which offers the whole of *Ulysses*," said Canby, "would be to hand over, in so many words, the whole affair to Mr Sumner."[11] John Saxton Sumner was secretary of the New York Society for the Suppression of Vice and the lawyer who had successfully prosecuted *The Little Review* for the "obscene" excerpt from the "Nausicaa" episode, which describes Bloom masturbating as he watches Gertie MacDowell lean back to watch fireworks. In the early 1920s, Sumner's power to interdict literature about sex, even if devoid of explicit description and "vulgarisms," was as strong as his power to impound underground pornographic pamphlets, photos, novelties, and prophylactics.

Realizing that the conviction of *The Little Review* made publication of *Ulysses* in the early 1920s quixotic (and filing away until later the recognition that it also compromised chances for American copyright of the novel),

Roth therefore published, with permission and with at first delayed payment, excerpts from "Work in Progress" in *Two Worlds* (although of course the complete work, *Finnegans Wake,* had not yet appeared) when it began publication in 1925. He had finally accumulated the necessary capital, with the success of the English Institute he began on Houston Street to teach English to immigrants.

Roth called his venture "an experiment in magazine publishing," explaining that a magazine, unlike a book, lets the reader see the writer's work as it develops. Ford Madox Ford, in accepting a contributing editorship, applauded this idea as one he had not previously realized was "quite true."[12] The idea of private subscription Roth attributes to the freedom that George Moore had in mind when he said he would publish his books privately because of difficulties he had had "in the moral business of publication." Roth wrote Cabell, Ford, Eliot, Huxley, Symonds, Santayana, and H.D., as well as Joyce, for contributions. He wanted the contributors to sign personally fifty copies, according to the 1922 letterhead (several contributors who lived outside New York wondered how that would be possible). Frequent revision of his letterhead prospectus column allowed the editor to publicize his efforts for prospective authors, advertisers, and agents. The prospectus on the letter dated December 2, 1926, stated that *Two Worlds* would become a collector's item, an "investment" as well as a "pleasure," which has already at "book sales" fetched more than the published price. The wording of at least one of these prospectus columns would cause Roth problems in the controversy to follow.

The plan for *Two Worlds* stressed the freedom of the writer, but as Adelaide Kugel said, her father wanted to publish "daring and erotic" pieces. As every publisher knew in the early 1920s, before the younger ones had begun to challenge Sumner's power to force expurgations or expensive obscenity cases, private printing was the way to handle what the anti-vice societies called "the virulence of sex." If the book were only available by subscription, it would not fall into the hands of people susceptible to being "corrupted." In 1920, John Quinn told Joyce that he had advised Ben Huebsch (before the conviction of *The Little Review*) to publish *Ulysses* privately at $8 a copy (over $100 today). It would be attractively printed, not for sale in stores, and the writer would collect a much larger royalty than with a trade edition. He referred, as did Roth, to George Moore's *Storyteller's Holiday.*[13]

Advertising in several leading literary magazines, including the *Times* (London) *Literary Supplement* (where Radclyffe Hall found a coupon and replied with a subscription),[14] Roth realized his goal of 450 subscribers.[15] This made it possible for him to pay his contributors to his first issue. He paid as little as he could: $25 to all but Joyce, who (eventually) received $50. But that was standard practice with literary journals.

Roth's prospectus capitalized on both the investment and the experimental literary value of *Two Worlds*. A finely printed work reflected a level of taste that raised the "risqueness, gaiety" from the indecent to the artistic. Those responsible for the production and distribution of "gallantiana" in the 1920s, whether unbarbered or "abridged," often profited from the aristocratic refinement the "gallant" experience embodied. The category of gallant literature was not a genre but rather a convenient way of marketing sexually focused literature, including that from the past and in the public domain. Much more so than the much later category "soft core," gallantiana included a lot of serious writing. *Two Worlds* contained a fair amount of this: Pierre Louys, Oscar Wilde, Boccaccio, Rabelais, Twain (*1601*), Mather's translations from *The Arabian Nights*, and shorter contemporary works that "could not be printed in the ordinary commercial magazine."[16] Even after Roth printed the *Ulysses* installments, Pound admitted that Roth started out "not merely as a man on the make but . . . also to rebel against and satirize something more vile than any possible act of an individual."[17] That would be the vast venality and smug morality of American censorship.

In his letterhead's marginal prospectus, Roth presented *Two Worlds* as a successor of *The Little Review,* the recently adopted motto of which was "the advancing point toward which the 'advance guard' is always advancing."[18] Conveniently, Roth did not mention the score of American Little Magazines with limited resources and a readership with literary and/or political enthusiasms. They flourished in the 1910s and after the war: Joseph Kling's *The Pagan, The Liberator* (which as a leftist political publication had a large number of readers and a belligerent attitude toward the censors, as did *The New Masses*), the eclectic *Poetry,* or the well-reputed *Contemporary Verse.* The goals of these magazines' editors and the scope of their interest in experimental forms were far in advance of those of *Two Worlds*. Roth featured a lot of material old enough to be in the public domain. Meanwhile, *The Little Review* had presented to its readers Vachel Lindsay, Djuna Barnes, Witter Bynner, Gertrude Stein, Malcolm Cowley, Edger Lee Masters, Yeats, Huxley, Dorothy Richardson, and H.D.[19]

Joyce had accepted $200, $50 apiece for four selections. That Pound had given Roth permission to publish this "new work [in progress]" while he was Joyce's literary agent is probable, three years before *Two Worlds* appeared. But Sylvia Beach, in 1925 Joyce's agent, denied that any proper permission had been forthcoming.[20] Did she mean she denied him permission? She could not have flatly denied his request if Joyce did not agree. In a March 5, 1926, letter to Weaver, who had tried to get excerpts from *Ulysses* included in *The Egoist*, Joyce writes that he had planned to do some revising of a segment of the Shem and Shaun chapters "for Mr. Roth" but was too tired to do so. Richard Ellmann annotates this statement by acknowledging that "a letter from Pound suggests that Joyce had made an arrangement of some sort with Samuel Roth."[21] Joyce may have heard positive evaluations from Pound, or perhaps H.D. or George Moore, who met Roth or communicated with him in London. Perhaps, too, the Savoy Hotel stationery Roth used to write letters upon arriving in London impressed some Joyce acquaintances, if not Pound himself.

No evidence shows that Roth paid in advance, as he should have. Beach's December 3, 1925, letter, in response to one of Roth's, upbraids him for publishing excerpts from "Work in Progress" without permission.[22] A month passed after her December letter before he sent a check for $100 for the first two "Work in Progress" episodes, dated January 2, 1926 (on the back Joyce has written "pay to an order of Sylvia Beach").[23] Such a delay was bad business even for a beginning editor, and Roth, in addition to being short of funds, was a bad bookkeeper as well as an inexperienced publisher. In any event, Joyce took the money when it was, tardily, paid for the first two episodes, and there is now good evidence that Roth did pay with dispatch for the other two.[24] The agreement for the "Work in Progress" selections was made in 1922. At the time, Roth invited Pound, Ford, and Arthur Symonds to be *Two Worlds'* contributing editors. All three agreed, Pound and Ford suggesting several young writers. A new literary publication presents to established men of letters an opportunity to cement their status and influence by getting promising younger writers' works before the public. Roth seemed at that point industrious and even financially sound.

Roth's "Magazine Empire" Expands; the *Ulysses* Excerpts (1926)

In April 1926, Roth launched a second subscription publication, *Casanova Jr.'s Tales*. He changed the rather puerile title to *Secret Memoirs of Gallant Men and Fair Women* for volume 2. Each issue of volume 1 contained lengthy segments of Gertrude Beasley's memoir of her west Texas upbringing, *My First Thirty Years*. Irresistible were Beasley's brooding, detailed descriptions of the violence, child abuse, bestiality, and incest in her large family and her vivid delineations of the regional dialect, outhouse graffiti, landscape, architecture, and character types. H. L. Mencken admired the book and noted that it could never be published in America. That partly explains its appearance in a Roth magazine, as does its original 1925 appearance in a limited edition in France by Robert McAlmon's Contact Editions (in plain binding to fool Customs). There is no evidence that Roth informed McAlmon of his serial reprinting. Nor did he approach Beasley, who when she returned to the United States early in 1928 tried to contact him for payment.[25] Many copies of the French edition were seized by British and American Customs as obscene.[26]

Casanova Jr. outsold *Two Worlds* by a wide margin, Roth stated, although a subscription and a single copy cost more than *Two Worlds.* One difference between the two magazines was that *Casanova Jr.* contained no Joyce, but more sex and scatology than the first. In a leisurely 1930 retrospective of his recent career as magazine editor—he was writing from prison—Roth said he published his second subscription magazine to prove he did not have to rely on the name of James Joyce to be successful. Using the pseudonym "Francis Page" as editor of *Casanova Jr.* further distanced the publication from *Two Worlds.*[27]

Five years after Roth first wrote to Joyce about *Ulysses,* a full-page notice appeared in a November 1926 number of the *Saturday Review* advertising both the subscription (*Two Worlds, Casanova Jr.*) magazines and two newer, newsstand ventures. One of the latter was *Two Worlds Monthly,* a feature of which was excerpts from *Ulysses.* Joyce, Beach, and Weaver wanted to know whether Roth was an aggressive new force in American publishing or merely a speculator seeking windfall profit. Those they asked to find out were predisposed to think the worst. Roth remembers an "outraged telephone call" from Lloyd Morris, author of a 1917 book on contemporary American writers such as those Roth had published. At Beach's request, Morris made six visits to Roth's office on Fifth Avenue near Forty-second Street, but Roth was out.[28] One of Gorman's letters to Joyce explained that he had tried to get a copy of *Two Worlds* but could not.[29] That is not surprising, since it was a subscription magazine out less than a month, but Gorman's comment about Roth being "very careful about letting 'TW' fall into antagonistic hands" is incisive. An American editor who knew Pound, John M. Price, wrote Beach a year later that he had found it difficult to get a copy of the first issue of *Two Worlds Monthly,* containing in expurgated form the first of the *Ulysses* excerpts. He had tried both letter and office visit.[30]

Although by 1929 Roth did have an office and warehouse on Fifth Avenue, and listed one in *Two Worlds Monthly,* the "office" Morris visited may have been only a small space or desk in a large room. Roth would have rented it because of the prestigious address. To use a Houston Street address would make writers and subscribers believe the enterprise could not have solid financial

Figure 10. Advertisement in *Saturday Review* for four of Roth's magazines. Sylvia Beach Papers, Manuscripts Division, Department of Rare Books and Special Collections, Princeton University Library. By permission of Fred Dennis.

footing or intellectual respectability.[31] Pound called this the "desk room" gambit used by entrepreneurs operating on a shoestring.[32] When Weaver wrote corporate lawyer John Quinn, who as an art collector and literary patron was a key New York contact, about Roth, he informed her that "Samuel Froth" was a cash-poor small-timer. Any attempt to publish *Ulysses* would land him in jail.[33]

The first issue of *Two Worlds Monthly* appeared on newsstands in July 1926. The man who convinced Roth to take the precipitous giant step from coterie to mass-market circulation was Morris Eisenman, a friend from Roth's

Samuel Roth, Infamous Modernist

own newspaper-selling days and Second Avenue's Café Royal who was now head of an important newspaper distribution outfit, the Metropolitan News Company.[34] Perhaps Eisenman was able to get *Two Worlds Monthly* displayed prominently (which he could not do without the expurgation), and it is possible there were newsstand posters. Roth wrote that his circulation was 25,000.[35] He deplored Weaver's and Hemingway's exaggerations (40,000 and 50,000, respectively), which they believed meant that he was making lots of money. However, Roth's own figure might be high also. In addition to *The Dial*, American magazines at the time containing contemporary literature included *The Bookman* (19,000), *The Nation* (30,000), *Scribner's* (75,000), and *Century* (25,000). Certainly the *New Yorker*'s circulation (53,000) and the *American Mercury*'s (45,000) were beyond Roth's capabilities.[36] His other newsstand venture, *Beau*, might have had a higher circulation than *Two Worlds Monthly*, due to its articles on theater, stories on sexual encounters, witty aphorisms and cartoons, photos of actresses and dancers, and advertisements for the finest in clothing, vacations, jewelry, and whiskey. However, it could not have been anywhere nearly as high as *Harper's Bazaar* (100,000), *Smart Set* (reported as 25,000 in 1925 but as 250,000 in 1928), or *Vanity Fair* (87,000). The nature of newsstand competition for both his entries ensured the rapid collapse of Roth's "magazine empire" by 1928.

Eisenman and Roth understood each other, and the business, well. Perhaps in their discussions, Roth had said that he had long admired *The Dial*, with a circulation of over 10,000 in the mid-1920s, including newsstand sales.[37] But *The Dial* had subsidies from wealthy supporters, which Roth did not.[38] Realizing the potential just beginning in America for finding investors for publishing ventures, Roth attempted to get some "angels" of his own. Conde Nast, publisher of *Vanity Fair* and *Vogue*, had recently put shares on the Stock Exchange, as had Curtis Publishing.[39] Of course, Roth's publications were not comparable. But he sensed the air, and lived in hope, and hype. The first two 1927 issues of his newsstand monthly featured full-page notices inviting "small investors as well as big ones" to purchase common stock. "This is our reply to the numerous requests."

Regarding distributing sexually explicit literature, if Roth lacked the status of an established publisher, he also had less to lose. Pound, an astute observer of Roth, warned Joyce that Roth was not only "quite clever" but had "a strong pull of avarice, bidding him to be BOLD."[40] Ben Huebsch, Alfred Knopf, or Thomas Seltzer would not take the risk of ignoring the wishes of a writer with Joyce's status by issuing an expurgated *Ulysses*, and thereby being considered untrustworthy philistines by modernist writers and their agents (*The Little Review*'s expurgations were another matter, considered necessary in view of police threats). Roth published the "Nausicaa" episode unaltered in *Two Worlds Monthly* in 1927, a fact, as I show below, that went unacknowledged by Joyce's supporters. In doing so he risked a court case brought by Sumner and confiscation of the magazine by the police. Pound, who liked Roth's defiance of the sex censorship, pointed out to Joyce that the publisher was "after all giving his public a number of interesting items that they would not otherwise get."[41]

Why would Roth attempt in 1927 what he was warned off doing, by Canby and others, in 1922? The answer is that, having been suppressed by court action, *Ulysses,* even in excerpt form, could only be published by a "BOLD" risk-taker. A luftmensch would do it, one hubristically willing to let bluenoses and litterateurs alike do their worst. Sumner's investigation of *The Little Review* had established precedent for censorship. Therefore, neither Customs nor the Copyright Office would have to request an investigation determining obscenity by the Department of Justice. It is extremely interesting to note that a book was not in fact denied copyright because of obscenity. As Professor Robert Spoo has shown, the Copyright Office was required to ask the Justice Department to determine a work's obscenity before refusing it copyright on that ground, but they had always eschewed taking advantage of this procedure. Roth did not much care. His chief reason for "boldness" was that there was no reciprocal copyright agreement between England and the United States. In its absence, Joyce would have had to have established interim copyright in accord with America's Manufacturing Clause, as set forth in the 1909 U.S. Copyright Act. The latter required filing of copyright notice and depositing the foreign edition in Washington. *Ad interim* copyright being thus established, printing or photolithographing the work in America was required within thirty days of the foreign edition having being deposited. *Ulysses,* in the absence of that, was in the public domain.[42]

The Little Review had its selections expurgated. Sumner had their "Nausicaa" episode censored nonetheless. (Paul Vanderham points out that Pound's reasons for barbering included avoiding court action on the basis of obscenity but also Quinn's possible withdrawal of financial support for *The Little Review* because of his personal objection to Joyce's coarseness and scatology.)[43] Roth certainly did not want a court case either, but he knew one could not be won based on violation of copyright. Legally, he was not a pirate. As for respecting protocols of British and American publishers, now, therefore, was the time—it

Samuel Roth, Infamous Modernist

was sink or swim with him—to publish *Ulysses,* not as a "privately printed" and carefully distributed unexpurgated volume (that came three years later) but in serial form. He needed a sensation to initiate the newsstand public into his mass-market magazine—with a notoriously modern, uninhibited European work, barbered of course. That fact, readers would have to discover for themselves.

Launched at the same time as *Two Worlds Monthly* was *Beau,* a glossy magazine about men's lifestyle, with beautifully executed art deco covers, attractive photos of actresses, erotically tinged stories, and Roth's own reviews of stage plays. The cover of the July 1927 issue featured a near-replica of the "running torchbearer" Modern Library logo, which had been introduced by Random House two years earlier. It was another of Roth's brash imitations of a successful symbol of high culture for his own readers. Two other examples are "The Literary Guillotine," a column copied from *Vanity Fair*'s "We Nominate for Oblivion," and, again on the cover of the first issue, a nineteenth-century dandy similar to *The New Yorker*'s Eustace Tilley. Roth later bragged than he had invented the genre of the "men's magazine." *Esquire* did covet his title, but that magazine's inception five years later was inspired by fancy advertisement brochures for men's haberdashery. *Esquire* was also quick to combine that interest with sophisticated erotica and skilled writing. Its sponsors in the clothing industry gave its editor, Arnold Gingrich, resources and contacts Roth could not dream of.[44]

"At the Sign of the Mocki-Grisball"

For his subscription magazines, *Two Worlds* and *Casanova Jr.'s Tales,* Roth adapted the accessories of the limited edition: the numbering of each copy, the limited number of copies printed, the abstract and art nouveau illustrations and decorations, and the use of a colophon (a decoration and brief production notes regarding the printing of the work). A colophon traditionally appeared on the last printed leaf in a book, but it was placed in *Two Worlds* on the front cover. What a colophon it was! It occupies the bottom third of the wrapper. In the center is a circular medallion around the edges of which are naked classical figures wrestling with each other. It was a typical decoration for gallantiana, depicting a health and vigor that could be explained as innocent and wholesome, not indecent. The sly implication was that if anyone was offended, it was a case of *honi soit qui mal y pense.* To the right of the medallion was a limitation statement (number of copies printed) and a handwritten number designating the copy in hand. To its left was the following:

PUBLISHED ONCE / EVERY THREE / MONTHS AT THE / SIGN OF THE / MOCKI-GRISBALL / 500 FIFTH AVE- / NUE, SUITE 405-8 / NEW YORK CITY / WHERE CONTRI- / BUTIONS, SUB- / SCRIPTIONS, AD- / MONITIONS, AND / INVITATIONS TO / TEA WILL BE / GRACIOUSLY RE- / CEIVED.

Roth used a similar statement for the two-volume bound compilation of *Two Worlds Monthly* in 1927. He explains that "mocki-grisball" was an in-joke. The man who served as registrar at Roth's English Institute school, "himself an immigrant," would mutter "grisball" when an Italian immigrant would decline to sign up for a course, and "mocki" if a Jew did not do so ("CMAM," 239–40). The word *mocki*, a Jew who speaks in a Yiddish accent, is similar to the Hebrew *machos*, which denotes in the Passover Hagaddah the ten plagues. There may be a suggestion of the libel on a Jew as him- or herself being a plague,[45] a lethal infection from which the healthy community must be cleansed. The irreverent linking of "mocki-grisball" with the respectable tradition of tea and conversation (but in this case, rebukes) is similar to the challenge Roth made in London with his affected British accent, Bond Street haberdashery, imposing fur coat, walking stick, bow ties, and, occasionally, lemon-yellow gloves and even spats, spouting Yiddish insults.[46]

Roth's daughter reports that her father "liked to boast that he was a Galician peasant, descendant of horse thieves and pirates."[47] Yet her father was no blunderer into the high-hat world. He had been to Columbia, where his teacher, John Erskine, was a prototype of the American man of letters. He had impressed Huxley, Zangwill, H.D., and J. C. Squire in London interviews. Further, he knew *Two Worlds* subscribers wanted reading matter that could show off their cultural and social bona fides.[48] It was not practical, but it was typically Roth, to use the mocki-grisball colophon, which negated the medallion itself. But the latter's clean-lined, cool, classical grace is itself undercut by the mundane reality of the text, and also by close inspection of what the two male figures might be up to with the female. The reader was made to wonder what manner of man was behind the magazine he held in his hands. The publisher had a multifaceted awareness of what he wanted to do—just as, much more discreetly, his readers had regarding what they wanted.

Early success as a poet and editor might have made Roth less wary than he could afford to be. It was hard to anticipate an International Protest, but he

THREE DOLLARS A COPY   TEN DOLLARS A YEAR

TWO WORLDS

A *Literary Quarterly Devoted to the Increase of the Gaiety of Nations*

EDITED BY SAMUEL ROTH

CONTRIBUTING EDITORS
ARTHUR SYMONS—EZRA POUND—FORD MADOX FORD

DECEMBER, 1925

CONTENTS

PUBLISHED ONCE EVERY THREE MONTHS AT THE SIGN OF THE MOCKI-GRISBALL 500 FIFTH AVE-NUE, SUITE 405-8. NEW YORK CITY. WHERE CONTRI-BUTIONS, SUB-SCRIPTIONS, AD-MONITIONS, AND INVITATIONS TO TEA WILL BE GRACIOUSLY RE-CEIVED.

500 COPIES OF THIS NUMBER WERE PRINTED AFTER WHICH THE TYPE WAS DISTRIBUTED. OF THE 450 COPIES SET ASIDE FOR SUBSCRIBERS THIS IS NUMBER

Figure 11. Front cover of Roth's *Two Worlds,* showing classical figures in sexual frolic, and the text featuring the "mocki-grisball" invitation. By permission of the Roth estate.

was a candidate for something like it. Like other thick-skinned, perseverant luftmenschen who had to take sometimes desperate risks, Roth blundered by defying warnings about the political and financial vulnerability of the middleman working in an underground economy. However, also like them, his will was not broken by setbacks, even by being branded a literary pariah who had cheated a great novelist out of money he badly needed for himself and his family.[49] Convicted of breaking parole in 1929, he emerged in 1931 from a term in the U.S. Detention Headquarters in lower Manhattan and then in a Philadelphia prison with new projects and sustained love of bookselling and publishing. He saw his temporary ill fortune as the result, first, of self-serving, vindictive colleagues, and then of hypocritical moralists, especially John Sumner. His reasoning, as morally questionable as it was self-serving, galvanized his spirit for a ferocious struggle ahead against competitors, detractors, and censors.

To characterize Roth as a luftmensch publisher distinguishes him from mainstream Jewish publishers of his generation. Thomas Seltzer, although a leading Village bohemian and the first editor of *The Masses,* was a graduate of the University of Pennsylvania. Temperamentally, Roth and Seltzer were opposites. The most telling example is Seltzer's fate as a publisher. He is responsible for establishing D. H. Lawrence's reputation in America. Eventually, Lawrence left him for Knopf. Seltzer's debts, incurred while fighting Sumner's attempts to prosecute him for publishing erotica, forced him out of business. Like Seltzer, Roth suffered bankruptcy in the late 1920s, but his response, in letters and editorials, to Joyce and his friends who engineered the Protest was as proudly, startlingly defiant as it was vulgar, or as Pound stated it, "damned impertinent." He had a rhinoceros hide, as Gorman put it, or, in the words of former employee Waverley Root, what seemed to be "supreme self-contentedness."[50] It was hard to categorize him. Horace Liveright was a more renowned "scoundrel" than the pirate of *Ulysses* (Liveright's reputation was cemented by a film with that title written by Ben Hecht). Donald Friede was thrown out of three Ivy League universities and forced a censorship case over Aldington's *Birth of a Hero* in 1929. Yet, these men and their colleagues (Huebsch, Simon and Schuster, Albert and Charles Boni) had more social and monetary advantages than Roth.[51]

There was another band of publishers who, like Roth, dealt in popular magazines and lending-library novels, banned erotica, gallantiana, and sex pulps during the 1920s and 1930s. They, like Roth, had to deal with the anti-vice societies, police action, and media attacks. Nat Wartels issued cheap "modern" novels of young people on the make. Sam Curl and Alex Hillman,

Wartels's partners, published detective magazines in the 1930s. Joseph Meyers, who co-owned the Illustrated Editions Company and other inexpensive reprint houses, created the "Forbidden Classics" (written in ancient Greece or Rome, the Renaissance, or the eighteenth century). Meyers, a former boxer, was tough inside as well as out. Ignoring the warnings of other publishers and the police, he planned a "piracy" of *Ulysses* in 1932, while Random House was working on getting its own edition legalized.[52]

What these publisher-booksellers and Roth shared was the nature of their offerings. They could get banned pornography for wealthy customers. Beyond that, they appealed strongly to people who wanted access to the titillation one could get from inexpensive books: entertainment that made appeals to mass audiences similar to those of magazines and movies. However, except for Sam Curl, of urban Irish background, and Joe Meyers, the boxer, even these erotica merchants seem to have been from more affluent family backgrounds than Sam Roth.

The book dealer with whom Roth worked most closely over several decades was Jacob (Jack) Brussel. The latter, a well-loved Fourth Avenue book scout, bookstore owner, and publisher of all kinds of erotica, had a disposition as sunny as Sam's was volatile. They shared three enthusiasms in addition to bookselling: their Jewish heritage, America's First Amendment freedoms, and passionate discussion of literature. They both employed Gershon Legman, aware of his encyclopedic knowledge of sex customs and practices. They had both seen the central Pennsylvania countryside—on the way to Lewisburg Penitentiary. Roth finished a term there in 1939, just before Brussel entered, for distributing an edition of *Tropic of Cancer*, which Legman was instrumental in publishing.[53]

The Great *Ulysses* Hullabaloo (1927–1928)

Two Worlds Monthly published twelve excerpts from *Ulysses* beginning with volume 1, number 1. (The final one, from the "Oxen of the Sun" episode, appeared in volume 3, number 4, which was published only in the second volume of the bound compilation of the magazine). Joyce's supporters presented Samuel Roth to his colleagues, customers, and readers as a scoundrel and thief with such indignation that their labels determined the rest of his career.[54] Roth, in response, played the victim of misrepresentations. This allowed him to retain his self-esteem and to prevent anyone from declaring the matter closed. His histrionic outrage more than matched Joyce's quieter one, and the publisher took advantage of the labyrinthine path he trod with *Ulysses* for thirty years. The slivers of doubt remained. One result was his being invited to address the James Joyce Society in 1950. Admitting that her father was manipulative, self-absorbed, and abrasive, his daughter nevertheless admired how her father "fought back and continued to fight back all his life."[55] Both sides were playing the same game of self-advertisement, the stakes in one case being a dramatic success in magazine publishing, and in the other, the ability to broadcast publicity about Joyce's plight and his genius in order to entice journalists, publishers, and readers to a modernist landmark.

"Impatient with Further Delays"

In August 1927, interviewed by the *New York Post*, Roth stated that he wrote Harriet Weaver for permission to publish *Ulysses* excerpts. His offer was turned down on June 8, 1922.[56] Significantly, in this interview he advanced the date of Pound's permission from 1922 to 1923. But its real date would have been about a month after Weaver's letter. This suggests that, still needing permission, he asked Pound for it; Pound's reply has disappeared. As I have stated, Roth "went ahead" in 1926; several years later, he wrote that he had become "impatient with further delays."[57] He took out the full-page advertisements in several magazines, including the one in the *Saturday Review* that spurred Joyce, Beach, and Weaver to find out whether he was at all professionally reputable. Literary critic and historian Milton Hindus, who respected Roth and in 1950 published an important book with him under his Boar's Head imprint, wrote that whatever permission Roth claimed, he slighted one of the greatest of contemporary artists by disdaining Joyce's financial need and not keeping him informed of his intent or actions.[58] Roth probably did not think he was actually patronizing Joyce. But he knew what he was doing, knew it was in any event not Joyce directly who gave him permission, and knew that the (now non-extant) letter he thought gave the permission was four years old when he deposited, with Arthur Garfield Hays, checks and promissory notes for *Ulysses*. The novel was a siren tempting Roth for that long at least. Joyce got his own back in *Finnegans Wake,* where Shem, like Roth, "with his unique hornbook [*Two Worlds Monthly*] and his prince of the apauper's pride," is described as "blundering all over the two worlds."[59]

Arthur Garfield Hays Writes to Joyce on Roth's Behalf (January 1927)

Roth had learned quickly what it takes for a booklegger to do business. A mainstream publisher like Huebsch or Knopf would have been much more forthcoming than Roth when Hays, a prestigious lawyer, conferred with him about Joyce's impending lawsuit to force *Two Worlds Monthly* to stop printing *Ulysses* segments. Hays was then Joyce's lawyer. At Joyce's request, Jane Heap had gotten Hays to represent him, but after she did so, Joyce got the firm Chadbourne, Stanchfield, and Levy to take over.[60] Roth apparently prevaricated regarding expurgation, as a long letter from Hays to Joyce in January 1927 praising the young publisher's "good faith" reflects.[61] Roth offered to pay Joyce $1,000; Hays wrote that he had asked Roth to come see him after a long hiatus in his contact with the young publisher. He informed Joyce that Roth was so great an admirer that "if he published anything he would do it without asking you to dot an i or cross a t." This must mean that Roth would not expurgate. He concludes by saying frankly that "as to the collection of these notes when they come due, it must depend largely on Mr Roth's future prospects." He also says Roth has shown "good faith [in depositing promissory notes totaling $800]" and that "there is some prospect of success with these magazines." Roth must have told Hays he hoped to be able to pay for future installments in cash, that the *Monthly*'s future prospects were good, and that, as Hays reported it to Joyce, "it takes a little time for a proposition like this to get on its feet." Therefore, if Joyce might be looking for a place to publish a new story, he should think of one of Roth's magazines. Roth must have impressed Hays greatly to elicit such a letter. Throughout his career, Hays was devoted to freedom of expression.

Of course, Roth fully intended to expurgate for not only newsstand but mail-order sales of his monthly magazine.[62] Morris Eisenman would have, if asked, advised just that. That Pound had expurgated for *The Little Review* several years earlier is not less but more reason for a scrupulous man to have observed publisher-author conventions. Roth knew Joyce would never allow him to expurgate. As Arnold Bennett put it soon after the Protest appeared, "The great mass of American publishers and editors behave far better than their copyright law would allow them to. They continually ask for and obtain the permission of British authors."[63] Publishers such as Boni, Knopf, and Huebsch would have proceeded as he described. Roth was not of their brotherhood, and could not afford to be.

The International Protest (February 1927)

Published in French and English, the Protest's stated intent was to "oppose to Mr. Roth's enterprise the full power of honest and fair opinion." How this could be done is left unstated, but the following were logical ways to use "full power" to stop the "pirate": publishers could refuse to allow him advertising space; writers could stop sending him material to publish; readers could boycott his magazines; distributors and bookstore and newsstand dealers could take Roth's magazines off their shelves; and the Post Office could declare his enterprise fraudulent. "We hope that this can be made to mean something," wrote the editor of *The Nation*.[64] Roth did suffer, financially and psychologically, from the first three of these methods. Beyond this, news dealers did not have to be pressured to take *Two Worlds Monthly* and *Beau* off their stands; declining sales made that a natural response. Roth would have been hurt by having his second-class mailing privileges revoked. Mail orders were important, but he could post by Railway Express instead of using the U.S. mails.

Roth had made himself a target at which Joyce, his associates, and, because of them, the international literary community could focus a public hating. The most egregious example never saw print. It was Ludwig Lewisohn's first draft of the International Protest. He said Roth had "the shamelessness of a highwayman but [was] quite without the highwayman's courage, since the law grants him a temporary immunity. The issue. . . . involves the good name of American publishing and of American literature." Those signing the Protest, Lewisohn stated, did so "in the name of common honor and honesty and of that security of the works of the intellect and the imagination without which art cannot live."[65] One of his generation's best-known writers about what the Jewish people had exchanged in America for the piety of the European shtetl, Lewisohn saw in Roth an epitome of amoral venality. Therefore, he had no trouble exorcizing him from legitimate company in a vehicle of unprecedented influence in the literary community. Whether he knew that Joyce had accepted payment for the "Work in Progress" excerpts in *Two Worlds* is doubtful. He did not hear it from Beach, Pound, or Joyce. So, maybe, he did not have to consider the possibility. Had he done so, he may have tempered the outrage in his draft. Nor did he consider Pound's belief—expressed in his 1918 article in *New Age*—that the real frustration experienced by European writers of sexually explicit literature was not piracy but the American copyright law, which prioritized moral platitudes and business profit over free expression.[66] Therefore, what Roth had done in dancing around and in breaking down the boundaries of fairness with the *Ulysses* excerpts, Lewisohn had done in drafting the Protest. Joyce excised the invective. Perhaps, since he had Archibald MacLeish use his Harvard Law expertise in reading the draft, he had been brought to understand the problem of slanderous assertions by one who was about to sue the person slandered.

Waverley Root's essay in the December 1927 issue of *transition* was a close second to Lewishon's draft. It followed an essay, "The Case of Samuel Roth," wherein *transition*'s editors' rhetoric identified Roth as "vermin," "lice," "liar and sneak thief," and "parasite." These were all classical epithets for the mythic International Jew, the pariah middleman whose enterprises enabled him access to money, sex, and power while weakening the moral values of the place where he resided. That explains the title *transition* assigned Root's reminiscence of his employment as an editor for Roth: "King of the Jews." It was obviously sarcastic, not only in suggesting Roth viewed himself as a martyr but also in focusing on Root's delineation of Roth's venality.

Root and Roth hated each other. The latter had dismissed his young editor because, he said, Root had tried to sell Roth's mailing list to *Vanity Fair*. Root's side of the story was that he resigned after he discovered that Roth had lied to him about having gotten Joyce's permission when he began the *Two Worlds Monthly* segments of *Ulysses*.[67] Root tells his readers Roth was Galician, which country "is reputed to produce probably the lowest recognizable specimens of the human race extant." Root asserted that he had heard Roth, that man of "supreme self-contentedness," declare that God might have chosen him to be the just man of his generation. However much the language of Root's essay, following the editorial that precedes it, egregiously reflects contempt for Roth as an exemplar of the degenerate racial outcast, even Roth's daughter would have to admit that Root's "self-contentedness" observation seemed on the money. Root had heard from Roth's friend Joseph Freeman about Roth's "King of the Jews" ambition as well as other of his ways of fashioning himself as a literary celebrity (the booming voice, fur coat, walking stick, stentorian pronouncements).[68]

Newspaper and trade publications reporting on the Protest (some British papers did not print it because they feared libel prosecution)[69] included the open letters, letters to the editor, and personal requests of Joyce's supporters. There were interviews with and statements from Joyce himself, Beach, and signers of the Protest such as Manuel Komroff, Ernest Hemingway, Eliot, and Bennett. The very mention of famous signers such as D. H. Lawrence, Maugham, Yeats, Walpole, Bridges, and Masefield—the *New York Times* article on the Protest named all of these—could not help but raise eyebrows. Certainly the name of Albert Einstein, considered a special prize by Joyce, lent immediacy and authenticity.[70] Beach had sent the Protest—signed by 167 writers, artists, and intellectuals—to approximately nine hundred papers in the United States. It precipitated two other humiliating revelations, by T. S. Eliot and a London literary agent on behalf of A. E. Coppard, H. M. Tomlinson, Middleton Murry, and G. K. Chesterton, about Roth's printing their poems and stories without permission or payment. Eliot revealed that Roth pirated his poem "Fragment of an Egon" (eventually part of *Sweeney Agonistes*). The contemptuous tone of Eliot and the editors of *transition* made it clear that they wished "to rid contemporary literature of this poisonous vermin." Roth's cavalier treatment of these five "contributors" was a matter of record.[71] Disingenuous misstatements in the wake of the Protest by Joyce's supporters, on the other hand, excessively dramatized the injustice done to him.

The power of the press was in their hands; that Joyce's justifiably well-reputed books were highly collectable investments was by no means incidental to this state of affairs. The media reported what Joyce's representatives said as facts. One wellspring of the latter's moral indignation was Roth's assumed lack of permission, regarding not only the *Ulysses* episodes in the monthly but the "Work in Progress" episodes in the quarterly. Beach's open letter to the literary press requested readers who had copies of *Two Worlds* to contact her regarding whether contributors had signed their work.[72] This aforementioned feature of Roth's project was discarded before publication, so there would be no such copies. That did not mean his project was fraudulent, but Beach made it appear to be an indication. Two of the newspapers that covered Joyce's troubles in detail carried her charge about lack of payment for the "Work in Progress" excerpts: the *International Chicago Tribune* (edited by Bernhardt Ragnar) and the *New York Post,* whose literary editor was Henry Seidel Canby. The *Tribune* wrote that "The new unnamed work, now running serially in *transition*, was also pirated by Mr. Roth when its first installments ran in an English quarterly."[73] (*The Egoist* was meant; it ran excerpts concurrently with *The Little Review*.) The *Post* quoted Beach's "without permission and without payment" mantra, part of her open letter.[74] Her letter to *This Quarter* declared that "some time ago" Roth published unauthorized excerpts of "Work in Progress" and printed (she referred to what Hemingway said) 8,000 copies, not 450. Her implication, left unstated possibly to ward off what would be an embarrassing libel suit, was that Roth was nothing but an egregious thief.

Ezra Pound: "Hell and Yet Again Hell" (1928)

The question of whether Roth may actually have had Pound's permission to publish selections from *Ulysses* or "Work in Progress" can only be answered tentatively. The missing July 3, 1922, letter aside, Pound's letter (from Vienna) to Bernhardt Ragnar, the editor of the *International Chicago Tribune*, dated May 23, 1928, states, "As I considered [in 1922] the law under which *Ulysses* was suppressed an outrage, the people who tolerate the law little better than apes, I approved the suggestion, that is to say, I wrote [to Roth], as nearly as I can remember that I approved any legal means of nullifying the effect of article 211 of the US penal code."[75] As I stated above in connection with the Copyright Office procedure and the Manufacturing Clause, it was the latter that often led to difficulty with copyright (although a work legally interdicted as obscene would be intercepted by Customs). The profit motive behind it infuriated Pound. In Kugel's judgment, the May 23 letter to Ragnar is "at last Pound's confession of permission."[76] She and others believed that Pound, when deposed in Genoa in the spring of 1928,[77] before the resolution of Joyce's suit against Roth to cease publishing *Ulysses,* stated he did not give Roth permission, thus perjuring himself. However, thanks to the research of Robert Spoo, it is now clear that Pound did not put anything on record regarding the injunction. He wrote Joyce: "Don't I owe you 20 or 30 simolean dollars, for not having my fingerprints taken v. Roth?. . . . wot became of it . . . gone to trial without my Alf.David.??"[78]

Pound wrote his May 23 letter, which appeared in the May 26 issue of the *International Herald Tribune,* because he was angry concerning what he called "slanderous" rumors about him. Presumably the Paris literary community was talking about his not signing the International Protest of February 1927 against Roth. They would have also been curious about his reluctance to give the deposition. Clearly, Pound did not like the idea of being deposed. He had done much to further Joyce's career and publishing prospects without any reciprocal interest on Joyce's part regarding his need to concentrate on his own writing. For a number of years he had regretted attending more to the careers of contemporary writers, and especially Joyce, than to own poetry; he did not want to stop what he was doing to prepare to testify.[79] Joyce relied heavily on friends to attend to his business affairs so that he could continue to write. A distraught Sylvia Beach finally wrote him in 1927 that "every time a new terrible effort is required of me and I manage to accomplish the task that is set me you try to see how much more I can do."[80]

Pound put it differently. "Hell and yet again hell," he had written to Ragnar on March 21, 1928, before he had apparently agreed to testify, "Have just recd. Bales of 'Depositions' in the suit of Joyce v. Roth. Suggest you play it up. Knock *hell* out of Article 211, out of copyright piracy, and out of consulate, bureaucracy, the thieving Roth and things in general. Interview with Joyce might also be staged."[81] The need to complete his account of what he did and did not do was a chief motive for the May 23 letter. It gave him a chance to suggest—and this is very true—that Roth took advantage of what he did say and did so three years after he said it. As stated above, whatever sanction Roth may have acquired was not timely and therefore not valid when Roth began *Two Worlds Monthly* in 1926. By all conventions of publisher-author relations, it should have been supplemented by either Joyce's own sanction or by that of his agent at the time, Sylvia Beach.

Joyce's Injunction against Roth (1928)

The December 24, 1928, lawsuit decision was in the form of an injunction prohibiting Roth from publishing anything by Joyce and from using the author's name in advertisements.[82] Roth agreed to this, since, due to losses he had incurred with *Two Worlds Monthly*, he was no longer publishing the magazine. Conde Nast Publications, for example, collected $1,569 for non-payment of advertisements in February 1928.[83] Roth, broke, had nothing to lose by accepting the injunction. Therefore, Herbert Gorman, Forrest Read, and Richard Ellmann are wrong in claiming that Joyce forced Roth to stop publishing by bringing suit.[84] Joyce knew, for at least one of his American friends or lawyers would have made it clear, that he had no case for violation of copyright. These three scholars' interpretations are results of the advertising campaign by Joyce's supporters that told the story of a brave, successful fight put up by an impecunious literary genius of established avant-garde reputation against a piratical parvenu publisher.

That publicity, leading up to and following the International Protest, made Joyce's case stronger when he applied for the injunction. He hoped it would afterward as well. It may seem rather anticlimactic to have the New York Supreme Court state that Roth could no longer use Joyce's name in any publication. But Joyce hoped a more significant precedent would be in the offing. It is therefore interesting to note that according to the law firm of Greenbaum, Wolff, and Ernst, the injunction had no force in law, since it was "granted by consent, and of course could have no binding force in any subsequent proceeding."[85] Joyce was banking on a very different interpretation. Carol L. Shloss, building on Robert Spoo's *Yale Law Review* essay and its discussion of copyright and obscenity law, explains Joyce's "European" conception of "moral right."[86] She quotes his 1937 speech at the PEN Club: the injunction, he said, implies a "juridical conclusion . . . that the bench can protect an author against the mutilation and publication of his work just as he is protected against the wrong use of his name." Shloss goes on to say that Joyce wanted to develop a legal justification for circumventing a piracy suit made futile due to lack of international copyright agreement, and also due to the concept that the creator of "obscenity" has "dirty hands" and thus cannot claim copyright. His basis was that creative work such as his *Ulysses* is an exception to the above strictures—as a work of imaginative power it represents his very identity as a person, to which he has a "moral right." He thought that the decision that Roth could not use his name in order to market his work, a personal possession greater than any commodity, could be extended to give Joyce power to prosecute anyone who would publish *Ulysses* without his permission. That the work was in the public domain was superseded by this principle of "moral right." This helps explain the intensity of Joyce's response to Roth's American publications of his novel.

Joyce's Fears That Roth Could Destroy His Livelihood

If *Two Worlds Monthly* presented a problem for the Vice Society, it was an equally serious one for the business that Joyce, Pound, John Rodker, and Weaver were in. As Roth published his *Ulysses* excerpts openly in 1926, Joyce's position was different than in 1922, when rumors of an unknown American pirate surfaced soon after *Ulysses'* first impression appeared. Then, Weaver wrote Quinn that he might "appeal to the aid of the Anti-Vice Society" to hunt him down.[87] She decided not to take this course, for Rodker had assured her that "American agents" who bought many copies had been receiving them. Therefore, the anonymous pirate would not have many customers. She thus avoided having to appeal to the Society for the Suppression of Vice, the aesthetic and political standards of which were the opposite of her own.

In 1926 many copies of *Ulysses* had been confiscated, hurting (Joyce thought) chances for an American publisher to risk a limited edition. Such a venture would be lucrative for the writer. He would not need to pay a professional agent. The book would not be wholesaled to distributors but sold directly to collectors and book dealers, especially those who, recognizing that its value would increase, would pay the high price. Nor would there be a 20 percent tax on printing, as there would have been for a book manufactured in England.[88] For the Shakespeare and Company edition, Joyce's royalties were to be 66 percent. This was not exceptional for privately published literature. Lawrence, who, although ill, was deeply involved in marketing *Lady Chatterley's Lover*, got 90 percent of all proceeds.[89]

Upon hearing the false reports that Roth was circulating 50,000 copies of

Two Worlds Monthly and "pocketing at least 1,000,000 francs a month," Joyce was ready to take sweeping action.[90] *The Little Review*'s circulation had been about 500.[91] He wrote to his brother, a few weeks before the International Protest appeared, "*Ulysses* sold well there [in the] last five years, but Roth has killed the sales here, too, and has, or will, pocket the proceeds of 25 normal editions. . . . If Roth carries this through, the pirates in America will make it the beginning of even worse."[92] His New York lawyers, when requesting the injunction, reiterated his complaint that if not for Roth's piracies, *Ulysses* would have brought Joyce at least $10,000 in profits.[93] Earlier, as Beach had made public in a letter to the editor of *This Quarter*, Hemingway had reported that, as mentioned above, as many as 8,000 copies of *Two Worlds* had been sold.[94] That was a wild exaggeration, but as Adelaide Kugel conjectured, her father exaggerated also, to impress Hemingway when they met for dinner one night in New York to discuss Roth's buying some stories for one of his magazines.

And Hemingway exaggerated further.[95] He wrote to Maxwell Perkins that "Joyce is all broken up about it. Roth has stolen his *Ulysses* without permission, never paid Joyce a cent, is publishing *Ulysses* in monthly installments and expurgating it. . . . Joyce is in absolute despair. The work of 13 years of his life being stolen from him by a man who not content with that trys [*sic*] to blacken Joyce's character and not content with stealing a man's life work and lieing [*sic*] about it then garbles it."[96] Hemingway was not only melodramatic but paranoid, adding that Roth had pirated every story he himself wrote in Paris.[97] Adelaide Kugel suggests that perhaps Hemingway was trying to impress Perkins, his new editor.[98] He also conceived a puerile plot to trap Roth by circulating in New York a small print run of "Today Is Friday," which he thought Roth would pirate, thus giving him a chance to "nab" the thief.[99] No work by the author is in Roth's periodicals.[100] There is an advertisement for a story in *Two Worlds Monthly*, but Hemingway was too expensive.[101] Nor should any have been advertised.

Hemingway's histrionics aside, Joyce mirrored his scorn of Roth and his kind ("Rothim," in the punny argot of *Finnegans Wake*). They would conflate prurient interest and sexually explicit literature to make money from hoi polloi, at the same time taking it from the pockets of serious writers by killing their prospects of experimental limited-edition sales. After Roth's unexpurgated book-length *Ulysses* appeared in 1928 or 1929 (it was based on the May 1927 impression of Shakespeare and Company's edition), Joyce's outrage increased. When, in March 1932, Milton Abernethy of *Contempo* magazine published a review by Roth (the magazine had earlier carried an advertisement and a review of some publications of his William Faro imprint), he earned Joyce's furious condemnation. Pound was then a contributing editor to *Contempo*. "How can you [Pound] possibly allow an honorable name like yours to be used as a shield for such a rascal? I consider it monstrous that he should be offered the hospitality of any literary paper."[102]

A "Nut Poet" or a Threat to the Marketing of Modernism?

Roth's credit was badly overextended by the time the Protest appeared. Five years earlier, when John Quinn informed Sylvia Beach that she needn't worry about "Samuel Froth," he said Roth had little money, owed creditors, and was known to New York publishers as a "nut poet . . . full of crazy ideas."[103] He underestimated Roth, who did not end in jail for his *Two Worlds* excerpts. But Quinn was quite realistic about Roth's prospects for ultimate success.

In view of the facts, Joyce and his friends responded to Roth's *Ulysses* excerpts with what looks like a surplus of bile and, as I hope to show, a good measure of dishonesty. It leads to an important question: Did Joyce and his publishers and agents think collectors of finely printed first editions, their primary customers, would be satisfied with the barbered excerpts Roth offered on newsstands and by mail order? It does not seem possible. Beach's Shakespeare and Company edition, published after subscribers reserved copies, was manufactured in France by a master printer on fine paper with one hundred "special" copies signed by Joyce.[104] Perusing Beach's sales records, Lawrence Rainey shows that less than half of the copies of her edition went to individual readers, while about 60 percent went to people who recognized their worth as a collectable investment. Privately printed copies of *Lady Chatterley's Lover* and *Ulysses* were not presented to the general public as a good read or to cognoscenti as exceptional contemporary writing. Instead, publishers and booksellers made them desirable to financially comfortable readers—"middlebrows," Rainey terms them—as avant-garde works worth understanding and keeping as prime examples of contemporary imaginative achievements, however sexually explicit in style or erotically shocking they may have been.[105]

Even so, Roth's *Two Worlds Monthly* excerpts may have made those well-off collectors think of their Shakespeare and Company copies as less significant. Beach's production was superior in design and integrity of text. But to have the work, or parts of it, available to a diverse audience of newsstand readers diluted its value as expensive object. Its scarcity had been compromised and thus its mystique as a rare artifact. Joyce, like other writers, may have felt *Ulysses'* reputation cheapened by exposure to bourgeois readers, including shopgirls, office workers, and college boys believed to be unsuited for appreciating anything more than the taboo words and risqué behavior.[106]

Roth presented another indirect threat: his knowledge of a group of middlemen entrepreneurs dealing in erotica. Joyce himself was too far removed from the realities of publishing and bookselling to be aware of how his books might get into diverse readers' hands. Otherwise, why would he have listened to a shrill, callow Hemingway? However, people like Weaver, Rodker, and Pound knew more. They may have seen clearly the danger Joyce dimly sensed. *Ulysses* and *Chatterley* were read by a diverse group of people in Europe and America, who were susceptible to various sales pitches and motivated in diverse ways (especially by word-of-mouth suggestion). These readers were not frequenters of upscale locations such as those on the Left Bank, Charing Cross Road, or midtown Manhattan, where store owners had legitimate first or otherwise authorized editions on hand. Many found unauthorized copies, above or under the counter, complete and expurgated, in the smaller general-interest and secondhand bookshops of Europe and America, where readers from indeterminate social backgrounds rubbed shoulders with not only with the elite but with undercover agents of the vigilant anti-vice societies searching out "dirty books" where they would most likely turn up, and where they could find booksellers, like Roth, more vulnerable to scorn and prosecution than those whose wealthy clientele could afford them protection. Many smuggled copies (acquired from bookleggers) were rented out from booksellers' back rooms as if they were running lending libraries, for in a few months one's investment could be recouped; profits could extend over a period of years.[107]

The publishing and distributing strategies of erotic booksellers like Roth seemed "monkeyish" to Lawrence, and predatory to Joyce. Being a professional writer was difficult enough due to arrangements with publishers, agents, and critics. Building a reputation with the general public and the academic literary establishment took time and effort. The legislation of morality sometimes required irritating revision. All that was part of the game, best left to one's admirers, patrons, and friends. But the "Rothim" represented a degeneracy that might make it impossible for the writer to continue to make a living.

At the bottom of Joyce's outrage was not the absence of copyright protection, regardless of the statements Weaver and Beach made to newspapers, and despite the high-flown wording of the International Protest. That document was motivated by a more personal, and of course interrelated, matter, as deeply involved in personal identity as was his reputation as an avant-garde writer: losing profits. Pound explained to Joyce that he did not sign it, because it was a "misfire."[108] That must have been dismaying to Joyce, who may have felt that Pound slighted his character. Richard Ellmann writes that Pound "thought Joyce was putting personal advertisement ahead of the general evil of the copyright and pornography laws and using 'a mountain battery to shoot a gnat.'" Joyce's attention, Pound thought, should be on what the latter had described several years earlier as "The Eunited, Eunuchated States of America" and, as Ellmann goes on to say, "with the whole American people who sanction the state of the laws."[109] Pound wrote H. L. Mencken that "you, confound you, with your columns on asinine legislation ought to dig out Article 211."[110] This law, equally with the Manufacturing Clause, was to Pound part of the capitalist tyranny repressing imaginative work.[111]

Pound's concerns were seen by Joyce and his supporters as both irrelevant to the business of decensoring *Ulysses* and as quixotic. Hemingway called them "moonshine."[112] That in itself suggests that either Pound had not made clear to them his growing quarrel with capitalism and America or that they did not sympathize with it. Their practical if not their aesthetic interests precluded their doing so. As Beach wrote regarding Joyce, this "great loveable but merciless man" was "a great business man, hard as nails," with "one-sided business methods."[113] The most lucrative way to publish *Ulysses* (in 1927; by 1930 the situation was different, as Huebsch and Bennett Cerf, among others, were realizing) was in an expensive limited edition that upscale booksellers' agents would sell to wealthy collectors.[114]

Joyce and his friends needed the International Protest to make clear that the *Ulysses* in *Two Worlds Monthly* was as textually as it was morally corrupt and therefore worth nothing to either general readers or collectors of finely printed as well as authentic avant-garde literature. The way to do that was to create in Sam Roth the archetype of a desecrater of literary expression. His friends and supporters could do that for him. Joyce had shaped his own image as a dedicated literary genius with little time for mundane affairs. Gordon Bowker tells us he seldom gave interviews, and instructed Gorman that he should leave out of his biography information that would fully reveal the novelist's problems: his reason for not returning to Ireland in 1912, his father's and his own drinking, his daughter's mental instability, his occasional carousing. Joyce insisted on reading Gorman's proofs.[115] The image of the retiring, dedicated writer ("the hero of the Paris cafes," Roth called him)[116] helped make the necessary contrast with the bumptious "pirate" against whom 167 literary and intellectual colleagues rallied on behalf of an icon.

The two worlds' worth of ignominy Roth acquired as a result of his Joyce publications was as much the result of spotlighting his barbering as it was of his piracy. Joyce's friends publicized, to the point of dodgy exaggeration, Roth's "mutilation" and "bowdlerization." In the course of his future career, the extent to which Roth expurgated was remarkable. He was also capable of bowdlerization, although he boiled with indignation when it was suggested. He did both with the 1930 "Samuel Roth" edition of *Lady Chatterley's Lover,* and so cleverly that it served as a basis for the Secker/Knopf authorized abridged edition two years later. "Miss Beach Plans to Sue Mutilator of Joyce's Work," read one *Chicago International Tribune* headline. But to what extent were the 1926–27 "mutilations" egregious?

In a letter to the *Saturday Review,* Beach wrote that Roth had lied when he said only "'a dozen words were left out of the first two installments by a subeditor.' [The statement] condemns itself upon comparison of the Two World's [*sic*] publication with an authentic edition. One hundred and thirty-one variations from the original appear in the first eight installments, . . . ranging from the changing or deletion of one word to the omission of twelve lines."[117] Did the twelve lines count as 1, 12, or 120 variations? Regardless, Roth expurgated less than did Pound and Margaret Anderson for *The Little Review,* which publication neither Beach nor any other commentator ever mentioned.[118] They were, as was convenient for making their point, comparing Roth's text with the 1922 Shakespeare and Company edition.

In his reprint of the "Telemachus" and "Proteus" episodes (volume 1, number 1 of *Two Worlds Monthly*), Roth's "mutilations" amounted to leaving out the phrase "is she up the pole"; six lines about men masturbating in the public baths; and a few sentences, which Pound also left out in *The Little Review,* involving dogs defecating. In the next issue of the *Monthly* came "Calypso," and a bowdlerization that Herbert Gorman and the Joyceans made a chief sign of Roth's perfidy. This is the substitution of "crater" for "cunt" ("the grey sunken cunt of the world"). Gorman fumed about the Mutilator's rib-nudging euphony, but Pound bowdlerized as well, substituting "belly." Is Roth's "p—d on his halldoor" (in "Scylla and Charybdis") worse than *The Little Review*'s substitution, a set of ellipses? In reprinting Bloom's visit to the outhouse, Roth leaves out more ("seated calm above his rising smell"; "and wiped himself with it") than *The Little Review.* Roth also bowdlerized ("crazy door" for "door of the jakes"), but Pound left out the entire paragraph in which the offending phrase occurred. That issue also contained "Lotus Eaters." Roth but not Pound leaves out "a stump of black guttapercha wagging limp"; Pound but not Roth leaves out "limp father of thousands." In Roth's next issue, reprinting "Aeolus," he commits another euphonic bowdlerization, "He can kiss my royal Irish aunt" (aunt for "arse"). Roth's version of "Lestrygonians" (volume 1, issue 4) expurgated two references to gonorrhea. "Always cutting my phrose to please his phrase," Joyce wrote in the *Wake*.

Interestingly, both Roth and *The Little Review* printed in full (including "fat nipples") Bloom's reverie about Molly and Bloom making love. Sumner did not complain to Heap and Anderson, but he was about to start a devastating harassment campaign. When *The Little Review* printed the "Scylla and Charybdis" episode, Anderson noted for her readers that certain lines had to be left out due to the Post Office surveillance. The most evident example was excision of the phrase "a honeymoon in the hand" after the mock title "Everyman His Own Wife." This episode appeared as Joyce wrote it in Roth's volume 2, issue 1. His "Scylla and Charybdis" and his "Cyclops" (issues 3 and 4) contain only minor cuts, while *The Little Review*'s are perforce expurgated. His "Cyclops" passage discussing erections in men who have been cut down after hanging is left intact, although Anderson told her readers that "some twenty lines" had been removed.[119]

Perhaps Roth made a point of giving his readers what *The Little Review* could not. However, he also leaves in some words and phrases that appear in the earlier magazine: "kick the shite out of him," "Their syphilization," and "tonguetied sons of bastards' ghosts," among others. "Nausicaa" (in the *Monthly*, volume 2, issue 4) was the last episode *The Little Review* published. Pound left out only one word: "wet" (with spilled semen). Sumner brought suit, and Anderson and Heap lost the case. Roth presents this episode nearly without abridgment. This includes passages about menstrual cycles, mutoscope pictures of the "for men only" kind (reproductions of images of women in lingerie, or of their bodies, in what looked like moving images), Bloom's opinion of female fantasies ("I'm all clean come and dirty me"; taking a man from another woman), fireworks and erect penises, and Bloom's gratitude to Gertie for providing him the relief of masturbation. The expurgation and bowdlerization that Beach had exaggerated had dwindled as *Two Worlds Monthly* proceeded, and as Roth got more desperate for newsstand sales.

There are several reasons why Roth might have only lightly expurgated "Scylla and Charybdis," "Cyclops," and "Nausicaa" (although several of the latter's passages had been vehemently objected to by a lawyer whose daughter had acquired a copy of *The Little Review*).[120] One is that erotica publishers had to take risks. Second, by 1927 the book trade and journalists had succeeded in reducing Sumner's power. Excellent lawyers—Sumner's special nemesis was Morris Ernst of the ACLU's National Council on Freedom from Censorship—had defeated him in court; thereafter, liberal newspapers had presented him as a snoop and an intransigent prude. These reversals, concern about contributions from supporters of the Society, and increased tolerances for sexual explicitness forced him to concentrate on obvious smut instead of literary classics.[121] By 1930, Joyce was making a renewed effort to get *Ulysses* published in the United States. Claude Kendall, Huebsch, and Random House seemed to be very serious about doing so.[122]

A final reason for Roth's boldness in the segments he published in volume 2 of the *Monthly* is that Sumner may have had to act with some restraint. Eisenman, and probably Roth, would have known that the "town censor" did not take action against retailers, distributors, or wholesalers who had contributed to his Society. This does not mean he was hypocritical any more than Roth, Joyce, or Beach was. Business is business. Sumner needed money to continue his crusade. That meant the recruiting of an impressive number of contributors to show his board of directors. It is possible that Eisenman's Metropolitan News Company bought Sumner's tolerance by becoming one of these contributors. This final point is relevant here because the politics of erotica, and modernist literary, distribution is complex, as the manipulation of facts equally by Joyce's supporters and Roth evinces.

Roth had begun by being very sensitive to potential censorship. Before publishing *Ulysses* he reassured the advertising manager of *The Nation*, which had accepted his notice, that there would be no trouble with the censors. "The work is being carefully expurgated by us and we have sent both the first and second numbers through the mails."[123]

In February 1927, when Sumner refused to allow the *Monthly* (and *Beau*) to be sold on newsstands, Roth, as many had before him, went to see him. The latter thereupon allowed the *Ulysses* excerpt, although he would not allow *Beau*'s reprinting of Ben Franklin's "Advice on Choosing a Mistress." That same month, Roth visited Boston to talk to the president of the Watch and Ward Society, Raymond Calkins, taking copies of these two magazines. Regarding *Ulysses*, a confused but not censorious Calkins exchanged a tentative approval for the elimination of articles on homosexuality, Charlie Chaplin's morals, and "Some of the Secrets of Becoming a Successful Mistress."[124]

What the Protest and its publicizers—including Joyce himself—stated about Roth has been universally adopted by writers on *Ulysses*, both in 1927 and since. R. F. Roberts, in his "bibliographical notes" in 1936, chortled over the "many [omitted] passages and phrases" in Roth's magazines but did not mention the barbering in *The Little Review*.[125] For Gorman, publishing in 1939, Roth was simply an "astonishing pirate," "a "callous thief."[126] Today, excellent scholars follow this line. Paul Vanderham states that to have *Ulysses* published by Roth would in itself warn authorities of its obscenity. But Roth, although by 1936 "much prosecuted," was known only as a writer and bookseller and had no citations for writing or publishing obscenity.[127] Bruce Arnold's comment shows the extent to which Roth brought this derision on himself. Arnold refers to the "New York publisher and religious crank who believed that he was called by God as a good man in his generation."[128] Roth actually wrote this in his introduction to the second volume of *Two Worlds*, by way of wondering why the clamor of Joyce's supporters should claim his attention. In 1974, Leo Hamalian wrote an influential essay, "Nobody Knows My Names: Samuel Roth and the Underside of Modern Letters." He based the piece on an interview with Roth. But he flatly describes the *Ulysses* excerpts as "cruelly bowdlerized to placate the censors."[129] How much crueler must *The Little Review* have been?

Samuel Roth and Cultural Capital

Joyce's supporters succeeded in determining Roth's pariah status for the rest of his career. A final example is his series of communications with book collector John Slocum in 1950, when the two met by chance in Ben Abramson's New York bookshop.[130] After Slocum was subjected to Roth's insistent self-defense, he wrote Abramson, "I think [Roth] would have been a world beater if he had ever been able to distinguish between right and wrong."[131] In contrast, the International Protest seemed an exemplary defense by "inspired talent spotters who, guided by their disinterested, unreasoning passion for a work of art have 'made' a painter or writer, or have helped him make himself, by encouraging him in difficult moments with the faith they had in him, guiding him with their advice and freeing him from material worries."[132] In Joyce's case these "talent spotters" included Beach, Weaver, Lewisohn, MacLeish, John Quinn, Arnold Bennett, Middleton Murry, influential Paris journalist Sisley Huddleston,[133] Eugene Jolas, translator Valery Larbaud, Rodker, and Pound.

The words are anthropologist and philosopher Pierre Bourdieu's, describing the work of establishing a writer's or artist's reputation in a particular culture. A few of these workers were rewarded in February 1927 by an invitation to celebrate with Joyce the publishing of the International Protest.[134] Bourdieu writes of "cultural capital": the power of prestige, not money, which media, other writers, publishers, and critics can bestow on an artist because they understand the system of ideas and behaviors by which prestige is established.[135] Marketers of modernism needed to establish legitimacy by setting critical standards and by pointing out a set of creative artists who have used them in a manner critics admire. "Gatekeepers of culture," such as Cerf and Random House, find people adept in translating, editing, and distributing works that the authors can attest are authentic. These people must fight off pressures to revise or redact the author's works from social conservatives offended by their sexual frankness or political implications. They must get texts printed in tasteful, well-crafted, and readable formats for "proper" readers, who will appreciate them for their creative, if iconoclastic, originality, not their prurience or propaganda value, and for their literary exclusivity, not for their mass appeal. All of these sophisticated criteria are also subjective and class based. They are accepted by wealthy "middlebrows" who have financial means to patronize great writers and their publishers.

Joyce's friends understood these criteria of cultural capital and knew how to get *Ulysses* marketed by showing it was an epitome of them. They were the discriminating and scrupulous arbiters of literature. A good example of a man they could respect was the Giorgio Joyce's brother-in-law, Robert Kastor, a New York stockbroker and book collector. Bennett Cerf, whom Kastor asked in 1931 to publish *Ulysses* and fight it through the courts, recalls the soft-spoken Kastor and his firm partner, famous "in Yale Crew annals" and for his expertise at sailing and bridge. Their office "might be mistaken for an old southern club, with a liveried old negro flunkey at the door, and a handful of distinguished old gentlemen watching the stock quotations."[136]

It was invaluable that Joyce's defenders had, in Roth, the opposite kind of entrepreneur, one they could stigmatize as a pirate, "mutilator," and "bowdlerizer": one who would without permission print the four-page excerpt from Eliot's "Fragment of an Egon" under the poet's working title for *Sweeney Agonistes*, "Wanna Go Home Baby?"[137] He thus cavalierly used Eliot's phrase as an apt, prurient wink at *Two Worlds Monthly*'s newsstand readers. With an obeisance faintly scented with irony (this was after the International Protest), he proceeded to dedicate this issue to Eliot, "who has given [!] us some excellent verses, several sound critical formulae, and one of the most charming literary personalities of our time." Roth's own ghostly voice, which modernist scholar Paul K. Saint-Amour, in a brilliant piece, has channeled from Elysium for readers of the *James Joyce Quarterly*, declared: "There is nothing like a pariah to galvanize the right-thinking. Put another way, ideas of privilege seldom go unaccompanied by ideas of punishment. . . . I became the *bête noir*

Samuel Roth, Infamous Modernist

of modernism, the king of its shadow realm."[138] That he used as colophon for *Two Worlds* "the sign of the mocki-grisball" is further proof. Respectability and privilege do not have the power they need if there is no impertinent "shadow side," just as the defender of decency, the moral entrepreneur, cannot gain and keep public attention without his or her symbiotic relationship to enemies such as the gangster, madam, gambler, or pornographer. Roth seemed to need to be and enjoy being the nemesis on the other side of the mirror. Another phrase for this is "cultural mutation." In 1927, Samuel Roth was an American cultural mutation, indeed a shadow side of modernism. Similarly, at the end of his life he worried that hard-core explicitness would bring a reversal of the liberalization of freedom of expression he took credit for. For him, the openly published hard-core paperbacks explicitly describing intercourse, homosexuality, and sadomasochism were the dangerous cultural mutation.[139] When he himself had distributed books about such subjects, he was much more restrained. He may have forgotten that his business as well as the law required that he be.

Roth knew how difficult it was to attain cultural capital without appearing to worm one's way into it like a *mocki*. The word was often applied to a Jew "on the make," especially in the garment industry, with an eastern European accent and "ghetto" manners. Sam Roth had both ambition and an accent, but he added a veneer of British inflection after his visit to London, when he added to his haberdashery the aforementioned walking stick ("to subdue my enemies," he joked to his daughter)[140] and spats. British names suggested to him Continental refinement, suitable for a bookseller serving the affluent with an erotica section in their gentlemen's libraries.[141] The alias under which he distributed his first piece of porno (1928) was "Roger St. Clair." The name suggested a man of taste and education, whose library could safely contain subversive and esoteric works. "St. Clair" reminded Roth of the Chicago book dealer St. George Best, who was an agent for the infamous Charles Carrington, publisher of classic banned erotica in beautifully printed editions.[142]

After his initial success with *Two Worlds*, Roth moved the family to the sumptuous Hotel Ansonia on the Upper West Side (where Stravinsky, Florenz Ziegfeld, and Theodore Dreiser stayed). The Roth apartment featured a bathroom with marble fixtures and a large refrigerator in the kitchen. He began purchasing status items for himself and his family: a writing desk, a highboy, a chest of drawers. From auction houses he brought home a Tiffany-inspired desk set and framed paintings. From clothing stores he got "white linen plus-fours probably inspired by Gatsby," and for Pauline "an ivory satin gown trimmed with mink which made her furious with him."[143] Gershon Legman, writing to Adelaide Kugel when she was collecting information for "In a Plain Brown Wrapper," warned her that she would have to deal with her enigmatic father's need to reinvent himself on his own terms:

> The essential problem was always an attempt to rid himself of his identity and be someone or something else, more snazzy, more admirable—also less Jewish, until his old age—without really wanting to go to the trouble involved. He therefore accepted anyone else's identity, and thus anyone else's literary identity and property with perfect calm, since in a way he felt he had a perfect right to it—needing it so. That's a very American ethic, as you know. A significant number of his magazine titles ("Two Worlds," "American Aphrodite," etc) are simply famous European magazine titles, appropriated to the American scene; and I imagine his unauthorized publications were similarly justified. . . . In that sense, SR's discussions of himself as a benefactor of literature (though admittedly not of authors!), can be fathomed.[144]

Man of letters, refined British gentleman, man about town, literary arbiter, cultural commentator welcomed into clubs, theaters, and cafés although Jewish and foreign-born: Roth desired all of these self-images. And yet, why use the mocki-grisball colophon, so antithetical to these goals? He wanted to retain that luftmensch-like strategy of creative independence. That's what made him a cultural mutation. However much it isolated him from success in the publishing community, it pleased that bedrock, stiff-necked element in his character that intertwined with creativity and energy: his "prince of a pauper's pride." It had been so with the first Roth in Nuszcze, Jerosh, and it seemed to be so with Samuel Roth in America. Of course it would prove disorienting to himself and his loved ones.

As his career developed, he proved with *Jews Must Live* to be, temporarily, a traitor to his own people. His clothing, many non-Jewish friends (outnumbering his Jewish ones), fascination with Jesus, and publishing of obscenity are other disorienting elements. But some of his best writing shows a deep appreciation of Hasidic folklore and ideals. His final novel was about the final assimilation of the Jewish and Christian religions, thanks to the sacrifice of a Jesus with a very Jewish belief system, with "menschlekeit" substituting for "mercy."

The more he resented Joyce, Pound, Eliot, and Lewisohn, the more he wanted what they had. He baited these fine writers in his magazines and excoriated them in letters to editors, with equal outrage as he did John Sumner, another arbiter and, in fact, patrician. Roth had trapped himself in a symbiotic relationship. The more he tried to drain off some of their charisma, repute, or cultural capital, in order to invest himself with some of it, the more these literary nemeses of his could use his fulminations to show their own legitimacy and the hubris of the churlish, jumped-up pirate named Samuel Roth. They were joined by middle-class people who wanted to separate themselves from disreputable fellow citizens whose shameful acts might call their own hard-won, still-insecure status into question. In March 1927, about a month after the International Protest, a Clean Books Committee of Hungarian Jews ("the Jewish edition of Mr Sumner," Roth called them) filed a complaint in Jefferson Court against Roth because of obscenity in *Two Worlds Monthly* and *Beau.* The *Ulysses* episodes were among their chief complaints.[145]

Roth regarded the Hungarian Jews with amused superiority. Another critic of his behavior regarding *Ulysses,* his friend Maurice Samuel, hurt him deeply, enraging him by making him feel beneath contempt. Asked to support Roth regarding the charges of the International Protest, Maurice wrote frankly about the "conventions" with which, as an aspiring member of the literary establishment ("my circle"), he had aligned himself. His *You Gentiles,* about differences between Jewish and non-Jews in American society, had been published by the well-established firm of Harcourt, Brace (previously known as World Publishing). In 1927 the same firm published his *I, the Jew.* "My reputation and my credit lie in a certain world which is altogether antagonistic to you," he wrote Roth, "and would be to anyone associated with you. . . . If I felt you had antagonized it in pursuit of something important, or something good, I would not hesitate. . . . But I learned nothing from you that might make me believe this."[146]

For Roth this was a crushing shock of recognition of what the International Protest meant. Maurice's response was an act of betrayal. Thereafter, the man was, to his former friend, "Moishe Schmeeil"; a "callow English youth whose real business in the United States was dodging the British military draft."[147] Maurice became Roth's personal scapegoat for all those who had denied him the status he felt due him in the world of literature and publishing: people such as Lewisohn, Root, Beach, Joyce, Eliot, Herbert Gorman, and Hemingway, all of whom had deprived Mr. Roth of New York of any cultural capital he may have acquired with his poetry or editorial work.

In 1925, Sam Roth was at the height of his career as commentator on contemporary Jewish life. Subsequently, Roth witnessed Maurice Samuel taking over that role for their generation of American Jews.[148] Maurice had the career as man of letters Sam had plotted out for himself, while he was relegated

Figure 12. Maurice Samuel, once Roth's close friend but later considered a nemesis. By permission of the Marcus Center of the American Jewish Archives, Cincinnati, Ohio.

to an outcast status as the pirate of *Ulysses,* and later as the self-hating Jew who wrote *Jews Must Live,* and as the middleman distributor of "schmutz." It was Maurice Samuel who wrote books about the life and works of the Yiddish writers he and Roth had both loved, particularly Sholem Aleichem and C. N. Bialik. It was Samuel, with his King's English acquired from fourteen formative years, not six months, in England, who became a leading lecturer, translator of Sholem Asch and I. J. Singer, and chronicler of the story of the aforementioned Mendel Beilis. Roth had published poems on Bialik in his twenties and read Aleichem's stories aloud, to his family and to patrons in his bookshop. He had a contract in 1925 to translate Beilis's account of his arrest and trial but did not complete the work, due probably to his labors to establish his *Two Worlds* magazines.[149] In 1966, Maurice published a book on the Psalms, based on his radio conversations with Mark Van Doren. At the same time, Roth was composing his last book of poems, the "Israeli Davidia or Psalms of David." He had little hope of getting it published and read.

Roth's ostracism from readers, writers, and publishers was not as complete as it seemed in 1927. He received letters from subscribers to his magazines as far away as California who had read of his troubles. Some canceled subscriptions;

Samuel Roth, Infamous Modernist

others requested explanations if they were not to do so. There were expressions of support also, some accompanied with requests for more readable banned books, such as Harris's *My Life*.[150] Roth had, with his wonted opportunism, established a Two Worlds Defense Fund, focusing on his troubles over sexual content rather than on the Protest. He was proud of supporters such as Marianne Moore of *The Dial*, who had decided against printing *Ulysses* excerpts; the physician and writer Ralcy Halstead Bell; George Whitsett, the editor of *Contemporary Verse*; and Jim Tully, who averred, "I would say that Mr. Joyce has been given a fair deal."[151] He also drew considerable comfort from the fact that some of the best writers, such as Aldous Huxley, George Bernard Shaw, George Moore, not to mention Pound, did not sign the Protest.

There was at least one modernist publisher who continued to do business with Roth. This was John Rodker, British contributing editor to *The Little Review*, who found the French printer for the second impression, by the Egoist Press, of *Ulysses*. A month after the Protest appeared, Rodker expressed his gratitude for Roth's interest in the erotica he published in Paris under his Casanova Society imprint. He had a New York representative call on Roth with a copy of *Eastern Love* and *Sara*.[152] Business is business. Perhaps this is why the wife of composer George Antheil, when she broached the subject of Roth and his pirated edition of *Ulysses* to Frances Steloff, owner of the Gotham Book Mart, was told that Steloff was "anxious not to be connected to this affair."[153] Roth was a distributor who could fulfill the needs of many readers of modernist works with sexually explicit passages. These were among the Gotham's best customers, as they were of Ben Abramson, whose friendship with Roth was cemented during his days of publishing Joyce, Lawrence, and others.

Frothing Lion: Roth at the James Joyce Society (1950)

At his Westchester bookshop in 1949, Abramson introduced Roth to John Slocum, who was interested in purchasing whatever Joyce items Roth might have. Abramson initiated the meeting with Roth, telling the latter that Slocum would be willing to absolve him of blame as a pirate of *Ulysses* if he could produce canceled checks proving he had paid Joyce.[154] He may have shown Slocum the February 26, 1927, letter from Hays listing the $800 in promissory notes he returned to Roth after Joyce had rejected his offer. Perhaps also he showed Slocum the check for $100, half the payment for the "Work in Progress" selections. In that check the date "1926" seems to have been reworked to make it look like "1925." If that is so—and it would have more foolish than cadgy—it might seem to Slocum that Roth did pay, through Beach, in advance of the "Work in Progress" excerpts.[155] As I have said, Roth was tardy in paying for the first installments.

Invited to speak to the James Joyce Society meeting at the Gotham Book Mart on December 6, 1950, Roth started out brilliantly, saying, "I feel like a lion in a den of Daniels." In Jewish imagery, the lion (*leib* in Yiddish, and his father's middle name) must not keep company with jackals, so he was getting his own back in more ways than one. Six years later he wrote that the lion represented "the unghettoed Jew of Europe."[156] Leopold Bloom had been one of those, an outsider resentfully and enviously fighting some of the same problems of class and race as Roth, sometimes (like Bloom) a lion, still was. But his talk went downhill from there. He chose to focus on nefarious enemies, extraneous attacks on certain signers of the Protest, and, more cogently, on the amount of money he did offer Joyce through Hays.[157] It was not a style that an audience of Joyce scholars, booksellers, and connoisseurs of modernism appreciated, although Roth said he got seat-edge attention and thunderous applause. Two justifications, despite their elements of truth, were especially abrasive. He asserted that his publications of *Ulysses* were in fact windfalls for the author, bringing him and his book the publicity he needed to make the literary marketplace accessible to his novel. He also challenged the audience to match his own generosity—did any of them donate money to Joyce or to his widow, as he averred he had done? The silence, he recalled, "grew desolate."[158]

Only an upstart outsider would have risked what Roth did with *Ulysses*. A final irony is the equivalency in professional tactics between Roth and Joyce's advocates. What he did in his rough-edged entrepreneurial game, they did in their polished one, fixing his identity as a mutilator and bowdlerizer, although in reality no more so than Margaret Anderson or Ezra Pound. We might say, redacting Falstaff, that in the case of *Ulysses,* Sam Roth was reckless enough to be not only irresponsible in himself but the cause of irresponsibility in other people, including James Joyce.

CHAPTER 4

1928–1934

Roth Must Live: A Successful Business and Its Bankruptcy

Sitting in his Welfare Island cell in 1929 and looking up from the gutter of a shattered reputation, Roth wrote, "I am not at all sure how much I am to blame. . . . But I am ashamed of what I have done."[1] He meant, first, that the public calumny of the moral outcast was insupportable. A second source of shame was that of professional and financial failure. At the same time, his ambition and belief in his abilities as publisher and writer were intact. He continued his prose writing and publishing career, but under a series of pseudonyms: Norman Lockridge, Daniel Quilter, David Zorn, Eric Hammond, Joseph Brownell, Francis Page, Michael Swain, John Henderson, William Hodgson, and perhaps even J. A. Nocross.[2]

The Secretary

John Saxton Sumner, the secretary for the New York Society for the Suppression of Vice, was a "one-hundred-percenter."[3] In this he was similar to other reformers of manners and morals. Like the postal authorities, he conflated Communist ideas, scatological language, disloyal talk, psychoanalytic probing of repressed desires, and explicit discussion of sexuality as dangerous destabilizing forces. In the 1927 annual report of the Vice Society he noted that New York "is the source and supply of so much questionable published matter" that officials have a "special responsibility" to remedy the situation.[4] His own efforts to fulfill that responsibility were skillful. Employing a few loyal and clever undercover agents instead of mendacious, fly-by-night petty thieves and con men, as did other cities' anti-vice societies, Sumner was consistently able to discover underground printers, mail drops and warehouses of distributors, and retailers of banned books. Therefore, federal government investigators and postal investigators often consulted him regarding suspects. No wonder Roth wrote a prospective customer for *Fanny Hill* that he needed a check or money order in advance, for he "could not keep such an account with safety, for you or for us."[5]

Although both Sumner and Roth disliked Joyce, Sumner arrived at his opinion of Roth's criminality from a radically different perspective than Joyce's supporters did. Root, Weaver, Beach, Hemingway, and Pound had hyperbolically told the world that Roth was a pirate and a thief, an enemy of creativity insofar as he not only appropriated literature and art but also reproduced it in contexts that demeaned it by stressing its prurient interest, not to mention stealing its readerships and thus making the writers' careers problematical. As the "Town Censor" (as some journalists called him), Sumner saw the publisher as inflaming a volatile human instinct that had to be not only refined by priestly teachers but also policed by secular authorities. Roth and other merchants of sex had commercialized the instinct, assuming a role authorities had deplored for centuries. The outsider middleman had dared compete, without knowing or caring, with responsible lawgivers, who recognized degeneracy when they saw it. What previously had been the province of sacred regulation was on display in "vulgar," "cheap" contexts. "A newly created class of addicts" had sprung up, ravenous for "thrills," Sumner was convinced.[6]

There was something, on the other hand, that Sumner shared with Joyce and his supporters. The institutions of both modernism and vice suppression saw themselves as upholding, respectively, artistic and moral integrity against barbarism. They had spent a long time training themselves for this struggle. To point out that Joyce was anxious to make money from an American edition of *Ulysses,* or Sumner to maintain his society's preeminence in the face of declining contributions, was considered the irreverent mudslinging of philistines. Without moral indignation and resentment, it would be difficult—for either the anti-vice societies or reputable modernist writers and their publishers—to finger a scapegoat.

For Roth, Sumner seemed the most dangerous shard in a kaleidoscope of enemies, all the more imposing because he spoke for many, and all New York knew of him. To Sumner, established publishers, other writers including Joyce, and editors who admired European modernism were just as contemptible as Roth. However, this brought no comfort to the publisher. In fact, it isolated Roth further, because the enemies of his enemy could never be his friends. Most modernist literati, like Joyce, were glad to see him go to prison. In *Finnegans Wake* Joyce alluded to Roth: "Ought to be depraved of his libertines . . . into some drapery institution off the antipopees [Welfare Island penitentiary?] for wordsharping."[7]

Ironically, Sumner was dependent on "pariah capitalists" such as publishers and distributors who used underground methods.[8] It was only through the success of the smutmongers' businesses that the authorities who indicted them on the charge of "sex for its own sake" could augment their ideological capital. Further, the bookleggers, even if, like Roth, aware of First Amendment principles and good writing, were themselves agents of repression—for their products were a safety valve providing fantasies the satisfaction of which allowed people to tolerate conventional ideals of decency.[9] Large numbers of consumers of erotica not only quietly siphoned off the frustrations caused by their culture's restrictions on sexual impulse but did so harmlessly, that is, without criticizing the ideology itself.

Sumner Sends Roth into Detention and His Brother to Welfare Island

Sumner had suspected Roth from the first issue of his first subscription magazine. His first jail term came when Sumner raided his Book Auction bookstore in May 1928. In January of that year the Post Office had discovered that Roth was mailing unexpurgated copies of *The Perfumed Garden,* published and distributed earlier by Jack Brussel. Sentence was suspended, and he opened the Book Auction using his wife's name as owner of the "A. R. Paulsam Company." A consignment shop, it would allow publishers to auction off their remainders, book lovers to auction their libraries, and booksellers to do the same with their overstock. He would then sell these items to people who could not afford new, finely printed—and possibly esoteric or erotic—books.[10] Sumner's May raid yielded erotic artwork and Roth's reprint of Carrington's bibliography of *Forbidden Books.* In mid-October Roth began a four-month term in Welfare Island (the Workhouse). Sumner probably suborned a fellow bookseller he had recently netted, Henry Klein, to help frame Roth by getting the latter's permission to store some artwork overnight on the premises. Klein, Roth noted, did avoid a prison sentence after the arrest.[11]

Sumner's methods were even more effective in the summer of 1929, when he used investigators and a lawyer member of his society to trap Roth's younger brother, Moe, into offering three strictly banned books (including *Lady Chatterley's Lover*) to the lawyer. But Roth was convicted only for violation of parole; he could not be directly linked to the erotica porno selling. It was Moe who was convicted of possession and sale of obscene books, a crime that would have been more serious for a repeat offender. The warehouse was leased not by Sam but by Moe, and Pauline Roth was legally the proprietor of the Golden Hind.[12] Roth wrote to the judge on the case, John C. Knox, explaining that he had no involvement in what he called "my brother's stock of obscene books."[13] However, It was clear to Knox, who relied on affidavits of postal inspectors as well as Sumner's testimony, that there was no record of Moe being a bookseller prior to his arrest, and that the stock was accumulated by Roth. Knox revoked Roth's parole, regarding the *Perfumed Garden* 1928 conviction, on the request of Roth's probation officer, only a week after Sumner's raid on the Golden Hind. Of course he knew about Roth's previous publications, culminating with his unexpurgated *Ulysses* and *Lady Chatterley* volumes, copies of which had been intercepted by postal inspectors. Roth served four months at U.S. Detention Headquarters (West Street and Eleventh Street) in Manhattan.[14]

Regarding the Roth publication of the unexpurgated *Ulysses* volume, it was not, as Joyce believed, "a photographic forgery of the Paris edition."[15] As the Slocum and Cahoon bibliography of Joyce states, the Roth piracy was a new edition, amateurishly edited and printed. Roth used the Loewinger brothers, Rudolph and Adolph, 230 West Seventeenth Street, who did later printing for Roth, as well as for other erotica distributors.[16] Sumner presumably found the plates for Roth's *Ulysses* edition in the Golden Hind warehouse, further incriminating Moe.[17]

The precipitous nature of Knox's action shocked Roth, or at least he professed to be in a pleading letter to him. But the judge wanted Roth to know that the authorities had his number.[18] He may also have been repulsed by how Roth had used his wife and brother to cover his tracks. The publisher also put in harm's way the substitute schoolteacher, objectivist poet, and Roth book salesman Henry Zolinsky, whom Sumner arrested at the Golden Hind office in 1929, when he walked in with a copy of *Lady Chatterley's Lover*. Roth had listed Zolinsky as co-owner of a related company that had the same address as Faro.[19]

The Vice Society raid on his warehouse showed Roth had quickly become an expert distributor, and probably a leading consultant, on the best-selling banned (and therefore desirable) erotica. Sumner confiscated order forms, bills, American Express shipping forms, and circulars. The Golden Hind was the imprint under which Roth issued his most attractively printed and expensive books. He had sold more than $700 worth of books per week in Chicago orders alone, and realized significant profits in cities in the Midwest and on the West Coast.[20] Roth's daughter writes that the majority of Roth's stock found in 160 Fifth Avenue was copies of *Lady Chatterley's Lover.* There might have been another storage room, at 166 Fifth, where most "flagitious" items were kept; the term was a favorite with moral entrepreneurs, roughly corresponding with the present label "hard core."[21] Roth was responsible for at least three unexpurgated piracies of *Lady Chatterley's Lover,* each of which had several impressions. One employee who, with Roth, went to a secret (possibly even from Sumner) storeroom at Fourth Avenue and Twelfth Street stated that Brentano's was one store that bought *Ulysses, Lady Chatterley's Lover,* and other flagitious works to sell under the counter.[22]

Roth's list of subscribers in the late 1920s would have been made up of the kind of men for whom a gentleman's library was both desirable and attainable. He would have used his customers for *The Lyric* and his subscription magazines, the list Jack Brussel provided for *The Perfumed Garden,* customers from the Book Auction, and people interested in his Golden Hind Press offerings. At the 1929 trial he had estimated his Golden Hind mailing list to include "2500 people, a certain percentage of whom always buy a certain number of books."[23] In March 1931 he told federal investigators that he had built up his mailing list "through the telephone book and had selected only professional people such as doctors and dentists, etc., because they were more apt to buy than the ordinary run [of customers]."[24] One could add scientists, nurses, sociologists and anthropologists, ministers, and certified public accountants.[25] The list was subdivided by level of sexual explicitness and scatology the customers wanted. "Hot" items would be delivered in person (as Moe Roth did). Especially because the *New York Times* (and possibly *The Nation*) would not place his advertisements after the International Protest,[26] sales resulting from mail-order solicitation of the borderline pornographic content were key.

By the standards of the early 1930s, it would be difficult, if not futile, to prosecute texts not either explicitly alluding to intercourse or using indecent language. Similar de facto permission applied to illustrations of bare-breasted females; these had proliferated in classic texts from Ovid to *Moll Flanders.* Roth knew how to avoid prosecution; but he also, especially for one or more of his private mailing lists, could sidle up to the line between erotic and pornographic in attention-getting and witty ways. An example is the Golden Hind's "privately printed for subscribers only" edition of Catulle Mendes's *Lila and Colette,* which for the occasion was titled *There Are 20 Good Ways of Doing It.* The paperbound cover is illustrated with a naked man and woman whose (hairless) pubic areas nearly touch. They are the closest parts of their bodies to each other, for the man and woman have each bent their bodies backward so that of the man (on the left) seems to form an inverted "C" and that of

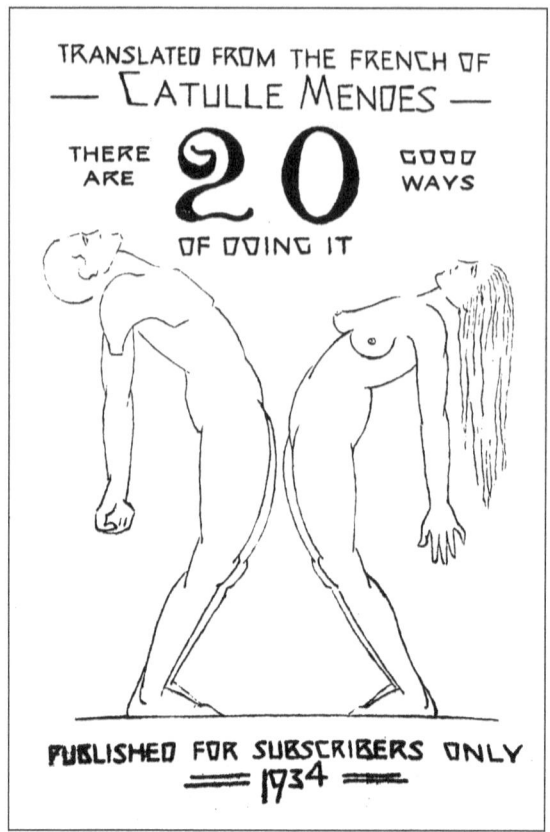

TRANSLATED FROM THE FRENCH OF
— CATULLE MENDES —

THERE ARE **20** GOOD WAYS

OF DOING IT

PUBLISHED FOR SUBSCRIBERS ONLY
1934

Figure 13. Front cover,
*There Are 20 Good Ways
of Doing It* (1934). By
permission of the Roth
estate.

the woman forms a conventional C shape. Now, this may be a very awkward way of doing it. However, they cannot do it, because neither figure has genitals—as was the case with a number of illustrations in books and magazines the publishers of which wanted to avoid flagitiousness. There were at least twenty good ways of twitting the bluenoses. But the works in the Golden Hind warehouse were clearly interdicted by the standards of the day, and obviously subversive of conventions of sexual expression.

Moyamensing Prison: A Test of Roth's Mettle

His daughter presents convincingly the persistence, resourcefulness, and hope for the future Roth displayed for his family during the four-month prison sentence, which began February 28, 1930. "Sam's identity was set for himself (and for the prison world) when addressing a piece of paper with his pen. And write he did. He wrote Pauline at least every other day, sometimes twice in the

Samuel Roth, Infamous Modernist

same day." For at least part of his sentence, the family lived in Jersey City, possibly because erotica distributors found the post office there not as assiduous as the ones in New York. Pauline might have maintained a reduced mail-order business.[27] Roth revised a book of short comments on public figures, which he published pseudonymously ("Joseph Brownell") in a folio deluxe edition in 1929 as *The Telephone Book as a Guide to American Culture*.[28] Realizing the number of pulp magazines paying for stories, he wrote fourteen of them. Critics who say Roth had ghostwriters because he was incapable of sustained concentration on writing himself do not know of his total body of work, much of which remains unpublished.

The news that Roth would have to stand trial for selling copies of *Ulysses* to a Rittenhouse Square bookstore reached him only days before his expected release from custody at Detention Headquarters.[29] Perhaps the fact that he could not be prosecuted for distributing the pornography in his New York warehouse (but only for violating parole) had something to do with his having to answer for a similar crime in Philadelphia. En route there he was warned that the police chief was a violent sadist who, according to rumor, had sodomized a patrolman with a night stick during an argument. The superintendent of police at the time was William B. Mills, known as a "shrewd disciplinarian" who had won respect as a fighter against gambling and other vice operations in 1918, and subsequently for his ability to keep order in the city's houses of detention. His career ended in 1939, after four prisoners at Holmsburg County Prison had suffocated in disciplinary cells where they had been placed during a heat wave, by officers serving under Mills. Mills was acquitted of wrongdoing, but the trial made clear that he must have known of the punishment.[30] As Roth tells it, he walked into Mills's office at the prison alone, without his lawyer.

At Moyamensing, Roth was ordered to plead guilty or face a longer sentence. He was at first allowed neither pen nor paper and was put to work in a mattress factory. When he was allowed to write, he told Pauline to contact a Philadelphia poet of talent, Ralph Cheyney (Roth later published a book of his poems), whose father was a professor. Possibly due to the professor's efforts, Roth found himself transferred to a better cell, was allowed to write, and was treated with respect by the guards. Roth explains this, however, as only he could: the warden had been given by the prison censor a letter in which "the poet had expressed [in a letter to the prisoner] warm sympathy with his plight, compared it to the plight of Jesus in Jerusalem, and prophesied that a day would come when Philadelphia would be proud to boast of his presence in it if only as a prisoner" ("CMAM," 302).

Roth's perseverance and self-dramatizations had their roots in this afore-mentioned sense of mission, or *taklis*. Eastern European immigrant Jews' sense of taklis was one of their sustaining forces. Their success in business was proof: their determination, enthusiasm, anxiety, malleability, and respect for education embody it.[31] But in a larger sense taklis is, as I have mentioned in connection to Roth's ambition to become a poet, the special destiny for a Jewish man in God's ultimate plan for his people. In Kabbalistic writings, especially in Isaac Luria's sixteenth-century interpretations, the word may reflect the process of cleansing the world of impurity, and the loving state of mind in which a person of refined devotion does so. Loving kindness, an attribute of the Tree of Life, is a necessary complement to knowledge, and as such is one of Yahweh's attributes. (Leopold Bloom probes this core belief when he braves the men, and growling Garryowen, in Kiernan's pub to proclaim that love, not hate, is "really life.") The created universe is radically impure and needs the tzaddiks (hidden wise men) to purify it, as Yeshea told Roth it was his destiny to help accomplish, thus preparing it for ultimate reintegration with holiness. That is *tikkun*, or "rectification."[32]

Roth lived in the two worlds of business success and spiritual destiny. In the former he was shrewd and pragmatic. In search of his Yeshea-inspired destiny he composed an alter ago sustaining a sense of purpose evident only to him. It motivated the zeal to write books and poems about Jewish history, and to overcome each fluctuation in his fortunes with the belief that bankruptcy, public disgrace, and incarceration were necessary preparation for fulfilling his divinely inspired conviction "that the accomplishing of great works awaits me outside this prison." The irrationality of this belief reinforces its mystical basis.

It might have a Hasidic origin. Gershom Scholem, the influential scholar of Jewish mysticism, writes of the concept of "redemption through sin." Rational intentions to holiness are constantly thwarted because of pathologies such as jealousy, vindictiveness, venality, or compulsive satisfaction of sexual desires (Roth's own "sweet state of chaos"). For a self-aware human being, his or her life as it has been lived appears to be driven by anarchistic demons. This experience of Scholem's "state of utter shamelessness" is essential; it leads to a "tikkun of the soul," even though one's mythic journey is a kind of apostasy ("I am ashamed of what I have done"), leaving behind the most comforting and sacred taboos of one's society and faith, the acceptance of which would mean not striving to forge a self open to redemption.[33]

A hopeful sense of mission was a good resource for surviving prison. But it was not always present. Writing to his nine-year-old son during his first prison term, and using a style certain to be difficult for any boy to decipher, he regretted that fathers pass on their faults to their sons. His, he stated, were "a selfish, grasping, aloofly independent nature, a love of lazy, luxurious living, and a strange, hostile soul."[34] He feared these might be Richard's heritage. They weren't. Sam and Pauline made sure that his compulsions did not impede his love for his children, although they did determine family finances and opportunities.

After Moyamensing's threats of violence and its ban on writing, Roth planned a set of books that could be sold openly, by mail order and in bookstores, as well as stocked in lending libraries. The Faro imprint was incorporated on August 6, 1930, with "a [bank] authorized capital of $25,000."[35] At least part of that money would have come from sales of books, either gallant or banned erotica. The stock of the Book Auction, and arrangements with Jack Brussel, may have provided other income. He may also have borrowed from relatives, including his in-laws. He now had the capital to start his climb to affluence and middle-class security, if not respectability.

Alrightnik for a Spell: "Wm. Faro, Incorporated"

The name for the new business was derived from a cellmate, William Paro, whom Roth tried to talk into being the titular president. But Bill, jailed for stealing mail, wanted no more trouble from the Post Office. Sam changed the "P" to an "F," telling Bill there wasn't time to change the papers of incorporation, and offering him a job.[36]

Faro titles centered on hot topics, not exclusively sexual. Many wholesaled gossip about strange careers and secret lives that captured the eyes and ears of hoi polloi in the first years of the Depression. Examples include *The Great Lindbergh Hullabaloo*; Clement Wood's biography of spy-adventurer Fritz Duquesne, *The Man Who Killed Kitchener*; *The Private Life of Frank Harris* (a biography on which Roth and Wood collaborated, and which extended Harris's amours to shocking practices of sadomasochism, pedophilia, and other fetishes);[37] *Woman's Doctor* (a novel about abortion);[38] *My Heart in My Throat: The Story of a Strange Captivity* (account by an opera singer of being forced into sexual slavery by a rich executive at the Met); *Lady Chatterley's Husbands* and *Lady Chatterley's Friends*, two anonymous "sequels" to Lawrence's novel, the latter by Wood; *The Intimate Journal of Rudolph Valentino*; and *Loose Shoulder Straps* (also by Wood, under the name "Alain DuBois"). There was also gallant erotica (sophisticated in subject matter and literary style, and eschewing explicitness), including *Celestine: The Diary of a Chambermaid*. This

CELESTINE

A CHAMBERMAID'S DIARY

What does she see?

What does she think?

What does she say?

There are her master's Mistresses

The son of the master

The coachman

and that fierce little captain who kills and eats all of his pets

FROM THE FRENCH OF

OCTAVE MIRBEAU

Figure 14. One dust-jacket variant for one of the steady-selling books in the Faro imprint. Note the keyhole motif. From collection of the author. By permission of the Roth estate.

early and steady-selling Faro number was "The Frenchiest of all the modern French novels," according to the dust-jacket blurb. Roth issued two memoirs by his friend Dr. Ralcy Husted Bell at Bell's own expense: *Memoirs and Mistresses: Colors and Odors of Love* and a later revision, *Amatory Recollections of a Physician,* a title Roth suggested because it was similar to the unpublishable Victorian classic *The Amatory Experiences of a Surgeon.* Perhaps that is why the American News Company would not distribute it.[39] When Bell died as a result of a gunshot wound (possibly from a shotgun he had himself rigged to fire at a suspected intruder), Roth attempted to put forward the story that Bell had been a murder victim.[40] The publisher's reason was that Bell had made enemies by scaring poachers off his land. However, that *Memoirs and Mistresses* might have provoked spousal vengeance was stated on various advertisements, both Roth's (while planning a posthumous version of Bell's memoirs) and wholesalers'.

The Faro list also included anthropological studies of fertility rites, marriage customs, and chastity belts. A set of titles designated as "The Ardent Classics" included his own dramatization of *Chatterley;* his stalwart friend Ralph Cheyney's poems *A Pregnant Woman in a Lean Age;* and two titles by Sacher-Masoch, *Venus in Furs* and *Venus and Adonis.* In addition, Roth "edited"—in fact, emasculated and redacted—an important privately printed collection of American scatological and bawdy humor, *Anecdota Americana* (1927, 1934).[41] It became "stories for the smoking car, stag, and the intimacy of your own parlor."

Despite the sneering of New York's men of letters and booksellers, as of 1931 Roth still had considerable allies. In addition to Mark Hellinger, Clement Wood, and Ralph Cheyney, there was the Detroit newspaperman Harold Auer, agent for Lord Alfred Douglas when Roth published his *My Friendship with Oscar Wilde.*[42] One of Roth's more clever ventures was a concept for a book club, Autographed Editions, one of the earliest in American publishing.[43] He was able to offer only one volume. It had a pretentious title, *Body: A New Study, in Narrative, of the Anatomy of Society,* and contained pseudonymous short stories the publisher had written in prison. Therefore the books were easily autographed, unlike the issues of *Two Worlds* where he first publicized the scheme. Finally, he issued several of his own books, including his satire of Sumner (*Diary of a Smuthound*)[44] and his lyric poetry (*Songs Out of Season*).

The Faro flagship was "The Samuel Roth edition" (i.e., expurgation) of *Lady Chatterley's Lover,* first published in 1930, and reprinted from the same plates in 1931 and 1932.[45] Milwaukee bookseller Harry Schwartz, who carried lots of erotica, recalls the Roth edition "sold by the thousands."[46] Throughout, Lawrence's descriptions of specific physical acts and responses to them are replaced with tamer and more conventional ways men and woman have of expressing their responses to bodily urges, and to one another. The two *Chatterley* "sequals" (that is actually the spelling on the title page of the first; Roth was proofreading-impaired) epitomize the meretricious. *Lady Chatterley's Husbands* (1931) and *Lady Chatterley's Friends* (1932)[47] are easily digestible, potentially profitable product: three sex pulps (including the expurgated

Chatterley). The sequels show Connie as a promiscuous flapper and creature of nightclubs and ocean liners who finally falls for a sheik of Araby. Mellors has long since gone back to game keeping.

Roth was also avid of copyright for *Chatterley*. Through his contacts with the Curtis Brown agency he spoke to Lawrence's widow in the fall of 1930, telling her of lucrative royalties if she would give him permission for his expurgated edition. She demurred, stating she did not want to be involved with such an "awful man."[48] She was probably referring to the International Protest and the rumors of Roth's unauthorized printings of *Chatterley*. The publisher offered $1,000 for permitting him to hold copyright in his play about Connie and Mellors.[49] That would have established a precedent for gaining copyright for *Lady Chatterley's Lover*.

Samuel Roth was "nominated for oblivion" in June 1932, by *Vanity Fair,* in the magazine's monthly feature with that headline. It explained the nomination thus: because Roth "is reputed to be a notorious book pirate; because, under the alias, William Faro, he published . . . a scurrilous attack of the President; because he has served two prison terms for publishing pornography, but still poses as a great champion of great literature."[50] Roth was grateful for any publicity. The *New Yorker* also ran a dismissive essay on his Faro imprint in its January 1932 "Books, Books, Books" column, subtitled "William Faro Incorporated." The writer, novelist "R[obert] M. C[oates]," confessed that he had not read any of the Faro review copies he had been sent. He must have skimmed some of them, for he finds them "unbelievably dull, but quite, quite harmless." As for the author of the Harris exposé, which is stated to be Samuel Roth, "R.M.C." is not quite sure this is so, given his number of aliases. "Mightn't Samuel Roth be a pseudonym, too? Then who would Samuel Roth be? Maybe he doesn't know himself."[51] This sneering pleased Roth. He embellished his own importance as a celebrity worth satirizing by asserting that its author was Dorothy Parker.[52] As R.M.C. implies, the only reality for a beginning publisher who needed dramatic exposure for himself and his books is fabricated sensation.[53]

Most of the titles of William Faro Inc. do not show any of the vitality and creativity that makes some examples of popular writing valuable. But Roth can take credit for publishing some of this latter kind of material as well, including his own short story ("Body," in the volume of that name) on the toxic effect of prurient spectatorship. William Faro Inc. tackled subjects such as flamboyant homosexuality, black-white sexuality, and the venality of a sitting president decades earlier than "gatekeeper" publishers dared to.

From Sex Pulps to Subversion of Racial and Gender Stereotypes

When necessary, Roth remaindered unsold Faro books to a number of smaller-scale mail-order distributors who themselves placed small ads in newspapers and pulp magazines for Faro titles.[54] He was relying heavily on the same points of sale as did other "sex pulp" publishers. The term "sex pulp" denotes a novel with titillating but not explicit sexual content. Pulp magazines of the interwar period specialized in such stories. The protagonists were young people striving for independent careers. They approach the borderline of the illicit by becoming gigolos or showgirls, partying, traveling, appearing on stage or screen, meeting celebrities, and dressing glamorously. Dangers such as excessive drinking, thievery, pregnancy, and abortion loom, but the story almost always ends with the principals finding their dream mates. The sex-pulp audience included many females: office workers, shopgirls, fans of topical films, and patrons of lending libraries. Conventional romantic sentiments are as essential to the genre as is titillation. But two Faro sex pulps upset the expectations of readers in order to comment ironically on the sexual and racial stereotypes of the 1930s, an as yet unacknowledged feat.

A Gentleman in a Black Skin

The dust-jacket illustration for *A Gentleman in a Black Skin* (working title: *Black and White*)[55] by Donna McKay depicts a shadowed male profile and a full-lipped female with closed eyes. The man's lips rest near the woman's right cheek, with his nose close to her right eyelid. There is a caption: "She was young, rich, beautiful. But she awoke one morning to find herself married to a negro—." The blurb on the flap of the dust jacket avoids sensationalism and indicates, in monosyllabic, clichéd, easy-to-read language, a novel on a contemporary urban problem: "That white women, moved by the controlling passion, marry negroes is nothing new. But how can the woman face her family and friends? How does she—a cultured woman—reconcile herself to the ways of a Negro?"[56] The gentleman is Paul Johnson, a Harlem dancer who has modeled for sculptress Susanne Dale (as in "dare"?). How they were married is unexplained; Sue awoke one morning in a Harlem hotel room after a one-night stand to be told it had happened. She tells Paul that before they live together, he must prove himself acceptable in an upper-middle-class social setting. She is convincing. She makes her living creating seductive surfaces.

Paul, an accomplished dancer who has enjoyed the high-hat geniality of white nightclub patrons, desires to escape Harlem as much as he wants to possess and live with Sue. So intent is he on these dreams that he is blinded to Sue's strategy of stalling him until he recognizes he can never emerge from Harlem's shell. She rarely demurs, and usually nods agreement, when her parents discuss their African American servants, almost always called "niggers," who, they say, must be disciplined as one would children, since the only way the white employer can make them work is to bully them. The exception, an intelligent housemaid, is soon fired. Only Sue's brother, Tony, a furtive, neurotic homosexual, recognizes that Paul is just a sex object to Sue. He sees that because he himself is helplessly in love with him. Therefore he gives him money to open his own club. Paul's creative decor and eye for talent make him successful. Paul finally realizes that Sue is actually horrified at the prospect of being his wife; his subsequent comment is just: "I have more respect for the lousiest black prostitute on Lenox Avenue than I have for you!" Unfortunately, he has been so contemptuous of Harlem's blacks, and so proud (Sue would say, above himself), that he is a lone wolf, and easy prey for white gangsters who control Harlem vice. While they are wrecking his club, he strangles one and is shot, with "an expression of dazed surprise" on his face. So ends the dream of equality for the gentleman of talent whose beauty and skills are unique, irresistible, and easily forgotten by those who have cultural capital, especially because his skin color makes discarding him simple and painless.

Paul is hardly blameless. His desires for the apparent material and aesthetic comforts of white Manhattan have distorted him into being as coldly manipulative as his false white goddess. Sue has sculpted a statue of Paul that she calls *A Gentleman in a Black Skin*. It brings her instant fame and fortune. She has embodied in it the sensual beauty of the man she could not see except as an object of lust. It's fitting that her benefit from their relationship is a material one, for sex is like money, and both are infinitely preferable, for Sue and her set, to actual humane contact with a "negro." The tragic implications of Tony's inability to make such contact are undeveloped. The ending of the novel is a strong reality check. When the gangsters invade Paul's club and apartment, Sue is relieved when they allow her to telephone Tony. Gazing at Paul's corpse, and seeing a replica of the statue of him she had crafted, she "shivers suddenly, as if awakening from a sleep." That statue, and the hope Paul nurtured from its popularity, has led to yet another black man's murder. Sue's shiver, however, seems to be from the close call she has had. The gangsters would have shot her too if she were black. She runs to the corner to meet Tony, and they drive back to Manhattan, peering through heavy rain.

According to Adelaide Kugel, "Donna McKay" is a pseudonym; she met the woman at her father's apartment in 1932.[57] Claude McKay, the Jamaican poet and novelist, had, of course, no such wife. Regardless, Roth probably liked the woman's dramatic appearance and willingness to stretch the truth for the sake of what looked like alluring publicity. The surname was sure to interest readers of *Home to Harlem* (1928), McKay's most famous work. The novel described street life in a way that appealed to readers curious about Harlem's prostitutes and nightclub licentiousness. The similar descriptions in *Gentleman* may have been done at Roth's suggestion. None of this precludes the strong possibility of a socially conscious ghostwriter being responsible for *Gentleman*.

Roth knew Claude McKay, who was a coeditor at *The Liberator* when Roth published a poem there in 1919. In 1932 or the next year, Roth contacted McKay about producing Roth's play *Lady Chatterley's Lover* in Harlem with a black cast.[58] In 1941 the publisher wanted McKay to ghostwrite a biography of his friend Dante Cacici's experiences in Harlem.[59] The Roth Archive contains a typescript of an unpublished McKay novel.[60] By 1940, McKay's rejection of Marxism had made him an outcast among activists and their publishers.[61] Perhaps he turned to Roth as an outcast novelist would to an outcast publisher.

A Scarlet Pansy

Wm. Faro's most successful, and subversive, sex pulp, "Robert Scully's" *A Scarlet Pansy*, begins, "Fay Etrange lay dying on a battlefield in France, dying in the arms of the man she loved." It ends with the same sentence, with the emendation of the last line to "the last man she loved." Dr. Fay is a practicing physician and a transvestite homosexual male. In the arms of her lover Frank on a World War I battlefield, and due only to the chaos of the Great War, she could openly express desire and its spiritual outcome, devotion. (The feminine pronoun is always used to identify her, and her male friends.) After the retrospective first sentence, the narrator delineates Fay's life story, starting with her childhood as a strong and brilliant boy in Kuntzville (pun?), in the hills of Pennsylvania (modern-day Kutztown is in Pennsylvania Dutch country). Turn-of-the-century Kuntzville is a place of almost primordial innocence as compared to the capitals of America and Europe where the adult Fay displays her hermaphroditic beauty.

Fay's life is a carnival, and the names of her friends are those of a dazzling sideshow: Billy Pickup, a playboy; Henry Voyeur and Percy Chichi, philosophical observers; Teddy Wemys Cocke, one of Fay's lovers; Bobby Dike,

Figure 15. Frontispiece (by "Rahngild") and title page for one of Roth's most successful Faro titles, published in a pirated edition after his 1933 bankruptcy. By permission of the Roth estate.

a "collar and tie woman"; the La Butsch family of high livers. They are not ashamed of being gay, transvestite, or lesbian, and are as proud of their hedonism as they are of their freedom of expression. Perhaps Scully's characters offer a subversive challenge to the straight world by enjoying themselves while absorbing and boldly claiming the grotesqueries that world sneeringly attributed to "inverts."[62] Fay seduces boxers, cops, ballplayers, and sailors. However, in the interest of keeping their subversive identity without suffering violence, she and her friends allow themselves to be treated with contempt. When one of Fay's friends, Sissy Beach, volunteers for the Navy, "she" is told that her lisp disqualifies her. "Young man . . . you wouldn't even make a first-class Yeomanette." Sissy breaks into "hot, scalding tears": "I think you are the meanest old things. So there!" Sissy becomes a song-and-dance man at Navy Yards. "I'm doing my bitterest bit." Is this subversion of the norm, or

Samuel Roth, Infamous Modernist

a backhanded, even heartbreaking, tolerance of it? The narrator's detached point of view dramatizes the pathos: poor Sissy is not only cruelly excluded from loving her country, but, bound by its ideals, as a result is selling herself cheaply in order to express her patriotism. Like the rest of the novel, this episode refrains from sentimentality or preaching, and the humor is objectively presented. This makes the despair behind it a tragic presence to the reader, and encourages him or her to think through what he or she has just read.

From Scully's detached style, in fact, innocence and kindness are banished, except when the romantic, teenaged Fay is virginal, and when she finally discovers the man she was meant for. After she was first seduced, "She felt her debasement and defilement. . . . She outlined a plan to go to New York—to New York, for reformation!" Behind the whimsical irony in this statement is the narrator's awareness of what his characters are made of. "Thus began her degradation. Morally, from then on, she was to go down, down, down." But she also becomes a physician. As much as Scully sets forth the genius of Fay and her gay urban enclave at creatively remaking the sensuality of their time in their own images, he knows their limits. As with the other pleasure seekers with whom Fay and her friends share nightclubs and ocean liners, the ethical dilemmas hidden behind the glamour appear only when fatal harm is at hand.

In the novel's concluding pages, the setting changes from chic Berlin cafés to the chaos of the battlefield, where all are equal in the shadow of death. Fay's homosexuality is unconditionally accepted by her lover and ignored by the other soldiers. Dr. Etrange, unlike Sissy Beach, is able to do her "bit," saving many lives amid the red chaos. Campy artifice disappears, the concept of sexy "rough trade" becomes trite, and "cruising" evolves into mutuality. Our hero dies happy, not for "God and country" but because she is in the arms of the man she loves, having saved Frank's life with her medical skills and then having taken the bullet meant for him.[63]

Is it poor Fay, still camping, therefore both self-stereotyping and also still loyal to melodramatic sentimentalities about love that exclude her beautiful transvestite gaiety? Or does Fay die bravely fulfilling herself in mutual love? Roger Austen, in his study of *The Homosexual Novel in America,* states that Fay, like many protagonists of 1930s gay novels, is "lost" in a vacuous although glittering pursuit of sensual pleasure that denies the reality of their loneliness.[64] I believe, however, that in the final chapters Scully shows a piercing awareness of the limitations Austen deplores, thus providing a fresh poignancy for an issue not openly discussed at the time. In its ending, *A Scarlet Pansy* breaks away from camp vivacity to shock readers in a different way than it had at the outset. War not only makes snobbery and prejudice irrelevant, it also administers a reality check with electric force: only in extremis can a "pansy" (a soft, unnatural, hothouse plant) break through an exclusionary moral consensus to capture the heart, not just the sex thrill of her lover. Austen's definition of "rough trade"—a soldier back from the hell of the front lines—is ironically apt.[65] War can make irrelevant even the macho either-or of the rough trade. But does that hard-bitten enlightenment last? The last page of *A Scarlet Pansy* brings the reader back to the beginning. The first paragraphs had described Fay's dying embrace, but also had stated that Frank "in his gratitude for her recent ministrations . . . thought he loved her. Perhaps he did. Perhaps he was broad-minded enough even for that. At least, in after years he was heard to speak reverently of Fay." The narrator begins as he will end, as a mature, admiring, yet laconic observer of ultimate realities beyond surfaces. His Fay is one of the most heroic of cultural mutations.

A Scarlet Pansy was one of Faro's most popular books, obviously purchased by members of the 1930s sexual underground as well as the sexually curious.[66] While the former could get it in stores that sold it, along with banned items, under the counter,[67] they could also buy it through mail order and in book- and specialty stores. The format and advertisements were those of other Faro titles, as were its points of sale. In addition, Roth issued (in 1932) what must have been a small press run of special copies, with title page and the "Rhangild" frontispiece in red in black. These copies might have been intended for Roth's special list of erotica customers, who would pay more for a deluxe copy.[68]

Pansy was one of four Faro titles pirated by "Nesor Publishing Company" from Roth after his 1933 bankruptcy. After Roth's release from Lewisburg Penitentiary in 1939 he abridged the novel considerably and sold it (in a sense, reclaimed it from the pirates) as part of his extensive mail-order operation, under the imprint "Royal." That Royal is not another imprint of those responsible for Nesor is indicated by the fact that the revisions for the abridgment were evidently Roth's work.[69] This abridgment excised much of the beautifully realized pre–World War I setting, perhaps because 1940s readers wanted sensation in an up-to-date context. Many of his mail-order circulars featured it for more than a decade.[70] He was nearly sent back to prison in 1941 when his parole officer discovered that he had been trying to sell erotica, including *Pansy*.[71]

As the "pansy craze"—tourists slumming in clubs where gay people put on their outrageous and intensively creative shows—was still alive in the early

1930s, Roth tailored his advertisements for his first edition to extend their prurient spectatorship to the book: "What THE WELL OF LONELINESS did for
the man-woman, this most unusual tale does for the woman-man—only that
the latter is a so much more wayward and more fascinating creature." There
were several novels about the gay or lesbian urban ambience before the one he
published. Blair Niles's *Strange Brother* (1931) is another. In fact, in the same
way that contact between Caucasians and African Americans increased in
the interwar years with the scintillating pleasures of uptown, contact between
the gay and straight cultures became greater with the pansy craze.[72] That, and
Roth's ability to generate sales by packaging novels as sex pulps, and to extend
this technique to good subversive writing, are what motivated William Faro's
Gentleman and *Pansy*.[73] These books helped, therefore, build respect for gays
and blacks with general readers.

A *Scarlet Pansy*'s pseudonymous author is quite possibly the expatriate
short-story writer and poet Robert McAlmon, in the mid-1920s a friend of
Gertrude Stein and Ernest Hemingway. Hugh Hagius has carefully assembled
evidence supporting this claim.[74] McAlmon married "Bryher" (Annie Winifred Ellerman), who was clearly having an affair with H.D.; the union was a
marriage of convenience for both (although McAlmon later maintained that
he was bisexual and wished intimacy with his wife, which she refused). The
marriage of Mason Linberg (who is a caricature of McAlmon himself) to Marjorie Bull Dike closely resembles the events at the McAlmon-Bryher nuptials.
Hagius states that McAlmon's "Miss Knight," in his volume *Distinguished Airs:
Grim Fairy Tales* (1925), is similar in characters and style to *A Scarlet Pansy*,
as are other works McAlmon published, some of them written in the period
1929–31. Although *A Scarlet Pansy* is set in the first two decades of the twentieth century, there are references to historical events that show it could not
have been completed before *The Well of Loneliness* appeared in 1928.[75]

While Scully might indeed be McAlmon, there are two caveats to keep in
mind. First, the signature on the contract bears some resemblance to that of
Robert McAlmon, but it cannot with any certainty be identified with his own.[76]
The second problem is a statement by Roth's daughter. She says that Robert
Scully was a pseudonym because the author "dared not use his name to write
about 'the love that dare not' in 1932 without losing some of his practice."[77]
That might explain why the contract states Scully's address as a post-office box
in Charlottesville, Virginia. He would not want even the pseudonym identified with his home or office address. There was a Robert Emmet Scully, born
in New Jersey,[78] listed in the records of the American Medical Association

beginning in 1918. A graduate of the University of Virginia (Charlottesville) School of Medicine, he was commissioned into the Navy's Medical Reserve Force in 1921. Subsequently, he practiced in U.S. veteran hospitals in Newark and (as of 1931) in Somerset Hills, New Jersey.[79] This information places this Robert Scully in locations where he might, possibly as a member of literary or social gay circles, have become acquainted with Roth when *A Scarlet Pansy* was being written and/or prepared for publication. If McAlmon, probably because of actions for libel, wanted not to be associated with the book, Roth could have asked Scully (in return for money or some other favor) to allow his name to be used as author. Royalty checks might be sent to the Charlottesville post-office box listed on the contract. Of course, another possibility was that Roth appropriated McAlmon's work due to lack of international copyright agreement, and published it under Scully's name. He was desperate to avoid bankruptcy in 1932.

Hagius writes persuasively that *Pansy* is a roman à clef.[80] In addition to the similarity between Linberg and McAlmon, Hagius notes that Fay is "a composite of McAlmon's best friends, Marsden Hartley and William Carlos Williams."[81] There is a whole family of Beaches and Beach-Butsches, which may be a nasty squib aimed at Paris booksellers Sylvia Beach (publisher of *Ulysses*) and her friend Adrienne Monnier. The "double meanings" for fruits and vegetables in *Pansy* parallel the more explicit gay slang in McAlmon's privately published *Distinguished Air*. The detached, laconic tone of the narrator of *Scarlet Pansy* might reflect McAlmon's own attitude. To supplement Hagius's observations: Fay's final lover, Lieutenant Frank, recalls Lieutenant Henry in *A Farewell to Arms*, though it is Fay who dies, not her soldier-lover.

McAlmon's friends noted his own detachment not only from his literary colleagues but also from the gay men and women whom he knew casually and invited to his tables at European cafés and bars.[82] Roger Austen writes of the author of *A Scarlet Pansy*, "He usually struck a tone that revealed more dismay than acceptance [of homosexuals] and certainly more detachment than identification [with them]."[83] The comment indicates a possible reason for that: his awareness of the tragic, eternal otherness of the era's flamboyant homosexual. Another reason could be McAlmon's criticism of gay men's hell-raising in nightclubs and after-hours dives. Stanford Smoller points out the debasement awaiting gay people after their anonymous sex, drugs, and drunken histrionics. Beyond the carousing was despair and death wish.[84]

By the 1930s McAlmon's reputation had declined, and his modernist friends were avoiding him. Joyce thought McAlmon was trying to irritate his friends in his memoir *Being Geniuses Together*. He called the memoir "the office boy's revenge."[85] Fitzgerald thought him a good man to stay away from.[86] However, fellow writers such as Kay Boyle, William Carlos Williams, Ezra Pound, Erskine Caldwell, and Louis Zukofsky were praising his work at this time.[87] Hagius maintains that McAlmon tried to place the novel with various respectable, mainstream publishers but with no success. Therefore, he argues, McAlmon sold it to Roth for "a lump sum."[88] The agreement would have included royalties.[89] When would the two men have made this agreement? McAlmon was in Europe from 1931 to 1934, but just before that he was in New York. At this time two book dealers and publishers of attractively printed erotica, Martin Kamin and David Moss, spoke to McAlmon about resuming Contact Editions under their auspices.[90] He refused. Kamin and Moss carried some books similar to those Roth published. If McAlmon had contact with them, he could easily have met Roth, and even might have been recommended to him by Moss and Kamin if he told them he was looking for a publisher for *A Scarlet Pansy*. It is possible that, in addition to seeing the Faro imprint as his last chance, McAlmon was indicating to his former friends—all fierce enemies of Roth—that if they were shocked by his doing business with the subject of their International Protest, he returned the contempt.

That McAlmon was Scully becomes increasingly plausible when one considers the similarities in the careers of Roth and McAlmon and how they would know about, and want to help, each other. Both were poets in the Village after World War I. Perhaps McAlmon visited the Poetry Book Shop on Eighth Street then (near Romany Marie's gathering place), where poets like Robinson, Reznikoff, and Zukofsky went. In his *Objectivists Anthology*, Zukofsky published several of McAlmon's poems. John Glassco was a good friend of both writers. McAlmon did not sign the International Protest, possibly, as he had told Joyce, because he did not like *Ulysses*.

Whatever the nature of a possible collaboration between the two publishers-authors, *A Scarlet Pansy* is a modernist project. The exploration of tabooed sexual behavior; the sense of entrapment hidden behind a glittering surface; the concealment of subversive beauty beneath a burlesque of high-society cavorting; the use of a "low" genre popular because of its mass entertainment value to treat a subject conventionally believed to be beyond dispute; and the embodiment of such a challenge in language that newsstand and lending library readers use, and the initiation of those readers into an illicit slang: all are exemplary of modernist writing. If McAlmon, Sylvia Beach, John Rodker, Harriet Monroe, Thomas Seltzer, and Eugene and Maria Jolas were modernist publishers, so also, when in his own unique manner he mixed iconoclastic literature, venality, and prurient titillation, was Samuel Roth.

"Body"

A Gentleman in a Black Skin and *A Scarlet Pansy* dramatize ways a culture's outsiders cannot help adopting its conventions: styles in dress, affectations in gesture, methods of seduction, and ways of refining desire into love. Roth's own collection of short stories, awkwardly titled *Body: A New Study, in Narrative, of the Anatomy of Society,* released in a Faro impression after his Autographed Editions Club version, contains one story that has equally strong observations about seduction, love, and the consequences of imitating conventions that can skew inner yearning into sadly limited destinies. In "Body," Roth adds to the stories of Paul Johnson and Fay Etrange another American success tragedy. He describes a successful, and famous, couple, and in the course of the story fires a broadside against his own business strategy of displaying beautiful young females to men who could not take their eyes off them.

"Body" consists of a conversation between a film producer and a psychologist. The former has fallen in love with, and married, a seventeen-year-old ingénue just attaining stardom. Their wedding night was a shock to him. The girl was not only unresponsive but also not *virgo intacta,* although she had never experienced intercourse. She had never been a victim of sexual abuse. Something malignantly unnatural had blighted what once was pure. Perhaps Roth remembered the warning of Dr. Blitz, his first employer: "Stop looking so hard at her or you'll wear her out." The only solution is for the producer to divorce her. "Wedded to her public," her attractiveness, says the psychologist, can only satisfy solitary sensualists, who themselves are producers only of corruption and sterility. He concludes that the "Orientals" make their women wear veils because they know "how much more damage a man can do with his eyes than with that ridiculous organ whose power of evil has been so grossly exaggerated in our society."

The "moral" of Roth's fable would not have given John Sumner an "I told you so" moment. It is not about "the virulence of sex," but about how regulation of sexual desire (Sumner's goal) and the exploitation of the consequent need for relief of repressed urges by the erotica merchants combine to make voyeurs out of modern men. Roth carries this insight further, into the most severe cynicism, directed at those whose business it is to provide the prurient entertainments that substitute for "natural" sexual fulfillment. Such people debauch themselves, and even their loved ones, when the loved ones are part of the business. In "Body," the victim is the ingenue wife of the film producer. Roth's wife was his partner, taking the role of head manager during his prison sentences. Roth's brother Moe, like Pauline, was listed as owner of Roth offices

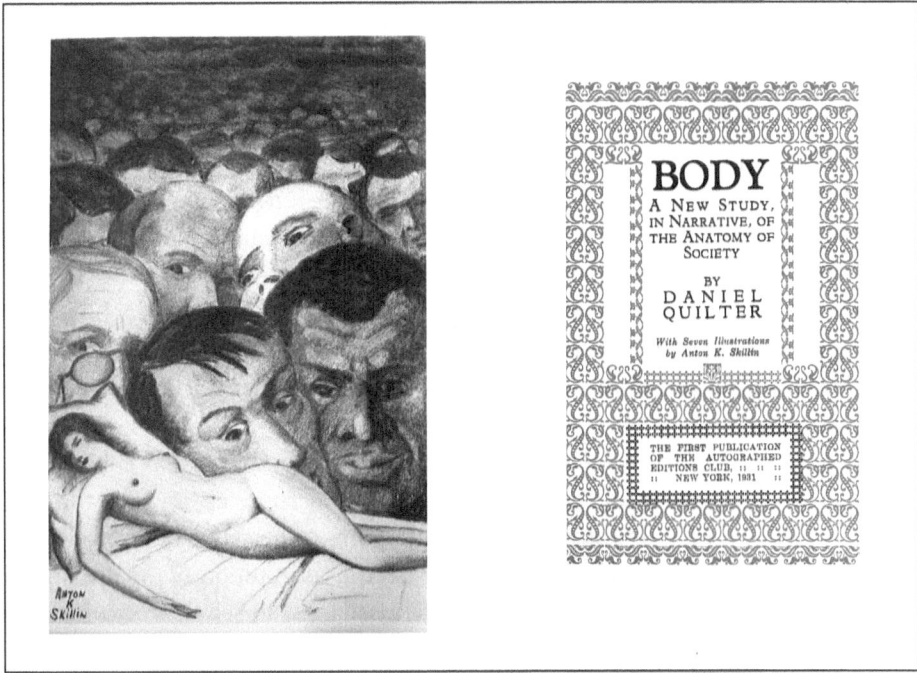

Figure 16. Frontispiece and title page for the Autographed Editions Club printing of
Body. The title story is about prurient spectatorship. By permission of the Roth estate.

and firms. The cynicism in "Body" might be partly self-directed, but Roth's
bland narrative style shows no sign of such an insight.

The frontispiece to the book-club printing of *Body* is a powerful depiction
of exactly what pandering means. A naked, nubile woman is lying on a bed
with her face averted and eyes closed. A sea of male faces strains to get the best
look at her. The features of the half-dozen men in front represent various races
and social classes; all are leering. The artist, A. K. Skillin, implies the legends
of Sleeping Beauty and Beauty and the Beast. There are sets of modernist images Skillin and/or Roth may have had in mind. One is a dream sequence from
Fritz Lang's *Metropolis* (1927). In the entertainment district of the city, crowds
are entranced by the robot-doppelgänger of the kidnapped heroine Maria,
here dancing as the Whore of Babylon, who is, as one entranced spectator
says before attacking his neighbor, all seven deadly sins. The joyless captiva-
tion in the faces of the wealthy men watching Maria's hip-swinging dance in
a diaphanous costume is similar to those Skillin draws. As she dances, the

men watching become, literally, all greedy eyes. Those eyes—evil eyes—then become a backdrop for the figure of Death, who prepares to "descend upon the city."

Perhaps both writer-publisher and artist knew of the drawings of the Polish writer and artist Bruno Schultz, which show groveling and usually middle-aged men adulating often-naked girls and preening women. Examples are "Procession," "Undula at Night," "Pilgrims," and "Suzanna and the Elders," all done in the 1920s and all projecting furtive pleasure and psychic unrest against a backdrop of thick, final darkness; some of the men's heads barely hide grinning skulls beneath a thin layer of skin. The religious aura of Schultz's titles may suggest deracination of the controls on the sex instinct. These used to be imposed by sacred but now defunct rituals.

Voyeurism often includes sadomasochism and fantasies of control. But even if it does not, it results in masturbation, or fantasies in which the consumer of images and narratives identifies him- or herself with a protagonist. Autoeroticism, a result of scopophilia (sterile substitution of the eye for the penis), induces shame. This explains the cruel irony in Schultz's drawings, the mad aggressiveness in Lang's film, and the callous rejection by her husband of his wife in Roth's "Body." The producer sees his wife as shamed by her admirers' voyeurism and divorces her in order not to be infected by that shame, for which he, in displaying her on stage and screen, is responsible. He washes his hands of her, and his psychologist encourages this betrayal. Here is a cynicism hard to stomach.

The conjunction of the young and beautiful with the aged and leering in both "Body" and in Schultz's drawings is suggestive of the Talmudic treatment of the expulsion from Eden.[91] Adam and Eve gained knowledge of good and evil and lost their instinctual, life-giving obeisance to the Tree of Life. The "Evil Inclination" is sexual desire after Eden. Compulsive attention to the heart (the serpent incites greed and envy—the Evil Eye—in both Eve and Adam) instead of the head binds one to it. The goal of the person indulging in sexual desire becomes control of the sex object. The stories and images of Lang, Schultz, and Roth/Skillin contain echoes of the rabbinic tales: innocence is destroyed, and the wiles of the demoness of surging sexual libido, Lilith, perversely supersede Eve in the heart of the man. In "Body" the youthful starlet has in fact become a Lilith in the heart of her husband, as the sorcerer Rotwang has created in the image of pure Maria her opposite, the Whore of Babylon, who drives mad the tuxedoed patrons of the café in which she performs her terrific dance of death. Moreover, like spectatorship in general, this public sinning is especially heinous in Talmudic lore because it embodies a Sodom-like communal degeneration. The latter is actually the sin of the film producer in "Body," who has paraded the starlet's beauty on many a theater silver screen.

Roth's personal experience with the responses of male audiences to women performing extended from nickelodeons, dance floors, and "Follies" stages (all depicted in his own magazines and books) to the prison auditorium in which he watched films such as *Camille*, starring Greta Garbo. Many men breathed obscenities, often while masturbating. He spoke with his daughter frankly about his "outraged reaction." "Dad felt very proprietary about Garbo, and saw [his fellow inmates'] activity as a violation of her personally."[92]

A short story by Delmore Schwartz, "The Heights of Joy," is an analogue of "Body." Both are products of observations regarding 1930s theatergoing.[93] Schwartz's probable source was an incident in the life of the brilliant, scintillating screen star Hedy Lamarr. In her late teens, she married a Viennese arms manufacturer who later attempted to buy up all copies of her film *Ecstasy* (1933), in which she indulged, naked, in the sports of swimming and running. In one scene she simulated orgasm. Schwartz's skills in the short story exceed Roth's as greatest does least. Roth's characters are largely vehicles in his didactic parable. A reader can feel contempt for the producer's callousness, although there are not enough details about him to encourage that. The teenage actress, the victim not only of the leering moviegoers but of her publicist husband (who has unwittingly been her pimp), never appears in Roth's story. Schwartz delineates his Hugh Baur as a financier of great power and fame who has single-mindedly accumulated his fortune and political status. He is shy, in fact afraid, of women, which is implied as a reason he has dedicated his life to sterile accumulations. No wonder he clearly assumes, without ever articulating it, that sex is like money. Magda Gehrhardt, almost twenty years younger, is a queen of the "motion picture cathedral" whose "image is everywhere."[94] Her sexuality is the perfect foil to Hugo's money. In the film *The Heights of Joy*, Magda runs and swims naked in sunlight, "moving like a breaking wave, with the same grace, joy and spontaneity." Her beauty awes the financier, making him shy in approaching her. They marry; Magda is lovingly attentive, although Hugo cannot arouse himself even on the marriage bed. It is her image in the film on which he dotes, and spends his passion.

"She was her own rival," much as Rotwang's false Maria is the chaste original's doppelgänger, and much as Roth's starlet's image on the movie screen is her sinister one, which destroyed her health. Skilled in accumulation, Hugo makes a trip to America to buy extant copies of *The Heights of Joy*. There the film exists in various states, some piecing together only the "hot" scenes (just as the volumes *My Love Life: A Love Autobiography* and *Observations of an*

Old Man in Love, both of which Roth distributed, contain only the banned chapters of Frank Harris's *My Life and Loves*). In Hugo's absence, Magda, with no understanding of her husband's mission, becomes interested in his male secretary and loyal confidante. But both are responsible adults who care for Hugo and whose desires are mature, and thus disciplined. When Hugo returns, because Magda and the secretary do not hide that "in their hearts" they have been adulterous, Hugo knows the truth. He feels relief. "The disease of love" has loosened its hold on the financier, who need no longer try to be part of any mutual contract. He can retire to his private theater where he has Magda just where he wants her. As the lights go down, he experiences "a serene exaltation."[95] Schwartz's Hugo is a victim of the scopophiliac inclination that Roth's producer, equally depraved, has spent his career energizing.

Roth knew well, from the pinups and kept women of the druggist he worked for, and then from his teenage crush on a film star whose movies he compulsively sought out, the consequences of fixation upon erotic images. And of course he made a good living from publishing such images and stories revolving around them. The real subject of some of these were the men who needed to fantasize that they could possess the kind of female beauty Roth's goods epitomize. How many of his Faro titles could claim, in fact, to be modernist? Roth's own short story and poems, *A Scarlet Pansy,* Ralph Cheyney's poems, and several others could be counted among them. The more numerous sex-and-scandal books appealed to the public's idle curiosity about forbidden passion, watched from at a safe distance.

Awareness of this haunted Roth, and it seeped into his advertisements: he told prospective customers of one circular that the books were sure to please them because of "the woman-juice that many [of them, young and old] like to lap up." Locked up for distributing pornography in the late 1930s, he wrote a novel the heroine of which was a renowned European actress. He wrote of her "lovely sorrowful life, ravished as it was, infested and plundered by the eyes of men longing away for her."[96] Possibly this insight was especially haunting because, as deeply as Roth thought about male spectatorship, he never acknowledged his own responsibility for employing it in his business, no more than did the impresario in "Body." He wrote fictions instead, some based on his own "cowardly dreaming," or daydreams. Always, Roth was writing about himself, even when doing versions (he called them "redactions") of Heine's poems or the Psalms of David. These fictions ended with him confessing some of his iniquities, and being gladly forgiven, even by women he had betrayed, and by his father.

When Sumner raided 96 Fifth Avenue in 1931, Roth's business must have become lucrative enough to allow him to hire a prestigious firm; his business associate and co-defendant, Julius Moss, employed Greenbaum, Wolff, and Ernst.[97] Sumner had charged Roth and Moss with mailing an indecent circular for books both obscene and purporting to be obscene. The defense's thoroughly documented brief demonstrated that the advertising matter contained nothing obscene, and the two books Sumner found and submitted as evidence were not obscene as a whole or by the mores of the current day. The case was dismissed.[98] Roth's victory statement does not acknowledge the stellar legal talent arrayed on behalf of the defendants; he glories in a triumph purely personal: "I was advised on all sides to sue him for false arrest, but I did not want that. I had beaten him beautifully and decisively. That was enough for me."[99] It was as if his vindication was destiny itself. This focus on his personal destiny explains why he does not mention a later victory that same year: his wife's acquittal in September of selling unexpurgated copies of *Lady Chatterley's Lover*.[100] Sumner was back from the "beating" in 1934, prosecuting the Faro *Anecdota Americana*. Not believing the expurgations excised the smut, he forced Roth to pay a $100 fine or serve twenty days.[101]

Roth's self-aggrandizing pride was soon to be probed by a kind of attack he had not before suffered. If the modernist literary community was capable of ostracizing him, the sitting president and his supporters could cause an equal amount of trouble. The occasion of the *tsouris* was a scandal book that, on the cusp of the 1931 election, helped in some way to defeat Herbert Hoover: John Hamill's *The Strange Career of Mr. Hoover under Two Flags*. It accused "The Great Engineer" of abusing Chinese mine workers, manipulating stocks, profiting from the relief of Belgium during World War I, and being complicit in the execution of the brave British nurse, Edith Cavell.[102] The White House certainly took the book seriously. The Republican Party contracted writers who revealed in the course of their rebuttals that Roth had spent time in jail for pornography. Three investigators acquired personal information about the publisher, Julius Moss, now Roth's office manager (alias "Richard Ross"), and Henry Zolinsky. Moss was not only distributing *The Strange Career* and other Faro books, but it seems Roth had been advising readers of his circulars to send their money to "Ross's" address. There was another address for the same purpose, that of "Norman Walters Associates," the address of which was the same as Faro.[103] That indicates Roth might have been using these shadow concerns to hide profits from the IRS. The Hoover men filed no complaint about this; their information was obtained through egregious abuses of judicial procedure and of a citizen's privacy.

One of the investigators worked for the IRS, and through his contacts with Salvatore Cotillo, who was the judge in a civil suit filed against Roth by a man who claimed Hamill had stolen his research, he got access to relevant court documents. He also accessed Roth's bank account. Then he offered the publisher financial help, with a view to getting the book withdrawn from circulation. Roth declined the money and stood firmly behind the book. The Hoover man who interviewed Roth reported: "Mr. Roth would be delighted to go to court on a libel suit as he figures it would be a great publicity stunt and would increase the sale of his book tremendously. He is further convinced that he could secure the services of any one of a number of prominent lawyers who would take the case gratis."[104] Roth was implying that although the Democratic National Committee would not risk sponsoring a book the documentation of which could be attacked, he could arrange for a sympathetic lawyer to publicize the Republicans' attempt to suppress freedom of expression.

However, Hamill, who only offered Roth his work when he could not get the Democratic National Committee to sponsor it, "took alarm," as Hoover put it in his autobiography, and allowed himself to be bought out.[105] Hoover reported that "one of my lawyer friends" contacted Hamill's lawyer, and the result was "a written confession . . . that he had fabricated every word of it." The president does not mention the operatives his personal secretary had appointed to read sealed court papers, nor the promise one of them made Hamill of a contract for a second book.[106]

Judge Cotillo issued a restraining order against sale of *The Strange Career* in New York State (later lifted, because the man who filed the suit, a disgraced cop and Tammany hanger-on, could not pay the required $500 contingency fee). Eventually, no damages were awarded either party, for, as the New York Supreme Court justice stated, they had "dirty hands." The only purpose of the book, he wrote, was for "persons of unsavory reputation" to make money by appealing to morbid curiosity. Seizing the moral high ground, the justice stated it was "unsportsmanlike" as well as immoral to take advantage of the president, who, given his position, could not file a libel suit.[107] It was at this hearing that Hamill took the stand and said he was sorry he wrote the book.[108]

The *New York Times* editorialized on the deplorable character of contemporary popular books that cared nothing for truth and aimed only to be "arresting and stimulating and challenging."[109] At this point the Republican National Committee, assured that no powerful Roosevelt supporter was backing Roth, might have rejoiced. Nothing short of disgust—and by the "Paper of

Record"—had been directed at the "smear book" publisher by a state supreme court justice and a newspaper the presidential endorsement of which was still problematical. Who, indeed, but opportunistic hacks could have issued *The Strange Career of Mr. Hoover*? The president could take the high road, and did. Hamill's last visit to Roth ended with his fleeing the office, according to Roth, to avoid being brained by the business end of the publisher's walking stick.[110]

If any of this probed the depths of Roth's self-doubt and cynicism, he showed no signs of it. As the sparring with the White House investigators indicates, he seems to have been at the top of his game. He made money; at least ten thousand copies were sold. He was able to play the part of an intrepid whistleblower. Hamill's work is not fair to Hoover. But he does provide documentation, however imperfect. Roth could legitimately take some credit for the defeat of the sitting president by Roosevelt. He, and friends who advised him, knew the potential for disaster if a small publisher with little prestige were to challenge entrenched wealth and power with such explosive material.[111] There was something about that challenge, despite the additional disadvantage of his prison record, that was irresistible to Roth. "There must, under the circumstances, be someone courageous enough to publish such things. If not I, who?"[112] He might have said the same, a few years later, for *A Gentleman in a Black Skin* and *A Scarlet Pansy*. Here, at least, were three episodes during which he did not let his enemies define him. More were to come.

There was a quixotic and essentially self-destructive side to his defiance. He also said, "I will continue to publish what appears to me to be true or beautiful, if I have to make a barracks out of every jail in the United States."[113] His complex self-image is rooted in a powerful aversion from what he senses, at some deep level of his psyche, is his status as a pariah capitalist and the political vulnerability to which it condemned him. Whenever contempt for his dubious right to publish a work or for his taste in advertisement and polemic reared its ugly head, he responded as a defiant, crusading martyr: "If I am to do this thing, I will do it the only decent way. Show myself in the open. Let me be a target, then, for their worst blows. Truth will survive in the end."[114] Such a histrionic reaction had the effect of making it inevitable that he would retain pariah status. It also suggests, along with the mocki-grisball colophon, that he found it irresistible to operate on the edge of illegitimacy. Paradoxically, he also craved worldly acclamation. Even more paradoxically, he felt Yeshea's presence inside his head as he proceeded in this midlife "sweet state of chaos."

Another, monumental crisis was on the horizon: bankruptcy. After a period breathing the heady air of the *alrightnik,* Roth found himself back where he had been after the collapse of *Beau* and *Two Worlds Monthly* in 1927:

thrown back upon surreptitious scheming and confronted by a new round of legal troubles. The destiny he had sought to avoid, that of a booklegger and pornographer, would catch up with him during the 1930s. Motivated by the bankruptcy, it loomed upon the very path to worldly security he had taken to avoid it. He had to retreat from affluence back into the outland that separates the civil, the reasonable, and the honorable from the rascal, and the man of letters from the coarse poseur. That followed by only a year the shame of being without the funds to support himself and his loved ones. But before that, he spent a despairing night on the Bowery. For the first time since his humiliation when Joan brought home street-walking money for him, Yeshea appeared. But Yeshea would never sanction what immediately followed: revenge against enemies in the form of a dire anti-Semitic diatribe.

CHAPTER 5

1934

Jews Must Live: "We Meet Our Destiny
on the Road We Take to Avoid It"

By 1932, Roth tells us, the effects of the Depression had forced upon him the necessity of liquidating William Faro Inc. He was confident of an orderly procedure, for he had ample credit, books, and copyrights. He approached his principal creditors, chief among whom were the owner of a bindery and the wholesaler who had supplied him with book paper. Arrangements were made to pay these men certain sums per month until debts were cleared. Because over $4,000 was owed to the "paper house," he "mortgaged" it the plates of eight of his "best books." Roth's terminology is inaccurate. He could not "mortgage" the plates; he could take a loan, using the plates as collateral. If he could not pay the loan back, the paper house could keep the plates, or it could force Roth to sell the business, the creditors sharing the proceeds of the sale. The stage was set for an act of betrayal—and later self-betrayal. Given the murky legalities, that there was betrayal was questionable. The self-betrayal was as clear as alarm bells, and they rang inside Roth's head very soon after he did the deed.

Act 1: The Great Unraveling

Roth turned the events that forced him into bankruptcy and drove him to write *Jews Must Live* into a melodrama. It was a set of scheming blackguards versus a businessman fallen on hard times after the Crash. Somewhat later, possibly during his 1937–39 prison sentence, he began a revenge fantasy,[1] in which he lured the people responsible for cheating him, among them the printer, paper wholesaler, and lawyer, to an old, dark house. These men constituted for him the Other, a poisonous, heartless set for whom decent dealings carried no weight in the scales of justice.

The confederacy of schemers who cheated him of his business, Roth wrote, were all Jews. And their "happy conspiracy" occurred exactly when "news of the Nazi warfare against the Jews of Germany blazed out on the front pages of the American Press."[2] He thought the coincidence remarkable, and one of the signs of his God-ordained destiny on this earth. So, we should introduce the dramatis personae of the first act, which ended with another vision of Yeshea, this one in a Bowery flophouse. He changed the names, probably to protect himself from the guilty ones' lawsuits. His daughter provides two of them in her memoir.[3]

The Villains

Parrach: the binder. The name connotes "low-down scheming scumbag" in Yiddish. He sold Roth's business to a party he contacted without consulting Roth.

Lousse: a financial officer, hired on Parrach's lawyer's suggestion to help Roth liquidate. This "Lousse" may have been Julius Moss ("Richard Ross"), the affiliate of Roth whom he used to help with secreting the profits from his underground books, many of which were found during the 1929 Vice Society raid on the warehouse for his Golden Hind Press. Moss helped do the same during the distribution of *The Strange Career of Mr. Hoover,* hiding monies in surreptitious accounts. Lousse had sworn an affidavit to the effect that William Faro Inc. was unable to satisfy creditors because the owner was misappropriating funds.[4]

Ratte: the man to whom "Parrach" sold Roth's business, possibly William Paro, whom Roth had given a job as a salesman after Paro rejected the idea of being the man who stood as shadow owner of "William Paro Inc." "Ratte" refused to return the many Faro books, in which Roth had copyright, being stored on Parrach's premises, until he received promissory notes for a certain amount; Roth had the checks written but would not hand them over until the books were delivered to his warehouse. That was not going to happen. A few days later, he was served papers requiring that his business be put into receivership.

Just before Roth was served these papers, he learned that the Faro stock,

Samuel Roth, Infamous Modernist

thanks to the machinations of Ratte, had been sold on the order of a marshal's writ of execution to the binder. The evidence for Roth's inability to satisfy creditors was a summons served by an unscrupulous bookseller with whom Parrach and Lousse had conspired, complaining that Roth had defaulted on a promissory note that not Roth, but Lousse, had issued in the first place, according to Roth. Parrach's lawyer suggested that, instead of bargaining for terms with individual creditors, Roth should sell the business to Parrach. He would be allowed to reincorporate after all debts were paid. Roth demurred. The harried publisher was able to solicit many other creditors to vouch for him, and issued a restraining order, but Parrach and the paper wholesaler were already selling his property. He was denied—through political influence, he believed—the right to any of the proceedings of voluntary bankruptcy.[5]

It is as impossible to believe all of Roth's account as it is to discount it. Taking him seriously means that we must believe that he went to jail for selling obscene books in 1929 because his lawyer was too incompetent to state that he had no financial interest in the store (*JML*, 151). In fact, he deflected culpability to his brother Moe by having him sign the warehouse lease, and served four months in jail because of violation of an earlier parole.

On the other hand, four of Roth's Faro titles were pirated and issued from 1933 throughout the rest of the decade under the "Nesor" imprint. The titles were the aforementioned *A Scarlet Pansy,* the expurgated *Lady Chatterley's Lover, Anecdota Americana,* and *Venus in Furs.*[6] In two letters to me, Gershon Legman—who by the late 1930s was participating in New York erotica dealing—wrote that "two remainder publishers" were involved, one being an owner of a Canal Street bindery named Rosen or Rose. "Nesor" is an anagram of "Rosen."[7]

Whether Nesor—which might have later become Crown Publishers—cheated Roth will never be ascertained.[8] Surely many publishers of erotica who could not pay the printer's bill when the books were ready for distribution were denied delivery. This was established "cash and carry" practice. The property of William Faro Inc. would have been desirable for young businessmen at the height of the Depression, if it could be had cheaply. Booksellers could fall into traps set by lawyers, political fixers, judges, and politicians—and fellow bookmen. However, Roth initiated the bankruptcy dealings himself. After three years the market for his steady sellers had shrunk, largely due to the Depression. That was likely to have been especially true of his expurgated *Chatterley* after the Grosset and Dunlap reprint, published shortly after his bankruptcy.

The "shame" to which Roth admitted as a response to the International Protest boiled over after the bankruptcy. The inability to provide for his family and the impossibility of continuing to build for himself a reputation as a legitimate publisher of popular, and occasionally subversive, literature became maddening. And so his revenge upon those conniving colleagues was to consider them as a degenerate species of creature and to generalize their venality as being foreign to him. So he wrote a jeremiad, *Jews Must Live,* in which he includes a chapter titled "The Life and Death of William Faro." It contains a description of a night he spent wandering on the Bowery. Deep in despair beneath the El tracks, he took a cot in a flophouse. What follows is depicted in a drawing in *Jews Must Live* titled "The Vision": Roth, head in hand, sitting on the edge of the bed. Next to him is a ghostly figure the caption does not identify, but which we are told in the text is a spirit Roth has seen before: Yeshea. "What you are learning now," Jesus/Yeshea tells Roth, "is to be hated, not feared." His God, he now knew, would not allow his enemies to fix his identity as a schlemiel, or an egomaniac living in a fantasy world. Many Old Testament prophets had been hated by their people. Roth returns home and writes his jeremiad, making it sound like a task from on high. But God's words are dark, and it is up to the fallible human to interpret correctly and act as he believes right. The epigraph of *Jews Must Live* is "To the first generation of Jews that will learn to pronounce my name softly." That is melodramatic, but the epithets Jews used with "Samuel Roth" were pronounced softly because they taxed a language's ability to wring bitterness out of the heart.

Act 2: *Jews Must Live*

"What I have set down here I had to or go out of my mind. . . . It struck me like a tidal wave" (*JML,* 11). Roth was fully aware of the self-destructive aspects of *Jews Must Live,* and the shame of signing "to it my tortured name" was especially searing while he was reading the proofs. He meant his American name; the persona Mishillim was reserved for stories with a more providential ending. One must give him credit for the courage to make a plainspoken declaration of what he knew would distance him from people and traditions he loved. *Jews Must Live* contains much of his best prose; abstract phrasing, forced allusions, strained efforts at erudition, inappropriate sarcasm, and other attempts to assume authority are largely absent.

The fervor for his task cannot be separated from the self-pitying role we see

BY SAMUEL ROTH

JEWS MUST LIVE

AN·ACCOUNT·OF·THE·PERSECUTION·OF·THE
WORLD·BY·ISRAEL·ON·ALL·THE·FRONTIERS·OF
CIVILIZATION

ILLUSTRATED BY JOHN CONRAD

New York
THE GOLDEN HIND PRESS INC

Figure 17. Title page of Roth's *Jews Must Live* (1934). From collection of J. A. Gertzman. By permission of the Roth estate.

so often in his editorial and autobiographical writings from the mid-1920s (in *Two Worlds, Beau,* and *Stone Walls Do Not*) to the 1950s (introductions and inserted chapters in various mail-order books). "It dawned on me suddenly, blindingly," he writes in the prologue to *Jews Must Live* (18), "that all the evils of my life had been perpetrated by Jews." That is melodramatic nonsense. Was Sumner a Jew, or was Joyce, Pound, Hemingway, Eliot, or Waverly Root, or the bullies he met en route to England who were offended by having to be in his company, thought Jews had no place in Europe, and threatened to beat him up before the boat landed? ("CMAM," 199–201). One does not have to know anything about Roth's life to recognize that he is skewing his actual experiences to pursue a thesis that is itself not only self-serving but, given the time he wrote, potentially lethal.

Spite and Hysteria

Roth's overriding reason for writing *Jews Must Live* was revenge. If an amoral cabal of businessmen have defeated a colleague, the latter can deride them and get open contempt, or continue to treat them decently, in which case they despise their victim secretly, telling themselves he was just a schlemiel. The victim loses either way. But if he writes a book that sullies the identity of his rivals by calling all of their people (their "race") dirty cheaters and spreaders of "moral gonorrhea," and if he writes about the shady and antisocial business tactics of his tormentors in a chapter titled "The Life and Death of William Faro," he *pisses them off.* And that's what Roth did.

Attributing so much covetousness and betrayal to American Jews, *Jews Must Live* was a special boon for the Nazis. Roth presented examples of Jews who escaped serving their country, were quacks, shysters, double-dealers, and rapists, and made themselves rich at clients' expense. Without doubt, he was relieving bitterness over self-destructive personal grievances that hurt him more than the people (Maurice Samuel, Henry Hurwitz, Louis Untermeyer) whom he had chosen to make adversaries. Even Frank Tannenbaum was cited as a betrayer for daring to believe that Roth did not pay John Erskine promptly. Another self-destructive display of spite was directed at Jack Brussel for not telling him that to attempt to sell *The Perfumed Garden* would cause the Vice Society to monitor Roth's future activity. That would have been more convincing if it was not perfectly evident that Sumner had taken notice after he published his *Two Worlds* and *Casanova Jr.'s Tales* two years earlier (*JML*, 146–50). Finally, his own lawyer Nathan Padgug, despite his past services, was scorned as a typical Jewish lawyer (145–47, 154). "If it's money," Roth quotes Padgug, "it's worth lying and fighting for." Roth calls him "Magog" and also says he abetted the people who robbed him of his copyrights in 1934 (Gog and Magog were either a nation or kings who fomented strife, and would return to do so preceding the coming of the Messiah). "Magog" (152–53) told Roth to plead guilty in the *Perfumed Garden* affair because he could get him a suspended sentence (which he did). Roth omits that he would have been convicted in any jury trial, as Padgug said. Instead, Roth asserts he wanted to plead not guilty, since he was "innocent," which he was not.

Jack Brussel took a sour revenge on Roth, saying that Roth did not write *Jews Must Live* at all, but merely edited Clement Wood's research; Brussel told an interviewer, and no doubt other New York bookmen, that Roth simply could not concentrate on such an intense writing task long enough to finish it.[9] When Roth dedicated *The Private Life of Frank Harris* to Clement Wood, "the only other man in America capable of turning this trick," many believed Wood was the real author of the book. His daughter plausibly explains, however, that each man wrote sections so that the work could be issued shortly after Harris's death.[10] Roth had, as a practicing poet and autobiographer during the period 1916–22, shown himself capable of composing complex work. And in prison, he was able to write copiously. In 1937 he told his wife that while in Lewisburg Penitentiary he had worked on eight book-length manuscripts, most of which he had started before being incarcerated and all of which he had finished, or would soon finish.[11] Once published, they were to provide a source of income for him and his family.

However, Brussel's comment is especially interesting in view of Roth's description of the dinner-table conversation with Wood and his wife the evening of Roth's later Bowery adventure. In *Jews Must Live*, Roth said the couple (the name he used was "The Harlans") had told him that they "do not like Jews, as you know, but we do like you." Mrs. Harlan went on to tell Roth that the people whom she had met at his apartment had been opportunists, had sold him out, and were representative of a "nation of leeches" that did not deserve Roth's allegiance. The couple felt that the Nazis had reasons to want the Jews out of Germany.

If Wood was anti-Semitic, it did not show in his writing. Nor would anyone have spoken so churlishly in a friend's home, especially before his wife. For Roth to imagine this indicates how self-destructive and thus self-hating he was at the time he was writing. If he wanted readers to recognize his state of mind, and thus his unreliability as a narrator (as opposed to his obviously dubious value as a historian or an evaluator of Jewish culture), the only other place where they could possibly do so is at the end of the last chapter. However, he does not maintain a consistent ironic perspective. Perhaps he did commission Wood, a person who could research and write quickly and cogently, to compile information for *Jews Must Live*, and possibly do extensive copy-editing, for which task Roth had little patience. At most a year separated the loss of his business and the appearance of the book. Wood had ghostwritten several chapters of *The Private Life of Frank Harris*, which Roth indirectly acknowledged in his dedication. Roth published it under his own name.[12] Whoever researched and edited *Jews Must Live*, there is much of Roth's idiosyncratic character in it, and he must be held solely responsible.

Many people, including Pauline (to whom he was wont to read sections of his writings), told the author not to publish his book.[13] Fat chance. But similar self-destructive acts seemed to have an element of calculated enhancement of personal reputation and, as well, more than a little idealism: publishing *Ulysses*, sending copies of banned erotica through the mail while on parole, writing a satire on John Sumner while in prison in 1930, or taking on Herbert Hoover a year later ("If not I, who?"). *Jews Must Live* offered no such calculation. Other Jewish writers of the period—Jerome Weidman, Samuel Ornitz, Michael Gold, Meyer Levin, Budd Schulberg—had presented to the nation negative portrayals of Jews as sharp businessmen or heartless politicians. But these occurred in literary works addressing important social issues. What Roth did was completely sui generis for an American Jewish writer, with the possible exception of Ben Hecht's 1931 novel *A Jew in Love*. Hecht's Jewish protagonist is a sadistic lover, a wealthy book publisher and "bottom dollar man" who sees Zionists, Jewish reformers, and "nice" Jews as equally inadequate. Sexually inadequate himself, he takes pleasure in murdering innocence as represented in his mind by the blonde shiksa (Jews must love). He has a pure Hebraic face, "in which race leers and burns like some biologic disease."[14]

Only Roth's most loyal supporter and employee, Herbert Diament,[15] from the Poetry Book Shop days, would tolerate the nature of *Jews Must Live*. Its prologue, a public letter to "Dear Herbert," is titled "The Genesis of Jew-Hatred." Who else might take the author of *Jews Must Live* seriously, except the Nazis and other anti-Semites, is hard to say. All of Roth's self-justifying, tortured explanations for his failures, his arrogance, and his inability to take responsibility for what he had done are on display, as is a dismal pessimism about the future. This pessimism ("I expect to be living when they will be roasting Jews alive on Fifth Avenue") and the deep-seated misanthropy ("Man? He is no better than a fox, a louse or a cucumber") had been prepared for in previous statements, including the advertising copy for some of the Faro titles. The misanthropy had been reiterated by his vicious words directed at Harry Hurwitz, Jack Brussel, and Maurice Samuel. It was usually sexual conduct, as in Samuel's case, that stimulated Roth's derision. For example, he proclaimed that doctors almost never perform abortions without "taking" the woman; "9 out of 10 prostitutes were first seduced by their physicians."[16] Attribution of vulturine sexual acts to people whom he envied, and on whose shoulders he therefore placed some of his own tabooed compulsions, was one of Roth's spiteful characteristics.

Roth never regretted such statements, but he immediately disavowed *Jews Must Live*. The pro-Nazi Silver Shirts had advertised the book in sky writing over Los Angeles, an event witnessed by Charles Reznikoff; a Nazi magazine reprinted (from a book introduced by Alfred Rosenberg) forty-three pages of Roth's *Now and Forever* to indicate that the earlier book also was a Jew's confession.[17] Adelaide Kugel recalls a *Daily News* photo of Nazi propagandist Julius Streicher at his desk, on which sat a copy of *Jews Must Live*.[18] Roth and his wife at one point destroyed many copies of the book themselves. He instructed Pauline to return orders for the book with the statement that it was out of print until the author could "clarify his objective better."[19] In federal prison in 1937 on an obscenity conviction and applying for parole, the author pled for "a chance to revise that tragic book of mine."[20] Meanwhile, although the *New York Times* ignored the book, it was reviewed in various city newspapers in the South, Midwest, New England, and San Francisco. Most reviewers praised the concise repertorial style and the writer's resolution in writing what must have pained him considerably to relate.[21]

The people who suffered most from the ostracism that followed *Jews Must Live*, as he might have realized in a rational mood, were his own wife and children. Fifty years later, Adelaide got a final blowback from her father's vitriol, when she wrote to Marie Syrkin requesting details of Sam's relationship with her. "From [*Jews Must Live*] on, Sam was avoided," wrote Syrkin. "You can appreciate the reasons. On the number of occasions [that] he sought to resume his acquaintance with Charles [Reznikoff] and me, we found that impossible. I don't think it would be wise to gloss over this act [the anti-Semitic book] as a 'tragic mistake.' It was not viewed as a mistake. . . . You will not help your objective if you seek to minimize what to most appears horrendous—a betrayal."[22]

Before he left prison in 1939, inspired by Jacques Maritain's *A Christian Looks at the Jewish Problem*, Roth composed an essay calling on the Catholics of Europe to save Jews from extinction. He bade them remember that Jesus was a Jew and "the epitome par excellence of the Jewish nature."[23] At about the same time, he wrote an essay titled "Anti-Semitism as a Necessary Condition in the Modern World."[24] It is as if *Jews Must Live* never existed, and that Sam Roth was only an outraged victim, not a perpetrator, of hatred of Jews. In this essay he mentions the physical attacks on him by Christians in Galicia and by Italians and Irish in New York City. Worse were the "bruises" to his spirit, incurred by reading anti-Semitic statements made by writers and musicians whose art he loved. Hurt and fascinated, he read many books about Jewish perfidy as a world problem, concluding that no writer had explained the basis of Jew-hatred. Pretending he would never have given the reasons he had five years earlier, he then gives his own explanation: their love of Torah inspires the Goy's jealousy. His chutzpah is startling. In a 1937 letter, he planned to publish a translation of a new edition of the Talmud, because so much Nazi propaganda "was based on lying reports of what the Talmud advocates as Jewish policy in relation to gentiles."[25] *Jews Must Live* had contained one of these reports. Roth reiterated from anti-Semitic scholars the charges that on Yom Kippur all debts incurred toward gentiles during the year were abrogated.

One of the apologies Roth gave for the book was that it was one of his "hysterical" responses to what he interpreted as attempts to nullify his identity. His previous impetuousness had likewise been motivated by the drive to maintain it. Examples include throwing a book at his suddenly scolding rabbi; the reading aloud of an evangelical pamphlet on the trip to America after the red-bearded rabbi's admonition never to read it; the impertinent responses to criticism of his *Two Worlds Monthly* reprintings of *Ulysses*. In each of these instances, Roth rejected common sense, gaining money, status, or identity, because as Legman said, "He needed it so." He was the opposite of Kafka's hunger artist, who passively accepted being stared at in a sideshow, and providing money for his boss, because he could find nothing in the world, or in his imagination, to fight for or desire. The ravenous panther who inhabited his cage after his death fetched much better admission fees.

What seemed like a storm of aggression in Samuel Roth was a kind of survival tactic, because it preserved his hopes for an eminent future, rather than that of a schlemiel. That word, it needs to be stressed, meant one with not only an unlucky, but an unfortunate destiny.[26] Roth would rather die than accept schlemiel-hood. Fear him or hate him (Yeshea had predicted the latter). Let his enemies attack him with words or fists, or cast him out from among them. At all costs, he would be taken seriously, like his ancestor Jerosh. The intensity lifted him, in his own mind, far above the cash nexus. His behavior would one day allow him to enter a realm of purifying light. His view of the world and his place in it was very different from the humble one of the Jewish wise man who lives most of his life in seclusion, as well as being the opposite of Kafka's hunger artist's.

"My Tortured Name": Who Did Samuel Roth Think He Was?

The self-importance Roth assumes, and his inability to admit that anything he does, however mistaken, is not part of some "high purpose," is remarkable. Either the persona of the poet, the publisher, the social reformer, or the family man was orbiting inside his head, his sensibility always capable of making one of them temporarily at home there. So who did the writer of *Jews Must Live* think he was? Stereotypical self-images predominated, as in, "If I am a criminal it is in the same sense in which Cervantes, Bruno and Jesus and many other men of ideals and courage before me became criminals in their days" (*JML*, 148). His claim of exceptionalism allowed him to feel that judgments such as "fanatic," "egotist," or "scoundrel" were irrelevant. Roth never scrupled to consider deeply and thoroughly the damage he did with any particular act, whether it be the struggles his behavior imposed on his family, the scurrilousness of some of his personal attacks, or the meretricious character of many (certainly not all) of the faux erotic mail-order books he pandered.

He came to believe himself after *Jews Must Live* to be one of a small group of provocative people who seemed to be traitors to their people ("hated, not feared") but were eventually vindicated. One of those was the Jewess Berenice of Cilia, a descendant of Herod the Great, whose life Roth wanted his daughter to research for him.[27] She was considered a harlot among Jews, and there were rumors of incest with her brother, with whom she ruled in Galilee and Jordan. She was a concubine, and almost the wife, of Titus, destroyer of the Second Temple. After his capture of Jerusalem, she walked through the Temple with him. According to Jewish legend, Titus did not want to sack the Holy of Holies, but Berenice convinced him to do it. Her reason was not, however, depraved, although it was thought traitorous at the time. She and her brother hoped the action would stop the revolt and save Jerusalem from obliteration.[28]

The other fancied predecessor of the author of *Jews Must Live* was the historian Josephus. He seemed to betray the Jews when he surrendered to the Romans and joined their forces, even adopting a Roman surname. The ultimate result of this, however, was his "magnificent history" of the Jews under the Romans. Roth imagines that the writer's motive was Roman citizenship, and therefore the leisure "to write a history of [his] people that would live as long as the works of Livy." And so his people in the end honored him, rather than immortalizing him as a Benedict Arnold.[29]

In his autobiography, Roth stated that *Jews Must Live* was "primarily an act of religious hysteria" ("CMAM," 311). Ever since he was a child, he had "held dialogues" with God. On one occasion he asked God to prevent his mother from finding out he had torn the pants he wore on religious occasions, and lo and behold, the puretz's house caught on fire, absorbing everyone's attention. What Roth remembers, in explaining how *Jews Must Live* came about, is a child's sense of specialness. But it was more than just specialness, which after all many children feel. Marie Syrkin concludes her 1982 letter to Adelaide Kugel by saying her father appears to her "in his contradictions of good and evil almost a Dostoyevskian figure." For her to say so, after his irresponsible forcing of a commitment from her when she was sixteen, and despite *Jews Must Live,* is a generous act by a person placing fairness above justified hostility.

"A Dostoyevskian Figure" Undertakes a Metamorphosis

The critic Isaac Rosenfeld has delineated, in his discussion of Cahan's *The Rise of David Levinsky,* the seriousness that secular Jews, especially those bred in circumstances of poverty or oppression, invest in any task touching on their inner life. Levinsky, like Roth, experienced in eastern Europe an intense religious training, provided by the sacrifice of a parent. Rosenfeld shows that Levinsky's dissatisfaction with his business success is part of an emotional insecurity that will never be alleviated. That was true of Roth as well. Like Levinsky, he got his business started with a risky bit of chutzpah, if not chicanery. Levinsky, like Roth, needed to reiterate, especially to himself, that he would never be satisfied with his worldly riches.[30] For both men, personal history was a nightmare they needed to escape. Neither, of course, when they were Stephen Dedalus's age, thought he would abandon the inner strength that his religious instruction had taught him. Neither Levinsky nor Roth developed Stephen's independence, but neither would ever allow anything to diminish his sense of Jewish inner life, even if his success in pursuing the American dream of status and security made it impossible ever to reach it.

That 1939 essay on the source of anti-Semitism, in which Roth is silent on his own book about "the persecution of the world by Israel," is surprisingly eloquent about the uniqueness of the Jewish sensibility. He finds it in the conviction that the Torah is "lovely and delightful and the fountain of all human purity and wisdom." When Joseph rejected the invitation of his benefactor Potiphar's comely wife, Roth said, and allowed her to take his coat of many colors rather than his body, it was because of the concept of loyalty, which he had been taught by the Law. His love was only for Torah, which is personified as "a woman infinitely more beautiful and more precious . . . than the sensual Mrs. Potiphar."[31] The shadowy visitor in Roth's deeply felt early poem "Yahrzeit" (1920), "as merciless as God," understands the danger of allowing Eros to replace desire for spiritual harmony. The visitor sends the speaker on an inner voyage to transform sensual passion into intoxication with what is too holy to be expressed directly. "Yahrzeit" embodies the beginning of a quest that for both David Levinsky and Samuel Roth became a road taken, if at all, very late.

Even *Jews Must Live* is invested with this kind of dark, forever tentative spiritual mission. Immediately after a passage about the enormous stress writing the book was causing him, Roth states that reading the proofs and preparing the book for publication was "a metamorphosis I am still agonizing through" (*JML*, 11). The metamorphosis was more complex than a conversion from committed Jew and Zionist to anti-Semite. Milton Hindus has suggested that one seminal philosophical influence on Roth's thought and behavior was Nietzsche.[32] Hindus notes that Roth's title for a collection of his poetry, *Songs Out of Season* (1932), is an allusion to Nietzsche's *Thoughts Out of Season*. The latter is an early work by the great philosopher, and Roth, with typical immodesty, implies his own significance in affixing this title to a volume of his early poetry (albeit published a decade after most of it was written). This metaphysical commitment to growth and metamorphosis is what Israel Zangwill admired in Roth: it may have its roots not only in Nietzsche but in the Jewish belief in taklis, or destiny.

In their study of the culture and lifestyle of the eastern European shtetl, Mark Zborowski and Elizabeth Herzog emphasize that "apparent contradictions, inconsistencies and irregularities" will be reconciled in the course of working out one's destiny, for they may be interpreted "as parts of a long-term process building toward ultimate integration."[33] Such an assumption allows people to maintain faith in themselves as they pursue spiritual as well as secular goals, however unconventional the goals may appear to one's contemporaries. Roth struggled to synthesize diverse strains of thought, including the Nietzschean (which, in order to say yes to life, rejected any Judeo-Christian Manichaean conception of God's contest with Satan) and Hasidic (erasing sensual pleasure in order to suppress the Evil Inclination and learn Torah).

Roth saw his taklis as helping repair the world for the coming of Yeshea, but also as respecting the promise of America. His fight for the First Amendment was at best only partly relevant to the mission that Yeshea gave him, but his secular and religious idealism indicate, as perverse as it sounds, that Sam Roth retained his Jewish head ("Yiddisher kop") despite all the titillating and sensation-seeking reading material he published.[34] That assertion, on the other hand, certainly rang false to various people who knew and worked with Roth, including Gershon Legman, Harry Roskolenko, Marie Syrkin, Waverley Root, Louis Grudin, and Ezra Pound.

Either taklis, or Nietzsche, or both, had been much on Roth's mind four years before, in his prison memoir *Stone Walls Do Not* (1931). The book carries one of the world's strangest limitation statements: "For himself the author will keep one copy in the hope that it may some day grow into a good book." Roth was fascinated by apparent paradoxes working themselves out over time. Again, taklis. What seems to be walking with demons might result in understanding and acceptance of what a godly path (destiny) entails. The epigraph for *Now and Forever* (1925) is Whitman's "Do I contradict myself?" One paradox he might have hoped for would be that a "cutthroat" businessman shunned by his contemporaries could turn out, like Josephus, to be a prophetic writer. That would be an example of the Hasidic concept of "redemption through sin," which some commentators use to explain a period of personal humiliation leading to final exaltation. Even the supposed messiah Sabbatai Zvi's apostasy in converting to Islam instead of dying a martyr's death could be an example.[35]

Guilty of everything, this "tragic book of mine" sheds light on many facets of Roth's complicated character. First, Roth incorporated the views of writers pivotal to the development of Nazi ideology, one of them a Jew who had lost faith in a future for Jewry. Second, it is another drama of father-son struggle. The sources of Roth's sense of vulnerability—the rabbinical exorcism, the punishment for masturbation, the diminishing of his father's fortunes and status in America, the warning that if Sam insisted on being a poet his father would throw him out of his house—were important. They reinforced the writer's aversion to being subject to victimhood, manipulation, and isolation. Third, *Jews Must Live* is also an astute, however hateful, analysis of the Jew as middleman minority. Several passages show how the vagaries of ethnic and financial struggle put a businessman, specifically the erotica dealer, in a humiliating symbiotic relationship with the authority figures who deplore what he does. Finally, the book epitomizes the neurosis that Sander Gilman, Peter Gay, and other Jewish scholars (including Maurice Samuel) have specified as Jewish self-hatred and self-division, or the lack of a coherent self. David Levinsky was aware of businesslike dissimulation that as a Jew he will never fully atone for. In *Jews Must Live*, Roth conceals self-division behind the jeremiad. Therefore he cannot control or cope with it. But it's there.

Roth's Sources for *Jews Must Live:* From Marx to Hitler

Jews Must Live consists of sixteen chapters and an appendix ("Do Jews Emit a Peculiar Odor?"). The first chapter, called a prologue, details the author's realization that he had been ill-treated not by Christians but by fellow Jews. Discussions wherever possible concentrate on the Jew in America. However, from beginning to end Roth uses the analyses of European sociologists and historians, most with solid German academic credentials, who express horror at the influence and behavior of contemporary urban Jewish participants in the professions, business, the arts, and politics of the era. Here, for the Jews, was a nightmare from which they would not awake in time. The most influential ideologue was Houston Stewart Chamberlain (*The Foundations of the Nineteenth Century*, 1899), philosopher, historian, Teutonic supremacist, and, posthumously, the chief ideologue of the Nazis. Another whom Roth (or Clement Wood, if he did do the research) echoes is Werner Sombart, sociologist, Marxist economist, and social activist (*Modern Capitalism*, 1902).

Two other anti-Semitic writers were Otto Weininger and Heinrich von Treitschke. The latter, professor at the world-renowned University of Berlin, was an admirer of Bismarck and hoped that idealization of Nordic character traits would insulate the country from love of ease, security, and sensuality, and from the formidable nations surrounding it. In his *History of Germany in the Nineteenth Century* (1879) he wondered if Jews, isolated from statehood for centuries, could understand the selfless and spiritual resolve inherent in national consciousness. In "A Word about Our Jewry" (1879–80) he deplored the satiric approach to patriotism in the Jewish press, the ghetto-based jargon of Yiddish that Jews brought with them to Germany during the Enlightenment, the insularity of Jewish financiers, and their power to silence their critics by pressuring the media. The sensation-driven schemes of Jewish promoters of popular entertainment horrified him.[36]

Weininger, born Jewish but a convert to Catholicism, was a recent Ph.D. at the University of Vienna when he published *Sex and Character* (1903) at age twenty-three. The book was admired by Jewish writers such as Kafka, Karl Kraus, Arnold Schoenberg, and Ludwig Wittgenstein.[37] Ford Maddox Ford recalls the book being a favorite topic of conversation, discussed in whispers because of its open expression of what many men suspected but did not want to say in mixed company.[38] Joyce read it, nourishing and transcending *Sex and Character*'s observations in his portrait of the Wandering Jew as Ulysses.[39] Weininger believed in Aryan racial superiority as strongly as he did in male intellectual power, Jewish effeminacy, and female inferiority. By "Jewishness" or "the Jewish spirit," Weininger, like Wagner and other writers, meant a state of mind as much as an ethnic group or race.

These writers' examples are all drawn, with careful selectivity, from Jewish history, customs, behavior, and speech. They disparage those Germans who they think have been captured heart and soul by Jewishness, which is sometimes made indistinguishable from modern culture. The Nordic spirit (not the French, Italian, or Russian) is the opposite of this "degeneration." The stateless Jews, Weininger said, embody a zeitgeist that has become dominated by feminine character traits, and in fact by Jewesses, who offer direction, consolation, and release from loneliness. Those may be nurturing traits, but the Nordic male would possess his own strength. The need of the Jew to depend on the Jewess indicates servility and lack of resolution. Like women, Jews are willful, spiteful, and incapable of moral resolution, genius, or originality. They have internalized submissiveness to non-Jews, who, they realize, are allowing them to live in their country on sufferance. Like women, they are not able to discipline their sensuality. It is voyeuristic and prurient, suitable for "the promotion business" but not for ethical commitment. Jews' ability to adjust to alien customs, like female pliability to men, is due to their not having an innate set of ideals that are stronger than their venality and their fear of annihilation.

Weininger writes that Jews are incapable of creativity. Obsessed with their survival, they have become fixated on the ineluctable decay of living matter and with bodily emissions and excrements. The Jew, like the female, has no soul, that is, no idea of the sublime and its prerequisite, immersion in the metaphysical entity of the "Volk." The Jewish physician had taken the place of the Messiah, the journalist that of the artist, and the male marriage broker that of the family and church patriarchs.[40] Weininger predicted that *Sex and Character* would either make his fortune or kill him. Both happened. The book became a best-seller, and Weininger committed suicide the next year, choosing Beethoven's house in which to do so, as a final tribute to the Germanic genius he despaired of reaching due to the innate Jewishness of his mind and heart. He believed Christ himself was the only Jew to have overcome that Jewishness.

A third writer critical of the Jews was a man whom Roth heard a lot about from his years of friendship with Frank Tannenbaum. Karl Marx was born

Samuel Roth, Infamous Modernist

into a family of converts, and became a Lutheran at age six. He did not, however, see the Jews as an inferior race, but as needing, as did the rest of the Western world, liberation from capitalism. That was the thesis of his "On the Jewish Question" (1843).[41] Other European writers who explored the nexus between capitalism and Jewish faith were in fact anti-Semitic, though *Jews Must Live* does not mention them. Roth refers by name only to Sombart and Chamberlain as authoritative. They as well as other sources Roth uses identified the Teutonic race with moral purity and equated "Jewish spirit" with predatory capitalism. It was as if there were no German bankers, industrialists, arms manufacturers, or stock speculators, except those who, through greed, had betrayed their heritage by adopting the spirit of Judaism.

Sombart, von Treitschke, and Chamberlain provided Roth with his ideas about Jews isolating themselves from German culture and mores, and rabbinic sanctioning of parasitic behavior toward non-Jews. Chamberlain asserts that the Jew will suffer every humiliation in order to bring about "the Messianic empire of supreme power."[42] For Sombart, Jews are a "nation within" the larger society; Roth's way of putting this is that the Jews want a sovereignty of their own, and that even "Kol Nidre" sanctions the cheating of goyim.[43] The title of Roth's chapter 9 is "Judaism Is Not a Misfortune to the Jews Alone," paraphrasing Ferdinand Lassalle, a socialist with connections to Bismarck. He was another nineteenth-century Jewish writer (born Lassal) contemptuous of the Jewish desire for security through accumulation of capital and German goodwill.[44] Roth states, however, that he is following Heine's statement, "Judaism is not a religion, but a misfortune." Von Treitschke's "Heine sneers at everything German" becomes, in *Jews Must Live*, "every synagogue we Jews build in Christian countries is a finger of scorn we stick into the eyes of our hosts."[45] Historian Amos Oz recalls, in discussing Weininger, the Viennese quip, "Anti Semitism never got serious until Jews started doing it."[46]

Roth relies on Marx in remarking on the Jewish responsibility for the spirit of capitalism. Jews are the master of haggling, done in *mauscheln,* German mixed with Yiddish and some Hebrew, which Sander Gilman shows Germans thought of as the antithesis of their own language, and as the "hidden language" of the eastern Jew.[47] Roth describes Jewish lawyers (inventors of the "divorce mill racket"), physicians (using his own example of a Yiddish physician who gave him the choice of an operation performed by himself or a lifetime of suffering), and land speculators, who he says have already raped the land in Europe (somehow, although most could not own property there), as well as America and eretz Yisrael (Palestine). Especially in the chapter on

"The Jew and the Land," phrases such as "beloused," "repugnant ghetto character," and "slovenly and degrading" (*JML*, 80–81, 172, 178, 183) are reinforced by the illustrations, which look like woodcuts and may have been influenced by those in Gold's *Jews without Money* (1930). Most depict a bald man with a swarthy complexion and a bulbous nose gesturing, shrugging his shoulders and grinning, chomping a cigar, and towering over office buildings as if he is moving them on a chess board. The artist, "Conrad," told Adelaide Kugel that his Jewish father-in-law was used as model for these drawings.[48]

Roth asserts, citing Chamberlain as an authority, that Jewish mothers make every effort to provide moral education for their sons, but they invariably become "unbearable merchants and swindlers" when they hit the streets. "Toward the man-power of America, Jewry contributes only what it catches in its own sweat-shops, as in so many rat traps—set by itself" (108). Jews do not "dig wells, plough fields, forge skyscrapers, lay bricks, cut out trenches . . . rivet bridges, hinge gates, or fight fires." Nonsense, and he knew it.

Jews Must Live's evidence that Judaism is a "moral gonorrhea" focuses on "the woman market." His discussion of the subject begins with a Jewish proprietor of a European house in which each girl was assigned a number (being typically dedicated to demeaning Christians, the only girls he would not employ were Jewesses). Roth compares him to an American Jew, Florenz Ziegfeld (*JML*, 224), using burlesque as an example of what Weininger described as the agile Jewish mind, which, because the members of the race possess no soul, respects no boundaries or taboos. For Weininger, whom Roth echoes here, creation was not possible for the Jews, who could only produce a kind of corruption.[49] One illustration in *Jews Must Live* depicts a man with a large, bulbous nose, bulging eyes, and thin lips peering through a keyhole. It is titled "The Jew's Contribution to American Literature," indicating the corruption of literature into prurient interest in the forbidden. Its inclusion is an allusion to Roth's own publishing strategies and therefore an example of self-hatred. So is his long-standing admiration of Ziegfeld, especially because Roth speaks of his use of his business to gratify his own secret desires ("CMAM," 174).

The assumption that the Jewish people are incapable of great art, and can only anthologize and copy, is one slander one would expect Roth, a poet and fiction writer, would eschew. But the appendix of *Jews Must Live* can only be another example, consisting of a seventeen-page excerpt from Sir Thomas Browne, to which is added an eleven-page selection from Voltaire, and finally his own translation of Heine's "The Disputation." The title of the appendix— "Do Jews Emit a Peculiar Odor?" (*fetor judaicus*)—shows what these three excerpts have in common: Jews stink. Sander Gilman specifies the wellspring of anti-Semitism and also Jewish self-hatred to be their "hidden language." Yiddish is, Jew-haters assert, as dirty as the breath in which it is uttered is smelly.

Self-hate is particularly evident when Roth describes the "new language" of the gossip column as "insinuating, clearly-hinting, spicy." This from a publisher who had recently flourished by issuing books exploiting current scandals and political sensations. Only "other Jews," said Roth, could do what Walter Winchell did, becoming king of what he himself lauded as the "col-yum." But Roth equally denigrates contemporary Jewish poets such as Alter Brody, James Oppenheim, and Emma Lazarus, as he does novelists such as Ludwig Lewisohn and Waldo Frank (102–6). The conclusion is that, in the absence of a context of nationhood, neither genius nor imaginative creativity is possible for Jews. It is von Treitschke, with his worship of militant nationhood, who seems to be the source for this, although Chamberlain and Weininger also expressed the idea. Others who stigmatize the Jewish mind as exclusively rational and thus without culture, imagination, or a sense of sublimity are Sombart and Chamberlain, for whom the Talmud "Signifies the victory of will over understanding and every further effort of creative imagination."[50]

German Race Doctrine, American Nativism, and *Jews Must Live*

The political context in which the German or Germanophile scholars created their work should have, but did not, suggest to Roth the contrast between European anti-Semitism, where one's "race" was a shibboleth determining status, and America, where democratic institutions (but not, of course, popular prejudice) precluded it. Part of the background for anti-Semitic thought in Germany was Bismarck's Second Reich. At the center of western Europe, surrounded by aggressive nation-states, the German people under Bismarck needed steely resolution, Teutonic pride, and unreserved will to act in rock-hard solidarity. Habits, modes of thinking, language, and gesture, and tastes in entertainment were some of the markers of national brotherhood. Jews were believed incapable of any of the traits of the emerging German national sensibility.

America was isolated from European national struggles. Among anti-Semites, the "Jewish Question" was pressing because the Jews were prosperous, due to their business and professional acumen. Thus they were believed to be cheating. Here they were, detractors said, a kind of bacterial infection among the U.S. "volk," or the 100 percent Americans, bringing their low cunning and "slovenly" ghetto habits of mind, body, and language with them. In some Jewish immigrants such hostility prioritized a need for obsequious "niceness," or genteel docility, a response also noted in Europe. That might remedy the government's cautiousness in protecting their hard-won social and financial security.[51] Similar behavior had been in favor in many European cities. Peter Gay asks whether many of Berlin's successful Jews, in feeling a pressing need to be indistinguishable from their German neighbors, were, "in their anxiety to present a good front and avoid untoward publicity, so different from Treitschke?"[52]

There is an interesting parallel between *Jews Must Live* and the famous turn-of-the-century Viennese journalist Karl Kraus. Kraus also respected Chamberlain, excoriated Jewish writers and businessmen, and advised his fellow Jews to assimilate. He singled out Jewish journalists, who he said produced mordant, one-sided essays, "feuilletons," that buried the complexity of serious issues under sophisticated repartee: "spin." Kraus feared that feuilletons, which cannily argue from one point of view, gave substance to von Treitschke's claim, in "A Word about Our Jewry," that there were "too many Jews in Journalism."

Roth's definition of what Gilman describes as "the secret language of the Jews," a foundation of anti-Semitism, is based on the kind of criticism of *mauscheln* that Kraus had made. For Roth, himself very good at spin, Walter Winchell is the exemplar of "insinuating, clearly hinting, spicy language" with which "You can practically manufacture your own sensations" (106). Kraus's most recent biographer, Paul Reitter, sees him as attempting to offer an alternative self-definition to urban Jews willing to examine themselves and their "niceness." Their material and artistic blessings are real, but hide from them how non-Jews stereotype them.[53]

Kraus wanted to reform his co-religionists by making them more self-conscious, proud of their Talmudic heritage, and aware of its complex delineation of personal responsibility.[54] Despite Roth's later avowals of trying to shock other Jews to reform, he does not suggest in *Jews Must Live* that Jews return to the ethical obligations of traditional Judaism (as Kafka does)[55] or the positive aspects of their pre-Enlightenment shtetl roots. Nor does he defend the Talmud against charges of its being a textbook in how to prepare oneself to accumulate money. Instead, he warns Jews that they must reform by assimilating with Christian America. Sumner would like that. In 1932, Sumner advocated laws even more stringent than those in effect regulating immigration and enforcing quicker assimilation.[56]

Samuel Roth, Infamous Modernist

Roth was far more intransigent than the head of the Society for the Suppression of Vice. The latter never spoke in terms of race, although he recorded it in his arrest ledgers, as did other reformist institutions, and the police. Nor did he refer to immigrants as intentionally malicious subversive influences. His policy of enforced dispersal and assimilation of immigrants was supported by Jewish groups, albeit by established "uptown" ones. The careers of Sumner and his colleagues also prove that American ideals, ambitions, and institutions were indeed not those of the Germany which Roth's sources envisioned. There is no indication that the writer of *Jews Must Live,* more intransigent, and certainly less practical than Sumner, recognized this essential difference. The fanatic spite machine was the writer of *Jews Must Live,* or one of his demons.

Gershon Legman wrote to Adelaide Kugel that *Jews Must Live* ruined her father, that any Jewish judge he came before would throw the book at him as a "Jewish anti-Semite," and that he said to Legman he must have been "insane" when he wrote it.[57] Legman was not trying to shock her, but to make her aware that her father felt such panic at losing his property that he had rejected the possibility of America protecting its Jewish citizens.[58] Several years earlier than his correspondence with Adelaide, Legman had written to Leo Hamalian that Roth's motive was that "he figured Hitler would win and wanted to jine 'em at the start. Jack Brussel . . . concurred in this explanation of *JML.*"[59]

Jews Must Live and Roth's Alienation from His Father

Despite acts of alienation like Sam's refusal to accompany his father to Sabbath services or to visit his ailing mother when Yussef was in the house, the most piercing instance of renunciation of the father is the passage in *Jews Must Live* in which Roth explains the significance of Kol Nidre, sung by the cantor at the start of Day of Atonement services. This was the "soul breath" the child Mishillim so admired Yussef for singing to the Nuszcze congregation.

> *Kol Nidre!* What the sound of that word means to a Jew from the first time he hears it in the white twilight of a tall-candled synagogue on the eve of Yom Kippur, and on through the wilderness of the ghetto years, only a Jew can understand! The most intimate memories of childhood, youth and manhood, twine themselves about that tune, and he hangs upon it, as upon the branches of a tree ["By the waters of Babylon . . . we hung our harps on the willows"], the choicest of his emotions, till to threaten sacrilege against *Kol Nidre* would seem to threaten life itself. (130)

It seems that the author has allowed a hallowed memory to distract him from his thesis. If so, he quickly dives back into it. Instead of noting that this opening hymn on the Day of Atonement unified the scattered Jewish community in the midst of enemies, or that on Yom Kippur the ethical basis of secular affairs is scrutinized in order to offer God a repenting heart, Kol Nidre is interpreted as meaning that Jews do not have to obey promises or contractual documents made to "the goyim" in the course of the year. The prayer in fact means "all vows"; it contains a plea to God to allow "vows" (meaning irresponsible decisions, not legal agreements) to be erased in the year ahead, as the individual grows both more scrupulous and more pious.

The illustration accompanying the Kol Nidre paragraph, a man in a prayer shawl singing and gesturing piously with a menorah in the background, is the only one casting Jews in a sympathetic light. Yet, the interpretation Roth gives it makes it the ultimate in renunciation of his people. Instead of undercutting the anti-Semitic thesis of the book, his conclusion about Kol Nidre overwhelms any other suggestion than that the Jewish people are swindlers and liars. It also defiles the purest example in Roth's memory of his father's strength and piety. *Jews Must Live* evinces a bitterness directed not only at possibly dishonest colleagues but also at a father.

Yussef Roth died the year before *Jews Must Live* was published. That may have been before his son started writing the book, since the Faro bankruptcy about six months later and the shock of vulnerability had not yet absorbed his consciousness. I have described his son weeping at his father's deathbed, and his belated awareness that natural affection cannot be dismissed. Yet a year later he wrote *Jews Must Live,* the most crushing blow he could deliver to the common faith of Sam and his father. How sad that Roth conceived as part of his mission in life that he needed to write a book that would make him "hated, not feared." And how ironic that instead of the Jewish father leading his son in the path the Torah and Talmud had delineated, it was Jesus who had taken his place.

Roth Encounters Judas: Betrayal and Self-Betrayal

Jews Must Live concludes with a debate between Roth and Judas. The writer decries Judas's ability to sell "offal" by pretending it has "beauty," which it might have had if his "grasping faculties" had not perverted it. He delineates Judas as abject in asking mercy for his deeds, and yet, he notes, he is Shylock-like in doing so. Judas has no intention of sacrificing anything. He represents

Samuel Roth, Infamous Modernist

"some unhealable disease in the blood of the race." Roth picks up a water glass to send it "crashing through [Judas's] horrible skull." He had been speaking into a mirror, which "fell in a thousand shattered fragments at my feet" (282–85). How much self-awareness is in this sentence? If Roth is a Judas, has he been challenging his readers all along to doubt him? Only a Judas would betray his own people. Is he warning his fellow Jews to be more resolute, less fearful, and above all more independent of the Nazis' desire to shame them, than the "Roth" who narrates *Jews Must Live* has been? It is possible that was his intention. Most probably, all he meant, deep in despondency and fear of the future, was that as a man, as a publisher of sex and scandal books, and as a Jew, he was inherently repulsive, and he knew it, just as Chamberlain and the others had said. He could not conceive himself apart from the Jewish culture in all its vulnerabilities, even in the Golden Land.

The counterargument would be that the narrator has such evident biases that one might think he is setting himself up as an example of a person to sneer at. Roth calling himself a Judas can be read as more than a self-hateful assertion that all Jews are Judases. It can also be taken as despairing. The image of throwing a glass at Judas and breaking a mirror is solid proof of self-division and self-hate. In a mirror, one might see a double, always a sign of bad luck, and of incompleteness. Dostoyevsky's *The Double* describes a man brooding about his social and professional ineptness. He is helpless to prevent his double from becoming his nemesis. Popular and more successful at scheming, Dostoyevsky's protagonist's double exiles him to a sanitarium. Even more threatening to identity is the dybbuk, a wandering soul looking for a body to take over. Has the ghost of Judas chosen Sam Roth? A reader alert to these suggestions need not know that Roth himself had been so dismissively treated by colleagues in 1927 and 1933 that he was in danger of drifting loose from his own identity.

That final chapter is nightmare stuff. It also invokes pity. The source of the despair is a deep insecurity, going back, perhaps, to the boy Mishillim, seeing the demon at the spring, subsequently defying the rabbi and his father by deciding that, despite the exorcism performed on him in his sickbed, he would let no authority inhibit his libidinous desire. Nor, on the boat to America, would he let an irate rabbi stop him from reading aloud a Christian evangelical pamphlet. These kinds of resolution, and rejection of fathers they entail, might be proof of a thoughtful iconoclast. But the defensiveness and sarcasm of the writer of *Jews Must Live* suggests a sense of exclusion, carrying with it a fear of being thrown into the lions' den or Leviathan's belly. The price of slashing barriers and striking out into unknown territory has been, for him, awareness of a terrifying vulnerability. In *Jews Must Live* this vulnerability is connected not to stoic self-awareness but instead to something despairing and pitiable.

In his *Jewish Self-Hatred*, Sander Gilman specifies neurotic desire for "identification with the aggressor" as a key to the phenomenon.[60] As Richard Sennett states in his discussion of repressive authority's effect on those who are dependent on it, "the superior controls reality."[61] There is evidence of this in the rationalization that Jews ought to be careful of how they behave toward Christians; the Jews in Germany, if they behaved as those who forced his bankruptcy, might deserve their fate. Roth also wrote that Jews prepare for their own demise when what they say or do makes the non-Jewish community wonder whether they are being devious. That causes distrust and "build[s] justification of some future pogrom." That is why, in *Jews Must Live,* "I figuratively placed my people over my knee and delivered it a thorough trouncing."[62] And attained near-perfect schlemiel-hood. Rather than free himself, the oppressed person sees himself as at the mercy of the authority. It becomes his nemesis. The man who addresses his readers in *Jews Must Live* is a perfect example of Gilman's and Sennett's statements. Gilman's discussion of Roth is short, but his statement that "Roth's language internalized the language of the anti-Semite about the discourse of the Jew" has its epitome in *Jews Must Live.* Gilman also states that Roth "seemed to separate the self-hating Jew as writer from all other Jews." It would be hard to find a more complete display than *Jews Must Live* of the kind of authoritarian control that makes its victim so devoid of self-worth (although full of insolent blustering), and so submissive to its will that the authority's doctrines completely override any individual analysis by the victim of specific cases, including his own. He allows himself or others no mercy. Therefore he cuts himself off from spirituality. And yet this is the same Samuel Roth who defied James Joyce and his supporters, the police, congressional committees, and a sitting president.

Business Is Still Business

Did not Roth think his book would make it impossible for fellow booksellers and distributors to do business with him? He might have answered that he did not care, that the "organic necessity" of penning *Jews Must Live* left no space for practicalities. However, he was too completely a perspicacious businessman to let this happen. He needed to feed his family, so he must have been distributing books to wholesale outlets while he wrote *Jews Must Live,* despite the Faro bankruptcy. Bookmen of all sorts sold erotica of various grades of explicitness during the Depression. Nothing else made as much money. As for carrying, below and above the counter, the goods of a man you despised, business, for most merchants, is business. By the early 1930s, Roth knew the following had not allowed the *Ulysses* affair and the International Protest to dissuade them from selling his literary erotica: Frances Steloff and David Moss of the Gotham Book Mart; James Delacey of Harvard Square's Dunster House bookstore; and John Rodker, modernist publisher and friend of Sylvia Beach and Harriet Weaver. As for the strictly banned pornography he was about to peddle, he did not need a large number of distributors, salesmen, bookstore owners, or printers in any case. He could personally contact clients he knew had bought this kind of material in the past.

Act 3: "We Meet Our Destiny on the Road We Take to Avoid It"

Samuel Roth might have served as a prototype for Otto Weininger's analysis of the insecure minority businessman. What Weininger describes as the actions of such individuals is exemplified by Roth's bitter attacks on rivals, real and perceived; his multiple excuses for extreme responses; his exploitation of popular entertainment and the "woman market"; his various self-images; his resentment and insolence; and his penchant for "showing off" his well-placed non-Jewish friends. Roth's respect for ancestors (as in his autobiography and his "Nustscha" sonnets) was another quality that might have exemplified Weininger's "Jewish spirit," because belief in one's resourceful and fearless ancestral models supports what Weininger says are "new hopeful dreams." Exploited or disenfranchised people often need to start over.

Whenever Roth defied the censors, political authorities, or the literary establishment, the immediate result was never admiration or vindication. Instead, he garnered increased hostility and further ostracism. As with *Two Worlds* or *The Strange Career,* so with *Jews Must Live.* It was as if he was exemplifying La Fontaine's observation that "a person often meets his destiny on the road he takes to avoid it." Writing the book was apparently the surest possible way to preclude becoming a Jewish wise man. However, Roth might have intuited Yeshea's plan—at present he must "be hated, not feared"—as enfolding him in a thick cloud of contempt, so that when he finally revealed his full destiny he would emerge from the murk to the glory of having his name pronounced "softly."

155

Samuel Roth seemed to be self-destructing at Columbia, in London, and as a fledging leader of a "magazine empire." That does not mean failure. It could lay a foundation for heroism. Strenuous efforts to make people pay attention result in derision. His destiny was to pass over the borderline beyond which only individuals thought to be madmen, revolutionaries, holy fools, or criminals existed. But such people continue to hope that they may one day be acknowledged heroes or seers. They are irrepressible. With *Jews Must Live*, Samuel Roth becomes a pariah to his own people and exists "absolutely alone." At least he could fancy himself to have "undergone a metamorphosis." However futile his pursuit of a goal seemed, in his persistence Roth would never be surpassed. Like Leopold Bloom, he would endure and speak. He would be mocked and despised for doing so (like Joyce's "Bloom Elijah"). He may be marked down as a schlemiel, but he would have the last word, whether the opponent be James Joyce, the president, Ernest Hemingway, Walter Winchell, or the Supreme Court—and whether or not anyone listened.

"Too Rebellious to Be Free"

Adelaide Kugel believed that Edwin Arlington Robinson's "The Wandering Jew" (1920) was influenced by the poet's acquaintance with her father.[63] I think it was the perverse pride, the perseverance, the indomitable sense of purpose, and self-imposed isolation of her father that she had in mind. "What [her father and Robinson] had in common were poverty, loneliness, the Village, a deep interest in the Bible. SR was not the *old* [italics hers] man of 'The Wandering Jew,' but the wild seer . . . especially as Robinson had seen in [Roth's] *Europe*."[64] Roth's daughter, writing in the 1980s, was probably not thinking only of *Jews Must Live* but of her father's defiance of his detractors after the *Two Worlds* printings of Joyce, the *Strange Career* anti-Hoover book ("If not I, who"), the tell-all *Secret Life of Walter Winchell*, and the public defiance of Senator Kefauver at his hearings on juvenile delinquency in 1955. The qualities Robinson describes in his poem would have struck her as especially relevant to the man who wrote *Jews Must Live,* mirroring therein the Wandering Jew's "manifold anathemas" and his compulsion to see "the world around him [as] a gift / Of anguish."

> He may have died so many times
> That all there was of him to see
> Was pride, that kept itself alive
> As too rebellious to be free. (ll. 81–84)

In fact, biographers think the poem was modeled on a brilliant, cantankerous Village intellectual of Robinson's acquaintance, a Jew turned Catholic named Alfred Hayman Louis, previously a politician, historian, and legal scholar but reduced in late middle age to living in a garret.[65] This is a compelling argument, because "The Wandering Jew" could hardly depict the Sam Roth who since the age of nine had a fascination with Jesus, even if Robinson knew of that interest (Adelaide thinks he did, as he might have). Nor would Robinson have often witnessed Roth's pugnaciousness or stubbornness; certainly he would never have been its target. But Robinson would have read *Europe* (1919), in which Roth does appear as a prophet of Europe's enervation and America's promise. In his mid-twenties when he first read "The Wandering Jew," Roth would not have recognized himself in an old, outcast Village bohemian, or in Captain Craig, the subject of another poignant poem about a ruined genius to whom the world had ceased to listen. But years later his daughter, surveying his career, would. The speaker in Robinson's "The Wandering Jew" describes a defiant, solitary, wrathful figure who disdains pity and demands only to speak. That figure recalls both the legend itself of one who must live and wander until the Second Coming, and more generally the horrible knowledge embodied in the line "What life has in it to be lost." Still intransigent and proud of it, he will never acknowledge, or perhaps recognize, a redeemed earth.

The poem is perceptively read as a depiction of the sin of pride. Pride is not honor, and blocks self-awareness; the prideful person thinks he or she is honorable. This reading sees its subject not as a Jew but as an intellectual who defies studies and opinions that differ from those he holds himself. A man of "old, unyielding eyes," he is as lonely as he is intransigent.[66] "If not I, who" is certainly the watchword on the banner of a prideful man. Roth's last published work, *My Friend Yeshea*, about the writer's time-traveling presence at Jesus' ministry and execution in Jerusalem, was dedicated "To Those Who Will Listen to Me."

For Roth's daughter, Robinson's poem not only depicts a heroically, and tragically, determined person of stature. For her, it also incited compassion, and a desire to show the world how superficial its contempt for her father was. The bond between father and daughter was growing firmer and denser during the 1930s, as challenges to Sam's ability to persevere intensified. "Dearest Chig" and "My Lovely Chig" are salutations on his letters from prison in 1938. Adelaide's and Richard's sense of responsibility for him increased then.[67] Roth tried to discount the pressures of the problems he caused in the 1920s and 1930s by thinking of his teenagers as "tots." By 1936 they had resolved to "get on with their own lives." And they did; but the bond with their father was strengthened all the more due to the pride that led to his vulnerability. If only he had been more careful before publishing *Jews Must Live* and conducting a pornography business that attracted an FBI probe. But he wasn't. In 1936 Sam Roth became prisoner number 5079 in the penitentiary at Lewisburg, Pennsylvania. A three-year prison sentence had followed his trial for distributing "flagitious" pornography.

CHAPTER 6

1934–1939

A Stretch in the Federal Penitentiary

It was New Year's Eve, 1935. Sam and Pauline Roth, per custom, arrived at the Café Royal on Second Avenue at Twelfth Street, the preferred meeting place for writers and actors on the Jewish Rialto. Adelaide Kugel, in writing about *Jews Must Live*, recalls that her parents were accompanied by Sam Cohen and his wife. A neighbor when Sam and Pauline lived on West Sixteenth Street, Mr. Cohen, a furrier, "had begun in that business as a strikebreaker": "Before they were waited on, a few of the loud talkers got up and approached their table. Sam Cohen rose heavily, and before they could speak, growled in Yiddish, 'Ice breck baine,' translated literally as 'I break bones.'" Roth, with Cohen's help having faced down the opposition, could not bring himself to stay. It was years before he would venture into the Royal again.[1]

Carrying On, 1934–1936:
The Fifth Avenue Book Shop, The Black Hawk Press

The spring of 1934 handed Roth another setback: Sumner's successful prosecution of the Faro *Anecdota Americana*, over which Roth fired his lawyer.[2] He was fined $100, even though his editing, he recalled in "Count Me among the Missing," had made the book "harmless to the point of inanity" (396). For example, in entry number 248, "Little Adelaide came shining out of the bathroom. 'I washed as far as possible, moms,' she explained, 'and then I washed possible.'" That his daughter might have come across this sentence apparently did not occur to Roth. Some financial relief came when two musical comedy entertainers took a $500 option on Roth's jejune dramatization of *Lady Chatterley's Lover*.[3] It's hard to imagine where they found the laughs.

Meanwhile, Roth carried on his mail-order business, circularizing as frequently as finances would allow. He also found three storefronts near subway stations to sell his Faro "Big Dollar" books: "$1—Any Book—$1," read the sign in the windows. Another serendipity, although Pauline had her doubts, was the arrival for an extended stay of Anne Landy, an attractive divorcée who had helped out when, during Roth's 1929 prison sentence, the family lived in Jersey City. In 1934, when he opened the Fifth Avenue Book Store at 41 West Forty-sixth Street, he was still in bankruptcy, so Anne, with a "perfect credit rating," became the owner.

On the shelves would have been copies of Roth's post-bankruptcy imprint, the Black Hawk Press. Eight titles were published under this imprint in 1935 and 1936. Roth had continued his practice of printing European writers whose works were not covered by international copyright agreement. Three titles are exceptional and intense stories about sexual intimacy, seduction, and the trauma of syphilis. They are by the Welsh writer Rhys Davies, a friend of D. H. Lawrence; the novelist and travel writer Norman Davey; and James Hanley, an Irishman who lived in Wales and whose novel *Boy* had been prosecuted by Sumner in 1934. No copyright papers were filed in the Library of Congress for any Black Hawk book.[4]

Black Hawk reprinted Havelock Ellis's *Kanga Creek* (the first edition was privately printed in England in 1922) twice: first in a one-volume edition, and second in a handsome edition with the Hanley, Davies, and Davey stories. *Kanga Creek* relates the protagonist's awakening to natural vitality while working in a remote corner of Australia. To this work "Norman Lockridge" added a sixteen-page "Biographical Memoir in the Form of an Imaginary Conversation between Havelock Ellis, a Young Doctor without a Practice, and Olive Schreiner, a Young Woman without a Husband." Lockridge was the WASPish pseudonym that, after the International Protest, hid the identity of the literary pariah Samuel Roth.

The work is the first example of Roth's practice of inserting himself, however awkwardly, into his edition of another writer's work. At the end of the "Imaginary Conversation," "Lockridge" has Ellis state that Schreiner will become a muse or inspiration to men and women struggling with "brutal and reckless forces." One of these is "an Austrian Jew [Galicia was under the control of Austria during Roth's boyhood there], at war with himself and his race,

[who] will some day humble himself before [her] image as a symbol of the utter futility of all human quarrels."[5]

Both in single volumes and the combined one-volume edition, these five books might contain photos of coquettes striking peekaboo poses and line drawings of large-breasted nudes. Their complete detachment from the texts themselves makes them especially specious. However, those in the know could send $10, for which consideration the pasted-in photographs in their copies would reproduce the full-frontal nudity characteristic of the work of artists such as Franz von Bayros or would be like those in the aggressively pornographic "readers" of the period (copulating couples or threesomes).[6] Roth's circulars for the four single-volume titles stressed the "sex angle" (May–December, rape, syphilis, adultery) and also offered his own editions of "Two World Famous Suppressed Books," Twain's *1601* and Lewisohn's *Case of Mr. Crump*.[7]

"Norman Lockridge" Is Lionized by the Literary Establishment

One of Roth's most admirable works, due to its breadth and organization, was his *Golden Treasury of the World's Wit and Wisdom* (1935). He sent copies to leading critics and writers; in fact, the first-edition colophon states that "Only 1,545 copies have been printed . . . 1,500 are for sale, 20 for our favorite reviewers." Literary lions such as Carl Van Doren ("impressive and satisfying"), James Branch Cabell ("tremendously enjoyed this book"), and Roth's old teacher John Erskine ("extraordinary amount of wisdom") took the time to write Lockridge. Roth had continued his practice of dedicating numbers of *Two Worlds Monthly* to fellow writers and critics by likewise dedicating sections of *The Golden Treasury*. That might well result in favorable reviews, or at least blurbs. Van Doren wrote, "you may quote my two adjectives if you like." Morris Ernst, who two years previously had won his case against the Customs suppression of *Ulysses,* wrote "My dear Lockridge" that "a few more volumes like this and the preparation of briefs will become really a simple matter."[8] The chapter dedicated to him is titled "Lawyers and Their Tricks." Roth would have used these encomiums, and the honorary membership extended to him by the Mark Twain Society for "outstanding contribution to belles-lettres,"[9] in a major ad campaign.[10] His imprisonment in 1937 rudely halted that, but the book was as lucrative as it was gratifying. The *New York Times* reviewer praised "the patience, discrimination and literary deftness with which the editor has made his enormous collection of aphorisms and epigrams. [He felt] awed by the vast amount of labor, pains and time he must have put into it."[11] It warmed the reviewer's heart, he said, to think of the value people would get from it. He was joined by reviewers all over the country, from the *Washington Post* to the *Sioux Falls Leader*.[12] And it would have warmed the compiler's heart even more so if and when anyone found out who lurked behind the estimable Lockridge.

The Golden Treasury contains ninety-eight chapters, each comprising passages from writers representing all nations and historical periods. Some are devoted to the apothegms of a particular individual (Pascal, Rousseau, Voltaire, Nietzsche, Shaw, Twain, Shakespeare, Disraeli, Zangwill), others to subjects such as "Widowers, Widows, and Weeds" or "In the Realm of Pure Fancy." Thoroughly indexed by subject and author, the compilation evinces Roth's wide reading, and his ego as well, for as with *Kanga Creek,* he has found a way of counting himself among the company of the world's wise, if not witty, men of letters. One section in *The Golden Treasury* is headed "Thoughts in Prison." These are excerpted from *Stone Walls Do Not.*

The post-bankruptcy books, and especially *The Golden Treasury,* were a family project of sorts. Richard drew the Black Hawk Press logo; Adelaide did the majority of the proofreading, and her father let her choose the aphorisms on the dust jacket.[13] While at the 1936 trial much was heralded about Roth's supposed use of his children in his pornography business, the fact that they did educational and rewarding work on projects such as the encyclopedic *World's Wit and Wisdom* went unstated. The book stands with his best poetry as proof that Samuel Roth was, when he chose to be and had time to be, a talented writer and literary anthologist. Roth reedited and expanded his *Golden Treasury* for the 1945 edition. His fervent energy and encyclopedic knowledge of his subject exemplify his pleasure in attaining comprehensive knowledge of the subject. The book retained its appeal, partly because Roth advertised it as a way to win friends and influence people with 5,902 sure-fire quotations on "Current Events," "Love," "Marriage," "Lawyers," and "Flirtation."[14]

Why should Roth's general readers have to be introduced to intelligent writing in the format he provided? His answer would have been that they were stimulated by it, and once they opened the book, they could read exactly what those with bona fides, that is, cultural capital, could. Of a different nature was *The Secret Places of the Human Body* (a version of the *Ananga Ranga*), offered at $6. It was published in 1935 under the Golden Hind imprint, which Roth saved for his more sumptuously produced volumes, but was advertised with the Black Hawk books. The circular described the contents of the book and was illustrated (ironically, given the work's description of lovingly offered mutual pleasure) with a reclining nude female watching apprehensively as a large

Samuel Roth, Infamous Modernist

sword held by a disembodied hand approaches her pelvic area. The volume itself continues the lubricity of the advertisement. It contains pasted-in photographs of semi-nude women on otherwise blank pages, scattered throughout the book. However, it is abridged, for Roth did not include more than a few pages of the original chapter 10, which delineated coital positions. Therefore, Roth's edition of the book managed to leave out the "secret places" of the title.

"Flagitious" Pornography; an Aggressive D.A.: Off to Prison

Despite Anne's help, the Fifth Avenue Book Shop was a failure. There was not much traffic on Forty-sixth Street, and the store barely made the rent. One day, Sam perked up his ears when an elderly lady with a Yiddish accent dropped in and asked, "Where is sex?" Adelaide recalls the story as her father liked to tell it: "I told her, 'You've come to the right place. All these books are about sex.' 'Not books,' she said impatiently. 'Sex. Sex Fifth Avenue.'"[15] Soon, Sam moved to Forty-seventh Street, near the Gotham Book Mart (he admired Frances Steloff's support for modernist writers and their Little Magazines).[16]

Roth's shifting fortunes meant eight changes of address between 1924 and 1934; his daughter notes that she went to at least four different elementary schools and two high schools.[17] By mid-1935 the family was able to leave Bay Parkway in Brooklyn for the Mayflower Hotel on Central Park West.[18] The reason, however, was not retail sales. Sam had begun dealing in underground "porno." Taking the same advantage of Anne Landy as he had his own brother, Roth put her in charge of personal delivery. Anne ended her stay with the family about a year after it began, before the move to the Mayflower.[19] Roth then used his "man Friday," Yussie Biren, and salesman Bill Lightner as part of the personal delivery system. He may also have used them, occasionally, for a scheme involving the use of storage boxes in various subway stations. The scheme was intended to avoid the snooping of inspectors at the Post Office and protect the identity of the wholesale supplier.[20] The boxes served as pickup points for Roth himself to collect the books. Very early in the morning, he would remove them from the locker (he held one key and the supplier the other) and wrapped and addressed them himself, finishing the task by 8 A.M., before his office staff arrived. He did this, his lawyer at the 1936 trial said, to keep his wife out of danger of involvement.[21] Had he told Pauline of his activities, she might have stopped him before the project involved him, herself, and the two children in a humiliating federal trial.

He must have sent out some or most copies of these books by common carrier. In 1934 and 1935 the Golden Hind Press used the U.S. mails to circularize for, and Railway Express to ship, a wide range of materials, including the most strictly tabooed books of the era, erotic playing cards, and photograph sets.[22] In 1936, Roth and his wife faced a twenty-four-count federal indictment for conspiring to distribute obscenity through interstate commerce. The books included strictly underground pornography, and many of them must have been expensive: the various counts of the indictment state only one price, probably a conventional one for the Depression era: $12.50. They brought Roth lucrative returns, which of course was his reason for risking their sale. Some were "Readers": sixteen- or thirty-two-page booklets, each with a few pornographic illustrations and a narrative.[23]

In December 1936, District Judge Grover Moscowitz sentenced Roth to three years and twenty days and fined him $2,000, the payment of which was suspended. Suspended also was his wife's three-year sentence, the judge citing her two teenage children. She had to post a $5,000 bond, to be forfeited if there was violation of her probation; Samuel was to post an identical amount upon his release. Both were to be on probation for five years.[24] The sentence was an extremely severe one for a misdemeanor.[25] The reason was not only the publisher's previous record, which was damning enough. In fact, this record may have been one of the reasons that the jury needed little time to deliberate before declaring Roth and his wife guilty.[26] But there were other factors as well. Their children had helped with office tasks.[27] Roth had also committed perjury during the trial. The publisher at first apparently testified that he had not actually marketed the flagrantly obscene books for which he had been cited, but had only given his mailing list to another distributor. Later he confessed that these books had been left for him in a subway locker.

Roth's own explanations for the harsh sentence show how embittered he was against the bureaucratic governmental machinery and judicial bias. As Gershon Legman wrote to Adelaide, after *Jews Must Live* Roth was at a disadvantage with Jewish judges. Other schemers against him were government agents. Roth said a "postal employee" confided in him (but why?) that his mail was being steamed open. After learning who the client and the delivery person were, an inspector would personally deliver the books "and badger their buyers into opening the package in their presence." The New York office of the FBI, he (and his daughter) stated, had, at the Washington office's request, been following him, and had conducted surveillance at the Ritz Carlton, across the street from his Golden Hind offices.[28] Adelaide states they set up "telescopes."[29]

Roth suspected that one of the G-men had approached a friend of Pauline's, Sadie, who clerked for them. Sadie, Roth writes, was suffering from mental problems and was susceptible, according to Roth, to the agent's amorous advances. Then she was picked up and grilled by the FBI "night and day." Sam, "acting as an agent of mercy," told her that "the books and pictures were there. You might have seen them without knowing it. If you tell them that you saw such a book in my place, they'll stop bothering you" ("CMAM," 313–14). Surely Sadie was questioned, and could help corroborate the post-office evidence, but would the FBI choose to have someone romance a mentally unstable woman? The prosecution had been able to avail itself of the postal inspector's decoy letters to determine which books Roth mailed.

The FBI may have thought that draconian measures were needed to suppress Roth's perseverant defiance of authority. Both as a distributor of erotica over a decade and as a publisher of political attacks on not only a sitting president but a former one, Warren Harding, Roth had won enemies of political, social, religious, journalistic, and literary note. Surveillance of writers suspected of subversive inclinations goes back at least as far as the post–World War I Red Scare, as does monitoring mail.[30] Hoover opened an "obscenity file" in 1925, since he equated pornography with leftist radicalism. Roth's 1931 "smear book" on Herbert Hoover would have made the publisher suspect both as radical and smut peddler. The bureau's awareness of *The Liberator* resulted in a file on Louis Untermeyer starting three years before J. Edgar Hoover took over in 1924. (Hoover had Untermeyer declared a security risk in 1951.) Pre-Hoover investigations may have included Roth in the files on Frank Tannenbaum as well. Any association with John Reed or Louise Bryant, whom Roth contacted regarding an autobiography in 1932, would have meant FBI attention.[31]

Adelaide's explanation of her father's harsh sentence stresses the outrage of the Catholic Church, and of Postmaster General James J. Farley, regarding Clement Wood's *The Woman Who Was Pope* (Faro, 1931).[32] The anger of the Jewish community was still smoldering from *Jews Must Live*. And he had given Sumner other reasons to want to punish him because of his part in the distribution of Nan Britton's *The President's Daughter*. Britton's book revealed she had given birth to Harding's love child. Roth was also involved in the distribution of Gaston Means's *The Strange Death of President Harding*, which was marketed by taking advantage of Means's declaration that Harding's vengeful wife arranged his death. Sumner, an influential Republican, had with the aid of "five burly men" tried to stop distribution of *The President's Daughter* by raiding the publisher's office. Guild Publishing, which released both books, had distributed some of Roth's Faro titles and may have had a financial arrangement with him.[33]

The FBI investigated Roth's mail-order business, and may have collected evidence about the underground pornography being distributed at the same time. J. Edgar Hoover was in the process of building his bureaucracy, hoping that the FBI would become a national police force. For obscenity prosecutions the bureau had for a decade kept current, but as yet not centralized, an "Obscene File." Hoover had maintained since 1932 his own crime lab, which would explain the FBI's detailed analysis (used by the prosecuting attorney in *United States v. Roth*) of Pauline Roth's handwriting (proving she had signed various Golden Hind Press documents).[34] In 1935 a federal indictment was being prepared for Roth and six other dealers. Hoover's men uncovered the suggestive circulars, and the books themselves (all of which had literary merit), which were mailed from the Fifth Avenue Book Shop. Their investigation, according to the papers in Roth's FBI files, was limited to these Black Hawk books. Circulars for them were photostatted for "the Director." On November 26, 1935, Pauline, as owner of the Golden Hind Press (the address given was the second location of the Fifth Avenue Book Shop), was indicted by a federal grand jury along with six other dealers. They were accused of distributing obscenity through the mails. Pauline and the other dealers were selling the same kind of erotica: well-reputed fiction or sexology advertised for its sexual interest but without explicitness. Her lawyer was Hugo Pollack, who was recommended by Anne Landy. Pollack had no previous experience with obscenity trials, but he correctly saw that the government has little chance of a conviction.[35] Pauline was acquitted on December 17.[36] That leaves open the question as to why she was indicted.

The answer may be that the Post Office and Justice Department were devising a way to keep prosecutions for obscenity viable after attacks by Morris Ernst and the ACLU's National Council on Freedom from Censorship, and especially because of the *Ulysses* decision in 1934. That case, thanks to Ernst's successful advocacy, made conviction problematic in the case of sexually explicit material with educational and literary value. Therefore an "absolute" standard, as Judge Learned Hand called it, was out of favor (at least temporarily). In response to this, the federal enforcers of obscenity began to spotlight the prurient appeal—the "pandering"—of the circulars and of the way the books themselves appealed to ubiquitous curiosity about sex. This would explain the FBI's careful accumulation of the Black Hawk advertising material. One of the attractive aspects of the pandering complaint was that it allowed the postal authorities to conflate fraud (if the books themselves were insufficiently sexually explicit) with obscenity.

The pandering accusation did not have to be used against the Black Hawk

Press, because Roth's distribution of what was legally obscene was enough to cause his arrest a year later. Actually, in 1935 this new tactic of federal prosecution was still being worked out. Certainly, the Roths were very interested in how the focus on prurient advertising could be used to convict. It was to become crucial to how Roth ran his mail-order business after he was released from Lewisburg in 1939. In the 1940s and 1950s it became the chief weapon that the Post Office used against him. The first major victims of the charge of "pandering" were the owners of the Falstaff Press, a mail-order firm specializing in nonfiction sexology. They were Ben and Anne Rebhuhn and Ben's brother Sam Raeburn, whose methods and materials were closely allied to Roth's. They had been arrested in November 1935 with Pauline. Their catalogues included advertisements for at least one, and possibly more, books published by either Roth or Jack Brussel, or both in collaboration.[37]

In 1936 the Post Office received aid and comfort from a court decision that clarified the relation between fraud and salaciousness. The immediate result of this clarification was that the Falstaff Press lost its appeal of a previous conviction, and Ben Rebhuhn and his nephew were sentenced to the federal penitentiary.[38] Because of the suggestive manner in which their circulars were written, the Rebhuhns were deemed to be aware—that is, they had "guilty knowledge"—that the books themselves could have been represented as having prurient instead of scientific interest. Pandering was, in Learned Hand's words, "the gravamen of the crime."[39] An understandable reason for the Roths' interest in the fate of the Rebhuhns was that it strengthened their belief that federal obscenity prosecutions were directed against the mail-order distributors like themselves who were targeted as smutmongers, as opposed to those booksellers who had gained the status of people of letters. An example is the open and unhindered sale by well-reputed publishers of such works as René Guyon's *The Ethics of Sex Acts,* advertised in 1934 by Knopf as "a discussion of onanism, incest, homosexuality, fetishism, and even such 'extraordinary' variations as necrophilia and coprophilia."[40]

The current headlines about "Rings" selling obscene books and the "war" against the "flood" of "risky [i.e., risqué] books" were similar to those in New York dailies about the Roths: "Mother of Two Held on Spicy Art Charge" (*New York Evening Journal*); "Arty Alibi Fails / Publisher Given 3 Years" (*New York American*); "Roth to Serve 3 Years for Vile Books / Publisher Is Sentenced in Face of Plea He Wants to Write Helpful Works / Court Calls Him Egotist" (Hearst's *Journal American*).[41] At this time, prosecutors' focus shifted from the work itself to the person doing the selling, who became a criminal exploiting the "widespread weakness for titillation by pornography." The style of the person or the firm, not the product, had become the "gravamen." Those were the rules of the game.[42] The *Journal American* report on the case took full advantage of this development, with its headlines about "Egotist" and "Vile Books." It focused on Judge Moscowitz's shock at the involvement of Richard and Adelaide. Before warning Pauline about her suspension of sentence being revoked if she and her husband resumed their pornography selling, he stated, according to the *Journal American,* "I cannot believe a mother would sink so low as to let her children know anything like that [marketing obscene books and pictures] about their parents."[43]

The United States versus Pauline and Samuel Roth

If Pauline's acquittal in late 1935 was a relief, it may also have been a warning shot regarding Sam's erotica enterprise. A year later, the Post Office obtained a court order against Roth and his wife and caused their arrest. One memo advised the director of the FBI that the Roths are "old offenders, having been previously convicted in the local and federal courts."[44] These memos are dated in September 1936, within a few days of the Roths' arrests. Heading the prosecution was Irving R. Kaufman, in 1951 the presiding judge at the Rosenberg trial. In 1935 he was an ambitious assistant district attorney.[45] He brought in handwriting experts to verify that Pauline's signature was on various receipts. These documents and the experts' analysis were in the FBI files, so some were probably on the Black Hawk, and some on the pornography, receipts. This raises the question of whether the FBI worked solely on the Black Hawk books or whether they also prepared evidence for the 1936 arrest for selling pornography.

If Roth and his daughter are correct in reporting that the publisher was followed and spied on by FBI agents, then the agency clearly worked on both cases. Adelaide Kugel states that the intent was to build a case that would send Pauline to prison, unless Roth himself responded to that pressure by taking major responsibility. It is not clear whether that pressure was to be caused by Pauline's conviction for the literary erotica, or for the porno. Nothing in the FBI memos either documents or suggests that there was surveillance, which does not mean their New York office did not provide it. Roth sensed he would be convicted and imprisoned. Perhaps the denigration of not only himself but of his family in most newspapers made him believe so. Only the *New York Herald Tribune* report on the case humanized the Roths. It described Roth as a "tall, bespectacled" figure, his wife as "a petite woman of pleasing appearance," and their children as "said to be highly talented."[46] Of course it was Kaufman and Moscowitz, not the FBI, whose rhetoric gave the other newspapers their cues to treat Roth harshly. But the implicit and explicit support of the FBI clearly helped them.

On December 16, 1936, Roth was sentenced to three years in federal prison, and Pauline's sentence, because she had two children to care for, was suspended.[47] In calling eighteen-year-old Adelaide and sixteen-year-old Richard to the stand and trying to make them say they knew the contents of the books they had addressed for customers, Kaufman embarrassed and angered them. The district attorney had told the press that Sam and Pauline Roth had, as the *Times* put it, "employed" their son and daughter "to distribute illustrated books which [Kaufman] described as the 'filthiest' he had ever seen."[48] Because Roth thought the FBI was following him, he had once had Richard deliver a book to a customer. Kaufman tried to get the boy to say that he had seen the book before it was wrapped. He felt he had "sent [his father] to jail." His sister suffered equally about her grand jury testimony.[49] The children had addressed some envelopes in the Golden Hind offices after school while waiting to go home with their parents. When Adelaide's "grilling" was over—Kaufman asked her how to abbreviate "Pennsylvania" in order to prove she wrote out receipts—a reporter remarked to her, in sympathy, that Kaufman was an ambitious guy.[50] She and Dick were under a lot of pressure, for Judge Moscowitz could have declared, as Gershon Legman has pointed out, that the Roths were unfit parents, and had the children placed in foster care. The district attorney was intent on destroying Adelaide's credibility, and for good reason. On Hugo Pollack's advice, she had burst into the courtroom and embraced her mother. It backfired when she took the stand; Kaufman asked her if she was an actress.[51]

In May 1937, Roth petitioned, unsuccessfully, for reduction of sentence. The district attorney assigned to the case, Lamar Hardy, stated that the authorities had heard at least some of these pleas before; this was the publisher's fifth offense. It was altogether likely, therefore, that he and his wife would continue their erotica dealings. Furthermore, Hardy was not impressed, after conferring with Chester Battles, the postal inspector, that Roth had given helpful information.[52] Roth remained in the Lewisburg penitentiary until mid-1939.

Prison Letters and Writings

Roth's letters home, the first of which was December 14, 1936 (from a holding cell in lower Manhattan), and the last April 26, 1939, are a kind of anatomy of his character. They concern his hopes for the future, his current and future writing projects, his business affairs, and his hunger for confirmation that his family loves and supports him. For all that, his most frequent subject was the requests he makes of Pauline and Adelaide ("Chig"). For example, the latter was to research many aspects of the life of the aforementioned Berenice of Cilia, mistress of Titus and sister of Agrippa II. Titus and she loved each other, but the emperor exiled her at the urgent requests of his counselors. Roth, smelling melodrama and perhaps a movie contract, was writing a historical novel on her life. His daughter was to read primary and secondary sources, not neglecting any reference to Berenice in Jewish historians and commentators.[53] During 1938 and 1939, Adelaide was pursuing acting jobs and working at various secretarial and retail positions. When her letters were late, or provided him with less than exhaustive research, he sounded hurt. "Don't you like Berenice?"[54] (Poor Berenice; don't let her down, Chig.) He also expected his daughter to visit editorial offices of magazine and book publishers with his manuscripts, which were voluminous.

To "My Poor [alternatively "Sweet"] Darling" fell the task of writing to or visiting publishers with copies of her husband's stories, and (with her daughter's help) retyping them, in some cases from the handwritten letters in which Sam had incorporated them. In addition, Roth entrusted her with two daunting tasks. One was following up on his schemes regarding the reprint publisher for *World's Wit and Wisdom,* Eugene Reynal. "The dog" needed to return the plates and revise the contract for the book to Roth's satisfaction. The second major time-consuming labor involved Sam's futile appeal for commutation of sentence. He had prepared a list of thirteen reasons.[55] This meant making phone calls, typing letters, and interviewing officials.

Roth's letters were usually full of blind conviction about this or that of his numerous writings. "You spoke of that mountain of lies that has been built up against me. One successful book will melt that mountain and send it down into the sewers where it belongs."[56] Once his "Queen of the World: The Princess Berenice" was published, he wrote Chig, a reputable publisher was sure to "subsidize me for a year while I work out the four sequels to it."[57] Referring to the moments of depression and futility beneath his luftmensch-like enthusiasm, Adelaide added, "But he knew they would not." This kind of awareness surfaced rarely in Roth's prison letters, but when it did it was all the more affecting: "I am set in this rickety one-hoss shay of mine on the rocky road to Dublin I know in my heart I will never reach. May most of the shame be mine."[58]

Failing to produce respected writing and placing his family in financial stress by being in prison are both implied in the sadness expressed in this manipulative and endearing statement. The chief medical officer at Lewisburg had diagnosed an increasing "psychoneurosis" in the prisoner. His daughter recognized that its fundamental reason was his frenetic desire to write something remarkable. He was obsessed with it, for it was his vision of eventual salvation and wholeness, offered him in every dream in which Yeshea graced him with an appearance. The act of writing brought the vision to life. "His febrile state may also be attributed to having stayed up all night writing in the washroom."[59] That would atone for what he put his family through. On September 6, 1937, he informed Pauline that he would have written half a million words by the time he was released. Later that month he wrote, "I am working day and night, this [letter] is being done at 2 a.m. since I cannot sleep. . . . I am writing this by the light that filters in through the bars from the vestibule." Several months earlier, he wrote that an idea for a story "came to me at midnight last night, and I had finished the first draft in the washroom by dawn."[60] Milton Hindus has perceptively stated that Roth depended on writing as William Carlos Williams, Walt Whitman, and Graham Greene have stated that they did: as a compulsive form of therapy, or as a "disease," as Hindus put it, echoing Proust, "that keeps us from suffering from an even more dangerous one."[61]

The day before his sentence ended, he needed the help of two prison officers to help him carry heavy boxes containing his manuscripts to the official in charge of "final censorship." He wrote that to his son, for whom, he said, he had "ambitious and numerous" plans. If that might have given Richard pause, what he wrote to Adelaide must have, equally, struck her with sadness, affection, and resentment as she commented on her father's "comfortable home away from home" before quoting in her memoir her father's last prison letter to her:

> I have just been taking a look around my cell, at my manuscripts which have swelled to such fearful proportions, to the photographs of you, mother, Richard, and Einstein, . . . and I am thinking that though I have never regretted any of the several beautiful homes we have had in gardens and skies, I shall probably some day remember this little white room in which I have done the only really useful work of my life with real homesickness. Take this as a warning, my dears. You've no idea how easily during the next nine months I can make my way back here.[62]

His family understood that it was essential to keep Sam's ego safe from the whispers of his own demons. Knowing that he had, despite all, been a careful, endearing provider, they dug in their heels and allowed him to keep his belief in himself. But despite the cheering up, Roth's frequent scenarios of persecution had the effect of spreading to his family the father's paranoia, something probably many people close to convicts must contend with. It might well have been partly realistic. Pauline would tell Richard and Adelaide that the FBI still had the Roths in its sights, searching for ways to prove to the world their unsuitability for decent society.[63] She and her husband certainly would believe such a scenario could come about. They themselves had not the power to control reality in public life. Roth had made daring decisions in the past that had allowed people of acknowledged literary and social significance to fix his identity as an outcast: Joyce and his supporters among the London and Paris literary modernists; and John Sumner, with his elite social connections, his Ivy League credentials, and his soft-spoken gentility. More recently it had been the district attorney, the judge, and the Post Office personnel who had testified at the 1936 trial. Where Roth stood in the hierarchy of respectability was clear from the tone of most newspaper articles on his 1936 arrest and trial.

Samuel Roth continued to believe he would fulfill his destiny. Some of this resolution strengthens the love letters he wrote Pauline from prison. He tells her he will reach his goals and present her with all she desires. "At forty you are as lovely as when I first saw you at fourteen. . . . And even if it has taken me nineteen years, I have made myself (except for getting myself into a penitentiary) good enough for the girl who married me and almost good enough for the woman who loves me."[64] "It was this sort of heady stuff," Adelaide concluded, "that induced [my mother] to carry out his instructions."[65] He could pontificate like an Old Testament hero, and somewhat less than that as well: "[These] arms of their father's are long [sic] to reach out and powerful to protect them. PS: Try to locate for me those 3 vols on the trial of Henry Ward Beecher. Telephone the few law bookstores in the classified."[66]

His daughter loved his corny, gallant encouragement of her acting career and praise of her poise, beauty, and intelligence. She certainly did not forget the research skills she had learned on the projects Sam had depended on her to do. "He was a born teacher. He would make his arguments so persuasive that you could not forget them."[67] The translations she sometimes attempted were put to good use also. In 1941 Roth published *My Uncle Benjamin*, which she had translated (at age twenty-three) under the pseudonym "Marie Lorenz." Roth loved Claude Tillier's novel and decided that in order to sell it by mail order to people who "did not know enough to ask for it," Benjamin should "have a love life. What was wrong with inventing [in the advertisements] one for him so long as it brought a happy book into [readers'] dismally sex-ridden

Samuel Roth, Infamous Modernist

lives" ("CMAM," 348). If the Post Office inspectors had read this they would have seen it as an example of deceiving readers without discerning taste and judgment, who only wanted "hot stuff." Roth was successful with both the book and the advertisements, which started him on his successful seventeen-year career as mail-order distributor. Adelaide described the translation as her "last filial act for dad's business."[68] She might have meant that she did not like her father's hyping the book by advertising that the translator was a "chorus girl." Adelaide was in fact dancing in the chorus line at Manhattan's Café Havana-Madrid in 1941, waiting for a break as an actress.[69]

"Transfiguration": Prison Novel

"Tranfiguration," later titled "The Master of Europe," was the big book Roth hoped would restore his finances and reputation.[70] The finished typescript, 829 pages, he sent to the Atlantic Monthly Press's 1938 novel contest. The contest editor, A. G. Odgen, sent Norman Lockridge of the Bronx a kind rejection letter stating that since his work was "so much better than the average contest manuscript," and among the finalists, the press would welcome future submissions.[71] Naturally, it got them; Adelaide and Pauline were set to work preparing other typescripts.

The setting is Germany, 1948. Magdalyn and Tina Carryl are film stars who were born there. Tina had been told she was a new Theda Bara: "her dark lustrous silk stocking type of beauty was calculated to draw about her a great harvest of eye-lust." Roth meant by the sentence what was implied in Skillin's frontispiece for *Body*, with its reclining nude and her motley army of admirers. But it was Tina's sister Magdalyn, or Maddy, who had "scored heavily" in the new hit movie *Dream World*. Early in the novel we are present at the meeting of Maddy, now acknowledged to be the most beautiful actress in Germany and the most publicized symbol of Aryan beauty, with the nation's most powerful man. It takes place in his town house, "run as a bachelor's establishment should be run." What the Master of Europe does not know is that the Carryl sisters are actually Jewesses hiding that identity under stage names. In fact, Hitler had sentenced their father to a concentration camp, where he was murdered. When the Führer meets the Carryl sisters, he is strongly reminded of a nefarious decision that put an end to his love affair with a woman named Margaret. He had gone along with his advisers in ordering her disposal. They had discovered, by investigating her shadowy past, that she was a Jewess. What the Führer allowed to be done to the woman causes him regret and self-doubt.

So even when we first meet the Master of Europe, he is not a monster, but rather a man who has done great harm and is mesmerized by a group of sinister advisers. Then, one auspicious night, in a cathedral, while listening to a famous clergyman's sermon, the Führer is confronted by a mysterious, ghostly figure in "Palestinian" garb. The figure has come down from a cross that appears only to Hitler as he sits transfixed in his pew. Jesus, or Yeshea— for it is, not surprisingly, he—begins by directly accusing the Führer of being an enemy of humanity, although he sympathizes with Hitler's response to the Treaty of Versailles. However, Hitler had projected himself as a second Jesus, a savior of mankind, and had installed a cult of Germanic worship of himself as God. Jesus (Yeshea) does not blame Hitler for what he did to "my people," but, having done it, for "establish[ing] your own worth by stealing it from an image as purely Jewish as I make in your eyes." When Hitler replies that scholars believe Jesus was of Aryan stock, Yeshea thunders that neither Hitler nor "the English renegade [Houston Chamberlain] who first thought of it, really believed it." Hitler has attempted to replace with his own person that of Yeshea, and to show what that means, and the depth of the sin, before the immobilized, horrified Führer, the Son of God bleeds. "Those four ugly red spots were there, moving down from his hands and feet like molten red lava; it was as if the fires of hell were burning invisibly under that image."

The punishment is that Yeshea will inhabit Hitler's place in the world, while Hitler's soul will be imprisoned in the crucifix, which will be imprinted with his face. Yeshea will live his life from now on, and finish the task of renewing Germany. Hitler begs for his life, not ignobly but because he wants to "live" and "love." He weeps, then bows his head. Again, Roth's training in Hasidic mysticism might be evident in this dramatic but awkwardly applied plot device. Transmigration of souls, especially of the wicked, into other souls or into animals or inanimate things is described in the Zohar. The person afflicted can in time regain his human status, as even sociopathic behavior can be part of the soul's ultimate journey from darkness to light.[72]

As others have seen this Palestinian figure, and as Hitler's face does actually appear on that crucifix late in the novel, the reader is left confused as to whether or not Hitler has had a dream. He does have a conversation about sleep with his manservant that night. And how can Yeshea allow himself not only political machinations, even if devoid of chicanery, but also to fall in love with the passionate Magdalyn Carryl? From this point forward Roth writes of the Master of Europe (now played by Yeshea) as vulnerable, passionate, tentative, and brave. His sensual as well as spiritual needs, especially for Magdalyn, are difficult to identify with Jesus.

　　　　　　　　　　　　　　Samuel Roth, Infamous Modernist

Assuming, then, that what we have for the rest of the novel is the transfigured man Hitler, not the Son of God, that man's transfiguration is marked by his almost-immediate efforts to find the Jews a homeland—as Roth in *Now and Forever* had advocated a decade earlier—in Tanganyika. There had, the novel asserts, already been a Jewish state founded in Palestine. The problem at hand (in 1948, as imagined by a writer in 1937) is a fight between the Jews of Germany and Poland to establish immigration quotas to the new land. It has created a Gordian knot, to disentangle which a transfigured Hitler rose in the League of Nations, to announce that the Jews of Germany will be able to establish a country of their own in Africa. Hitler's metamorphosis from destroyer to savior of the Jews is consummated by the love of Maddy, who brings him peace. Now we see that the name Magdalyn, assumed to help disguise her identity behind a brilliant actress's glamour, is profoundly ironic. A politician turned savior but not martyr takes her for his helpmate. That the beloved of the newly transfigured Master of Europe is Jewish but bears the name of Jesus' female disciple provides a fine shock of recognition. Unfortunately, the writer's attempt to infuse mysticism into this couple's mutual recognition of what they mean to each other is awkward:

> [Hitler] fell on his knees before her and buried his head in her soft lap. For a while the quiet darkened theatre [they are visiting a nobleman's *schloss*] reverberated to a sobbing that had not been heard on earth for nearly two thousand years. When he finally raised his head, Magdalyn was startled by its sudden youngness. The man's face shone like a planet of light.
>
> She framed his face in her happy hands. "You're so young and handsome!" she cried.

The figure she is addressing has the body of Hitler but the soul of Yeshea, who sobs with awareness that two millennia of hate can be stifled by the conundrum of selfless statecraft.[73] If Yeshea could transfigure Hitler, he could do the same for the author of *Jews Must Live*.

Transmigration of souls is a topic that intrigued Roth, as it did Leopold Bloom and Stephen Dedalus in *Ulysses*. What happens between Hitler and Yeshea is a strange variation on the concept of the dybbuk. Here, Yeshea, a pure—not an impure or unfulfilled—soul, enters the body of an evil man. It does reflect the Kabbalistic belief that an iniquitous soul must suffer and redeem itself in the body of another creature. Perhaps in having Hitler redeem himself as chancellor, care for Magdalyn, and provide the Jews a homeland,

Roth is alluding to these beliefs. Thus the Hitler of the conclusion (if it is he) is both handsome and surrounded by light.

The Jewish Messiah will be astonishingly handsome. Still, the reader is left confused as to who is whom at this point. At the end, Hitler and Maddy meet outside the parliament, now restored to *das Volk*. A second world war will not take place. This part of the novel holds one's attention despite the tailored-to-please melodrama:

> "I offer you once more peace on earth, good will to men." When he reached the top of the long gracious steps that led down from the Reichstag, the whole city seemed empty of everything except the magic panoply of winter—cold clear air, and a frozen fiery sun that could caress a whole rainbow of icicles in the sky without hurting them. "Marvelous, isn't it," breathed Magdalyn, who joined him on the very last step.

Roth conceived "Transfiguration" in 1933. Oddly enough, he was writing *Jews Must Live* the same year. In his foreword he called it a "quasi-religious, quasi-mischievous" work. Five years later, he wrote Adelaide, "Some Jew must make of his heart an armory for the destruction of the forces gathering against our people. I feel that I am that man—and the only one. I say this not in vain pride but in utter humility—for there must be tens of thousands of Jews cleverer, wiser, more learned, and better than I am. But is there any stronger in soul? I doubt."[74]

This tone of high purpose, perseverance in the face of adversity, and crass salesmanship pervades all Roth's schemes. In a story of Adolf Hitler finding true love, and of his eventual transfiguration from dictator to democrat, there is a faith in benevolent destiny, his and others, which it is likely the author deeply craved, especially as this faith was often overpowered by gloomy fatalism. He hoped he could release his imagination from his rational suspicions that he may have been done for ("the rocky road to Dublin"). He needed to stop his heart from keeping him awake with its nervous palpitations.

Why did the *Atlantic Monthly* contest's judges make Roth's novel one of the finalists? One reason of course is the occasional eloquent passages and the all-embracing panorama the author had worked out. It is also important to note that popular publishing houses, like movie distributors, welcomed scenarios of a peaceful end to the current world crisis. The Roosevelt administration realized that the country, bristling with anti-Semitic spokespeople, was far from ready to face a belligerent Germany with a Depression still raging. Most Jews preferred to be quietly apprehensive rather than stir up more prejudice.[75]

That also may have been prudent from a business standpoint. The film industry did not want to flaunt an overly belligerent position when it depended on Europeans for distribution;[76] the same might be true for the book business.

While Roth's novel was too convoluted to be popular, the work did show a good feel for what might catch the attention of adult readers. "Transfiguration" combined elements of several popular genres: spy and mystery stories, the glamorous settings (movie studios, imperial balls, aristocrats' Great Houses), secret lives and hidden motives, and clandestine meetings between the unlikeliest pairs of lovers. Having no stomach for reticence in the face of danger, Roth wanted to alert, not anesthetize, readers to the crisis of his time. The fairy-tale ending, however reverent, was overly cozy for a political thriller. A final fault is the clichés straight out of Hollywood's Poverty Row, which include the stilted dialogues between Maddy and the Master; the clichéd spy intrigue that provides a husband for Tina; and the stock villain, an anti-Semitic newspaper editor, lecher, and conspirator named Herr Gleichner.

Roth's faith in redemption, so inconsistent with some of his previous writings, for the human capacity to shake down from the heavens a divine benevolence, is one of the attractions of "Transfiguration." It also once more embodied his lifelong desire to reconcile Jews with non-Jews. The Jewish actresses are not his only vehicle in this regard. A more original plot element is the adaptation, for the denouement, of motifs from Hasidic folktale. These climactic events are effective. But first, a little Nazi-of-the-Opera stage business. During a key Reichstag meeting, Herr Gleichner appears on an auditorium balcony and declares that the Führer has been replaced by a Zionist demon, through the black magic of the Palestinian Jew who somehow gained entrance into Hitler's inner chamber. It is true that since that Jew's visit, the chancellor has radically changed his political goals. Gleichner produces the crucifix on which is the face of Hitler. Now we are told that it had been made in hell, and as the howling madman grasps it, it pollutes his blood. Roth's somewhat murky symbolism suggests that Gleichner dies, not at the hands of Jewish demons, but at Satan's, whose plan for world war the publisher has failed to bring about. Here is an instance where the concepts of Chamberlain, Sombart, and Weininger in *Jews Must Live* are presented as ineffective fanaticism. Roth had stated his intent to atone for "that tragic book of mine." "Transfiguration" is as close as he came, but he failed to get it published, nor did he self-publish it. One reason might have been that if the Jewish population, blood already boiling by *Jews Must Live,* discovered that Roth had written a novel that conflated Hitler with Yeshea, they might make scenes like the confrontation in the Café Royal in 1935 look polite.

It is after Gleichner's burial that motifs of Yiddish folklore lend a poetic and rugged allure to the story, one integral to a conviction that the universe bears divine signals of universal moral integrity, if they can be read. These motifs come in two forms, both using magic and impressing on the reader the hand of God in forming redemptive insight out of despair and evil.[77] One such motif is the story of Gleichner's body, which the devil releases from its grave, disfigures with an expression of extreme agony, and then reclaims by opening a shaft of ragged darkness beneath its coffin. It's a reverse Resurrection, intended to inspire terror, not reverence. Hitler/Yeshea orders the corpse to be dropped into the ground so as to cover the hellish opening. When it disappears into the void, "At the contact of the body with the dark arm that seemed stretched forward to embrace it, there was a flash of pure black. . . . The smoke once more disappeared as mysteriously as it had on its first pouring forth from its hiding place in the earth, and everything was once more as though there had not been a sign of evil in that Hall."

To the motif of allowing the devil to reclaim an evil human is added one of redemption through treasuring a holy reality hidden in a seemingly venal exterior. Hitler may have learned this parable from the "Palestinian" who transformed him. A poor Jewish boy rises from poverty to become rich, but the acquisitiveness renders him emotionally frozen, even to his family. He does not really care about his money, and so colleagues find ways to transfer it to themselves. He goes in search of a tantalizing gold coin, glowing with a strangely beautiful light, that he once saw on the dirt floor of his childhood home. It was the Sabbath, so he could not pick it up until sunset, by which time it had vanished. Some of the details suggest those from Roth's life: his birthplace, bankruptcy, and failure to provide for his family. Paradoxically, the coin represents, not money, but something that can break down his paralysis and reinvigorate him. His search has been for his boyhood identity with nature (as in the first four "Nustscha" sonnets) and his adult care for his family. He joins a group, like himself, "drifting tidelessly. . . . For the sheer warmth of not turning the corners of the earth alone, he joined them." He turns east, entering a wilderness, and prays for a long afternoon, since night will find him with no prospects for survival. But after sunset he finds the "fine color and delicate design" of that Sabbath coin, "a round shining disk that radiated just enough light for him to see the road by." Soon the wilderness recedes, and behind the first door he knocks on are his wife and children.

A similarly reborn chancellor uses this story to explain how, after a spell of being used by Satan, he has humbly aligned his will to the ebb and flow of human contact. There are also arresting vignettes of people who, like the eastern

Samuel Roth, Infamous Modernist

European grotesques in the Yiddish folktales, are weak, sick, and yet dignified by a gritty endurance that outfaces their own suffering. A Reichstag foreman, for example, is "one of those thin, bespectacled little men whose faces seem all hair and glass."

Once again, as with his reverential early poetry about Moses, Sinai, and Kol Nidre, Roth can write about humility and the quest for peaceful wholeness. He distills into parts of "Transfiguration" a pious meditation, affecting in its plainspoken renunciation of the power to harm, and offering in the place of power politics a benevolence glowing with the clarity of pure winter sunlight, which might be an allusion to Shekinah, the light of God's presence. It is the duty of a wise man to help restore that clarity to the fallen world.

Prisoner Number 5079 Acquires a "Prison Wife," Enters the "True World," and Warms Up a Corpse

Roth had insomnia during his first month at Lewisburg, during which time new prisoners were quarantined to make sure they had no communicable diseases. When he did manage to fall asleep, it was worth it; he found an attractive young woman by his bedside. In his dream he had entered a universe where souls, even those attached to still-living bodies, were tried and met their just fate. This was the True World. "Mishillim Brings News from the True World" was the full title of the 265-page typescript in which Roth tried to interest Eugene Reynal. Using the pseudonym David Zorn, he stated that the work deserved close attention because of its "artistic treatment of the subconscious" and because "the plot is a natural for the movies." Using the same pseudonym, he had Pauline submit a shorter version, "Prison Wife," to various magazines.[78] Much of this True World story appears in "Count Me among the Missing."

The woman by his bedside was named Tanya (it might be relevant to state that "Tanya" is the title of a fundamental tractate delineating ideas about loving kindness, which the Baal Shem Tov popularized). The term "prison wife" (used in the title of chapter 15 of "Count Me among the Missing") indicates a fellow prisoner, helpmeet, and lover. To employ the phrase in reference to a female the writer knew in the past and now is part of a dream fantasy is awkward, even if the irony is understood. Roth tells us he met Tanya on Armistice Day, 1918. For Roth, who had been married on May 18 of the previous year,[79] it was a serendipitous overnight party. But Tanya got pregnant. Roth made it clear by arranging a meeting between her and another office worker that he was abandoning the young woman. Tanya had urgent need of a husband. But she had a supreme need, apparently, for the love and protection of Samuel Roth. Until her eighth month, Tanya "continued to come to the office to haunt me with her eyes. . . . The first day she did not appear I read on the front page of my newspaper that she had flung herself out of a window of her sixth floor apartment."[80]

The concept of a world where souls are tried is suggestive, once again, of Yiddish folktales. Some of the best-written sections of the "True World" novella have settings, as well as spiritual reckonings, relevant to the genre (and of course Dante's *Purgatory*). Here and elsewhere, Roth's fiction adopts with striking originality many motifs of this genre. Roth once stated, disappointed with his failure to become known as a writer, that he should have written in Yiddish, his first language. A chief reason for not doing so was that he wanted to become widely recognized in America. He would thus be able to support his family. He promised Pauline in several letters from prison that he would one day succeed in producing acclaimed work. The public recognition would be proof that he had been able to become an American success story. Along with most other sons and daughters of Lower East Side immigrants, the American dream was as much a part of their upbringing as poverty and synagogue.

In the True World, Tanya explains, almighty justice had decreed that Sam Roth would spend three years in prison for cavalier, callous behavior, which resulted in Tanya's suicidal despair. Is Tanya contemptuous toward the man who abandoned her? In Roth's dreams, not at all. She calls him "darling." They have long discussions on the value of the wisdom of the True World versus sensual pleasure in the mundane one. And Tanya introduces him to his "ghostly daughter," Nora (born in the True World, of course). Nora tells her dream father that they had met a few years before in a cafeteria on Forty-sixth Street (people from the True World can appropriate human bodies when they need to). Roth added a footnote in his text to the effect that if "skeptics" doubt the meeting took place, they will find it recorded in "the note-books of the FBI who were then following me about night and day" ("CMAM," 250). How they, or Roth himself, could access these notes is not suggested.

Nora looks very much like Chig. She introduces him to her fiancé, Simon Lerner, who is modeled upon the young editor Gershon Legman. The publisher and writer did develop some sort of bond. When Nora tells her "father" Simon loves him and that "in the most real sense of the word you're his father," he weeps. In "Count Me among the Missing," Roth says insightfully of "Lerner" that "his prose was scholarly without being dry, incisive yet spicy, quite

Figure 18. Gershon Legman, c. 1939. Legman was an editor and ghostwriter for Roth in the 1940s and early 1950s. By permission of Judith Legman, La Clè des Champs, France.

utterly irresponsible [being replete with four-letter words] but as Jewish as English writing can be" (246).[81]

Roth expanded his True World adventures when he prepared the typescript to submit to Reynal. It contains one episode in which the protagonist's own mother administers a severe tongue-lashing regarding his relationship in the True World with Tanya. His father is there also, but he merely listens and reads the paper. He's waiting—to Sam's distress—to take up the subject of *Jews Must Live* with his son. Meanwhile, Hudl has a go at him. She had kibitzed with another "good old fashioned Jewish Mother," who happens to be Tanya's. Why, Hudl asks, is Sam shaming Tanya by living with her—in the True World yet—and not marrying her? Did she not tell her son, when he had gotten himself engaged to the girl next door, "Can't you find yourself some *shiksah*? Why should you pick on a sweet Jewish girl like Pauline?" She concludes with a remark that leaves Sam's "world rocked to its very foundations": whenever her son has tried to do something independent of convention, he has "found what may have been called the way of the devil."

Tanya softened the blow. She is dismayed that he is applying for early release. Roth, in a distant echo of the title of his 1930 *Stone Walls Do Not,* suggests he could not love Tanya so well if he did love his honor, or his destiny, more. Tanya's response is "As always you are right. . . . You are so good to love—even in a dream." The situation recalls Sam's with Joan in London. He never tells us Joan's response to his leaving her to return to America. Perhaps he liked to believe she would have responded as Tanya did. But what happened in London was real abandonment, not a comforting interpretation of a dream.

A final display of egotism takes place when Roth describes his behavior in the last days of his father's life. Instead of showing up only when Yussef was on his deathbed, Roth states in his "True World" narrative that he and his father were "somewhat" estranged. Further, he says he spent time and money to arrange an operation that almost saved his father's life. Undoubtedly, this account is dishonest. Adelaide says that Roth did not even see his father since his mother's death. The probability that Yussef sent his son money for passage home after his London visit increases his eldest son's callousness. Was he conscious of the level of dejection Yussef Lieb might have experienced, thinking in Seagate of his firstborn son's contempt for him? In the "True World" manuscript, Roth invokes the spirit of his mother to make him, but only temporarily, aware of who and what he is at age at age forty-five, sitting in federal prison. "'Have you any idea,' asked my mother in the midst of my growing confusion, '[to] how few of the really important things in your life you have given any thought?'"

It mitigates Roth's guilt that it is his own Yiddish momma, as a result of a "Hartsvaitik" (heartaching) talk with a confidante, who scolds him. Sam Roth, however effectively he sometimes writes of this earlier life, in his "True World" narratives too often seems to be "shedding his sicknesses," as D. H. Lawrence put it, by cheering himself up, rather than enduring under the weight of, or atoning for, his choices and their consequences. Perhaps that is what Roth meant when he characterized these stories as "this cowardly dreaming of mine" ("CMAM," 357). However, when Roth finished writing "Count Me among the Missing" in the 1950s, he did not change, but only shortened, the events he wrote of in the "True World" narrative, and left out any reference to his parents, suggesting another evasion of his own guilt.

Another episode in the "True World" story recounts a similar evasion of guilt. The individual involved, Tanya tells him, has a grievance that Roth has little time to rectify before the case is brought to the True World's judges of final destiny. Despite all the melodrama, there is one section of this episode, and another unrelated one, where Roth seems to have mastered the use of dialogue as exposition, and some of the plain diction with which the Yiddish parable worked its magic. The narrator travels through a set of desolate small tenements inhabited by what seem to be demons. "Where people in our world have noses these creatures have single bulbous eyes, each as intense as the headlight of an interstate truck. Where people as we know them have foreheads, this strange race displayed a particularly thick growth of hair." He meets "a shabby, skinny female" with an "unbearable stench"; a "live rat rose out of her grey muddy hair." The death-bearing crone, somewhat akin to the Demon of the Spring Mishillim saw when he first felt sexual arousal, leads him to a fetid dwelling with an earthen floor the color of "dung," furnishings so decrepit that they look like singed paper, and a roof so damaged that it barely obstructs the sky. The house is a decayed version of his father's inn, which burned down soon after Mishillim's birth, with an eastern wall identical to that from which the Roth family, led by Yussef, used to pray. The Kabbalists state that those who have done wrong "will return to the days of their youth to correct their crooked ways."[82] Roth was almost thirty when he disdained one woman's plea for empathy, but because of the way his story ends, he may have had this statement in mind.

The narrator now beholds the body of a female laid out on a table. A wind gust removes the shroud. The shame of death (or is it female nakedness?) is so vivid that Roth almost bolts from the dwelling, until he realizes it is Myrna Darby, a Ziegfeld girl who died at twenty-one in 1929. Roth first saw Myrna in Ziegfeld's office. It was her shoulders that stunned him. Her full-page photograph appears in *Beau*'s March 27, 1927, issue, inscribed to Roth. The caption reads, "Myrna Darby, of *Rio Rita*, who has written for your editor across the loveliest shoulders in captivity" (see fig. 8). Soon after, Myrna asked him what she should do about the demeaning gossip that showgirls were call girls. All Roth could do was tell her to marry a rich man. He regretted this callousness deeply when Myrna died two years later, possibly from a heart defect. But she had been despondent about her career and her love life.[83] In the "True World" episode, he "applied" himself to her mouth and to "the lower orifice—which I tremble to name [but wishes to allude to] by the feeding of which a woman immortalizes her race."[84] The passage combines fleshly, solipsistic gratification with a spiritual ritual that replaces death with the most precious of gifts.

Perhaps there is an allusion to Elijah here as in the story of his failed attempt to revive the brokenhearted girl on the ship to America. But this time (as in 2 Kings 13–21) he is successful. He does not have to make a painful, humiliating atonement. It gives another resonance to his phrase "this cowardly dreaming of mine." Further, it seems to have been written during one of those sleepless nights by the dim light of the prison washroom, where masturbation would in the predawn hours not be observed.

"Esther," a Magic Parable of Two Worlds

The one episode where True World justice does not involve Roth's own deeds is titled "Estherki Guttkind." Here he can afford the objectivity of a detached narrator. A man still living is "called forth" to answer a complaint by a dead woman. He, or his ghostly essence, his soul, appears before the *bezdin*, or judge.[85] Roth's True World is a place where, although a human conducts his mundane life as is his wont, he must inevitably face a judge both just and inexorable, as in "Transfiguration," where Jesus/Yeshea comes down from his crucifix to confront Hitler. While visiting Warsaw, a wealthy American Jew had convinced Esther, a poverty-stricken, innocent young woman, to run away with him. In New York he finds a shabby apartment for her, giving her no chance to think about how her integrity would be compromised thereby. His shrewish wife circulates evil rumors about Esther's being hired as a secretary and seducing her husband, who does not dispute the story. The couple see to it that their lies are published in newspapers. Esther, her reputation and self-image destroyed, is deported back to Poland. Although her seducer has sent her some money, Esther can get no help or respect in Warsaw, due to the lies the man and his wife have perpetrated about her. She lives in poverty in the red-light quarter until she dies. When the bezdin examines the defendant, he admits everything. The judge asks if anyone "remembers something relating to his crime that might soften—however little—the sentence I must pass against him." His son Walter, a toddler, answers that he had overheard his parents discuss their strategy and suggests that they have at least been partially punished:

> "As soon as I could do it unobserved I went to the bathroom, found a bottle marked poison and drank all of it."
>
> A woman's shriek rent the atmosphere of the Court.
>
> "I didn't know, Walter, I didn't know!" cried the voice. "I didn't know or I would have let her stay. I didn't know!"
>
> The voice of the Bezdin waited until the woman's crying had ebbed out. "You're not too young, my son," mused the voice, "to realize that there are times when even the powers of this Court seem feeble against the demands made on it. Is there anything we can do for you, Walter Leipzig, to make up to you for the untimely severance of your life?"

The boy appeared to hesitate—but only for words. . . ."I want to live again," the voice of the boy said. "I want to be born to the woman whose posterity in the True World was destroyed by my father."

Walter will become his father's double, replacing him, not as predatory lover but as loving son, and atone for him, perhaps a bit like Yeshea does for Hitler. Walter's return to life, echoing the Baal Shem Tov's "Two Souls" parable, could be an example of the Kabbalistic doctrine of metempsychosis. He will be able to show in another body the benevolence his early death prevented him from exercising. He will also possibly prevent his sinning parents' souls from being dispatched after their deaths into either diseased bodies or even into beasts.[86]

The motif of a world where one is confronted with the consequences of what he has set in motion, and either suffers or rejoices on a cosmic scale, is beautifully exploited in Jewish writers of great talent. In I. B. Singer's "A Wedding in Brownsville" and "Short Friday" (both written c. 1963), lovers faithful to each other and stoically accepting of the world's cruelties are rewarded. In the first story, the black-icy November streets of Brooklyn and in the second the empty universe of snow oppressing a Polish shtetl merge with the swiftest harmony into a True World eternity. A physician recovers his lover, who was murdered by the Nazis, at a wedding that he and the reader at first are led to believe is taking place in a Brownsville synagogue. In "Short Friday," a shtetl-bound loving husband and wife, asleep after a Sabbath meal, seemingly awake to an unearthly darkness, and are led into Paradise by a fearsome archangel.

S. Ansky's *The Dybbuk* (1914) is the most famous example of the transmigration theme. The play dramatizes how a man loses his daughter, Leah, because he justifiably, but also conveniently, believes he has been released from an oath made to his best friend many years ago. Then, he swore to his friend he would give his daughter in marriage to his friend's son. He had heard that the man to whom he swore it died childless. But that man, now dead, did have a son, Chonen, whom Leah, knowing nothing of any oath, met. The couple fell irrevocably in love. Chonen dies, and Leah is forced into a marriage of convenience with a foolish youth from a wealthy family. On the wedding night, Chonen's spirit takes possession of the bride's body, as a dybbuk (here understood to be the wandering ghost of a person that, having suffered so much pain in life, attaches itself to a living soul). A rabbi exorcizes him, on pain of excommunication, but the True World, once invoked, will not be denied. Leah dies so she and Chonen can be together. In Ansky's play (and in Tony Kushner's moving 1998 adaptation), the young people of one generation have redeemed their fathers' oaths that they be together, but to the ruin of Leah's father. Cosmic justice means, for that unfortunate, that he has lost his daughter, a much more precious possession than his wealth. He wanted to increase that wealth through the arranged marriage—with intent to benefit his family as well as himself in the only way he knew—materialistically. But he had become so focused on worldly security that he could not realize the depth of his daughter's desire for Chonen, whose parentage he could not have known. He is helpless (as were Walter's parents) before what is the mystery of a thwarted destiny. That mystery is the driving force of God's justice. For Ansky, as for Roth, its home is the True World. In act 4 of *The Dybbuk*, a character returns from the "True World" to make an accusation. Ansky made heroic efforts before World War I to record for posterity the Galician folklore that saturates Roth's poems and stories.

A human is responsible for himself in a universe the contingencies of which he has not been able to think through. If, for his own security, Samuel Roth can advise only self-destructive marriages of convenience to two women who open themselves to him (Tanya and Myrna), a moral judgment weighs heavily against him, as it does to Leah's father, and to the parents of Walter, who killed himself to give Esther fulfillment, since his parents, to escape fear of the world's judgment, had destroyed her. "The only whole heart," said Rabbi D. J. Wolpe, "is a broken one, because it lets the light in."

Compare their loss to Roth's loss, as he conceives of and writes it in "True World": three years in prison, with a fantasy "prison wife" to comfort him until he is released to a loving family. Compare Roth's adventures in the True World to Kafka's projections of himself as the meek, withdrawn, therefore disposable "Hunger Artist" or the too-humble petitioner for entrance into enlightenment ("Before the Law"). Or compare them, considering Legman's assumption that Joyce identified with the wandering Jew Leopold Bloom, with the latter's visit to Nighttown for a(nother) session in verbal abuse, a few hours after his wife had an assignation, in Bloom and Molly's own bed, with her suitor and manager Boylan. Molly and Leopold have not made love since the death of their eleven-day-old son. Roth never sensed—at least never admitted to—that abyss of personal loss, in the Bowery or the Thames embankment.

That there is a True World was perhaps Samuel Roth's most persistent metaphysical belief. In his last years he acquired a friend and sincere admirer, the journalist William Ryan. Ryan's memoir of Sam concludes with the burial service at Paramus, New Jersey, in 1974. "As I turned my back on Samuel Roth for the last time I remembered what he once told me, word for word: 'You acquire in the dream world distant relationships which you must come to recognize, and if you don't come to recognize them you stifle creativity.'"[87] Taklis. Roth had begun "Count Me among the Missing" by stating, "The most important events in our lives break before we are born." Destiny. Despite all the cupidity, his relationship to God was intense. He knew it must be his source of ultimate atonement. However, in America he lives in his "own sweet state of chaos."

Philosophical Treatise in Support of the True World

Before leaving prison, Roth wrote at least part of a scientific dissertation on space, time, relativity, and matter which he published in 1945 under the title *The Peep-Hole of the Present: An Inquiry into the Substance of Appearance.* What ties this treatise to the "True World" narrative is the True World concept itself. The idea of "the Substance"—a world closer to God's own mind and more real that the mundane one ("Appearance"), and yet contemporaneous with it—is at the heart of the book. Human beings can and in fact are destined to break through a psychic door or peephole (a word chosen at least partly because of its usefulness in prurient advertisement) and become conscious of the True World, as Roth tells us he did with the aid of Tanya while in prison. He does not mention among his many sources the late-nineteenth-century philosopher Rudolf Steiner, in whose anthroposophy the narrator of Bellow's *Humboldt's Gift* (1975), Charlie Citrine, believes. It offers a method of transcending American capitalist materialism.

The book is extremely dense; Gershon Legman told me that it deserved the terrible review it received in the *Saturday Review of Literature,* which, when Roth saw it, was shattering; he told Legman it "aged" him.[88] *Peep-Hole* is easy to sneer at. The author referenced so many scientific postulates that it leaves one reeling: Heisenberg's indeterminacy principle, Einstein's relativity, Descartes' influence on Spinoza, Leibniz's monads. Roth writes, rather skillfully, in the style of an informal essay, as if he is doing a "philosophy made easy" book. But it isn't easy reading, but opaque.

Legman declared that when sixty-two-year-old Cambridge Don Sir Arthur Eddington saw a preface to *Peep-Hole* in his name, he "dropped dead."[89] On the other hand, Milton Hindus was impressed with the book, admiring *Peep-Hole* for the breadth of Roth's reading in physics and philosophy and his ability to develop the most difficult subject to book length. He rejects the theory that the preface was either forged or edited by Roth, although there is some Roth-like diction and phrasing.[90] Hindus was especially interested in "Roth's prophetic vein" in the final pages, and tried to get it thoughtfully reviewed.[91] He points out that Roth predicted correctly that birth control would be important, especially to the Chinese, in the second half of the twentieth century, at which time atomic physics will be the source of fearsome atomic weaponry that will make previous warfare obsolete. Roth also says that war will break out again once Japan and Germany are neutralized. These statements echo Reiser's arguments for restraining powerful nations' belligerent excesses of capitalism and imperialism, especially their monopolizing new technologies of propaganda and weaponry. He wanted these motives replaced with "planetary democracy." As with Roth's admonitions about the future in *Now and Forever* and *My Friend Yeshea*, those in *Peep-Hole* are made in the spirit of promoting peace and restraining the predatory nature of mankind.

Roth awakens from the True World on the day of his release from Lewisburg. One year later, a violation of parole almost landed him back in prison.

CHAPTER 7

1940-1949

**Roth Breaks Parole, Uncovers a Nazi Plot,
Gives "Dame Post Office" Fits, and Tells His Own
Story in Mail-Order Advertising Copy**

"Get your *Wit and Wisdom of the Week* here," shouted the dozen girls in red aprons and white caps. Pauline had hired them, and they were led by Chig, reluctantly. Mother and daughter would have guessed that Sam's release from federal prison would not end the requests he made of them. Upon his release from Lewisburg, Roth had Pauline design, and Adelaide and a dozen other young women wear, a costume (red apron, white cap) to hawk a twenty-five-cent newsletter in Foley Square. It detailed the charges against federal judge Martin Manton.[1] In 1939, Manton, the tenth-longest-serving federal judge in the country, was convicted of "selling" his federal judgeship by accepting bribes, and remanded to prison.[2] This was the man who had refused Roth's petition for bail prior to transportation to Lewisburg. By Roth's account, he had been placed in a holding cell with mobsters Gurrah Shapiro and Lepke Buchalter, convicted in November 1936 for labor racketeering in the fur trade (not murder, as Roth reported, although Lepke was a member of Murder, Inc.). Judge Manton granted bail for the two organized crime men, although they faced sentences of four years and $20,000 each. He did not allow Roth to be so released. Roth says Gurrah and Lepke bribed Manton ("CMAM," 376). It is possible, although newspaper accounts of Manton's bribery and solicitation of "loans" refer to dealings with powerful corporations, not organized-crime hard men. If Roth was in the same facility as Gurrah and Lepke, it would have to have been in late December. Roth was sentenced on December 16 and arrived at Lewisburg on January 8, 1937.[3] He probably would not have been in the same holding cell, as they were very small.

Having lost his assets in the Crash, Manton had taken bribes to make favorable rulings in certain patent cases. He was eventually convicted and sent to Sam's alma mater, Lewisburg. Roth's *Wit and Wisdom of the Week* stunt, for which he could not immediately pay the printer, was particularly foolish for a man on parole. But it was vintage Roth—a display of vindication but at the same time a threat not only to his own freedom but that of his wife, whom Judge Moscowitz had warned not to become involved in his publishing activities. With his parole officer fully aware of this *Wit and Wisdom* stunt, the immediate future, as Adelaide knew, seemed to indicate a return to prison, just in time, it must be noted, to confront a chastened Manton.[4]

It definitely would have meant Lewisburg, if not Atlanta or a worse hole, if the parole authorities had known of his role in the distribution of the underground "Medvsa" edition of *Tropic of Cancer*. It is possible that he was contacted by the book's publisher, Jack Brussel, when Brussel needed money to finish the printing. Brussel's plan was to send five hundred copies to Ben Abramson in Chicago and an equal number to the Gotham Book Mart. Miller's bibliographers state that Roth agreed to advance the money, in return for Brussel printing an overrun that Roth distributed to customers, "over the years," on Roth's special mailing list of interested parties for banned erotica.[5] One of their sources for this story is Gershon Legman. Additional evidence for it is that Richard Roth told his sister that his father had made this deal.[6]

According to Legman, at the time Roth had quite a few writers in his "stable" of underground porno hacks, who would provide the customers on his special list with what they wanted. The program was similar to that by which the agent for the Oklahoma collector Roy M. Johnson received erotic stories from his New York agent. Legman writes that one of these employees was a writer and reviewer of sex pulps, Robert Maxwell Joffee. Another was Jack Hanley, known as the writer of *Let's Make Mary*, a lighthearted instruction manual for Broadway-type make-out men (in their dreams). A third was Legman himself. "We all wrote smut for Roth," Hanley said. "He's the only book publisher really in the center of the sex business."[7] He meant before the war. But if Roth was able to provide his special customers with copies of *Tropic of Cancer*, he might also have commissioned new porno stories from his "stable" in the early 1940s.

If Roth did take some sets of Medvsa sheets, they would have to have been hidden somewhere. It may have been several years later that he offered his *Tropic of Cancer* overrun for sale. Another problem was how to put his hands on the money to give Brussel. He was forced to ask the printer, Max Spiegel, to let him have on credit the copies he needed of *Wit and Wisdom of the Week* ("CMAM," 377). Perhaps the answer is that Roth was fortunate in having very kind and responsive in-laws. Also, associates may have held funds Roth had accumulated before Lewisburg in various accounts opened under their own names, or aliases, as Julius Moss had done at the time of *The Strange Career of Mr. Hoover.*

Roth's parole was almost revoked in 1941. His FBI files indicate that it came to the parole board's attention that he had been trying to sell copies of erotica, including *A Scarlet Pansy.*[8] The Roths say the ostentatious revenge on Judge Manton was the reason, and that in fact Judge Moscowitz did order his return to prison for breaking parole. The reason that order was countermanded is one of the strangest occurrences in Sam's career.[9] "Mrs. [Violet] Jerzivit, the parole officer to whom he reported monthly, was—luckily for Mishillim—a liberal minded person of charm and understanding. Mrs. Jerzivit . . . opened the way for him to perform a signal service to his country."[10]

Roth Stays Out of Prison; Fritz Duquesne Goes to Leavenworth

In a biographical statement he prepared in 1955, when he was trying to keep from being sent to prison after a federal indictment for interstate distribution of books advertised salaciously, Sam Roth pointed out a patriotic service he had done his country, quite apart from his work in bringing good books to ordinary people.[11] In writing of that service in the autobiography, Roth writes of a meeting he attended that took place before he was arrested and sent to Lewisburg.[12] Although he does not say so, it might have been that the meeting was part of a conspiracy to sabotage military operations in case of war between Germany and the United States. It would have had to take place in the first part of 1936, or before then. Deeply involved was Frederick ("Fritz") Joubert Duquesne, the subject of Clement Wood's 1932 *The Man Who Killed Kitchener.* Duquesne's indictment stated that the conspiracy began in April 1936. Fritz would have been the man who informed Roth about the group. The FBI would have been interested in which pro-German individuals were in New York before the conspiracy was hatched.[13]

Roth writes in 1941 that a representative of the FBI's Brooklyn office asked the parolee to bring him to the meeting place Roth had visited. Instead, Roth suggested he himself return there, despite the danger. He learned over the next fortnight the identity of the chief conspirators, and informed the FBI. The spies were arrested. Transcripts of the Attorney General of the Eastern District of New York, where the case was tried, include the testimony of all the principal defendants.[14] At the trial, that testimony identified those present; Roth was not mentioned. He may have identified individuals attending certain meetings of Nazi sympathizers in New York, and relayed names to the FBI. Those names may have included conspirators, but probably only as corroborative evidence. The FBI, which had planted listening devices at various apartments, including Fritz's and his friend Mrs. Evelyn Lewis's,[15] would have had a good idea prior to summer 1941 who was involved.

Regardless, Mishillim (the persona Roth adopted whenever honor, not profits, was in the offing) was back in the good graces of his country, and had, he believed, partially made up for *Jews Must Live.* He had attempted to reshape himself in the image of the Humphrey Bogart of *All through the Night, Casablanca,* or *Passage to Marseilles*—all films released after mid-1941, but valid analogies, perhaps, since they all deal with risking one's life while revealing a patriotism that most people find inconceivable in a Main Stem gambler, a saloon owner, or a convict framed for murder. That kind of patriotism would be deemed equally unlikely in a man imprisoned for pornography.

The investigation Roth is referring to was a broad-ranging one, and involved Nazi-inspired activities that aimed at stealing American documents regarding ship movements and military top-secret weaponry. After the FBI's two-year investigation, thirty-three German espionage agents were indicted (sixteen were in the United States) and arrested on June 29, 1941. An intrepid double agent (and telegraph specialist) was instructed by the FBI to communicate secret messages from Germany to its agents in the United States, so that the FBI could trace them. In 1945 an acclaimed film about the case was released, *The House on 92nd Street.* One of the principal operators in the cabal was Fritz Duquesne. Duquesne was probably recruited by the Silver Shirts, the pro-Nazi group that had advertised *Jews Must Live* in skywriting over Los Angeles. He unwittingly gave the double agent valuable information about American ship movements and munitions, and was sentenced to eighteen years in prison in January 1942.

When he was transferred from Leavenworth in 1945, where he had been scapegoated by fellow prisoners and suffered debilitating illness, Fritz was a broken man. He may have experienced what the military now euphemistically calls "interrogation." After being thrown down a flight of stairs, he became increasingly paranoiac. He was released after nine more years in a medical facility, during which time he tried to make amends to Evelyn Clayton Lewis, whom he had convinced to help him in his espionage activities (Ms. Lewis

Samuel Roth, Infamous Modernist

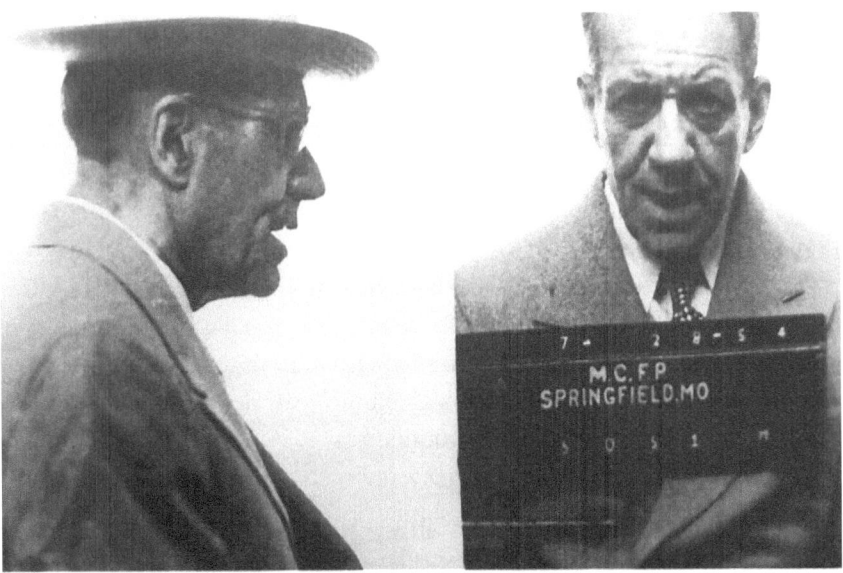

Figure 19. Fritz Duquesne in 1951, after ten years' imprisonment. Bureau of Prisons Records, The National Archives.

would not see him). Duquesne died two years later at a home for the indigent on Welfare Island.[16] Writing to Roth from prison as his release neared, he asked to meet with Adelaide and see her children. Her father decided the family should not communicate further with Fritz.[17]

Fritz was closer to Clement Wood than Sam Roth. His daughter reports that Clem introduced Roth to him, at one of Clem's penthouse parties at his apartment in the west 50s.[18] Subsequently, Roth and his family found Fritz to be one of the most entertaining of the circle of friends, including Wood and his wife, who were invited to Sam and Pauline's Friday-night "at homes" in the early 1930s. They knew him as "Major Craven"; Adelaide remarks on his fashionable dress, wavy hair, piercing blue eyes, enrapturing stories ("big-game hunting with Teddy Roosevelt"), and attempts to hide his small stature. "At fourteen I may have been gawky but the Major merely looking at me made me feel like a femme fatale."[19] He taught Richard martial arts.[20] "Major Craven" was cordial with the Roths throughout the late 1930s, visiting Roth's Fifth Avenue Book Shop with various women. Both men were short on funds at the time, and sometimes met in Chinese restaurants, Fritz, Adelaide remembers, using copious amounts of condiments to make any meal as filling as possible.[21] He lived on West Forty-sixth Street with a "sweet, quiet southern lady" named

Henrietta Jacobs.[22] One day Duquesne introduced Roth to a wealthy, elderly woman who wanted him to write more books like *Jews Must Live*. That, Fritz wordlessly suggested to his friend, would definitely help him financially. Roth, according to Adelaide, who was present, told her politely he was at the moment too busy to discuss the matter. Clearly, therefore, the FBI would have been interested in discovering what Roth could tell them about Fritz and his friends.[23]

There is little reason to doubt the basis of Roth's story of undercover activity at the request of the FBI. Adelaide remembers a mysterious visitor to their apartment who spoke with her father in private. Roth told her the man was with the FBI and she was "not to talk about the visit. He [Roth] had just been informed about their success in the roundup of the Nazi saboteurs."[24] Another person who worked undercover was one of Fritz's mistresses, who might have been Henrietta. Her situation was similar to Roth's in that she was Jewish, and was determined to help by reporting whatever she could overhear about Duquesne's plans. The G-men had much information on the spy ring in any event, for, as mentioned above, its double agent was working as a telegraph operator in league with them. But in such an important case, any corroborating evidence was invaluable. That the FBI would have agreed to let Roth work on his own to determine the identity of the Nazi spy ring is, however, highly questionable.[25]

In his autobiography, Roth does not present nearly as much detail about the spy ring as his daughter does in her memoir. He does not even mention Fritz's name. That indicates that he did not want to confront his betrayal of his and his family's friend. Fritz and Sam had a lot in common. They were both very good at public relations. Fritz worked successfully with Joseph P. Kennedy during his Hollywood ventures, and with RKO. In 1930 he was writing reviews of films and vaudeville for various movie magazines, as Sam had done with stage shows when he was publishing *Beau*. Both affected a British gentleman's style of speaking and sartorial elegance. Both wore well-cut suits, accessories such as a walking stick (Fritz walked with a limp), and in Fritz's case a monocle. Sam was showing off his unique approximation of social capital and status as man of letters; Fritz was deflecting suspicion. Both men used various aliases. Both men's self-assurance was enough in itself to command attention. Yet they harbored deep resentments. Both demanded freedom forcefully to assert their ideas, and thus were very interested in American constitutional protections, especially those granted under the First and Fourth Amendments. To this end, both had employed the services of Arthur Garfield Hays.[26] Both had liaisons with many beautiful women. Neither could work as part of a group without assuming a chief place within it.

Both men's eccentricities were as prominent as their need to take radical and dangerous chances with their personal safety and reputation. Both had vast faith in themselves. Both assumed they were justified, even destined, to take the lead in cauterizing civil society's moral decay and in reforming human behavior. Both lacked balanced perspective and often refused to consider the victims of their actions. This was much clearer in Fritz's case, because the sinking of Kitchener's ship meant the drowning of hundreds of people; aiding the Nazis needs no elaboration. But Roth chose to be an unfaithful husband, to write *Jews Must Live,* and to publish erotic material, all of which he knew would hurt his family's chances for success and self-respect. Both undertook missions guaranteed to bring them severe punishment and ostracism. Contradictory behavior was an outstanding trait of both men. Roth took his duty as Jew and American very seriously, yet befriended Nazi sympathizers. Duquesne worked for the Nazis, yet had many Jewish friends. Phyllis Keller, in her essay on George Sylvester Viereck, brilliantly summarizes his psychology in terms we could apply both to Fritz Duquesne and Sam Roth: "narcissistic self-absorption and self-over-evaluation (together with an exaggerated regard for members of his family, perceived as extensions of himself); the use of fantasy as a bridge to the outside world; unrestrained exhibitionism and self-dramatization; failure to integrate thought and feeling; and a sense of guilt which continually led [them] both to seek punishment and to justify [their] beliefs and actions."[27] Vulnerability and resentment are the keys to both men's temperaments. Fritz, as a boy, had to watch, he asserted, as his mother and sister were raped during the British "pacification" strategy of the Second Boer War. "God aids a just vengeance" was the Duquesne family motto. Roth absorbed his father's resentments, resulting from his having to appeal to the Polish lord of the manor to house his family, then having to work as middleman for that *puretz,* and finally having to immigrate for fear of the consequences of arguing with him. Roth himself explained his lifelong need to defy repressive authority by his own early patriarchal trauma, having to undergo a rabbinical exorcism and being suspected by father and rabbi of masturbating, and of course he resented Joyce and his supporters.

According to Clement Wood's *The Man Who Killed Kitchener,* Fritz's most dramatic story was that he arranged for the ship on which Lord Kitchener was sailing to Russia in 1916 to be sunk. "Fritz's life was spectacular, scintillant, adventurous, thrilling to its last detail."[28] It was therefore prime film material.

Roth sent out so many copies of Wood's book, including one to each major studio (RKO and Warner Brothers showed interest), that he ran out of review copies for newspapers. If *Kitchener* could be bolstered by an attention-getting event, one occurred on May 23, 1932, when the police arrested Fritz, intending to have him extradited to England to stand trial for the murder of Kitchener thirteen years earlier. Wood himself arranged bail.[29] Roth incorporated a clipping from a *World Telegram* story about the arrest in an advertisement for *The Man Who Killed Kitchener.*

This kind of exploitation makes it all the more interesting that Sam Roth would not mention Fritz by name, or even allude to him, while describing his service to the FBI in 1941. He was proud of that service, but unlike his daughter, he seems not to want to put on record his role in Fritz's fate. Roth took responsibility in his autobiography for other acts that led to the suffering of friends. But Legman's observation, that he was blinded to the hurtful consequences of what he did when a significant personal "need" (here, the amending of his own low repute) was attained by his action, is true. Whatever his patriotic motives might have been, he did betray Fritz Duquesne. If one does not acknowledge an act as disastrous to a friend, he has no hope of inhabiting a blissful True World. That is a form of tikkun, or recovery, and has to begin with humility, as a prelude to prayer.

Early 1940s Successes

After Lewisburg, Roth continued the Faro formula: erotica, gossip, and politically topical books. He published under a variety of imprints, because if the Post Office found a particular book unmailable, it would not deliver any mail sent under that book's imprint or trade name. He started with a slim book of "Confucius say" witticisms, *Confucius Comes to Broadway* (Wisdom House, 1940), by "Francis Page."[30] Angling for a notice in his column, Roth dedicates the book to Walter Winchell, "the columnist sage." To flush out, so to speak, a readership for the book, he included in a punny chapter titled "Wisdom in a Bathhouse," "Man got more hair on his chest than woman, but on whole, woman got more."[31]

The renascent publisher had two early successes, Krueger's *I Was Hitler's Doctor* (1941) and David George Plotkin's *Rage in Singapore* (1942), in addition to *My Uncle Benjamin* (Coventry House, 1941), for whom, in his circulars, he "invented a love life," as Adelaide put it. *A Golden Treasury* was reprinted under the Biltmore imprint. *Bachelor's Quarters: Stories from Two Worlds* (1944) was an excellent selection of short stories by a large number of contemporary writers; it showed once again Roth's skills as a voracious reader and an anthologist.[32]

"Kurt Krueger's" *I Was Hitler's Doctor* (originally titled *Inside Hitler*) was the result of an office supplies salesman turned literary agent offering Roth a set of notes. He told the publisher they were written by a German physician who immigrated to Canada after having known and treated Hitler in the late 1920s. The story is suspicious, but Adelaide confirms it, and knew the physician's name, which he did not want used when the book was published.[33] Roth wrote that *Hitler's Doctor* was valuable not as a scandal book with lurid allegations, such as those he published a decade earlier, but because it gave a profile of a species of psychological sickness that leads to negation of individuality and world war. The introduction, "Hitler as I Knew Him," was by Otto Strasser, another Canadian exile, and a former Nazi cited by Berlin as public enemy of the Reich in 1940.[34] There was a preface by "K. Arvid Enlind, M.D., Lt Col. Medical Reserve, USA." Probably, Roth did not know that in 1922 Dr. Enlind had been arrested with a confederate in a notorious confidence swindle involving wealthy women.[35] In his preface he acknowledges that *Hitler's Doctor* will provide a "vicarious kick" but that its larger interest is in revealing the modern neuroses that led to Hitler's rise and to the phenomenon of mass murder. The sensational "kicks" include reports of Hitler having an affair with Ernst Röhm, and his inability to maintain erotic desire when with his niece Geli Raubal, because he saw in her the image of his mother. There is also the revelation that the Führer once thought of curing his impotence by having a wasp bite his penis.

Roth noted in September 1941 that he had paid David Plotkin "$30 to date for *translating* [my italics] Hitler manuscript."[36] He had commissioned Plotkin to translate the physician's notes and assemble them into a text. The publisher almost closed a deal with John Lane for the English rights, but the firm was put off by fears that in England the book might be attacked as pornographic. In 1946, Roth sold the European translation and serialization rights for $10,000.[37] Thanks to Plotkin's hard work (especially if it was he who commissioned the three prefatory essays), *Hitler's Doctor* was "one of Dad's best selling books," according to Adelaide Kugel, "even in Brazil in Portugese." Roth wrote to the Curtis Brown agency that within the first year of publication he sold "nearly six large printings" at $3.75 per copy. Upton Sinclair complained to Plotkin about Roth's dilatoriness in paying him for his foreword, but his positive review of the book for *The New Republic* must have been largely responsible for its popularity.[38]

Plotkin's work involved dividing the manuscript into short chapters with provocative titles ("Oedipus Due North," "Dream Blitz and Nightmare," "An Odyssey of Torture"), something he also did for his own novel *Rage in Singapore* (1942), which Roth issued soon after the Hitler book and which takes place in Singapore, Kuala Lumpur, and the Malay Peninsula. The book was published soon after Pearl Harbor, and this, in addition to the comprehensive depiction of the customs, religions, and British colonial influence in Southeast Asia, made it a success. Harry Roskolenko groused that Plotkin never was anywhere near Singapore. On the grounds that everyone has to be somewhere, Roth's "Publishers' Note" tells the reader "we have had the additional disadvantage of not being able to consult the author [regarding editing], who, at this writing, has not yet managed to get back to the United States." Roth failed to sell the film rights, but three studios did show interest.[39]

Plotkin's next effort was the exposé of Senator Burton Wheeler, an "America Firster" and thus an opponent of American participation in World War II. Roth had passed on it, probably because Plotkin now considered himself a successful writer and Roth would not meet his price.[40] Wheeler asked the FBI to investigate Plotkin and find out who was behind him. The trail led to Roth, partly due to Pauline's mischievous answers to questions put to her. She could not resist giving the investigators a false scent. The FBI turned over Roth's file to the House Un-American Activities Committee regarding his possible connection with Plotkin.[41]

In 1948, Roth wrote to Alger Hiss's attorney, offering to testify in the trial of Hiss for espionage. Whittaker Chambers had admitted to being at one point a Communist, and accused Hiss of being one. Roth stated that he knew Chambers under the pseudonym George Crosley, which was the name Hiss recalled Chambers had used on one occasion when identifying himself to Hiss. Chambers maintained he had never used any but his birth name in identifying himself. Roth knew better, for Chambers had sent him poems to publish in one of his magazines in 1926 or 1927, requesting him to publish them under the name "George Crosley" (*Two Worlds Quarterly*'s June 1926 issue contains one poem, "Tandaradei," under the name Whittaker Chambers). Roth was deposed, but Hiss's attorney decided not to use the testimony, because of Roth's obscenity convictions, which he freely stated. Roth's motives, as Adelaide Kugel states in her excellent account of the case, included his "impulsiveness," but also his "hatred of Communism and Communists."[42]

Plotkin continued to work for Roth, producing most notably either a fine editing or creative-writing job on the still-controversial *My Sister and I*, purportedly by Nietzsche (1957). Plotkin was one of Roth's most skilled editors, in length of service and in other respects being similar to Gershon Legman.

Figure 20. David George Plotkin. Dust-jacket photo from Plotkin's *The Plot against America* (Missoula, Montana, 1946). From collection of the author.

Semi-erotic hack work was part of both men's responsibilities. Roth took a liking to both. Upon Plotkin's death in 1968, Roth's letter consoling his widow, Rachel, reveals that he saw David, as he did Gershon, as similar in profound ways to himself. What he said in tribute, he might well have said of himself: "He loved the world so much, and the world yielded so little."[43]

Roth must not have seen the first story in "Kin's" *Women without Men: True Stories of Lesbian Love in Greenwich Village* (1958). The title may echo "Bodenheim's" *My Life and Loves in Greenwich Village,* largely Plotkin's hack work published four years earlier. He may have resented such tasks, or perhaps that he did not benefit much from lucrative sales, especially those of "Nietzsche's" *My Sister and I.* "The Last Virgin in the Village" is about Saul Sutton, a "bourgeois bohemian," who, although a philanderer and a successful publisher of mail-order pseudo-erotica, insists that his daughter Irene, with aspirations to be a dancer and actress, remain a virgin. She therefore turns to loving other women. Saul runs a "literary sweat-shop," has soirees in which gangsters, prostitutes, and gamblers revel, is able to interest all kinds of women in sleeping with him, and has been in jail several times. In youth a devout Jew, Saul retained a belief in destiny, but "he was caught in the jaws of his own lawless life." Despite occasional flashes of authenticity, there is less here than meets the eye; the story is mostly bitterish rib-nudging. One thing is for sure: Plotkin would not have enjoyed meeting Roth, who with or without walking stick would have smote Plotkin to the ground for writing this story (the publisher had begun his second term at Lewisburg).

Plotkin, son of a rabbi and trained as a lawyer, had started out much as Roth had, with skillfully written poetry. His publisher was even more prestigious than McBride or Boni and Liveright. *Ghetto Gutters* (1926) was the last book issued by Thomas Seltzer Inc. The book contains many lyrics similar to Roth's, as well as those of poets both men modeled themselves after: Charles Reznikoff, Alter Brody, George Oppen, and Louis Zukofsky. The forty-page-long "Rubaiyat of a Brownsville Sheik" is similar to Roth's *Europe,* and even more strident. But the speaker in *Ghetto Gutters,* clearly a Marxist, never equates his destiny with the awestruck piety of the speaker in Roth's "Yahrzeit," "Kol Nidre," or the "Sonnets on Sinai."

Sam Roth versus "Dame Post Office": Early Rounds

In a November 1941 letter to his federal court probation officer, Roth declared that he was about to close down any direct mail-order bookselling. He pointed out the value of *I Was Hitler's Doctor* as evidence that he was now a legitimate trade-book wholesaler.[44] This declaration, for three reasons, is either sophisticated equivocation or a total lie. First, just three months later his Psychic Research Press received a permit to enclose business-reply cards or return envelopes in mailings, although it was forbidden to have these items sent to a "fictitious name" (the return address being one the Post Office had cited as "unmailable" because the company with that name was engaged in fraud or obscenity).[45] Second, Roth's daughter observed that her father, unable to publish new books because of the paper shortage, had been selling remainders by circular.[46] Third, in his autobiography he states that he had decided, despite the problems with postal inspectors, to conduct his business by mail order. He had learned that bookstores would not buy items that were "widely circulated by advertising copy" (with return addresses at which to order). The more books he sold by mail order, the fewer he need try to wholesale to stores. "A complete immersion in coupon advertising became inevitable" ("CMAM," 383). He started with a full-page advertisement for *My Uncle Benjamin* in the *Tribune* Sunday book review, receiving many coupon orders. Following that up, he "soon found himself with 400,000 mail-order buyers of books who could be trusted to absorb an edition of almost any book he published."

The remainders Roth sold during the war were varied, but several came to the attention of the Post Office inspectors. Examples include the digest-sized newsstand paperbacks with covers of handsome dressed-for-success, or uniformed, men and seductive women, often wearing low-cut gowns. Their authorship was attributed to "house names" such as Perry Dale, Gail Jordan, and Peggy Gaddis (*Army Widow, Week-End Husbands, Convention Girl*). In a circular titled "Joyful List of Books for Adults"[47] (with the decorated initial J featuring a tiny naked woman), Roth circularized many hardcover books sold inexpensively at the time or available in rental libraries at specialty stores ("5 and 10s," drugstores, cigar stores). Examples include *Gone with the Wind,* D. H. Clarke's *Threesome* ("just spills over with the woman-juice the older, and some of our younger, of our readers like to lap up"), as well as Roth's own *Hitler's Doctor,* and the four Black Hawk "Hot Classics" (as he now called them) from 1936.

In April 1941, Judge Moscowitz received the aforementioned petition that Roth be sent back to prison.[48] The probation officer did not mention the Medvsa *Tropic of Cancer* or any of the "flagitious" titles that occasioned the 1936 sentence. Those would not have been advertised through the mail. Neither does the officer mention *Wit and Wisdom of the Week,* which both Roth and Adelaide say caused the complaint that almost sent the publisher back to prison. Instead, cited were borderline circularized titles, some of which we have stated, but also books such as *Chinese Love Tales, Girls on City Streets,* and a joke book titled *Ain't Love Gland?*

The best indication of Roth's strategy for selling books as "hot stuff," even if there was absolutely zero sexual content to them, was how he advertised his own philosophical treatise *The Peep-Hole of the Present* (1945):

> What went haywire when the famous movie director married his pretty sixteen year old star? . . . Marriage found her as worn-out as a streetwalker of forty.
>
> What was wrong with the dazzling follies beauty abandoned successively by 3 husbands the morning after? Each had threatened suicide,

if she refused to marry him; yet, after the wedding night, each brought her back, with such unholy haste, to the doorstep of her poor parents.

What does an actress mean when she says she is "wedded to her public"?

This advertisement is truly remarkable, not only because of the misrepresentation of his own book, which cost him so much intellectual energy and physical discomfort to write in prison. The postal authorities' hackles must have been fluttering, but for Roth there is something other than capitulation to The Big Dollar involved, although there certainly is that. Each of these outrageous come-ons refers clearly to that provocative 1931 short story "Body." In it, as in the circular copy just quoted, an apparently pure young woman had been mysteriously debauched. The contrast is between what we are puzzled by when we see it and what is the destiny of the female performer whom the male spectator sees (as if through a peephole) as an object of masturbatory desire. This ultimate explanation provides the shock of recognition that makes "Body" interesting. Now we see the full import of his use of "Peephole"; the working title was "The Restless Universe."[49] Roth, in acquisitive and amoral advertising of his own devising, had found an unconventional way to communicate his message, while selling some of the print run of a very badly reviewed, and subsequently ignored, book. It is this sort of cheeky *mishegoss* that Maxwell Bodenheim laconically highlighted many years earlier (with a nod to taklis) when he inscribed a copy of his *Minna and Myself* to Roth:

> To Samuel Roth
> Who tweaks the grimly lascivious nose of the Philistine, and somehow manages to escape his vengeance. Only a Jew can adroitly maneuver toward the stars, without losing his smile.
> From another Jew, Maxwell Bodenheim.[50]

"Dame Post Office's Minions" Train Their Guns on Samuel Roth

None of Roth's mail-order offerings had been legally banned, but the postal authorities made subjective judgments, and enforced them by *ex parte* decisions. That is, after learning about a decision, a publisher or distributor could plead his case at a hearing. However, it was devoid of adversarial procedure, because the "trial [i.e., hearing] examiner," of course a Post Office employee, made the judgment. The decisions, therefore, were made by one party—the Post Office—exclusively, and were never overturned. Moreover, the postal judges were not nearly as forthcoming before banning a book or magazine as Sumner's Society for the Suppression of Vice or the Watch and Ward Society. Both institutions at their discretion would give opinions to publishers asking for advice about whether a particular book would be prosecuted or not if published. The Post Office told the publisher that everything depended on whether a particular postal inspector who saw it thought it could be mailed. Roth nailed this practice in a single precise sentence, noting that inspector and hearing examiner were on the same payroll: "The Post Office Department granted itself the order it asked of itself, and banned the book" ("CMAM," 387).

By 1945, Roth had moved with his family to 11 West Eighty-first Street, near Central Park West and across the street from the Museum of Natural History and its surrounding green space. The mail-order operations that caused his affluence presented a special problem for the postal bureaucracy. During the war, Roth had queried the postmaster (Albert Goldman) and the solicitor general, learning that he would not be told whether or not the postal inspectors would interdict either a circular or a book prior to the mailing.[51] Roth's Avalon Press received a letter from Goldman in 1945 stating that the press must submit the books *Parisian Nights, The Harlot's House,* and *About Women* to determine mailability in view of the advertisements he had sent.[52] These were posted third-class mail and thus were subject to being opened by an inspector. Later that same year, Goldman wrote Arrowhead Books that while circulars for five books, including *Bubu of Montparnasse,* were "acceptable for mailing at this time, it [is] understood that in depositing this matter in the mails, you are using the mails at your own peril."[53] With a shrug of his shoulders, Roth was quite willing to deposit his books first and learn the postal decision later.

Late in the 1950s, journalist John N. Makris told the story of the postal service's "silent investigators" and their efforts to combat "merchants in filth." One of their "great untold stories" was the tauntings these protectors of public morals endured from Samuel Roth.[54] His FBI files reveal that the Post Office had received so many complaints about Roth's mailings—it claimed their number reached five thousand—that a special form letter was devised to answer them.[55] The Post Office totaled the unmailable orders against Roth's books at seventeen in all during the 1940s and 1950s.[56] His circulars got progressively bolder and more suggestive, and some of them contained sneering references to the "blue noses" who have repressed "vital" novels and magazines, and who tell his customers their reading matter is indecent. "Don't let them worry you," one of his circulars assured his customers, "your morals are all right."[57] Roth would request he be present at hearings regarding "unmailable" rulings against his books and flyers; he kept a list of the names the inspectors used in decoy letters. In 1947 he decided to let loose his friend, the Irish poet Shaemas O'Sheel, on a particularly irritating trial examiner. He chose the hearing on *Waggish Tales from the Czechs,* since he believed it was the satiric stories on the Catholic Church that had motivated the obscenity decision. It was almost worth losing the case, the publisher wrote, to see Shaemas's lively performance as an expert witness ("CMAM," 386). At one point Roth told a presiding officer at a hearing that postal inspectors had ordered so many of his materials that they were paying his postage bill.[58] The scope of his business is reflected in his postal meter bill for 1952: $32,930 (equal to $282,000 in 2012). When Roth appeared before the Kefauver Subcommittee investigating juvenile delinquency in 1955 he stated that he took from his business a salary of $10,000 a year and his wife received $3,000 (that would equal $110,000 in 2012). He employed about fifteen people.[59]

In 1947, Roth was receiving about fifty pieces of mail daily at his Arrowhead Press offices.[60] At that time, fraud orders were issued against two of his books, one of them his expurgated *Ananga Ranga,* with the body's "secret places" expunged, the other his own novel, *Bumarap: The Story of a Male Virgin.*[61] The *Bumarap* circular promised the excitement of the hero's first sexual encounter, which he starts by kissing a certain "Countess's" toes (an echo of the nine-year-old Mishillim's own meeting with his childhood sweetheart at the spring in Nuszcze, and of his way of being tender with his mistress Joan in London). Thus ends chapter 25. Bumarap, as the next chapter begins, had reached the countess's face. "You Must Be There in Person," stated the circular, "the book sweeps you right into it as if you were actually there."[62] (But you weren't, and it's not often one gets a chance to be present for a male's deflowering, dammit.) Foreseeing a good sale for *Bumarap,* Roth filed an injunction against the postal unmailable ruling. The postal counsel argued that the episode with the countess excluded any lovemaking. In view of this, the four-page advertisement was fraudulent. One page of the circular had suggested that Bumarap's losing his innocence was hotter than anything in *Forever Amber,* and a bold headline touted both "The Passion of Male Innocence" and "The End of the First Spasm" as well as "be[ing] there in person." Roth's argument that there were few people who asked for refunds was also considered irritating.

We have discussed the evolution of the fraudulence-obscenity linkage while describing Roth's 1936 legal problems. It was very important for the Post Office.[63] Inspectors had legitimately applied that charge to hundreds of schemes and offers (cures for "lost manhood" or for baldness, or gadgets for increasing breast or penis size) that could be objectively proven to be swindles. Obscenity was much harder to determine objectively, for it was complicated by the question of "the mores of the present time," the need for adults to be informed in sexual matters, and the hazy borderline between art and salacity. Therefore, it was easier to deny a distributor of a book with erotic but not obscene passages the use of the mails if it was pruriently advertised ("pandered," as stated in the previous chapter). The fraudulent ruling was an end run around the subjectivity of defining obscenity. The postal authorities could choose whether to indict a book as obscene or to declare unmailable not only a book but all advertisements distributed under a particular trade name (such as Bridgehead or Arrowhead). They could do so by declaring the circulars themselves to be fraudulent. Correspondence from customers would be returned to the senders. In many cases the book itself could have been cited as obscene, but the inspectors were on surer ground with the fraudulent designation.

Roth v. Goldman (1949): Sam Roth Stands Firm for the First Amendment

Few "operators," as the Post Office called them, had the resources to force an appellate case. In 1949, Roth had the money to pay a lawyer to do so. The result was *Roth v. Goldman,* argued in the U.S. Court of Appeals, Second Circuit. As the distributor of books under five trade names, the publisher challenged therein the New York postmaster Albert Goldman, pleading that, as a result of the Post Office mail block, Roth had received no orders for the books advertised under the business names Candide Press, The Monthly Book-Gem, Psychic Research Press, Arrowhead Books, and Hogarth House. His business was "at a standstill," he said, and his considerable investment was lost.[64] The Post Office had been required to follow an Administrative Procedure Act in 1940, which would allow due process of law to mail-order distributors of printed material. But it asserted that if it waited until after the hearing to block an offender's mail, that operator would have already profited from his scheme.[65] They were correct. But their intransigence, which the government allowed (possibly because enforcing a law stifling a government bureaucracy might eventually be used to make the future uncertain for all such governmental offices), meant the business Roth was in was denied a basic democratic First Amendment protection.

Roth's affidavit was a judicious and deeply felt statement. He speaks for all mail-order booksellers who had spent their money remaindering or reprinting books, placing advertisements in reputable magazines and newspapers, building up mailing lists by renting or purchasing them, selling books that obviously please customers—and then losing their business because one postal inspector and trial examiner made a decision that, as the district judge's "Show Cause" order in *Goldman* put it, was "arbitrary, capricious, and unwarranted in fact and law."[66] The Post Office inspectors, the order pointed out, do not concern themselves with the question of any actual harm that would come to citizens if they were able to read a book such as *Waggish Tales from the Czechs* before the hearing as to its mailability took place. This was a set of ninety-six men's smoking-room stories, not scatological or pornographic in any way. The publisher may have assigned Harry Roskolenko to redact it from a work Roth purchased.[67]

Walker v. Popenoe had touched on this question of arbitrary obscenity rulings four years before. That decision asserted that suspension of a company's mail before a hearing was unconstitutional and that an obscenity decision determining whether or not a company would succeed or fail must be a "judicial not an executive function." But the judges did not recognize that the time span between decision and hearing could in itself be fatal to profits. The Post Office often stated that it was too dangerous to public morals to allow material they interpret as obscene to be distributed prior to the hearing, despite the vagueness of the concept of "public morals."

The appellate judges denied Roth an injunction. They felt that since the postmaster general had reviewed the evidence and ordered the books banned, "review should not be over exhaustive."[68] Roth had argued that he had done only what other businesses do to sell products. Should not they be judged by the tolerances for sexually explicit materials of the average intelligent adult of the community? But the Post Office had no jurisdiction over how a film, clothing, or motor vehicle corporation used media such as showroom displays, billboards, marquees, radio and TV programs, or coming attractions to purvey its high-priced goods. It had congressional mandate to police the mails.

Judge Jerome Frank concurred with the denial of the injunction, but did so with "bewilderment." In a lengthy opinion referred to in later censorship cases, he questioned whether there was a "clear and present danger" that required suppression of writings deemed obscene. Frank also stated that he could see nothing "less obscene in [Balzac's] *Droll Stories* [allowed circulation for many years] than in *Waggish Tales*." That implied a criticism of the paternalism that prevented average people without the bona fides of physicians, psychologists, and literary scholars from accessing erotic material that those elites thought valuable. Roth had long been telling his customers that they had every right to read both what the elite had access to and also what they themselves thought of interest. Postal inspectors chalked these statements up as irresponsible sales

Samuel Roth, Infamous Modernist

pitches. But Frank, a federal judge, was now giving a highly professional, impartial affirmation of Roth's assertions. Frank went on to question the lack of safeguards against "arbitrary official incursions" on freedom of expression, given the evolution of the obscenity test (which Dame Post Office seemed to assume did not exist). If the postmaster general knew that a published work would debauch the morals of hoi polloi, how had he arrived at that conclusion, what were his criteria, and why was he not specific about how they apply in the case of *Waggish Tales*?[69]

"As a matter of course," as Roth put it ("CMAM," 387), he lost such cases despite his protestations and the reservations of people like Judge Frank. The ACLU took close interest in this case, regretting that the Supreme Court had decided not to review the negative decision.[70] The organization had been protesting postal administrative policy since the attorney general's 1940 staff report on the department.[71] In 1954 it filed an amicus curiae brief in *Summerfield v. Sunshine Book Company*, whose nudist magazines had been denied use of the mails because of the photographs, although the genitals of the nudists were shown as sparingly and indistinctly as possible. This time the outcome was favorable to the ACLU.[72] Perhaps *Roth v. Goldman* helped pave the way for this decision.

Roth fought the same battles with the Post Office until the year before his federal indictment on twenty-four counts of distributing obscene materials in 1956. By this time he had begun circulation of a hardcover periodical, *American Aphrodite*. The publication included illustrated excerpts from erotic classics (some of which Roth had previously published) and modern stories and poems, by skilled writers, about sexual desire. Some were considered obscene, as were a book about lesbianism (*The Scorpion*) and books of "NUS" photographic studies of nudes.

Roth brought experts to testify at the hearing, but they were ignored. Why did he bother? One answer is the one he had often given before: he was right. Another is that bureaucrats do sometimes respond to shrill opponents like Roth in order to prevent their complaints from embarrassing the institutions in which the bureaucrats work. Wonder of wonders—just once, for about fifteen minutes—Roth may have brought Dame Post Office around to his perspective. In 1949 a postal solicitor informed him that, after a "Hearing before a Trial Examiner on May 17, 1949," a "case pending here" against his Book Bargain Counter had been dismissed. The books were Sadlier's *Forlorn Sunset* (advertised as "a city of sin in all its depravity"), Morton's *Yankee Trader* ("literally sizzles with the flesh of men and women burning shamefully under the cruel sensual examining fingers"), and Collins's *The Doctor Looks at Love and*

Life).[73] "Upon consideration of the entire record in this matter, it has been decided that the evidence is insufficient to warrant the issuance of a fraud order."

There was another signal victory for Roth two years later, one that encouraged him to continue publishing controversial books.[74] In March 1951 the U.S. District Court acquitted Roth of a charge of mailing a copy of the "obscene" book *Beautiful Sinners of New York*.[75] Roth brought expert witnesses, the writer John Cournos, and two psychiatrists to testify regarding the minimal effect of this book on the libido or moral scruples of any citizen who had read the current best-sellers *From Here to Eternity* and *Washington Confidential* or the pages of the *New York Daily News* ("CMAM," 390–91). The judge was the highly respected Edward Weinfeld, who was to serve with distinction for thirty more years and gain a legendary reputation for "never ducking the tough ones."[76]

Forlorn Sunset; Nightmare Alley

To return to the 1949 victory regarding Sadlier's novel, on the flaps of the dust jacket Roth explained that the original publisher's edition had not been selling well, because distributors and readers shied away from the gritty subject of a school where little girls were taught to be prostitutes. The book would have "disappeared from the book-shelves of this generation if our [the Boar's Head Press's] editor [Roth], who helped establish the reputations of most of our more daring classics, did not point out its merits to us [i.e., the imprint's owner, Roth]." If the reader turns to the back flap, he or she finds that Boar's Head Books fought the postal fraud ruling, which was based on the fact that *Forlorn Sunset* had been salaciously touted as "lewd, lascivious, obscene, and indecent. Out of this hearing came a complete vindication of our position." What had raised the hair on Dame Post Office's pate was the dust-jacket blurbs about the corruption of little girls "for the trade." The front cover of the jacket depicts an Edwardian man in top hat over which is superimposed the horrified face of a girl in pigtails. It is an example of Roth's resourcefulness at both triumphing over the postal inspectors and getting a good sale for "our" book in a way that was indeed salacious. But he eventually paid the piper for his boldness with a return ticket to Lewisburg.

Roth's defense of *Nightmare Alley*, which he distributed in 1949, was as apposite as his affidavit in *Roth v. Goldman* the previous year. The book was a classic noir crime novel published by Rhinehart in 1946 (made into a fine film the next year). It concerns the inevitable downfall and moral degradation of a sideshow "Geek" (the most degraded of the carny performers, who bites the heads off chickens to titillate the spectators). His schemes, which include encouraging a man to drink himself to death and a lucrative clairvoyance racket, lead him back to the degraded carny stage where he started. What could be melodrama is given depth by the author's refusal to make any contrasts between good and evil, for only the greater subtlety and social status of the former Geek's female nemesis cause his ambitions and identity to implode. Roth's own defense of the book at the postal hearing shows his best critical acumen: "*Nightmare Alley* is a natural outgrowth of our society. If it seems to a limited vision to be spittle, believe me it is spittle important for the healing of wounds which no other herb or drug will heal."[77] Reputable publishers such as Sun Dial, Triangle, and Signet/New American Library, as well as Heinemann in England, issued the book in hardback, movie tie-in, and paperback editions before Roth bought remaindered copies from Rhinehart. Why, he asked in his brief to the postal trial examiner, was no action taken against any of these firms but only against Roth, after he had been selling the book for only six weeks? While the previous publishers had not primarily used mail order, certainly that was for them a possible, if minor, method of distribution. The paperback must have appeared on newsstand display. Is this "the equality of all individuals before the law"?[78]

Many companies protested the Post Office's "unmailable" decisions, and many heads of such companies attended the postal hearings in Washington. But Roth may have been the only victim of the "fraudulent and unmailable" labeling to point out that the consequences of a fraud order did not end with the loss of revenue from one or more books. After the fraud order had been issued for *Bumarap*, he wrote a fifteen-hundred-word memorandum explaining that several of his banks had told them they would close his account, naming the institutions.

> As of this moment, I have no means of banking the money which my customers send me for books. What is happening here? Is it possible for the Post Office Department to put a man out of business by sending its agents to his bank every time he opens a new account [i.e., a new business name, the mail from the previous one having been blocked] and suggests to him [*sic*; the context suggests the bank president] that it was not a good idea to get this account?[79]

If what Roth refers to were standard procedure for the Post Office, there would have been more complaints about it than his. Even so, the possibility of this kind of treatment was shared by many capitalists in the underground economy. In their cases, as in Roth's, it was the man, not the books he published or other services he provided, who was at issue. Roth was appealing to a large audience with a "low" form of enticement, doing so in direct, monosyllabic language, the suggestiveness of which was as clear as the nose on any reader's face. His mail-order books had garish covers and illustrations often as suggestive as their titles and subtitles. His income came from people who, although they knew what they wanted, had disreputable tastes. That politicians, physicians, and captains of industry shared them, as any erotica dealer could testify, was immaterial to the legal argument, especially because it weakened it. But postal inspectors must have known, for erotica dealers would be glad to document it from their mailing lists, that professional people bought erotic materials just as office workers and manual laborers did. It's true that Sam Roth was fraudulent in his prurient advertising, but no more so than movie posters and coming attractions. Roth's cultural capital was the wrong sort.

A final example is the Post Office's response to his small-format (8" high × 5" wide), slick-paper newsstand magazine, *Good Times.* The objection was to notices in several issues for books the titles of which, as well as images used in the advertisements, suggested that flagellation was a theme. The appeal to alternative sexualities was clear; it was deceptively used as a selling point. There was very little about "perversions" in the texts. Hal Zucker, editor of *Good Times,* testified that the magazine contained stories by reputable writers (Roskolenko, James Wycoff, G. S. Viereck) and that he had adopted his *Tattooed Women and Their Mates* from his Brooklyn College thesis. But the hearing examiner would not accept any analysis about obscenity from the editor because *Good Times* was not intended for a specialized or academic audience but for "general distribution, and advertisement was made for these books." He was right. But his implication was that for this readership, literary merit is not relevant, because the purchasers cannot be trusted to distinguish good literature from smut.[80] For alternate sexual expression, one needed to prove his or her scientific credentials. That, apparently, revealed the cleanliness of one's imagination from prurience.

In a 1954 response to a hearing designating *Good Times* as "unlawful," Roth submitted a list of subscribers with professional credentials: physicians (287), lawyers (191), priests (46), rabbis (28), ministers (32), and executives (321). The figures submitted, he said, amounted to 40 percent of the whole. He wanted his lawyer, Nicholas Atlas, to stress the fact that various classes and professions read *Good Times* and that the Post Office had no right to decide on their morals. Atlas made that point, and then turned to *Walker v. Popenoe*. The basic right of due process was involved. But, of course, the argument was made in an *ex parte* postal hearing, where it could be ignored.[81]

Putting an exclamation point to the publisher's fifteen-year battle with Dame Post Office, the *Good Times* hearing was April 19, 1956, four months after Roth's federal conviction for distributing obscenity through the mails. That conviction, and a five-year penitentiary sentence, was based on postal inspectors' test letters (determining that the publisher intended to distribute questionable material) and a conspiracy charge for actions during the years 1953–55. It led to his appeal in the landmark *Roth v. United States* in 1957. The spring of 1956 must have been a time of acute pressure for him. But he still pursued the *Good Times* appeal. He never gave in. In the 1957 appeal case, he was just a few years ahead of his time. Those few years, and of course Roth's previous career, meant a second federal conviction. In 1959, Barney Rosset won his federal case, clearing his edition of *Lady Chatterley's Lover* for distribution by mail as a book club selection. Rosset had the right sort of capital, both financial and cultural—as well as, like Roth, fire in the belly, astute appreciation of modernist art and writing, and the bravery to defy governmental and legal authority.

Self-Advertisement:
"A Perversity in the Mind of Sam Roth"?

Roth's friend, the journalist William Ryan, records this waspish comment by Harry Roskolenko. The poet, journalist, and memoirist told Ryan that he had refused to ghostwrite books attributed to Kiki (*The Education of a French Model*, 1954) and Maxwell Bodenheim (*My Life and Loves in Greenwich Village*, 1954) because both were pseudo-memoirs in which Roth ordered the "editor" (i.e., ghostwriter) to put Samuel Roth into the accounts. Roskolenko deplored Roth's "tendency to do something better than the original. Phony things up. It was a perverse kind of literary imagination. . . . He would actually *fuck-it-up!* Distort it so it would become a perversion of everything." Harry concluded, "It's going to be an important element in getting a moral picture of the mind of Sam Roth—a perversity in the mind of Sam Roth."[82]

Roskolenko saw things as they were. He also lived in two worlds: creating imaginative work and providing for his everyday needs by writing to order. He confessed, "under five pseudonyms, I wrote a variety of [borderline] novels [in the 1950s] for various publishers." He stated the number to be fifteen. Under Harry's given name appeared poems, memoirs, travel books, and novels (some with a Trotskyite perspective)[83] justifiably praised in high-profile and literary media. The erotica sapped energy he needed for his poetry, but he realized "about a thousand dollars per contribution, including small royalties."[84] It's doubtful that he got that much from Roth for his book *The Rape of the Heart* (1953), a novel about an American and his Japanese mistress trying to find their places in a world of alien cultural values.

But he could not be a party to the editorial "fucking up" of two books in the way Roth wanted it done, which had nothing to do with practicality and everything to do with the mind of Sam Roth. It had begun soon after the Faro bankruptcy, when "Norman Lockridge" inserted that "Imaginary Conversation" into his reprint of Havelock Ellis's *Kanga Creek*. That kind of "perversity" came about because Roth seemed to have extended his sense of mission to his business acumen as a sex-and-sensation mail-order book distributor. Perhaps he thought the former would sanitize, or justify, the chutzpah required for the latter.

Allowing for the possible element of satire in Roth's self-referential encomiums, we should remember that chutzpah suggests a trait one can either deplore or admire, and possibly both. In penning (or requiring ghostwriters to cook up) most of these "perversities," he had a lot of fun. There are elements of both cynicism and bemusement in observing the world from a disadvantaged position and without the absolutes a culture instills in native citizens. In a person of incisive intelligence like Roth, the chutzpah involved in self-advertisement would produce not only repressed self-hatred but also an ability to let one's guard down and laugh. It's a trait more readily found in a mocki-grisball than in the composer of an International Protest, an anti-vice crusader, or a postal inspector who must declare mail-order sales either fraudulent or obscene.

The "Maxwell Bodenheim" *My Life and Loves* contains a chapter titled "Public Bohemian No. 1." After reading this chapter, George Sylvester Viereck wrote the bohemian with the walking cane and Yiddish accent that "your character is so complex that it is impossible for anyone, even for you yourself to analyze it adequately."[85] In plainer language (which Viereck did not use, wanting Roth to hire him as a writer for *American Aphrodite*), too many roles: aggressive Lower East Side striver (Samuel Roth, Joseph Brownell), man of letters (Norman Lockridge, Francis Page, Roger St. Clair), and devout Jewish poet with a special destiny (Mishillim, David Zorn).[86] The columnist for the

New Yorker (Robert Coates) concluded more than twenty years before that Sam Roth did not know himself who he is. Viereck is closer to the truth.

"Bodenheim," or the book's ghostwriter, continues: the publisher "masterminded his own defense" of a book titled *Beautiful Sinners of New York* (the title suggests a Carrington offering, *Beautiful Flagellants of New York*), a fictitious listing of the habits and preferences of "models" with whom a certain "flesh peddler" had slept. Roth did so by reading passages to the jury, thus making so obvious the book's prosaic dullness in recording "erotic life" that the jury laughed the case out of court.[87] The rear panel of the dust jacket states that *Beautiful Sinners* was originally published privately at a high price (not true) and has been "reproduced without expurgation for the pleasure and relaxation of a troubled world." Apropos of Greenwich Village, "Bodenheim" concludes that Roth's real bohemianism lies in his commitment to artistic freedom. Further evidence of his service to letters are his Friday-night gatherings, which equal those of Charles and Mary Lamb in bringing together writers and artists (but only those who had published with Roth) in America's counterpart of Bloomsbury, Greenwich Village. Now that is laughable, even to Roth.

Exit "Bodenheim." Enter Roth's friend Dante Cacici with an afterword, "Introducing the Author of *Bumarap*." Cacici and Roth may have met at Roth's Houston Street school for teaching immigrants English in the early 1920s, or before that, at gatherings of leftists when Sam was rooming with Frank Tannenbaum. It's also possible that they met in prison, for Cacici was arrested on counterfeiting charges in 1930 (police stated he and several confederates in the elaborate scheme were "Communists").[88] Above the title of Cacici's essay is a vignette of Roth with jutting chin, determined, assured expression, vest, striped pants, and walking stick. Cacici says that in London, Roth interviewed the most beautiful women in the country; his trailblazing allowed Bennett Cerf to get *Ulysses* published in America; he succeeded where Mencken failed with Boston's Watch and Ward bluenoses (by getting *Two Worlds Monthly* accepted at newsstands there); he put columnist George Sokolski in his place when he dredged up "a new parcel of old lies" regarding Roth's alleged piracy of *Ulysses*. At present—and all of this is indisputable—Roth is thinking of writing stories for children, as he did in his youth, and continuing his favorite recreations of walking in the city and girl watching.[89]

In several other Roth imprints the publisher makes briefer, but equally dramatic, appearances. A chapter inserted in Roth's 1954 edition of Kiki's *Memoirs* describes his lunch with the famous "French model" at which he tells her to remind Ernest Hemingway (whose introduction to the Paris first edition he uses) that Roth owes him a punch in the nose.[90] Perhaps it was the popularity of this title—Roth said in 1956 it had sold half a million copies—that encouraged him to insert himself into the edition.[91] We also learn that the texts of *Ulysses* Roth published in *Two Worlds Monthly* were expurgated without Roth's knowledge by a perfidious editor—another crack at Waverley Root, then a Paris correspondent for the *Washington Post*.[92] This was yet another attempt to declare his innocence of, and victimization by, the 1926 Joyce piracies and their aftermath. In his earlier edition of Kiki's *Memoirs* he recounts his decision "to publish anything offered me that seems good or beautiful."[93] In an (imaginary?) conversation with George Moore, prefaced to Moore's translation of *Daphnis and Chloe* (1954), he uncovers Moore's impotence, but diplomatically allows him to save face. Moore's translation of Longus's poem, Roth conjectures, might have been the result of their talk.[94] In London, Norman Lockridge interrupts his story of *Lese Majesty: The Private Lives of the Duke and Duchess of Windsor* (1952) to relate how he picks up pretty nannies in order to learn their rich employers' secrets.[95] An epigraph appearing on an otherwise blank preliminary page in these revelations declares "*I DEDICATE THIS BOOK TO ALL THE SLANDERED ONES OF MY TIME AMONG WHOM I HAVE NOT BEEN INCONSPICUOUS*" (caps and italics in source).

What is especially remarkable is a small but bitter stream of contempt for his customers that surfaces in some of his advertisements. One example has been quoted: "the woman-juice the older, and some of our younger, of our readers like to lap up." A circular for *I Was Hitler's Doctor* headlines "Hitler flows into the madness of this age and the madness of this age flows into Hitler." The draft of this advertisement reads, "underneath it all isn't it the same bestial foe rising out of the moral slime of modernity?"[96] Many of Roth's advertisements for his Bridgehead and Boar's Head offerings adopt this vein of misanthropy. A book about a couple who board a "lesbian" will show people that "abnormal passions in any household can poison even the most pious family life." The headline of this flyer is "Our Sinful World." In another section he asks, "Why do so many men find sexual delight in acts of brutality toward women?" One of his trade names, Woman's Secret Press, takes the novel approach of having a woman as its director. Offering *Venus in Chains*, she says, "Taking place in the South, the action is reflective of one segment of our population—but I wouldn't be surprised if all men acted that way if we gave them the chance."

If Not Him, Who? Misanthropic Philosophy
in Mail-Order Circulars

Roth had been resorting to this corrosive assessment of modern man for at least twenty years. It is reflected in *Jews Must Live* (Americans will one day "roast Jews alive on Fifth Avenue") and in an advertisement for the Faro *Lady Chatterley* that refers to "the sweet decadence which is eating our society to the bone. . . . *Lady Chatterley's Lover* . . . is an exposition of this very world in a state of decay. Nowhere else is the debacle of the moral world pictured with such honesty and excitement." Sources of this gloominess were the strictness of his Hasidic upbringing, his observations of a world war, the homelessness, emotional trauma, and wage slavery on the Lower East Side, his own bankruptcy, and his prison sentences. The idiosyncratic nature of articulating such cynicism in the specific phrasing of mail-order advertisements increases because it had a literary source: Max Nordau's *Degeneration* (1895). Nordau, a physician and, after the Dreyfus affair, a Zionist, thought modern humanity was becoming increasingly self-obsessive, addicted to sexual titillation, reliant on escapist entertainments, and tolerant of homosexuality and sadomasochism. "Duty," "obedience," and "discipline" were giving way to what he diagnosed as an emotional overstimulation, a "neurasthenia," which he thought scientific study of mind and body (he was intrigued by Lombroso's work) could remedy before the degeneration had progressed to a pandemic. Nordau did not examine class injustice, the strains of poverty, wage slavery, exploitation of underclass children, or the lack of opportunities for females (leading to mass prostitution) as causes. He found illustration for his claims in modernist authors like Nietzsche, Zola, and Ibsen, who, he said, had betrayed their culture and national ideals, destroying altruism and spirituality. Nordau deplored what he characterized as the self-defeating misanthropy of a "cardboard" Übermensch, the obfuscating symbolism of expressionist poetry, the Marxists' self-hating admiration for the underclass, and the hedonism of effete aristocrats (Wilde) or bohemian decadents (Baudelaire).

Sam Roth's publishing career would seem to represent the essence of Nordau's diagnosis of modern obsessions as driving civilization into steep decline. Roth made money on books on transvestites, flagellants, padlocks and girdles of chastity, self-amusement, prostitutes, the legendarily insatiable Messalina, the friends of Lady Chatterley, the three trials of Oscar Wilde, and "the dark surmise" about Nietzsche and his sister. But Roth ignored the irony. He had himself diagnosed the illness of Europe in his prophetic poem with that title ("let me be your doctor"). In "Body" he probed the damage to the female psyche when a woman became the object of prurient spectatorship. When he wrote about that, he relied on his own work as erotica distributor but gave no indication that his own erotic photos of showgirls had caused him, his customers, or the actresses and dancers whose careers he publicized any degeneration.

In his visit to the True World he did examine his culpability, but he resumed his publishing after prison. That did not stop him from writing, apparently under the influence of Nordau, an (unpublished) novel, "Helen Thy Beauty," in which his protagonist, a Greenwich Village poet, rejects modernist skepticism, with its elitism, obscurantism, and sexual libertinism. His examples of these attitudes are Gertrude Stein and Henry Miller.[97] Yet Roth was at the time publishing books by and about Jean Genet, Kiki of Montparnasse, Aubrey Beardsley, "the erogenous zones" and "sexual extremities" of the contemporary world, and his own *Beautiful Sinners of New York.*

All of this Roth did while amalgamating Nordau's analysis of the modern world into his pandering circulars and his writings in a way that would have caused Nordau, if he could have come back from the True World with a copy of *Degeneration,* to brain him with it: "The Gutter in the Sky: and in the human mind"; "[D. H.] Lawrence sees the rottenness of our life, but loved it nevertheless." The books Roth was selling were Genet's *Our Lady of the Flowers* and Lawrence's *Lady Chatterley's Lover,* two books Nordau would have raged against.

In the 1950s, Roth would make the work of other writers serve his own purposes by integrating them into his own vision. He did so by revising, with more respect for the authors to be sure, works that could not be more diverse: by Heine, Dio Cassius, Antonin Artaud, and King David. These (unpublished) writings of his he called "redactions." The plasticity and reinvention of the self are part of the American dream. A consequence is the temporary stifling of the still, small voice of God (1 Kings 19:12) echoing not out of earthquake or fire but protesting within the soul. Considering the entire course of Sam Roth's zigzag career, he seems to have made a more pragmatically successful adjustment than fictional semi-delusional American dreamers who did hear the still, small voice: Abraham Cahan's David Levinsky, I. B. Singer's Herman Broder, Henry Roth's Ira Stigman, or Delmore Schwartz's Shenandoah Fish.

The writer Samuel Roth who wrote about a final reckoning in the True World, and later *My Friend Yeshea,* is a bizarre doppelgänger for a publisher who implies in his advertisements that he is appealing to people who not only want to read about predatory sensual desires but would participate if given the chance. That Roth was actually pandering to attain solvency in his business is something he was unable to face. And yet (although it does not justify postal authorities' selective use of the term so as to exclude people with credentials such as college degrees and wealth), it is clearly true. The harshest example, one that would be most difficult to acknowledge, is an approach he took to purveying his daughter's engaging *Tina and Jimmy Learn How They Were Born,* a children's story attractively illustrated and printed, and explaining discreetly and in appropriate language for preteens the process of gestation and birthing. Adelaide published it under her "Marie Lorenz" pseudonym. "Sex Crimes against Children Usually Begin at Home," reads the hard-sell headline in one set of advertisements. What must his daughter have thought if she saw that circular—that she should have stood by her earlier promise to herself to make *My Uncle Benjamin* her last piece of work done to help her father? She might have sardonically asked herself, what price profits? Alternatively, she may have understood that sex crimes can certainly result from ignorance and fear of sexual desire. That, in fact, as several reviewers understood, would be the best reason for reading *Tina and Jimmy.*[98] As for Roth's advertising circulars, reading them can be a Kafkaesque experience, especially when one recalls that the writer of their disdainful judgments also told his customers their "morals were all right."

The specter of the writer who had abandoned his art for financial security haunted Roth. He had only to look in a mirror to see such a person. Instead he looked around him and identified such people as he judged inauthentic: Joyce, Pound, Lewisohn, Hemingway, Untermeyer. In an afterword to the Bodenheim book he mentions a "Poet-turned-Businessman . . . who had grown a little fat in his comparative prosperity" and who criticized Bodenheim for selling his poems to indiscriminate passersby on the streets of Greenwich Village. The poet in question was Louis Grudin, and the incident Roth accounts is garbled. In fact, Grudin, an accomplished poet, artist, writer on aesthetics, and longtime friend of Bodenheim, had another reason for criticizing the latter. He did so because Max in 1954 had gotten involved with Roth. Bodenheim explained to Grudin that he could not deliver a chapter a week of his autobiography to Roth, and he wanted returned what he had already given the publisher—which does not mean Roth had refused to do so, or had stopped paying Bodenheim, albeit not enough to relieve his derelict condition. Grudin had himself worked for a time, when he was a struggling young writer, with Roth in the Poetry Book Shop. He was probably grateful, since it paid some, however small, salary. But he was glad when Max "liberated" him from Eighth

Street, and he regretted that Bodenheim had accepted the arrangement with the publisher.[99] Who, really, was the poet who had become, as the years rolled by, a hardheaded businessman? Sam Roth. But he could recognize the behavior implied in such a change only in a person of whom he was jealous, a person with a solid and long-standing literary reputation, who was well liked, never fat, and never a businessman.[100]

CHAPTER 8

1949–1952

Times Square, Peggy Roth, Southern Gothic, Céline, and Nietzsche

In the 1950s, one of the features of Times Square was the "record-and-book-shops that offer titillation first and culture second" that film critic Judith Crist described.[1] "Tourist bookstores" was the epithet newspapers often used. The first of these, Louis Finkelstein's Times Square Book Bazaar, was founded in 1940, at about the same time Sam Roth had begun his mail-order operations.[2] Finkelstein was the advance guard. After the war began, servicemen headed for Forty-second Street as they did earlier to the girlie shows, hookers, gambling venues, and porno distributors at the honky-tonk circus sideshows back home.

Roth's Model: The "Tourist Bookstores" on the "Main Stem"

Roth was not part of the network of backdate magazine, remainder, and erotica dealers of the tourist bookstore kind, which were found in the mass-entertainment areas of major cities. But there were congruencies in materials, personnel, and prospective customers. Harry Roskolenko, Clement Wood, and David George Plotkin wrote tourist bookstore erotica. Roth used a chief jobber for tourist stores, G.I. Distributors, for *Good Times*.[3] More important than those facts, however, is the similarity in subject matter and literary tastes between Roth's readers and those of Times Square's bookstore and newsstand browsers. Roth's customers were people from small towns or rural areas across the eastern United States, as the postal inspectors well knew. Their "test letters" to obtain circulars and books as evidence for the 1956 federal indictment were mailed from Parma, Canfield, and Alliance, Ohio; Dearborn, Michigan; Cordell, Georgia; Old Greenwich, Connecticut; Aiken, South Carolina; and Rochester, New York.[4] If people could browse the shelves of tourist bookstores for images and texts (and novelties such as photo sets, sex toys, and erotic playing cards), Roth's mail-order catalogues allowed his customers to do the same. Rubber blow-up dolls—a "honey for your bedside"—anyone?

Tourist stores carried materials about homosexuality, sadomasochism, flagellation, and other sexual alternatives. Irving Klaw, on Fourteenth Street near Third Avenue, learned about niche audiences in the earlier 1940s, and his photo booklets on bondage, flagellation, wrestling girls, high heels, and other fetish clothing were also available in tourist bookstores as well as in his mail-order catalogues. Robert Harrison enhanced the interest of his girlie magazines in the later 1940s with fetish images. When mass-market paper-back publishers commissioned general-interest genre fiction not originally printed in hardback form in the late 1940s, their "paperback originals" with lesbianism and lesbian protagonists found an enthusiastic audience.[5] Sex pulp hardbacks also published such fiction. Samuel Roth knew that men living far from downtown mass-entertainment districts had curiosities just as strong as those of urbanites.

Roth as Purveyor of Alternative Sexualities

Roth knew that innovative magazines of general appeal, such as *Confidential* and *Playboy* in the early and mid-1950s, spawned many imitators, including Roth's own short-lived *The Earth* (modeled on Harrison's *Confidential* and Lyle Stuart's *Exposé*) and *Good Times:* sexy cartoons, bare-breasted pinups including a centerfold, issues devoted to high life in various cities (as well as in outer space), short stories, and celebrity reportage.[6] He was also aware that a smart publisher always had another title in reserve if one was banned by a municipality or by the Post Office.[7] The first magazine, or paperback book, purchase was impulse-motivated; when the subject was prurient curiosity regarding sex, private lives of celebrity, or violence, this was especially true. Subsequent purchases occurred because the customer wanted similar mate-rial. The niche market for gay, flagellation, and fetish materials was more re-sponsive to this strategy than a more diffuse one.[8] Roth had sensed the buying potential of gays and transvestites when he published *A Scarlet Pansy,* which he republished in shortened form after his 1940 return from Lewisburg. His ads in the girlie magazines allowed him to add some elements of the market for sexually alternative works to his mailing lists.

Samuel Roth, Infamous Modernist

To establish his own niche market readership for borderline erotic materials in the early 1950s, Roth published his mail-order catalogues listing the novels *Finistere* ("homosexuality rampant") and *Strange Brother,* Gide's *The Secret Drama of My Life,* and Proust's *Cities of the Plain* ("frank study of homosexual men and women in their daily lives"). In the circulars, hermaphroditism, sadomasochism, bondage, and female domination are all represented, both in text and illustrations. Flagellation was another topic given special emphasis. He advertised remaindered copies of *Justine* with a drawing of a naked girl lying on her stomach with her face in her hands. The caption asked, "Would you beat, whip, kick, or in any other vile and violent ways molest this beautiful and helpless girl?" An image in one circular, seemingly unrelated to the books advertised, is of a woman flailing two crawling men with a whip; she has a foot on each man's back.

By far the most remarkable aspect of the Roth advertisements is the spotlight they occasionally throw, in pictures and text, on pedophilia. Such items include *American Aphrodite*'s stories and illustrations. In a draft for an advertisement for the magazine, he wrote that he would in 1952 publish "a dozen stories of attacks on children, including Dostoyevsky's delineation of the rape of a little girl."[9] In Morton's *Yankee Trader,* customers are told that they can read of women and children "ravaged to the tenderest [*sic*]"; in Dale's *You Scratch My Back,* the appeal is that women and children are victims of corrupt school officials. Even Lawrence's *Sons and Lovers* is touted as "danger in a mother's caress." *Forlorn Sunset* and Windham's *The Dog Star* are headlined as "The Love-Affairs between Children and Adolescents." As for Radiguet's *Devil in the Flesh*: "Don't miss this, if you've ever desired someone younger than yourself."

Not only some of the advertisements for the Bridgehead or Boar's Head books but also the works themselves featured information, or stories, about sexual deviation or erotic violence. As J. B. Rund, publisher and scholar of erotic materials and their distribution, points out, Roth would never have rivaled the explicitness of under-the-counter publications dedicated to this subject that could be had on Forty-second Street. "Whatever he was peddling as S/M certainly would have delivered less than it promised."[10] Mr. Rund, who knew Roth, adds, "That was his nature." Roth deserved that comment. His awareness of the tolerances of the audience and of the postal system is another kind of explanation. His prices were higher, as well. The artwork in *Beautiful Sinners* had appeared in the stylish German art nouveau magazine *Jugend* ("CMAM," 387). These include a sketch of a prisoner in a dungeon whose buttocks bear scars from being sadistically whipped. The dust jacket of Jamison's

Figure 21. Roth circular for books concerning prostitution and pedophilia, c. 1950. By permission of Kinsey Institute for Research in Sex, Gender, and Reproduction (Vertical File, Erotica Producers, 20th Century, Samuel Roth).

Venus in Chains (1953, rpt. 1964) features one of Mahlon Blaine's many erotic illustrations; work by this popular draftsman was familiar from having appeared in popular in books and magazines. For *Venus*, Blaine drew a naked woman with wrists chained, standing next to a demon who is holding the chains as if they were reins.[11]

Peggy Roth

Roth's publications were by no means limited to erotic hackwork acceptable only because inoffensive to "the mores of the present day." He was able to find excellent editorial assistants and ghostwriters who could recognize talent. He did not have far to seek for one of his best. It was his daughter-in-law, Peggy Roth. As Margaret Gruen, she was a novelist (the well-received story of a theatrical family, *Moonset*, 1943) and Hollywood scriptwriter, whose credits include a leading story credit for *Roadhouse* (1948), a highly respected noir starring

Ida Lupino. Mrs. Gruen was one of the victims of the House Un-American Activities Committee (HUAC) in 1951, having been put on a blacklist because she was present at meetings of a Communist Party organization, the American Peace Mobilization, and its subsidiary, the Motion Picture Democratic Committee. HUAC thought interest in these groups to be tantamount to advocating violent overthrow of the government. That was all it took to ruin a person. Upon Peggy's death in 1973, Dalton Trumbo, one of the Hollywood Ten who spent a year in federal prison for refusing to cooperate with HUAC, wrote a condolence letter in which he recalled her sympathy with his cause while they were both members of the Writer's Guild in 1949. "She could have saved herself from the social, economic, and political consequences of taking sides. . . . But she didn't do it, then or ever. It seemed she was incapable of abandoning herself."[12] Her informer was a fellow member of the Writer's Guild.[13]

It would have been impossible for Peggy to stay in Los Angeles without seeing former co-workers who were afraid to speak with her. Adelaide writes that her brother, Richard, had met Peggy in California, where Richard had gone after his discharge in 1946. The GI Bill gave him the chance to enter art school. While working for MGM he met Peggy, in 1948, on a picket line.[14] After Peggy divorced her first husband, she and Richard arrived in New York in 1951, on money sent by the bridegroom's parents, and married.[15] She worked for Roth's Seven Sirens Press, although she most likely did not appreciate the low wages he habitually paid. She was on staff when Roth started his *American Aphrodite* hardcover literary magazine and the newsstand publication *Good Times*.[16] Working with writers such as Harry Roskolenko, George Sylvester Viereck, and Dorothy Canfield Fisher (with whom Roth arranged to publish a story in an early number of the *Aphrodite*) was obviously rewarding.

However, tired of Sam's "caprices and obfuscations," as Adelaide put it, Peggy moved on in the mid-1950s to become, at the time of her death, an editor in chief at Dell Publishing, working with paperback acquisitions, rights, and permissions. She told colleagues that everything she knew about publishing, she learned from Sam Roth.[17] At her death in 1973, a memorial service at Lincoln Center's library included the editorial director of Dell, vice-presidents of Putnam's, and David McKay.[18] In addition to Trumbo's letter of consolation, novelist Joseph Heller's was read; the latter owed the publication of *Catch-22* to Peggy's defense of the manuscript. Richard was inconsolable for a long time.[19]

Roth, despite his professed hatred of Communists, must have sympathized with Peggy's blacklisting due to the International Protest. He could not have helped being aware of the contempt engendered by having been named an enemy of American values. He was himself "King of the Pornography Racket," "one of the biggest and most notorious pornographers."[20] Winchell wrote that he was "an ex-convict publisher who publishes trash," adding, "His son and daughter-in-law (Richard and Peggy G. Roth) have red front affiliations."[21] There is an interesting congruence in tone and attitude between the files the FBI compiled in the early 1950s on both the HUAC findings and on Samuel Roth. Both sets of documents contain newspaper articles and letters from concerned citizens that denigrate, respectively, Communists and pornographers. The former set notes HUAC's approval of Director Hoover's statement that Communists "espouse a cause that is alien to the religion of Christ and Judaism."[22] The FBI's Roth files detail the publisher's criticisms of McCarthy's and Kefauver's beliefs that Communists are attempting to increase juvenile delinquency by distributing pornography.[23] The bureau's concern about that issue goes back at least as far as 1944, when it cooperated with Detroit police in declaring Lillian Smith's delineation of mob lynching of blacks, *Strange Fruit*, obscene. The real fear was that the novel would stir up racial tensions, due to numbers of young African Americans (somehow) getting copies of the hardback best-seller. Most of the bureau's information justifying surveillance of supposed disloyalty is based on impressions about religious beliefs, good taste, proper deference for authority, and racial fears rather than actual cases of violations of law. But the director had in mind, as previously mentioned in connection with his own crime lab, the expansion of his power as head of a well-funded national law enforcement bureaucracy.[24]

Southern Gothic at the Boar's Head

Peggy Roth had the ability to work sympathetically with writers, encouraging them to develop in the direction that would display their talents as well as make them most marketable. Her correspondence with "Perry Dale" (Dale Sawyer) resulted in a fast-moving novel (*You Scratch My Back*, 1952) about an exploitation of a rural Oklahoma town's schools by an evil duo of redneck and college grad. Peggy wrote the author, "If you will observe closely the editing of *Scratch* you will see that my main effort was to preserve the strength and originality of the work and to cut down on the conventional love-story plot. Your strength as a writer lies in your access to extraordinary material and a willingness to report what you see." She encouraged Sawyer to remember his value as a "regional" writer and quoted Roth's instructions to her: "Tell Sawyer that his writing is like a documentary motion picture as compared to a typical Hollywood product."[25]

There is no regional dialect in *You Scratch My Back*. That would make quick reading difficult for Roth's customers. However, the early 1940s setting of Clear Creek, with its "small, dirty, ramshackle, muddy Main Street," is as authentically drawn as the characters and plot are lurid. James Smith is accepted by the community because he is a successful girls basketball coach and because his cohort, Jessie Arnold, and his free-wheeling, free-loving, pedophiliac three-hundred-pound wife, Ruby, have friends in the board of education and the county seat. James's wife, Mildred, rather improbably trusting of her husband despite his viciousness, realizes early that the inbred meekness of the Clear Creek residents makes it impossible to fight her husband's corruption and at the same time protect her two children. The climax features Mildred's kidnapping and torture by Jessie, Ruby, and James and her rescue, after which a mob of citizens, emitting "a deep rasping snarl" that drowns the search dog's baying, pummels the three villains into pulpy messes. "They were afraid to look [at the bodies] until their blood lust had died down and they became human beings again." Sawyer's direct, monosyllabic language restrains the sadism, giving it the flavor of documentary realism. Sam expertly highlighted the sexual violence in his circulars.

Roth's Boar's Head offerings *Scratch* and *Venus in Chains* (1953) had southern Gothic settings similar to those of Erskine Caldwell (the first issue of *American Aphrodite* was dedicated to him), Tennessee Williams, and Flannery O'Connor. The jewel in this crown was William Faulkner's *Sanctuary* (1931). Written to sell by sensationalizing entrapment in sexual sterility and vengeance, it was re-created as a pulp thriller, *No Orchids for Miss Blandish* (1939), by the prolific James Hadley Chase. Roth's regional novels were building on accounts of the degenerate underside of southern life, one of the genres with which the "paperback original" customers were enticed. The paperback firms were struggling among themselves for customers, and their reputations had been sullied as a result of congressional hearings concluding they were encouraging juvenile delinquency and sex crimes. Meanwhile, Roth's mail-order customers in the heartland could order his books without worrying about the local newsstand being forbidden by police and preachers from handling his competition, the "seamy" paperbacks.

You Scratch My Back is not hack work, thanks in good part to Peggy Roth's suggestions and encouragement. There's no evidence that she worked with H. F. Jamison's *Venus in Chains, Under the Lash of Devil's Law,* but it is a similar book. The regional details, narrative drive, and documentary force are writ large. In addition, the sadism and sexual brutality increase exponentially and include bondage, lesbianism, torture, and flagellation. The latter is implied in the title and suggested by the illustrations in the advertisements. The title was originally simply *Devil's Law*. There are many episodes featuring whipping. One describes the way the lash splits open scars and moles on a man's back, another the technique by which the skilled flagellator can produce rosettes instead of lines, and a third defines "Apache masochist" females: the breed can only be aroused by flagellation ("that's the high-sounding name they give it over in France").

The setting is a privatized prison on a plantation in the Deep South (Jamison's address was Beebe, Arkansas),[26] where people arrested by the police, mostly petty thieves and poverty-ridden African Americans, are forced into slave labor and live in filth, being given straw mattresses and scraps of food left uneaten by farm animals. Leetha Grey and her blind mother are picnicking near the Clay Beecham Plantation when an African American preacher comes tumbling out of the underbrush, his body covered with whip scars. He is captured, and with him the mother and daughter. Other abused prisoners include Fingers (he is missing a few), a noble, educated British thief who has endured the conditions and whippings in order to find extensive loot he has buried. The victims are kept in line by the chief guard and flagellator, Hunter, who masturbates when he sees a man flogged, and by an illiterate sex addict with rotting teeth named Tush. The star caricature is Leetha, a damsel in distress with a pure heart and a peaches-and-cream complexion. She endures being trussed and gagged, whipped, raped, forced into a chastity belt, and sold to a lecherous hanger-on at the plantation. In addition, she has been forced to smoke marijuana, although she does so only because if she did not, her mother would be shot—"weird, brain-demoralizing cigarette spawned in the lower pits of hell."

Jamison is a good writer. The dialogue epitomizes the tang of southern life as imagined by pulp writers: "I wants to size ye up frum tooth to hoof, lak I does whin buying a cow"; "Ye ain't nothing but the drizzle end uv a drunk, Kaiser Bill wet-dream." The descriptions themselves are as "documentary" and as plainly spoken as the publisher and editor would desire. They flash vivid melodramatic pictures before the readers' eyes, as in this description of a rapist's corpse: "his wide-open and distorted mouth, from which protruded those awful tushes [dog's teeth]—tushes covered with stagnated food in further-fermented, bacterial pus-pockets of diseased gums." There are echoes of *Sanctuary* and especially *Miss Blandish*: resourceful, kindly African Americans (in *Venus*, their "grapevine" brings the evil to light), the kidnapped, wealthy beauty, the syphilitic impotence of the subhuman rapist, the identification of orgasm with pain, flogging, torture, and the isolation of the terrified victim. But both books have very different endings than Jamison's. Faulkner's Temple

Samuel Roth, Infamous Modernist

Drake is paralyzed by her ambivalence about shame and desire, and at the end, recuperating in Paris with her mother, is as aloof from any kind of connection with other people as she was in Mississippi. Miss Blandish feels her brutal captor, although dead, still possesses her; she jumps out of a window. The sinister side of human behavior is by no means overcome at the climax of these stories.

But in *Venus in Chains,* all the perpetrators are dead. Fingers and Leetha have fallen in love in captivity, and they produce a child. Fingers, imprisoned for his theft, is put in a cell from which he can actually see the place where his loot is buried, until, due to a construction project, it plunges into a river. This latest irony drives him mad. Leetha, on the other hand, is lifted from (understandable) depression by a fellow sufferer on the plantation. So here, squareness and decency reign, which would warm the heart and stay the hand of Dame Post Office. I hesitate to give the child's name, for it does not seem to reflect well on the writer, his publishers or editors: "Fingertips." "You must shield forever those precious, priceless, baby fingertips." Sam? Peggy? H. F.? Might this whole southern-fried *megillah* be some sort of send-up? Is that the reason for the author's drooling, fanged perverts, sultry Creole, decadent mayor and plantation owner, sex-crazed, whip-wielding prison guards? Is that why Leetha rhymes with screecher? Hollywood agents, prick up your ears.

Bringing Good Books to the Heartland by Mail Order

In addition to reprints of erotica—by the Greek writers, de Maupassant, Catulle Mendes, Charles-Louis Phillipe—Roth published editions of other writers he admired, including John Masefield, Mario Uchard, and Giovanni Comisso, being careful in each case to get proper permission. He published some impressive nonfiction as well, including an edition of Viereck's prison memoir *Men into Beasts,* first issued as a Fawcett Gold Medal Paperback Original; his nephew Arthur Sainer's essays on the current theater, *The Sleepwalker and the Assassin;* and *Diaitis,* a book on cancer prevention through proper nutrition. His correspondence related to *The Peep-Hole of the Present* resulted in his publishing Professor Oliver Reiser's *The World Sensorium.* Reiser was a prolific author of studies in the relation of mind to body, and orgasmic as well as ratiocinative ways of knowing the world.[27] Denys Val Baker, whose novel *A Journey with Love* Roth published in 1955, brought many English and Welsh writers to public attention in the United States. "Norman Lockridge's" *The Sexual Conduct of Men and Women: A Minority Report* (on Kinsey's recent publications) was mostly by Gershon Legman and is one of the best examples of his inimical colloquial energy and challenging wit. Legman's translation, done with his first wife, Beverly Keith, of Alfred Jarry's *Ubi Roi* appeared in a handsome edition under the title *King Turd*. It contained all three plays. These books emphatically do give proletariat and lower-middle-class readers a chance to develop a consciousness about what their tolerances are for expressive writing.

There were plenty of exceptions. They would include his contribution to the sensational Mickey Jelke case. Roth at first tried to get Denys Val Baker to write on Pat Ward, whom Jelke pimped to Garment Center executives. When that did not happen, Roth issued Emmanuel Trujillo's *I Love You, I Hate You: My Six Weeks of Free Love with Pat Ward* (André Levy, 1955). It could have been an interesting report on the way New York business executives and Café Society entertained themselves after they left restaurants and nightclubs in the early 1950s.[28] It might also have replicated the kind of sympathy for the degraded woman that is a variation on one of Sam Roth's favorite themes. Sadly, the book is insubstantial.[29]

Roth's Financial Arrangements with Writers

The writers of Roth's mail-order texts were not well paid. Harry Roskolenko was critical of Roth's treatment of Maxwell Bodenheim. He was thinking of the pittance of an advance that made it necessary for the by then ill and alcoholic poet and his young wife to continue to live on the streets. He was also repulsed by Roth's use of Bodenheim's name as writer of *My Life and Loves in Greenwich Village*, which Roth published in 1954.[30] Some of the writing is by Bodenheim, but his contribution was thin.[31] The bulk of the book was probably ghostwritten by David George Plotkin and "puffed up" with section titles and vignettes. Roth's policy regarding author's salaries was to pay a prospective writer a small per diem until it was clear he or she could produce work he could use. Of the eighty-three people who subjected themselves to these conditions, Roth employed six on his staff. Bodenheim was the only one with previous writing success, but it was far from recent.[32] When Winchell was attempting to smear Roth due to his publishing *The Secret Life of Walter Winchell*, the columnist got a letter stating, "Ruth Bodenheim told me some time ago that Roth offered Max the magnificent sum of $25 for the reprint rights to Max's first novel. . . . Roth wants to cash in on the death of Max and Ruth, and he is one of the tightest men in the book publishing field." He goes on to say that the only money Roth paid Bodenheim was $25 a week for "re-write work," and perhaps an occasional advance of $5 or $10.[33] This contrasts to Adelaide Kugel's version. She recalls Bodenheim visiting the office regularly, writing only occasionally, but still being paid $10 per diem. A biographer of Bodenheim writes that Roth did provide the writer with an office and therefore "helped when few could or would."[34]

A charge even more contemptuous of Roth than Winchell's correspondent is that the "charlatan" Roth "plied" Bodenheim with whiskey so that he could get a number of the novelist and poet's recollections down on paper. Then the "sleazy" publisher ghostwrote and published the *Life and Love in Greenwich Village* farrago.[35] The author, Ross Wetzsteon, a long-term *Village Voice* reporter, does not specify his source for this information. Perhaps he came across the story in an interview. Who would think that if an alcoholic were "plied" with whiskey, the result would be a set of reminiscences, as opposed to incoherent babble and delirium? Not even the venomous short story by David George Plotkin based on Roth and his daughter, or Gershon Legman in his warts-and-all description of Roth, or the letter to Winchell about his treatment of Bodenheim, hints at this level of viciousness. What is interesting is the persistence of the image of Roth the unprincipled scoundrel and thief perpetrated by Joyce and his friends, Herbert Hoover's agents, the egregious *Jews Must Live,* the FBI, the Post Office, skilled federal prosecutors, Walter Winchell, and some Joyce scholars. Wetzsteon is careful to state that Roth published *Ulysses* without permission (he avoids saying it was pirated) and that he distributed erotica from his Lafayette Street office (although it was not a "fleabag"). Despite the accuracy, the depiction of Roth is a caricature of a sewer-dwelling petty criminal, just as President Hoover's operatives, the Post Office, and Winchell would have it. Stories need villains.

Roth in fact did egregiously exploit the lack of an international copyright agreement. Otherwise, he did not cheat authors, and paid promptly—but very little. His typical fee for a book-length work varied. He paid Jack Woodford, who had a large following, an advance of $500, not for his specialty, borderline sex fiction, but for a book titled *Drink and Stay Sober* (1954), with a 10 percent royalty on the first 5,000 copies retailed. A more common figure was a distinctly ungenerous $300, whether the writer was Jamison, Dale, Trujillo, or George Sylvester Viereck.[36]

Professor Milton Hindus Chooses Sam Roth

Milton Hindus chose Roth over an academic journal to publish his *The Crippled Giant* (1950), partly because he was impressed with Roth's reputation for controversial books. He also admired the publisher's ability to reach a general audience similar to the one for which Louis-Ferdinand Céline wrote. Céline's skill at describing underclass entertainment, factory labor, and lack of inhibitions in seizing the pleasures of sex, aggression, dance, and drink surpassed even those of one of his favorite writers, Paul Morand, whom Roth knew and published. Céline's sympathy, especially in *Journey to the End of the Night*, flowed toward proletarian workers and the kind of prostitutes who enjoyed sex. He thought no better of priests, politicians, generals, poets, and artists (art being the opposite of pure experience) than he did of gossip columnists, movie stars, circus impresarios, and popular singers. This leveling might have interested Roth, as might Céline's misanthropy, because the publisher's wide reading in contemporary literature included Antonin Artaud's work. Céline's worship of indeterminacy over hierarchical value judgments and of inspired eccentricity over gentlemanly decorum might have made Roth see in Céline a fellow iconoclast.[37] Any admiration would not have been mutual. Céline would have regarded Roth as a promoter, a wizard of hucksterism, and bourgeois in his need for material security despite his contempt for many judges, politicians, and writers. The French writer despised Jews precisely for these reasons, although by writing his Jew-hating pamphlets he may have been trying to bring receptive readers to understand the Hitlerian depths to which such reasoning leads, if in the service of political propaganda.

Roth encouraged Hindus to write something about Céline that fit his own publishing program. The two men had known and admired each other for several years, ever since Roth attended the young man's lectures at the New School. In 1947 the publisher suggested that Hindus observe what if anything was left of European culture and art after Hitler (he did not mention any advance).[38] In a remarkable but unpublished essay, "Samuel Roth," Hindus states he was impressed with *Jews Must Live* because of Roth's willingness to call down heaven itself on his Jewish enemies, and to take whatever retaliation he would suffer.[39] In the summer of 1948, Hindus undertook a difficult journey to Denmark, where Céline had taken himself, his wife, and his twenty-year-old cat to protect all three from death threats. There, he acquired a dog, then a porcupine. Céline was very interested in the porcupine, which rolled itself into a prickly ball to prevent injury. This reminded Céline of the people around him and their attitude toward him. "If I uncurl I'm lost."[40] Hindus was repulsed, of course, by Céline's anti-Semitism, and also by his host's slovenliness, his overuse of the words "merde," "shit," and "shitty" (40 percent of his vocabulary!), his saliva-punctuated outbursts, his constant degradation of any moral system, and insistence on pagan spontaneity. He preferred laughing children over the most intellectually accomplished adult, and dancing over writing.

In describing Céline as he did, Hindus reveals a lot about himself. His class sensibility and his desire for status as a public intellectual define him. He hates the dirty condition of Céline's rooms, changes his own hotel because the first was too cramped and dusty, yet is proud of Céline's classing them both as "hobos." He insists that although he is not like Céline, "a man of the people," they are both "mavericks." Shocked at recognizing that his visit had revealed contradictions within himself, he found the courage to write an excellent—and intensely felt—piece of critical and biographical analysis. After daily exposure to Céline, Hindus found himself no longer trusting any value judgments, including his own. He pointed out much irrationality on Céline's part, but his opinions are clearly subjective, colored by the crisis he is going through. It shook him physically as well as mentally. At one point he confesses, "he's made me as crazy as himself. My eye tics, the muscle in my right leg pulls and gives me pain." And again, "Celine and I can not basically affect each other. We can only witness each other's shame."[41] Céline had really gotten under his skin. Part of that shame may have been because he considered Céline, before he was exposed to the French writer's slovenly presence, the equal as a stylist to the supremely disciplined poet John Milton, whose epic combined ancient, biblical, and Renaissance culture to justify God's purposes, not sneer at any cosmic benevolence. Hindus wanted to meet an intellectual giant who had fought his own countrymen (as did Milton) and even the Nazis for the right to express his ideas. He had not expected a man who thought time-honored aesthetic ideals worth only being shat upon.

The Crippled Giant impressed Henry Miller, Alfred Kazin, and Dwight Macdonald for its quest to understand the way this "splinter" in Hindus's mind had unsettled the writer's sense of identity. Indeed, Hindus later conceded that he admired people who (like Roth in fact) "have had the courage I lacked to go to extreme length in exploring the possibilities of life."[42] Miller wrote Hindus that it "is a dreadful, horrible, painful thing to read. It must have taken courage to do it. Of course, I laughed outright a number of times." Hindus's favorite comment was from the writer (and friend of Delmore Schwartz) Maurice Zolatow: "it is a story of yourself—of the struggle within yourself—it is an intellectual biography in miniature." Mark Van Doren, Upton Sinclair, Sidney Hook, and Peter Viereck (George Sylvester's son) also were complimentary.[43]

The title refers to the one-eyed monster Polyphemous, from *The Odyssey*. This giant could see farther than mortals, but he had no perspective, being one-eyed, and thus lacked contact with the reality of the puny, crafty Odysseus and his men. They blinded Polyphemous and ran for their lives while "all he could do was rage in futility in his cage."[44] Céline, of course, did not physically attack Hindus, although when he read *The Crippled Giant* in manuscript he called him a traitorous ingrate, liar, and scoundrel and tried to prevent its publication. Hindus's book did injure Céline and his reputation, instead of giving him some renewed credibility. And Hindus did sail back to America with notes for an important book. He felt some guilt and fear at that, which is reflected in his choice of title. Polyphemous did almost hit Odysseus's ship with a rock, and Céline's words "came very near to my moral center."[45] That too says a good deal about the young author.

Hindus almost withdrew the work before publication. It was not Céline's imprecations but his avowal that he would bring suit for defamation of character that made Hindus sweat. He says that Roth "reluctantly agreed" with this decision and that he himself decided to continue.[46] Roth, however, has a different story, and if it is true, Hindus was lucky to have chosen a hard-nosed publisher instead of the editor of a scholarly journal. Roth told him:

> Obviously, despite the ocean of rage which separates you from him racially, you love Celine. After his own work, this love is today his most shining attribute. . . . But he fails to realize that your championing his work is the only defense-line behind which his own art can survive in a world of resentments of which he was one of the architects. . . . At the most crucial point in his life as an artist, Celine reverts to the behavior of the least heroic of his cowardly soldiers, and you, who can save him, go chicken-hearted. You should be ashamed, both of you. . . . Let us have no more of this nonsense, and on with the work.[47]

Unfortunately, the book sold poorly, at least partly because Roth did not advertise it as it deserved. In saying so to the author, his excuse was that problems with the Post Office had absorbed his attention, and probably strained his finances.[48]

A 1955 issue of *American Aphrodite*, coedited by Hal Zucker, was dedicated to Céline. In the lead editorial, Zucker explains why.[49] While Knut Hamsun's and Ezra Pound's support of fascism was ideological, Céline never tried to express a coherent position on that or any other political ideology. He was always falling into whirlpools along with the rest of the earth's inhabitants who could not make it to the lifeboats in time to avoid two world wars with a depression in between. An existential victim of a horrible century, Céline survives like a clown in a cartoon, "a writer writing the odyssey of humanity through the screen of schizophrenia." The image is especially appropriate in view of the allusion to Polyphemous in Hindus's title and the advertising accompanying the original edition of Céline's *Bagatelles pour un massacre*: "For a good laugh in the trenches."[50] There's a nagging admiration of one writer for another here that Hindus, with five years to ponder what he published about his experience in Denmark, would understand.

A Worm-Eaten Manuscript—Nietzsche's Last Work?—Is Redacted, and Shown to the World

In 1924, as Roth tells it, he acquired a manuscript the existence of which he had to take on the word of an impulsive, desperate man in return for Roth's part in a dangerous caper that allowed the man to recover his wife from her parents, who disapproved of the marriage. Roth received the manuscript three years after he had done the favor. He advertised it in his *Two Worlds* magazines in 1927 as "The Dark Surmise: Concerning Friedrich Nietzsche and His Sister," but his funds ran out before he could publish it. Then came the 1929 Sumner raid on his Fifth Avenue offices and storerooms, and the manuscript—he thought—disappeared somewhere among the materials the police removed. However, in the course of an inventory taken during the 1940s, Pauline found "brittle, vermin-eaten carbon copies of the translation and introduction."[51] The introduction is signed by the translator, Dr. Oscar Levy, who exclaims that he had thought all of Nietzsche's work had been accounted for when Roth sent him in 1924 a copy of this manuscript, supposedly written during the philosopher's stay in an asylum in Jena near Weimar following his nervous breakdown in Turin in 1889. "Imagine my astonishment," he says in his introduction.

Thirty years after Roth's London visit, the wormy manuscript in Nietzsche's handwriting became *My Sister and I* (Boar's Head, 1951). Going through fourteen impressions in the next two years (according to the publisher's reprint statement on the back of the title page), the book drew the ire of Thomas Mann, Nietzsche scholar Walter Kaufmann, and the reputed translator's sister. Whit Burnett (who published excerpts in an anthology of "great confessions")[52] and Wilhelm Reich admired the work. The latter thought Nietzsche spoke honestly therein and thus listed the book among his bibliographical sources in *The Murder of Christ*.[53] The editors of Amok Books published a 1990 "revised and updated" version, including Roth's "publisher's belated explanation," two of Kaufmann's four critical reviews, and Professor Walter Stewart's analysis of the controversy, which he has since expanded into *Nietzsche "My Sister and I": A Critical Study* (2007). An excellent afterword by Yeshayahu Yariv to the Hebrew edition appeared in 2006.[54]

The story of incest is at the heart of *My Sister and I*. No scholar supports this story. However melodramatic are the book's passages on incest, and however they can be deprecated as bearing "the leer of the sensualist," they can also be seen as consonant with the outsider Nietzsche's interest in the idea of incest as a mark of the Other, and possibly of his own experience with it. A fascinating allusion to Nietzsche's megalomania and its alliance with the incest motive is historian and psychiatrist Sander Gilman's "Heine, Nietzsche, and the Idea of the Jew."[55] Gilman does not discuss *My Sister and I*. He writes of the contemporary German belief among psychiatrists that the Jew is disposed to madness, because of inbreeding. At the time, movements of Jews from eastern Europe to the West were increasing. The identity of the degenerate Jewish "Other" was founded on the eastern Jew's observable odiousness to western Europeans and their suspicions of hidden malice as (supposed) carriers of disease and mental instability. Nietzsche himself has some of these traits: He was often ill, given to indisposition of the stomach and bowels (a German who did not enjoy beer) and to nervous instability. He was morose, reclusive, defensive, and preoccupied with sexual fantasies. He liked playing with words, twisting them into unconventional contexts. He was proud of his difference, conceiving of himself as the Other (even asserting he was descended from Polish nobility).

Gilman continues, "For not only was the model of 'degenerative' madness present within Nietzsche's fictive self . . . but the potential contextualization for this madness, the transgression against the incest taboo, was also present. (The implicit charge of incest stood at the center of the understanding of the pathology of the Jew)." Gilman also writes that the situation in which Fritz and Elizabeth Nietzsche found themselves after their father's death (he was five, she three), since it left the household without an adult male, was the kind that might produce sister-brother incest.[56]

Oscar Levy's daughter, Maude Levy Rosenthal, wrote the *Saturday Review* a letter spiked with indignation when the magazine published a review of *My Sister* in 1951. Her father, she assured the magazine's editor and readers, never wrote the introduction or translation, the style and inaccuracies in both of which were unlike him. Nor did he deliver the work to the publisher.[57] A broadside from a source as reliable as Oscar Levy's daughter might sink Roth's project, which he had carefully organized with mail-order advertisements in various periodicals with solid newsstand sales. He had received an advance proof of the Rosenthal letter from his advertising agency, and wrote Norman Cousins immediately, requesting either equal space in the issue in which Rosenthal's letter appeared or its removal.[58] He didn't get either. In subsequent weeks the cannonade continued. Dr. Alfred Werner called the book "definitely fiction" in *The Nation*, although his opening sentence, "perhaps the

Samuel Roth, Infamous Modernist

most sensational book of the winter season," should have helped sales.[59] In the *Aufblau,* "serving the German Jewish Market," Thomas Mann wrote a short commendation of a long article, published in two parts, by his friend Ludwig Marcuse, who had treated "the perpetration [of the "hoax"] in the only way it can be treated by literary men, with utter contempt." Professor Marcuse's essay continues Mann's tone of aristocratic contempt for a lowlife.[60] He questions why Roth would risk danger in 1921 for a manuscript he had not seen, and why he didn't identify the passages that needed reconstruction.

Roth's immediate response was typical of him. Mann and Marcuse had used the same language of class and professional elitism as Joyce's friends. They referred to the "previous career" of the "gentleman": "trashy," "pornographic," and "cagy." Returning the favor, Roth wrote insolently of Mann and Marcuse as weak, self-interested, and cowardly, or, in Werner's case, as acting like a cheap detective in trying to get the goods on him (Werner had contacted Roth when he was writing his review of the book for *Commentary*). Although Roth does well in answering the questions Marcuse posed in his piece and in detailing the good books he had published, he evades with invective the real issues of authenticity and narrative.

Roth's indignation, as always, was real enough. Unlike, however, in the case of his *Ulysses* publications, with *My Sister* a lot more potential sales were in the offing. He sensed that many of his own readers resent professors and famous novelists telling them what was not worth reading. Mann may have sensed this also. He seemed content to hand off the issue of *My Sister* to Werner and Marcuse. That way he did not have to risk both being locked in a skirmish with a disreputable individual or risking the contempt of general readers. Roth's sales may well have been helped by the articles and letters that followed in the middlebrow periodicals. That, after all, was the publisher's intention.

The definitive scholarly criticism of *My Sister and I* was, and for many still is, Princeton professor Walter Kaufmann's essays, especially those that appeared in *Aufblau* and *Partisan Review*.[61] One reason there were four was that Kaufmann, as the most recent Nietzsche authority, wanted to improve on points that Marcuse and Werner had made.[62] He points to the anachronisms, and the improbability of Levy as translator. He stresses the (to him) probable fact that the "American author" of both the introduction and text had referred to his own ideas in his *Nietzsche: Philosopher, Psychologist, Antichrist* (1950). He wrote to Roth (who responded with an extremely respectful letter of his own),[63] and discovered, he told his readers, all about the man whom Gorman said had the hide of a rhinoceros, who was subject of the unprecedented International Protest, who published the risible sequels to *Lady Chatterley's Lover,* who wrote *Jews Must Live,* and whom Kurt Kreuger contacted to publish the "filth which he uncovered" about Hitler. That, Kaufmann implied, was all *Partisan Review*'s readers needed to know.

Walter Stewart's recent *Critical Study* of *My Sister and I* examines in detail the truths and half-truths in Kaufmann's attack.[64] Stewart perhaps allows Roth too much credence regarding his story of the loss of the original manuscript (why did Roth not reproduce a page from the worm-eaten one that he used as copy text?). He asserts that academic hostility to *My Sister* rests partly on the fact that the narrator openly and dramatically discussed his syphilis. Academics feared the potential harm it would do to the philosopher's reputation. Stewart thinks Kaufmann is motivated by the same concern, but the latter, as Stewart acknowledges, does state, with documentation, that it is a "very probable" cause of Nietzsche's madness.[65] Also, Stewart questions Kaufmann's placing in a footnote the statement that in 1965 Plotkin confessed in his office at Princeton to writing the book "for a flat fee." This was in the 1968 "revised and enlarged" edition. Why did not Kaufmann reproduce Plotkin's signed confession, especially since he took Roth to task for not being able to document the original *My Sister* manuscript? It's a very valid point, but by 1968 the controversy, which was not directly related to Kaufmann's now-renowned biography, was almost twenty years old, and Plotkin had died.

Stewart's arguments are otherwise convincing. He shows that Kaufmann's statements regarding *My Sister*'s presumed ghostwriter's indebtedness to his *Nietzsche* are clearly overstated. Stewart documents very well a fair degree of carelessness on the professor's part regarding certain of Nietzsche's essays and letters and says that "both critics [in the reviews, not in Kaufmann's book] were wrong about Nietzsche's knowledge of Marxism." One of Stewart's best arguments concerns Kaufmann's assertion that the book was forged because in early impressions (corrected in later printings) the introduction stated Nietzsche had not read Schopenhauer when he wrote *The Birth of Tragedy*.[66] However, even without the later correction, there are so many references in the text itself to Schopenhauer's influence on Nietzsche that Kaufmann gives Roth the opening to say, in the latter's "Publisher's Belated Explanation" inserted after Levy's introduction (beginning with the 1953 impression), that Kaufmann's "deduction from this error is pedantic as well as impudent."

Why would such a brilliant scholar make that mistake? One answer is that he did not think a book Roth not only published but might have "forged" himself was worthy of careful reading. After all, the man had "almost always been ignored by scholars." Another factor is his proprietary interest in his own fine work, which had recently resulted in his exhaustive *Nietzsche: Philosopher,*

Psychologist, Antichrist. He would have been well advised, or concluded on his own, not to give Roth publicity by writing no less than four attacks on his Nietzsche "hoax." Kaufmann's attitude gave aid and comfort to the contrarian in Roth to do what he could not refrain from doing: take his own pedantry and insolence and present it with a sardonic bow to an established authority. Once again, as with the *Ulysses* hullabaloo, what Roth had done in some of his insolent defenses of his publications, his adversary, in this case Kaufmann, had also done. It was authority versus its relentless enemy, the grasping "vulgarian," in a struggle to a standstill that kept both parties' respect among people attracted to them, and their products, flourishing.

There may be a contrasting explanation for Kaufman's persistent attacks on the Nietzsche book. Roth, as we have mentioned, did indeed have a kind of status in the literary world at the time. In 1951 he was important because he had developed a following, not only by the mail-order circulars but by the advertisements he put in trade journals, magazines, and newspapers. If Kaufmann did know of Milton Hindus's publication with Roth, as he did know of Roth's *Ulysses* piracies, it might have convinced him that the publisher was capable of attracting many general readers interested in Nietzsche. *My Sister and I*'s sales proved him correct.[67] His daughter said that *My Sister and I* was so popular that whenever her father was short of funds, he printed more copies.[68]

Why, as his critics queried, would the publisher wait until 1951 to release *My Sister and I?* There were both business-related and literary reasons. Roth was expanding his list in the late 1940s and early 1950s, emboldened by his legal victories in 1949 and 1951 and his ad campaign in periodicals. Now it was time to enlighten Arthur Hays Sulzberger, publisher of the *Times.* Roth wrote him in 1953, complaining about the Paper of Record's refusal to print any of his advertisements. He pointed out that magazines such as the *Saturday Review, Harper's,* and *Atlantic Monthly* were happy to accept his "space advertising" for *My Sister and I. Esquire* also did so, and at least one other newsstand magazine. Through such middlebrow periodicals, "and many other media, I've sold more copies of *My Sister and I* than have been sold of the rest of the works of Nietzsche, since he has been first published in English at the turn of the century."[69] That puffery is impressive, regardless of the sensational and prurient advertising tactics.

Roth had prepared various notices touting the book for various magazine audiences. Some of these, for literary periodicals, avoided any mention of incest and quoted from favorable reviews from seven sources, including the *Saturday Review.*[70] A variation, perhaps for popular fiction magazines, is headlined "The boy who grew up in a house full of manless women." It stated that Nietzsche and his sister "grew to love each other physically as children." The copy was prepared with three thumbnail-sized images, any one of which could be inserted. One of these featured a naked mermaid, back, buttocks, and tail prominent, pressing herself against a copse of bushes and peering over the top. Roth also had illustrator Mahlon Blaine prepare a striking, cross-hatched drawing of Nietzsche writing at a desk while a woman peers intently over his shoulder. In the background are the mountains the philosopher loved, and a sphinx—Nietzsche's symbol of the joy and danger involved in saying "Yes to life," with all its sunlight and shadows. Below the desk, a snake winds around the torso of a figure seeking to disentangle himself from its length while its head approaches his. The snake head is similar in contours to the head of the woman. This drawing had been reproduced as a frame in which advertising copy could be inserted.[71] Both the peeping mermaid and the Lamia-like seductress would seem to be warnings against involving oneself with the forbidden. It's a powerful sales pitch. *Femmes fatales* are irresistible.

A biography of a writer Roth had always admired was a keystone to his building his case for legitimacy. Roth had read Nietzsche with care and insight. Like Schnitzler, Kafka, Werfel, Döblin, and Walter Benjamin, among others, Roth was one of the European Jewish intellectuals who identified with Nietzsche because they were outsiders both to the non-Jewish population of their countries and to their co-religionists. Nietzsche wrote of loneliness, and a way out of it, in a way that resonated.[72] It would have been an important step toward being taken seriously in 1951 if Roth could point to a respectful review from the Princeton scholar about his new addition to the Nietzsche canon. It would have been equally so to lunch and network with Sulzberger of the *Times,* or Cousins of the *Saturday Review,* as he suggested in his letter asking equal time in the issue carrying Oscar Levy's daughter's opinion of *My Sister.*

Neither Adelaide nor Richard believed the book was genuine. Richard was doing art work for the Seven Sirens Press at the time. He told his sister that he did not want his wife associated with the book.[73] Peggy had been unhappy at being involved in the swirl of angry denials in 1952 that *My Sister and I* was by Nietzsche. She had written a letter to the editor of the *Saturday Review,* obviously at Roth's prompting, identifying herself as one of his editors, and declaring her assurance that the work was genuine ("Nietzsche or nothing"). Richard and Peggy were aware that in the same year *My Sister* appeared, Roth published André Gide's confessional work *Et Nunc . . . Manet In Te,* which he titled *The Secret Drama of My Life.* Richard had contributed a signed frontispiece, depicting with understated somberness an old man writing his secret: inability to accept the intimacy of a loving wife. Roth issued the book despite

Figure 22. Proof for advertisement, *My Sister and I.* Note Nietzsche's Sphinx symbol, his beloved mountains, and the snake-like woman (his sister?) peering over the writer's shoulder. By permission of the Roth estate.

having had warning letters from the American copyright holder. Why did he do it? In 1952 he had to give a large sum to the latter in order to avoid a suit for copyright infringement. All "copies on hand" were to be destroyed.[74] To have published two original posthumous texts by famous writers in one year would have been quite an attention getter for Roth's "small publishing house."

His daughter, equally wary of her father's habits regarding the mysteries of sex (in the case of *The Secret Drama,* regarding Gide's homosexuality) and of his need for publicity (the book had an afterword about Roth's publishing enterprises), clearly did not believe in *My Sister* any more than did her brother and sister-in-law. She concluded mordantly that "a book that goes into fourteen printings cannot be all bad." How many readers did believe it to be the work of Nietzsche is an imponderable. But two recent writers, one an Israeli reviewer and the other a psychotherapist, do believe that it is genuine.[75]

The Argument for *My Sister and I* as Nietzsche's Final Publication

The psychotherapist reviewer, Heward Wilkerson, extols what he sees as an exemplary inmate asylum narrative, which demonstrates the thought process of a man in whom episodes of lucidity alternate with madness. He especially likes the open-minded humility of the philosopher who, on the brink of insanity and facing the loss of his power, can reassess himself so painfully.[76] Therefore, *My Sister* does parallel *Ecce Homo*, as Roth's "Belated Explanation" asserted. "Let us at least welcome *My Sister and I* into the post-modern, if not the classical, canon."[77] Yeshayahu Yariv begins his 2006 review by acknowledging many of the earlier criticisms. He considers the book to be a set of "unpublished notes," and he suggests "Last Pages" as an appropriate title. Perhaps his best passages are those that show how movingly the prose reflects a man who knows his present lucidity is coming only in flashes, bordered by insanity and despair. And not just any man, but a writer who, having declared that God is dead, fears he will be known only for that, and as being "the philosopher with a hammer," not for his brave self-awareness of the limitations of his insights, both in *Ecce Homo* and these notes jotted down in the asylum in Jena.

How could any but a great writer, Yariv asks, approach the phrasing in passages where Nietzsche contemplates the "frozen horror" of sleeping through a billion years of the sun rising against his beloved mountains, or where he "walks as a living corpse through a world without faith in life or in the future" and yet still gropes for the "intoxication of sensuous pleasures"? The "Last Pages" continues the pursuit of "rip[ping] away every mask." Nietzsche stages a high drama in which a physically and mentally sick man, once uniquely defiant of restraints upon human potential, is able to address his existential failure to experience freedom, and that failure's source in the most demeaning of personal, sexual experiences. Whether or not the "Last Pages" are "factual, accurate, or 'truthful,'" the writing, Yariv concludes, equals that of Nietzsche's "finest" work.

My Sister and I, as Yariv explained, contains powerfully written passages that may well surpass the talents of the editor or publisher. If it is not genuine, then Roth may have commissioned another writer to whose prose Plotkin and Roth might have added their own passages. This writer would have to have been as conversant with Nietzsche if not more so than Roth, but with greater talent at dialogue and dramatic description of human angst. Roth never wrote of a person who, like the speaker in *My Sister*, cannot conceive of himself as experiencing sexual arousal without thinking compulsively of his inhibitions, and of his intense and conflicted yearning. There are enough hints, in fact, of the neuroses haunting *My Sister and I* to make one think that it was not the philosopher describing them but rather a writer who had studied Lawrence's or Schnitzler's works, and Freud's as well. Nietzsche, despite his Zarathustra persona (another was that of a circus trickster), was supremely conscious of his fallibilities. Later in the book, surveying his emotional paralysis and his inability to keep his beloved Lou Salome's affection, "Nietzsche" declares, "Dionysos has been torn to pieces by the wild Maenads—the Lama [his sister], Mama, and Lou! Dionysos is bleeding to death. Help, Keepers, help!" (234). There is no such character in any of Roth's fiction or poems. Nor is there any in Plotkin's fiction.

One of the most puzzling statements in the Roth Archive is William Ryan's. This dedicated friend of Roth and his wife in their later years wrote Pauline soon after her husband's death that he had been speaking with Abraham Bronson Feldman, author of *The Unconscious in History* (1939). Feldman "explained to me what he believes to have been Sam's highly ethical purpose in ascribing *My Sister* to Nietzsche."[78] This seems to suggest that Roth did write, or partially write, *My Sister and I*, and that ascribing it to the philosopher was sure to bring him derision. But what should the publisher have done—issue it as fiction? If he did, the book would have been less likely to receive angry criticism and, as a consequence, pass unnoticed.

There are certainly parts of *My Sister and I* that, in style or topics of interest, bear the stamp of Roth. Nietzsche describes God visiting him at age twelve, and at two other times, and when God did "break in" on him, he appeared as "a glaring fusion of the portraits of Abraham, Moses, and the Young Jesus in our family Bible."[79] There would have been no image of Jesus in Yussef Leib's Bible, but Roth was only ten when he discovered Yeshea in the evangelical pamphlet he read on board ship. Roth, as his *Golden Treasury* and other works demonstrates, loved and wrote aphorisms; there are many in *My Sister and I*. His method stressed puns (sometimes sexual), ironic repetition, and contrast of the abstract and mundane. Whether or not the passages indicating Roth's hand attempt humor, "Nietzsche's" tone is often sardonic. An example is, "When I first came face to face with [Elizabeth's anti-Semitic husband] I discovered that, as with his likeness in the dust, the human worm is at his best when he wriggles."[80] Another example shows a robust vulgarity and a wincing pessimism that is more Roth than Nietzsche. In fact, it is a summary of Roth's public life: "If I have one talent it is to make people angry. I make a rainbow of

241

urine over the world, and in such matters, the world is never slow to retaliate" (122). At times, "Nietzsche's" word choice is one Roth favored in his own writing. Throughout his career he used "sweet" to refer to his sexual response to female beauty, as when he thinks of his first girlfriend, he "saw as well as felt the sweetening of my secret flesh." One of the drafts of his autobiography has the title "Chapter Two. The Sweet Pain" (masturbation). In *My Sister* the word is used when Nietzsche sees an attractive woman passing his hospital room. He states that when he could no longer follow her with his eyes, "I was outside the pale of sweetness" (p. 115). All his "tenderness" left him, perhaps for the last time.

My Sister and I's narrative voice seems at times consistent with the personality of the great philosopher, and at others to echo that of one or more writers whose purpose might be to suggest the source of responsibility for German anti-Semitism, or to explain to readers a horrific example of the sadomasochistic consequences of sibling incest. Therefore, there is no unified impression of the narrator's character. This deepens the mystery, making one wonder who indeed is telling the story. Three of Roth's obsessions were women, Jews, and destiny. It is unlikely that Nietzsche's "Last Pages," if they were his, would focus so closely, and repetitively, on these topics. *Ecce Homo* was less concerned with them, although those were public not private revelations about the man's life and works.

As the skeptics note, *My Sister* adds a Russian "Countess" (not, of course, Lou Salome) as a lover. Her desire for the philosopher when he was an adolescent is motivated, according to the narrator's heated account of her, by her need to humiliate "to the point of blotting out my manhood." He writes of an occasion when "to retrieve my human dignity I flogged her with the riding-crop which she kept in her boudoir along with her riding boots." The narrator speaks of approaching women with a whip lest they reverse the natural order and emasculate a man's body and soul. However, he writes like a decadent when he describes the Countess's sadomasochistic delight as her back arched cat-like against the whip, the glow of her naked body "like the moon-eyes of a night owl that is wrapped in an amber gauze, a yellow that has the hint of death in its dull effulgence." Such melodramatic passages are hardly Nietzsche's, unless emotional breakdown makes its victim imitate Huysmans. They do help explain the popularity of *My Sister and I*, especially with readers of the literary magazines in which Roth placed advertisements. The publisher needed to do a powerful job of salesmanship, and he certainly, and very effectively, did so.

The narrator's state of mind is a puzzle that calls for careful contemplation and empathy. Some passages suggest deep childhood traumas resulting in reticence regarding opening one's body to intercourse and resultant sadomasochistic fetish. If Marcuse and Kaufmann had noticed these, they might have thought of them as pornographic trash that proved their point. They did cite the descriptions of six-year old Elizabeth fondling her brother's genitals as deplorable. While this kind of writing cannot help but arouse prurient interest, that fact only reflects a cultural link between sex and furtive curiosity. When Whit Burnett included passages of *My Sister and I* in his paperback anthology, *The Scarlet Treasury of Great Confessions,* he included the passages cited above, since they were "self-revelations" such as those of writers like André Maurois, Havelock Ellis, George Sand, St. Augustine, and Oscar Wilde.

There are fine passages in which Nietzsche faces the repression and secrecy that he had allowed to seep into his own sexual relationships, poisoning the love he could have more openly expressed to Lou Salome and even Cosima Wagner, binding him to his sister and the mother whom he resented for depriving him of a substitute for his dead father. His direct addresses to both women, now lost to him forever, are enthusiastic and plaintive at the same time. His praises are not of Salome's body or of their sexual intimacies, except for a few passages that refer to "the naked ritual of her passionate body" and "the electric energy of her vibrant, eloquent flesh" (248, 249). Having seen her naked, he became, "in her high silken bed . . . merely a naughty child: Caesar with the soul of a diapered infant" (248). It's a brutal piece of self-analysis. That it comes on the cusp of his mental illness makes it even more remarkable. Unfortunately for the text's claim to authenticity, Nietzsche and Lou were not lovers. The passages can be accepted as autobiography only if Nietzsche is engaged in erotic fantasizing. Further, why would Nietzsche refer to Salome as "a Jewess" (206)? That was a rumor started by Elizabeth, who despised her, as Nietzsche knew.[81]

Nietzsche's writings, despite his defense of Jews from German zealots, often speak of the eastern Jews as degenerate.[82] The commendatory remarks on them in *My Sister* might reveal the influence of Roth. They imply defiance of Prussian anti-Semitism, and of the "big mouths" who wallow in it, such as Heinrich von Treitschke, who is mentioned several times, and of Elizabeth's ur-fascist husband. This Nietzsche describes himself as "a champion of massacred Jewry" (225). He predicts how far Bismarck's goose-stepping troops will take their resentment. In addition, the philosopher states the only real antecedents of himself to be Solomon, because of his will to power, and Samuel, whom God called three times in youth to his service. In addition to the passage about God's appearance to him as a child, in a kind of fusion of

Abraham, Moses, and Jesus, all Jews (184), the Nietzsche of *My Sister* contrasts the "weeping and pity of Calvary" with the "thunder of Sinai" and admires the "roll of Jehovah's thunder" (225–26).

Nietzsche, never more clearly than in his later writings, whether or not those include *My Sister and I*, knew what his destiny would be: he had looked into the void, it had stared back at him, he had reviewed his life, and he knew where he was going. With or without his chimera Zarathustra, the Überman, and the Lou in whom he believed "though she slay me" (113), he would lose his reason. Roth knew from his visions of Yeshea who he was, what his duty amounted to, and that nothing would prevent it from happening. He had prepared a conundrum of a book for ambitious marketing to various audiences. It would help him maintain a successful publishing business, which, despite its appeals to prurient sensation, he could claim was a legitimate provider of ideas. *My Sister and I* presented a picture of multiple Jewish influences in a great man's life and thus helped Roth atone for *Jews Must Live*. Now, is this the kind of man who would publish a hoax?

CHAPTER 9

1952–1957

The Windsors, Winchell, Kefauver: Back to Lewisburg

Tuesday, April 13, 1954, was supposed to be a pleasant day for Sam and Pauline Roth. They were to join their daughter, her husband, John, and their daughter-in-law in Connecticut for their granddaughter Candy's birthday party. Arriving home at 11 West Eighty-first Street, they found two detectives waiting for them. Policemen were searching the apartment for obscene books; at the same time, Roth's Lafayette Street office was being ransacked, and the six-person office staff questioned and released. Confiscated items included boxes with paid orders, seven cabinets with information about customers, post-office bags full of packages ready for mailing, 70,000 books, mailing lists and stencils with 300,000 names, and the "stock, minutes and seal of the Seven Sirens corporation"; all this gear was roughly packed up to be carted off.[1] Thus Roth would be unable to fulfill his obligations to his customers, who of course would think he was a cheat. The assistant district attorney in charge of the case, according to Roth, told one of the employees that "as far as I am concerned, your boss is out of business."[2]

Telling Roth his home was being searched to find evidence of a conspiracy "to conduct an illegal business," the detectives would not let him call his lawyer, and held him, Pauline, and Richard, as Roth puts it, "incommunicado for an hour and a half while his library, the bureau drawers of his bedroom, his clothes-closet and even the pockets of the clothes on his person were ransacked." Roth, when the detectives' attention was elsewhere, left the apartment to phone his lawyer, Nicholas Atlas. He was also concerned that if the police

Figure 23. Result of police raid on Roth's Lafayette Street office in 1954, implying a warning of draconian measures to come. By permission of the Roth estate.

found a sum of money he kept in the apartment, he would never see it again.[3] As he tells it, one detective discovered his absence, intercepted him on the street, and grabbed him around the neck, pinning him against a parked car. The policeman said Roth punched him; thereupon he arrested the publisher for assault. Roth's explanation: "The use of a telephone—granted even murderers—was still denied him." Roth is writing in the third person ("Mishillim"), which, in this case, provides distance from the humiliation dealt out to himself and his wife and son ("CMAM," 392–93). It also promotes skepticism. More important, it creates a context for the event: Roth's destiny as one who suffers for behavior which one day will reveal itself as part of a divine mission to restore light and justice to his world.

Adelaide recalls that Richard eventually made it to the party but the grandparents of the birthday girl did not. They were held on bail of $8,000 for Roth

Samuel Roth, Infamous Modernist

and $7,500 for his wife. The headlines in the *World Telegram and Sun* and the *Journal American* were exultant: "Police Throw the Book at Publisher of Filth" and "Roth in Toils Again on Obscene Books."[4] These articles, and those in the *Times* and the *Post,* reproduced the detective's complaint that Roth had hit him in the neck, after a struggle on the street following Roth's unauthorized exit from the apartment while under guard. Both accounts described Roth's previous record, the "hundreds of complaints" about his publications, and the "obscene literature" that motivated the police action. As a result of the latter, they stated, Roth had been subpoenaed to appear at the Kefauver hearings on juvenile delinquency. "No newcomer to the courts," said the *Post;* "convicted previously for sending obscenity through the mails," explained the *Times.*[5] No paper suggested that any violation of Roth's civil rights might have occurred. Nor was it made clear that the raid on home and office was carried out, not by the Justice Department or FBI at the request of the Post Office, but, oddly enough, by the New York police at the behest of the district attorney's office, even though interstate distribution of pornography was the charge.[6] Adelaide Kugel recalls "there were (and are [as she researched her father's life]) certain words that jump out at me from a newspaper: 'smut,' 'lewd,' 'obscenity,' 'pornography' and 'Samuel Roth.' As they did once again in 1954 on April 14."[7] They continue to jump out, as in *The Amazing Adventures of Kavalier & Clay*, where Michael Chabon specifies Roth as "a walleyed loser" and "comically shifty-looking."

The dismissal of all charges, however, thirteen months later, indicated that the police used draconian measures that precluded a case being brought. The warrant was declared deficient: "the affidavits on which it was based were too vague." The judge concluded that despite his contempt for obscenity, he had to dismiss the charges due to the unconstitutionality of "unlawful searches." That no books taken had been declared obscene had to be inferred.[8] Even more revealing is the fact that a March 1955 memo to J. Edgar Hoover from one of his New York agents, informing him of the raid, stated merely that the *New York World Telegram* had reported the previous year's obscenity raid on Roth's apartment and that according to the *Brooklyn Eagle,* he had been "indicted" two weeks after the raid for mailing "obscene, filthy, and indecent literature."[9] As is typical of FBI research, only information regarding a subject's culpability is recorded, for that is what can be used. A subsequent indictment unrelated to the raid followed Roth's testimony before the Kefauver subcommittee in late May 1955.[10]

Roth had worked calmly and cleverly to bring the dismissal about, despite the high bail and, according to Roth, the suggestion of the assistant district attorney that "his wife and son were being charged, and that their immediate future depended on his *cooperation*" ("CMAM," 394). He was annoyed by his attorney's postponements of a hearing, while editorial writers and politicians, not to mention J. Edgar Hoover, were describing "pornography" (by which they meant books and magazines with sexual content) as not only a major cause of juvenile delinquency but as part of a conspiracy of Communists to demoralize the youth of the country. Roth wrote a letter to District Attorney Frank Hogan that described the events of April 13 in a tone that implied, if it did not overtly state, that the letter was written because the district attorney's reputation as an honest and compassionate administrator made Roth believe Hogan was his best chance at obtaining justice. Before sending it, Roth contacted his friend from Joyce's attempt to sue him, Arthur Garfield Hays, and another smart, sympathetic lawyer, Hugo Pollock, getting their approval.[11] Probably, Hogan saw that the irregularities in the conduct of the raid could be embarrassing. In any event, it worked.

But Hogan could not have been unaware of the raid in the first place, and of the manner in which it was carried out. He, like Hoover, was friendly with Walter Winchell, whose coverage of crime stories could make or break a district attorney's reputation. In 1949, when a suspect in a murder case wanted to surrender to Winchell, Hogan told him he "had absolutely no objection."[12] The raid on Roth's home and office was a signal that powerful enemies were going to make life miserable for him. He could indeed, along with his family and employees, be frightened and humiliated and find himself "out of business." The latter would not happen as a result of the behavior of officers making the arrests on the night of April 13. That was just for starters. But he had better be prepared. Gershon Legman got wind of this just before he left New York to settle in France in 1953. He was talking at Roth's Lafayette Street office with his pals and fellow Sam Roth and Jack Brussel employees, artist Mahlon Blaine and writer-translator Keene Wallis. They and Legman comprised the "gleesome threesome." Wallis told him, with a piercingly meaningful stare, to "get out."[13]

What had Roth done to deserve this? He had stung renowned public figures and institutions where it hurt most: their reputations.

Norman Lockridge, Reporter, Uncovers the Prince of Wales's "Homosexualism"

In 1952 the Duke and the Duchess of Windsor were minor celebrities in New York and London. They were leading a comfortable life, partying with members of Café Society, enjoying the best shows, restaurants, and travel accommodations. They were easy targets for the gossip columnists and popular entertainment magazines, and the previous year Walter Winchell, who disliked them enough to snub them on one occasion at the Stork Club (perhaps because of the Duke's liaison with Hitler after his abdication), reported on the frequent rumors of the Duchess's affair between herself and a gay playboy with a vicious way of expressing aggression toward people.[14] Celebrity hostess Elsa Maxwell and columnist Louis Sobel were discussing the possibility of the Duke and Duchess finally separating. This tittle-tattle accounted for the sales potential of "Norman Lockridge's" *Lese Majesty: The Private Life of the Duke and Duchess of Windsor.* The book ignored the recent controversies and publicity, focusing instead on the author's findings regarding the glamorous "Wales" being a closet homosexual. The Duchess's biographer notes the book's "readable scurrilousness," and that "there was no suit for libel."[15]

The "Lockridge" pseudonym had been used, until now, for works that would not diminish the image of the author of the acclaimed *A Golden Treasury of the World's Wit and Wisdom.* As editor of a good literary anthology, *Bachelor's Quarters* (1944), and a "biographical memoir" of the relationship of Havelock Ellis and Olive Schreiner (1930), Lockridge had shown once again how much modernist writing was about human sexuality. It seems self-destructive to dust off this pseudonym for what was bound to be a vilified attempt to provoke a scandal. Both epigraphs to *Lese Majesty* are clues, ones that Harry Roskolenko among others saw as a "perversion." Roth needed to impose his presence on a work, either as a kind of playful self-mockery or, conversely, as a wise man might appear suddenly, to enlighten people about its true import: "Open this book as if you were entering a sacred temple. Do not shut it. Let its pages come to a soft closing. This is only one of the many ways to keep your integrity in the age of the Bomb."

"Lockridge" begins by describing his success in gathering evidence during his 1921 stay in London regarding the sex life of Edward Prince of Wales. He interviewed London nannies, journalists, Sir Edmund Gosse, and a psychologist. As a result, he pulls a possible truth out of thin air: Mrs. Simpson has found a way sexually to satisfy the deeply inhibited Prince so powerfully that he had become dependent on her. As a boy, Wales, like so many British nobility, received no affection from his father. Young David was surrounded by little girls toward whom the king, since they did not need the hardening necessary for a future leader of the Empire, could afford to be affectionate. He concluded he should be like his sisters. He is (QED?) a practicing "homosexualist." It is true that the Duchess could have appealed to him by dominating him in a way that might have reminded him subconsciously of his father, and was perhaps therefore a substitute for male sex partners. There is an interesting story here, but Lockridge misses its complexity, just as he misses the pathos in the Duchess's story. Wildly ambitious and manipulative, she found herself unable to enter the royal family, and bound for life to a man of stunted inner life whose only real pleasure, despite his elegant charm and solid administrative skills, was to keep himself bound to her, uxoriously. Roth knew the book's audience, and that they were looking for not only information but especially for titillation, and reinforcement of the caricatures of celebrity reporting.

If there was no libel suit, since that would increase conjecture about the Duke's sexual orientation, there were, instead, attempts to suppress. Roth stated that he was requested to visit a district attorney's office, where he was asked amiably, although with a hint at his vulnerability as a mail-order operator, to withdraw the book. "Any other small publisher with a grain of common sense would have agreed." Subsequently, Roth continues, plainclothes men daily invaded his office, without warrants, searching his premises for obscene books and magazines. Since Winchell's attack on Roth's publications was a year later, he may be exaggerating. What is certain is that he invited the most severe response from vested authority possible. That too was his nature. Not only did the publisher refuse the district attorney's request, he published a paperback edition of *Lese Majesty* in 1953. It is reset, and in digest-sized format suitable for newsstand display.

The illustrations were very much in the style of Mahlon Blaine, one of the "gleesome threesome" working wisely for the occasion under a pseudonym ("Hannibal St. Elmo"). The first drawing delineates a snarling woman with the Duchess's facial features; a forked tongue protrudes from her teeth and she displays a hand with two fingers, both with the concave nail of a feline about to strike. In the left background is the pale head of the Duke, eyes closed as if he is either disdainful of his surroundings or moribund. Others do not caricature the Windsors but rather satirize gossips, especially newspaper reporters, who gleefully chatter and mock. That first drawing is an insolent attempt to increase indignation and thus sales, regardless of any warnings.

On October 26, 1952, the Sunday Pictorial section of London's *The Guardian* discussed *Lese Majesty* under the headline "An Outrageous Insult to Our Royal Family." *The Guardian* demanded the British ambassador take action against "the most nauseous publication of the year." This was pure gold. In his circular for *Lese Majesty,* Roth reproduced the article, with his own rebuttal.[16] He admitted that many of his publications "rotate about sex—even as every individual does in his real life." He spoke truer than he intended. Roth catered to people who cautiously circle around an object of desire, deciding whether or not it might be worth the consequences of contact, and often replacing the hunt with a printed fantasy. The second half of the circular lists several erotic titles. "Don't let [the politicians] worry you—your morals are all right."

Walter Winchell's Private Life Is Exposed; Roth Gets Newspaper and Radio "Pub-lousity"

Lyle Stuart was one of the American luftmensch publishers whose career paralleled Roth's.[17] Disillusioned by what he was required to do as a reporter for a Hearst newspaper, and then for *Variety,* he became a maverick in the tradition of George Seldes. Like Roth, Stuart had the chutzpah to sell himself as an inspired truth-teller and to ignore the contempt of established publishers whose tastes and methods were genteel. Stuart, again like Roth, "love[d] the game, the battle of wits, the winning, but not what I've won."[18] He could respond with stubborn confidence to the aggression of police raids, and to being a defendant in a lawsuit. The money for his publishing enterprise—Lyle Stuart, Inc. began in 1959—was a result of a libel case he won against Winchell for slandering him five years earlier on his radio program.[19]

This preeminent gossip columnist had been on the FBI Special Correspondents list since the mid-1930s.[20] His innuendos could kill reputations, and his personal irritability was deeply resented. In October 1951 he became embroiled in a nasty contretemps with dancer Josephine Baker about her claim that she, as a black woman, had received poor service in the Stork Club. Stuart had started a monthly political newsletter, *Exposé,* in late 1951. With smoke from the Stork Club firestorm still in the air, Stuart quickly reedited his November *Exposé* and had the staff hand-distribute copies to Times Square newsstands. Within an hour he received calls for more. Eventually, 91,000 copies were sold. According to Stuart, Roth called him and asked if he could expand the articles into a book, offering him $1,000 (more than twice Roth's usual fee at the time). *The Secret Life of Walter Winchell* appeared in 1953. Steam flowed from the columnist's ears as he read Stuart's tell-all: Winchell's false reporting, thin skin, jealousy of his daughter's suitors, vindictive smears, Commie-baiting, and diminishing reputation. Finally, Stuart taunted the "frenetic" columnist with the eagerness with which the public had snapped up his *Exposé* articles.[21]

After the book appeared, three thugs from New York's waterfront attacked Stuart one morning near his home. It was not at Winchell's instigation; the men foolishly wanted to bring themselves to the powerful man's attention. It was the last thing Winchell would do, not only because he was above such clueless thuggishness himself but because the headlines brought the book more attention, in which his many enemies luxuriated. It was more pure gold for Roth. The back of the *Secret Life* dust jacket reproduced some of the newspaper coverage of the attack on Stuart.

Roth must have made money from the Winchell exposé. He used some of it to publish his own imitation of a political newsletter, *The Earth* (1955). *The Earth* was a one-shot flop, but *The Secret Life of Walter Winchell* was one of the foundations upon which was built the enmity that led Samuel Roth for the second time to the gates of federal prison. Peggy Roth's observation, with which her sister-in-law agreed, was "If Sam doesn't like someone he writes [or publishes] a book at 'em."[22] He was indeed appalled by what Stuart had unearthed about Winchell, as were many New York writers and publishers.

Editorial writers and politicians, not to mention J. Edgar Hoover, were describing erotica as not only a major cause of juvenile delinquency but as part of a conspiracy of Communists to demoralize the youth of the country. In the vanguard was, and had been since the Iron Curtain descended, Walter Winchell. "I and my family were called Communists." Winchell wrote, "His son and daughter-in-law have been dealt with in Calif. for Communist activities." "Every week in his nationally syndicated columns and his weekly TV broadcasts," Roth recalled, Winchell decried him as a publisher of dirty books. He demanded to know why Mr. Hogan . . . did not arrest me and close my business. Finally Mr. Hogan acted."[23] The harassed publisher was not exaggerating this time. His FBI files contain reports on what Winchell broadcast on several occasions. Exalting over Roth's 1956 federal conviction, he used the epithets "louse," "filthy bum," "public enemy," and "vulture." In 1957 he praised the Internal Security Committee's conclusion that Communists have circulated "pornographic pamphlets and books." Citing Roth, and Philip Foner, whose Citadel Press had distributed *Good Times,* he crowed, "I said at the time the money had come from 'commies.'"[24]

Considering that Roth's shrewdness was sometimes erased by his impetuousness, perhaps he does not deserve full marks for deciding to fight Winchell's power. Still, he does deserve some credit. Sensational books for

Samuel Roth, Infamous Modernist

the general public can educate as well as titillate, and can do so with a "reality check" from which established media with corporate advertising revenues shy away.

Pornography, Sexual Deviance, Juvenile Delinquency, and "The Louse of Lewisburg"

The information about the Roth family's Communism came from Howard Rushmore. By the early 1950s, at Winchell's suggestion, Rushmore was *Confidential* magazine's chief reporter on Communist infiltration into the entertainment industry.[25] Rushmore wrote several reports for Winchell in early 1954 concerning the Roths, and Richard and Peggy.[26] These memos were written less than six weeks before the April 1954 raid on Roth's office and home. They were used almost verbatim: "That ex-convict publisher, who publishes trash (by an ex-convict extortionist) also published a book by Hitler's ex-helper, George Sylvester Viereck. His name is Samuel Roth of New York and Lewisburg Federal Penitentiary. This louse (in 1948) was quoted as saying that Alger Hiss was telling the truth. (I have the proof, Chump.)"[27] Rushmore also sent Winchell a *Confidential* article titled "America on Guard! Sam Roth the Louse of Lewisburg," which he might have written. It focused on Roth's 1950s porno and his attempts to help Alger Hiss. Winchell also used the aforementioned letter written to him by a possible acquaintance of Ruth and Maxwell Bodenheim. From it he paraphrased the paragraph on Roth's failure to give the penniless couple more than a pittance.[28]

There was a chorus of opinion in the mid-1950s declaring that sex publishers were aiding and abetting the Communist strategy of using prurient books, magazines, comics, and movies to weaken young Americans' moral resolve. The leading shapers of public opinion were part of this chorus. Professors could always be found to ratify this notion, as they could the erotica/juvenile delinquency nexus. The day before Roth's testimony at the subcommittee investigating the effect of obscene material on juvenile delinquency, a memo readying the press and subcommittee for that day's session reminded that "Benjamin Karpman, famous criminologist, stated [for the subcommittee] that a definite correlation existed between pornographic materials and juvenile delinquency. . . . As part of its investigation of the many factors contributing to Juvenile Delinquency, the Subcommittee undertook an intensive investigation of the distribution to children of pornographic materials."[29] While the phrase regarding the "many factors" was explicitly cautionary, the word "children" to indicate teenagers was a hint that the criterion for unlawful pornography was that of the Hicklin Standard, which defined obscenity as what might debauch the morals of the most susceptible, immature members of the community. That standard, despite the 1934 *Ulysses* decision, had since that date remained the measure of unmailability used by the postal service.

The media enthusiastically supported the notion that "perversion" was being taught to adolescents by greedy criminals with subversive connections. Blaming adolescents' neurosis on the pornographers, occasionally in league with the Reds,[30] was an easier sell, and more likely to retain customers and advertisers, than criticism of parental problems such as compulsive gambling, alcoholism, infidelity, divorce, or anxiety about maintaining a standard of living that would sanction conspicuous consumption. The "Commie" smear was certainly a roadblock to Roth's hopes of establishing himself as a well-reputed publisher. It dovetailed with the danger of "muck merchants" (Hoover's term) in our schoolyards. "Cites the 'Danger from Within,'" ran the caption of a quarter-page *New York Times* photograph of "The Rev. Daniel Egan, a youth worker," who testified just ahead of Roth at the 1955 Kefauver hearings on juvenile delinquency. "He said pornography posed a greater threat to the nation's youth than Communism."[31] There was no need, apparently, for an accompanying article.

It needs to be stressed that to many liberals, even to First Amendment heroes such as Morris Ernst and Heywood Broun, Communism's threat to American democracy was an immanent concern. Broun and Ernst combined in the late 1940s to halt what seemed to be a Communist takeover of the Newspaper Guild. Apparently, Ernst maintained a long correspondence with Hoover about the dangers, despite the director's belief, as rock solid as it was indiscriminate, that sexually explicit materials were undermining the country's morale and that the Post Office and the churches were our front line of defense against that and other "Red" initiatives.[32] The New American Library would not publish any book by a Communist. Little, Brown similarly dropped the popular and prolific Howard Fast after he refused to identify his political party when asked by a Senate subcommittee. Secular and religious institutions declined to fight against that kind of repression, constrained by the need to maintain their status. They preferred to place trust in their government to protect its cultural institutions.

In 1956, when Philip Foner was co-director of Citadel Press and Remainder Book Company, he was subpoenaed to appear before a Senate subcommittee investigating the "Scope of Soviet Activity in the United States." They quizzed

Samuel Roth, Infamous Modernist

him about his "conspiracy" with Roth and G.I. Distributors to distribute obscene materials published by Roth, including *Good Times*.[33] Foner took the Fifth Amendment two dozen times, refusing to state whether he published articles by Communists, whether he was a Communist, why he lost his teaching position at City College, and why he was on the faculty of three schools on the attorney general's "subversive list." At the conclusion of his testimony, the subcommittee's chief counsel placed on record an article from a recent *Counterattack* ("facts to combat Communism"), declaring that the question of a link between "pro-Communist interests" and pornography had been proven by the fact that Roth's "obscene magazine" had been distributed by the Citadel Press. A list of Citadel Press publications was placed on record to indicate Foner published books by Communists. The list included ten titles about sex and sexuality, three of which focused on homosexuality.[34]

The language of the promoters of the filth merchant/Communist nexus is similar to that used earlier in the century to scapegoat immigrants as a source of cultural infection or state subversion. James Gilbert, in his study *Cycle of Outrage: America's Reaction to the Juvenile Delinquent in the 1950s,* writes that in discussions of causes of the problem, "The predominant metaphor was one of contagion, contamination, and infection."[35] That kind of rhetoric was more familiar to Roth than to anyone. It had been used against him during the *Ulysses* protest, particularly by Waverley Root in *transition,* where it was identified specifically with Jewish immigrants from Galicia. And he used it himself, egregiously, in *Jews Must Live.*

Roth Lectures Senator Kefauver; Indictment Follows

The Kefauver subcommittee heard Roth's testimony on May 31, 1955, along with that of Irving Klaw, the "Pin-Up King" and leading distributor of fetish photographs. Eddie Mishkin, "Porn King" of Times Square and six others eventually joined Klaw. Roth was a unique witness. Lyle Stuart advised him to leave town and to state that he was sick and could not appear.[36] Four other witnesses invoked their Fifth Amendment protection. That was not Roth's nature. In fact, he stated that it would be fifty years before a defendant could do so without being stigmatized. He volunteered more information than any other New York witness, and did so in such a way that even experienced politicians were frustrated. They found it hard to know how much was factual and how much was filtered through this particular man's consciousness of himself:

255

"There isn't a company like mine. My business is unique, there is nothing like it in the world."[37]

Coincidentally, Roth was subpoenaed by the subcommittee the day after the April 13, 1954, raid of his Lafayette Street office. The subpoena was served while Roth and his wife "were questioned in District Attorney Hogan's office after a raid on their apartment."[38] It seemed another "we'll get you" moment. On April 22, Roth told the subcommittee that because of his arrest on April 13, and that because charges were pending, his lawyer had told him not to answer questions unless he was granted immunity.[39] (Charges were filed on April 29; he posted a $200 bond.)[40] Kefauver would not give immunity, and Roth was temporarily dismissed. He appeared on May 31. A few weeks earlier, in preparation for the three-day hearings in New York, a memo from subcommittee researchers identified Roth and the Woodford Press, after an interview with the city postal inspector in charge of obscene material, as the largest mail-order dealers, with Roth by far the one in business longest.[41]

Faced with public exposure as a corrupter of youth, Roth returned in full measure the subcommittee's indignation. His loyal journalist friend, Bill Ryan, in attendance at Sam's appearance before the subcommittee, describes the witness as "growling" his answers to the litany of questions about his arrests over the years. At one point, when Kefauver asked about his wife's past involvements in his business, "Sam Roth shot up out of his seat at the brink of doing bodily harm."[42] Ryan must have been approximately correct, because the official transcript has Roth standing up, saying, "All I can tell you is that we were right." He might have walked out if Kefauver had not ordered him to sit down.

Counsel Peter N. Chumbris's interrogation had started with a list of Roth's most sensational titles, most of which he had remaindered from publishers of digest-sized newsstand pulps. These were the books the *Times* listed in its coverage of the hearing. After a paragraph on Cornell professor George W. Henry's testimony regarding "the definite correlation between the spread of suggestive booklets and pictures and the rise in juvenile delinquency," the *Times* article explained that "this view was disputed by Samuel Roth of 110 Lafayette Street."[43] His real address, near Central Park West, would have increased his stature over the one given, in Chinatown. If Professor Henry's words were statistically without merit, the basic belief of the subcommittee was equally so. The latter was that Roth and other mail-order distributors' "natural bent, as far as advertisement was concerned, would lie in the juvenile trade." The reason given for this statement, made during Roth's brief appearance before the subcommittee's investigation of comic books, was that "adolescence represents an

Samuel Roth, Infamous Modernist

age, as the psychiatrists say, during which a youngster's normal sexual activity reaches a high point."[44] Apart from the telling point Roth often raised—that his books were too expensive for teenagers—his circulars referred often to authors about whom adolescents would not have heard, let alone read, and also to deviant, not "normal," sexual practices. But what right does a Lafayette Street publisher of erotica have to question a Cornell professor and psychiatrists chosen to testify before senators?

While Roth's claim that he published "only fine books" detracted from any credibility he had, the *Times* article's failure to mention that some of his arrests did not lead to convictions and his claim that he did publish impressive modernist works indicate that he had as little cultural capital as an Eddie Mishkin, Irving Klaw, or Abe Rubin, dealers in sadomasochism booklets, flagellation, and bondage photos. The *Times* avoided the melodrama of the *Daily News,* "New York's Picture Newspaper." Its story, "Dirty-Pix Probers Entangle 3," included three small pictures of a troubled Klaw in bowtie, a "cool" Mishkin in dark glasses, and Rubin, looking like someone caught with his mitts in the till, covering his mouth with his hand. Directly under the headline, and three times larger, was a photo of Roth in profile, jaw thrust forward and mouth open in a snarl as he discussed a circular he was holding.[45] That facial expression was very familiar to Adelaide Kugel. She had seen it many times, as her father was arguing a friend into a corner and about to deliver the coup de grâce. But however good it made him feel, in this case, his daughter wrote, it was "a small, dearly bought victory."[46]

On several occasions, Roth insisted that he had superior ability than the subcommittee to distinguish good literature from obscene hack work. Then he questioned their reasoning in connecting books about sex with juvenile delinquency. "It is just that the juveniles of our time have no respect for the religion of their elders." He added, waspishly, "This goes to high office as well as to the home."[47] Who on the subcommittee, the press, or the "decent" community would swallow that home truth from a "muck merchant?" The *Daily News* story followed Roth's "truculence" with the Cornell professor's alarm at the fetish images, and socialist Norman Thomas's assertion that "pornographers" were hiding behind the First Amendment. Later, when Kefauver asked Roth if he would question J. Edgar Hoover's judgment that "juvenile delinquency is caused by pornographic literature," he said that Hoover might know more than he "if he [Hoover] made a study of it."[48] When the chairman asked why he would try to publish a book about the showgirl Pat Ward after the Mickey Jelke trial, the reply was on a par with Roth's best epigrams: "I believe the

New Testament rotates around just that kind of woman."[49] The Hearst-owned *Journal American* used the subject as fodder for a demeaning headline: "Pat Ward Barred Book on Her Life."[50] Roth concluded by telling Kefauver that many people have criticized his business and that "you are a great deal more wrong than they are, because you have been sitting in judgment of me." In other words, he was claiming a great deal of cultural capital.

Now he would have to prove in court that books could provide purchasers educational improvement and artistic pleasure even if advertised salaciously. A superseding indictment of twenty-five counts of sending obscenity through the mails and one count of conspiracy (with Foner's Remainder Book Company) to do so was filed against him on July 20, less than two months after his testimony.[51] The *Times* article on the indictment concluded, with quiet astringency, by reminding readers that at the Kefauver hearings, Roth had said that "no youth could be corrupted by the books and pictures he handled."[52]

United States v. Roth, Followed of Course by *Roth v. United States*

The twenty-six-count indictment, filed in the District Court of the Southern District of New York, named "Wallet Nudes," "Stereoptic [*sic*] Nude Show," "2 Undraped Stars," *Good Times* numbers 5, 8, and 10 of volume 1, and several issues of *American Aphrodite*, including volume 1, number 3, featuring Beardsley's *Venus and Tannhauser,* with the illustrations. These materials had been ordered by postal inspectors, on two occasions using the names and addresses of a children's home and a registry for nurses. The original trial was in mid-January 1956 and was followed by the appeal the same year. Roth's lawyer, whom later he would vilify but who earlier had done well for him, was Nicholas Atlas. Roth was annoyed that Atlas had agreed with George Leisure pretrial that the "community standards" criteria for obscenity would be accepted.[53] The publisher realized that the prosecution wanted to describe Roth's customers as underage boys. The standard is vague enough to allow the government lawyer to appeal to the jury's understanding of the average adult's need to stop adolescents from being sexually stimulated. But Atlas did make salient points. By the standards of the time, books by such writers as Norman Mailer, John O'Hara, and Thomas Mann (*Confessions of Felix Krull*), published by Random House and Knopf, had been allowed to circulate, as had been *Ulysses,* all with more explicit passages than *Venus and Tannhauser*. He reminded the jury of

Samuel Roth, Infamous Modernist

the testimony of experts, including Albert Ellis (*Sex without Guilt* [1958]), a psychologist of whom Lyle Stuart thought highly. Ellis had insisted that words such as "impure" are subjective and unfit for any unbiased legal definition. Atlas discussed the tenuousness of any connection of juvenile delinquency with sexually explicit material. He may have been a bit patronizing with the jury when he stressed the learnedness of the defendant's expert witnesses or when he told them they had to be analytical, like professors.[54] Furthermore, he should have explained more fully that nothing in *Good Times,* and only *Venus and Tannhauser* in *American Aphrodite,* was legally borderline pornographic. Such texts and photos could be found openly displayed on most Times Square newsstands and bookstores. Perhaps he did not want to make a distinction that could invite Leisure to describe in detail the masturbation scene in the Beardsley story and one illustration in it showing a child servant's penis.

George S. Leisure Jr., for the government, was (as Atlas pointed out) a much younger, less experienced man than Atlas, but his appeals to the jury were highly skilled. His success was evidenced by the verdict in both the original and the appellate cases. It possibly gave the Roths a chill of déjà vu, for the young and ambitious Irving Kaufmann had achieved a similar result twenty years earlier. In Leisure's summation of the government case, he needed to rehabilitate to a degree the credibility of the government witnesses whom Atlas had shown through his cross-examination to have complained about Roth's circulars either without reading them, or having been ignorant of the authors in his list, some of whom were famous. One woman had stated, "Where my son is concerned . . . I am one mother out of a million that feels" the books in Roth's circular should not be sold. "Where your son is concerned," Leisure pointed out, "your opinion should be the law of the land."[55] Suggesting the jury put themselves in the place of such upright, respectable folk, he said, "It isn't any fun to get up and be cross-examined." He told the jury that the government witnesses had done their best and that they reminded him of the men and women of the jury. Now it was up to them to uphold decency.

As for the defense's expert witnesses, Leisure opined he would take the "plumber from Alliance, Ohio" over Dr. Ellis, who believes there is no such thing as obscenity. That was not what Ellis said, but the distortion, and the "just folks" gambit, served Leisure well.[56] He knew the inner world of the representatives of what Paul Goodman called "the organized society," and the truths they held inviolate. Writing a few years later, Goodman stated that the "delinquent" believes his first orgasm convinces him of its rightness. The boy is told he must stop. Whether or not he does—and if he does not he is labeled "delinquent"—he feels the hostility that shame and betrayal incite. (This was Mishillim's case in Galicia, where father and rabbi received the boy's resentment.) Goodman explains that parents, teachers, and friends give the adolescent a chance to "belong." If this does not work, the hostility is explained not on the evidence that orgasm is irresistibly pleasurable but on expert wisdom regarding "insecure affection at home, slum housing, comic books, and naughty companions: tensions and conditions."[57] Leisure appealed to the belief that parents and others responsible for teaching mature behavior are the backbone of the social order. That their approach might be inadequate is a hard assumption to make. Better to assume that delinquency results when parents are thwarted by "tensions and conditions," as they to a degree are. The people responsible for these conditions have to be punished—that's what "the law of the land" was for. By implication, Roth was a kind of Fagin, replacing family togetherness with words and pictures that produced antisocial, reckless youth.

"Can you imagine the audacity of that man, mailing that envelope to the Ulrich's Children's home? That wasn't addressed to an adult there." Actually, it was not addressed to any person, just the home. If it had gotten into a child's hands, an official have to have been careless about what he did with it. As for Roth's "Lexicon of Love" in the *Aphrodite,* the man "takes natural and normal words and puts terrible connotations on them." That is, with more forthrightness than most of the era's editors of dictionaries, he explains their erotic connotations. Had Roth managed to put the pocket-sized *Good Times* before the public from coast to coast, as Leisure said? Not nearly to the extent the Hearst newspapers had put Winchell's column before the public. His wording—"flooding the country" and "terrible connotations"—moved the jury in just the right way, and its vagueness helped.

Leisure made much of Beardsley's deathbed wish to have his erotic works burned, as he did of the biographer Haldene McFall's characterization of those who thought such a decision a loss to the world of arts and letters. McFall had called them "Jackals." The epithet was tailor-made to fit the defendant, as was McFall's rhetoric regarding *Venus and Tannhauser:* "bent only on satisfying every lust in a dandified way that casts but a handsome garment over the barest and most filthy license." Atlas was much amiss in not objecting to the introduction of McFall's outdated work. Leisure concluded that if the jury did not want the Post Office to continue to "fight this kind of thing [he had characterized *Venus and Tannhauser* as "filth"], then acquit him, and I can assure you the sewers will open." When Roth stood for sentence, Leisure reminded Judge

John M. Cashin that not only was he one of the Post Office's most persistent offenders, but that his business activities had increased after his indictment. Postal officials had reported to him that 1,650 complaints had been received after July 20, 1955.[58]

Only an experienced lawyer, like Atlas and indeed Cashin himself, would be aware of how many changes Leisure had rung upon the theme of civic duty to preserve decency. In the post-verdict session before Judge Cashin, Atlas pointed out the difficulty of a publisher losing his business and going to jail because he could not know what was likely to be judged obscene by a jury. Then he made a thorough, accurate, analytical review of Leisure's tactics.[59] It made no difference. For the appellate case (decided in September 1956), Roth replaced Atlas with Phillip Wittenberg; Leisure again handled the government argument. But the issues that Atlas had originally addressed were raised only in the opinion of a liberal, although concurring, judge on the three-man panel, Jerome Frank. Presiding, Judge Charles E. Clark ruled that there was nothing incitative in Leisure's summary, and, further, that the government's adjective "filthy" was not a prejudicial, class-based value judgment but merely a designation for the broad concept of "indecent" (which includes obscenity). "Filthy" and "indecent" were bias-free only in comparison to all the other snarl terms sanctioned by the Comstock Laws. Clark affirmed the original sentence; he did point out that the vagueness of words such as "obscene" and "filthy" might in other contexts have been a problem: "A serious problem does arise when real literature is censored; but in this case no such issues should arise, since the record shows only salable pornography. . . . We are hardly justified in rejecting out of hand the strongly held views of those with competence in the premises as to the very direct connection of this traffic with the development of juvenile delinquency."[60]

Judge Frank's doubts about the obscenity statute, and the distinction between literature and whatever might be obscene, had been aired in his reluctant consent to the ruling in *Roth v. Goldman* (1947), regarding *Waggish Tales from the Czechs*. Frank understood that the real value of the obscenity law was to address a social problem—the random exposure of unwilling citizens to erotically stimulating material, including that purveyed for commercial gain. He concurred in the 1956 appellate case, with as much reluctance as in 1947. His opinion, however, stressed that it is impossible to determine whether or not obscene publications affect behavior, either of children or adults. Therefore exposure to such material could not be categorized as a "clear and present danger."[61] He also made an implicit criticism of Judge Clark regarding the effect of obscene materials on juvenile delinquency. Citing the leading experts on the subject, Sheldon and Eleanor Glueck, he explained that juvenile delinquents do not read very much, which might explain why for them aggression is not sublimated by vicarious means. (A dealer in comic books, citing another authority, made exactly this point before the Kefauver subcommittee in 1954).[62] Frank quoted an article by a superintendent of a school for girls: "Adults have always sought a panacea which would cure the problem. It is sufficient to note that delinquency has always risen during periods of stress and strain, and the era in which we are living is no exception. . . . Neither do restrictive measures such as . . . censorship of reading matter . . . prevent delinquency."[63]

What would it have taken for Roth to win a 1957 obscenity case? Nothing would have helped; the man was on trial, not the books, and his audience as well—"we know who buys that," just as clearly as we decent people (who would never buy it) know the "jackals" who want it published. The circulars made part of the trial's exhibits show the teasing language that sold books about sex to average people. They gave authorities charged with protecting public order a glimpse of the imagination of the ad writer who knew his audience. Titles of digest pulps such as *Frisco Dame, Red Light Babe, Over Night Blonde,* and *Waterfront Hotel* embody the language of common men.[64] Roth's advertisements also speak their language: "along comes this rich beautiful woman. . . . Yes, the men are as willing as she is passionate"; "Who is this Peggy, the white girl, who has so many black men grasping for her sexual magic?"; "Weird female life behind bars."[65] If Roth's rib-nudging sales pitches are, in fact, more a safety valve for the daily frustrations of "making a living" than a threat to public order, they nevertheless are a challenge to the church and state authorities who routinely teach buttoned-up restraint. It should be noted that the circulars on exhibit were not those with allusions to sadomasochism, bestiality, and incest. The federal prosecutors limited themselves to ones about which several hundred recipients, their indignation boiling upon first glimpse of the headlines and line drawings, had written letters of complaint.

The Justice Department had a much more salable notion of guilt than Roth's lawyer had to work with, when he attempted to present abundant evidence that best-selling authors had featured as much scatology and sexual explicitness as Roth's books and magazines contained. That the issues of *Good Times* on which Roth was convicted (numbers 5, 8, and 10 of volume 1) featured writing by Pierre Louys, H. E. Bates, John Cournos, Henry Miller, and Sylvia Townsend Warner meant nothing when weighed against the newsstand format of the magazine, the colloquial language about "fun," "babes," "Broadway" and "Hollywood," the bare-breasted models, and the advertisements for *The Sexual Conduct of Men and Women* and *King Turd. American Aphrodite,* as Atlas showed, contained literature that was on a par with contemporary best-selling novels.[66] Leisure's reply—the latter were not for a general audience—is illogical (how did they get to be best-sellers?), but he got away with it. Adults who buy these well-reviewed novels were assumed to be superior in character to Roth's mail-order customers.

"We can understand all the difficulties of censorship of great literature," Judge Clark pronounced, "without feeling justified in casting doubt upon all criminal prosecutions, both state and federal, of commercialized obscenity." The latter pertained supremely to Roth, with his previous federal sentence, his jail time in two cities, and his many unmailable rulings and subsequent demands for hearings regarding postal inspectors' decisions. That Roth was manipulating interest in sex for secular riches must have been clear to the jury that had just heard government witnesses who knew nothing about the sexual passages in the Bible and also believed that it was written by a "holy spirit." Americans had been taught, as Atlas had made painfully clear, that "sexual deviance" caused "broken homes." If Leisure's witnesses were representative, the average citizen would not have believed differently unless President Eisenhower, General MacArthur, Billy Graham, or Estes Kefauver had told them so. What a dizzying reversal of field that would have been.

Hannah Arendt writes that "for the man who is in any case suspect, there is no relation between the offense he commits and the price he pays. . . . The innocence of the suspect which Chaplin so consistently plays in his films is . . . an expression of the dangerous incompatibility of general laws and individual misdeeds. . . . Because Chaplin is suspect, he is called upon to bear the brunt of much that he has not done. . . . Yet because he is beyond the pale, unhampered by the trammels of society, he is able to get away with a great deal. Out of this ambivalent situation springs an attitude both of fear and of impudence, fear of the law as if it were an inexorable moral force, and familiar, ironic impudence in the face of its minions."[67]

Roth's daughter stated that Charlie Chaplin was one of her father's favorite performers.

"Whereas the Books Are Good I Am Bad"

Writing from prison in 1958, Roth had predicted "the book will win," and that the victory (he had only one more year to wait for the Grove Press's success in the case of *Chatterley*) would protect other books from censorship. But, he acknowledged, there would remain an "everlasting insistence (as a bone thrown to my enemies) that whereas the books are good I am bad."[68] That was another result of the American success tragedy he courted. If Roth were not the opportunistic, irascible, and sometimes megalomaniacal idealist he was, the early 1960s advances in freedom of expression would not have happened when they did. He concluded his May 1959 appeal for reduction of sentence by writing: "I am not complaining. It took only ten years of my life to ease the laws of my country toward the tenderer organs of its literature. I said, *Let our books live,* and now they live."[69] The awkward image aside, who compares himself to God creating the universe? Perhaps a man who sees himself as suffering, Prometheus-like, to bring freedom to his fellow citizens—at considerable personal cost. That is the person who could write to Pauline, by way of cheering her (and himself) up while serving in federal prison, "However little I have accomplished for myself, I have won the greatest victory against book censorship in modern times."[70] Lest this be judged another Rothian broadside, constitutional lawyer Frederick Schauer, writing in 1976, stated, "The Roth case remains the cornerstone of American obscenity law."[71] It should also be stated that the Supreme Court deliberations ignored the books such as *Venus and Tannhauser* on which Roth had been peremptorily convicted. It focused instead on the Comstock criteria, LAPS (literary, artistic, political, or social) value, and "clear and present danger." But Roth, who often criticized his lawyers, had none for those who argued at the Court. He would have been proud of the amicus curiae briefs filed by the Authors League of America, Inc. (Morris Ernst et al.), Greenleaf Publishing (Abe Fortas et al.), the American Book Publishers Council, Inc. (Horace D. Manges), and the American Civil Liberties Union (Emanuel Redfield).[72]

Sam Roth's Contribution to America's Freedom to Read

Sam Roth's status in fighting censorship in America is unique, and will probably never be replicated. In *Grove Press v. Christianberry* (1959), Barney Rosset and his staff at Grove Press realized that they had to convince Judge F. Van Pelt Bryan at the Second Circuit of the Southern District of New York that they were not appealing to shameful and degenerate curiosity about the taboo: that they were not men like Sam Roth. This required that they define their tactics and distribution methods very differently from how Roth had done. Behind this necessity lay the assumption that the publisher had to make sure the right kind of people bought the book. Rosset distributed by mail through the Readers' Subscription Book Club, the clientele of which was largely academic. He hired a leading advertising agency, Sussman and Sugar, who had represented Random House, Simon and Schuster, and Harvard University Press.[73] It prepared notices for leading newspapers, and a "Digest of Public Opinion" that quoted editorials criticizing the Post Office's unmailable ruling on *Chatterley*. That ruling was the reason for Rosset's civil suit.

Charles Rembar, Rosset's brilliant lawyer, knew how to convince Judge Bryan that Grove was going to push back the boundaries of the taboo in an acceptable manner, by limiting its audience. He cited the criteria of the LAPS test and argued that in the Grove edition, insights into the nature of sexual instinct replaced prurient interest as a criterion for determining whether or not a book or magazine was obscene. Although most citizens would not make the distinction, an "'average' notion of what is objectionable" should not control the freedom "to write and be read" if the book was not sold, or read, with appeal to prurient curiosity, Rembar said. He relied on the principle of "variable obscenity": if the audience for a work was carefully defined, and if the text were not advertised with appeal to prurient interest, it could not be banned, although it might have been by the standards of a past time and place.[74] Bryan wrote, "the format and composition of the volume, the advertising and promotional materials, and the whole approach to publication, treat the book as a serious work of literature."[75] Three years later, while getting *Fanny Hill* decensored, Rembar adopted Eberhard and Phyllis Kronhausens' term "erotic realism" (in contrast to pornographic thrill) to specify what sexually explicit art and literature had legitimately to offer. It was another allusion to the concept of variable obscenity.[76]

It needs emphasizing that no one was more aware of the barriers to personal identity and creativity that Comstockery presented than Barney Rosset. No one, including Samuel Roth, did more to fight it. (In addition, Rosset's chutzpah in going ahead with his decision to publish *Chatterley* in America despite his being forbidden to by the Lawrence estate equals Roth's own.)[77] It is one of the ironies of American publishing history that in order to be in the vanguard of this "de-censorship" fight, Rosset's Grove Press had to make a legal argument that rested on distrust of the reader who could not separate erotic realism from prurient sensation. He must have known it was an argument of pragmatic use only. His paperback editions made available to millions not only *Lady Chatterley's Lover* but also other erotic classics banned in the United States before 1959, from *Tropic of Cancer* to *Naked Lunch*.

Two faulty impressions form the foundation for the cultural assumption that the legitimate audience for sexually explicit literature is an educated elite. One is that such readers are above base, self-indulgent motives for reading it.[78] The second, related impression is that people who lack cultural capital are without the discipline to restrain themselves from vicarious desire while reading or observing. That is, they are not responsible enough to appreciate art or analytical enough to absorb knowledge from it. What follows from that? A democracy that works—that is, a democracy with proper social control—must have the right kind of shibboleths ("obscenity," "salacity," "erotic realism") to enforce those restraints that it labors to embed in the minds of its citizens. For example, Anthony Comstock and his colleagues and successors in the anti-vice societies all believed that birth control information would only be used by the masses for sybaritic purposes. Of course, in 1959 the courts would not accept Comstockian prejudices about what constituted clear and present danger to the country's moral health. We've seen how Judge Jerome Frank questioned, in demurring from Roth's 1949 conviction for *Waggish Tales from the Czechs,* whether obscenity was a criterion for banning printed matter as a clear and present danger in any case. The minority opinion in *Roth v. United States* concurred. It took two more years, and a different sort of iconoclastic publisher, to make that the basis for a constitutional principle protecting erotic texts. But finally it happened. Its major facilitator, who always believed in the common man's right to read what the elite read, was still in prison.

A Short Sentence? No Thanks

If the vessel of Samuel Roth's life lay shattered at one's feet, some pieces would glow with a reverential white, others would be a deep vibrant pink, others an angry blood red. Still others would reflect the subtle beauty of actresses' gowns, others the somber black of the judge's robe, yet another the brightly colored vivacity of Mahlon Blaine's dust jackets for Bridgehead and Boar's Head books. But one fragment would be so stunningly bizarre as to have no recognizable color, yet it would be far from transparent. That one would represent a single utterance of Roth's in 1956, one that sealed his fate for the next five years. Adelaide Kugel writes:

> Between 1/13 (the jury's verdict) and 2/5 (sentencing), Richard Roth, thru an intermediary, promised Judge Cashin $5000 [equivalent to

Samuel Roth, Infamous Modernist

almost $400,000 in 2009] for a light sentence. SR was to meet him at a certain place at a certain time. The judge rolled up in a car to keep the appointment and waited half an hour. SR never showed. When Dick wanted to know why, Dad said, "I don't want to know that I live in a country where a judge can be bought for $5,000."[79]

The family believes Cashin's harsh sentence was the result of Roth's standing him up. John M. Cashin was on recess appointment as U.S. District Court judge until January 12, 1956, at which time he was nominated for a full commission. He was confirmed by the Senate on March 1 and served until his death in 1970.[80] In his autobiography, Roth states that Cashin's not being as yet confirmed made him vulnerable to pressure from any senator, such as Kefauver, who wanted Roth put away. Roth says nothing about Richard's bid on his behalf, which, considering not only his son's gentle nature but his having been attacked as disloyal by HUAC and Winchell, was a heroic act on his part. The father who had inspired this sacrifice makes only a wry, indirect comment: "There had been excitement of an indeterminate nature when [Cashin] moved to Ulster County into a judgeship, and it was said that attaining a judgeship had made a poor man of him" ("CMAM," 369). Of course, Roth could not have published any information about the attempted bribe. But he might have found a way to allude to Richard's remarkable sacrifice.[81] He might have been too enraptured with his own. Not even his own wife and children could be privy to what Roth had going on inside his head. Something else, related to but much stronger than defeating any opponent, guided the publisher in late middle age. It had nothing to do with his publishing business.

It was *taklis*, his destiny in the Real World. Yeshea had told him that he needed to be cast out of his community in order to fulfill his mission. In his second prison opus, *My Friend Yeshea* (written 1958–60), he finds himself present at Christ's final trip to Jerusalem. Late in the book, Mishillim has a vision of the Most High, who tells him that his destiny included "publish[ing] books of such a degree of sensitiveness that they would be sure to bring you condemnation by the ignorant and prurient. . . . This would lead you into a jail whenever I needed you in one, as surely as if you were a born thief."[82] The epigraph for the Windsor book, and Roth's statement before Kefauver that he never published anything but books of serious import, are thus sanctioned by the very highest authority. Immortal accuracy would have been better served if Yeshea had added "some" before "books," or clarified "sensitive." However that might be, with the Winchell book and its blowback, Roth had stumbled into the perfect sinkhole leading inexorably to federal prison, where the prisoner wrote his redemption and destiny.

When Sam Roth was finally released from Lewisburg in 1961, an equally shrewd and much better funded publisher for whom Roth helped pave the way, Barney Rosset, invited him to lunch. "He seemed a bit wacky," Rosset noted, "too interested in occult ideas."[83] Roth was still in the grip of his True World adventures with Yeshea. The need to complete his earthly mission had been present for many years, and became urgent as Roth got older. He had established a good home, a comfortable living for Pauline and himself, and saw his children marry and find their own way in the world. Confrontations with divine presence, and atonement with it, may be occult preoccupations. If they force one at last to look into oneself with authenticity instead of self-justification (his assertion that he only published books of serious import, for example, and had never abandoned poetry for success in business), they can also be healing experiences, producing peaceful forgiveness.

The Return to Lewisburg

Roth was held longer than expected at West Street, since bail, granted between the January 13, 1956, guilty verdict and the February 7 sentencing, was denied after that date.[84] On his first night there, Yeshea appeared to him, for the fifth time, in a dream that took place on the shores of the Sea of Galilee, where Mishillim was about to accompany the rabbi on the month-long journey to Jerusalem. Cheered, he cheered Pauline up, writing that he would make it all up to her after he redeemed himself with his book on Yeshea.[85] While at West Street, he worked on plans for selling razor blades.[86] The letterhead read, "Man Comfort. Creators of Shaving Ease." The initial "M" was decorated with a naked female walking through the V portion of the M. Who else but Sam Roth would do this? Possibly, he could use his purchases of the blades and printed advertisements (but hardly the letterhead) to convince judges that he would not reenter erotic bookselling upon his release. Another scheme he worked on in prison was marketing a lamp that would eliminate glare from TV screens and thus preserve children's eyesight.[87] In the fall of 1956, a full-page notice appeared in several magazines in which Pauline Roth stated that she was putting her husband's business up for sale, because "I simply feel that my husband's business and character were so falsely and maliciously treated by the press ... that whether the U.S. Supreme Court finds for him or against him I do not want him to find himself in business when he is finally released."[88] That, in view of the way the case unfolded, was a reasonable position for a loved one to take. It would also reinforce an appeal for early parole.

Roth arrived at Lewisburg at the beginning of May; he was sixty-one or sixty-two years old. He was relieved to be sent back to the minimum-security facility, a clean, well-ordered place.[89] One of the administrators remembered him from 1938. There was the mandatory first month in quarantine, during which the staff was polite and helpful. With the exception of a painful outbreak of boils, requiring hospitalization, he had a comfortable stay. As always when in captivity, this lion, hoping to roar in his writing, was pliant with prison authority, and they smiled back. He wrote Pauline and Chig that he enjoyed the meals, the weekly films, the ball games, discussing various authors at the prison literary society, winning a prize in a short-story contest, writing a manual on "Basic English for the Illiterate Adult," presiding at the Literary Forum with discussions of *Lolita* and the film *The Ten Commandments* (both right up his alley), and taking a leading part in High Holiday services, just as he had done during his first stay. He enjoyed the company as well, since Lewisburg housed white-collar criminals. David Greenglass and Harry Gold, principal witnesses in the Rosenberg case, were members of the Forum.[90]

At Lewisburg when Roth arrived was the radical sex therapist and psychoanalyst Wilhelm Reich, who was also a victim of a federal agency, in his case the Food and Drug Administration. An injunction had been ordered on his orgone energy accumulator, and Reich defied the injunction. He was convicted and sent to Lewisburg in late March 1957, where he died on November 3. It is hardly possible that Roth had lunchtime conversations about sex and censorship with Reich, as one source has claimed.[91] Reich was obviously depressed by the government's destruction of his books and his orgone installations. He did not have much contact with other prisoners. Although he lost considerably more of his creative work than had Roth, there is a valid comparison. Both men, and their writings, were treated as too dangerous to society to be allowed to exist in its midst. Both men would rather face prison than be given leniency for apologizing to representatives of a closed-minded and cliché-ridden state apparatus. For Roth, as opposed to Reich, it was another example, of which the International Protest was an earlier one, of a contempt that he never doubted was unfair and which he believed it was his destiny to overcome. For Reich it meant a final martyrdom. Having no access to Yeshea, Reich had to confront the suppression of his work as psychologist and writer with only humiliating mundane realities, and the sanctimonious vigilance of the federal bureaucracy, in view.

Since Adelaide Kugel was living with her own family in Connecticut, and could not run over to the Forty-second Street research library for him, there were less letters to her than during his first stretch. Otherwise, the whole scenario was familiar from the late 1930s. "I believe that much can be accomplished here that we could not accomplish in New York."[92] "We," of course, meant "I." Sam wrote Pauline that "I have written our life—yours, mine, Richard's, and Chig's," in *My Friend Yeshea*.[93] As published, *Yeshea* contains no mention of his wife or children.

It is clear that the government case against Roth was weak, and the draconian sentence was at least partly due to the enmity of Winchell, Hoover, and especially Senator Kefauver, who would have to approve Cashin's permanent appointment to the second circuit. Interestingly, the assistant district attorney in charge of the case refuted Roth's claim that the Legion of Decency or the National Office of Decent Literature reviews or censors adult material. The former, he wrote, "arous[es] Catholic opinion against the low moral tone of the films, and the latter is *not* concerned with the field of adult reading." That is nonsense, as Paul Blanchard's *The Right to Read* had proven four years earlier.[94] Roth's querulous appeal, replete with section headings such as "The Lie Is Sanctified" and "A Pretense at Truth Is the Canker of the Rose," made his cause seem hysterical. It is as if the writer wants to solidify martyrdom for himself at the hands of a hostile world. The larger freedom-of-expression issue he fought for was quixotic—in his hands. So was a bizarre proposal to the FBI. Roth would go to Mexico to spy on Communist expatriates living there, of which there were many since the HUAC hearings and McCarthy's activities.[95] The FBI investigated Roth's publishing career and decided he had little acquaintance with Communists but was looking for a way out of prison. They ignored his request.[96]

A Life "Painfully Repoured"

Sam Roth's need to have time to write about Mishillim and his mission resulted in his final prison opus, in which he revealed when and where his destiny was ordained. In his first letter to Pauline from Lewisburg, he told her, "Whether you believe it or not, I work better here than in my beautiful library." That was a chief reason why he was back in Lewisburg. He promised a creative breakthrough the astonished world would revere, and for which it would pay lots of money. It all rang hollow with bad faith and boasting. But "life is and." There is bravado, but also bravery, not the kind that requires an existential choice to carve subjective meaning from chaos but a struggle to conform to a preexisting but elusive divine reality. The perseverance that led to the completion of *My Friend Yeshea* is very real. So is the faith in a destiny that, implicit in the ideal of a True World, restores integrity and wholeness. While writing the "Resurrection" section of *My Friend Yeshea*, Sam quoted for Pauline verses in which "I've written my heart out."[97] Lazarus chants them as he dances at the weddings of Mary and Martha that Roth imagines taking place at the synagogue in Capernaum on the Sea of Galilee. Lazarus is "like a living corpse floating along the floor," singing in a honeyed whisper with his arms enfolding an invisible partner:

> Turning, turning in my narrowing furrow
> I feel the speculative flight of air fowl
> . . . .
> I'll keep on turning till I
> Wear out. Deep in me, seeds of wings are pushing
> To break through flesh and blood.
> . . . .
> Can I be said to live, whom death made such a meal of?
> May a peach-pit, spat out as indigestible,
> Hope to return a peach tree? Let all peach trees
> And their peri-wigged sisters-in-law plum trees
> Bow heads in shame and hide their savory faces.
> Take it on your own terms, fighter in darkness.
> If you can't spare the blood, fill my arteries
> With the sap of woodcombs loused up with combing
> The diseased coiffures of Theban Pharaohs.
> I'll dance on that. I'll make an orange do for
> A sun, an apple for a moon, a cloudburst
> For a deluge, and I'll wait. Someone, somewhere
> Must be as tired of promises as I am.

A wrinkled peach pit is an occasion for bravura lightheartedness due to the irony of its being able to produce a whole new fruit tree, after being spit out as of no account. Why should a tree be ashamed to have owed its life to such an artifact? A turning corpse absorbs enough tiny earthy vitalities to endure the burgeoning of wings in its flesh. It draws tiny increments of new life from fruits of the earth and air, and waits, sensing its loved ones are as tired of promises as it itself is. But now the corpse is awakening. As Lazarus chants and the narrator of *My Friend Yeshea*, Mishillim, watches, the latter swears that his own life was being "painfully repoured—as was the case with Lazarus—from the vats of the *Real World* into those of the *True*."

CHAPTER 10

1958-1974

"It Had Been a Long Time since Someone Like You Had Appeared in the World": Roth Fulfills His Mission

In a key moment in *My Friend Yeshea*, Yeshea explains to Roth ("Mishillim"), "Imprisonment will preserve your latent possibilities and replace your vanished credit with an invincible authority. . . . And you'll bring back to your world . . . its only hope for a peaceful life among the races and nations."[1] In one of the promotional drafts for his book, Roth explains,

> Mishillim turned his back on Yeshea. He fled from the task and from his own people. Yeshea followed him, searching him out in every hiding place, from New York to London and back. Still Mishillim fought Yeshea until, sentenced to prison for five years, he could fight no more. There, through miraculous visions, Yeshea allowed Mishillim to become a witness to the whole of the Nazarene's earthly life and to rediscover his own mystic origin on a shore of the Dead Sea.[2]

A Final Prison Opus

It took Roth at least four years in Lewisburg to write the book of his destiny. During that time he read the Bible, the Talmud, various historical novels, works on the life of Christ, sermons, and Hasidic philosophy. In a sense, he was continuing what he had done originally in 1916 with group of Universalists on Twenty-third Street, who met every Sunday to "remind themselves that God is not confined within one religion."[3]

My Friend Yeshea, however, is a novel about a Jewish destiny. God follows man and asks the fugitive, as he first did of Adam hiding after eating the apple, "Where art thou?" It's a fundamental Hasidic concept, as Martin Buber points out, and uses prominently the image of turning one's back to God. There comes a time when the believing Jew has to turn again to God and account for himself.[4] But the book has another, complementary, subject. It is a story—actually, a recorded dream—of an American Jew who needed to write it because his secular life, despite his going to prison for an "idea," left him psychically unfulfilled. The story of Sam Roth and *My Friend Yeshea* is uniquely American, modernist, and even Joycean, although certainly not in style or subtle allusiveness. It is so in its author's belief in the ability of commonplace, worldly behavior to coexist with the deeply spiritual. Keene Wallis, one of the editors on Roth's staff and translator of *The Divine Comedy* for *American Aphrodite,* wrote a blurb suggesting its Jewish yet also multi-ethnic American tenor: "My own Jesus was a Missourian South Presbyterian, admirable but not imaginabl[y] warm and tender. I love this Jew Jesus, the more as he is most Yiddish."[5]

Roth and other contemporary Jewish writers exploring Jesus as a great rabbi were drawing on two religions' premodern value systems, both of which deplore subversion of the absolutes on which they were founded millennia ago. These other writers, such as Henry Roth and Lamed Shapiro ("The Cross"), were modernists.[6] Along with Sholem Asch (*The Nazarene*) and Israel Zangwill (*The Melting Pot*), their assimilation of Christian with Judaic doctrine was experimental. *My Friend Yeshea* is an iconoclastic work, overlooking, as these other writers do, the medieval and eastern European Jewish belief in Jesus as a blasphemer and sorcerer. Like the other writers, Roth suggests a modern way in which Jews could define themselves in relation to other Americans.[7] The mission God gives Roth's narrator, Mishillim, in *Yeshea*'s closing pages is about maintaining the democratic spirit.

Mishillim intends to, and wishes that he had previously been able to, use the symbols of the Hebrew Bible and Talmud in order to make his contemporaries in the modern city aware of who and what they are. His goal is not far from what Reznikoff and his objectivists were attempting. However, dedicated to making his readers recognize the ageless vitality of a world infused with monotheistic spirituality, he saw his own creativity, and its sources, in the arcane, complex, and universal—the roots of which were in the literature and the religious sensibility of the past, and supremely in the classical and biblical past. He described his inspiration as "a fierce holy flame boring into the inner significance of nature which is not red and ravenous in tooth and claw but the living garment of God himself."[8]

Published by "The Friends of Mishillim"

Roth certainly employed all his ingenuity to find readers for *Yeshea*. He had sent drafts to various publishers—Macmillan, Association Press, Harpers, Heinemann—but the result was polite rejection letters.[9] After deciding to publish it under his Bridgehead imprint, he was unsuccessful in his attempts to find advertising agencies to handle publicity. He placed notices in trade publications, and even arranged for 11″ × 21″ posters ("streamers") above the windows of New York's IRT subway cars. These implied that the book had already caused a sensation and was on sale at "Doubleday's, Brentano's, Scribners, Department Stores, and all neighborhood book shops." Translations were in progress. The posters suggested people give the book to friends of different faiths, urging, "If you own a bible you must have *My Friend Yeshea*." A draft of one advertisement included the statement "Don't go on keeping the door of your house closed to your last hope"; another told people, "Jews give Christians *My Friend Yeshea*." He prepared pre-publication statements for various periodical book review editors, including one for *The Jewish Leader*.[10] A sermon preached in St. Patrick's in early 1962 encouraged him. It was titled "Israel and Christ" and was about the Jewish antecedents of Christianity and the Jewishness of Jesus.[11]

A membership application for "The Friends of Mishillim" appeared on the back flap of the dust jacket of the book. He could not organize a Billy Graham–like crusade, but he did plan a lecture to be given in Times Square. "Hear God's voice / Through the voice of / Samuel Roth, Author of / MY FRIEND YESHEA."[12] The original "friends of Mishillim were at his side when his mission was revealed to him." Now that the book, "the foundation-stone of *Mishillimism*," had appeared in the world, his new friends would "become the princes, cardinals, and deacons of the new religion." This is something new: an evangelical Jew. But so it had been decreed.

The carefully posed photo of himself chosen to accompany the publication of *My Friend Yeshea* shows a nervously alert, trim person, severe with a touch of elegance, looking not quite directly at the viewer. This is the pose of a man who has searched out an awareness of life, experienced harsh tests, found his destiny, and desires to share that knowledge and how it has enriched him. This serene but determined fellow-feeling is reflected in a tender smile.

He has his arms crossed so that an expensive watch, well-tailored suit, and well-positioned bow tie are equally prominent with thick wrists, long fingers, determined mouth, and piercing, deep-set eyes. Not only equanimity but affluence and learning indicate a worthiness that has been hard-earned, and with which he is therefore comfortable.

"He Was Dreaming His Better Self"

This is Arthur Sainer's title for his essay in honor of his uncle. He says that for his uncle, a place to stay, whether in the Catskills on vacation or at Lewisburg in his cell, was a place to write. "More than a challenge, Sam was a familiar mystery, but impenetrable nonetheless, a whole cloth of mystery."[13] Whatever the literary merits of Roth's account of the ministry of Christ from the Sea of Galilee to Golgotha, his nephew's comment is discerning: "There is a largeness of spirit in Sam's serious writing, certainly a concern for humane values, and a commitment to stand in righteousness, somewhat in the manner of the Prophets." The published 628-page version was illustrated with stark line drawings for each section suggesting ancient longing, pain, and redemptive prayer.[14] Roth's book was about Yeshea's plan for Mishillim; his "better self." "Every one of us leads two lives: the life we plan, and the life planned beyond us."[15]

The book is intended to round out Roth's prophetic career by bringing to mankind what was promised in that pamphlet he read aloud in the steerage section of the *Praetoria* a half century before. The heart of *My Friend Yeshea*'s first two sections, "The Journey to Jerusalem" and "The Crucifixion," consists of Yeshea's acts of humility, his free gift of love, and his healing of mind and body. Many pages are given to his discussions with thieves, lepers, and Roman authorities such as Pilate and Caiaphas, the chief priest of Jerusalem. Rabbi Gamaliel, head of the Sanhedrin, adviser to Herod, and a teacher of Paul, is also prominent. Like other Jewish writers on Jesus, Roth avoids questions of Incarnation and Trinity, which run contrary to Jewish monotheism.[16]

With Rabbi Yeshea in Galilee and Jerusalem

For Roth, Yeshea's greatness lies in his love of life, laughter, and people, whether they be centurions, thieves, farmers and fisherman, his devout followers, or learned rabbis. Yeshea seems to thrive on imparting God's presence as embodied in the holy light of Shekinah. A rabbinical term for the glory radiated throughout the Holy of Holies in the Second Temple, and throughout

Figure 24. Roth in 1960, from the dust jacket of *My Friend Yeshea*. By permission of the Roth estate.

a redeemed world, Shekinah is at the center of the vision of another Jewish writer, whose eight-year-old protagonist intuits a need to assimilate Jesus' love and assurance into his Yiddish teachings, especially family history. In Henry Roth's *Call It Sleep*, David Schearl is fascinated with the light in a painting of

Christ in a Catholic playmate's apartment. At the climax of the novel, the light (from an electrical circuit) floods the boy's soul (as it did that of Elijah when his lips touched the burning coal) and symbolizes pure creative joy. Shekinah—spiritual, life-giving, and creative—is conceived as a feminine attribute. In *My Friend Yeshea,* Roth envisions Shekinah as Yeshea's gift to mankind, and the distinguishing feature of Yeshea himself. He radiates it not so much in his discursive speech as in a "genialness so deep, so rich and so widesweeping" that it could only be defined as "an all-conquering love of life." Compassion is inseparable from it. Yeshea's implicit invitation is to join him in a harmony not possible in isolation from other humans. Communal solidarity in worship is a prerequisite for many acts of sacrifice and piety. Such ideals of human potential are exemplified by the Hasidic masters.

A majority of the most appealing characters in *My Friend Yeshea* are women, as might be expected given its author's admiration for them. His guide in the journey to Jerusalem is "the woman of all women," Lilith. "Hers were the flowering breasts, the full haunches and the moving hips of nymphs out of mind."[17] He was "thrilled to his toes." Yeshea had obviously approved if not arranged this pairing. There is no trace of irony in Roth's Mishillim-Lilith matchup, despite the unfortunate mention of toes. Lilith makes him forget his loneliness and reminds him that the senses have a complementary purity to the divine presence. Roth had once conjectured that the story of Lilith proves one of the "Talmud-makers" was a "sensualist" and that a person who did not meet Lilith had suffered "one of the major punishments in creation" ("CMAM," 337). Most Jewish readers, naturally, would be quite censorious at Mishillim's joy in having Lilith as a companion.

In the rabbinical literature, after the appearance of Eve, Lilith became, and remained, a threat. The female and male elements were equal in man when he first became a living soul. But after a submissive Eve replaced Lilith, she hid herself in glowering darkness, spawned demons, and killed human babies. In glaring contrast, Roth, in *My Friend Yeshea,* makes no identification of the female principle with the Evil Inclination, as the biblical commentators do in regard to both Eve and Lilith. Those scholars would undoubtedly disdain the connection Roth does make between the joy of beholding a world that is God and a delight in the ephemeral universe in which the senses are a snare. It is present in Roth's lavish description of Veronica's beauty: "Flesh more blonde than the flesh of the wild peach, of the wild apricot, and sweeter than the wild strawberry"; "she stopped the clouds in their tracks"; "the flowers quivered and grew rigid." The sensual seems to overpower, not merge with, the metaphysical in these passages. Only in his early religious verses does Roth express a conviction that happiness means replacing sexual pleasure with the ascetic discipline through which one intuits that everything in the world is God's love.

People who are conflicted regarding sensual satisfaction and obligations to other people do not "give joy to God," as Buber puts it. Such contradictions are not present in "a holy rest in God."[18] Mishillim was warned of this when, in "Mishillim Brings News from the True World" (c. 1938), the Lord tells him he has "kept so close to her [Lilith] all your life. Never have I seen a man so hot in pursuit of the ancient bitch as in your sad feverish life."[19] The ideology is very different in *My Friend Yeshea*, where Moses said God made Lilith "nine parts fire and one part ice" (382), implying a criticism: didn't God see her independence before creating her? Lilith tells Mishillim that her excision from the Bible is due to her being the first human rebel. That, God could not abide, having seen it, as Roth imagines, in the second Adam he created, when he danced with his back to God. So, God banished her to the night hinterlands. The poisonous root of the Evil Inclination is rebellion against familial and social order. This is the Lilith of the Talmud and Jewish folklore. Mishillim's guide greatly resembles the accounts of the ideal female in Gnostic writings, and perhaps in the Zohar, where a woman completes the soul of the man she loves.[20]

The version of Mary Magdalene and Yeshea that Roth offers is also built on the premise that piety and carnal desire were not incompatible. While he does not make Mary Magdalene Yeshea's bride, his narrative states that Yeshea wanted to marry her. This is not an unreasonable interpretation, given that at the time Jewish men were supposed to be married in order to complete their awareness of human potential. Even the apostles were admonished to go out teaching in pairs; husband and wife may have been meant.[21] In any event, Yeshea's love of Mary began when he first saw her in her father's house. She rejected him, and became a prostitute whose beauty made her wealthy and powerful in northern Galilee. In Phasaelis, Mary approaches Yeshea, sounding like Samuel Roth: "The last shreds of my pride trail in tatters behind me. Whatever virtues I was born with have been scared out of my nature. The seven demons who replaced them have dug their claws into me and hold me in pawn" (*MFY*, 111). This effective passage is followed by others graphically depicting the howls of the demons, in despair and anger as Yeshea exorcized them from his beloved's body.

Some of Roth's most successful writing is in this vein. *Yeshea*'s narrator, as in Roth's autobiography, suggests a modicum of sympathy with the demon's "half-sob, so that it was difficult to decide whether its grief was for itself or on behalf of the endangered woman" (115). Here is another example of the writer's insistence that sensuality is congenial to human nature. And that to deny it has torturous consequences for the psyche and body. However, if Yeshea showed such hesitancy, he would never have saved Mary. Roth describes Yeshea as performing this and other miracles without any scrolls, books, wands, or human or supernatural helpers. These abilities are further indication that Rabbi Yeshea is the son of God. Mishillim therefore gives testimony not only to the career of the greatest of rabbis but also to the birth of a new religion. Roth further tries to reconcile Christianity to Judaism by making the third part of his novel about the Resurrection. He was aware of the problem for Jewish readers, and when, at the climax, Mishillim gets his mission, he gets it directly from Yahweh and climbs Jacob's Ladder to be examined. Sholem Asch got into the same difficulty, not in *The Nazarene* (1939) but in another of his novels about New Testament figures, *The Apostle* (1949), a copy of which Roth asked his wife to send him.[22] Favorable reviews of *The Nazarene* pointed to Asch's attempt to stress similarities between Jesus' teachings and Jewish messianism, with its values of sacrifice, suffering, and atonement.[23] His premise was that Jesus had undertaken to preach Yahweh's Covenant, as had Moses and the Patriarchs.

A Jewish writer on Jesus has to walk a sky-high tightrope about the amount of Christian doctrine he puts in his work. Christianity posits a dualism between God and Satan. The devil is not defeated, and evil does not leave the world, until the Apocalypse. Hasidic Judaism posits that any human can celebrate his or her unity with God, who as the *Ein Sof* permeates all things.[24] For Roth, it is feminine beauty that makes this unity immanent in the world. This metaphysics is at odds with both Hasidic and Christian thought.

There are two indications that Roth did take care to avoid the entanglements of using Christian eschatology, to the extent he could. He at first intended, but decided to exclude, the Ascension, as well as the Resurrection. He also decided to keep the latter word as title for the third and final section of his work, which describes Jesus' visit to the faithful, including Mishillim, sometime during the forty days following his death. Roth had been toying with using the Greek word *Perousia* instead, which means "Second Coming."[25] He had no doubt that his purpose was a deeply, and uniquely, Jewish one. "To be devoted to something is to want to understand it, to resist any misunderstanding of it, and be prepared to fight for it. I feel that way about the books I love, the ideas I live, my wife and my people." So Roth wrote in a letter to Pauline as he was finishing the first section of *My Friend Yeshea*.[26]

Roth Dreams a Final Examination, and a Revelation of Identity

In the final pages of the novel, Mishillim finds himself on the ivory steps of the Enthronement. "It was a long time since someone like you had appeared in the world," God greets him, "and the routine of prophecy needed shaking and awakening in a new milieu." Yahweh himself proclaims Mishillim a tzaddik, one of the "secret thirty-six" of any generation with a potentially earth-saving message to convey. Yeshea's statement comes after another "True World" trial (as in the 1930s' "Mishillim Brings News"). This time, Mishillim, climbing Jacob's Ladder, listens to an accusing seraph report on his past sins. At his side is an appointed defending angel, Azrael (*MFY*, 480–91). Mishillim's sins—that is, those of the adult Samuel Roth—include the plot against the lives of the five men responsible for his Faro bankruptcy and the desire to have them caught in a pogrom, if one resulted from the Jew-hatred in *Jews Must Live*. Mishillim admits the "hatred, lying, the evil intent." The guilt is clear enough, as is his confession of "insatiable sensualism." It is also clear in his recounting of how he ignored his father for the last seventeen years of his life, and would not pray for his soul from the day he became angry at the synagogue's sexton, who was enforcing a rule barring entrance to anyone who did not contribute to its maintenance. The self-importance of course was Mishillim's. The Kaddish is a symbol of the continuance of the faith from generation to generation. At this point, Azrael, "wings drooping, his eyes circled by rings of black smoke," can hardly bring himself to take his place at Mishillim's side. "Azrael" means "whom God helps."

He will need lots of help defending this sinner, and in fact he gets it, from Yahweh himself, who, like a Hasidic holy man, insists on believing in Mishillim's better self, a self that triumphs behind all the ambition, petulance, neurosis, philandering, belligerence, and self-division. Sam wrote to Pauline, as he was working on *Yeshea*, that "There are such unutterable things in my heart, too, in spite of my deadly verbosity. We are not afraid of those things or of each other. They are, in a word, mysteries—*sacred* mysteries—which we do right not to violate."[27] It may be that he is referring to his many infidelities. He does confess his "insatiable sensualism," but could not, in print, go further. He had been more specific in "Mishillim Brings News," but that was unpublished. He could not hide his infidelities from Yahweh. Roth might be inferring that

God himself was close enough a friend to see Roth's better self, even in spite of these. He, and Yeshea, might realize that the ambition, self-doubts, gloominess, and hostility are all-too-human traits that Roth/Mishillim could use as a ladder to reach a level on which he could fulfill, as a tzaddik, a holy mission.

One mystery the existence of which Sam Roth was at best only occasionally aware was the inevitability of a divided self when one balances the worldly utopia of the American dream and the spiritual oneness offered to the pious believer. If conscious of such self-division, Roth could not proclaim himself, or write that Yeshea had proclaimed him, a tzaddik—unless and until, that is, he could redeem all of those iniquities which made Azrael's wings droop. He might climb the ladder resolutely fashioned from the experience his grasping neediness and hostile soul had given him. *My Friend Yeshea* was itself a key step in that process. Roth has Veronica say to Rabbi Jesus that he taught her "a little more than my soul can bear, for the octopus of knowledge has more claws than eyes" (351). The ego-tearing dilemma of reconciling worldly pleasures of power, respect, and security with self-transcendence, sanctity, and innocence are the topic of much American Jewish literature, including Roth's early poetry. He believed America's spirituality was grounded as deeply as its acquisitiveness.

Mishillim's parents, present at the trial, forgive their son, of course, and so does Yeshea, with explanations that veil too thinly the need of the author to justify rather than humble himself, and convincingly atone. Recalling *Jews Must Live,* Yeshea explains that the first obligation of a writer is not to please but to produce something that expresses a truth flowing from the author's passion, one that was based in Roth's case, the publisher swore, on an unprovoked betrayal. Perhaps Roth's Friend did not listen carefully to Mishillim's own epithet for *Jews Must Live* at his heavenly trial: "ugly" (*MFY*, 582). Its benighted author has now apologized. Has Mishillim been lascivious? Then like David, he is "a man of desire." In *Apotheosis: The Nazarene in Our World,* a long poem Roth had self-published in 1957, the narrator has Yeshea give him his marching orders as a prophet by saying, despite his objections, "You are the one—you are the one and only!" There's a possible allusion, given this call to Roth to fulfill his destiny, to God's sending Nathan to force King David to repent for his sins against Bathsheba's husband (2 Samuel 12). "Thou art the man," Nathan says, after detailing in a parable David's perfidy in taking from Uriah, a faithful soldier, the one beloved person in his life. Roth may intend Yeshea to say, in both *Apotheosis* and *My Friend Yeshea,* that there have been humans before Roth, greater than he, but both venal and powerful, who were able to recognize their base acts and persevere.

Roth had made his living as a middleman providing a mass American male audience with disreputable reading material. Now he is to be a mediator (the title of a 1907 novel about unifying the Jewish and Christian faiths),[28] like the prophets of old, even Moses, Isaiah, Samuel, or Jeremiah. It is a humbling moment. Throughout biblical narrative, the fearful chosen one tries to state he is unworthy.[29] Roth also: he is old, no one listens to him, he has weak eyes, weak hearing, heart palpitations yet. This section of *Yeshea* replicates *Apotheosis*. There, Jesus, clad in workshirt and "patternless" coat and pants, takes Roth on a tour of the earth's nations in crisis and predicts disaster unless Roth raises a warning voice. In *My Friend Yeshea*, Mishillim remembers that Jesus came to him because, in his words, "your life spells nothing if not humiliation." Therefore, he is suitably "disenchanted."[30] It's the typical attribute of a hidden wise man.

The Nazarene, Sholem Asch, and Samuel Roth

The possibility of reconciling the Jewish and Christian peoples received its most powerful literary form as Hitler marched into Poland and France, in the best of the novels about Jesus and the Jews, the Yiddish writer Sholem Asch's *The Nazarene* (1939). Asch was first impressed with the spirituality of Jesus during a trip to Jerusalem, thirty years before he wrote the novel. Roth had revered Yeshea almost twice as long, dating from his voyage in steerage to America. Both *The Nazarene* and *My Friend Yeshea* have a three-part structure, although only Roth would make his last part about the Resurrection. The narrator of *The Nazarene* is a yeshiva student who, in the company of an aged, mysterious, anti-Semitic scholar, finds himself in Jerusalem; in *My Friend Yeshea* it is Roth, by himself, who does so. Roth writes of an anti-Semitic centurion: "it was the Jewishness of this particular Jew [Yeshea] that had led [the centurion] into such an extravaganza of hatred" (428). But the centurion reconsiders. In a haunting passage, Roth suggests the ineffable human motivation that led to the centurion's hate/love of Yeshea:

> What had transpired which had altered his feelings toward this one—a Jew? . . . He found himself in that mystic region where the roots of hatred and love feed one stalk. . . . At the heart of all the creative elements in our nature there is an indeterminate entity—half fraction, half symbol—under whose influence all of our agencies realize that they live by one law, that this law is served equally by love and by hate, and

that love and hate can substitute for one another without loss to either, or to the law itself. (427)

This is a perfectly cogent explanation of the kind of religiosity that Asch was delineating. In *The Nazarene,* a cruel adviser to Pilate lifts a sponge of vinegar to Jesus' lips; his fate is to wander the earth in various guises, unable to die until he undergoes a moral reversal. This is the old scholar, who finally, because of his two-millennium journey, becomes aware of the law "served equally by love and hate" that fueled it. Recalling the Passion of Yeshea, the old man says, "I struggled with him. He conquered me! . . . He took me as one takes a pot and breaks it." He is "like a fish which is caught on a hook. . . . And so I am fastened to him."[31] If hate can be so transfigured, can Roth's own chaos of venal desires also be?

The similarities are clear, and so are the differences. Asch's novel sold two million copies and produced a firestorm of praise and dismay. His champions included Alfred Kazin and Lionel Trilling. On the other hand, many Jewish luminaries, including Abraham Cahan, who had previously published the famous writer in *The Forward,* ostracized Asch. That was Sam's case with the Jewish community after *Jews Must Live,* but he had no literary reputation to lose, no defenders, and hardly any sales.[32]

Ironically, *The Nazarene*'s translator was Maurice Samuel, for whom the obvious model in *Yeshea* is the swinish and double-dealing teacher's assistant, Moise Schmeel. In these passages, Samuel Roth, in all his boorish vindictiveness, emerges behind his persona Mishillim. Far from harboring the humility or tolerance of Yeshea or Hasidic Judaism, Roth's heart still contracted with bitterness, even while writing an intensely religious work about his mission as a tzaddik. That's a sure sign of unacknowledged self-division. Yet he could put into the mouth of God the statement that it had been ages since anyone like Mishillim/Roth had drawn breath on earth. Did he think he could hide the presumption from the Master of the Universe?

At age sixty-four, Roth had not yet traveled far enough on the path of becoming a wise man. Perhaps there were too many roles, and dreams, profane and holy, that were too incompatible with each other. A tzaddik has opened himself in all humility to what he knows is cosmic justice. He does not desire to succeed in attaining a reputation as man of letters and making his family proud of him for that reason (as he had told Pauline she would one day be). Nor does he hide from the light what is in the deepest level of his soul. If he retains anger, fear of punishment, pride, or a compulsion to prove his virtue

Samuel Roth, Infamous Modernist

to his community, he needs to cleanse and heal himself. Only "a simple or unified soul" can show his contemporaries what peace in God is, and bring Shekinah to his world, helping repair it for the Messiah. His task is to reach a divine place where, as a disciple of the Baal Shem Tov put it, "all contradictions vanish."[33] Instead, Roth seems like almost everyone else to have evaded that "octopus of knowledge that has more claws than eyes" in order to fend off its soul- and intellect-rending but potentially salutary claws.

What Roth hid from was the subject of a powerful, and also censored, play by Asch, *God of Vengeance* (1918). It takes place in nineteenth-century Russia; Donald Margulies's 2000 adaptation is set in the Lower East Side. Yekel (Margulies fittingly Americanizes the name to "Jack Chapman") is a wealthy owner of an apartment house, the lower floors of which he runs as a brothel. On the top floor he lives with his wife, Sarah, and his daughter, Rifkele. Yekel, delegating to the young procurer Shloyme the management of the brothel, is a respected figure in the Jewish community, and it is essential for him, as provider for his family, which is the center of his universe, to retain this status. To this end he orders a holy scroll to be kept in his daughter's room. It was a tradition for parents without a son. When she marries, the groom can use it to help fix the couple's place in the pious community. That part of Rifkele's identity that inheres in her status as a decorative Jewish object and a marriage prize (like the scroll) in the home of an alrightnik makes her a commodity of a different sort than the girls in his lower-level brothel.[34] The family does not see this as commodification, of course. To marry a daughter to a respectable husband is a part of parental duty, as it was in Jewish shtetl culture, where, however, lack of opportunities prevented awareness of more fulfilling worldly vistas. With Americanization would come this awareness, and increased rebellious bitterness on the part of those designated for an arranged marriage. It would take a lot of agonizing generational conflict before the parental duties of the old country began to lose their strength.

The comparison between Yekel and Sam Roth has of course nothing to do with their daughters. Both men live with a divided consciousness. They make money by exploiting sex, and at the same time strive openly, as they understand the concept, to please God. Roth's *My Friend Yeshea* is certainly an exercise in piety far nobler than Yekel's conspicuous display of his holy scroll in the room of his daughter. But Roth knew, and had been expressing since "Body," that solitary erotic satisfaction became a kind of Medusa, paralyzing the human need for connection and mutuality. But he would not examine this contradiction as he wrote about his God-given mission. The way his business forestalled devotion, as he had learned the latter from his Hasidic teachers and from his studies of the Gospels, remained an imponderable to him.

The Jewish concept of vocation means something antipathetic to commerce: *menschlekeit*. It denotes work that helps prepare other people and therefore oneself for the return of the Messiah (tikkun). It would require withdrawing from mundane security for oneself.[35] It would definitely be foreign to the work of providing male customers with safety valves to drain off, thus escape from, their sexual frustrations. Despite Roth's steady awareness of this failure, he knew he could not give up his business, not only for his sake but for the sake of his family. The contradictions would never vanish; they are inherent to the American dream. That awareness, when it comes to Yekel, tortures him as well.

Ironically, Yekel reaches further toward atonement, although, or because, he suffers more. He is fated not to retain his double function, his divided self. Rifkele meets and falls in love with Shloyme's girlfriend Hindel, one of the prostitutes. Yekel's daughter disappears from her gilded cage. Yekel has only wife, Sarah, to defend him as his twin sanctuaries, lucrative business and modern American home, lower and upper story, collapse into each other, leaving his secrets, and the pseudo-pious lie he has been living, exposed. Now perhaps, in humility and suffering, he will be open to Shekinah, and build for himself a unified soul consonant with authentic human needs. He dismisses his daughter's suitor and divests himself of the facade of respectability, including the scroll. He is advised not to be hasty: "penitence, prayer, and charity" is his friend's advice. In his mouth it is a platitude. But the threefold admonition, to be practiced during the ten days between Rosh Hashanah and Yom Kippur so that the Book of Life may be open to the penitent, might be all that remains for the suffering Yekel, and it could make a new man of him.

Roth was headed for prison, but he did not face a catastrophe. He did not give up the worldly security his work gave him, running his business successfully, thanks to Pauline's love and loyalty, during both his federal incarcerations. Can, therefore, *My Friend Yeshea* substitute for, or be counted as, penitence, prayer, and charity? It's almost tragically harsh to conclude that Roth came before Yeshea with unclean hands, despite his confession, because he was not able to let the light of full awareness penetrate his novel about his destiny. But he did not have to humble a broken self. He did not lose loved ones, health, and safety, as did Asch's brothel owner, or the old wandering scholar in *The Nazarene*, or the emotionally frozen lost soul in Roth's own parable of the Sabbath coin. The latter had accepted his own imminent death in snowbound isolation before he found the lost coin, and with it, light, warmth, and his abandoned family. That lost soul was brought to understand what the perfect moral stringency of the True World's bezdin (judges) required.

Sam Roth was back in business after his release from Lewisburg, and living comfortably among his books in his Upper West Side apartment. Wherever Ezekiel Rubinoff, protagonist of Reznikoff's *By the Waters of Manhattan*, might be in 1960, it is possible he solved the problems his prototype, Samuel Roth, was writing of at that time. Or perhaps he was still wrestling with them, still exerting his powerful will to succeed, without attempting to discard either the worldly success or the spiritual discipline. Could there be atonement in that course of action? One thing is certain: no matter how far Ezekiel or Sam would wander to find his destiny, neither man would ever believe he would die a swindler.

Back in Business

In his final statement of Mishillim's sacred mission, God instructed him to communicate to Russia, America, and the world the bases for world peace: self-determination for their respective satellite states, ethnic and racial equality, arms control, and standardized wages worldwide. As for Israel, she must find a way to coexist with her neighbors. Yahweh insists that Mishillim ("peace bringer")[36] find a way to advocate peace with Egypt as a way of starting the process. And Roth did try to publicize his ideas; as we've seen, with the "streamers," the projected lecture in Times Square, and the "Society of the Friends of Mishillim," he gave it his best entrepreneurial shot.

If *My Friend Yeshea* seemed to be bringing Jews and Christians together so that they might fight against the tide of Communism, Roth foresaw giving up his book business and becoming, not a razor blade or lamp wholesaler, but an advocate for the cause upon release from prison.[37] But in fact *My Friend Yeshea* was only an obscure novel, based on vivid dreams. In the book, and not for the first time, the author projected himself onto a cosmic background. The act of writing itself was the atonement, as it was when he visited the True World during his first stay at Lewisburg, dreaming his better self. If that is harsh, by writing about such a high mission Roth invites strict judgment upon his accomplishments or lack of them after he received his mission. On the other hand, a tzaddik need not show, after his enlightenment, dramatic external changes in conduct. That is a modern expectation, based on the need for revealing in public a quantum change and observable results. There had been some of these. Roth had been an underground publisher of key modernist texts, a trade publisher of some very good ones, an excellent anthologist, and an iconoclast. In the latter role he successfully attacked a sitting president, an ambitious senator, and a malicious gossip columnist who relished destroying careers with insinuations of Communism. Above all, Samuel Roth sacrificed money, status, and personal freedom to liberate freedom to read from political bureaucracy and its exploitation of social taboos to prevent change.

Roth found the money necessary to resume his business in part from selling to Belmont Books the paperback rights to five of his previous publications.[38] In 1965 he received royalty checks totaling $1,500 for two titles.[39] Another source of revenue would have been from books advertised from 1961 to 1963 under the heading "Shopping for Life and Pleasure."[40] These were just the stuff that the 1957 prosecuting attorney, hands held in horror at *Venus and Tannhauser,* would have excoriated as opening the sewers, but thanks in part to *Roth v. United States,* books like these were acceptable. Roth's censorship troubles were over. But he remained on guard. That too was his nature, the hostile, distrustful part. He frequently requested the Library of Congress to ascertain if titles he was considering reprinting were still under copyright.[41] When he opened a package from the Copyright Division returning copies of *Violations of the Child Marilyn Monroe* (1962) that he had sent as part of the application, he opined, "Someone in your office is using his or her job to carry on a small vendetta with me." So many "enormously pornographic books . . . daily receive copyright," he fumed. "I can't believe that this harmless little book is being subjected to rejection." It wasn't. He had sent too many copies, and the division was kindly returning them.[42]

Violations, by Monroe's "Psychiatrist Friend," was published after the star's death in August 1962 (the body was discovered by her therapist).[43] The book exploits the same interest in pedophilia, child sexual abuse, and attacks on innocent femininity that Roth's circulars featured in connection with such books as *Forlorn Sunset, The Devil in the Flesh, Yankee Trader,* and *You Scratch My Back.* "Children have sex-troubles as interesting as those of adults!" *Violations* has an appendix titled "The Child Chasers." It consists primarily of an excerpt from a story by Robert M. Coates in *American Aphrodite.* Coates was a novelist and expatriate, friend in Paris of Hemingway, McAlmon, and Nathaniel West, and the man who wrote the dismissive 1932 piece on Wm. Faro in the *New Yorker.* "The Child Chasers" describes what goes on in the mind of a man who has furtively molested a little girl in a movie theater. When he is discovered he flees, snarling, from an outraged snarling mob. He dies beneath the wheels of a Sixth Avenue El train. The thud not only reverberates in the mind's eye of the reader but also challenges his or her empathetic consciousness. Coates took on a tabooed subject and "made it new" by (potentially) subverting readers' preconditions about the proper application of justice to a child molester.

An ad for *Violations* appearing in the *Confidential* spin-off *The Informer* promises that the book reveals the name of a "high U.S. official" as one of Marilyn's paramours. It does not, but the question regarding why, after the star's death, she aroused "deification" is interestingly addressed. The frontispiece consists of two photos of stars, Elizabeth Taylor and Marilyn. The "Psychiatrist Friend" predicts correctly that Marilyn will become an American icon while Taylor's fame will not outlast her career. Taylor was in charge of her life. Marilyn was conditioned as a child to fend off, if and when she could, indifferent foster parents, lust-crazed molesters, and manipulative employers. She always felt the impulse to escape those whom she thought wanted to possess her, as her violators did when she was a child. In the films for which she became famous, male audiences could fantasize that they could capture her in ways she would have understood to be similar to those of her violators. That fantasy is the kind of response that popular mass entertainment has created for society's vicarious release of repressed sexual desire. Roth had believed this for a long time, and its restatement in 1962 is an ironic judgment on newspaper journalism and the entertainment industry. That judgment applies to himself as well, although he does not say so, here or elsewhere.[44]

Violations of the Child Marilyn Monroe contains the most wickedly puzzling endpapers of any book in the history of the known universe. They consist of a manipulated photograph covering the front and rear pastedowns and free leaves. A voluptuous, smiling Marilyn, at a window, seems to point to her right breast. In the background is an excavation site. On the right is a camera pointed at the star. In the middle of the photo is a smiling Papa Hemingway. There is a sentence in the text in which Marilyn states that she is a "man-made, self-reinforced excavation, always ready and happy to receive whatever byproduct of masculine spilling that may come her way." That gross but resonant utterance is likely Roth's. It alludes to Marilyn's fate as a goddess on view. It reveals what the endpapers might be about. But it primarily functions, for Roth, as a substitute for the fact that he will never get to punch Hemingway, who had died the previous year, in the mouth.

As late as 1968, Roth was placing classified advertisements in men's magazines for back issues of *Good Times,* with its "ravishing nudes and other stimulants." The name of the company listed over a Broadway mail drop was "Living Dolls." The three-foot-high inflatable honeys were one of the other stimulants.[45] After that last gasp, the time had come to retire. One trial advertisement he wrote is poignant, in that it hints at regret at, not reconciliation to, inevitable age and illness. It also carries a trace of disappointment that neither Richard nor Chig wanted to take over an enterprise for which they had little time and which was no longer competitive: "A half a century inoffensively pornographic publishing business. Original founder and present owner is too old and ill to carry on. A wonderful opportunity for the father of an ambitious son or daughter to expand the vision of his family and set them going toward lofty goals."[46] He sold his stock of trade books in January 1970 to one Bernard Shaw.[47]

Heine's "Hebrew Melodies," "Redacted" from the English, Hebrew, and Yiddish Translations

It was Heine's poems on Jewish themes that Roth wanted to work with, and the unpublished manuscript is titled "The Hebrew Melodies of Heinrich Heine, in a Redaction by Samuel Roth."[48] He could not read German well, due to his conservative father not wanting him exposed to modern European culture. Therefore Roth worked with Yiddish, English, and Hebrew translations. Redactions also freed him from literal translation, permitting him to exercise what Roskolenko called his "tendency to do something better than the original."[49] The author had no ability to self-publish at this very late stage in his career (the Book Awards imprint issued only reprinted erotica). He sent the work to Athenaeum in 1969, under the name Francis Page, opining that in addition to its "commercial prospects" it might "cop" the Book-of-the-Month Club award for "best translation from a foreign language."[50]

Privately, Roth admitted his redaction was a battle that neither he nor Heine survived: "Heine appeared to be preparing an organized withdrawal." He tries to justify himself by summarily dismissing the translations of Emma Lazarus and Louis Untermeyer as unworthy of engaging in any struggle for victory on the Heine front. Their poems and essays had in fact been warmly welcomed in America. Untermeyer was known as "the American Heine," and both poets were important in establishing Heine's twentieth-century American reputation.[51]

Roth did not explain why he admired the German poet, but there were several reasons. The redactor wrote that he believed "all my life" in communication between the living and the dead. "In that faith," wrote Samuel Roth, the explorer of the True World, "I felt that I could not only reproduce Heine in English, but that, when I chose to, I could write like him."[52] Heine had a complex, inconsistent self-image. He knew the destructiveness that rage, fear, and resentment unloosed. Roth also well knew that response, in himself and others. Both men had isolated themselves for a time from their religion, Heine by converting to Protestantism so that he could practice law, and Roth by publishing *Jews Must Live.* Both experienced guilt and self-hatred. Heine wrote of leaving Germany for France (where he spent the last twenty-five years of his life) because of "the impossibility of washing away the Jew" in his native land.[53] Both writers made significant compromises, making many enemies yet managing to lead comfortable daily lives. Both accepted their outsider status, Roth by his self-proclaimed "mocki-grisball" epithet; Heine by his interest in Marx, his residence in France, and the innovative mixture of romanticism and sharply satirical passages in his poems. His harsh criticism of Christianity and of contemporaries also isolated him. Both men bristled with what Roth called Jewish belligerence, sometimes narcissistic and sometimes heroic.[54]

Roth added several stanzas to the beginning of Heine's renowned "The Princess Sabbath." They describe the Jews and "Arabs" as competing in ugly fashion with each other six days a week, shouting for the attention of pass-ersby, "carping" with each other, and grubbing for money even in the gutters. The world of trade was Roth's far more than Heine's. But Roth's description of poverty-stricken ghetto Jews "pidd[ling] through slime and slops" six days a week to find salable items does echo Heine's language and theme. Also, writing about Isaac and Rebecca, he juxtaposes the sordid with the ethereal, much in the spirit of Heine's romances:

> Moving through the golden star-dust
> Toward the trail of trade before him:
> Dreamers of the dust and dreamers
> Of the flesh that tremulously
> Wait behind a stirring curtain
> For a bloodied consummation.

Also successful is the redaction of a poem Heine wanted to write but did not, a second part of "Donna Clara," a haunting story of Donna Clara's rejection of a Jew, Don Romero, with whom she shares a consuming passion. (Lazarus had written her own version.) She marries a knight, as her father instructed her. At the wedding, she sees Romero and, dancing with him, recognizes how cold his hands are, how dry his cheek, and how he carries a carrion odor. Roth, redacting, then tells us he had only hours ago "died a Jew's death," presumably at the hands of the Inquisitors. Roth eschewed a comforting love-conquers-all finale. Clara's politic family could do what they did to remove Romero from the scene because the naive, romantic daughter was playing out a Romeo and Juliet script. Romero expected to become Clara's husband due to his success at fighting Arabs and because he had left his beloved with child. His fate is a bitter one.

Roth admitted that in his redaction of Heine he was "shooting blindly at moving targets."[55] A miss, largely. He adds nothing significant to most poems, even the most faithful redactions, such as "The Will," "Affrontenburg," and "The New Israelite Hospital at Hamburg." But Roth seems to be recovering a precise and forceful, because plainspoken, American voice, which allows him both to be colloquial and to write provocative, because slightly eccentric, images. He is becoming skilled at the implications of irony. His stanzas from "Prologue to *The Rabbi of Bacharach*" are effective in this way. In Heine's unfinished novel, planted evidence of ritual murder forces the rabbi and his wife to flee the city on Passover. Roth's impassive, sardonic narrator dismisses a sentimental response that would soften the viciousness:

> Such a painful story, really!
> Ladies dab their eyes and sigh.
> Even God is having trouble
> Keeping Heaven's porches dry.

"Heliogabalus: His Sunhood"

Roth was over seventy when he wrote this 341-page manuscript, under his pseudonym Norman Lockridge, about the teenage second-century A.D. Roman emperor.[56] As the use of the pseudonym suggests, he wanted to publish the work, and in May 1968 he sent it to Hill and Wang.[57] The eponymous protagonist was, as a child, a royal priest of the sun god Eliogabalus in Syria. He came to the Roman throne at fifteen as a charismatic prodigy, renowned as the handsomest man in the empire. He indulged in sybaritic revels that revealed him to be a transgender (possibly even transsexual) person with two "husbands" (both slaves). In addition, he performed in "barbarian" Phoenician rites devoted to his god, wore outlandish costumes, assumed effeminate gestures and speech, and violated such taboos as having sex with vestal virgins. At nineteen he was murdered by a mob incited by the next emperor, his cousin Alexander Severus. Roth apparently relied on various sources: Dio

Cassius, the *Scriptores Historia Augustae,* and the novel by Antonin Artaud, *Heliogabalus: Or, the Crowned Anarchist* (1934).

Roth's "Heliogabalus" is another redaction. There is much of interest, especially including another piece of evidence of Roth's early appreciation of a modernist writer whose present-day reputation far exceeds what it was when Roth knew of his work. His grandson, a university literature student and poet, was especially appreciative of learning about Artaud. The Frenchman's vision was the opposite of Roth's; schizophrenic, he spent as much time in an insane asylum as Roth did in prison. He was an anarchist, desiring a total dismantling not only of religion and spirituality but also of linguistic cues regarding syntactic and lexical order. Literature, to Artaud, was commodity and status, therefore "shit." Roth wanted to be considered a man of letters, while to Artaud that was just another name for copriphiliac. But there were two shared realities that had bedeviled both men. First, and probably most important to Roth, was the repression of Artaud's "obscene" work. The French radio broadcasting authorities withdrew Artaud's radio play, *To Have Done with the Judgment of God,* from its scheduled performance in 1947 on grounds of incoherence, obscenity, and blasphemy, all three, to Artaud, characteristic of twentieth-century culture under the ego-strangling restrictions of a Judeo-Christian deity.[58] There was a second similarity: both men were regarded as unbalanced and without cultural or symbolic capital. Artaud's self-invention, like Roth's, was unmarketable to any particular coterie. Both were objects of derision, or were ignored, by journalists and academics.

While it would be fascinating to report that Roth seems to have understood what Artaud was suggesting about the holiness of anarchy, and its radical self-affirmation, these final pages of Roth's "Heliogabalus" show nothing of the sort. Artaud had cruelly served up a nightmarish stew of a sun without shadows, ecstasy, violation, helplessness. Roth merely titled his final pages "The End."

The "Israeli Davidia," or "Israeli Book of Psalms"

In April 1967, at the age of seventy-three, Sam asked his grandson to copyedit a set of poems titled "The Israeli Book of Psalms" (an alternate title was "The Kingdom"; "Israeli Davidia" was apparently an earlier version), which represented his personal adaptation of the 150 Psalms of David.[59] (In quoting from this work, I give the number the poet assigned each poem, and indicate if I am quoting from the "Davidia," which contains some notable lyrics not in the

Psalms.) "Please don't discuss it or mention it in conversation with anyone," he wrote. "I've never liked anything I've done as much as I like this. I'll really miss it—if I ever decide that it's all done."[60] Despite the request for secrecy, he sent the manuscript titled "The Kingdom" during 1967 and 1968 to Harper and Row, Allen and Unwin, Viking, Secker and Warburg, and the Jewish Publication Society.[61]

Roth's early poetry had resonance, discipline, and assurance. It avoided sentimentality and hollow declamations. It was, above all, about something—a receding spirituality for which the poet and his audience could not help grasping, even despite themselves. His redaction of the Psalms of David retained the discipline, and were written in the colloquial language of the streets, workplaces, and homes of the American city. Humility and thankfulness mark these twentieth-century psalms. But these feelings coexist with challenges to the Almighty—"I want to know, and now"—although (not too decorously) restrained by awareness of to whom he is speaking.[62] The psalms are thus sometimes marked by the impatience that led to Roth's early undoing as man of letters. Nevertheless, he comes to terms with his personal flaws with irony and reflective distance. The frequent deference was an infrequent note for Roth, and suggests that these late poems were the occasion for a personal discovery. That was a chief reason for the poet's enjoyment in writing them.

Psalms were originally a nonliterate culture's communal prayers in times of danger, and had evolved into personal communications recited in synagogues and wherever private individuals needed inner strength. They were supplications meant for relief of the speaker's people, rather than an answer to the poet's own grievances; they praised God's power and his mercy toward a community of penitent sinners.[63] Roth's poems are addressed to "The Lord" and are personal declarations, or sometimes further questions, in answer to the divine question, "Where art thou?" This is as true of the most querulous as it is of the most pious of them.

Roth is not the only writer to have supplemented belief with direct challenges to the Lord in twentieth-century American Jewish literature. I. B. Singer wrote that the devout "have often dared to question His justice, and to rebel against His seeming neutrality in man's struggle between good and evil."[64] In *Europe* ("Thus Saith the Lord"), written more than forty years before his "Davidia," the poet describes God humbling himself for allowing, in revulsion at humanity, his "keys of creation" to fall into the abyss. The final lines of Roth's first psalm assert, "This is a / little rebellion, Lord. / Are you with it?" He was hoping to incite a dialogue, as difficult as that would be in the nuclear age, by which time it would take enormous fervor to make God acknowledge a human being. Often, as in his first poem, questions were posed in a poem's concluding line. The speaker does not appear egotistical or hubristic, but as an older man with a spark of King David's courage, sometimes used waywardly. David once fought on the side of the Philistines; Roth's psalmist confesses having walked with sinners and unbelievers. This poet, like King David in his psalms, often succeeds in creating a worshipful tone, but that is often tentative. Roth did not live in a world of uplifted armor and war cries, or communal hymns, but in one that necessitated irony, careful assessment of people and opportunities, and quiet remorse. "Dad always felt guilty about something," Adelaide notes, giving examples of self-assertion and self-indulgence such as his adulterous affairs and his rejection of his own father.

The speaker iterates his little rebellions throughout the psalm sequence. His fallibility, which is the source of his insistence, was never more on display, or more ironically expressed. "If I'm to be delivered, the time is now, Lord" (number 6). The biblical Psalm 6 is a supplication to the Almighty to effect a merciful rescue of Israelites helplessly besieged by foes.[65] Roth's allusion to it helps us place him in his own world, that of a still-uncertain retired business-man. An unnumbered poem in the "Davidia" invents a story about the angel sent to expel Adam and Eve from Paradise. He was the only one who would do so, and since then he perpetually weeps. In this poet's universe, angels as well as flesh and blood are allowed "little rebellions," if they are willing to pay a price. God has shrewdly quarantined the weeping angel from the others. So it appears to the poet, whose intelligent worldliness cannot conceive of a pious explanation. In number 80, after describing the contempt for Jews throughout the Diaspora centuries, the speaker asks, "Why have you broken down our fences / so all who pass may pause and pluck her" (the vine at Kadesh, from which the Jews drank during the Exodus). In his psalm 27, Roth complains that Jewish poets and philosophers have to live so close to their enemies, the Amelikites, referring to Jews' own bankers. "Can't you provide more space between us?" Again the direct address, as impossible as it is to look directly into God's eyes. The irony is clear: the supplicant here is a narrowly focused pragmatist. But he is still wondering about a very large subject, and is learning that for him, history as nightmare is, finally, a subject with spiritual roots and branches.

Roth's number 36 is a rebellion of a different sort. The original contrasted materialistic with spiritual people and, as translator Robert Alter comments, is a confident supplication to God to impose justice.[66] In fact, the justice has already been applied: "There did the doers of mischief fall." Roth, setting the contrast as between the Jews, or at least the pious ones, and other people, is just as confident of God's power. However, he doubts the ability of the pious to reform the worldly: "Is there anything left that we can teach them?" he concludes. A further contrast between an ancient, pious supplicant and the modern halfhearted one is a shocking image: the poet compares the teachings of the pseudo-pious man to "a red light / outside a tenement wherever / power and pleasure are the subjects / of their ["the gentiles"] exclusive convocations." The image of a whorehouse in this context is not a strange one for Sam Roth to use. It reveals, somewhat ironically, his cynicism as well as his benighted moral state. But he's implicitly confessing, and asking the readers to think through the questions his psalms pose. In that sense, he tries to provide a communal context.

Another notable set of redactions is about the speaker's fascination with sex, his misanthropy, and his fear of aging and death. David had these problems also; his need for Bathsheba led, at least indirectly, to God's barring him from having a hand in the building of the First Temple. For his ordering the death of Uriah and his company of soldiers sent to the hottest part of the battle, David's own son dies. Now he must live continually in a state of war-readiness. In Psalm 51, David offers God, for relief, "a broken spirit: a broken and contrite heart."[67] Roth's own experience is as unheroic as the language in which he expresses it is commonplace. Nor had he experienced the broken heart that, as Rabbi Nachman of Breslov said, "lets the light in." One of his most self-loathing verses is number 59, in which the speaker writes of his "woman fever" preventing him from other pursuits, "leaving your otherwise devoted servant slave to a hole, a small enough hole, but a hole that knows no end of filling."[68] That he asks God why this is so completes his debasement. Roth's version of Psalm 38 retains the images of the impure, diseased body from the original (twisted, with running sores, dizziness, painful internal organs, and pounding heart) but attributes the infection, and consequent self-hatred, to a non-biblical "Arab strumpet" in order to identify the impurity with David's own undisciplined lust. "Pluck the wanton out of my flesh," he writes. These two poems are helpless whines, not pious supplications. They do embody existential doubt, which two poems in the "Davidia" collection explore forcefully. The first describes a dream that comes as close to a death experience as one can have and wake up.

> The moon vanished, lost in a drizzle.
> She wasn't missed till I remembered

Seeing her arch and fall, and melt in
Falling . . .
. . . .
As if to remind us of our condition,
The stars like giant pebbles dropped down
Into our atmosphere and fizzed out.
It was something that called for fury.

The process was so sudden and inevitable that there was not time for anyone to express concern. As "the universe" retorted to the man who insisted "I exist" in Stephen Crane's poem, that fact instilled no "sense of obligation." It's the nightmare of one who knows he will die, and so cannot be content to be part of a natural process with no metaphysical purpose. Roth's psalm 38 is as different from David's suffering as David's contrition is from Roth's fear of nothingness. But the modern as well as the biblical sufferer's panic results in their turning to the Lord as the only possible refuge.

God is not mentioned in this poem. What this may indicate about the writer's soul is explained in his psalm 144. A similar statement, number 108, is about how the speaker's life work has "made a mock of his Jewishness." Now the angel of death approaches. In 144 the speaker is walking with his "Guide" through a snowstorm, on a quest for his "long lost soul." The atmosphere clears, wolves turn into lambs. The Guide tells the speaker he has worked in his life with a precious metal (money?) but not with people. It's a moment of brutal clarity, not peace.

Look around you. What do you notice? And I answered
"Nothing. There's nothing here. Certainly
no people."
"But you don't need people,"
he insisted. "Without a soul you've
no need of people."
"Then what were we
Searching for?" I insisted.
"Nothing,"
He answered. "And we've found it."

This poet's being might be empty of soul, but the universe in this empty space at which he has arrived is not empty of spirituality, nor is he without a guide.

The latter seems to be asking "Where art thou?" Now it is the speaker who, enlightened about as much as a stiff-necked human being can be, has to answer for himself. The most repeated word in this mysterious poem is "secret."

The speaker in Roth's redaction of Psalm 38 is both a modern version of David and Roth himself. Confronted with personal weakness, both must learn to use it as they find, painfully, the road to holiness. A similar poem, and its original, number 41, is about physical torture (David's, and the speaker's, enemies would "pour him out like so much water"). The poem is also about the distance between God and the world Jews have had to struggle with since the days of the Judges and Kings. In the biblical Psalm 17, David pleads that God hide him "in the shadow of thy wings" from his enemies who would "cast us down . . . like a lion that is eager to tear in pieces." That horror in Roth's psalm 17 is symbolized by the sufferings of the Diaspora as imprinted in "anatomical afflictions / induced into me by Amalek" (the invention of the Jew's body, as Sandor Gilman analyzes it):

> tell me if my millennia
> In your bloody, perspiring ghettos
> did or did not transform me into
> something other than the creation
> fashioned by you out of the starlit
> Mesopotamian mud, named Adam?

This poem, and others almost as rebellious, might explain why one draft of Roth's "Psalms of David" was signed "David Zorn." The biblical David's next prayer is of thanksgiving for deliverance. Few poets could come closer to the awesome glory of the God of Battles, coming down in fire, darkness, lightning, and cloud out of which his "brightness" thundered hail and tornado: "the foundations of the world were laid bare." But the poet Roth, from his study near Central Park West, sends forth an irascible question, and never waits for an answer he knows he has to find in his very mundane self. He "wants to know and now." Then he hopes God will "go and break his [Amalek's strutting] legs for him." Armchair warriors are moral cowards.

The "stiff necked" all-too-human querulousness Roth believes characterizes Diaspora Jews is the topic of two other poems. The first, set in the time of the Exodus from Egypt, delineates the desire of one faction of the mixed multitude to return to the "flesh pots" rather than observe the laws Moses brought from Sinai. For this nation, childlike faith in a God who can produce honey from rocks cannot compete with the inductive evidence of the difficulty of the trek through the wilderness. The second, number 21 in the "Davidia" (a completely different poem from the biblical psalm), reimagines Jacob's deathbed prophecy to his sons, the Children of Israel (Genesis 49:1–2). In Roth's version, the patriarch finds that he cannot predict the ultimate future, for God's vision at that moment departed from him. Roth tells us what Jacob saw but could not report: six Jew-killing monsters, including Hitler and Stalin, a "monumental meanness." Could the battle God Jehovah, the earth-shaker who so gloriously vanquished the pagan idols, let his Children of Israel contemplate such a desultory future? Roth seems close here to what James Kugel described, apropos of the Book of Lamentations, as "God as the enemy." Jeremiah "unflinchingly" stares at the possibility that the Lord, if "responsible for everything," is responsible for "even the cruelest evil."[69]

Roth never considered, with Nietzsche's prophet, that "God is dead"; he reproduces sometimes the original Psalms' royal praises and thanksgivings in the spirit of the singing congregation, often those specifically attributed to the biblical David. But his tone is that of a twentieth-century urban outcast. His will to say "I exist," to resist authority and demand explanation, is ground deeply into his soul. In this final work, Roth meant to explore himself as he had lived out his days in both his worlds, as venal, titillating publisher and as God-seeking iconoclast haunted by his own venality and sexuality, yet fighting to erase the hypocrisy of people who suppress ideas they find offensive.

His linking himself with the epic yet all-too-human warrior-poet David is like Joyce's linking of his Leopold Bloom with Ulysses. Both Leopold and Samuel are representative members not of a heroic age but of modern times. Both were more advertising man and girl watcher than warrior, and neither was capable of making his contemporaries fear and respect him. But they could directly confront Amalek, in American courtrooms or in an Irish pub. They never lost their guilt, humor, sense of adventure, love of sensual and divine beauty, their curiosity (note the mutually irresistible topic of the transmigration of souls), and, even more importantly, their seeking to realize their destinies in squalid and hostile circumstances.

Psalm 150 is both David's and the modern speaker's "leave-taking." In this poem God makes answer, and has the last word. The poem opens with "David's leaving. It's high time I / put away this substitute living." No more poems, but one more question, or complaint. Why will not the Lord explain to him the mystery "in the songs of / birds, the smiles of women, the perfumes / of flowers." But one thing the speaker knows, for which awareness he has "unutterable devotion" to God, is the ultimate reality. That he can express, in admirable simplicity: "*Death was, is, and takes all.*" God answers, giving his legacy:

> So when the universal silence
> descends on everything, swallowing
> the last of the towers of Zion,
> it will be possible for them [the faithful] to
> turn and remember that a peaceful
> end to all things was all I ever
> saw or promised.

The original Psalm 150 is a hallelujah, a joyous praise of God, using lute, lyre, and cymbal. There is little in Roth's lines that qualifies as song, and nothing of elevated speech, or of the formality in prosody, diction, or image that conveys the solemnity or devotion of divine revelation. But that is a great strength of this poem. Its unheroic facts-on-the-ground bluntness gives it finality, one that erases all hopes, all anxiety, all questions, and all doubt. It's both a communal psalm and an American acceptance, after all, of an eternal presence into which even a "little rebellion" will ineluctably flow. For a man who was willing to put away his love of writing to make money, publish books that made him a villain of indecency and a hero of free expression, and then isolate himself in a prison cell to find time to write his destiny, it is a humbling acceptance. Artaud, from his sanitarium room, would sneer, "You are not free." Heine, from his "mattress grave," would end years of suffering still writing, with penetrating self-awareness of his own "split" between two worlds of bodily pain and astute evaluation of romantic dreams ("Whoever boasts of his heart that it has remained whole, only owns that he has a prosaic, remote nook heart. The great world split has gone through mine").[70] Samuel Roth need write no more. His American success tragicomedy and its struggle, its energy, promise, sexiness, comic gaiety, disparagement, betrayals, compromises, regret, and loneliness had reached its denouement. History, for him, would not be judged a nightmare from which one awakes screaming. What could such a man, in his old age, want, and finally find, more than a peace that he lost during his childhood in "Nustscha," where "one golden dawn / I sang like any bird on any tree / My Song of Songs" (sonnet 2)?

Roth's psalms take their place, with his earlier verses, among the meditative Jewish American poems of the mid–twentieth century. He wasn't quite fair to himself when he wrote his daughter-in-law in 1958 that "I sing [to the world] in the wrong language and the wrong key."[71] Writing at about the same time, Karl Shapiro composed "The 151st Psalm,"[72] the four stanzas of which encapsulate Roth's entire "Davidia": God "whimper[s]," "take[s] wages," read-ies his people for his "hungry Hand." The final two stanzas, with their won-drous contradictions, are especially relevant:

> Immigrant God, You follow me;
> You go with me, you are a distant tree;
> You are the beast that lows in my heart's gates;
> . . . .
> Shepherd of the flocks of praise,
> Youth of all youth, ancient of days,
> Follow us.

The End

There were two literary acknowledgments left for Sam Roth. In 1972 a passage from *Stone Walls Do Not* was selected for inclusion in an anthology of prison writing titled *Imprisoned in America: Prison Communications, 1776 to Attica*, which was published by Harper and Row the following year. It included let-ters, poems, drawings, songs, and petitions from inmates. The editor, in writ-ing for permission, wrote that "I have become an admirer of your work while researching."[73] She had become used to uncovering strong writing ignored or disdained because of the writers' lack of status. Roth was right back at her, with a suggestion that she consider adding a four-page poem in *Stone Walls* to his contribution. In 1973 the *Journal of Modern Literature* published his ac-count from "Count Me among the Missing" of his 1920 visit to London during which he met many of Britain's leading men of letters. It accompanied Leo Hamalian's witty but often disdainful essay on his career.

In 1968, the year of his retirement, Roth's health was failing. By 1973, diabe-tes made it difficult to see, and heart disease weakened him, leading to minor strokes. In August 1973 his daughter-in-law, Peggy, died. Everyone loved her for her open-heartedness, intelligence, empathy, and complete authenticity, as her public memorial service showed. Frank Tannenbaum, a man whom Samuel Roth loved, and to whom he was greatly indebted for the encourage-ment that started his career as a writer, died in 1972, as did one of his most pro-lific writer-editors, David George Plotkin. How Roth responded to the death that year of the man he loved to hate, Maurice Samuel, is unknown. He and Pauline enjoyed three visits from his journalist friend Bill Ryan and his wife, Sharon, in 1973. On one of those occasions, Sharon photographed the couple, Pauline still handsome, Sam frail, perhaps blind, but still well dressed, and, as the Ryans found, talkative. Bill Ryan wrote, that he was, as always, courtly, and still able to reveal his "storehouse of knowledge."[74]

In late June 1974, Roth was hospitalized. In those final several weeks, he remained himself. Adelaide Kugel writes about one of her last visits. Her father had been restrained to his bed because he would walk the corridors. "Oh Chig, Chig," he said when he saw her, "I thought you would make it all right." His daughter, remembering Sam's many pleas for his wife and daughter's succor, took this as a reproach. "The implication that I had failed him was so wounding that the obedient child in me . . . could not question him." She brooded, realizing that "he had done just what he wanted in his willful life, consulting no one, least of all me." While she was arguing with the attending physician, Roth changed his approach: "Forgive me, but does either of you have a scissors?"[75]

He died on July 3, 1974. Bill Ryan reports his last words to Pauline: "Father Time has come round for me at last." The Alters, the Kugels, and the Roths gathered at Riverside Chapel for the memorial service, at which Richard read "Kaddish" and other poems from *Songs Out of Season*. Eulogy was given by First Amendment lawyer Jerry Olitt, another admirer who befriended Roth after his release from Lewisburg. Samuel Roth is interred with Pauline at Cedar Park Beth El Cemetery in Paramus, New Jersey.

The obits were standoffish but not unkind. Some attention, they conceded, should be paid. They put him in his proper place, according to the rules of the game. The *Times* acknowledged Roth's editorial success with *The Lyric*, and his poetry and speculative writing during prison sentences, but not his acclaimed youthful religious poems. The obituary noted his importance in liberalizing the "definition of obscene material" but also his "piracy" of *Ulysses* and Pauline's and his "conviction" for "disseminating" *Lady Chatterley's Lover*. *Ulysses* was not copyrighted in the United States, but this fact was not part of the existing narrative of events. The *Times*' statements, therefore, can be stated to be "fair enough." Finally, *The Strange Career of Mr. Hoover* did not become "controversial" because the author, Hamill, repudiated it.[76] It sold well not only because of the upcoming presidential election, the first since the Crash, but also because Roth knew how to excite curiosity in the lives of celebrities. To say that is to be fair enough.

What do obituary writers know, and what do they think their readers should know? I would hope that Samuel Roth/Mishillim/David Zorn went directly to the True World, to be called forth and judged. With Jerosh the Red and Yussef the cantor and Hudl of the long hair and the exorcist rabbi; with Bones the neglected and Mary the sugar bum and Frank the anarchist;

Samuel Roth, Infamous Modernist

Figure 25. Pauline and Samuel Roth in 1974. Photo accompanying William Ryan's "The Passage of Samuel Roth," *The Rosslyn Review* (Arlington, Va.), September 19, 1974. By permission of the Roth estate.

with Pauline the beloved and Marie the beautiful and Maurice the schmeeil and Erskine the teacher and Herbert the loyal and Robinson the poet and Reznikoff the objectivist; with Joyce the ungrateful and Bloom the wanderer and Pound the despicable and Root the bigot; with Joan the sacrificial and mocki the grisball and Myrna the showgirl and Helen the actress and Sumner the smuthound; with Viereck the critic and Fritz the dashing spy betrayed and Clement the friend and the president and his strange career; with whoever told the stories about the irrepressible pansy and the smart gentleman from Harlem; with Adelaide the adoring and Richard the gentle and his Peggy; with Tanya the abandoned and the parents in the True World forgiving; with Harry the world traveler and Gershon the mordant sage of laughter and pleasure; with a honey for your bedside and whipping Devil Law and Hindus the scholar and Celine his legpuller; with Nietzsche and his sister and Plotkin the ghost and the gleesome threesome; with Winchell the bully and Kefauver the inquisitor and Leisure the thunderer and Cashin the hardhearted and Barney the beneficiary; with Lilith the thrilling companion and Yeshea the supreme guide and Marilyn the violated child and sublime, split-souled Heine and the transgendered emperor. All these go with Mr. Roth of New York, carrying his redaction of the Psalms wherein David Zorn, Mishillim, Francis Page, Roger St. Clair, and Norman Lockridge finally transfigured into a peaceful, reverential Samuel.

Yes. Destiny.

Roth Imprints and Business Names

Roth Imprints (1919–1966)

This preliminary and tentative list of the various imprints Roth used on the title pages of his books was compiled from various sources. The imprints are listed in chronological order. Please note that these are imprints, not trade names, which are much more numerous. The Library of Congress catalogue records were extremely helpful in making this checklist, as were the WorldCat online database and the titles in the Roth Archive at Columbia University and in the New York Public Library Research Division printed catalogues. Also important were the comments of booksellers, and colleagues and relatives of Roth: C. J. Scheiner, Arnold Levy, Anton Gud, William Ryan, Adelaide Kugel. The essays on Roth by Ryan and Hamalian cite many titles and imprints, as do the Kefauver Hearings ("U.S. Senate. Subcommittee to Investigate Juvenile Delinquency of the Committee on the Judiciary"), although Roth denied having anything to do with several of them, and the following court cases: *Samuel Roth v. Albert Goldman,* U.S. Court of Appeals (1949); *United States v. Samuel Roth,* C-53-79 (1929); *United States v. Samuel Roth,* Cr 148-9 (both the original and appellate cases, 1956 and 1959); *United States v. Pauline Roth and Samuel Roth,* C99-114 (1936). The Vertical File of the Kinsey Institute for Sex Research (s.v. "Erotica Producers, Twentieth Century, United States, Roth, Samuel"), in Bloomington, Indiana, has many of Roth's circulars from the 1950s, which are useful in corroborating titles of books he published, although the circulars list books for sale, including remainders from other publishers, as well as his own imprints. Extensive holdings of Roth imprints are found at the Humanities Research Center (University of Texas at Austin), the Morris Library of Southern Illinois University, and the Library of Congress.

Roth's bookselling and publishing career evinces many complex and interesting bibliographical problems that can only be implied in this list. The large number of separate imprints is due to various factors, among which are the ebb and flow of his financial situation, his desire to publish various kinds of books for various audiences, and the need to counter both the interception of certain titles by the Post Office and the reluctance of newspapers and magazines to accept advertisements. In a few cases, legal injunctions regarding subject matter necessitated new imprints.

The imprints are listed chronologically, each entry beginning with the books issued in the first year the imprint began publishing. I have provided each publication (several titles were reprinted under more than one imprint) with a number. These numbers run consecutively.

Lyric Publishing Company (1919)

Roth continued this imprint name when he reestablished *The Lyric* on his own. It had been used for the 1917 and 1918 issues of a Little Magazine under the auspices of Columbia University.

The second number of volume 2 (January 1918) gave the address of the publisher as 1353 Clinton Avenue, the first of Roth and Pauline's two Bronx addresses after their marriage. After the war they resided at 1425 Grand Concourse. There were five numbers of volume 3, the first being issued January 1919 and the last May–June 1919. The first and second numbers of volume 4 were issued as a double number from Roth's Poetry Book Shop at 49 West Eighth Street and dated July–August 1919. There were no more issues after 1919.

1. *The Lyric* (magazine) (1919)

The Poetry Book Shop (1920)

The Poetry Book Shop issued supplements to *The Lyric* as follows. It is possible, as Adelaide Kugel states, that numbers 2 and 4 were never issued (carton 51, s.v. "1919," Roth Archive).

2. Bellamann, Henry. *A Music Teacher's Note Book* (1920). The Sign of the Lyre series, no. 3.
3. Gorman, Herbert S. *The Fool of Love* (1920). The Sign of the Lyre series, no. 2.
4. Long, Haniel. *Students* (1920). The Sign of the Lyre series, no. 4.
5. Reznikoff, Charles. *Poems* (1920). The Sign of the Lyre series, no. 1.
6. Robinson, Edwin Arlington. *Lancelot: A Poem*. New York: Seltzer, 1920. Roth stated that he arranged to have 400 copies run off for him, to commemorate the poem's winning The Lyric Society's $500 poetry prize.

The following may have been published with subvention from the author:

7. Bell, Ralcy Husted. *Her New Lovers* (1919)
8. Connell, Harriett. *The Song of the Waukarusa: A Book of Love* (1920)
9. Crane, Elizabeth. *Poems* (1920)
10. McCormick, Virginia. *The Hermit and Other Poems* (1920)

Two Worlds Publishing Company (1925–1927)

11. *Beau: The Men's Magazine*. October 1926 (no. 1)–October 1927 (no. 7). Originally published under the imprint Beau Publishing Company, with the February 1927 number the imprint became Two Worlds Publishing Company.
12. *Casanova Jr.'s Tales*. April 1926–January 1927. Stated as "privately printed" in no. 1, but the phrase "Published for One Thousand Subscribers by the Two Worlds Publishing Co." appears on the title page beginning with no. 2, and advertisements ask subscriptions be sent to Two Worlds Publishing Company.
13. *Love's Secrets*. "spring number," 1927. The sheets are identical to those of the 3rd

and 4th numbers of *Two Worlds Monthly*, but "the sheets are bound in reverse order" (G. Thomas Tanselle, "Note 282. Samuel Roth's *Love Secrets*, 1927," *The Book Collector* 15, no. 4 [Winter 1966]: 486–87).

14. *Secret Memoirs of Gallant Men and Fair Women*. 2, no. 1 (March [?] 1927)–3, no. 12 (January 1929). A continuation of *Casanova Jr.'s Tales*. (I am grateful to Kathryn Hodson, Special Collections Department Manager, University of Iowa Libraries, for confirming the dates for me.)

15. *Two Worlds* (quarterly): 1, no. 1 (September 1925)–2, no. 8 (June 1927)

16. *Two Worlds Monthly*: 1, no. 1 (1926)–3, no. 4 (October 1927)

Coventry House (1929–1941)

This imprint seems to have been reserved for books either finely printed or which Roth especially liked.

17. "Brownell, Joseph" [Samuel Roth], ed. *The Telephone Directory as a Guide to American Culture* (1929)

18. Donnelly, Robert. *Just Like the Flowers, Dear. A Botany for Parents* (1932) (the book possibly was self-subsidized by author).

19. Douglas, Lord Alfred. *My Friendship with Oscar Wilde, Being the Autobiography of Lord Alfred Douglas* (1932)

20. Goddard, Gloria. *The Last Knight of Europe: The Life of Don John of Austria* (1932)

21. Jarry, Alfred. *The Garden of Priapus* (1932). "Privately printed for subscribers by Coventry House." Trans. Louis Coleman. Introduction by Matthew Josephson. Illustrated by Arthur Zaidenberg. See Black Hawk.

22. O'Sheel, Shamus. *Ballads of the B.E.F.* (1932)

23.———. *It Never Could Happen, Or, The Second American Revolution* (1932)

24. Voltaire. *A Philosophical Dictionary* (1932). "Ten volumes in Two."

25. Tillier, Claude. *My Uncle Benjamin* (1941). Trans. "Marie Lorenz" [Adelaide Roth]. Illustrated by Mahlon Blaine.

Golden Hind Press (1928–1935)

Note: This was the name Roth used in the late 1920s and 1930s to designate his business operations, and it rarely appears as an imprint; more often it is used in the phrase "privately published by the Golden Hind Press." Pauline Roth filed papers to conduct business under this name at the County Clerk's office in Manhattan in April 1928.

26. "Jenks, Anton Shrewsbury" [Samuel Roth?]. *A Dead President Makes Answer to the President's Daughter* (1928)

27. Bell, Ralcy Husted. *Self-Amusement and Its Spectres* (1929). "Published in a limited edition for subscribers." See Big Dollar.

28. [Bonneau, Alcide]. *Padlocks and Girdles of Chastity* (1932). See Big Dollar Book Co.

29. Nafzawi, Umar ibn Muhammad, and Sir Richard Burton. *The Perfumed Garden for the Sweet Recreation* (1933). Illustrated. "Privately published for 500 subscribers."

30. [Roth, Samuel, ed.] *Anecdota Americana. Five Hundred Stories for the Amusement*

of the Five Hundred Nations That Comprise America (1933). Verso title page: "New Revised Edition." The text differs from the Faro version, although there is a statement at the end of both versions reading "this is the end of the first five hundred." See Wm. Faro.

31. Twain, Mark. *1601, or Conversation as It Was at the Fireside in the Time of the Tudors* (1933)

32. Roth, Samuel. *Jews Must Live: An Account of the Persecution of the World by Jewry on All the Frontiers of Civilization* (1934). Illustrated by John Conrad.

33. Mendes, Catulle. *There Are Twenty Good Ways of Doing It: An Acccount of the Sweet Adventures of Lila and Colette, behind the Little Red Lights of Paris* (1934). Illustrated by Rahngild. Paperbound. Stated to be "Privately Printed" on title page verso: "copyright 1934 by The Golden Hind Press, Inc." On cover: "Published for subscribers only." Colophon: 975 copies. See Faro, Boar's Head.

34. *Secret Places of the Human Body, Known as the Ananga-Ranga or the Hindu Art of Love* (1935). Trans. Sir Richard Burton. "Privately Printed."

William Hodgson (1930)

35. "Wakem, Hugh" [Samuel Roth]. *Diary of a Smuthound* (1930). Imprint: "William Hodgson, Philadelphia" (copyright verso title page: 1930). See Faro.

John Henderson (1930)

36. Lewisohn, Ludwig. *The Case of Mr. Crump* (1930). See Black Hawk.

William Faro, Inc. (1930–1933)

Note: In addition to the books listed below, Faro is stated to be the publisher of the paperback review *Plain English* ("The News-Politics-Books-Plays and movies in Plain English"), vol. 1, no. 1 (June 1932).

37. Lawrence, D. H. *Lady Chatterley's Lover* (1930). Modern Amatory Classics no. 1. Verso title page: "Revised 1930, by William Faro, Inc." 2nd impression, 1930. 3rd impression, 1931. 4th impression, 1932. The dates 1931 and 1932 are on the title pages. Frontispiece by A. K. Skillin not in 1st impression.

38. Mirbeau, Octave. *Celestine: Being the Diary of a Chambermaid* (1930). Trans. Alan Durst. Modern Amatory Classics no. 2. Title page states there were "printings" 1930 (Modern Amatory Classics), 1931, 1932, 1933.

39. "Wakem, Hugh" [Samuel Roth]. *Diary of a Smuthound*. Impr.: "William Hodgson, Philadelphia" (copyright verso title page: 1930). Dust jacket gives publisher as William Faro, Inc. Perhaps copies with this jacket simply represent a later issue or state.

40. Anon. [Anthony Gudaitis]. *Lady Chatterley's Husbands: An Anonymous Sequel to the Celebrated Novel Lady Chatterley's Lover* (1931). Illustrated (by Rahngild) and unillustrated impressions were issued.

41. Anon. *The Intimate Journal of Rudolph Valentino* (1931)

42. Bell, Ralcy Hustead. *Memoirs and Mistresses: Colors and Odors of Love* (1931)

43. Cheyney, Ralph. *A Pregnant Woman in a Lean Age* (1931). The Ardent Classics, no. 5.

44. Hamill, John. *The Strange Career of Mr. Hoover under Two Flags* (1931). This being one of Roth's most notorious and best-selling books, there were many impressions, and a paperback.

45. Hellinger, Mark. *Moon over Broadway* (1931)

46. Mendes, Catulle. *Lila and Colette* (1931). "The Ardent Classics," no. 3. See Boar's Head. Another edition or impression is as follows: *There Are Twenty Good Ways Of Doing It; An Account of the Sweet Adventures of Lila and Colette, Behind the Little Red Lights of Paris.* Illustrated by Rahngild. New York: Privately Printed, 1934. See Golden Hind.

47. Roth, Samuel. *Lady Chatterley's Lover: A Dramatization of His* [i.e., Roth's] *Version of D. H. Lawrence's Novel* (1931). "The Ardent Classics," no. 2.

48. Roth, Samuel [and Clement Wood] *The Private Life of Frank Harris* (1931)

49. Roth, Samuel. *Stone Walls Do Not: The Chronicle of a Captivity* (1930 [vol. 1], 1931 [vol. 2]). 2 vols.

50. Sacher-Masoch. *Venus and Adonis* (1931). "The Ardent Classics," no. 4. Another edition, Privately Printed, 1934 but issued not as an Ardent Classic but at the same time as *Lila and Colette* and *Venus in Furs.*

51. Sacher-Masoch, Leopold. *Venus in Furs* (1931). "The Ardent Classics," no. 1. Trans. Alan Durst. There is another edition under the Faro imprint, stated verso title page to be "copyright 1932, The Big Dollar Book Co." "The Rahngild edition."

52. Wood, Clement. *The Woman Who Was Pope: A Biography of Pope Joan, 853–855 A.D.* (1931)

53. Anon. [Clement Wood]. *Lady Chatterley's Friends: A New Sequal [sic] To Lady Chatterley's Lover and Lady Chatterley's Husbands* (1932)

54. Bell, Ralcy Husted. *Memoirs and Mistresses: The Amatory Adventures of a Physician* (1932)

55. "Dubois, Alan" [Clement Wood]. *Loose Shoulder Straps* (1932)

56. Dickinson, G. Lowes. *Hands Off China! The Letters of a Chinese Official* (1932)

57. Dutcher, Mary Lee. *Circulation: An Uncensored Study of a Newspaper Office* (1932)

58. Gudaitis, Anthony. *A Young Man about to Commit Suicide* (1932)

59. Lindgren, Lydia. *My Heart in My Throat: The Story of a Strange Captivity* (1932)

60. McKay, Donna. *A Gentleman in a Black Skin* (1932)

61. "Quilter, Daniel" [Samuel Roth]. *Body: A New Study, in Narrative, of the Anatomy of Society* (1932). Modern Amatory Classics, no. 3. Another impression of the 1931 edition (see Autographed Editions Club), with a different frontispiece and illustrations by A. K. Skillin.

62. Roth, Samuel. *Songs out of Season* (1932)

63. Vitray, Laura. *The Great Lindbergh Hullabaloo: An Unorthodox Account* (1932)

64. Wood, Clement. *The Man Who Killed Kitchener* (1932)

65.———. *Warren Gamaliel Harding: An American Comedy* (1932)

66. Anon. [Samuel Roth, ed.] *Anecdota Americana: Five Hundred Stories for the Amusement of the Five Hundred Nations That Comprise America* (1933). See Golden Hind.

67. Lennox, Walter. *Women's Doctor* (1933). Dust jacket has subtitle "A Story of the Abortion of Human Life."

68. Scully, Robert. *A Scarlet Pansy* (1933). The "special" copies with colored title page dated 1932.

Autographed Editions Club (1931)

69. "Quilter, Daniel" [Samuel Roth]. *Body: A New Study, in Narrative, of the Anatomy of Society* (1932). Frontispiece and illustrations by A. K. Skillin. See Faro.

Michael Swain (1932)

70. Wood, Clement. *Herbert Clark Hoover: An American Tragedy* (1932)

Big Dollar Book Company (1932)

Although there are three titles with this imprint, Big Dollar is really a trade name under which Roth tried to reduce his Faro stock shortly before the Depression caused him to declare bankruptcy. The back panel of the dust jacket of *Padlocks and Girdles of Chastity* lists twenty-three Faro titles, and that of *Sacred Prostitution and Marriage by Capture* lists twenty-five. The three titles listed below do not have Faro imprints.

71. Bell, Ralcy Husted. *Self-Amusement* (1932). See Golden Hind.
72. [Bonneau, Alcide]. *Padlocks and Girdles of Chastity* (1932). See Golden Hind.
73. Wake, C. S[taniland]. *Sacred Prostitution and Marriage by Capture* (1932)

The Black Hawk Press (1935–1936)

No copyrights are on file in the Library of Congress for this imprint. Most of the books are stated verso the title page, or at the bottom of it, to be "privately published for subscribers only, 1935" or as "published for the subscribers of the Black Hawk Press." The first four titles, stated to be limited to 900 copies, were advertised with three "banned" books: *1601* (New York: Golden Hind Press, 1933), *Ananga-Ranga* ("Copyright 1935 by the Golden Hind Press"), and *The Case of Mr. Crump* ("NY: John Henderson, 1930"). The circulars, headed "Four Privately Printed Books," "Two World Famous Suppressed Books [*Crump, 1601*]," and "Secret Places of the Human Body," were used as evidence in *United States v. Pauline Roth and Samuel Roth* (1936).

74. Ellis, Havelock. *Kanga Creek: An Australian Idyll* (1935)
75. Davey, N. *The Penultimate Adventure* (1935)
76. Davies, Rhys. *Bed of Feathers and Tale* (1935)
77. Hanley, James. *A Passion before Death* (1935)

The above four titles were also published together as one volume with no inclusive title (except on spine and dust jacket). *Kanga Creek* includes "Biographical Memoir in the form of an imaginary conversation between Havelock Ellis . . . and Olive Schreiner . . ." by Norman Lockridge [Roth].

78. Grant, John Cameron. *The Ethiopian: A Narrative of the Society of Human Leopards* (1935). Possibly a photolithographic impression of the Carrington edition.
79. Franklin, Benjamin. *The Suppressed Letters of Benjamin Franklin* (1936)
80. Jarry, Alfred. *The Garden of Priapus* (1936). See Coventry House.
81. "Lockridge, Norman" [Samuel Roth], ed. *A Golden Treasury of the World's Wit and Wisdom* (1936). See Biltmore Pub. Co. Other imprints for this title are Halcyon House, Herald Publishing, and "Dorene Publishing Company." Title page, half title, and spine of the latter read "World's Wit and Wisdom." Dust jacket has entire title. Verso title page

states "Copyright 1936, Black Hawk, 1945 Biltmore, 1945, Dorene." Dust jacket, however, reads "Biltmore" on back flap and spine.

Wisdom House (1940–1942)

Note: This imprint may have been used because of a magazine Roth issued titled *The Wit and Wisdom of the Week* (1940?)

82. Page, Francis [Samuel Roth]. *Confucius Comes to Broadway* (1940)

83. Anon. [Roth, Samuel]. *Dear Richard: A Letter to My Son in the Fighting Forces of the United States* (1942). An advertisement for this book on the rear panel of the dust jacket for *Rage in Singapore* states that *Dear Richard* was "printed as a gift book with a place on the page facing the title page for the photograph of the sender."

84. Gautier, Theophile. *The Wife of King Candaules* (1942). Illustrated by Richard Roth.

85. "Kin, David" [David George Plotkin]. *Rage in Singapore: The Cauldron of Asia Boils Over* (1942)

The Biltmore Publishing Company (1941–1945)

86. "Lockridge, Norman" [Samuel Roth], ed. *Bachelor's Quarters. Stories from Two Worlds* (1944). Some reprinted in *Shadow in the Rose Garden,* by arrangement with Belmont Books in 1961. Verso title page: "17 stories reprinted complete from *Bachelor's Quarters,* edited by Norman Lockridge."

87. ———. *Golden Treasury of the World's Wit and Wisdom* (1945). See Black Hawk.

88. Kreuger, Kurt. *I Was Hitler's Doctor* (1943 [1942?]). "From the German of Kurt Krueger, MD, Foreword by Upton Sinclair, Introduction by Otto Strasser, Preface by K. Arvid Enlind, MD, Lt. Col. Medical Reserve, USA." See Avalon (*Inside Hitler*), Boar's Head. Verso title page: "Copyright 1941, 1942, by Avalon Press, Inc. copyright, 1943, by Biltmore Publishing Co., Inc."

Avalon Press, Inc. (1941–1951)

89. Anon. *The Greater Omnibus of Private Books* (1942). Contains H. A. Manhood, *Marriage and the Use of Passion* (frontispiece by Mahlon Blaine); Leonid Andreyev, *Abyss,* trans. John Cournos, woodcut illustrations probably taken from the Nonesuch edition; A. E. [H. E.]. Bates, *Mrs. Esmond's Life,* "first published . . . by the White Owl Press, London"; and *The Greek Anthology,* illustrated with line drawings. See Paragon.

90. de Maupassant, Guy. *The Parisian Nights of Guy de Maupassant* (1945, 1951). "A new redaction by Marie Lorenz [Adelaide Roth Kugel]. The 1951 impression is the only Avalon imprint dated later than 1945. The dust jacket carried advertisements for 10 Unusual Books, most of which were issued with imprints used for books issued later than 1946.

91. Gautier, Theophile. *The Wife of King Candaules* (1942). See Wisdom House.

92. Kreuger, Kurt. *Inside Hitler* (1941). See Biltmore, Boar's Head, under the later title, *I Was Hitler's Doctor.*

93. "Philistina." *Alec the Great: An Account of the Curious Life and Extraordinary Opinions of the Late Alexander Woollcutt* (1943). "With Special Emphasis on An Affair of the Heart, Known Only to Three Survivors, of Whom the humblest signs herself 'Philistina.'"

94. Phillippe, Charles-Louis. *Bubu of Montparnasse* (1945). "In a new redaction." Translator Marie Lorenz [Adelaide Roth]. See Boar's Head.

95. Reiser, Oliver L. *The World Sensorium: The Social Embryology of World Federation* (1946)

96. Roth, Samuel. *The Peep-Hole of the Present: An Inquiry into the Substance of Appearance* (1945). See Boar's Head, Philosophical Book Club.

97. Underwood, William J. *Self-defense for Women* (1944)

Paragon Publishing Company (1942)

98. Anon. *The Greater Omnibus of Private Books* (1942). See Avalon.

The Philosophical Book Club (1945)

99. Roth, Samuel. *The Peep-Hole of the Present: An Inquiry into the Substance of Appearance* (1945). See Boar's Head.

Herald Publishing Company (1946)

100. "Lockridge, Norman" [Samuel Roth], ed. *A Golden Treasury of the World's Wit and Wisdom* (1946?). Title page states Herald, but "Biltmore" is on the spine.

Arrowhead Books (1947)

101. Roth, Samuel. *Bumarap: The Story of a Male Virgin* (1947). See Boar's Head.

Candide Press (1947)

102. Lockridge, Norman. [Samuel Roth; possibly ghostwritten by Harry Roskolenko]. *Waggish Tales of the Czechs* (1947)

Boar's Head (1947–1954)

103. Morton, Stanley. *Yankee Trader* (1947). "Copyright 1947 by Sheridan House." Apparently Roth purchased either the unbound sheets or the plates and ran a new impression, with his own imprint on the title page and with his own dust jacket (with list of his "unusual books" on the back panel). See Bridgehead.

104. "Lorenz, Marie" [Adelaide Roth]. *Tina and Jimmy Learn How They Were Born* (1948)

105. Anon. *An Omnibus of Passionate Women* (1949)

106. Anon. [Samuel Roth]. *Beautiful Sinners of New York* (1949). "Foreword by Louis Berg, M.D. From the Diary of a Flesh Peddler." There was a paperback issue, "special price $1."

Pasquerello and Madonna Babetta, Beautiful Sinners of New York, Lila & Colette, Bubu of Montparnasse, and *Sexual Conduct of Men and Women* are provided with a uniformly designed paper dust jacket with an illustration of a satyr and a naked woman occupying the right third of the upper cover and the phrase "Library of unusual books edited by Samuel Roth" at the top left.

107. Mendes, Catulle. *Lila & Colette and the Isles of Love* (1949) "With illustrations by Rahngild (Susan Inez Aguerra?) and decorations by Valentin de Campion." See Faro, Golden Hind.

108. Boccaccio, Giovanni. *Pasquerello and Madonna Babetta* (1949). Illustrated by Fabio Farbi. "Library of Unusual Books."

109. Sadlier, Michael. *Forlorn Sunset* (1949). From sheets of the Farrar ed.

110. Hindus, Milton. *The Crippled Giant: A Bizarre Adventure in Contemporary Letters* (1950)

111. "Kiki" [Alice Prin]. *The Education of a French Model: The Loves, Cares, Cartoons, and Caricatures of Alice Prin. . . .* (1950). Copyright attributed to Edward Titus, 1929 and 1930, and to Seven Sirens Press, 1950. Trans. Samuel Putnam. Intro. Ernest Hemingway. In addition to Kiki's drawings, and photographs of her, there are photos of nude models. For another edition, see Bridgehead. The front dust jacket is modeled on that of the 1930 Black Manikin edition, save for the title and the blurb "Kiki tells all—including an attempt on the virtue of her grandmother by an American soldier."

112. Krueger, Kurt. *I Was Hitler's Doctor* (1950). See Avalon, Biltmore.

113. Philippe, Charles-Louis. *Bubu of Montparnasse* (1950). "In a new redaction." Intro. T. S. Eliot. See Avalon.

114. Gide, André. *The Secret Drama of My Life . . . Et Nunc . . . Manet In Te* (1951). Copyright for "translation and additions." Some copies contain a six-page essay by Roth titled "Innovations in Publishing" as an afterword (pp. 123–28). Although very careful about copyright law at this stage of his career, Roth was forced to withdraw this book from circulation, copyright having been held by another publisher.

115. Nietzsche, Friedrich. *My Sister and I* (1951). One of Roth's most popular books, *My Sister* went through fourteen impressions in two years. See Bridgehead.

116. "Dale, Perry" [Dale Sawyer]. *You Scratch My Back* (1952). See Bridgehead.

117. Heartman, Charles H. *Cuisine D'Amour: A Cook Book for Lovers . . .* (1952). A reprint of a 1942 "Limited Edition." Verso dust jacket of Boar's Head edition: "Limited Edition Reprint," although the back panel of the dust jacket states "Limited Private Edition."

118. Hecht, Ben, and Maxwell Bodenheim. *Cutie, A Warm Momma* (1952)

119. "Lockridge, Norman" [Samuel Roth]. *Lese Majesty: The Private Lives of the Duke and Duchess of Windsor* (1952). A different edition of the same title, in digest-sized paperback, with illustrations after the manner of Mahlon Blaine, was issued by "Continental Books" in 1953.

120. "Crozier, H. R." [Harry Roskolenko]. *The Rape of the Heart* (1953).

121. Jamison, H. F. *Venus in Chains: Under the Lash of Devil Law* (1953). See Bridgehead.

122. Jarry, A. *King Turd* (1953). Trans. Gershon Legman and Beverley Keith.

123. Nass, L[ucien]., and G[ustave].-J[oseph] Witkowski. *The Nude in the French Theatre* (1953). "Copyright 1953, by Samuel Roth." There were French editions in 1909 and 1914. The book offers no identification for the English translator.

124. Roth, Samuel. *The Peep-Hole of the Present: An Inquiry into the Substance of Appearance* (1953). Verso title page: "First popular edition, 1953." See Philosophical Book Club

125. Stuart, Lyle. *The Secret Life of Walter Winchell* (1953)

126. [Longus]. *The Pastoral Loves of Daphnis and Chloe* (1954). Trans. George Moore. Intro. Samuel Roth.

Hogarth House (1948)

127. "Lockridge, Norman" [G. Legman?]. *The Sexual Conduct of Men and Women* (1948). Another impression, in a different binding, gives the date on title page as 1949. See Bridgehead, Book Awards.

The bulk of this book is in Legman's inimitable style, although the title page attributes to him only an introductory essay, "Minority Report on Prof. Kinsey." See Bridgehead, Book Awards. There is an abridged version, titled *Sex without Tears,* attributed to "Lockridge," with cartoons by VIP, published in paperback by Fawcett under its Crest imprint in 1956, which credits copyright to Roth, 1948 and 1956, and states that the book, under the title SEXUAL CONDUCT OF MEN AND WOMEN, "was originally published by Bridgehead Books."

Good Times Publishing Company (1953)

Roth identifies this company as the publisher of the first six issues of *Good Times* magazine, at 110 Lafayette Street. After that, the name of the publisher was stated to be Picadilly Books. Of note is the alternate contents and covers of several of the early issues, including numbers 1 and 4. The staff changed also: for number 1, Arthur Sainer was listed as Managing Editor, and Associate Editors were Mahlon Blaine, Denys Val Baker, David George Kin, Norman Silverman, Dante Cacici, Rhea Baskin, and Keene Wallis. In number 3, Ellen Ellsworth was Managing Editor and Richard Roth, Kin, Sainer, and Irwin Tuck were the Associate Editors.

128. *Good Times* (digest-sized magazine; see Picadilly)

Picadilly Books Company (1954–1956)

Roth identifies this company as the publisher of *Good Times* magazine, at 110 Lafayette Street, beginning with volume 1, number 7, and with *Everybody's Pleasure,* which apparently appeared in only one issue, January 1956.

129. *Everybody's Pleasure* (magazine)

Bridgehead Books (1954–1964)

Note: While *American Aphrodite* (1953–56) is copyright in the name of Samuel Roth, its companion magazine, *London Aphrodite* (1955–56), is copyright in the name of Bridgehead Books. *London Aphrodite* was published with *American Aphrodite,* but edited not by Roth but by Denys Val Baker.

130. Bodenheim, Maxwell [with David George Plotkin and Samuel Roth?]. *My Life and Loves in Greenwich Village* (1954). "Illustrations by a Group of his Friends." A paperback edition was published by Belmont Books in 1961, "by special arrangement with the Seven Sirens Press."

131. Comisso, Giovanni. *Loves of the Orient* (1954). See Boar's Head

132. Crébillon Fils. *The Lady on the Sofa* (1954). "With etchings by Robert Bonfils"

133. "Kiki" [Alice Prin]. *The Education of a French Model* (1954). "Copyright 1955 by Seven Sirens Press, Inc." This is a different edition from the 1950 version (see Boar's Head),

with added chapters about Kiki's visit to New York (not written by Kiki) and an entirely different set of photos. There are also illustrations by Mahlon Blaine. This version was issued in paperback without the illustrations in 1962 by Belmont Books: "published by special arrangement with the Seven Sirens Press, Inc."

134. Masefield, John. *The Everlasting Mercy and the Widow in the High Street* (1954). Reprinted from the plates of the Macmillan edition, with permission.

135. Richardson, Eudora Ramsey, and Josiah Pitts Woolfolk ["Jack Woodford"]. *Drink and Stay Sober* (1954).

136. Washburn, Charles. *Come into My Parlor: A Biography of the Aristocratic Everleigh Sisters of Chicago* (1954). Verso title page: "Copyright 1934, National Library Press." Some copies with the latter imprint are in Roth bindings and dust jacket with "Bridgehead Books" printed on spine of dust jacket. Belmont paperback edition states "published by arrangement with Seven Sirens Press."

137. Baker, Denys Val. *A Journey with Love* (1955). Fawcett published a paperback ed. in 1956 under its Crest imprint, attributing copyright to Bridgehead Books, 1955.

138. Nietzsche, Friedrich. *My Sister and I* (1955). Copyright Boar's Head verso title page ("Twelfth printing May 1955").

139. Viereck, George Sylvester. *Men into Beasts* (1955). Appeared as Gold Medal Books no. 260 in 1952 (reprinted 1956). This is acknowledged verso the title page of Bridgehead edition.

140. "Lockridge, Norman" [G. Legman?]. *The Sexual Conduct of Men and Women* (1956). See Hogarth House, Book Awards. Front flap of dust jacket: "We did not plan to publish the contents of this book for some time to come—until we had some assurance that American readers were prepared to enter into a free and frank discussion. . . ." This is the same copy that appeared in the 1949 Hogarth House edition.

141. Roth, Samuel. *Apotheosis: The Nazarene in Our World* (1957)

142. Angelo, P. John, and "Robert Browne" [Samuel Roth]. *Diaitis: Anti-Cancer Nutrients In Cancer Prevention and Research* (1961). John provided the notes; Roth wrote the text. They were fellow prisoners at Lewisburg. ("Statement by Angelo John," carton 44, folder 13, Roth Archive). Intro. Robert D. Barnard. Preface M. Stern. Copyright card states that Browne is a pseudonym of Samuel Roth.

143. Roth, Samuel. *My Friend Yeshea* (1961). "Published for the Friends of Mishillim by Bridgehead Books. Decorations by Chester Kalm."

144. Anon. *Violations of the Child, Marilyn Monroe. By Her Psychiatrist Friend* (1962)

145. "Lind, Bruno" [R. C. Hahnel]. *Vagabond Scholar: A Venture into the Privacy of George Santayana* (1962)

146. Jamison, H. F. *Venus in Chains: Under the Lash of Devil Law* (1964). See Boar's Head.

147. Sainer, Arthur. *The Sleepwalker and the Assassin: A View of the Contemporary Theatre* (1964)

148. James, Beauregard. *The Road to Birmingham* (1964). "Published for Society for Racial Peace of Washington, D.C., by Bridgehead Books, N.Y., 1964."

149. "X, Dr. Jacobus" [Jacobus Sator]. *The Erogenous Zones of the World: Descriptions of the Intra-Sexual Manners and Customs of the Semi-civilized Peoples of Africa, Asia, America, and Oceania. . . .* (1964). See Book Awards.

André Levy (1955)

150. Genet, Jean. *The Gutter in the Sky* (1955). The book is a retitled and slightly expurgated version of *Our Lady of the Flowers*. Portrait of Genet by Richard Roth. Trans. Bernard Frechtman.

151. Trujillo, Emmanuel. *I Love You I Hate You: My Six Weeks of Free Love with Pat Ward* (1955)

152. Zucker, Hal, ed. *Tatooed Women and Their Mates* (1955). "World Folk Arts Series, no. 1"

Note: Each of these titles has the same statement verso title page: "copyright 1955 by Deux Maggots."

Earth Publishing Company (1955)

153. *The Earth: A Newspaper for Its Men and Women.* Apparently there was only one issue of this newsstand tabloid, October 1955.

Wynkin de Word Books (1962)

154. "Harmon, Harry" [Samuel Roth]. *Picasso for Children.* "Copyright 1962, by Bridgehead Books." Copyright card states Harmon is a pseudonym of Roth. See Book Awards. Two other titles in the series, *Daumier for the Young* and *Chagall for the Young*, by "Francis Page" [Samuel Roth], were advertised with other remainders offered on the rear panel of Bridgehead offerings. There is no indication of these two books being published.

Book Awards (1964–1966)

155. [Bloch, Iwan]. *The Sexual Extremities of the World. Taken from the Uncensored Notes of a French Army Surgeon* (1964). 2 vols. in 1. Intro. Norman Lockridge.

156. Klein, S. *A Guide to a Successful Honeymoon* (1964)

157. *The Suppressed Poems of Ernest Hemingway* (1964?). "Number one of The Library of Living Poetry." There is an entry in WorldCat for this title and publisher, although copies I have seen do not state a publisher. Hanneman (A26B) states that Roth may have been the publisher of this twenty-six-page pamphlet, which was issued in several impressions and states in the 1950s and 1960s. It might have been given away as a premium for various orders.

158. "X, Dr. Jacobus" [Jacobus Sator]. *The Erogenous Zones of the World: Descriptions of the Intra-Sexual Manners and Customs of the Semi-civilized Peoples of Africa, Asia, America, and Oceania.* . . . (1964). See Bridgehead.

159. Marchand, Henry L. *The French Pornographers: Including a History of French Erotic Literature* (1965)

160. Block, Iwan. *The Marquis De Sade's 120 Days of Sodom. His Anthropologia Sexualis of the 600 Perversions Practiced in the School for Libertinage. The Whole French Age of Debauchery* (1966)

161. Cabanès, Augustin. *The Eroticon* (1966?) Trans. from the French by Robert Meadows. Intro. N. Lockridge. The book may not have appeared under this imprint. A copyright application was filed October 18, 1966 (in name of Cabanes and Lockridge as authors.)

Pioneer Books (1966)

162. [Roth, Samuel?]. *A Proposal to Jacqueline Kennedy* (1966)

Business Names Used by Samuel Roth (1941–1966)

These are the names under which Roth sent—or intended to send—his mail-order circulars and books from 1941 to 1966. Some are the names of imprints; most—although some are designated as "presses"—are names Roth used to distribute circulars and books and to receive orders after a previous name had been declared unmailable (i.e., interdicted) by the Post Office. That meant mail addressed to it, or with the name on the letterhead, would not be delivered.

Roth kept his Business Certificate forms, required by the Manhattan County clerk or by the corresponding administration in Newark, New Jersey. The year in parenthesis indicates when he used the name. If there are two years listed, it may be because the address (offices or mail drops) to which mail was to be delivered had changed. Alternatively, he may have decided that the Post Office would drop its vigilance for a particular business name after a few years of flagging it as unmailable.

There are sixty-five business names in this list.

The abbreviation KI indicates that the business name is not one for which a Business Certificate was filed. It is one that the Kinsey Institute has written on a circular in its vertical file, when Dr. Kinsey received it.

1. Coventry House (1941)
2. Wisdom House (1941)
3. Avalon (1941)
4. Authors and Publishers (1944)
5. Philosophical Book Club (1945)
6. Arrowhead Books (1946)
7. Books of Wisdom Club (1946)
8. Monthly Book Gem (1946) KI
9. Candide Press (1947)
10. Rise and Shine Books (Newark, N.J.) (1947, 1954)
11. Boar's Head Books (1948, 1952)
12. Bridgehead Books (1948, 1962)
13. Personal Books (1948, 1952)
14. Psychic Research Press (1948?)
15. Psychology and Self Aid Club (1948)
16. Secret Life Books (1948)
17. Seven Sirens Press (1948)
18. Book Fair (1949, 1952)
19. Gay Books (1949)
20. Ideal Books (1949)
21. Unusual Books (1949)
22. Beacon Books (1950)
23. Broadway Bargain Counter (alternatively, Book Bargain Counter) (1950?) KI
24. Continental Books (1950)

25. Joy Bookery (1950)
26. Paper Book Sensations (1950)
27. Star Books (1950)
28. Amourette (1951)
29. Black Hawk (1952)
30. Boar's Head (1952)
31. Book Leads (1952)
32. Golden Hind Press (1952)
33. Joy Bookery (1952) KI
34. Lunar Books (1952)
35. Smart Set Books (1952)
36. Book Gems (1953)
37. Broadway Books (1953) KI.
38. Coventry Books (1953)
39. Doric Books (1953)
40. Falstaff Books (1953)
41. Gargantuan Books (1953)
42. Gargoyle Books (1953)
43. Good Times Pub. Co. (1953)
44. Paragon Books (1953)
45. Utopia Press (1953)
46. Book Offers (1954)
47. Confidential Books (1954)
48. Derby Press (1954)

Certificate is in name of Helen Ungar, 1201 Shakespeare Ave., Bronx, N.Y.

49. Golden Road Books (1954)
50. Piccadilly Books (1954)
51. Special Books Club (1954)
52. Amazon Books (1955)
53. André Levy (1955)
54. Amative Press (1955)
55. Adore Books (1955)
56. Book Service (1955?) KI
57. Rover Books (1955)
58. Caustic Books (1955)
59. The Earth Pub. Co. (1955)
60. Vital Books (1955)
61. Chocolate of the Month (1960)

At this time, the Business Certificate did not require identification of the nature of the business. The form and its duplicate copy, dated November 29, 1960, bear Roth's signature.

62. Living Dolls (1961)
63. Book Awards (1962)
64. Harvard Books (1964)
65. Pioneer Books (1966)

Abbreviations

AK   Adelaide Kugel

"CMAM"   SR, "Count Me among the Missing"

HHMF   Misrepresentation Files, Herbert Hoover Presidential Library, West Branch, Iowa

JML   SR, *Jews Must Live*

MFY   SR, *My Friend Yeshea*

"PBW"   AK, "In a Plain Brown Wrapper"

PR   Pauline Roth

RA   Samuel Roth Archive, Rare Book and Manuscript Department, Columbia University

SR   Samuel Roth

Chapter 1. 1893–1916

1. Ryan, "Samuel Roth," 59.

2. "Count Me among the Missing," typescript, Chapters 3–5, RA. The archive contains not only also drafts of Roth's autobiography (cartons 1–3) but also of his daughter's memoir of her father, "In a Plain Brown Wrapper" (cartons 16–20). Both works, save for part of one chapter of the autobiography, are unpublished. The autobiography is hereafter cited as "CMAM," the memoir as "PBW." When it is necessary to document page numbers from "CMAM," I do so in parenthesis in the text. There are eight different typescripts of this work. I have used principally the complete version typed on thin paper (in carton 1, folder 7 [carton and folder numbers hereafter given in form 1.7]), but when another version describes an incident more carefully I have used that version and so indicated. None of the versions can be dated, and so to identify the one with final revisions is impossible. Throughout his career, Roth wrote stories in which he used events described in the autobiography. Three of these appeared in *Two Worlds: A Quarterly* . . . under the pseudonym David Zorn ("Prologue," "White Streams," and "Open Plumbing") and are referred to below. References to Roth's early life can be found in other of his works (including *Stone Walls Do Not, Jews Must Live,* and *My Friend Yeshea*), as well as in essays he had others write introducing him to readers of his publications.

3. In *Jews Must Live* (1934), Roth states the real name of the shtetl to be "Ustcha," but in the 1952 map drawn by Mahlon Blaine the name is spelled correctly. I am indebted to Krzysztof Willmann, a Polish scholar with a special interest in Galicia, for his help. Helpful in locating the region of Galician Jewish settlements are Mokotoff and Sack, *Where Once We Walked*, and Weiner, *Jewish Roots in Poland*.

4. Descriptions of shtetls at the end of the nineteenth century can be found in S. Miller, *Dobromil*, 6–7; Kriwaczek, *Yiddish Civilization*, 290; and Schoenfeld, *Jewish Life in Galicia*, 11–13. For a description of the market square and the products sold there on fair day, see Kugelmass and Boyarin, *From a Ruined Garden* 30–36. Regarding poverty, see Mahler, "The Economic Background," 255–64.

5. Bartal, "Imagined Geography," 179–87; Hundert, "The Importance of Demography," 35.

6. "Nustscha," sonnet 4, in SR, *Songs Out of Season*, 47, 49.

7. Miron, "Literary Image of the Shtetl"; Kassow, introduction, 17–23.

8. "CMAM," 30, 74. On p. 30, Roth states that each male was given ten lashes before entering the synagogue.

9. The distinction is described in Meltzer, *World of Our Fathers*, 87–92.

10. Miron, introduction to Sholem Aleichem, *Tevye the Dairyman*, xxvii.

11. SR, *Stone Walls Do Not*, 1:48; SR, "The Editor at Home," n.p.

12. Hindus, "Samuel Roth," 30. His introduction is in Linetzki, *The Polish Lad*.

13. I am again grateful to Krzysztof Willmann for referring me to the site of the Bukovina Society of the Americas, which describes this personage.

14. "Notes for My Literary Biography," quoted in Dawidowicz, *The Golden Tradition*, 277.

15. 7.1, RA.

16. Weininger, *Sex and Character*, trans. Willis, 402.

17. SR, *Stone Walls Do Not*, 1:15. In reality, according to Roth's nephew, the late playwright and critic Arthur Sainer, it was not Yussef Leib but one of Yussef's brothers who ran the tavern. Also, Sam seems to have borrowed for himself the situation of his sister, Soori, later Mr. Sainer's mother, then five years old. Arthur Sainer, e-mail to the author, December 10, 2006.

18. I am grateful to Dr. Benjamin Nathans of the Department of History, University of Pennsylvania, for describing the position of Jewish contractors for the Polish lords, in an e-mail to me of August 20, 2007.

19. Fuks et al., *Polish Jewry*, 32–41; Rosman, *The Lord's Jews*, 48–56, 77–81; Kugelmass and Boyarin, *From a Ruined Garden*, 25–29; Himka, *Galician Villagers*, 145–59. The importance of Jewish agents to Polish lords is carefully described in Kotik, *Journey to a Nineteenth Century Shtetl*, 218–23, 259–65, 352–55.

20. Roth, *The Peep-Hole of the Present*, 240; "The Hebrew Melodies of Heinrich Heine," Introduction, p. 1, 4.3, RA. Unpublished. Undated but probably 1966 or 1967.

21. Dawidowicz, *The Golden Tradition*, 24.

22. Eliach, *There Once Was a World*, 83. Eliach writes of the town of Radun, in the Vilna province of Russia, where the rabbi allowed an exorcism to be recounted only on the Purim holiday.

23. The phrase is that of Dan Miron in his *The Image of the Shtetl*, 338.

24. See J. Roth, *The Wandering Jews*, 27–50.

25. Samuel, *Prince of the Ghetto*, 123.

26. Elbogen, *A Century of Jewish Life*, 174–75; Ezra Mendelsohn, "Jewish Assimilation

in Lviv," in Markovits and Sysyn, *Nationbuilding,* 107; Leila P. Everett, "The Rise of Jewish Politics in Galicia," in Markovits and Sysyn, *Nationbuilding,* 155.

27. [Samuel Roth] "David Zorn", "White Streams," 177.

28. Feige's statement is made in a revision of chapter 2 of "CMAM" with penciled corrections to the typewritten text. It is located in 3.2, RA. The name of the protagonist in the revised chapter 2 is "David" [Zorn]. The chapter heading reads "Chapter Two. The Sweet Pain." Below that is "White Streams" underlined, and crossed out. Perhaps this is evidence that when Roth revised the "CMAM" passage, he used as a base text his *Two Worlds* story instead of the "CMAM" one. That would suggest the latter was written before 1925, no earlier than 1919.

29. I am using here the revision of chapter 2 of "CMAM," 4–15, in 1.10, RA.

30. The detail, like the one about the summer heat noted above, is reported in the story "White Streams" that Roth wrote for *Two Worlds Quarterly,* 200.

31. "CMAM," chapter 2 revision, pp. 4–20.

32. Mintz, *Legends of the Hasidim,* 132.

33. [Roth] "Zorn," "White Streams," 202.

34. Ibid., 201.

35. Saul Bellow's *Humboldt's Gift,* based on the life of Delmore Schwartz, contains a passage on page 119 in the Penguin edition of the novel referring to the "tight lips, mumpish or scrofulous cheeks, . . . and look of enraged, ravaged childhood" in the photo accompanying the *New York Times'* obituary of the poet ("Delmore Schwartz Dies at 52; Poet Won 1959 Bollinger Prize," July 14, 1966, 35). This image is of a disheveled, depressed Schwartz late in life, but it bears some resemblance to the photo of Schwartz looking into the mirror. It is reproduced in the unpaginated gallery of photos bound in Atlas, *Delmore Schwartz.* Roth possibly showed it to Blaine when he commissioned the drawing. Roth does not mention Schwartz in "CMAM." He could not help but know of his brilliant poetry and short stories, and therefore he probably knew that he and Schwartz were fellow dropouts from Townsend-Harris High School.

36. "CMAM," chapter 2 revision, 4–19 (the passage includes penciled additions).

37. Roth planned an edition of *White Stains* as a capstone of his publishing career, in 1966. Ryan, "Samuel Roth," 39–42; Hamalian, "Nobody Knows My Names," 903; "PBW," "The Poetry Book Shop," 18.

38. The Ellis Island records are at http://www.ellisisland.org. Krzysztof Willmann wrote me that a man named Israel Roth was a landlord living near Kasimirowka.

39. SR, *Stone Walls Do Not,* 1:18; "CMAM," 81–82. For the *landsmanshaftn* see Sachar, *History of the Jews in America,* 197–98.

40. S. Miller, *Dobromil,* 37–38.

41. Note s.v. "1903," unbound set of notes in 23.13–14, RA.

42. Typescript headed "Every Jew and Christian will want to read this extraordinary account. . . . ," 8.11, RA, on advertising of *MFY.*

43. Rischin, *Promised City,* 87, referring to findings of the Board of Health and the United Jewish Charities.

44. E-mail, Arthur Sainer to the author, December 10, 2006; Bradley and Kosak, "Manhattan Kosher Foods," n.p. For butcher shops on Catherine Street, an unidentified newspaper article in the Print Room of the Museum of the City of New York (folder: Catherine

Street) from circa 1900 states that the decline came after the construction of the East River bridges and the influx of a new population. Then, "the new style [kosher?] of meat market invaded every block."

45. Rischin, *Promised City,* 56, 272.

46. SR, *Stone Walls Do Not,* 1, 29.

47. Howe, *World of Our Fathers,* 128–29. Roth discusses this event in "CMAM," 99. He places the event, which occurred on July 30, 1902, during his "first week" in America. That would make his arrival earlier than believed.

48. Howe, "The Lower East Side," 11–14. See M. R. Cohen, "A Dreamer's Journey," 43: "This intensity of life, this striving for perfection in diverse fields . . ."

49. Introduction to Hapgood, *The Spirit of the Ghetto,* 2.

50. Asch, *East River,* 240–43; Ornitz, *Bride,* 92, 116–19.

51. "PBW," "Willett Street," 6, 7–12.

52. Ibid., 5.

53. "CMAM," 100, "David Zorn" [Samuel Roth], "Open Plumbing," 368. The latter is a novelette Roth published in *Two Worlds,* March 1926, 367–96. This version probably preceded "CMAM," but that is not certain, as Roth said he began his autobiography in 1919.

54. Ornitz, *Bride,* 46 (for sugar in gin); Chotzinoff, "Life on Stanton Street," 273 (Mary Sugar Bum). Roth describes the iceboat incident and the invectives in "CMAM," 104–7, and "Open Plumbing," 370, 373–75.

55. Roskolenko, *Cherry Street,* 4.

56. "Saving the Children of New York's East Side," *New York Times,* August 2, 1908, Part 5, 3.

57. "CMAM," 121–22, 130; "1906 to 1914," list by AK, 23.1, RA.

58. Hamalian, "Nobody Knows My Names," 890; SR, *Stone Walls Do Not,* 1:33.

59. "Betty Grable and the Street Walker," *Exposé,* 8. Reprinted in Roth's *American Aphrodite,* 1, no. 5. *Exposé* was Lyle Stuart's political newsletter. Roth published Stuart's *Secret Life of Walter Winchell* in 1953.

60. SR, "The Hunt," 1–2; copy in 48.1, RA.

61. "CMAM," 120; SR, "Open Plumbing," 388.

62. Lucille Wilson, according to the Web site *International Movie Database,* starred in five short romance films in 1914, directed by Wallace Reid.

63. SR, "Open Plumbing," 390–91. This novella goes into considerably more detail about the nickelodeons than "CMAM."

64. Ibid., 391–92.

65. Unsigned letter to PR, May 4, 1954, 35, 20. The letter gave Pauline Roth advice on what she should do after the city police raided the Roth home and office.

66. "PBW," "96 Willett Street," 13–14; "CMAM," 98. Soori worked as a milliner's assistant, then in a sweatshop until she was married.

67. SR, *Stone Walls Do Not,* 1:29. Another reason might have been that, while waiting for his family, Yussef may have visited Lower East Side prostitutes ("PBW," "96 Willett Street," 11–13.)

68. "96 Willett Street," 6.

69. "He was a user." Sheet labeled "Notes—9," "Notes" (for "PBW"), s.v. "1962," p. 6, 24.3, RA.

70. "PBW," "Friendships," 12.

71. "PBW," "The Making of Jews Must Live," 13–14, and "Antisemitism, Love/Hate"; "CMAM," 143–44 (for Hudl's death).

72. The will, about a paragraph long and signed only by typewritten name and those of two witnesses, is in 47.13, RA.

73. "PBW," "Friendships," 6.

74. A copy of "The Poet's Sufferings" is in 11.7, RA. "Published by the Students' Aid League, Inc. 81 Second Avenue."

75. The translation was of "The Maggid's Seventh Drashah," *The Maccabean,* January 1919, 13–14.

76. "PBW," "Higher Education," 14. His daughter says the editors accepted whatever Roth sent. I have found stories about the boys in the following issues of *The Jewish Child* for 1915: March 26, April 9 and 16, June 4 and 11, and December 17 and 31; in 1917, stories in issues for September 21 and 28. There were several other stories, set in Galicia and based on happenings among the people of Nuczsze and Pidlipitz.

77. "PBW," "Higher Education," 11–12. Adelaide Kugel says these stories were published in *The American Hebrew,* but this is not so. I have found six stories by Roth in *The American Hebrew* from 1914 to 1918, but none are about his boyhood friends in America. They are set in eastern Europe.

78. Imprint reads "The Judean Press." Reprinted in *The Lyric* 3–4 (January/February 1918).

79. A copy exists in 1.3, RA. There is no copy in the Library of Congress, and no copy listed in the OCLC First Search database.

80. "PBW," "Friendships," 9D.

81. Sanders, *The Downtown Jews,* 80–83.

82. Weatherhead and Maier, *Frank Tannenbaum,* 8–9; Foner, *History of the Labor Movement,* 448; Avrich, *Anarchist Voices,* 216, 263, 352. The events are discussed by Adelaide Kugel in her chapter on Frank Tannenbaum, "PBW," "Friendships," 7–10.

83. "PBW," "Friendships," 2.

84. Michels, *A Fire in Their Hearts,* 72–74.

85. SR to Frank Tannenbaum, April 6, 1945, 38.3, RA.

86. "CMAM," 150. There is a note by Adelaide Kugel (51.1, RA) to the effect that "through Frank he meets John Reed and Louise Bryant."

87. The account of Frank in Bayonne is based on newspaper accounts, especially in the *New York Herald,* summarized by Adelaide Kugel in "PBW," "Friendships," 14–17. Roth covers the events in "CMAM," 150–53.

88. Weatherhead and Maier, *Frank Tannenbaum,* 8–12; Hirschhorn, *Democracy Reformed.*

89. The Columbia University catalogue for 1916–17, 336–37, lists Samuel Roth of New York City and Frank Tannenbaum of Bayonne, New Jersey ("Candidate for Honors"), among eighty-five "non-matriculated students." Frank is the only honors candidate. Since neither Frank nor Sam had graduated high school, they could not actually matriculate. But how Frank could, therefore, be an honors student is unclear. Perhaps it was due to his having arranged with the warden to be admitted to Sing Sing prison to study inmate behavior before he took classes. He was planning to write a book.

90. Roth's transcript is on file in the Columbia University Office of the Registrar. His courses were listed for me by Bill W. Santin of that office in an e-mail of March 28, 2008.

Roth discounts that Frank's influences had anything to do with his success in getting Sam admitted.

91. "PBW," "Friendships," 20–24; "CMAM," 153–54.

92. Most of these contributors' letters are in 35.15–16, RA. For Erskine see also 36.11.

93. Several letters in the file labeled "1917" in 35.15, RA, confirm this. Erskine's book, printed at The Trow Press, cost him $199 for 500 copies, with each additional 100 costing $16. The format was identical to a book Santayana had recently had printed there.

94. Roth could not have had the money to pay for it. Since he did not of course have an established reputation, who actually did finance *First Offering* is a mystery. His daughter thinks the October 1917 offer to "Friends of the Lyric" of a bound and inscribed volume of the first five issues for five dollars explains it ("PBW," "133 Clinton Avenue," 13–19). It is possible that Frank got Mrs. Childs to contribute to its costs of production.

95. It is at least equally likely, as Professor Christopher Pollnitz, of the University of New South Wales, N.S.W., Australia, and editor of Lawrence's poems, suggests, that Roth was successful in contacting Lawrence in Cornwall. Pollnitz thinks this a very likely scenario, partly because Lawrence was always willing to help out beginning writers and editors and was not always considerate of an agent's wishes. I am most grateful to Dr. Pollnitz for his e-mail of June 10, 2007, and to Dr. Paul Poplawski of the University of Leicester, U.K., coeditor of the third edition of *A Bibliography of D. H. Lawrence,* for his e-mail of June 9, 2007. How did Roth get the revised versions? There is no surviving correspondence between Roth and Lawrence from 1917. That does not mean that none existed, for as we have seen, Roth was quite conscientious about contacting contributors. Perhaps Roth could have had the three poems from Huebsch, but only if he had access to revised versions by midyear and if Roth knew this.

96. "Some Recent Books of Poetry," *New York Times,* July 7, 1918, 5:310.

97. Frank Tannenbaum to SR, October 2, 1917, 35.15, RA.

98. "PBW," "London," 1.

99. John Erskine to SR, September 27, 1917, 35.15, RA.

100. Tannenbaum to SR, October 2[?], 1917, 35.15, RA.

Chapter 2. 1917–1925

1. Kessner, *Marie Syrkin*, 83.

2. Quoted in "PBW," "Higher Education," 22.

3. Maurice Samuel to SR, August 1, 1916, 51.1, s.v. "1916," RA (this letter is in a file of transcriptions, arranged chronologically and filed in a shoebox, of her father's papers that Adelaide Kugel made while researching her biography); Marie Syrkin to AK, December 1, 1984; Samuel's original three-page letter is in 37.14. Roth's treatment of the Syrkin-Samuel-Roth affair is in "CMAM," 147. Adelaide Kugel discusses it in her "Higher Education" chapter in "PBW," 18–23.

4. 51.1, s.v. "1942," RA. Carton 51 is a set of index cards organized by Adelaide Kugel. It contains some notes about, and writings of, her father.

5. "PBW," "The Lyric," 13.

6. Rascoe, "Judaic Strain," 173.

7. AK, blue spiral notebook, s.v. "The NYPL," 25.7, RA.

8. Hindus, *Charles Reznikoff: A Critical Essay,* 30–34. Hindus calls the attempt to sell

books on consignment for publishers "harebrained." But since Roth also used consignment at his Book Auction in the late 1920s, it must have been sensible strategy.

9. A letter to Roth from Carl Van Doren on February 26, 1920 (35.17, RA), on *The Nation* stationery indicates that he knew Roth at that time.

10. "CMAM," chapter 9; AK, blue spiral notebook, s.v. "The NYPL," 25.7, RA.

11. His memory may be faulty regarding its location, and must be regarding its duration. Adelaide says ("PBW," "Poetry Book Shop," 1) it began at 61 West Eighth and moved (exact date not given but late in 1919) to 49. But Poetry Book Shop letterhead dated June and October 1919 ("Announcement," June 1919, folder "Joseph Roth," 37.10, RA) gives number 49, not 61. The book catalogue issued from the shop dated January 1, 1920, also gives the address 49 West Eighth. A copy of the newsletter is also in 37.10.

12. Roth lists these in *Stone Walls Do Not*, 1:84, 90, in which he devotes chapters 16 and 17 to the shop.

13. "Catalogue of Samuel Roth at the Poetry Book Shop 49 West 8th Street New York," 16 pp., issued "January 1st, 1920," 37.10, RA.

14. SR, *Stone Walls Do Not*, 1:85–86; "PBW," "The New York Poetry Book Shop," 7.

15. "PBW," "The New York Poetry Book Shop," 12.

16. Kling, *From Bohemia to Utopia*, 11.

17. SR, *Stone Walls Do Not*, 1:95; AK, notebook with blue cover, s.v. "Poetry Book Shop."

18. Mondlin and Meador, *Book Row*, 27, 36.

19. The first number of volume 2, in December 1917, noted the resignation of Frank and states that it was published at Columbia. So does the second (January 1918), but the address of the publisher is given as 1353 Clinton Avenue, the first of Roth and Pauline's two Bronx addresses after their marriage. There were five numbers of volume 3, the first being issued in January 1919 and the last in May–June 1919. The first and second numbers of volume 4 were issued as a double number from Roth's Poetry Book Shop at 49 West Eighth Street and dated July–August 1919.

20. A four-page undated pamphlet titled "The Lyric Society," laid into a copy of volume 4, numbers 1 and 2, of *The Lyric* in the Roth book collection in Columbia University's Rare Book Department, announced this plan. The archive also contains a holograph draft by Roth (37.10, RA) titled "The Lyric Calendar," to be printed "May 1, 1919."

21. "PBW," "More Poetry," 7–8.

22. They were announced in the February 1920 number of *Poetry*: E. A Robinson for *Lancelot*, David Morton for "Ships in Harbor," and Clement Wood for "Jehovah."

23. "PBW," "More Poetry," 8–10, 16–19.

24. SR, "Edwin Arlington Robinson," 507–11.

25. Robinson to SR, December 8, 1920, 35.17, RA. Robinson's recent biographer writes that Robinson, "not having read the fine print," did not know that winning the $500 meant that Roth had the right to publish *Lancelot*. Donaldson, *Robinson*, 336. Roth's description of the contest stated that he would publish the winning poems.

26. Robinson to SR, May 17, 1921, 35.17, RA.

27. A letter, Squire to SR, February 21, 1921 (35.17, RA), thanked him for the books (probably about Robinson); another letter, referring to those books, stated, "I am not as enthusiastic as I hoped to be." For Robinson's London trip see Donaldson, *Robinson*, 380–85.

28. SR, "A Bookshop Night's Adventure," 140–46. *The Bookman* also published a short Roth piece titled "Robinson-Bridges-Noyes" in 1920.

29. SR, "Edwin Arlington Robinson," 510.

30. Robinson to SR, May 17, 1921.

31. This comment appears in a light blue spiral notebook in Adelaide Kugel's handwriting, 25.7, and in another holograph note in 25.10, RA.

32. M. Wilkerson, *New Voices*, 347 (also included in the 1922 edition); Coblentz, *Modern American Lyrics*, 91; Untermeyer, "Jewish Spirit in Modern American Poetry," 131; Zangwill, "Watchman, What of the Night?" 26.

33. Syrkin to SR, n.d. but 1920, 51.1, RA.

34. Syrkin to SR, n.d., 35.17, RA, accompanying typescript of three poems.

35. Syrkin to SR, January 22, 1919, 51.1, "1919," RA. The Giovannitti poem "New York and I" appeared in the September 1918 *Liberator*, pp. 14–15. Roth's rejoinder "From a Bus," playfully taking "Arthur" to task for too vehement criticism of New York City, is in the February 1919 *Liberator*, p. 40. Sassoon to SR, June 27, n.d. but probably 1921, 35.18, RA.

36. SR, "Yahrzeit," *The Nation*, May 8, 1920, 622; SR, "Kol Nidre," *Poetry: A Magazine of Verse*, June 1918, 126–29.

37. Eliade, *Eternal Return*, 105–10.

38. Wilkerson to SR, March 4, 1919, 35.17, "1918–19," RA.

39. Rittenhouse to SR, [July] 1918, 51.1, RA.

40. *Menorah Journal*, December 1917, 288–89.

41. Crawford, "Poet or Prophet?" 341–42. Reviews of *Europe* also appeared in the *New York Sun* (Herbert Gorman), *The Dial*, the *Hebrew Standard* ("N.K."), and newspapers in St. Louis, Philadelphia, Detroit, Salt Lake City, and Chicago. These clippings are pasted into a dummy (otherwise blank) bound copy of *Europe*, 42.7, RA.

42. "M.V.D.," "Books," 886a; "Lithmus," 118; Lieberman, "A New Jeremiad," clipping pasted in copy of *Europe* cited in note 41 above.

43. Scholem, "Redemption through Sin," 97–98.

44. Biale, *Gershom Scholem*, 31, 48.

45. "A Letter to Mr. J. C. Squire."

46. Urofsky, *American Zionsim*, 185, 186, 201.

47. SR, *Now and Forever*, 95.

48. Ibid., 122–27. A poem probably published during the late 1910s or early 1920s titled "Isaiah" is in 10.9, RA. It states that the gift of Zion is replacing conflicts between nations with "bold and lofty destinies / Beyond the bounds of tribe and clan."

49. Urofsky, *American Zionism*, 207–8; Sachar, *History of the Jews in America*, 248–51, 258–61.

50. Kahn-Paycha, *Popular Jewish Literature*, 92–97.

51. SR, *Now and Forever*, 139–40.

52. SR, "Life and Letters," 7.

53. "Looking into Jewry's Future."

54. *Now and Forever* (review), *Boston Evening Transcript*, Dec. 1, 1925, part 6, p. 3.

55. "PBW," "Avenue A," 8. I have not found this speech. A book with an introduction by Rosenberg is by George Liebbrandt (*Judische Weltpolitik in Selbstzeugnissen*), published in Munich in 1938. It contained excepts (in German) from *Now and Forever*.

56. Gordon, "A Playboy Prophet in Israel," 294.

57. "New Books in Brief Review," 136.

58. "PBW," "Avenue A," 9. The only translation is not Roth's, but Harrison Goldberg's.

Adelaide says Beilis offered Roth $150 for the translation. Samuel's *Blood Accusation: The Strange History of the Beiliss Case* appeared in 1966.

59. Zangwill to SR, June 16, 1925, 35.18, "1925–26," RA.

60. "Life and Letters," 8. In September 1926, Roth wrote a eulogy for Zangwill in his *Two Worlds* Little Magazine in which he admitted that Zangwill's gifts with language far exceeded Roth's own.

61. Tannenbaum to SR, October 2 [?], 1917, 38.3, RA.

62. SR, "Why Critics Should Be Educated," 249, in response to Untermeyer, "Why a Poet Should Never Be Educated."

63. Wood to SR, July 5, 1921, 35.17, s.v. "1921," RA.

64. Marie Syrkin to SR, n.d. but in file marked "1920," 51.1, RA; Moulton to SR, May 26, 1921, 35.17, RA.

65. Fried, "Creating Hebraism, Confronting Hellenism," 149: "*The Menorah Journal* became a forum in which a politics of the American-Jewish imagination emerged." See also Wald, *The New York Intellectuals*, 28–30.

66. SR, "A Bookshop Night's Adventure," 145: "Think of us as a people who began the building of a national culture at a time when culture had a better reputation than life, and discovered in the midst of our enterprise that culture had gone bankrupt."

67. Zangwill to SR, July 6, 1921, 35.17, s.v. "1920–21," RA.

68. "PBW," "The English Institute," 4.

69. Roth's story of an imaginary conversation involving Gilbert Chesterton, Edmund Gosse, Hilaire Belloc, George Moore, and Zangwill appeared in the June 1922 *Journal*. SR, "Mr Edmund Gosse Entertains on the Occasion of His Seventieth Birthday."

70. SR to Hurwitz, November 26, 1921, postscript, 35.17, RA.

71. This passage is crossed out in the handwritten draft, which is preserved in a set of materials Roth carried with him to show prospective British publishers. These materials are contained in the casing of a copy of *Robinson Crusoe* with "Stories" written on the cover, in 10.9, RA.

72. SR, *Stone Walls Do Not*, 1:89.

73. Freeman to SR, October 20, 1921, 35.17, s.v. "1920–21," RA.

74. Handwritten letter to Roth signed "Herbert," March 21, 1921, 35.17, s.v. "1920–21," RA, states that he has kept track of Sam's mail and has found "nothing but bills and bills."

75. "PBW," "London," 3.

76. Ibid., 21. A tentative contract he made with J. M. Dent for an anthology of American poetry contained a clause that half his royalties should go to his creditors.

77. This phrase occurs in a handwritten "Dedication" Roth wrote to an unknown set of poems. It and six letters written by either Jackie or Roth to each other are in 36.9, RA. There is one letter from Sam addressed to her at Long Eddy, New York. She wrote two letters to Roth in 1926 sent from Louisville, Kentucky (35.17, s.v. "1925–26"). Roth published a set of eight poems "To Dear Jacqueline from London" in *Two Worlds Monthly*, April 1927, 93–95.

78. "PBW," "London," 2.

79. Hindus, "Samuel Roth," 48.

80. Legman to AK, July 20, 1988, p. 5, 38.13, RA.

81. "PBW," "Mae West, Joyce, and Pound," 5–7. A play he hoped West would star in, "The Heavenly Babe," is in 10.4, RA.

82. Gahagan to SR, n.d.; text transcribed by AK in 23.1, RA.

83. Letter (TLS), n.d., but 1926, reproduced by AK, in 35.1, s.v. "1926," RA.

84. "CMAM," 228–29. In London, Roth wrote five poems he published in his *Songs Out of Season* (1932) under the heading "Songs Written for the Entertainment of My Lady Joan."

85. "CMAM," 232. He said he tried to find her "every year" since, but has failed. There is one letter to Roth, from the London artist signing herself "Alma C. M.," that mentions Joan as looking "charming. . . . She has a loveable generous nature." Alma to SR, June 1, 1922, 35.1, s.v. "1922–24," RA. Alma wrote that she had seen Joan at least once in London. Alma C. M. to SR, June 1, 1922, 35.17. Adelaide Kugel discusses Joan in "PBW," "London," 19, 22.

86. The Dent contact stated the title to be "The Imperial Motive in Contemporary American Poetry." Writing a decade later (*Stone Walls Do Not*, 1:103), Roth gives its title as "The Spirit of Modern American Poetry." He describes it as a "survey": "a combination of quotation and criticism."

87. A letter from Pound, in 36.31, RA, tells Roth that he is not pleased with Roth's plans. The concept of the book may have originated in a set of lectures by Roth titled "Some Reflections on American Poetry" that Roth announced in the January 1, 1920, catalogue of the Poetry Book Shop; see 37.10, folder "Joseph Roth," RA.

88. "CMAM," 219; "PBW," "London," 20. Dent to SR, June 15, 1921; Richard Wilson (editor at Dent) to SR, May 20, June 5, 15, 28, July 3, 1921. The latter is the letter in which Wilson says he is returning the manuscript. All letters in 51.1, s.v. "1920–21," RA. Roth repeats Dent's negative view of Pound in a draft of his London year ("Adrift in London") that he wrote c. 1972.

89. Richard Wilson, editor of Dent and Sons, to SR, May 20, June 20, 25, 28, 1921; Dent to SR, June 15, 1921; all in 35.17, RA. In *Stone Walls Do Not*, 1:103–4, Roth describes his project. A one-page undated typescript in the Clement Wood Papers at the Brown University Library, Providence, Rhode Island, outlines the work. A letter from Roth to Wood of May 21, 1921 (also at Brown) states the book had been accepted by Dent, provisionally, if an American publisher could be found; Pound to SR, May 11, 1921, 36.31, RA; "PBW," "London," 20. J. M. Dent's aforementioned letter to Roth stating "I feel that you have gone to the extreme of the erratic, and depend too much on Ezra Pound" suggests that Pound did agree to work on the project, but that is not clear.

90. "H.D." to "S.R.," May 27, [1921], 35.17, RA. There are six letters from H.D. to Roth in 35.17, dated May or June 1921. Dent, Duffield, and Leonard Woolf all declined to publish it.

91. A photocopy of a letter from Roth to Joyce, February 12, 1921 (35.17, RA), ends by asking him "why is *Ulysses* not yet in book form?" Adelaide Kugel made this copy at the SUNY Buffalo collection of Joyce material.

92. "Ulysses: A Commentary by Samuel Roth," nine-page computer printout, transcribed from the original by Adelaide Kugel, is in 24.3, RA.

93. "PBW," "The English Institute," 1.

94. Freeman, *An American Testament*, 207–9. At the bottom of page 6 in "PBW," "The English Institute," is a handwritten note by Adelaide Kugel: "The police at Bow Street station took a mug shot of him—and it is just as Joe [Roth, a cousin] said." I have not found the "mug shot" in the Roth Archive. Nor is there a painting done in London that also corroborates Freeman. Kugel writes that she found it in one of her father's desk drawers ("PBW," "The English Institute," 1).

95. Eliot to SR, February 22, 1921, 35.17, RA. Roth's comments on Eliot are in "CMAM," 219–20.

96. These notes are in the casing of a copy of *Robinson Crusoe* with "Stories" written on the cover, 10.9, RA.

97. "PBW," "English Institute," 1; "CMAM," 235.

98. "PBW," "English Institute," 3–5; "CMAM," 236–39; Scroggins, *The Poem of a Life,* 50.

Chapter 3. 1925–1927

1. Gorman, *James Joyce,* 306–7.

2. "PBW," "The Peddling of *Ulysses,*" [4], 22.6, RA.

3. Joyce's reply was dated February 18, 1921, from Paris, 51.1, RA (not in Ellmann, *Letters,* volume 3).

4. Weaver to Quinn, September 15, 1921, John Quinn Papers, New York Public Library, Manuscript Division.

5. Dorothy Richardson to SR, June 31 and August 1, 1922, 35.18, RA. Of course, Richardson had already published her eighth novel in the series by 1925, when he started *Two Worlds.*

6. This "cycle" was advertised in a December 2, 1926, letter to subscribers headed "Beau Publishing Company," in 35.22, RA.

7. He did publish what his table of contents called novels: in *Two Worlds*, Zorn's "Open Plumbing" (March 1926; 30 two-columned pages), and in *Two Worlds Monthly*, Jules Lemaitre's *Myrrha* (January 1927; 15 pages).

8. AK, "Wroth Wrackt Joyce," 243. A reproduction of the July 4 letter from Paris (no date but clearly 1922) is in 36.31, RA.

9. "CMAM," 240; SR, *Stone Walls Do Not,* 1:106; "PBW," "Ulysses Beached," U-13. See AK, "Wroth Wracked Joyce," 243.

10. De Grazia, *Girls Lean Back Everywhere,* 7–17; Spoo, "Copyright Protectionism and Its Discontents," see section on "Serial Publication in the United States: The Little Review."

11. Canby to SR, July 18, 1922, 35.17, RA

12. Ford to SR, July 7, 1922, 35.17, RA.

13. Quinn to Joyce, August 15, 1920, 6, Quinn Papers.

14. Hall to SR, October 29, 1925, 35.18, RA.

15. SR, *Stone Walls Do Not,* 1:108. In "CMAM," 249, Roth places the advertising expenses for the first issue at $1,650.

16. SR, "Writing Finis to Volume One of Two Worlds," 564. F. J. Hoffman's bibliography of Little Magazines rightly credits Roth with interest in printing translations of modern Russian and French writing, noting his "eclectic tastes" and his "interest in foreign literatures" (F. J. Hoffman, Allen, and Ulrich, *The Little Magazine,* 279, 282).

17. Pound, Letter to the Editor, *The New Statesman,* April 16, 1927, 10.

18. In the spring 1922 issue; quoted in Churchill and McKible, *Little Magazines and Modernism,* 73.

19. Chielens, *American Literary Magazines,* 181–85; F. J. Hoffman, Allen, and Ulrich, *The Little Magazine,* 59–60.

20. Sylvia Beach, "Letter to the Editor," *This Quarter,* Spring 1926, copy in 51.1, RA. Adelaide Kugel transcribed part of the letter from the Sylvia Beach Papers, Department of Rare Books and Special Collections, Princeton University Library.

21. Ellmann, *Letters,* 3:139. Adelaide Kugel discusses the "Work in Progress" excerpts

in *Two Worlds* in "Wroth Wrackt Joyce," 245, and in an unpublished typescript describes what she thinks are corrections Joyce made for Roth's June 26, 1926, issue of his *Quarterly* on page proofs for *This Quarter's* autumn/winter number, which contained the same except ("Backup for Joyce/Roth Agreement," 22.6, RA).

22. A photocopy of this letter, on Shakespeare and Company stationery, is in 26.2, RA.

23. There is a photocopy of two checks, one a replica of the other (placement of signature, rubber stamping, and amount are in exactly the same position on both) made out to Joyce, dated January 2, 1926. Below Joyce's signature is Beach's. The rubber stamp of the French bank contains the date of "9 Fev." Along with the letter A. G. Hays wrote to Joyce on February 26, 1927, regarding Roth's offer to Joyce concerning *Ulysses*, the photocopy is in 23.3, RA: Hays states he is returning "check for $200." The January 2 check is not related to the offer Roth made to Joyce regarding *Ulysses*.

24. A letter in a private collection dated March 18, 1926, states Roth sent $100 for the March *Two Worlds* segment from "Work in Progress" and for the June selection. Information supplied courtesy of Professor Robert Spoo of Tulsa University. I am grateful to Dr. Spoo for his e-mail to me of February 12, 2011.

25. In 1927, seriously in need of funds, Beasley tried to contact both McAlmon and Roth to pay her for their printings of *My First Thirty Years*. She felt they both owed her money. I am grateful to Alison Tartt of Austin, Texas, who is researching Beasley's life, for sending me a copy of a letter from Beasley to the Secretary of State in Washington dated January 7, 1928, which she received from the National Archives and Records Administration. I am also grateful to Ms. Tartt for her e-mails of March 9, 10, and 14 and April 12, 2011.

26. Levesque, "Where Did You Go, Edna Beasley?"

27. SR, *Stone Walls Do Not*, 1:109.

28. Morris to Sylvia Beach, November 1, 1925, Beach Papers.

29. Gorman to James Joyce, November 17, 1925, 35.18, RA.

30. *Modern SAN Review*, August 1926, reprinted a letter from Price to Beach: "I sent the man three one-dollar bills early last October for the first number. I wrote seven letters and made four calls to his office (finding him "out" each time) before I obtained my copy." Box 129, folder 1, Beach Papers. Price informed Pound that Roth was using his name on the masthead of *Two Worlds*: Wilhelm, *Ezra Pound*, 21–22.

31. "PBW," "Ulysses Beached," U-2.

32. Pound to Joyce, November 19, 1926, Paige, *Letters of Ezra Pound*, 203.

33. Quinn to Weaver, July 27, 1922, 1–2, 5, Quinn Papers.

34. "PBW," "Seven," 1. Eisenman's *New York Times* obituary (April 20, 1948, 23) identified him as president of "one of the largest newspaper distributing agencies in the country." In 1897 he was co-founder of the newspaper *Abendblatt* and helped found the *Daily Forward*. Late in his life he founded a publishing company in Israel that employed C. N. Bialik.

35. Page 3 of 5-page typescript by Roth headed "The Letters," probably in response to Ellmann's *Letters* (1966), in 23.4, RA.

36. These circulation figures were found in N. W. Ayer and Son, *American Newspaper Annual*. The directory indexes only one of Roth's magazines, *Beau*, in 1927 and 1928, but neither lists it with the other magazines or provides circulation figures for it.

37. SR, *Stone Walls Do Not*, 1:106.

38. Rainey, "The Price of Modernism," 35–36.

39. Denner, "Publishing Business," 943. "Mr Roth Is Building the Most Powerful Magazine Group In America," states a full-page notice in several issues of *Two Worlds Monthly*.

40. Pound to Joyce, December 19, 1926, Paige, *Letters of Ezra Pound*, 203.

41. Pound to Joyce, December 25, 1926, ibid., 206.

42. I am extremely grateful, once again, to Professor Robert Spoo for his help, not only for his articles "Copyright Protectionism and Its Discontents" (see 633–39, 644–45) and "Ezra Pound's Copyright Statute" (1786–87) but for his letter of March 27, 2011.

43. Vanderham, *James Joyce and Censorship*, 18–19.

44. See Peterson, *Magazines in the Twentieth Century*, 274–76.

45. I want to thank my friend Madeline Kripke, an expert on and collector of entomological works, for this suggestion.

46. On page 50 of his unpublished essay "Samuel Roth," Ryan describes Roth's idiosyncratic dress. Hindus's "Samuel Roth" (10) notes Roth's gloves, spats, well-tailored suits, and glasses. He first met Roth in the mid-1940s and thought he was imitating a "1890s dandy."

47. AK, 4-page typescript headed "Joyce/Roth," p. 1, 16.5, RA.

48. See Bourdieu, *Field of Cultural Production*, 162–67.

49. In a letter to Pauline from Lewisburg Penitentiary (n.d. but spring 1958, 37.4, RA), Roth says that he cannot live for expensive vacations or hobnob with alrightniks, for he is "not only your husband, I am a child of the world."

50. Root, "King of the Jews," 181.

51. Gilmore, *Horace Liveright*, 64–80; see also Dardis, *Firebrand*, and Madison, *Jewish Publishing in America*, 253–54, 258–59, 263–64.

52. Bennett Cerf to Morris Ernst, October 20, 1932, file box 270, Morris L. Ernst Papers, Humanities Research Center, University of Texas at Austin.

53. K. C. Davis, *Two Bit Culture*, 48–50 (Meyers; I am also indebted to Allan J. Wilson [interview of January 29, 2002]); Bill Pronzini, "Footnote," http://www.lendinglibmystery .com/Phoenix/1950-52.html (Phoenix Press, Wartels, Curl); Crider, *Mass Market Publishing in America*, 143–44 (Hillman); "Book Dealer Is Held," *New York Times*, April 3, 1930, 5; "Bookseller to Leave Jail," *New York Times*, May 23, 1930, 25; Edwin McDowell, "Nat Wartels, 88, Chairman of the Crown Publishing Empire," *New York Times*, February 8, 1990, B15; Dzwonkosky, *American Literary Publishing Houses*, 15, 101–2; Gertzman, *Bookleggers and Smuthounds*, 24, 66–72 (Curl, Hillman, Wartels), 313 n. 21 (Meyers), 26–28, 87, 209–16 (Levine, Rebhuhn); "Obituary Notes," *AB Bookman's Weekly*, December 10, 1979, 4008–11; Mondlin and Meador, *Book Row*, 225–29; interview with Mina Brussel, New York City, December 21, 1991 (Brussel).

54. AK, "Wroth Wrackt Joyce."

55. "Sum Up," notes by Adelaide Kugel on her memoir, 21.1, RA.

56. Robert W. Potter, "T. S. Eliot Reopens Roth 'Piracy' Row," *New York Evening Post*, August 11, 1927, 26. For Weaver's publication of *Ulysses* excepts, see the online catalogue of the University of Tulsa Library Special Collections exhibit of Joyce items, item 27, http:// www.lib.utulsa.edu/speccoll/collections/joycejames/trieste_zurich_paris.htm.

57. SR, *Stone Walls Do Not*, 1:108.

58. Hindus, "Samuel Roth," 56.

59. This is Adelaide Kugel's interpretation. Her analysis of Joyce's references to her father is in 21.1, RA.

60. Ellmann, *James Joyce,* 585 (citations are for the original edition unless otherwise noted); "PBW," "Seven," A-4. Hays's February 26, 1927, letter to Roth informing him that Joyce had refused his offer of $1000 is in 23.3, RA.

61. Hays to James Joyce, January 14, 1927, 26.2, RA.

62. SR to David Boehm, advertising manager of *The Nation,* August 5, 1926, 35.18, RA.

63. "U.S. Piracy of Ulysses," *Sunday Express* (London), March 27, 1927, copy found in 51.1, s.v. "1927," RA. Adelaide Kugel found the article in the Collection of James Joyce's Manuscripts and Letters at the University of Buffalo.

64. [Oswald Garrison Villard], Editorial, *The Nation,* March 16, 1927, 277.

65. The Lewisohn draft is reproduced in Ellmann, *Letters,* 3:151.

66. See Spoo, "Ezra Pound's Copyright Statute," 1776–87.

67. "CMAM," 244; SR to Slocum, December 27, 1950, and Root to Ben Abramson, November 20, 1950 (transcript of letter from Beinecke Library), 23.2, 23.3, RA. Root's essay is in *transition* 9 (December 1927): 178–84.

68. Freeman, *An American Testament,* 207–9.

69. Bowker, *James Joyce,* 360.

70. "Printing of 'Ulysses' Here Causes Protest," *New York Times,* February 18, 1927, 21; Ellmann, *Letters* 3:150.

71. Peters, "Mr Roth of New York," 10 (the editor adds that Roth has never paid for an advertisement in the magazine); Robert W. Potter, "T. S. Eliot Reopens," *New York Evening Post,* August 11, 1927, 26; T. S. Eliot to editors of *transition* (9 [December 1927]), "Correspondence" section, July 26 and August 22, 1927, 185–86, 190; "The Case of Samuel Roth," 177.

72. "Open Letter," in Gorman, *James Joyce,* 308.

73. "James Joyce Makes Deposition against Roth for Pirating Work," *International Chicago Tribune,* March 20, 1928, 51.1, s.v. "1928," RA.

74. Repeated in "Miss Beach Plans to Sue Mutilator of Joyce's Work," *New York Post,* November 1, 1926, 51.1, s.v. "1926," RA. For *This Quarter,* See note 94.

75. Quoted by Adelaide Kugel in "PBW," "The Fifth Avenue Hotel and the Book Auction." Pound's May 23, 1928, letter to Bernhardt Ragnar can be found in the New York Public Library's Berg Collection, s.v. "Pound, Ezra Loomis." The May 29 letter to Pound from Ragnar, telling him his letter was printed "in Saturday's paper on Page 4," is in the Pound Archive at the Beinecke Library, Yale University. I have used the copy in 23.13, RA. Kugel points out that *Ulysses* had been published several months before Pound would have "approved the suggestion" and that therefore Pound had no authorization to give permission at that time. Only the publisher, Sylvia Beach, could have done so. Perhaps that helps explain the circumspection in Pound's letter to Ragnar.

76. "PBW," "Mae West, Joyce, and Pound," 13.

77. Joyce to Weaver, March 28 and April 8, 1928 ("Pound has agreed to give evidence against Roth"), Ellmann, *Letters,* 3:174.

78. E-mail, Robert Spoo to the author, February 6, 2011, citing Pound letter of October 24, 1928. Dr. Spoo had published this letter in his "Unpublished Letters of Ezra Pound." I am extremely grateful to him for his help.

79. Nadel, *Ezra Pound* 106; Scott and Friedman, *Pound/The Little Review,* xxx, 266.

80. Beach to Joyce, April 12, 1927, Banta and Sherman, *James Joyce's Letters to Sylvia Beach,* 209.

81. Pound to Ragnar, March 21, 1928, Berg Collection, New York Public Libary.

82. Benjamin H. Connor [Joyce's Paris lawyer] to Herman Ould, Esq., December 6, 1929, p. 2, in 23.4, RA. Ellmann, *James Joyce,* gives the date as December 27 (p. 587).

83. *Satisfaction of Judgement,* City Court of the City of New York, February 8, 1928, 33.11, RA.

84. Read, *Pound/Joyce,* 227; Gorman, *James Joyce,* 312; Ellmann, *James Joyce,* 587: "the legal net of Joyce's attorneys had begun to close in on Roth, who suspended publication."

85. Alexander Lindey to Bennett Cerf, March 31, 1932, Ernst Papers, file 270. The firm also felt that since *Ulysses* was not copyrighted, anyone could publish it and use the author's name in advertising, even though the New York State Civil Rights Law says using a person's name without his or her permission is unlawful.

86. Shloss, "Privacy and Piracy in the Joyce Trade"; Spoo, "Copyright Protectionism and Its Discontents."

87. Weaver to Quinn, November 15, 1922, Quinn Papers.

88. Worthen, *D. H. Lawrence,* 144.

89. Ibid. Worthen notes Lawrence was "author, organizer, and paymaster" for the Orioli *Chatterley.*

90. Joyce to Weaver, November 5, 1925, and Joyce to Stanislaus Joyce, November 5 and December 15, 1926, and January 8, 1927, Ellmann, *Letters,* 3:131, 145, 148; Ellmann, *James Joyce,* 585.

91. Rainey, "The Price of Modernism," 35.

92. SR to Stanislaus Joyce, January 8, 1927, Ellmann, *Letters,* 3:149.

93. "Joyce-Roth Suit Goes to NY Supreme Court," *New York Herald Paris Edition,* May 21, 1928; "The Wrong People," *Vancouver, B. C. Daily Province,* May 29, 1928, and "Joyce Testimony on Ulysses Here," *New York Times,* May 20, 1928: 12. The first two of the articles are clippings found in 51.1, s.v. "1928," RA.

94. Sylvia Beach, "Letter to the Editor," *This Quarter,* Spring 1926, copy in 51.1, s.v. "1925," RA. Adelaide Kugel transcribed part of the letter from the copy at Princeton University's Beach Papers.

95. AK, "Wroth Wrackt Joyce," 246. In a prison letter of September 18, 1960 (37.6, RA), Roth wrote that the meeting took place at the Café Royal, that he could not speak because of dental work earlier in the day, and that Hemingway "left in a huff."

96. Hemingway to Maxwell Perkins, November 16, 1926, Baker, *Ernest Hemingway,* 225.

97. Ellmann, *Letters,* 3:145, 148, 149; Ellmann, *James Joyce,* 585.

98. "PBW," "Seven," A5.

99. Hemingway to Perkins, December 7, 1926, Baker, *Ernest Hemingway,* 237–38.

100. None are listed in Hanneman, *Ernest Hemingway.* The 1975 supplement does not list any either, nor does L. H. Cohen's *A Bibliography of the Works of Ernest Hemingway.*

101. "CMAM," 251. Either because of the entrapment plan or Hemingway's anti-Semitism, Roth tried to tell the world of his contempt for Hemingway. In *Lady Chatterley's Husbands* (Faro, 1931) there is a character named Cyril Stitchlane, a bullying, sybaritic novelist. As G. Legman points out in a note in his copy of the novel, a very nasty paragraph on pp. 185–86 is in a style very different from that of the anonymous writer of *Husbands,* and that style is Roth's.

102. This letter is quoted as part of a notice by the Gotham Book Mart of "An Archive of Major Literary Importance," the *Contempo* papers, to be sold "en bloc." The first appearance of Pound as a contributing editor to *Contempo* was in number 14 (December 15, 1931). This is

the first issue that lists such editors. It was in number 19 (March 1932) that Roth contributed a short essay as part of a group of eleven writers and editors who were asked to contribute their opinions about a review of Frank Harris's *George Bernard Shaw.* An undated copy of Pound's letter to Abernethy, photocopied by Adelaide Kugel during a visit to the Humanities Research Center, University of Texas, is in 51.1, RA.

103. Quinn to Weaver, July 27, 1922, 1–2, 5, Quinn Papers.

104. Ellmann, *James Joyce,* 504.

105. Rainey, *Institutions of Modernism,* 42–76.

106. Bourdieu, *The Rules of Art,* 121–23, 254–61.

107. For rentals and other strategies of secondhand and general booksellers in the period see my *Bookleggers and Smuthounds,* 61, 77, 80–81, 90, 95.

108. For an excellent analysis of Pound's opinion, see Spoo, "Ezra Pound's Copyright Statute," 1776–87.

109. Ellmann, *James Joyce,* rev. edition, 586. The quotation is from Scott and Friedman, *Pound/The Little Review,* 267 (Pound to Anderson, April 22, 1921). See also Tytell, *Ezra Pound,* 206–7; Pound to Joyce, December 25, 1926, Paige, *Letters of Ezra Pound,* 206.

110. Pound to Mencken, April 27, 1927, Paige, *Letters of Ezra Pound,* 211.

111. Tytell, *Ezra Pound,* 206; Wackiewicz and Witemayer, *Ezra Pound and Senator Bronson Cutting,* 6–8, 9–11, 24–29; Wilhelm, *Ezra Pound,* 56–61.

112. Ellmann, *James Joyce,* 586.

113. Fitch, *Sylvia Beach and the Lost Generation,* 326. Bowker, *James Joyce,* describes Beach's and Adrienne Monnier's anger at Joyce's plans to publish an American edition, and the obstacles she put in his way after he signed over the world rights of *Ulysses* to her (407, 425–27, 433, 447).

114. Rainey, *Institutions of Modernism,* chapter 2.

115. Bowker, *James Joyce,* 347, 512.

116. "CMAM," 253. On Joyce's occasional "profligacy," see Bowker, *James Joyce,* 227, 310.

117. Sylvia Beach to editor of the *Saturday Review* (N.Y.), May 23, 1927, p. 2, Beach Papers.

118. Vanderham's *James Joyce and Censorship* contains an appendix ("The Censor's *Ulysses*") that lists "passages expurgated by the editors of *The Little Review,*" and also passages noted by John Sumner, by a New Yorker who contacted Sumner about passages he deplored in his daughter's copy, and by U.S. Attorneys Martin Conboy and Samuel Coleman.

119. Vanderham, *Joyce and Censorship,* 234.

120. Ibid., 37.

121. Gertzman, *Bookleggers and Smuthounds,* 160–69.

122. Ellmann, *James Joyce,* 641; Lawrence Pollinger (of Curtis Brown Ltd.) to Joyce, June 15, 1931; B. W. Huebsch to Sylvia Beach, May 16, 1931, both in James Joyce Archive (Feinberg Collection), Special Collections, Southern Illinois University.

123. SR to Boehm, August 5, 1926, 35.18, RA. The text was to be read, "installment by installment, by Mr Sampliner of the Eastern Distribution Corporation."

124. Raymond Calkins to SR, February 14 and 15 and March 28, 1927, 51.1, s.v. "1927–28," RA.

125. Roberts, "Bibliographical Notes," 573.

126. Gorman, *James Joyce,* 312.

127. Vanderham, *James Joyce and Censorship,* 83–85.

128. Arnold, *The Scandal of "Ulysses,"* 59.

129. Hamalian, "Nobody Knows My Names," 894. The Hadrian Press version, "The Secret Careers of Samuel Roth," was published in 1969. This is a revision of the article of the same title that appeared in the *Journal of Popular Culture* 1, no. 4 (1968): 317–38.

130. Sources for Roth's appearance at the James Joyce Society and attendant events are in 23.3, RA: Minutes of Joyce Society Meeting, December 6, 1950 (from Berg Collection, New York Public Library); Slocum to Abramson, December 30, 1950; Root to Abramson, November 20, 1950; Slocum to Root, December 30, 1950 (all from James Joyce Collection, Beinecke Library); SR to Slocum, December 27, 1950; Slocum to SR, February 3, 1951. Roth's own story of his Joyce Society appearance is in "CMAM," 247–48.

131. Slocum to Abramson, December 30, 1950, Joyce Collection, Beinecke Library.

132. Bourdieu, *Field of Cultural Production,* 77.

133. Deming, *James Joyce,* 2:548–49, reproduces Huddleston's appreciation of *Ulysses* in his *Back to Montparnasse* (1931).

134. Ellmann, *Letters,* 3:151.

135. Bourdieu, *Field of Cultural Production,* 77–83, 113–14.

136. Cerf, "Publishing *Ulysses*," 1–2. Bowker says Kastor was "acting for Joyce in New York" (*James Joyce,* 433).

137. See Spanos, "'Wanna Go Home, Baby?'" 12.

138. Saint-Amour, "Soliloquy of Samuel Roth," 468.

139. Hamalian, "Nobody Knows My Names," 92.

140. AK, four-page typescript headed "Joyce/Roth," p. 1, 16.5, RA.

141. For an extended description by poet Walter Mehring of the "poison cupboard" in his father's library, see his *The Lost Library,* 59–66.

142. Legman, *The Horn Book,* 34, discusses Best. In his introduction to Kearney's *The Private Case,* 48, Legman states that Best was "Carrington's secret salesman in America." Sumner's 1929 raid on Roth's office uncovered letters Roth wrote to and received from Best, indicating that Roth "was practically the publisher" (of the impression of the Carrington edition of *Forbidden Books*). *United States v. Samuel Roth,* C53-79, Stenographer's Minutes, pp. 28–29. There is a letter from Best to SR, March 12, 1926, 35.22, RA.

143. AK, "Notes" (compiled for her memoir of her father), p. 11, 24.2, RA. "PBW," "The Ansonia," 2–6. AK describes her father's British affectations upon his return from London in "PBW," "The English Institute," 1.

144. G. Legman to AK, July 20, 1988, 38.13, RA.

145. "Mr Roth Is Hailed into Court," *Two Worlds Monthly,* April 1927, 1–2; "Roth's Magazine Accused," *New York Times,* March 10, 1927, 2.

146. Samuel to SR, April 19, 1927, 37.14, RA.

147. SR to Abba Eban [about conversations he heard regarding the Russian Revolution in 1916], March 18, 1969, p. 4, 36.7, RA. For Schmeeil, see *MFY,* 82–83, 497–98.

148. Alter, "Maurice Samuel and Jewish Letters," 50.

149. S. Slutsky, Secretary of Mendel Beilis Publishing Co., to SR, July "23/25," 192[5?], 35.18, RA. The company would pay Roth $150 for the translation.

150. Arthur Doyle (California) to SR, April 27, 1927; L. J. Salter (New York) to SR, May 2, 1927; John B. Barnhill (Pennsylvania) to SR, May 28, 1927; R. W. Denney (California) to SR, May 4, 1927; Alexander Benger (n.p.) to SR, May 4, 1927: all in 51.1, RA.

151. Moore to SR, April 25, 1927; Bell to SR, April 23, 1927; Tully to SR, April 28, 1927; Whitsett to SR, May 2, [1927?]: all in 51.1, s.v. "1927," RA.

152. Rodker to SR, March 15 and May 13, 1927, 51.1, s.v. "1927," RA. Rodker wrote Weaver that "you will subscribe my name with pleasure to your protest." The letter, found by Adelaide Kugel in box 50 M-83 in the Houghton Library and transcribed by her, is in 51.1, s.v. "1926," RA.

153. Böske Anthiel to Sylvia Beach, June 9, 1931, box 129, Beach Papers.

154. "PBW," "Peggy and the Lion," p.6–10.

155. Professor Robert Spoo (e-mail to the author, February 12, 2011) suggests this explanation for the check being attached to the letter from Hays, for Roth would have been interested in convincing Slocum he had been slandered by Joyce and Beach. I agree that Roth was capable of acting in this way.

156. SR, *Apotheosis,* 33.

157. Roth wrote about what he said in "CMAM," 247–48, and his December 27, 1950, letter to Slocum contains the gist of his argument, including invective directed at Waverley Root, Konrad Bercovici, and a "lady poet." Saint-Amour, "Soliloquy of Samuel Roth," 476, traces the phrase "Lion in a Den of Daniels" to an 1888 Oscar Wilde letter.

158. SR to Peggy Roth, March 6, 1960, 37.9, file "Prison Letters-Peggy Roth," RA.

Chapter 4. 1928–1934

1. SR, *Stone Walls Do Not,* 2:334–35.

2. "Nocross" is stated verso the title page to be the holder of copyright of the privately printed *The Strange Confession of Monsieur Mountcairn* (1928), a time when Roth would not want to use his name own name, because of the International Protest. The author might have been Benjamin Musser (Austen, *Homosexual Novel in America,* 47).

3. Hofstader, *Anti-Intellectualism in American Life,* 118–34, discusses the "one hundred per cent" mentality of the 1920s.

4. "Vice Society Seized Ton of Books in 1927," *New York Times,* May 3, 1928, 29.

5. *United States v. Samuel Roth,* C53-79, Stenographer's Minutes, p. 93. Sumner had found this note on Roth's desk during the October 1929 raid of the Golden Hind offices.

6. John S. Sumner Papers, State Historical Society of Wisconsin, Madison, contains essays titled "Literature and the Law," MS44-[p]1, and "The Thrill Addict and the Theater," MS40[?], pp. 5–10. A note states that the latter article appeared in the *North American Review* in July 1927.

7. *Finnegans Wake,* 421.35–422.2. Adelaide Kugel has brilliantly analyzed this and other Roth-related passages of the *Wake*: 24.4, typescript headed "Wroth Wrackt [sic] Joyce," RA.

8. The sociological concept of "pariah capitalism" was inspired by such classic statements about outsiders as those of Georg Simmel ("The Stranger") and Max Weber ("Judaism, Christianity, and the Socio-Economic Order"). Weber analyzes the responsibilities of the Diaspora Jew toward those with whom he is engaged for economic survival. Simmel discusses the behavior of, and the nature of hostility toward, "the stranger."

9. For the concept of commercialized outlets for repressed instincts in modern societies, and of these outlets as themselves a kind of social control, see Herbert Marcuse's "surplus repression": *Eros and Civilization,* 37–48, 87–91.

10. "PBW," "The Fifth Avenue Hotel and the Book Auction," 8–9.

11. The ledgers for the New York Society for the Suppression of Vice for 1926 state that a

"West 15th Street" dealer (Klein) was sentenced to fifty dollars or thirty days in jail for giving a Sumner agent an "obscene circular" for Harris's *My Life and Loves*. Names and Records of Persons Arrested Under the Auspices of the New York Society for the Suppression of Vice, microfilm reels 1 and 2 (shelf number 19,359), MS Division, Library of Congress.

12. In April 1929. Adelaide Kugel wrote the author on December 7, 1988, "Pauline Roth was made proprietress of GHP."

13. SR to John C. Knox, February 23, 1930, 31.19, RA.

14. In the transcript for *United States v. Samuel Roth,* C53-79, p. 17, a postal inspector testified that he wrote "test" letters in February 1929 under assumed name to order copies of *Chatterley,* and received a copy. Judge Knox wrote that Moe's warehouse at 160 Fifth "enable[d] the other addresses to be kept relatively free," C53-79, p.5.

Sumner's ledgers for 1929 state that Max Roth was sentenced to from six months to three years in the penitentiary.

On the "jacket" of the indictment in the mailing of *Perfumed Garden,* filed January 27, 1928, Judge John C. Knox has written, "Feb 28, 1930—Deft. surrendered to the court, for violation of Parole. Deft. Sentenced to four months imprisonment." There is a six-page statement by Knox revoking Roth's probation in 31.19, RA, dated January 28, 1930. Judge Knox had specified Roth was to be held at Detention Headquarters (Roth states its address in "Second Preface," *Stone Walls Do Not,* 1:[13]) for his violation of parole.

15. "A Letter from Mr. Joyce . . . ," *Ulysses* (New York: Modern Library, 1934), xvii. The *New York Times* obituary of Roth, possibly following Joyce's lead, states that "In 1928 [*sic*] police raided the premises of his publishing company and seized plates containing 'Ulysses,' which Mr. Roth had pirated from Paris" ("Samuel Roth, 79, Tested Obscenity," *New York Times,* July 4, 1974, 22).

16. Slocum and Cahoon, *A Bibliography,* 28–29; Roberts, "Bibliographical Notes," 573. Roth submitted an application for copyright of his Faro *Celestine,* on which he noted that the Loewingers were the printers (Application for Copyright, November 15, 1930, 36.3, RA), as do the *New York Sun* ("Seize Obscenities Worth $70,000," April 10, 1934, 18) and the *Times* ("2 Tons of Books Seized," April 10, 1934, 21). Sumner's ledgers for 1934, and the *New York Sun,* report some of the books involved as *Crimson Hairs, Anecdota Americana, Randiana,* and *My Secret Life.*

17. Frances Steloff wrote to Sylvia Beach that since the plates for the Roth edition had been confiscated, there were not many copies of *Ulysses* in circulation: March 10, 1932, box 129, folder AM 18348, Beach Papers. Neither the newspaper accounts, the Sumner ledgers, nor the transcript for *United States v. Samuel Roth,* C53-79, mention plates. It is possible that the information about the confiscated plates was a rumor.

18. Knox to SR, February 25, 1930 (response to Roth's to him two days before), 31.19, RA.

19. A fifteen-page Post Office report was prepared by C. H. Saffell for Hoover's "smear book" investigators. It is in HHMF and is titled "New York, NY: Publication and sale of a book entitled 'The Strange Career of Herbert Hoover Under Two Flags'" and is dated November 28, 1931 [hereafter cited as "Saffell report, HHMF"]. It contains memos, letters, affidavits, and reports about various charges John Hamill, author of *Strange Career,* made against Hoover. Information about Zolinsky is in "Post Office Investigation," December 4, 1931.

20. New York Society for the Suppression of Vice, "Periodical Letter" (to members of

the society) signed John Sumner, "New York, Oct. 28, 1929." These letters are in the New York Public Library, The Research Libraries, under the author "Society to Maintain Public Decency, N.Y." ("Periodical Letters" 1925–39).

21. AK to the author, December 7, 1988.

22. AK, interview with Yussie Biren, December 6, 1986, summarized in "Telephone Interview," 24.3, "Notes," p. 15, RA.

23. *United States v. Samuel Roth*, C53–79, Stenographer's Minutes, p. 39.

24. Memorandum (unsigned) dated November 12, 1931, p. 3, HHMF.

25. Regarding physicians and especially dentists being large consumers of mail-order erotica: interviews by the author with the following: bookseller of erotica and professor of erotology C. J. Scheiner, June 5, 1987, and November 14, 1991; Mrs. Adelaide Roth, July 3, 1987; New York bookseller and editor Arnold Levy, June 3, 1987; Gershon Legman, June 17, 1990; and Mrs. Mina Brussel, Jacob's widow, December 21, 1991.

26. Hamalian, "Nobody Knows My Names," 903.

27. "PBW," "Jersey City," 4–14.

28. "Edited by Joseph Brownell." Dedicated to Morris Eisenman. S.v. Pound, Ezra: "poet, critic; one does not ask of a clown whether he is an actor, married, or even human."

29. "Prosecutor Raids a Philadelphia Bookstore," *New York Times*, January 25, 1930, 1. The owner was Horace Townsend. Roth does not mention the reason for his being incarcerated in Philadelphia. There are no records in Philadelphia of this case.

30. "Mills to Quit as Police Head; Is 'Disgusted,'" *Philadelphia Bulletin*, December 7, 1932; "Mills' Trial Opens for Jail Deaths," *Bulletin*, April 24, 1939; "New Board Plans Mills Inquiry," *Bulletin*, January 27, 1939; articles found in Urban Archives Newspaper Clippings Collection, Paley Library, Temple University, Philadelphia.

31. Kligsberg, "Jewish Immigrants in Business," 254–60.

32. Unterman, *The Kabbalistic Tradition*, 67, 152, 224, 262–63, 285.

33. Scholem, "Redemption through Sin," 119–29; Biale, *Gershom Scholem*, 83–84.

34. SR to Richard Roth, November 15, 1928, 36.33, RA.

35. The statement regarding Roth's start-up capital for Faro is in a memo headed "Samuel Roth," p. 2, Saffell report, HHMF.

36. *JML*, 190–92. Paro's criminal record is recorded on pp. 4–5 of the Saffell report, HHMF.

37. Harold Barber to SR, October 4, 1932, and SR to Barber, October 11, 1932, Harris-Ross Correspondence, box 2, Arents Library, Syracuse University, Syracuse, New York.

38. A contract in RA states that the author, "William Lennox," is a pseudonym of Samuel Roth.

39. "PBW," "200 W. 16th Street," 200–210.

40. "Scout Murder Hint in Gun Trap Death," *New York Times*, June 4, 1936, 56; "Burglar Gun Trap Kills Dr. R. H. Bell," *New York Times*, June 2, 1931, 31. Roth wrote an essay on "The Death of Dr. Bell" (36.5, RA).

41. Legman, *The Horn Book*, 485–86.

42. Harold C. Auer, a friend and admirer of Roth and at the time circulation publicity director for the *Detroit Free Press*, was acting as American agent for Douglas. Correspondence between Auer and Roth is in 36.6, RA.

43. Tebbel, "Main Trends in Twentieth-Century Book Clubs," 408.

44. The book was published while Roth was serving his prison sentence in Philadelphia,

and the imprint is "William Hodgson." "William Faro, Inc." is printed on the dust jacket: this suggests there were two impressions.

45. A ledger book Roth prepared in 1933 lists sales for his various Faro titles (43.4, RA). The four best-selling titles are his expurgated *Lady Chatterley, Celestine, A Scarlet Pansy,* and *Anecdota Americana.* Roth kept a tally of royalties to be sent to Frieda Lawrence if she sanctioned his expurgation of *Chatterley.* As of January 1, 1933, they totaled $3,865.95.

46. H. Schwartz, *This Book-Collecting Racket,* 6.

47. For authorship of the sequels, see my *Descriptive Bibliography,* 239–43.

48. H. T. Moore and Montague, *Frieda Lawrence and Her Circle,* 34.

49. Frieda was not clear on what she could or could not do as her husband's beneficiary, since the estate had not yet been settled. Regarding Roth's opinion of Frieda: AK, handwritten note attached to photocopy of H. T. Moore and Montague's *Frieda Lawrence and Her Circle,* 22.11, RA.

50. "We Nominate for Oblivion," 42.

51. "R.M.C.," "Books, Books, Books," 76–77.

52. Hamalian, "Nobody Knows My Names," 906.

53. SR, *Jews Must Live,* 202. What did incense Roth was the literary world's ignoring his labor of love, a deluxe two-volume edition of Voltaire's *Philosophical Dictionary* (Coventry House, 1932), about which he complained, "The whole edition fell dead at my feet the very first week I issued it."

54. For example, *Bedtime Stories,* June 1933, 65; *Pep,* February 1933, 60; *Spicy Stories,* August 1933, 61. Information about *Strange Career*'s points of sale is in the HHMF, p. 10.

55. So stated in a contract signed by Donna McKay in 42.13, RA.

56. I want to thank Bill Stevens of Books of Choice, Bloomington, Minnesota, for providing a photocopy of the dust jacket.

57. "PBW," Friday Nights at Home," 9. This contrasts with her earlier "notes": a typewritten document headed "1932," notes by AK re Faro titles, p. 108, 23.14 RA.

58. AK, notes for "PBW," 21.1–2, RA.

59. McKay to SR, October 6 and 8, 1941, 36.26, RA.

60. The letters are in 29.7 and 29.8, RA, as is the typescript, titled "Amiable with Big Teeth: A Novel Concerning the Love Affair between the Communists and the Black Sheep of Harlem." Set in Harlem, it concerns efforts to publicize the assaults of Mussolini on Ethiopia.

61. Wintz, "Politics and Poetics of Claude McKay," 179–81; Giles, *Claude McKay,* 142–49.

62. Fone, *Columbia Anthology,* 710.

63. As Fone suggests (ibid., 649). For analysis of the novel see ibid., 649, 654, 715; "Words on Homo Words"; Hagius, "The Mystery," 35–39. I want to thank Ewa Wolynska of the Special Collections Department of Central Connecticut University for sending me a PDF of the typescript, where it is in the Canon Clinton Jones Papers (item 51, box 3).

64. Austen, *Homosexual Novel in America,* 42–46, 62–64. Austen states that the copy of *Scarlet Pansy* he read was the Royal edition.

65. Quoting McAlmon's "Miss Knight": "a war-made queer one" (Austen, *Homosexual Novel,* 44).

66. A handwritten ledger book for the Faro business, compiled early in 1933, gives the number of copies of the book sold in January of that year as 68, and Scully's royalties as $117 (43.4, RA). That, of course, was early in the year of publication. RA also contains (42.13) a copy of Faro's contract with Scully.

67. Le Grand, "The Golden Age of Queens" [6], reports that *A Scarlet Pansy*, which is described as "the first truly gay book done in English and printed in America," had a "good sale" (in San Francisco), but mostly "under the counter."

68. The collection of books in RA includes a copy with the red and black title page; the frontispiece is monochrome. I am grateful to Neil Pearson, author of *Obelisk: A History of Jack Kahane and the Obelisk Press,* for his e-mail of March 5, 2011, informing me of the existence of the special 1932 impression with the colored frontispiece and title page.

69. Gershon Legman writes, on the endpaper of his copy, that Roth made "expurgations" in 1946 "to steal back copyright." I want to thank Steven Gertz, then of Dailey Rare Books, Los Angeles, for sending me photocopies of selected pages of this Roth-revised and Legman-annotated copy.

70. There is a typed note laid into the copy of *A Scarlet Pansy* (the 1932 edition) in RA. Possibly a draft of advertising copy or of a note meant for purchaser of Roth's business (c. 1968), it concludes, "The book had a big sale for years in the present [unexpurgated] form, and still sells in a condensed edition of 223 pages."

71. Leo T. Clark, Probation Officer, to Hon. Grover Moscowitz, "Petition for Revocation of Probation," *United States v. Samuel Roth,* U.S. District Court, Southern District of New York, April 7, 1941, appended to *United States v. Pauline Roth and Samuel Roth,* C99-114, 1936. It is likely that, if the book that came to the parole officer's attention was not the 1933 Faro edition, it was the abridged version.

72. Clancy, *Gay New York,* 324; Bullough, *Before Stonewall,* 5.

73. SR, *Stone Walls Do Not,* 2:259–61. Roth had no special sympathy for homosexuals. When he published serious books about the subject, such as *The Strange Confession of Monsieur Montcairn* in 1928, he was responding to a demand for writings about this tabooed sexual behavior. In his prison memoir *Stone Walls Do Not* he referred to these individuals, in and out of prison, as "abortions of Nature."

74. Hagius, "The Mystery," 8–24. Fone says only that there is "slight evidence" that McAlmon was Scully, but does not elaborate. Fone, *A Road to Stonewall,* 227. I want to thank Mr. Hagius for his insightful comments in e-mails to me, October 26–29, 2010.

75. Hagius, "The Mystery," 38–39. The character Marjorie Bull Dike physically resembles Radclyffe Hall. In an e-mail of March 13, 2011, Hagius informed me that there are works in which incidents from *Pansy* may be found. One is a manuscript McAlmon mentioned to Sylvia Beach as "My Susceptible Friend Adrian." Others are "Jennie June's" *Autobiography of an Androgyne* (1918) and *The Female-Impersonators.*

76. I am grateful to Lucia Begg of Contact Editions, Toronto, Canada, to Dave Stewart of Between the Covers Book, Gloucester City, and to Bauman Rare Books, Philadelphia, for examples of McAlmon's handwriting.

77. Typewritten document headed "1932," p. 108, 23.14, RA. Scully is also mentioned in "PBW," "Friday Nights at Home," 18.

78. "Robert Scully Missing," *New York Times,* May 16, 1897, New York Times internet archive, accessed May 2009.

79. I want to thank Sonya Coleman, Historical Collections Specialist, Moore Health Sciences Library, University of Virginia, for this information, sent to me in an e-mail of July 17, 2009.

80. Hagius, "The Mystery," 10–15; Sussman, "Words on Homo Words: *The Scarlet Pansy* 2."

81. Hagius, "Fay Etrange," 4.

82. Smoller, *Adrift among Geniuses,* 190–92, 211–16.

83. Austen, *Homosexual Novel in America*, 42.

84. Smoller, "Berliners for Sale," 30–31.

85. Vidal, foreword, x.

86. Fitzgerald told Perkins that McAlmon was a "bitter rat" to be avoided. Hagius, "The Mystery," 33–34.

87. Smoller, *Adrift among Geniuses,* 237–38.

88. The statement about "lump sum" is from "Words on Homo Words," the author of which interviewed Hagius. Hagius, in "Fay Etrange in Sex Change," 2, states correctly that Roth published the first edition.

89. In his earlier "The Mystery of *A Scarlet Pansy*," Hagius had not yet recognized Faro as an imprint of Roth, and states that the first edition of *Pansy* was unadvertised and not listed in any publisher's catalogue, although it sold well (2).

90. Smoller, *Adrift among Geniuses,* 237–38.

91. A. Cohen, *Everyman's Talmud,* 66, 90–93, 102–6.

92. AK, notes for "PBW," 2 pages, headed "SR's letter of May 17, 1937," point 9, p. 2, 17.5, RA.

93. Roth's story and others in *Body* were probably written during his 1930 prison stay. Delmore Schwartz's "The Heights of Joy," the story "Screeno," and the collection of stories and poems called *Screeno* were not published in his lifetime. See the Selected Bibliography in McDougall, *Delmore Schwartz,* 143–49.

94. D. Schwartz, "The Heights of Joy," *Screeno,* 73–74.

95. Ibid., 88.

96. "Transfiguration" (unpublished novel), typescript found in 13.4 (part 2) and 13.5–6 (part 1), RA.

97. *People v. Samuel Roth and People v. Julius Moss*. Roth was represented by Bushel and Gottleib. Newman Levy and Alexander Lindey of Greenbaum, Wolff, and Ernst argued the case for Moss.

98. "Clears 2 on Indecent Book Charge," *New York Times,* May 8, 1931, 4.

99. SR, *Jews Must Live,* 194.

100. "Denies Selling Banned Book," September 10, 1931, 22, and "Acquitted on Obscene Book Charge," September 11, 1931, 14, both in *New York Times.*

101. Sumner to C. S. Bodwell, June 30, 1934, Paige Box 3, Papers of the New England Watch and Ward Society, Special Collections, Harvard University Law Library, Cambridge, Massachusetts; Sumner's ledgers for 1934 (states thirteen books were involved).

102. See my *Bookleggers and Smuthounds,* 251–55.

103. Three-page memo, "Status of Bank Account," April 29, 1932, HHMF.

104. Memo to Mr. George Barr Baker, October 13, 1932, item 6, HHMF.

105. Hoover, *Memoirs,* 3:224.

106. The contract, in HHMF, provides for a generous allowance to Hamill for research purposes, and an advance of $75 per week. It is appended to a letter from Robert J. Phillips to Edgar Rickard dated December 16, 1931.

107. "Court Throws Out Hoover Book Suit," *New York Times,* January 13, 1933, 124.

108. "Author Repudiates Anti-Hoover Book," *New York Times,* January 5, 1933, 23.

109. "The Truth About—" and "Spirit above Facts," *New York Times,* January 6, 1933, 18.

110. Hamalian, "Nobody Knows My Names," 904; Gershon Legman, in a letter to Leo

Hamalian and the present writer, November 11, 1986, reminisces about "the cane he always carried, à l'anglaise."

111. SR, "Seeing Mr. Hoover Through," 5–14. *Plain English*, "Copyright 1932 by William Faro, Inc.," seems to have been published solely to give its publisher a platform to explain his actions regarding the Hoover exposé.

112. SR, *Jews Must Live*, 197.

113. SR, "Comment," *Plain English*, June 1932, 3.

114. SR, "Seeing Mr. Hoover Through," 7.

Chapter 5. 1934

1. Five-page manuscript beginning "Chapter I," in ledger book quarter bound in leather, 14.3, RA; *MFY*, 580–82.

2. Roth, *JML*, 14 (cited in text as *JML* with page number or, if context is clear, simply by the page number).

3. "PBW," "JML," 2.

4. Three-page memo, "Status of Bank Account," April 29, 1932, HHMF.

5. The Index on file in the Archives of the Bankruptcy Court of the Southern District of New York lists William Faro Inc. as applying for bankruptcy on June 5, 1933 (vol. 122, case no. 57489). Records of cases for that period, however, are no longer available.

6. A search of the WorldCat shows that these four titles have Nesor as well as Faro imprints.

7. G. Legman to the author, August 4, 1985, September 6, 1988. The Rose Bindery at 200 West Street is listed in the *Phillips Business Directory* for New York City, 1928–29 edition. The relevant documents in HHMF are as follows: three-page memorandum headed "Post Office Investigation," December 4, 1931, signed C. H. Saffell, p. 3; HHMF, item 4.

8. See "Crown Publishers: The First Ten Years," *Publishers Weekly*, November 11, 1946, 2806–10; Edwin McDowell, "Tight Grip on a Rich Empire," *New York Times Biographical Service* (New York: The Times, 1981), 1448–49.

9. William Ryan, "Clement Wood," unpublished essay, copyright 1990, pp. 27–28. *JML* mentions "A Jew who will here remain nameless" (148), but whoever read *JML* among the Fourth Avenue booksellers would know the nameless man was Brussel.

10. AK to C. J. Scheiner, May 7, 1991, 39.1, RA.

11. SR to PR, June 7, 1937, 37.2, RA.

12. Hamalian, "Nobody Knows My Names"; Ryan, "Samuel Roth," 49.

13. Ryan, "Samuel Roth," 51; "PBW," "The Making of Jews Must Live," 6–7. There is a MS draft in Roth's hand in 10.8, RA, in a otherwise blank brown copybook with "Books to Read H.C." gold-stamped on the spine.

14. Harrap, *Creative Awakening*, 154–56. There may be one other example of similar contempt for co-religionists. Saul Bellow ("A Jewish Writer in America," 28) refers to a "famous literary figure" of his acquaintance who believed "his fellow Jews . . . had plunged the world into war, and that the goyim were cattle driven to the slaughterhouse by Yids."

15. "Diament" or "Diamant" is the spelling Roth uses when he gives Herbert's full name. "CMAM," 168.

16. SR, *Now and Forever,* 139–40; SR, preface, *Now and Forever,* 27; SR, *Stone Walls Do Not,* 1:85; "CMAM," 213; *Beau,* October 1927, 92, 117.

17. Hindus, "Samuel Roth," 6 (says Reznikoff told him of the incident); AK, shoebox file, 51.1, s.v. "1938," RA. The book, by George Liebbrandt (*Judische Weltpolitik in Selbstzeugnissen*), was published in Munich in 1938 and contained excerpts (in German) from *Now and Forever, The Protocols of the Elders of Zion,* and an essay on Horst Wessel.

18. AK, "Notes" for her memoir, p. 11, 24.3, RA.

19. "PBW," "1939," 7.

20. *United States v. Pauline Roth and Samuel Roth,* Memorandum in Support, 7. In several letters (October 4 and 11, 1937), Roth instructed Pauline to get back from the printer the plates of *Lady Chatterley's Husbands, Lady Chatterley's Lover* (presumably his expurgation), and *JML.* He most likely did not want another impression of *JML* to appear, which would destroy any chances for parole.

21. Roth collected the reviews he could find. They are in 42.9, RA.

22. Marie Syrkin to AK, December 11, 1984, file "Personal Letters, 1981-," 38.22, RA.

23. "Counsel of Thunder: A Call to Catholics to Return to Their Original Faith," holograph 1-page MS, 31.18, RA.

24. Seven-page typescript, 1.2, RA.

25. SR to PR, May 17, 1937, 37.2, RA.

26. Rank, *Double,* 41–42.

27. SR to PR, April 25, 1938, 37.2, RA.

28. "Essay on Berenice," http://www.falcophiles.co.uk/characters/berenice.html.

29. SR, *Stone Walls Do Not,* 2:197–202. Roth states (198) that Josephus surrendered at Masada, confusing that with Josephus's action at the city of Jotapata.

30. Rosenfeld, "David Levinsky," 273–81.

31. Seven-page typescript, "Roth's Views on AntiSemitism in Prison," p. 6, 24.3, RA. When Roth wrote about Joseph's fleeing from Potiphar's wife's advances, scholars believed that it was the garment that he left behind. James Kugel, in *The Bible as It Was,* 259, says that Joseph was able to resist the wife's advantages because of the wisdom that his father, Jacob, taught him regarding self-control and the sin of adultery. This is not far from Roth's interpretation.

32. Hindus, "Samuel Roth," 4, 17–19, 27–28.

33. Zborowski and Herzog, *Life Is with People,* 409.

34. Ibid., 424.

35. Scholem, "Redemption through Sin," 98–99.

36. Von Treitschke's *History of Germany,* vol. 7, and "A Word about Our Jewry." See Elon, *The Pity of It All,* 217–18; Gay, *Freud, Jews, and Other Germans,* 114.

37. Robertson, "Historicizing Weininger," 23.

38. Ford, "Women and Men" (1919), quoted in Byrnes, "Weiningerian Sex Comedy," 270.

39. Bowker, *James Joyce,* 224.

40. Weininger, *Sex and Character,* trans. Löb; Robertson, "Historicizing Weininger," 23–28; Byrnes, "Weiningerian Sex Comedy," 267–81; Elon, *The Pity of It All,* 236–37; Gay, *Freud, Jews, and Other Germans,* 195–96.

41. Marx, *A World without Jews.* See Gilman, *Jewish Self-Hatred,* 188–208.

42. Chamberlain, *Foundations of the Nineteenth Century,* 288.

43. Deuteronomy 15 states that every seven years a fellow Jew is to be released from any debt incurred, while non-Jews need not be released. The concept is that a loan to fellow Jews is charity, not a business transaction, but to a non-Jew, a visitor to Israel, the loan is part of a business transaction.

44. Gilman, *Jewish Self-Hatred,* 205.

45. Von Treitschke, *History of Germany,* 177–78; *JML,* 129.

46. Elon, *The Pity of It All,* 237.

47. Gilman, *Jewish Self-Hatred,* 188–208, describes Marx's discussion of "The Jewish Question," or the way Jewish behavior is the spirit of capitalism.

48. "PBW," "The Making of Jews Must Live"; *JML,* 3.

49. Weininger, *Sex and Character,* trans. Löb, 163–277, 281; Byrnes, "Weiningerian Sex Comedy," 268–73; Steinberg, "The Source(s) of Joyce's Anti-Semitism," 63–64.

50. Chamberlain, *Foundations of the Nineteenth Century,* 488.

51. Slezkine, *The Jewish Century,* 116.

52. Gay, *Freud, Jews, and Other Germans,* 114–19, 184.

53. Reitter, *The Anti-Journalist.*

54. Gilman, *Jewish Self-Hatred,* 233–38; Reitter, *The Anti-Journalist,* 73–87, 157–74.

55. Robertson, "The Problem of 'Jewish Self Hatred,'" 105.

56. See my *Bookleggers and Smuthounds,* 14–15, 28–29, 119–21.

57. Legman to AK, March 12, 1981, 38.13, RA.

58. Actually, FDR, early in his presidency, began to appoint Jews to high positions in his administration: Dinnerstein, *Anti-Semitism in America,* 104, 108.

59. Gershon Legman to Leo Hamalian, "First Day of Spring 1976," author's collection.

60. Gilman, *Jewish Self-Hatred,* 18–19, quoting Anna Freud.

61. Sennett, *Authority,* 100. The discussion of authority and its effects in this paragraph follows Sennett's discussion, especially on pp. 46–49, 80–82, and 100–104.

62. SR to Milton Hindus, March 25, 1950, and undated (1945?), p. 4, box 8, Milton Hindus Papers, Farber University Archives and Special Collections Department, Brandeis University Libraries.

63. This comment appears in a light-blue spiral notebook in Adelaide Kugel's handwriting, 25.7, s.v. "The NYPL," RA.

64. AK, note s.v. "Robinson," 24.9, RA.

65. Donaldson, *Robinson,* 351.

66. Ibid., 171–79.

67. AK, handwritten note in blue spiral notebook with contents ("Edel . . . Erskine"), 25.7, RA.

Chapter 6. 1934–1939

1. "PBW," "The Making of Jews Must Live," 3–4.

2. Affidavit of Assistant District Attorney Mark F. Hughes (*United States v. Samuel Roth,* Cr 148-49, U.S. District Court, Notice of Motion for New Trial, 1959, pp. 3–4.) Re firing the lawyer: Oberwager and Oberwager to Roth, April 28, 1934, 33.14, RA.

3. "PBW," "The Making of Jews Must Live," 5.

4. Several titles state that two extra copies were printed on special paper for the libraries

of Norman Lockridge and "Lazar," a name affected by Roth's dentist (and possible investor in the Black Hawk Press).

5. Ellis, *Kanga Creek,* 126.

6. Chester Battles [Postal Inspector], Memorandum to Lamar Hardy [U.S. Attorney], September 9, 1938, U.S. Dept. of Justice, Central Files, File No. 33S251-1, National Archives. Battles states that such copies were purchased by distributor Maurice Fryefield from Pauline Roth in 1935. Legman noted von Bayros's art inserted in certain copies of the 1940 *Tropic of Cancer* (Shifreen, 13).

7. Roth's FBI files contain a memo "for Mr. Tamm" headed "RE: The Fifth Avenue Book Shop, 77 West 47th Street, New York City" dated July 17, 1936. Appended is the circular headed "Four Privately Printed Books." FBI files available under FOIA from U.S. Department of Justice (Office of Information Policy), Washington, D.C.

8. Morris Ernst to Lockridge, May 26, 1936; Carl Van Doren to Lockridge, May 30, 1936; John Erskine to Lockridge, June 2, 1936; James Branch Cabell to Lockridge, June 17, 1936; all in 36.12, RA.

9. Cyril Clemens to Norman Lockridge, June 18, 1936, 36.12, RA.

10. "PBW," "The Mayflower," M-7.

11. Quoted in ibid. The review appeared in the March 29, 1936, issue of the *Times.*

12. There is an extensive set of clippings in 53.15–16, RA.

13. "PBW," "Enter the FBI," 6.

14. Advertising copy found in 48.8, RA. In 1967, Roth sold the copyright to the Markus-Campbell Company, "publishers of self-improvement books and home study courses," for $1,000. Letters from Markus-Campbell to Norman Lockridge, August 25, 1966, and their lawyer, March 15, 1967, 36.12, RA.

15. "PBW," "The Mayflower," M-2.

16. "PBW," "The Making of Jews Must Live," 13.

17. Her lists are headed "Where They Lived" and "Where I Lived and Went to School," 23.1, RA.

18. "With the profit he made on the erotica he put out four [Black Hawk] books. . . . He was also able to move us out of Brooklyn to Central Park West and Sixtieth Street." "PBW," "The Mayflower," M-2.

19. "PBW," "The Making of Jews Must Live," 6, 7, 10, 12–13.

20. "PBW," "The Cape to the Bull," 4.

21. *United States v. Pauline Roth and Samuel Roth,* 1936, Memorandum in Support, June 22, 1937, p. 4.

22. *United States v. Pauline Roth and Samuel Roth,* C99-114, pp. 2–30 (counts of indictment).

23. Some titles: *Pageant of Lust* (illustrated), *Amatory Adventures of a Surgeon, Episodes of Life* and *Wide Open* (explicit in their illustrations), *Nirvana* (a favorite for reading at smokers), *The Horn Book* (a classic of erotology), *The Lustful Turk, The Romances of Blanch La Mare* (illustrated with drawings of various intercourse positions), and *Fanny Hill.*

24. *United States v. Pauline Roth and Samuel Roth,* 1936. The sentences were recorded in a letter from FBI Special Agent Whitley to J. Edgar Hoover, December 31, 1936 (letter is part of Roth's FBI files).

25. "U.S. Indicts Couple Over 'Obscene' Mail," *New York American,* October 2, 1936,

Archives of the ACLU, Mudd Manuscript Library, Department of Rare Books and Special Collections, Princeton University, box 879, folder 164 [hereafter cited as ACLU Archives]. If maximum sentence was enforced on all twenty-four counts of the indictment, Roth could have faced 117 years in jail and a fine of $125,000.

26. "Publisher Found Guilty," *New York Times*, December 10, 1936, 8.

27. "Roth and Wife Held Anew for Pornography," *New York Herald Tribune,* September 4, 1936, ACLU Archives, box 879, folder 164.

28. "PBW," "Building the Case and Conviction," [B5–6, 10–11]; "PBW," "Enter the FBI," 7; "CMAM," 313.

29. "PBW," "Enter the FBI," 7.

30. Williams, "The Bureau of Investigation and Its Critics," 570.

31. Robins, *Alien Ink*, 42–44 (mail openings), 67 (obscenity file), 57, 281–82 (Untermeyer), 35–36 (Reed, Bryant).

32. "PBW," "The Mayflower," M-5; "CMAM," 383.

33. The "five burly men" statement is printed on a preliminary leaf in what is probably the second impression of *The President's Daughter.* It states that plates and printed sheets of the first edition were confiscated by the police at the printer's. The case was dismissed and the material returned.

34. Charles, *FBI's Obscene File,* 20–26. The "Laboratory Reports" (handwriting analyses) and various memos, with cover memo from Lamar Hardy to Special Agent in Charge, FBI N.Y. Office, August 1, 1936, re US v. Pauline Roth et al., are in Roth's FBI file.

35. "PBW," "The Mayflower," M-5.

36. "7 Book Sellers Indicted," *New York Times,* November 27, 1935, 19; "Mrs P. Roth Acquitted . . . ," *New York Times,* December 18, 1935, 29.

37. The book was Felix Bryk's *Dark Rapture.* Roth had distributed the author's *Circumcision in Man and Woman.*

38. *U.S. v. Rebhuhn et al.,* Point 9, appellate court report.

39. *U.S. v. Rebhuhn,* 109 F2d [*Federal Reporter, 2nd Series*] at 515 (point 9).

40. Advertised in *The Nation,* April 11, 1934, 423, under the heading "An important contribution to the literature of that 'New Morality' which is growing up among thinking people."

41. *New York Times,* December 10, 1936: 8; *New York Evening Journal,* September 4, 1936; *New York American* December 17, 1936; *New York Journal American,* December 17, 1936, 3. Adelaide Kugel found the *Evening Journal* and *New York American* articles in the Humanities Research Center "morgue" (clippings file) of the *New York Journal American.*

42. See Paul and Schwartz, *Federal Censorship,* 65, 218.

43. Page 4 of the Affidavit, notarized May 14, 1937, in *United States v. Pauline Roth and Samuel Roth,* C99-114, 1936.

44. The memos in question are W. B. Lindquist to Mr Tamm, July 17, 1936; Hoover to Agent in Charge, September 2, 1936; B. Whitely to Director, September 9, 1936; E. A. Tamm to The Director, September 17, 1936, all in Roth FBI files.

45. From December 2009 through March 2010, I attempted to get permission to view Judge Irving R. Kaufman's papers at the Library of Congress. Despite the helpfulness of the MS reference librarian, there was no response from the estate.

46. "Roth and Wife Guilty on Vile Book Charges," *New York Herald Tribune,* December 10, 1936, article found in 51.1, s.v. "1936," RA.

47. Adelaide Kugel reproduces the the *New York Evening Journal* article in "PBW," "The FBI Building Their Case," B-11. "3 Years for Samuel Roth," *New York Times,* December 17, 1936, 11, reports the judge warned Pauline she would be sent to jail if she involved herself with her husband's business. A photocopy of a page titled "Criminal Docket" in 31.19 related to the case states dates of indictment, trial, and sentencing.

48. "PBW," "The FBI Building Their Case," B-11; "Obscenity Charge Heard," *New York Times,* September 4, 1936, 7.

49. "PBW," "The FBI Building Their Case," B-11.

50. AK, "Notes II" [for "PBW"], 23.14–15 (this note dated 1935), RA.

51. "PBW," "The FBI Builds Their Case," B-10, B-11.

52. Hardy does say, on page 3 of his Memorandum in Opposition to Defendant Samuel Roth's Application for a Reduction in Sentence, June 22, 1937 (*U.S. v. Pauline and Samuel Roth*), that Roth did give one name which led to the arrest of that person.

53. SR to AK, January 12 and February 20, 1939. The prison letters for 1936–39 are in 37.2.

54. SR to AK, January 12, 1939.

55. SR to PR, May 2, 1938.

56. SR to PR, January 17, 1938.

57. "PBW," "1939," 13.

58. Roth to AK, January 6, 1939.

59. Adelaide Kugel, first of two unnumbered pages of notes on "SR's Letter of May 17, 1937," inserted between pp. 20 and 21 of "Number 5079," "PBW."

60. SR to PR, May 17, 1937.

61. Hindus, "Samuel Roth," 21.

62. SR to Adelaide Roth, April 24, 1939; "PBW," "1939," 13, 18.

63. "PBW," "Love, Sam," 18.

64. SR to PR, May 24, 1937.

65. "PBW," "Love, Sam," 9.

66. SR to PR, January 14, 1937.

67. "PBW," "Notes," 16.

68. "PBW," "Roth Renascent," 4.

69. Ibid., 5.

70. A more compact version, a sixty-one-page single-spaced typescript titled "The Leader," is in 8.6, RA.

71. A. G. Ogden to Norman Lockridge, April 28, 1938, letter preserved in prison letters for 1936–39, 37.2, RA.

72. Scholem, *The Messianic Idea in Judaism,* 346–49.

73. Gitenstein, *Apocalyptic Messianism,* 42.

74. SR to AK, October 10, 1938.

75. Dinnerstein, *Anti-Semitism in America,* 123–27.

76. Gabler, *An Empire of Their Own,* 341–44.

77. Yassif, *The Hebrew Folktale,* 352–57.

78. SR to PR, November 21, 1938, contains the draft of a letter Roth wants Pauline to send Reynal. The typescript (incomplete), which bears the return address "693 Broadway New York City," is in 8.8. The story in "CMAM" occupies most of chapter 15 in the version with the sidenotes (pp. 233–80). In the version with no sidenotes it is on pp. 357–81. For magazine submission of "Prison Wife," see SR to PR, January 10, 1939.

79. City of New York, Certificate of Marriage Registration, 15539-1917. The groom's parents are listed as Joseph and Hudel Gluck; the bride's as Joseph and Rose Hertzberg.

80. "CMAM," 236. I am using here a draft with typed sidenotes, because it is a bit richer in detail. This event would have been July 1919. There is no record in the *New York Times* of such a suicide.

81. In his autobiography, the as yet largely unpublished "Peregrine Penis," Legman states that although Roth discouraged any liaison with Chig, the publisher "buil[t] up a whole imaginary arranged marriage in his mind, unbeknownst to me, in which I would become his imaginary son in law and marry Chig." Gershon Legman, "Samuel Roth," chapter 24, "Peregrine Penis," 259. Unpublished. Copyright Kryptadia, Inc. 2006. I would like to thank Judith Legman, La Clè des Champs, France, for permission to quote this passage.

82. Unterman, *The Kabbalistic Tradition,* 250.

83. See http://findadeath.com/forum/showthread.php?p=92972. This Web site is devoted to deaths of celebrities and contains much information and various pictures of Myrna Darby.

84. "CMAM," 373 (draft with sidenotes).

85. As in I. B. Singer's use of the word, *Mayn tatns bezdin shtub,* the Yiddish title of *In My Father's Court.*

86. *Jewish Encyclopedia.* The defense of these characteristics of metempsychosis are attributed to Isaac Abravanel. The article on transmigration of souls can be found at http://www.jewishencyclopedia.com/articles/14479-transmigration-of-souls.

87. Ryan, "Samuel Roth."

88. Gershon Legman, telephone interview with the author, May 6, 1987; Legman, "Samuel Roth," in "Peregrine Penis," 268. I want to thank Judith Legman, La Clè des Champs, France, for allowing me access to this chapter.

89. Legman said (telephone interview) Roth published only the parts of what Eddington wrote that were positive. Two letters from Winifred Eddington, dated January 1 and February 6, 1945, are in 40.9 and 48.13, RA. Sir Arthur died in November 1944, so he could only have seen the galley sheets; the book was published in 1945. A brief correspondence between Roth and Eddington's sister early that year (he had sent her a check for $50, presumably for a "MS") was cordial.

90. Legman, "Peregrine Penis," 268. Legman states that the preface was "almost entirely faked."

91. Hindus, "Samuel Roth," 41–46. The prophetic passages in *Peep-Hole* Hindus quotes are on pp. 259–61.

Chapter 7. 1940–1949

1. "CMAM," 376–77; "PBW," "Roth Renascent," 2–3.

2. "Justice for Sale" [editorial], *New York Times,* June 5, 1939, 16.

3. Notation handwritten on back of Indictment papers, headed "Dec 16, 1936"; *United States v. Pauline Roth and Samuel Roth,* Memorandum in Support, 6. See "Dewey Hails Verdict in Fur Racket Case," *New York Times,* November 9, 1936, 8; "$228,000 of Loan Is Traced to Judge Manton's Properties," *New York World-Telegram,* January 27, 1939, 1, 17; "Judge Manton Is Convicted by Jury of Selling Justice," *New York Times,* June 4, 1939, 1, 2.

4. "PBW," "Roth Renascent," 4.

5. Shifreen and Jackson, *Henry Miller*, 11–12.

6. AK, "Notes" for "PBW," 21.1–2, RA.

7. Legman, "Samuel Roth," in "Peregrine Penis," 258–61.

8. Leo T. Clark, Probation officer, to Hon. Grover Moscowitz, "Petition for Revocation of Probation," *United States v. Samuel Roth*, U.S. District Court, Southern District of New York, April 7, 1941, appended to *United States v. Pauline Roth and Samuel Roth*, C99-114, 1936.

9. Handwritten notes regarding Roth's record from a Criminal Docket in 31.19, RA, record a "Hearing on violation of probation" for Pauline and Samuel Roth on May 14 and 20, 1941. Arguments for "dismissing the proceedings" were made, and the "proceedings [were] adjourned without date." Seven months later, January 9, 1942, Roth and his wife were found guilty and, instead of return to prison, Roth's probation was extended until December 16, 1944, and Pauline's for eight months.

10. "PBW," "5079," 8. Adelaide spells her last name "Jersawit."

11. "If I Take the Witness Stand," p. 5, in 6.4, RA; "CMAM," 378.

12. He writes in one version of "CMAM" (378) that because of *Jews Must Live* he was invited to a meeting by people with whom Duquesne was friendly.

13. Indictment, *U.S. v. Frederick Joubert Duquesne*. Duquesne and thirty others, sixteen of whom were in the United States and thus subject to indictment, were charged with violating Section 233 of title 22, U.S. Code: acting as foreign government agents.

14. There are eight boxes of Attorney General's transcripts in Record Group 21, EDNY 38425. They are listed as *United States v. Herman Lang et al.* There were, during the summer of 1941, several meetings at which the two or three conspirators present discussed micro documents, troop movements, documentation regarding military airplane technology, and plans to communicate with other members of the conspiracy.

15. Duquesne so stated in his testimony, which does not make it true, but it does seem likely.

16. Ronnie, *Counterfeit Hero*, 240–60, App. D, 194, 310–21. Duquesne may not have been the only contact American Nazis used to contact Roth. Another suspect is George Sylvester Viereck, a close friend of Roth who spent World War II in federal prison, on suspicion of being a German operative.

17. AK, "Notes" for "PBW," p. 14, RA.

18. "PBW," "1932," 6.

19. "PBW," "Friday Nights at Home," 14–15.

20. "PBW," "The Making of Jews Must Live," 11; Diamond, *Nazi Movement*, 109, 194.

21. "PBW," "The Man Who Killed Kitchener," 2, "Notes, 1932."

22. "PBW," "The Making of Jews Must Live," 6.

23. Ibid., 12: "Sam . . . found himself at what turned out to be a Nazi conclave and by listening and watching gathered some valuable information."

24. "PBW," "Roth Renascent," 8.

25. Suppose his intentions would have been discovered, and he was held, perhaps on instructions by the Abwehr, as a bargaining chip in negotiations. That might have been fatal to the FBI probe as well as highly embarrassing, even if the public knew nothing of it.

26. Ronnie, *Counterfeit Hero*, 196–97, 182–83, 188.

27. Keller, "George Sylvester Viereck," 64.

28. Wood, *The Man Who Killed Kitchener*, 23.

29. Manager of Bail Bond Bureau to SR, June 7, 1932, 36.21, RA.

30. "PBW," "Roth Renascent," 10.

31. In my copy, page 48 has a single line blacked out by some censorious hand, or else by someone in the Wisdom House office. The line reads, "Gal [who] wear mink in day, fox by night."

32. A letter from John Cournos to Roth dated July 7, 1944 (35.13, RA) states that Cournos would write the introduction. The working title was apparently *The Bedside Companion*.

33. "PBW," "Roth Renascent," 11–13.

34. One early impression of the book has a frontispiece photo of Hitler in lederhosen posing with Strasser and his family.

35. "Women Say Lindsay Looted Even Walls, Widow Declares Plaque Adorns Promoter's Home—Says Dr Enlind Has Her $1,200 Harp," *New York Times*, March 7, 1922, 14.

36. Plotkin note signed by him, September 22, 1941, 36.24, RA.

37. "Agreement between Samuel Roth and . . . Dr. F. Gellé," September 30, 1946, 35.13, RA.

38. Upton Sinclair to Dr. Kurt Krueger (in care of Avalon Press), January 28, 1942, 38.3, RA; "PBW," "Roth Renascent," 13.

39. Maximilian Becker of AFG Literary Agency to SR, July 9, 1942, 35.13, RA.

40. "CMAM," 379–80; "PBW," "Roth Renascent," 14–17.

41. Note in Adelaide Kugel's card file, s.v. "1946," 51.1, RA, states that "FBI furnished a copy of Roth's identification record to HUAC with regard to Plotkin's identity." This is recorded in Roth's FBI files: "Memorandum to Mr. Nichols," March 4, 1954, pp. 3–4.

42. "PBW," "Mr. Roth Goes to Washington," 12. She describes a 1983 TV dramatization of the Hiss-Chambers case in which the actor playing Roth opens a briefcase containing copies of *Fanny Hill, My Life and Loves*, and *The Perfumed Garden*. The deposition can be found in 33.23, RA.

43. SR to Mrs. David George Plotkin, April 1, 1968, 36.29, RA.

44. SR to Frank Aranow, November 5, 1941, 31.19, RA.

45. "Permit to Send Out Business Reply Cards . . . Under Section 510, Postal Laws and Regulations," 32.4, RA.

46. 51.1, s.v. "1944," RA.

47. The Kinsey Institute for Sex Research, Bloomington, Indiana, maintains an extensive vertical file of printed circulars, letters, catalogues, brochures, and other documents. The collection of relevant circulars is filed under "Erotica Producers (United States) (20th Century)—Roth, Samuel."

48. Leo T. Clark, Probation officer, to Hon. Grover Moscowitz, "Petition for Revocation of Probation," *United States v. Samuel Roth*, U.S. District Court, Southern District of New York, April 7, 1941, appended to *United States v. Pauline Roth and Samuel Roth*, C99-114, 1936.

49. "PBW," "1939," 14.

50. The inscription is undated (the book is part of RA). It is likely that Bodenheim wrote this when he renewed acquaintance with Roth in the 1950s. At the Poetry Book Shop, he and Louis Grudin worked for Roth c. 1920, before he had any quarrel with censors.

51. Office of the Solicitor to Irving Kolman, August 11, 1942, 32.4, RA. This was in response to a letter to the Solicitor General from The Psychic Research Press, July 21. Roth probably used the name "Irving Kolman" because, still on parole, he did not want to be identified.

52. Albert Goldman to Avalon Press, January 23, 1945, 32.4, RA.

53. Goldman to Arrowhead Books, October 15, 1945, 32.4, RA.

54. Makris, *The Silent Investigators,* 289–99.

55. "SAC, New York," memorandum to J. Edgar Hoover, January 30, 1956, in Roth's FBI files.

56. Affidavit by Mark Hughes, *United States v. Samuel Roth,* Cr 148-49, U.S. District Ct, So. District of N.Y., #24030, p. 4, date-stamped March 4, 1959.

57. Circular from Coventry Books, advertising *Lèse Majesty: The Private Lives of the Duke and Duchess of Windsor,* Kinsey Institute files.

58. Makris, *The Silent Investigators,* 292.

59. U.S. Senate, Subcommittee to Investigate Juvenile Delinquency . . . , 1955, 205–6 ("Testimony of Samuel Roth, New York, NY").

60. So stated on the New York Post Office form denoting delivery of its letter regarding its accusation of using the mails to defraud, attached to the Transcript of Proceedings.

61. Transcript of Proceedings Before the Solicitor, November 7, 1947. This is the Fraud Order Hearing for *Bumarap.*

62. The circular is included as Exhibit 6 in *Roth v. Goldman,* 172 F2d. 788 (1949), *Transcript of Record.*

63. United States, Senate, Attorney General's Committee on Administrative Procedure, *Administrative Procedure in Government Agencies,* 15–41. This section of the report is on fraud orders. There are two relevant documents in RA: "Postal Laws Relating to Lotteries, Schemes to Defraud, Etc." (32.4), 3 pp., and "A Fraud Order: What It Is and How It Affects the Delivery of Mail and Payment of Money Orders," 2 pp. (32.4). Both are undated.

64. "Complaint," pp. 2–13, *Roth v. Goldman, Transcript of Record.*

65. Paul and Schwartz, *Federal Censorship,* 94–97.

66. Alfred C. Coxe, "Order to Show Cause," *Roth v. Goldman,* 172 F2d 788, p. 35.

67. Gerson Legman, in his chapter on Roth from "Peregrine Penis," 267–68, states that Roskolenko "re-ghosted" the book from a work by the humorist Roy McCardell. However, there are letters to and from De Lysle Ferree Cass and Sam Roth that discuss a book of Czech stories in 38.8, RA. A letter of April 3, 1933, from Cass to Roth states he has enclosed the manuscript of *Gesta Czechorum* and refers to "the similarity of idea between your recently-published 'Anecdota Americana' and my enclosed manuscript."

68. Quoted in F2d, p. 788.

69. The text of Frank's opinion is reproduced in Bosmajian, *Obscenity and Freedom of Expression,* 56–61.

70. Herbert M. Levy to SR, July 11, 1949, 31.19, RA.

71. The Humanities Research Center, University of Texas at Austin, has extensive documents of ACLU campaigns against postal censorship in the Ernst Papers, especially file 827.

72. *Summerfield v. Sunshine Book Company,* 1954.

73. These titles and their descriptions are listed in U.S. Post Office Department, "In the Matter of the Complaint that Book Bargain Counter . . . ," 31.7, RA.

74. "PBW," "Beautiful Sinners, etc.," 5.

75. Affidavit by Mark Hughes, *United States v. Samuel Roth,* Cr 148-49.

76. Arnold Lubasch, "At Age 79, Judge Weinfeld Is Still Building on a Legend; Judge's Exacting Standards Decisions Are Cited Bow Tie, No Overcoat," *New York Times,* August 10, 1980, 20. He may have ruled differently had he suspected that the foreword, by Louis Berg,

M.D., was not by Berg but by Roth. Gershon Legman's statement to this effect is made on the front cover pastedown leaf in my copy.

77. "Before the Solicitor of the Post Office Department," Respondent's Brief, p. 6, 31.12, RA.

78. Respondent's Brief, p. 4. The copy of *Nightmare Alley* in RA has penciled notations of explicit passages containing slang words and phrases referring to intercourse of various types. Some of these notes suggest that Roth was planning an expurgated edition.

79. "Memorandum," undated, 32.4, RA.

80. U.S. Post Office, *Official Transcript . . .*, in the Matter of Samuel Roth d/b/a Special Books and Special Books Club, . . . 1956.

81. Atlas's brief for the defendant is in 31.14, RA.

82. Ryan, "Samuel Roth," 63.

83. Hindus, in "Samuel Roth," praises Roskolenko's work, stating that he made his acquaintance when both were in the "Trotskyite movement" (52).

84. Roskolenko, *Poet on a Scooter,* 276. In 1960, Roskolenko, testifying under oath at the trial of Eddie Mishkin, gave his real name as "Hyman Rosen" to protect his reputation. *People v. Mishkin*, p. 1207.

85. Viereck to SR, June 5, 1954, 38.1, RA.

86. Psychoanalysts use terms such as projection, doubling, and paranoia to explain this phenomenon. See Rogers, *Psychoanalytical Study of the Double,* 10–17.

87. Roth was arrested for mailing *Beautiful Sinners* in March 1951, and acquitted on May 28 (*United States v. Samuel Roth,* Cr 148-49; affidavit of Mark F. Hughes, p. 4).

88. "Arrest of Six Foils Counterfeit Plot," *New York Times,* January 19, 1930, 27.

89. Cacici, "Introducing the Author of *Bumarap*," *Bumarap: The Story of a Male Virgin,* 233–56. For Cacici's counterfeiting arrest, see "Arrest of Six Foils Counterfeit Plot," *New York Times,* January 19, 1930, 27.

90. "Kiki" [Alice Prin], *Education of a French Model* (1954), 118. This is a revised text of a book first published by Roth in 1950, possibly through arrangement with the original Paris publisher, Edward Titus. A publisher's note states that "the second half of this book . . . is not to be taken too seriously."

91. "Norman Lockridge" to Paul Kohner Inc., August 16, 1956, 36.20, RA.

92. *Education of a French Model,* 1954, 110–11.

93. SR, "Advertisement," *Education of a French Model* (1950), 6.

94. SR, Introduction, *The Pastoral Loves of Daphnis and Chloe.* The verso of the title page states that Roth copyrighted the title in 1953; there is no acknowledgment of agreement with the London publisher.

95. "Norman Lockridge" [Samuel Roth], *Lese Majesty,* 24–29. The epigraph is on p. [6].

96. Both the draft and the printed ad are in 40.2, RA.

97. These statements are from section 8 of the typescript, titled "When Beauty Rode the Tiger."

98. A file of reviews of the book is in 53.15–16, RA.

99. Three-page letter (p. 1 missing), Louis Grudin to unstated recipient, undated but after 1954, box 2, folder 13, Maxwell Bodenheim Papers, Rare Book and Manuscript Library, Butler Library, Columbia University.

100. See *My Life and Loves in Greenwich Village,* 252–54. I am indebted to Michael Swee-

ney of Holland, Michigan (letter of May 14, 1997), for identifying Louis Grudin and for describing his career.

Chapter 8. 1949–1952

1. Crist, "In the Dark and after Sunset," 58.
2. The Manhattan County Clerk's Office has on file the Permission To Do Business form, signed by Finkelstein on January 3, 1940.
3. *United States v. Samuel Roth*, 1956, Count 26, and court transcript, pp. 257–73.
4. *United States v. Samuel Roth*, Grand Jury Indictment, pp. 4a–26a.
5. L. Miller, "The 'Golden Age' of Gay and Lesbian Literature."
6. Roth thought of working up a British equivalent of *Good Times*, as a mockup found among the books in his library (in RA) tentatively titled "L'Amour: The French Magazine Written in English" suggests.
7. Peterson, *Magazines in the Twentieth Century*, 378–80.
8. Brady, *Hefner*, 47–54.
9. Page 2 of 3-page typewritten sheet, section beginning "To the subscribers . . . ," 9.7 (folder of "loose pages—various texts"), RA.
10. J. B. Rund, e-mail to the author, February 16, 2010.
11. Bookseller C. J. Scheiner reports seeing a copy of *Venus* with "7 full page illustrations from 1930s French flagellation books." Scheiner, *Compendium*, item 691, p. 69.
12. Typed letter, "Dalton Trumbo," 2 pp., undated, 30.12, RA.
13. U.S. House of Representatives, *Communist Infiltration . . .* , 1731 (Her informer stated Gruen's name on 1727). Navasky, *Naming Names*, 136–37, states she might have cooperated because, having a child, she could not afford to be blackballed.
14. "PBW," "Peggy and the Lion," 2–5.
15. Candy Kugel, e-mail to the author, February 21, 2010.
16. "PBW," "Beautiful Sinners, etc.," 8. Although "Margaret Meehan" was not listed in the masthead, her editorial work was implied in the name of her grandmother, "Ellen Ellsworth."
17. Ibid., 9–10.
18. Linda Greenhouse, "Peggy Roth, Editor for Dell Publishing," *New York Times*, August 11, 1973: 22.
19. "PBW," "Peggy," 1.
20. M. Morgan, "King of the Pornography Racket," 24–25.
21. Makris, *The Silent Investigators*, 290–99.
22. Memorandum, E. R. Glavin to Mr. Tolson, April 23, 1951, and letter, "A Loyal American" to Sen. William Knowland, September 21, 1951, *FBI File on the House Committee on Un-American Activities*.
23. Articles from the *Times* (July 21, 1955) and the *World Telegram and Sun* (July 25, 1955); memos SAC New York to Director, January 30, 1956, M. A. Jones to Mr. Nichols, March 4, 1954, and A. H. Belmont to A. F. Boardman, January 15, 1956; all in Roth's FBI Files.
24. Charles, *FBI's Obscene File*, 25, 28 (expansion of FBI power), 30–31 (*Strange Fruit*).
25. Dale Sawyer to Margaret Meehan, September 11, 1952, and Margaret Meehan to Dale Sawyer, October 1952, 38.1, RA.
26. Certification of authenticity of a story "Three Hoots of an Owl," signed by Jamison on January 2, 1954, 38.1, RA.

27. 37.8, RA.

28. Trujillo to SR, 38.1, RA.

29. Lyle Stuart, who had knowledge of surveillance activities on Nazi groups, suggested that Roth contact Trujillo (interview with the author, February 19, 2001).

30. SR to PR, June 4, 1959, 7.3, RA. Roskolenko, when interviewed by journalist William Ryan, expressed annoyance at Roth's treatment of Bodenheim ("Samuel Roth," 63).

31. "PBW," "Max and Estes," 2.

32. "Norman Lockridge" (Roth), "Helen Thy Beauty: An Adventure in Letters," n.p. (first page in typescript), undated draft, 4.8, RA. The two Bodenheim typescripts are in 26.8–9: "The Borderlands of Passion" and "Clara: A Novel."

33. I have in my possession a set of letters, memos, photos, clippings, and lists of Roth's arrests that I purchased in 1994. These papers contain a letter to Winchell over the name Paul Plotkin (undated). I have not been able to discover if he is any relation to David George Plotkin.

34. J. B. Moore, *Maxwell Bodenheim*, 171. Kugel's per diem statement is in "PBW," "Max and Estes," 3.

35. Wetzsteon, *Republic of Dreams*, 387, 390.

36. Roth's contracts with various authors are in 42.13–15, RA.

37. Many of these points are from Hindus's analysis in *The Crippled Giant*, and also from Stanford Luce's introduction to his translation of Céline's *Conversations with Professor Y*, xi–xxiv.

38. SR to Hindus, September 23, 1947, Hindus Papers. There is also at Brandeis a 5-page muddled account by Roth on encounters with Joyce and with the conspirators who caused his bankruptcy.

39. Hindus, "Samuel Roth," 2–7, 11–14.

40. Hindus, *The Crippled Giant*, 88.

41. Ibid., 80.

42. Hindus, "Samuel Roth," 59.

43. Hindus, *The Crippled Giant*, 147.

44. Ibid., 129.

45. Ibid., 151.

46. Hindus, *The Crippled Giant: A Literary Relationship*, 156.

47. Ibid., 152.

48. SR to Hindus, May 12, 1950, Hindus Papers.

49. Zucker, "Why Celine?" 3–4.

50. Mason, "Uncovering Céline," 16–18. Mason concludes that Céline might best be understood as "a humorist."

51. "Publisher's Explanation," 16. The explanation was added after the attacks on the book's authenticity by Walter Kaufmann of Princeton University, among others.

52. Burnett to PR, June 3, 1958, 36.27, RA.

53. Reich, *The Murder of Christ*, 226.

54. Yariv, "Nietzsche contra Nietzsche." Another interesting, negative, article on the book is Dutton, "Nietzsche Dreams of Detroit."

55. Gilman, "Heine, Nietzsche, and the Idea of the Jew," passim.

56. Ibid., 80.

57. Placzek, "Nietzsche Discovery"; Meehan, "Rediscovered Nietzsche"; Rosenthal, "Rediscovered Nietzsche."

58. SR to Cousins, May 6, 1952, 42.20, RA.

59. Werner, "That Nietzsche Book," *The Nation*, May 31, 1952, 526; Roth responded in "That Nietzsche Book: Fiction or Nonfiction?" *The Nation*, June 21, 1952, 611–12. Werner's "That Nietzsche Book: Definitely Fiction" appeared in the July 19 Letters to the Editor column (p. 66).

60. An English version of Mann's and Marcuse's articles was sent to Roth by the *Aufblau* Advertising Department editor on May 15, 1952, 42.20, RA. The Mann piece appeared on May 16, 1952, and the Marcuse essays on April 18 and 25, 1952. See also Werner, "Who Wrote *My Sister and I*?" and "The Pseudo Nietzsche."

61. Kaufmann, "Nietzsche and the Seven Sirens"; Kaufmann, "Re: Nietzsche's *My Sister and I*."

62. Stewart, *Nietzsche*, 24–26.

63. SR to Walter Kaufmann, undated (ribbon copy?), 42.20, RA.

64. Stewart, *Nietzsche*, 22–71.

65. Kaufmann, *Nietzsche*, 69–70.

66. Stewart, *Nietzsche*, 30–32.

67. Laura Bailey of New York City told me that when she worked at New York's large and prestigious Strand Book Store in the mid-1950s there were always "stacks" of *My Sister and I* kept in stock because there was such a large demand for it.

68. "PBW," "Beautiful Sinners, etc.," 7.

69. SR to Sulzberger, October 5, 1953 (carbon copy, probably on Seven Sirens Press letterhead), 42.20, RA.

70. *Atlantic Monthly* (June 1952, [5]) and *The Nation* (April 19, 1952, 387) were two magazines in which the full-page ad appeared.

71. One place it appeared was *Good Times* 1, no. 1 (1953): 53.

72. Golomb, "Nietzsche and the Marginal Jews," passim.

73. "PBW," "Beautiful Sinners, etc.," 7–8.

74. Stern and Reubens to SR, April 16, 1952, 38.1, RA; Hamalian, "Nobody Knows My Names," 914. Hamalian says Roth thought the book was in the public domain, but Knopf filed an injunction and proved that they alone held American copyright. Of course, the client (Richard Heyd) of the law firm that sent Roth the letter may have given rights to Knopf. *The Nation*'s review, "The 'Zone of Silence,'" appeared on April 19, 1952, 386.

75. Yariv, "Nietzsche contra Nietzsche"; H. Wilkerson, "Retrieving a Posthumous Text-Message."

76. H. Wilkerson, "Retrieving a Posthumous Text-Message," 56.

77. Ibid., 55, 67.

78. Ryan to PR, September 18, 1974, 37.13, RA.

79. *My Sister and I*, 184.

80. Ibid., 77, 81, 122, 193. Page numbers are hereafter given in the text.

81. Mandel, *Nietzsche*, 164.

82. Gilman, "Heine, Nietzsche, and the Idea of the Jew," 76–80, 94–97.

Chapter 9. 1952–1957

1. SR to Nicholas Atlas, May 18, 1954, 31.19–20, RA. The information about the mailing list comes from "Court Dismisses Obscenity Charges against Samuel Roth," 2359. It reports the number of books taken as 50,000.

2. "CMAM," 397; Talese, *Thy Neighbor's Wife,* 103.

3. "PBW," "Beautiful Sinners, etc.," 14.

4. Clippings of these and of the *Times* piece are in 51.1, RA.

5. "US Subpena [*sic*] Follows Raid on Publisher," *New York Post,* April 14, 1954, 9; "Publisher, Wife Seized," *New York Times,* April 14, 1954, 10.

6. The 1954 arrests of Samuel (assault, conspiracy) and Pauline Roth (conspiracy) are recorded in the *Record of Cases 1952–66,* Office of the District Attorney, New York County (microfilm file H-N 1954 to A-G 1955), New York City Municipal Archives (R. No. 338,442). The *Record* notes that the motion to dismiss the charge of assault was granted on May 23, 1955.

7. "PBW," "Beautiful Sinners, etc.," 12.

8. "Publisher Is Freed," *New York Times,* May 21, 1955, 15; "Court Dismisses Obscenity Charges," 2359.

9. Memo, SAC New York to The Director, March 4, 1955, Roth FBI Files.

10. "Publisher Accused in New Indictment," *New York Times,* July 21, 1955, 48.

11. Seven-page typewritten essay, discussing Roth's grievances against his lawyer, Nicholas Atlas, pp. 2–3, 31.16, RA.

12. Gabler, *Winchell,* 392.

13. Legman, "Mahlon Blaine," in "Peregrine Penis," p. "4:3." I want to thank Judith Legman for telling me of Blaine's, Wallis's, and Legman's employment with Jack Brussel in her e-mail of December 27, 2011.

14. King, *The Uncommon Life,* 433–35.

15. Higham, *The Duchess of Windsor,* 384–85.

16. A copy of the circular is in the vertical file of the Kinsey Institute for Sex Research.

17. In the offices of Barricade Books, Fort Lee, New Jersey, are copies of *Exposé* and *The Independent,* files of information used to research the articles, and files of letters written to, and by, Lyle Stuart relevant to the stories he published. I wish to thank Lyle's widow, Carole Livingstone, for giving me access to this material.

18. "Wild Genius of Merchandising the Bizarre," 66.

19. *Lyle Stuart v. Walter Winchell, American Broadcasting Company, et al.*

20. Gabler, *Winchell,* 200–202.

21. Ibid., 466–67; Stuart and Whalen, "The Story of *Exposé,*" 4–5; Lyle Stuart, interview with the author, May 26, 2006, Fort Lee, New Jersey; [Samuel Roth], "Epilogue in Advance," in Stuart, *The Secret Life of Walter Winchell,* 7. Stuart said that although many stores were afraid to stock the book, fearing Winchell's Red smears, the Copacabana, which Winchell had been savaging in his columns, bought fifty copies a day to give to its patrons.

22. "PBW," "Beautiful Sinners, etc.," 11.

23. Ibid., 12. Adelaide is quoting a "preparation for Trial" paper prepared by her father.

24. Memos, H. L. Belmont to L. V. Boardman, January 16, 1956, and January 20, 1957, re Walter Winchell broadcasts, both in Roth's FBI files.

25. Gabler, *Winchell,* 459, 468; Jay Maeder, "Turncoat: The Estrangements of Howard

Rushmore," http://www.nydailynews.com/archives/news/2001/02/26/2001-02-26_turncoat
_the_estrangements_0.html.

26. I have in my possession a set of letters, memos, photos, and lists of Roth's arrests
which I purchased in 1994. These papers—hereafter cited as "Winchell Roth file"—contain
a February 26, 1954, letter to Winchell (signature indecipherable but it might be "Howard")
on Twentieth Century Fox stationery stating he had just received details on Richard and
Peggy Roth. A separate document states their affiliations with suspect groups: "Howard" to
"Walter," March 2, 1954.

27. This statement, made on March 4, is quoted in Makris, *The Silent Investigators,* 294.

28. Letter to Winchell over the name Paul Plotkin (undated), Winchell Roth file.

29. Subcommittee to Investigate Juvenile Delinquency, "Background on Hearing of U.S.
Subcommittee to Investigate Juvenile Delinquency," May 31, 1955, box 413, General Letters,
U.S. Congress, Judiciary Comm., Juvenile Delinquency Subcommittee 1955, General Files,
Pornography Investigation 1955, Record Group 46, National Archives, Washington, D.C.

30. "Dope and Smut Used by Reds, Senators Told," *New York Daily News,* March 1, 1957,
15; William Golder, "The Big Business of Pornography," H. Lynn Womack Papers, box 1,
folder 7, Rare Book and Manuscript Collections, Kroch Library, Cornell University, Ithaca,
New York ("At a Moral Leadership Workshop on salacious literature, the chaplains expressed
wide belief that there was obvious Communistic influence in these magazines"); "Action for
Decency" (pamphlet), Chicago: Americans for Moral Decency, n.d., ACLU Archives, box
783, folder 23 ("The record shows one known Communist after another engaged in publishing, mailing, and distributing pornography"), p. [8].

31. *New York Times,* May 25, 1955, 28.

32. Salisbury, "Strange Correspondence," 575–77.

33. U.S. Senate, Subcommittee to Investigate the Administration of the Internal Security
Act, 1196–99.

34. Lawrence Van Gelder, "Philip S. Foner, Labor Historian and Professor, 84" [obit.],
New York Times, December 15, 1994, B20; "Jefferson Book Banned in Overseas Libraries,"
New York Times, February 17, 1953, 29.

35. Gilbert, *A Cycle of Outrage,* 75.

36. Lyle Stuart, interview with the author, August 10, 1995, New York City.

37. U.S. Senate, Subcommittee to Investigate Juvenile Delinquency [hereafter cited as
"U.S. Senate–Kefauver"], Hearings on Juvenile Delinquency (Obscene and Pornographic
Materials), "Testimony of Samuel Roth," 197.

38. "U.S. Subpena [*sic*] Follows Raid on Publisher," *New York Post,* April 14, 1954, 9.

39. Ryan, "Samuel Roth," 10.

40. Memo from Marvin Fuller to "Files," headed Subcommittee to Investigate Juvenile
Delinquency, May 4, 1955, Record Group 46, box 415, folder "Post Office," National Archives.
"Publisher Accused in New Indictment," *New York Times,* July 21, 1955, 48.

41. Memo from Fuller to "Files," May 4, 1955.

42. U.S. Senate–Kefauver, Hearings on Juvenile Delinquency (Obscene and Pornographic Materials), "Testimony of Samuel Roth," 202. Ryan's quotation is on p. 32 of his
"Samuel Roth" essay.

43. "Smut Held Cause of Delinquency," *New York Times,* June 1, 1955, 35.

44. U.S. Senate–Kefauver, Hearings on Juvenile Delinquency (Comic Books), "Testimony of Samuel Roth," 196.

45. James Desmond, "Dirty-Pix Probers Entangle 3," *New York Daily News,* June 1, 1955, 5 ("3-star final" ed.).

46. "PBW," "Max and Estes," 10.

47. U.S. Senate–Kefauver, Hearings on Juvenile Delinquency (Obscene and Pornographic Materials), "Testimony of Samuel Roth," 188.

48. Ibid., 205.

49. "PBW," "Max and Estes," 10.

50. *Journal American,* May 31, 1955, 4.

51. *United States v. Samuel Roth,* Cr 148-49, pp. 1–27.

52. "Publisher Accused in New Indictment," *New York Times,* July 21, 1955, 48.

53. "PBW," "Max and Estes," 16.

54. Appendix to Appellee's Brief, *United States v. Samuel Roth,* 237 F.2d 796, U.S. Court of Appeals, "Defendant's Summation," 38a–51a.

55. *United States v. Samuel Roth,* Cr 148-49, stenographer's minutes, January 3–4, 1956, pp. 38–69.

56. Appendix to Appellee's Brief, "Government's Summation," 52a–61a.

57. Goodman, *Growing Up Absurd,* 36–39.

58. *Samuel Roth v. United States,* U.S. Court of Appeals, Southern District of New York, Appendix to Appellant's Brief, p. 2a.

59. *United States v. Samuel Roth,* C. 148-49, Before Hon. John M. Cashin, District Judge, N.Y., February 7, 1956, pp. 8–27.

60. *United States v. Samuel Roth,* U.S. Court of Appeals for the 2nd Circuit, 237 F 2d 796, p. 4.

61. *United States v. Samuel Roth,* U.S. Court of Appeals, pp. 15, 31, 68; *United States v. Samuel Roth,* 237 F.2d 796, 1956, paragraph 15.

62. U.S. Senate–Kefauver, Hearings on Juvenile Delinquency (Comic Books), "Testimony of Alexander Segal," 194.

63. *United States v. Samuel Roth,* U.S. Court of Appeals, endnote 34.

64. William Ryan ("Samuel Roth: A Lion," 14) deplores the interrogator at the Kefauver hearing mentioning these titles, which he thought was a lie calculated to smear Roth. Ryan did not know that although Roth did not print such books, he did offer them in his circulars. The titles are listed in "Brief of Samuel Roth," written in late 1955 or 1956. Found in Record Group 46, box 415, folder "Post Office," National Archives.

65. "United States District Court Southern District of New York, Affidavits I–VI, 1960," 32.11, RA.

66. Roth had plans to publish some of the stories, including his own, in book form. RA has unpublished bound volumes of two such collections, one with trial publication information.

67. Arendt, *Jew as Pariah,* 80.

68. SR to PR, January 22, 1958, 37.4, RA.

69. *United States v. Samuel Roth,* Cr 148-49, An Appeal from the District Court of the Southern District of New York, July 29, 1959, p. 15.

70. SR to PR, January 22, 1958, 37.4, RA.

71. Schauer, *Law of Obscenity,* 39.

72. FindLaw for *Roth v. United States,* 354 U.S. 476 (1957): http://caselaw.lp.findlaw.com/cgi-bin/getcase.pl?court=us&vol=354&invol=476#f5.

73. Rembar, *The End of Obscenity,* 70; Caffrey, "*Lady Chatterley's Lover,*" 66. The Arents Library, Syracuse University, has a Grove Press archive that collects legal briefs, news clippings, correspondence, and advertising copy. I have used these documents to prepare this section and wish to thank the staff of the library for their help.

74. Rembar, *The End of Obscenity,* 94–99, 118–26; Schauer, *Law of Obscenity,* 92–95. For "erotic realism," see Kronhausen and Kronhausen, *Pornography and the Law,* 25–29, 249–60.

75. *Grove Press v. Christianberry.*

76. Kronhausen and Kronhausen, *Pornography and the Law,* part 1. See Rembar, *The End of Obscenity,* 286–87; Schauer, *Law of Obscenity,* 92–95.

77. Caffrey, "*Lady Chatterley's Lover,*" 58–63, 75–76; Gertzman, *Descriptive Bibliography,* 126, 230.

78. However, Learned Hand knew better. In 1936 a mail-order sexology publisher wanted to introduce into evidence his mailing list, with customers divided into sections such as "professors," "doctors," "army officers," and "reverends." Hand refused the request as irrelevant to the press's guilt or innocence, stating, "even respectable persons may have a taste for salacity." Hand's reversal of the conviction of Esar Levine is given in *United States v. Levine.*

79. I have reproduced the handwritten note found in 54.1, RA, laid into a copy of stenographer's minutes of the 1956 *United States v. Samuel Roth* trial. There is another note regarding this incident, in notes Adelaide Kugel made for her biography, 24.2 ("Notes," p. 5). She does not mention Roth's explanation for not showing up at the rendezvous. "The judge was taking a considerable chance in keeping this rendezvous. He waited in his car for half an hour."

80. "Judges of the United States Courts," http://www.fjc.gov/servlet/nGetInfo?jid=395& cid=999&ctype=na&instate=na.

81. Nor was that all his son did for his father at this time, according to Adelaide Kugel. Despite his father's truculence, Richard again used contacts to get his father a temporary release from prison in order to prepare for the Supreme Court review of his conviction. The note to this effect, which uses the phrase "greased palms up to the Supreme Court," is in an index card headed 10/5, in 51.1, RA. However, the Supreme Court had greater laxity than other courts in granting bail during their deliberations. Justice Harlan granted bail: http://appeals.uslegal.com/appellate-process/applications-to-individual-justices.

82. *MFY,* 588.

83. Ryan, "Samuel Roth," 60.

84. The back of the "jacket" of the Indictment for *United States v. Samuel Roth,* Southern District of New York, lists in longhand the dates of the trial, verdict, and sentencing.

85. The letters Roth wrote from prison during his second stay in Lewisburg are in cartons 23, 26, and 37 in RA. This one, dated February 17, 1956, is in 37.3.

86. SR to PR, February 17, 1956, 37.3, RA.

87. Typed sheet headed "The Eyes of Your Children," laid into typescript of "Prince Hal and the Jewish Proposal," 11.9, RA.

88. 39.7, RA.

89. There were excellent facilities for psychotherapy. Greenfield, *Wilhelm Reich vs. the U.S.A.,* 268.

90. Two clippings on the Forum from a prison newsletter, mentioning Gold and Greenglass, are in 37.2, RA. Roth mentions the manual on teaching English in a letter to Pauline, January 26, 1960 (37.6).

91. Martin, *Wilhelm Reich and the Cold War*, 412, 420. Lichtman and Cohen's *Deadly Force and the Informer System in the McCarthy Era*, 154, mentions Reich only in that he managed the library at Lewisburg. The somewhat unreliable source for the lunchroom discussions is Harvey "Job" Matesow, an actor, producer, and a witness who gave false testimony to HUAC. Greenfield (*Wilhelm Reich vs. the U.S.A.*, 268) writes that Matesow himself said Reich had little contact with other prisoners. Sharaf's *Fury on Earth* (471–72) also states that in prison Reich did not seek contact with others. Sharaf does not mention Matesow or Roth.

92. This first letter from Lewisburg, May 1, 1956, is in 23.6, RA.

93. SR to PR, February 12, 1958, 37.2, RA. On February 16 he wrote, "The Resurrection gives such as picture of our foursome that I may hold it back."

94. Blanchard, *The Right to Read*, 181–94.

95. Anhalt, *A Gathering of Fugitives*, 52–63.

96. Memorandum from SAC Philadelphia to Director, FBI, December 26, 1957, to which is appended Roth's proposal, Roth FBI files.

97. SR to PR, November 6, 1959. The poem appears on pp. 550–52 of *MFY*. In the letter, where of course it stands by itself, it had a title: "Lazarus after the Fact."

Chapter 10. 1958–1974

1. SR, *My Friend Yeshea*, 10. See also p. 588. Hereafter cited parenthetically in the text as *MFY*.

2. 40.5, RA.

3. "If I Take the Witness Stand," 1, in 6.4, RA.

4. Buber, *Hasidism and Modern Man*, 133–35.

5. 23.13, RA.

6. M. Hoffman, *From Rebel to Rabbi*, 2–12, 113–39.

7. Ibid., 4, 86, 125.

8. "Helen Thy Beauty" (typescript), p. 137, 4.8, RA.

9. These letters are in 40.6, under a secondary file labeled "My Life with Jesus," an earlier title for *MFY*.

10. 40.5 and 42.19, RA.

11. Gleason, *Israel and Christ*, [1]. See especially pp. 7 and 29.

12. 23.13, RA.

13. "He Was Dreaming His Better Self," unpublished essay, copyright Arthur Sainer, p. 3.

14. A three-page set of descriptions for eighteen in-text illustrations (not in the printed volume) is in 40.5, RA.

15. SR to PR, January 7, 1958, 37.4, RA.

16. Cohn-Sherbok, *The Jewish Messiah*, 74–76.

17. The passages regarding Lilith's nature in *MFY* are on pp. 21 and 381–82.

18. Buber, *Tales of the Hasidim*, 2.

19. "Mishillim Brings News . . . ," 222, 8.8, RA.

20. A. Cohen, *Everyman's Talmud*, 267; Berg, *The Essential Zohar*, 226–27.

21. "Jesus and Mary: Their Sacred Marriage in Gnosticism."

22. Norich, "Sholem Asch and the Christian Question," 255–56. The letter requesting *The Apostle* is dated January 17, 1958.

23. M. Hoffman, *From Rebel to Rabbi*, 195–96.

24. Konigsberg, "The Only 'I' in the World," 30–33; Buber, *On Judaism*, 82–92.

25. SR to PR, March 28 and February 5, 1959, 37.6, RA.

26. SR to PR, April 15, 1959, 37.5, RA.

27. SR to PR, June 28, 1959, 37.5, RA.

28. Fine, "American-Jewish Fiction, 1890–1930," 21. The author is Edward Steiner.

29. James Kugel discusses the "prophetic call narrative" in *The God of Old*, 46–50.

30. SR, *Apotheosis*, 54, 10–11.

31. SR, *The Nazarene*, chapter 29 (the passage quoted is on 695–96); Siegel, *The Controversial Sholem Asch*, 137–39.

32. Umansky, "Asch's Passion" (April 24, 2007, accessed July 27, 2010).

33. Buber, *Hasidism and Modern Man*, 88–94; Lamm, *Religious Thought of Hasidism*, 255.

34. Siegel, *The Controversial Sholem Asch*, 35–40; Seidman, "Piety and Scandal," 56–60.

35. A. Cohen, *Everyman's Talmud*, 193–96. There is a precise explanation of this concept, using the Hebrew word *Avodah*, on the Web site *My Jewish Learning*, http://www.myjewishlearning.com/practices/Ethics/Business_Ethics/Themes_and_Theology/Value_of_Work/Work_as_Calling.shtml (accessed September 4, 2011).

36. Ryan, "Samuel Roth," 59.

37. SR to PR, May 14, 1956, 23.6, RA, and June 22, July 7, July 20, 1958, 37.2, RA.

38. The titles were *The Education of a French Model* (the cover makes it seem that Hemingway was the author), *The Shadow in the Rose Garden* (seventeen stories from *Bachelor's Quarters*), *My Life and Loves in Greenwich Village, Come into My Parlor,* and *The Ambassador* (sixteen stories from *Bachelor's Quarters*). He sold the paperback rights to *Celestine* to Universal in 1965. Before entering prison he sold *The Sexual Conduct of Men and Women* (published in abridgment as *Sex without Tears*) and Denys Val Baker's *A Journey with Love* to Crest.

39. 43.8, RA.

40. 48.15, RA.

41. 36.3, RA. He was oddly interested in several titles of interest in the 1920s but hardly in the 1960s, as well as several gallant titles. That he thought *Sons and Lovers* and *The Virgin and the Gypsy* might be out of copyright is also strange.

42. SR to Chief Librarian, January 15, 1962, and L. H. Mumford to SR, January 23, 1963, 36.3, RA.

43. 43.12, RA, contains a ledger book into which Roth pasted clippings about Monroe's death. The one from the *New York Daily News*, August 7, 1962, 6, contains a photo of Dr. Ralph Greenson. Roth also kept a separate set of clippings (42.4).

44. The publisher collected over fifty World Wide photos of Monroe, captioned for one-time reproduction in newspapers. These photos are in 44.15, RA.

45. The ads appeared under the heading "Sophisticated Men's Classified," sent by an advertising company to magazines such as *Cavalcade, Dude, Uncensored,* and *Monsieur,* as well as to distributors of multiple men's magazines. 43.1, RA.

46. This handwritten paragraph is in Adelaide's shoebox file under the date 1964, 51.1, RA.

47. An acknowledgment of receipt for $4,000 from Shaw, January 15, 1970, is in 46.6, RA. That is a very low figure. Roth stated the business to be worth $52,000 ("Miscellaneous Property of Seven Sirens Press, Inc." n.d., 38.1–2, RA).

48. 4.3, RA. Other folders in this carton contain drafts of the work, several of which folders carry the date 1960s. Adelaide Kugel's handwritten chronological list of notes for her

biography (24.5–9, RA) states that this was a late, post-Lewisburg work of her father's (red spiral notebook, s.v. line numbered 66: "1960 . . . retirement, Heine, Heliogabalus, Psalms").

49. Ryan, "Samuel Roth," 63.

50. So stated in a note on his Literary Properties stationery, March 14, 1968, laid into the black unpaginated copybook ("MS Records" on cover), 44.7, RA.

51. Sammons, "Jewish Reception as the Last Phase," 206–7, 209–10.

52. SR, introduction to "The Hebrew Melodies of Heinrich Heine, in a Redaction by Samuel Roth," p. 4, 4.5, RA.

53. Rose, *Heine,* 117.

54. Sammons, "Who Did Heine Think He Was," 202–6, is brilliant in presenting Heine's contradictions and originality.

55. SR, introduction to "Hebrew Melodies," 5.

56. Typescripts are in 5.1–7, RA.

57. So noted in black unpaginated copybook ("MS Records" on cover), s.v. "Heliogabalus," 44.7, RA.

58. Barber, *Antonin Artaud,* 156–58.

59. The "Davidia" are in 8.1–4, RA. They are not in order, and show corrections in Roth's hand. The "Psalms" are in 7.4–7. Those in file 6 are in numbered order 1 through 50 and are preceded by the letter from Roth to Kugel. The "Davidia" contain some poems not in the "Psalms," and some of these, not included in what seems to be the final set, the "Psalms," are very skilled.

60. SR to his grandson, April 19, 1967, 7.6 ("The kingdom, with letter 1967"), RA.

61. So noted in black unpaginated copybook ("MS Records" on cover), 44.7, s.v. "The Kingdom," RA.

62. Similar questions appear in two versions of chapter 15 of "CMAM," which concern Roth's prison thoughts during his second stay in Lewisburg. His psalms are his refined version of them.

63. J. Kugel, "Topics in the History of the Spirituality of the Psalms," 115–24, 132–36.

64. Singer, "Author's Note," 116.

65. Alter, *The Book of Psalms,* 15–17.

66. Ibid., 126.

67. Pinsky, *The Life of David,* 109–12.

68. "Notes," p. 19, 24.3, RA. Adelaide remembers that her father often ruefully said "man is a hole-filling animal" when referring to his infidelities. She notes this when mentioning the "Where did I go wrong?" conversations Sam and Pauline had late in life.

69. J. Kugel, *The Great Poems of the Bible,* 227.

70. Quoted by Kaufmann, *Twenty Five German Poets,* 101.

71. SR to Peggy Roth, August 10, 1958, 37.4, RA.

72. Shapiro, *Poems of a Jew,* 6.

73. Cynthia Owen Philip to SR, June 27, 1972, 35.11, RA. Roth replied, suggesting she add a poem of his, on July 4, 1972.

74. Ryan, "Passage of Samuel Roth," unpaginated, 46.6, RA.

75. "Notes" for "PBW," unpaginated ("1972/3" written in margin), 24.2, RA.

76. "Samuel Roth, 79, Tested Obscenity," *New York Times,* July 4, 1974, 22.

"Action for Decency" (pamphlet). Chicago: Americans for Moral Decency, n.d.

Alter, Robert. *The Book of Psalms: A Translation with Commentary.* New York: Norton, 2007.

———. "Maurice Samuel and Jewish Letters." *Commentary,* March 1964, 50–55.

Anderson, Margaret. *My Thirty Year War: The Autobiography.* New York: Horizon Press, 1969.

Anhalt, Diana. *A Gathering of Fugitives: American Expatriates in Mexico, 1948–1965.* Santa Maria, Calif.: Archer Books, 2010.

Ansky, S. *"The Dybbuk" and Other Writings.* Ed. and intro. David G. Roskies. New Haven: Yale University Press, 2002.

Arendt, Hannah. *The Jew as Pariah: Jewish Identity and Politics in the Modern Age.* New York: Grove, 1978.

Arens, Egmont. *The Little Book of Greenwich Village: A Handbook of Information Concerning New York's Bohemia.* New York: E Arens, 1918.

Arnold, Bruce. *The Scandal of "Ulysses": The Sensational Life of a Twentieth-Century Masterpiece.* New York: St. Martin's 1991.

Artaud, Antonin. *Heliogabalus: Or, the Crowned Anarchist.* Trans. Alexis Lykiard. 1933. London: Creation Books, 2003.

Asch, Sholem. *East River.* New York: Putnam, 1946.

———. *God of Vengeance.* 1907. Adaptation by Donald Margulies. New York: Theatre Communications Group, 2004.

———. "Kola Street." In *A Treasury of Yiddish Stories,* ed. Irving Howe and Eliazer Greenberg, 260–75. New York: Penguin, 1990.

———. *The Nazarene.* New York: Putnam, 1939.

Ascheim, Steven E. "'The Jew Within': The Myth of 'Judaization' in Germany." In *The Jewish Response to German Culture from the Enlightenment to the Second World War,* ed. Judiah Reinharg and Walter Schatzberg, 212–41. Hanover: University Press of New England, 1985.

Atlas, James. *Delmore Schwartz: The Life of an American Poet.* New York: Farrar, Straus, and Giroux, 1977.

Austen, Roger. *The Homosexual Novel in America.* Indianapolis: Bobbs-Merrill, 1977.

Avrich, Paul. *Anarchist Voices: An Oral History of Anarchism in America.* 1995; Oakland, Calif.: AK Press, 2006.

———. *The Modern School Movement: Anarchist and Education in the United States.* Princeton: Princeton University Press, 1980.

Ayer, N. W., and Son. *American Newspaper Annual and Directory.* Philadelphia: N. W. Ayer and Son, 1925, 1926, 1927, and 1928.

Baile, David. *Gershom Scholem: Kabbalah and Counter-History.* Cambridge: Harvard University Press, 1982.

Baker, Carlos, ed. *Ernest Hemingway: Selected Letters, 1917–1961.* New York: Scribner, 1981.

Banta, Melissa, and Oscar A. Sherman. *James Joyce's Letters to Sylvia Beach, 1921–40.* Bloomington: University of Indiana Press, 1987.

Barber, Stephen. *Antonin Artaud: Blows and Bombs.* London: Faber and Faber, 1993.

Bartal, Israel. "Imagined Geography: The Shtetl, Myth, and Reality." In *The Shtetl: New Evaluations,* ed Steven Katz, 179–92. New York: New York University Press, 2007.

Bellow, Saul. *Humboldt's Gift.* New York: Penguin Books, 1984.

———. "A Jewish Writer in America." *New York Review of Books,* October 27, 2011, 26–28.

Berg, Rav P. S. *The Essential Zohar: The Source of Kabalistic Wisdom.* New York: Bell Tower, 2002.

Biale, David. *Gershom Scholem: Kabbalah and Counter-History.* Cambridge: Harvard University Press, 1982.

Blanchard, Paul. *The Right to Read: The Battle against Censorship.* Boston: Beacon, 1955.

Bloch, Michael. *The Duchess of Windsor.* London: Weidenfeld and Nicolson, 1996.

Bodenheim, Maxwell [David George Plotkin and Samuel Roth?]. *My Life and Loves in Greenwich Village.* New York: Bridgehead, 1954.

Bosmajian, Haig, ed. *Obscenity and Freedom of Expression.* New York: Burt Franklin, 1976.

Boulton, James T, ed. *The Letters of D. H. Lawrence.* Vol. 5. Cambridge: Cambridge University Press, 1979–2000.

Bourdieu, Pierre. *The Field of Cultural Production: Essays on Art and Literature.* Ed. Randal Johnson. Cambridge, U.K.: Polity, 1993.

———. *The Rules of Art: Genesis and Structure of the Literary Field.* Cambridge, U.K.: Polity Press, 1996.

Bowker, Gordon. *James Joyce: A Biography.* London: Weidenfeld and Nicolson, 2011.

Boyer, Paul S. *Purity in Print: The Vice-Society Movement and Book Censorship in America.* New York: Scribner, 1968.

Bradley, James, and Hadassa Kosak. "Manhattan Kosher Foods." http://www.nyfoodmuseum.org/kosher.htm.

Brady, Frank. *Hefner.* New York: Ballentine, 1975.

Britton, Nan. *The President's Daughter.* New York: Guild, 1927.

Bryk, Felix. *Circumcision in Man and Woman.* New York: American Ethnological Press, 1934.

———. *Dark Rapture: The Sex-Life of the African Negro.* New York: Walden, 1939.

Buber, Martin. *Hasidism and Modern Man.* New York: Harper and Row, 1966.

———. *On Judaism.* Ed. Nahum N. Glatzer. New York: Schocken, 1967.

———. *Tales of the Hasidim: The Early Masters.* New York: Schocken, 1947.

Bullough, Vern. *Before Stonewall: Activists for Gay and Lesbian Rights in Historical Context.* Binghamton, N.Y.: Haworth Press, 2002.

Burnett, Whit. *The Scarlet Treasury of Great Confessions, by World-Famous Diarists, Letter Writers, and Lovers.* New York: Pyramid Books, 1958. 189–207.

Byrnes, Robert. "Weiningerian Sex Comedy: Jewish Sexual Types behind Molly and Leopold Bloom." *James Joyce Quarterly* 34, no. 3 (1997): 267–81.

Cacici, Dante. "Introducing the Author of *Bumarap*." In *Bumarap: The Story of a Male Virgin*, 233–56. New York: Arrowhead, 1947.

Caffrey, Raymond. "*Lady Chatterley's Lover:* The Grove Press Publication of the Unexpurgated Text." *Syracuse University Library Associates Courier* 20 (Spring 1985): 49–79.

"The Case of Samuel Roth." *transition* 9 (December 1927): 177.

Céline, Louis-Ferdinand. *Conversations with Professor Y.* 1986. Champaign, Ill.: Dalkey Archive Press, 2006.

Cerf, Bennett. "Publishing *Ulysses*." *Contempo,* February 15, 1934, 1–2.

Chabon, Michael. *The Amazing Adventures of Kavalier & Clay.* New York: Random House, 2000.

Chamberlain, Houston. *The Foundations of the Nineteenth Century.* 2nd ed. London: John Lane, 1912.

Chandler, Charles. "The Influence of Rudolf Steiner on *Humboldt's Gift*." *Saul Bellow Journal* 18, no. 1 (2002): 15–30.

Charles, Douglas. *The FBI's Obscene File: J. Edgar Hoover and the Bureau's Crusade against Smut.* Lawrence: University Press of Kansas, 2012.

Chielens, Edmund, ed. *American Literary Magazines: The Twentieth Century.* Westport, Conn.: Greenwood, 1992.

Chotzinoff, Samuel. "Life on Stanton Street." *A Lost Paradise.* 1955, rpt. Harold U. Ribalow, ed., *Autobiographies of American Jews.* New York: A Commentary Classic, 1965.

Churchill, Suzanne, and Adam McKible, ed. *Little Magazines and Modernism: New Approaches.* Hampshire, U.K.: Ashgate, 2007.

Clancy, George. *Gay New York: Gender, Urban Culture, and the Making of the Gay Male World, 1890–1940.* New York: Basic Books, 1995.

Coblentz, Stanley. *Modern American Lyrics.* New York: Minton, Balch, 1924.

Cohen, Abraham. *Everyman's Talmud: The Major Teachings of the Rabbinic Sages.* 1949. New York: Schocken, 1995.

Cohen, Louis H. *A Bibliography of the Works of Ernest Hemingway.* New York: Random House, 1931.

Cohen, Morris Raphael. "A Dreamer's Journey." In *The Old East Side: An Anthology*, ed. Milton Hindus, 39–48. Philadelphia: Jewish Publication Society of America, 1969.

Cohn-Sherbok, Dan. *The Jewish Messiah.* Edinburgh: T. and T Clark, 1997.

Columbia University. *Catalogue* for 1916–17. New York: [Columbia University] Printing Office, 1917.

"Court Dismisses Obscenity Charges against Samuel Roth." *Publishers Weekly,* May 28, 1955, 2359.

Crawford, Nelson. "Poet or Prophet?" *Poetry,* October 1920–March 1921, 341–42.

Crider, Allen Billy, ed. *Mass Market Publishing in America.* Boston: G. K. Hall, 1982.

Crist, Judith. "In the Dark and after Sunset." In *The New York Herald Tribune Presents New York New York*, ed. Tom Wolfe et al., 45–59. New York: Delta, 1964.

"Crown Publishers: The First Ten Years." *Publishers Weekly,* November 11, 1946, 2806–10.

Dardis, Tom. *Firebrand: The Life of Horace Liveright.* New York: Random House, 1995.

Davis, Kenneth C. *Two Bit Culture: The Paperbacking of America.* Boston: Houghton Mifflin, 1984.

Davis, Susan. "Key to the Fields: Gershon Legman, Folklorist of the Unspeakable." In *Everything You Know about Sex Is Wrong,* ed. Russ Kick, 61–67. New York: The Disinformation Company, 2006.

Dawidowicz, Lucy S., ed. *The Golden Tradition: Jewish Life and Thought in Eastern Europe.* New York: Holt, Rhinehart and Winston, 1967.

de Grazia, Edward. *Girls Lean Back Everywhere: The Law of Obscenity and the Attack on Genius.* New York: Vintage, 1993.

Deming, Robert H., ed. *James Joyce: The Critical Heritage.* Vol. 2. London: Routledge, 1997.

Denner, R. "Publishing Business—A Virgin Field for American Investors." *The Magazine of Wall Street,* September 24, 1927, 942–44.

Diamond, Sander A. *The Nazi Movement in the United States, 1924–1941.* Ithaca: Cornell University Press, 1974.

Dinnerstein, Leonard. *Anti-Semitism in America.* New York: Oxford University Press, 1994.

Donaldson, Scott. *Edwin Arlington Robinson: A Poet's Life.* New York: Columbia University Press, 2007.

Doran, George. *Chronicles of Barabbas, 1884–1934.* New York: Rhinehart, 1952.

Dutton, Denis. "Nietzsche Dreams of Detroit." *Philosophy and Literature* 16 (1992): 244–49.

Dzwonkosky, Peter, ed. *American Literary Publishing Houses, 1900–1980: Trade and Paperback.* Dictionary of Literary Biography no. 46. Detroit: Gale, 1986.

Elbogen, Ismar. *A Century of Jewish Life.* Philadelphia: Jewish Publication Society of America, 1945.

Eliach, Yaffa. *There Once Was a World: A Nine-Hundred-Year Chronicle of the Shtetl of Eishyshok.* Boston: Little, Brown, 1998.

Eliade, Mircea. *The Myth of the Eternal Return.* Princeton: Princeton University Press, 1971.

Ellis, Havelock. *Kanga Creek: An Australian Idyll . . .* New York: Black Hawk Press, 1935.

Ellmann, Richard. *James Joyce.* London: Oxford University Press, 1961.

———. *James Joyce.* Rev. ed. New York: Oxford University Press, 1982.

———. *The Letters of James Joyce.* Ed. Stuart Gilbert. Vol. 3. New York: Viking, 1966.

Elon, Amos. *The Pity of It All: A History of the Jews in Germany, 1743–1933.* New York: Holt, 2003.

FBI File on the House Committee on Un-American Activities. Wilmington, Del.: Scholarly Resources, 1985.

Fine, David Martin. "American-Jewish Fiction, 1890–1930." In *Handbook of American Jewish Literature,* ed. Lewis Fried, 15–34. New York: Greenwood, 1988.

Fischtal, Hannah B. "Reactions of the Yiddish Press to *The Nazarene.*" In *Sholem Ash Reconsidered,* ed. Nanette Stahl, 266–78. New Haven: Beinecke Library, 1994.

Fitch, Noel Riley. *Sylvia Beach and the Lost Generation.* New York: Norton, 1983.

Fone, Byrne R. S. *The Columbia Anthology of Gay Literature.* New York: Columbia University Press, 1998.

———. *A Road to Stonewall: Male Homosexuality and Homophobia in English and American Literature, 1750–1969.* New York: Twayne, 1995.

Foner, Philip S. *History of the Labor Movement in the United States.* Vol. 4. New York: International Publications, 1965.

Foucault, Michel. *Abnormal: Lectures at the College de France, 1974–1975.* Ed. V. Marchetti and A. Salomomi. New York: Picador, 2003.

———. *Discipline and Punish.* Trans. Alan Sheridan. New York: Vintage, 1977.

Freeman, Joseph. *An American Testament: A Narrative of Rebels and Romantics.* New York: Farrar and Rhinehart, 1936.

Fried, Lewis. "Creating Hebraism, Confronting Hellenism: *The Menorah Journal* and Its Struggle for the Jewish Imagination." *American Jewish Archives Journal* 53, nos. 1 and 2 (2001): 147–74.

Fuks, Marian, et al. *Polish Jewry: History and Culture.* Warsaw: Interpress, 1982.

Gabler, Neal. *An Empire of Their Own: How the Jews Invented Hollywood.* New York: Anchor, 1989.

———. *Winchell: Gossip, Power, and the Culture of Celebrity.* New York: Knopf, 1994.

Ganz, Marie. *Rebels: Into Anarchy and Back Again.* New York: Dodd Mead, 1920.

Gay, Peter. *Freud, Jews, and Other Germans: Masters and Victims in Modernist Culture.* Oxford: Oxford University Press, 1978.

Genet, Jean. *The Gutter in the Sky* [*Our Lady of the Flowers*]. Philadelphia: André Levy [Samuel Roth], 1955.

Gertzman, Jay A. *Bookleggers and Smuthounds: The Trade in Erotica, 1920–1940.* Philadelphia: University of Pennsylvania Press, 1999.

———. *A Descriptive Bibliography of "Lady Chatterley's Lover": With Essays toward a Publishing History of the Novel.* Westport, Conn.: Greenwood, 1989.

Gilbert, James B. *A Cycle of Outrage: America's Reaction to the Juvenile Delinquent in the 1950s.* New York: Oxford University Press, 1686.

Giles, James R. *Claude McKay.* Boston: Twayne, 1976.

Gilman, Sander L. "Heine, Nietzsche, and the Idea of the Jew." In *Nietzsche and Jewish Culture,* ed. Jacob Golomb, 76–99. London: Routledge, 1997.

———. *Jewish Self-Hatred: Anti-Semitism and the Hidden Language of the Jews.* Baltimore: Johns Hopkins, 1986.

Gilmore, Walker. *Horace Liveright: Publisher of the Twenties.* New York: David Lewis, 1970.

Gitenstein, R. Barbara. *Apocalyptic Messianism and Contemporary Jewish-American Poetry.* Albany: State University of New York Press, 1986.

Glassco, John. *Memoirs of Montparnasse.* 1971. New York: NYRB Classics, 2007.

Gleason, Robert W. *Israel and Christ.* New York: Beacon Books, 1962.

Goldberg, Harrison. *The Story of My Sufferings.* New York: Beilis, 1926.

Golder, William. "The Big Business of Pornography." *General Federation Clubwoman,* February 1960, n.p.

Goldman, Emma. *My Life.* 1931. Reprint. Vol. 2. New York: Dover, 1970.

Goldsmith, Emmanuel S. "The Education of Maurice Samuel." In *The Other New York Intellectuals,* ed. Carole S. Kessner, 228–46. New York: New York University Press, 1994.

Golomb, Jacob. "Nietzsche and the Marginal Jews." In *Nietzsche and Jewish Culture,* ed. Golomb, 158–73. London: Routledge, 1997.

Goodman, Paul. *Growing Up Absurd: Problems of Youth in the Organized Society.* New York: Vintage, 1960.

Gordon, Franklin. "A Playboy Prophet in Israel: Samuel Roth Takes Issue with Zangwill on the Jews and Their Future." *American Hebrew,* July 10, 1925, 294.

Gorman, Herbert. *James Joyce.* New York: Rhinehart, 1939.

Grant, John Cameron. *The Ethiopian: A Narrative of the Society of Human Leopards.* New York: Black Hawk Press, 1935.

Green, Arthur. "Typologies of Leadership and the Hasidic Zaddiq." In *Jewish Spirituality*, ed. Green, 2:127–56. New York: Crossroads, 1987.

Green, Nancy L., ed. *Jewish Workers in the Modern Diaspora*. Berkeley: University of California Press, 1998.

Greenfield, Jerome. *Wilhelm Reich vs. the U.S.A.* New York: Norton, 1974.

Griedler, Egon. "Heine: Father of Secular Judaism." jbooks.com, http://jbooks.com/seculaarculture/Friedler.htm. reprinted from *Contemplate: The Journal of Cultural Jewish Thought*, 2006.

Grove Press v. Christenberry. 175 F. Supp. 488 (Southern District of New York, 1959).

Hagedorn, Hermann. *Edwin Arlington Robinson: A Biography*. New York: Macmillan, 1938.

Hagius, Hugh. "Fay Etrange in Sex Change." N.p.: Biliogay.com, [1994?].

———. "The Mystery of *A Scarlet Pansy*: An Underground Gay Novel of the Lost Generation." Typescript. 1982.

Hamalian, Leo. "Nobody Knows My Names: Samuel Roth and the Underside of American Letters." *Journal of Modern Literature* 3, no. 4 (1974): 889–921.

Hamill, John. *The Strange Career of Mr. Hoover under Two Flags*. New York: Faro, 1931.

Hanneman, Audre. *Ernest Hemingway: A Comprehensive Bibliography*. Princeton: Princeton University Press, 1967.

Hapgood, Hutchins. *The Spirit of the Ghetto*. 1902. Reprint, New York: Schocken, 1976.

Harrap, Louis. *Creative Awakening: The Jewish Presence in Twentieth-Century American Literature, 1900–1940s*. New York: Greenwood, 1987.

Hecht, Ben. *A Child of the Century*. New York: Signet, 1954.

Higham, Charles. *The Duchess of Windsor: The Secret Life*. New York: McGraw-Hill, 1988.

Hill, Oliver. *Pan's Garden*. London: Philip Allan, 1928.

Himka, John-Paul. *Galician Villagers and the Ukrainian National Movement in the Nineteenth Century*. New York: St. Martin's, 1988.

Hindus, Milton. *Charles Reznikoff: A Critical Essay*. Santa Barbara, Calif.: Black Sparrow Press, 1977.

———, ed. *Charles Reznikoff: Man and Poet*. National Poetry Foundation, University of Maine Orono, 1984.

———. *The Crippled Giant*. New York: Bridgehead, 1950.

———. *The Crippled Giant: A Literary Relationship with Louis-Ferdinand Celine*. Hanover, N.H.: University Press of New England, 1986.

———. "Samuel Roth." Unpublished essay. Circa 1980.

Hirschhorn, Bernard. *Democracy Reformed: Richard Spencer Childs and His Fight for Better Government*. Westport, Conn.: Greenwood Press, 1997. Accessed at http://www.h-net.org/reviews/showrev.cgi?path=5720942611822.

Hoffman, Frederick J., Charles Allen, and Carolyn Ulrich. *The Little Magazine: A History and Bibliography*. Princeton: Princeton University Press, 1947.

Hoffman, Mathew. *From Rebel to Rabbi: Reclaiming Jesus and the Making of Jewish Culture*. Stanford: University of Stanford Press, 2004.

Hofstader, Richard. *Anti-Intellectualism in American Life*. New York: Vintage, 1961.

Hoover, Herbert. *Memoirs: The Great Depression, 1929–41*. Vol. 3. New York: Macmillan, 1952.

Howe, Irving. "The Lower East Side: Symbol and Fact." In *The Lower East Side: Portal to*

American Life (1870–1924). ed. Allon Schoener, 11–14. New York: The Jewish Museum, 1966.

———. *World of Our Fathers.* 1976. New York: Bantam, 1980.

Howe, Irving, and Kenneth Libo, eds. *How We Lived: A Documentary History of Immigrant Jews in America.* New York: New American Library, 1979.

Hundert, Gershon. "The Importance of Demography and Patterns of Settlement." In *The Shtetl: New Evaluations,* ed. Steven Katz, 27–38. New York: New York University Press, 2007.

"Jesus and Mary: Their Sacred Marriage in Gnosticism." Llewellyn Worldwide, http://www .llewellyn.com/journal/article/659.

Jewish Encyclopedia. 1906 edition, s.v. "Transmigration of Souls."

Kahn-Paycha, Danièle. *Popular Jewish Literature and Its Role in the Making of an Identity.* Lewiston, N.Y.: Edwin Mellon Press, 2001.

Kassow, Samuel. Introduction to *The Shtetl: New Evaluations,* ed. Steven Katz, 3–26. New York: New York University Press, 2007.

Kaufmann, Walter. "Nietzsche and the Seven Sirens." *Partisan Review* 19 (May/June 1952): 372–76.

———. *Nietzsche: Philosopher, Psychologist, Anti-Christ.* Princeton: Princeton University Press, 1950.

———. "Re: Nietzsche's *My Sister and I.*" *Aufblau* 19, no. 9 (1952): 8.

———. *Twenty Five German Poets: A Bilingual Collection.* New York: Norton, 1975.

Keller, Phyllis. "George Sylvester Viereck: The Psychology of a German-American Militant." *Journal of Interdisciplinary History* 2, no. 1 (1971): 59–108.

Kellman, Ellen. "Power, Powerlessness, and the Jewish Nation in Sholem Asch's *Af Kidesh Hashem.*" In *Sholem Asch Reconsidered*, ed. Nanette Sthal, 106–20. New Haven: Beinecke Library, 2004.

Kessner, Carole S. *Marie Syrkin: Values beyond the Self.* Waltham, Mass.: Brandeis University Press, 2008.

"Kiki" [Alice Prin]. *The Education of a French Model.* New York: Bridgehead, 1950. (Second, revised, edition, 1954).

Kin, David George [David George Plotkin]. *The Plot against America: Senator Wheeler and the Forces behind Him.* Missoula, Mont.: John E. Kennedy, 1946.

———. *Women without Men: True Stories of Lesbian Love in Greenwich Village.* New York: Brookwood, 1958.

King, Greg. *The Uncommon Life of the Duchess of Windsor.* Secaucus, N.J.: Barricade, 2000.

Kligsberg, Moses. "Jewish Immigrants in Business: A Sociological Study." In *The Jewish Experience in America,* vol. 5 of *At Home in America,* ed. Abraham Karp, 249–84. Waltham, Mass.: American Jewish Historical Society, 1969.

Kling, Joseph. *From Bohemia to Utopia.* New York: Joseph Kling, 1953.

Knoll, Robert E., ed. *McAlmon and the Lost Generation: A Self-Portrait.* Lincoln: University of Nebraska Press, 1962.

Konigsberg, Ira. "The Only 'I' in the World: Religion, Psychoanalysis, and *The Dybbuk.*" *Cinema Journal* 36, no. 4 (1997): 22–42.

Kotik, Vekhezel. *Journey to a Nineteenth Century Shtetl.* Ed. David Assaf. Trans. Margaret Brister. 1913. Reprint, Detroit: Wayne State University Press, 2002.

Kriwaczek, Paul. *Yiddish Civilization: The Rise and Fall of a Forgotten Nation*. New York: Vintage, 2006.

Kronhausen, Eberhard, and Phyllis Kronhausen. *Pornography and the Law: The Psychology of Erotic Realism and Pornography*. New York: Ballantine, 1959.

Kugel, Adelaide. "In a Plain Brown Wrapper." Unpublished typescript, c. 1980–1989.

———. "Wroth Wrackt Joyce: Samuel Roth and the 'Not Quite Unauthorized' Edition of *Ulysses*." *Joyce Studies Annual* (1992): 242–48.

Kugel, James. *The Bible as It Was*. Cambridge: Harvard University Press, 1997.

———. *The God of Old: Inside the Lost World of the Bible*. New York: Free Press, 2003.

———. *The Great Poems of the Bible: A Reader's Companion with New Translations*. New York: Free Press, 1999.

———. "Topics in the History of the Spirituality of the Psalms." In *Jewish Spirituality: From the Bible through the Middle Ages.*, ed. Arthur Green, 113–44. New York: Crossroads, 1987.

Kugelmass, Jack, and Jonathan Boyarin, eds. *From a Ruined Garden: The Memorial Books of Polish Jewry*. New York: Schocken, 1983.

Lacy, Gerald M., ed. *D. H. Lawrence: Letters to Thomas and Adele Seltzer*. Santa Barbara, Calif.: Black Sparrow Press, 1976.

Lamm, Norman. *The Religious Thought of Hasidism: Text and Commentary*. Hoboken, N.J.: Yeshiva University Press, 1999.

Legman, Gershon. Introduction. *The Private Case: An Annotated Bibliography*. By Patrick Kearney, 11–60. London: Landesman, 1981.

———. *The Horn Book*. New York: University Books, 1964.

———. "Peregrine Penis: An Autobiography of Innocence." Unpublished autobiography, copyright Kryptadia Inc., 2006.

———. ["Norman Lockridge"]. *The Sexual Conduct of Men and Women: A Minority Report*. New York: Hogarth House, 1948.

Le Grand, Toto. "The Golden Age of Queens" [Part 1]. *The Bay Area Reporter*, September 4, 1974, [6].

Levesque, Sidney. "Where Did You Go, Edna Beasley?" *Abeline On Line Reporter News*, March 4, 2007, http://www.reporternews.com/news/2007/Mar/04/where-did-you-go-edna-beasley.

Lhevinne, Isadore. "Napoleons All." *Contempo*, April 15, 1932, 2.

Lichtman, Robert M., and Ronald D. Cohen. *Deadly Force and the Informer System in the McCarthy Era*. Urbana: University of Illinois Press, 2004.

Lind, B. [R. C. Hahnel]. *Vagabond Scholar: A Venture into the Privacy of George Santayana*. New York: Bridgehead, 1962.

Linetzki, Isaac Joel. *The Polish Lad*. Trans. Moshe Spiegel. Philadelphia: Jewish Publication Society, 1975.

"Lithmus." "America and Europe: Two Arraignments by Present-Day Prophets." *Menorah Journal*, April 1920, 116–20.

"Looking into Jewry's Future." Review of *Now and Forever*, by Samuel Roth. *New York Times Book Review*, August 23, 1925, 2.

Lyle Stuart v. Walter Winchell, American Broadcasting Company, et al. Examination before Trial of Walter Winchell. Supreme Court, New York County, November 7, 1955.

Madison, Charles A. *Jewish Publishing in America: The Impact of Jewish Writing on American Culture*. New York: Sanhedrin Press, 1976.

Mahler, Raphael. "The Economic Background of Jewish Emigration from Galicia to the United States." *YIVO Annual of Jewish Social Science* 7 (1952): 255–67.

Makris, John A. *The Silent Investigators: The Great Untold Story of the United States Postal Inspection Service.* New York: Dutton, 1959.

Mandel, Siegfried. *Nietzsche and the Jews: Exaltation and Denigration.* Amherst: Prometheus, 1998.

Marcuse, Herbert. *Eros and Civilization.* 1955. Reprint, Boston: Beacon Press, 1974.

Markovits, Andrei, and Frank E. Sysyn, eds. *Nationbuilding and the Politics of Nationalism: Essays on Austrian Galicia.* Cambridge: Harvard University Press, 1982.

Martin, Jim. *Wilhelm Reich and the Cold War.* Ft. Bragg, Calif.: Flatland Books, 2000.

Marx, Karl. *A World without Jews.* 1844. Reprint. Ed. and trans. Dagobert Runes. New York: Philosophical Library, 1959.

Mason, Wyatt. "Uncovering Céline." *New York Review of Books,* January 2010, 16–18.

McAlmon, Robert. *Being Geniuses Together, 1920–1936. Revised and with Supplementary Chapters by Kay Boyle.* New York: Doubleday, 1968.

McDougall, Richard. *Delmore Schwartz.* New York: Twayne, 1974.

McKeever, William A. "The Moving Picture, A Primary School for Criminals." *Good Housekeeping,* August 1910. http://www.thehenryford.org/museum/ypit/nickelodeon/nick.html.

Meehan, Margaret. "Rediscovered Nietzsche." Letter to the Editor. *Saturday Review of Literature,* April 5, 1952, 22.

Mehring, Walter. *The Lost Library: The Autobiography of a Culture.* New York: Bobbs Merrill, 1951.

Meltzer, Milton. *World of Our Fathers: The Jews of Eastern Europe.* New York: Dell, 1976.

Mencken, H. L. *My Life as Author and Editor.* Ed. Jonathan Yardley. New York: Knopf, 1993.

Messick, Hank, and Burt Goldberg. *The Mobs and the Mafia: An Illustrated History of Organized Crime.* New York: Crowell, 1972.

Michels, Tony. *A Fire in Their Hearts: Yiddish Socialists in New York.* Cambridge: Harvard University Press, 2005.

Miller, Henry. "Obscenity and the Law of Reflection." In *Literary Censorship: Principles, Cases, Problems,* ed. Kingsley and Eleanor Widmer, 31–38. Belmont, Calif.: Wadsworth, 1961.

Miller, Laurence. "The 'Golden Age' of Gay and Lesbian Literature in Mainstream Mass-Market Paperbacks." *Paperback Parade,* February 1997, 40–48.

Miller, Saul. *Dobromil: Life in a Galician Shtetl, 1890–1907.* New York: Loewenthal Press, 1980.

Mintz, Jerome R. *Legends of the Hasidim: An Introduction to Hasidic Culture and Oral Tradition in the New World.* Chicago: University of Chicago Press, 1968.

Miron, Dan. *The Image of the Shtetl and Other Studies of Modern Jewish Literary Imagination.* Syracuse: Syracuse University Press, 2000.

———. Introduction. *Tales of Mendele the Book Peddler: Fiske the Lame and The Travels of Benjamin the Third.* By Mendele Moykher-Sforim. New York: Shocken, 1996.

———. Introduction. *Tevye the Dairyman and Motl the Cantor's Son.* By Sholem Aleichem. London: Penguin, 2009.

———. "The Literary Image of the Shtetl." *Jewish Social Studies* 1, no. 3 (1995): 1–43.

Mokotoff, Gary, and Sallyann Amdur Sack. *Where Once We Walked: A Guide to the Jewish Communities Destroyed in the Holocaust.* Rev. ed. Teaneck, N.J.: Avotaynu, 2002.

Mondlin, Marvin, and Roy Meador. *Book Row: An Anecdotal and Personal History of the Antiquarian Book Trade.* New York: Carroll and Graff, 2003.

Moore, Harry T., and Dale B. Montague, eds. *Frieda Lawrence and Her Circle.* London: Macmillan, 1981.

Moore, Jack B. *Maxwell Bodenheim.* New York: Twayne, 1970.

Morgan, Malcolm. "King of the Pornography Racket." *Top Secret,* February 1956, 24–25, 43–45.

Morgan, Ted. *Literary Outlaw: The Life and Times of William S. Burroughs.* New York: Holt, 1988.

"M.V.D." "Books: Anglo-Saxon Adventures in Verse." *The Nation,* June 1920, 886a.

Nadel, Ira B. *Ezra Pound: A Literary Life.* New York: Palgrave Macmillan, 2004.

Names and Records of Persons Arrested Under the Auspices of the New York Society for the Suppression of Vice [Ledgers of the Society]. Manuscript Division of the Library of Congress, shelf no. MSS 19,359.

Navasky, Victor S. *Naming Names.* New York: Penguin, 1981.

"New Books in Brief Review." *Independent,* August 1, 1925, 136.

"Nickel Madness." http://www.thehenryford.org/museum/ypit/nickelodeon/nick.html.

Nietzsche, Friedrich [Samuel Roth and David George Plotkin?]. *My Sister and I.* Trans. Oscar Levy. New York: Boar's Head, 1951.

Nin, Anaïs. *Diaries.* Vol. 3. New York: Harcourt, Brace, Jovanovich, 1969.

Nordau, Max. *Degeneration.* New York: Appleton, 1895.

Norich, Anita. "Sholem Asch and the Christian Question." In *Sholem Asch Reconsidered,* ed. Nanette Stahl, 251–65. New Haven: Beinecke Library, 1994.

"Now and Forever: A Conversation on the Future of the Jews." *Boston Evening Transcript,* Book Section, August 1, 1925, 3.

N.W. Ayers and Son's American Newspaper Annual and Directory (1880–1969). Philadelphia: N. W. Ayers and Son's.

Official Transcript of Proceedings before the Post Office Department, in the Matter of Samuel Roth d/b/a Special Books and Special Books Club. New York, April 19, 1956.

1000 Pin-Up Girls. Text by Harald Hellman. Cologne: Taschen, 2002.

Ornitz, Samuel. *Bride of the Sabbath.* New York: Rinehart, 1951.

———. *Haunch Paunch and Jowl.* 1923. New York: Marcus Wiener, 1986.

Paige, D. D., ed. *The Letters of Ezra Pound: 1907–1941.* New York: Harcourt Brace, 1950.

Paul, C. N., and Murray Schwartz. *Federal Censorship: Obscenity in the Mail.* New York: The Free Press of Glencoe, 1961.

People of the State of New York v. Edward Mishkin. 26 Misc. 2d 152 (1960). Court of Special Sessions of the City of New York. Transcript of Record.

People v. Samuel Roth and People v. Julius Moss. Memorandum for the People (Magistrates Court), 1931, Morris Ernst Papers, Humanities Research Center, University of Texas at Austin. File 90, pp. 2–4.

"Personette." *Atlanta Journal,* April 1, 1920, n.p.

Peters, A. D. "Mr Roth of New York." Letter to the Editor. *The New Statesman,* March 26, 1927, 10.

Peterson, Theodore. *Magazines in the Twentieth Century.* 2nd ed. Urbana: University of Illinois Press, 1964.

Phillips Business Directory of New York City. New York: W. Phillips and Sons, 1927.

"Picking on the Little Fellow," *Publishers Weekly,* February 1, 1936, 604–5.

Pinsky, Robert. *The Life of David.* New York: Schocken, 2005.

Placzek, A. K. "Nietzsche Discovery." *Saturday Review of Literature,* February 2, 1952, 19–20.

Plotkin, David George. *The Plot against America: Senator Wheeler and the Forces behind Him.* Missoula, Mont.: John E. Kennedy, 1946.

Pois, Robert. *Race and Race History and Other Essays.* New York: Harper and Row, 1970.

Pound, Ezra. Letter to the Editor. *New Statesman,* April 16, 1927, 10.

Pronzini, Bill. "Footnote." http://www.lendinglibmystery.com/Phoenix/1950-52.html.

Rainey, Lawrence. *Institutions of Modernism: Literary Elites and Popular Culture.* New Haven: Yale University Press, 1998.

———. "The Price of Modernism: Reconsidering the Publication of *The Waste Land.*" *Critical Quarterly* 31, no. 4 (1989): 21–49.

Rank, Otto. *Double: A Psychoanalytic Study.* Chapel Hill: University of North Carolina Press, 1971.

Rascoe, Burton. "The Judaic Strain in Modern Letters." *Menorah Journal,* August 1923, 170–76.

Read, Forrest, ed. *Pound/Joyce: The Letters of Ezra Pound to James Joyce, with Pound's Essays on Joyce.* New York: New Directions, 1967.

Reich, Wilhelm. *The Murder of Christ.* New York: Noonday, 1953.

Reitter, Paul. *The Anti-Journalist: Karl Kraus and Jewish Self-Fashioning in Fin-de-Siecle Europe.* Chicago: University of Chicago Press, 2008.

Rembar, Charles. *The End of Obscenity: The Trials of "Lady Chatterley's Lover," "The Tropic of Cancer," and "Fanny Hill."* New York: Random House, 1968.

Rischin, Moses. *The Promised City: New York's Jews, 1870–1914.* Cambridge: Harvard University Press, 1962.

"R.M.C." [Robert M. Coates]. "Books, Books, Books: William Faro Incorporated." *New Yorker,* January 9, 1932, 76–77.

Roberts, R. F. "Bibliographical Notes on James Joyce's 'Ulysses.'" *Colophon,* n.s., 1, no. 4 (1936): 565–79.

Robertson, Ritchie. "Historicizing Weininger: The Nineteenth-Century German Image of the Feminized Jew." In *Modernity, Culture, and the "Jew,"* ed. Bryan Cheyette and Laura Marcus, 25–39. Stanford: Stanford University Press, 1998.

———. "The Problem of 'Jewish Self Hatred' in Herzl, Kraus, and Kafka." *Oxford German Studies* 16 (1985): 99–108.

Robins, Natalie. *Alien Ink: The FBI's War on Freedom of Expression.* New York: Morrow, 1992.

Rogers, Paul. *A Psychoanalytical Study of the Double in Literature.* Detroit: Wayne State University Press, 1970.

Ronnie, Art. *Counterfeit Hero: Fritz Duquesne, Adventurer and Spy.* Annapolis, Md.: Naval Institute Press, 1995.

Root, Waverley Lewis. "King of the Jews." *transition* 9 (December 1927): 178–84.

Rose, William. *Heinrich Heine: Two Studies of His Thought and Feeling.* Oxford: Clarendon Press, 1956.

Rosenfeld, Isaac. "David Levinsky: The Jew as American Millionaire." In *An Age of Enormity: Life and Writing in the Forties and Fifties,* ed. Theodore Solotaroff, 273–81. Cleveland: World, 1962.

Rosenthal, Maude Levy. "Rediscovered Nietzsche." Letter to the Editor. *Saturday Review of Literature,* May 5, 1952, 28–29.

Roskies, Diane K., and David G. Roskies. *The Shtetl Book*. N.p.: KTAV Publishing House, 1975.

Roskolenko, Harry. *Poet on a Scooter*. New York: Dial, 1958.

———. *When I Was Last on Cherry Street*. New York: Stein and Day, 1965.

Rosman, Murry. *The Lord's Jews: Magnate-Jewish Relations in the Polish-Lithuanian Commonwealth during the Eighteenth Century*. Cambridge: Harvard University Press for the Center of Jewish Studies, 1990.

Roth, Joseph. *The Wandering Jews*. Trans. Michael Hoffman. 1937. Reprint, New York: Norton, 2001.

Roth, Samuel. "Advertisement." *The Education of a French Model*. By "Kiki." New York: Boar's Head, 1950.

———. *Apotheosis: The Nazarene in Our World*. New York: Bridgehead, 1957.

———, ed. ["Norman Lockridge"]. *Bachelor's Quarters: Stories from Two Worlds*. New York: Biltmore, 1944.

———[?]. *Beautiful Sinners of New York*. Preface by Louis Berg. New York: Boar's Head, 1949.

———. "Betty Grable and the Street Walker." *Exposé*, October 1953, 8.

———. "A Bookshop Night's Adventure." *The Bookman*, October 1923, 140–46.

———. *The Broomstick Brigade*. New York: Bloch, 1914.

———. "Count Me among the Missing." Unpublished autobiography.

———. "The Editor at Home: Fallen Worlds." *The Lyric* 3, no. 4 (1919): n.p.

———. "Edwin Arlington Robinson." *The Bookman*, January 1920, 507–11.

———. "Epilogue in Advance." In *The Secret Life of Walter Winchell*, by Lyle Stuart, 7. New York: Boar's Head, 1953.

———. *Europe: A Book for America*. New York: Boni and Liveright, 1919.

———. *First Offering*. New York: The Lyric Publishing Company, 1917.

———. "From a Bus" (poem). *The Liberator*, February 1919, 40.

———. *Golden Hair: A Dramatization of the Several Legends of Helen of Troy in Six Scenes*. Printed Pamphlet, n.p, n.d.

———, ed. ["Norman Lockridge"]. *A Golden Treasury of the World's Wit and Wisdom*. New York: Black Hawk Press, 1936.

———. *Halfway: A Poem of Our Time*. New York: Privately printed, 1946

———. "The Heavenly Babe." Unpublished play.

———. "The Hebrew Melodies of Heinrich Heine, in a Redaction by Samuel Roth." Unpublished. 1966 or 1967.

———. ["Norman Lockridge"]. "Helen Thy Beauty: An Adventure in Letters." Unpublished.

———. "The Hunt." *Hebrew Standard*, July 14, 1914, 1–2.

———. "If I Take the Witness Stand." Six-page typescript. Unpublished.

———. Introduction. *The Pastoral Loves of Daphnis and Chloe*. Trans. George Moore. New York: Boar's Head Books, 1954.

———. *Jews Must Live: An Account of the Persecution of the World by Israel . . .* New York: Golden Hind Press, 1934.

———. "Joyce, Ulysses, Roth, the Van Dorens, and Villard's 'Nation.'" *Two Worlds Monthly*, May–June 1927, 119–20.

———. "The Kingdom: A Book of Israeli Davidia." Unpublished.

———. "Kol Nidre" (poem). *Poetry: A Magazine of Verse*, June 1918, 126–29.

———. "Leaders in Zion." In *Secret Memoirs of Fair Men and Gallant Women*, April 1927, 7–9.

———. ["Norman Lockridge"]. *Lese Majesty: The Private Lives of the Duke and Duchess of Windsor*. New York: Boar's Head Books, 1952.

———. "A Letter to Mr. J. C. Squire." *The Nation*, November 10, 1920, 526–27.

———. "Lexicon of Love." *American Aphrodite* 1, nos. 1–4 (1951): 1–65.

———. "Life and Letters." *Two Worlds Quarterly*, September 1926, 7.

———. "Mr Edmund Gosse Entertains on the Occasion of His Seventieth Birthday." *Menorah Journal*, June 1922, 171–78.

———. "Mr Ludwig Lewishon Commits Literary Murder." *Two Worlds Monthly*, September 1927, 187–90.

———. "Mr. Sumner and Beau." *Two Worlds Monthly*, March 1927, 359–61.

———. *My Friend Yeshea*. New York: Bridgehead, 1961.

———. *Now and Forever: A Conversation with Mr. Israel Zangwill on the Jew and the Future: With a Preface by Mr. Zangwill, the text by Samuel Roth*. New York: McBride, 1925.

———. "Nude Ascending a Staircase." *American Aphrodite* 3, no. 9 (1953): 39–51.

———. ["David Zorn"]. "Open Plumbing." *Two Worlds*, March 1926, 367–96.

———. *The Peep-Hole of the Present: An Inquiry into the Substance of Appearance*. New York: The Philosophical Book Club, 1945.

———. "Prince Hal and the Jewish Proposal" (unpublished play).

———. "Publisher's Advertisement." *The Ethiopian: A Narrative of the Society of Human Leopards*, by John Cameron Grant, v–xii. New York: Black Hawk Press, 1935.

———. "The Publisher's Belated Explanation." *My Sister and I*, by Friedrich Nietzsche [David George Plotkin?], 15–18. "10th Printing." New York: Boar's Head, 1953.

———. "Publisher's Introduction." *Men into Beasts*, by George Sylvester Viereck, 7–11. New York: Bridgehead, 1955.

———. "Robinson-Bridges-Noyes 1920." *The Bookman*, December 1920, 361–62.

———. "Seeing Mr. Hoover Through." *Plain English* 11, no. 1 (1932): 5–14.

———. *Songs Out of Season*. New York: Faro, 1932.

———. *Stone Walls Do Not: The Chronicle of a Captivity*. 2 vols. New York: Faro, 1930.

———. ["Joseph Brownell"]. *The Telephone Book as a Guide to American Culture*. New York: Coventry House, 1929.

———. "That Nietzsche Book: Fiction or Nonfiction?" Letter to the Editor, *The Nation*, June 21, 1952, 611–12.

———. "To Dear Jacqueline from London." *Two Worlds Monthly*, April 1927, 93–95.

———. "Two Poets on the Lower East Side." *The Maccabean*, December 1918, 356–57.

———. "*Ulysses*: A Commentary by Samuel Roth." Nine-page computer printout, Roth Archives.

———. "What the Boys Read and Talk About." *Sentinel*, March 1918, 12.

———. ["David Zorn"]. "White Streams." *Two Worlds: A Literary Quarterly . . . ,* 1, no. 2 (1925): 177–252.

———. "Why Critics Should Be Educated." *The Dial*, March 14, 1918, 249.

———. ["Norman Lockridge"]. "The Women of Plentipunda." *American Aphrodite* 1, nos. 1–4 (1954).

———. "Writing Finis to Volume One of *Two Worlds*." *Two Worlds*, June 1926, 564.

———. "Yahrzeit" (poem). *The Nation*, May 8, 1920, 622.

Roth v. Goldman. 172 F.2d 788 (1949). U.S. Court of Appeals, 2nd Circuit, Southern District of New York. *Transcript of Record.*

Roth v. Goldman. Civ. 62-397. District Court, Soouthern District of New York, 1951.

Ryan, William F. "Clement Wood." Unpublished essay. 1990.

———. "The Passage of Samuel Roth." *The Rosslyn Review* (Arlington, Va.), September 19, 1974, n.p.

———. "Samuel Roth: A Lion in a Den of Daniels." Unpublished essay. 1977[?].

Sachar, Howard M. *A History of the Jews in America.* New York: Vintage, 1992.

Saffell, C. H. "New York, NY: Publication and sale of a book entitled 'The Strange Career of Herbert Hoover Under Two Flags.'" November 28, 1931. "Misrepresentation Files," Herbert Hoover Presidential Library, West Branch, Iowa.

Saint-Amour, Paul K. "Soliloquy of Samuel Roth: A Paranormal Defense." *James Joyce Quarterly* 37, nos. 3–4 (2000): 459–77.

Salamander, Rachel. *The Jewish World of Yesterday, 1860–1938: Texts and Photographs from Central Europe.* Trans. Eileen Walliser-Schwarzbart. New York: Rizzoli, 1990.

Salisbury, Harrison E. "The Strange Correspondence of Morris Ernst and J. Edgar Hoover." *The Nation,* December 1, 1984, 575–77.

Sammons, Jeffrey T. *Heinrich Heine: A Modern Biography.* Princeton: Princeton University Press, 1979.

———. "Jewish Reception as the Last Phase of American Heine Reception." In *The Jewish Reception of Heinrich Heine,* ed. Mark Gelber, 197–214. Tubingen: M Niemeyer, 1992.

———. "Who Did Heine Think He Was?" In *Heinrich Heine: Alternate Perspectives, 1985–2005,* 189–206. Wurzburg: Konigshausen and Neumann, 2006.

Samuel, Maurice. *Blood Accusation: The Strange History of the Beiliss Case.* New York: Knopf, 1966.

———. *I, the Jew.* New York: Harcourt, Brace, 1927.

———. *Little Did I Know.* New York: Knopf, 1963.

———. *Prince of the Ghetto.* 1948. Reprint, New York: Schocken, 1973.

———. *You Gentiles.* New York: Harcourt, Brace, 1924.

Sanders, Ronald. *The Downtown Jews: Portraits of an Immigrant Generation.* New York: Harper and Row, 1969.

———. *The Lower East Side: A Guide to Its Jewish Past . . .* New York: Dover, 1994.

Schauer, Frederick. *The Law of Obscenity.* Washington, D.C.: Bureau of National Affairs, 1976.

Scheiner, C. J. *Compendium.* Brooklyn: C. J. Scheiner, 1989.

———. Introduction. In *White Stains by Anais Nin & Friends,* iii–xi. London: Delectus, 1995.

Schoenfeld, Joachim. *Jewish Life in Galicia under the Austro-Hungarian Empire and in the Reborn Poland.* Hoboken, N.J.: KTAV Publishing House, 1985.

Scholem, Gershom. *The Messianic Idea in Judaism and Other Essays in Jewish Spirituality.* New York: Schocken, 1971.

———. "Redemption through Sin." In *The Messianic Idea in Judaism and Other Essays in Jewish Spirituality,* 78–141. New York: Schocken, 1971.

Schwartz, Delmore. *Screeno: Stories and Poems.* Intro. Cynthia Ozick. New York: New Directions, 2004.

Schwartz, Harry. *This Book-Collecting Racket.* Chicago: Normandie House, 1937.

Scott, Thomas L., and Melvin J. Friedman, eds. *Pound/The Little Review: The Letters of Ezra Pound to Margaret Anderson.* New York: New Directions, 1988.

Scroggins, Mark. *The Poem of a Life: A Biography of Louis Zukofsky.* Berkeley, Calif.: Shoemaker and Hoard, 2007.

Seidman, Naomi. "Staging Tradition: Piety and Scandal in *God of Vengeance.*" In *Sholem Asch Reconsidered*, ed. Nanette Stahl, 51–61. New Haven: Beinecke Library, 2004.

Sennett, Richard. *Authority.* New York: Vintage, 1981.

Shapiro, Karl. *Poems of a Jew.* New York: Random House, 1958.

Sharaf, Myron. *Fury on Earth: A Biography of Wilhelm Reich.* New York: St Martin's, 1983.

Sherman, Mary. "The National Consumer's League." *Charities and The Commons* 15 (1906): 669–73.

Shifreen, Lawrence J., and Roger Jackson. *Henry Miller: A Bibliography of Primary Sources.* N.p.: Shifreen and Jackson, 1993.

Shloss, Carol Loeb. "Privacy and Piracy in the Joyce Trade: James Joyce and Le Droit Moral." *James Joyce Quarterly* 37, nos. 3–4 (2000): 447–57.

Siegel, Ben. *The Controversial Sholem Asch: An Introduction to His Fiction.* Bowling Green, Ohio: Popular Press, 1976.

Simmel, Georg. "The Stranger." In *The Sociology of Georg Simmel*, ed. Kurt H. Wolff, 42–48. New York: Free Press of Glencoe, 1950.

Singer, Isaac Bashevis. "Author's Note." *The Penitent*, 167–70. New York: Fawcett Crest, 1985.

Slezkine, Yuri. *The Jewish Century.* Princeton: Princeton University Press, 2004.

Slocum, John, and Herbert Cahoon. *A Bibliography of James Joyce.* New Haven: Yale University Press, 1953.

Smoller, Sanford. *Adrift among Geniuses: Robert McAlmon, Writer and Publisher of the Twenties.* University Park: Pennsylvania State University Press, 1975.

———. "Berliners for Sale. *Gay and Lesbian Review*, May–June 2012, 29–32.

Sontag, Susan. Introduction to *Antonin Artaud: Selected Writings*, ed. Sontag, xvii–lix. New York: Farrar, Straus and Giroux, 1976.

Spanos, William V. "'Wanna Go Home, Baby?': *Sweeney Agonistes* as Drama of the Absurd." *PMLA* 85 (1970): 8–20.

Spoo, Robert. "Copyright Protectionism and Its Discontents: The Case of James Joyce's *Ulysses* in America." *Yale Law Journal* 108, no. 3 (1998): 633–67.

———. "Ezra Pound's Copyright Statute: Perpetual Rights and the Problem of Heirs." *UCLA Law Review* 56, no. 6 (2009): 1775–1834.

———. "Unpublished Letters of Ezra Pound to James, Nora, and Stanislaus Joyce." *James Joyce Quarterly* 32, nos. 3–4 (1995): 533–81.

Steinberg, Erwin R. "The Source(s) of Joyce's Anti-Semitism in *Ulysses.*" *Joyce Studies Annual* 10 (Summer 1999): 63–84.

Sternlicht, Sanford. *The Tenement Saga: The Lower East Side and Early Jewish American Writers.* Madison: University of Wisconsin Press, 2004.

Stewart, Walter. "*My Sister and I*: The Disputed Nietzsche." In *My Sister and I,* by Friedrich Nietzsche, xxxviii–lxiv. Los Angeles: Amok, 1990.

———. *Nietzsche My Sister and I: A Critical Study.* N.p.: Xlibris, 2007.

Stuart, Lyle. *The Secret Life of Walter Winchell.* New York: Boar's Head, 1953.

Stuart, Lyle, and Joe Whalen. "The Story of Exposé." *Exposé*, December 1953, 3–6.

Summerfield v. Sunshine Book Company. U.S. Court of Appeals. District of Columbia Circuit, 22 F.2d 42; 95 U.S. App. D.C. 169. 1954.

Supreme Court New York County. The New York Society for the Suppression of Vice Against Macfadden Publications, Inc. and Bernarr Macfadden. File Box 387, Morris Ernst Papers, Humanities Research Center, University of Texas at Austin.

Sussman, Matt. "Words on Homo Words: *The Scarlet Pansy* 2." http://www.queerty.com/words-on-homo-words-the-scarlet-pansy-2-20061011.

Sutin, Lawrence. *Do What Thou Wilt: A Life of Aleister Crowley.* New York: St. Martin's, 2000.

Talese, Gay. *Thy Neighbor's Wife.* Garden City: Doubleday, 1980.

Tanselle, G. Thomas. "Note 282. Samuel Roth's *Love Secrets,* 1927." *The Book Collector* 15, no. 4 (1966): 486–87.

———."The Thomas Seltzer Imprint." *Papers of the Bibliographical Society of America* 63 (1964): 380–448.

Tebbel, John. "Main Trends in Twentieth-Century Book Clubs." In *American Literary Publishing Houses 1900–1980: Trade and Paperback,* ed. Peter Dzwonkoski, 407–16. Dictionary of Literary Biography 46. Detroit: Gale Research, 1986.

Trujillo, Emmanuel. *I Love You I Hate You: My Six Weeks of Free Love with Pat Ward.* Philadelphia: André Levy [Samuel Roth], 1955.

Tytell, John. *Ezra Pound: The Solitary Volcano.* New York: Anchor Doubleday, 1987.

Umansky, Ellen. "Asch's Passion." *Tablet Magazine,* http://www.tabletmag.com/arts-and-culture/books/801/aschs-passion.

United States v. Frederick Joubert Duquesne. Indictment. U.S. District Court for the Eastern District of New York. Trial Docket Cr. 38425, RG 21, National Archives.

United States v. Levine. 83 F.2d 156, 2nd Circuit 1936.

United States v. Pauline Roth and Samuel Roth. C99-114, U.S. District Court, Southern District of New York (1936). Memorandum in Support of Application for Modification of Sentence. June 22, 1937.

United States v. Rebhuhn et al. 109 F.2d 512, 2nd Circuit 1940. Appellate court report.

United States v. Samuel Roth. C53-79. U.S. District Court, Southern District of New York (1929). Stenographer's Minutes.

United States v. Samuel Roth. Cr 148-49. U.S. District Court, Southern District of New York. 1956.

United States v. Samuel Roth. 237 F.2d 796. U.S. Court of Appeals, 2nd Circuit. 1956.

United States v. Samuel Roth. Cr 148-49. U.S. District Court, Southern District of New York. Notice of Motion for a New Trial. On Appeal from the U.S. District Court, Southern District of New York. 1959.

Unterman, Alan, ed. *The Kabbalistic Tradition: An Anthology of Jewish Mysticism.* London: Penguin, 2008.

Untermeyer, Louis. *Heinrich Heine, Paradox and Poet.* New York: Harcourt Brace, 1937).

———. "The Jewish Spirit in Modern American Poetry." *Menorah Journal,* August 1921, 121–32.

———. "Why a Poet Should Never Be Educated." *The Dial,* February 14, 1918, 145–47.

Urofsky, Melvin I. *American Zionsim from Herzl to the Holocaust.* New York: Anchor Books, 1976.

U.S. House of Representatives. *Communist Infiltration of Hollywood Motion-Picture Indus-*

try. Hearings before the Committee on Un-American Activities. 82nd Congress, 1st Sess., September 20, 21, 24, and 25, 1951. Washington, D.C.: Government Printing Office, 1951.

U.S. Post Office Department. In the Matter of the Complaint that Book Bargain Counter . . . is conducting a scheme for obtaining money through the mails by means of false and fraudulent pretenses." F & L Docket 17/354. (Post Office Hearing)

———. Official Transcript of Proceedings before the Post Office Department, in the Matter of Samuel Roth d/b/a Special Books and Special Books Club, New York, April 19, 1956.

———. Transcript of Proceedings before the Solicitor for the Post Office Dept., in the Matter of Arrowhead Books, November 7, 1947. U.S. Dept. of Justice, Central Files, No. 145-5-301, National Archive and Records Administration. (Post Office Hearing).

U.S. Senate. Attorney General's Committee on Administrative Procedure. *Administrative Procedure in Government Agencies*. Pt. 12: *The Post Office Department*. S. Doc. 186, 76th Cong., 1st sess. Washington, D.C.: Government Printing Office, 1940.

———. Subcommittee to Investigate Juvenile Delinquency of the Committee on the Judiciary. Hearings on Juvenile Delinquency (Comic Books). 83rd Congress, 2nd session. S. Res. 190. Washington, D.C.: Government Printing Office, 1954.

———. Subcommittee to Investigate Juvenile Delinquency of the Committee on the Judiciary. Hearings on Juvenile Delinquency (Obscene and Pornographic Materials). 84th Congress, 1st session. S. Res. 62. Washington, D.C.: Government Printing Office, 1955.

———. Subcommittee to Investigate the Administration of the Internal Security Act . . . Hearings on Scope of Soviet Activity in the United States. Committee on the Judiciary, 85th Congress, 1st session. Washington, D.C.: Government Printing Office, 1956.

Vanderham, Paul. *James Joyce and Censorship: The Trials of "Ulysses."* New York: New York University Press, 1997.

Vidal, Gore. Foreword. *Miss Knight and Others*. Albuquerque: University of New Mexico Press, 1992.

Violations of the Child Marilyn Monroe. "By Her Psychologist Friend." New York: Bridgehead, 1962.

Von Treitschke, Heinrich. *Treitschke's History of Germany in the Nineteenth Century*. Trans. Eden and Cedar Paul. Vol. 7. New York: AMS Press, 1968.

———. "A Word about Our Jewry." Trans. Helen Lederer. *Readings in Modern Jewish History* no. 6. Cincinnati: Hebrew Union College, 1958.

Wackiewicz, E. P., and Hugh Witemayer, eds. *Ezra Pound and Senator Bronson Cutting of New Mexico: A Political Correspondence, 1930–35*. Albuquerque: University of New Mexico Press, 1995.

Wald, Alan M. *Exiles from a Future Time: The Forging of the Mid-Twentieth-Century Literary Left*. Chapel Hill: University of North Carolina Press, 2002.

———. *The New York Intellectuals: The Rise and Decline of the anti-Stalinist Left from the 1930s to the 1980s*. Chapel Hill: University of North Carolina Press, 1987.

Weatherhead, Richard W., and Joseph Maier. *Frank Tannenbaum: A Biographical Essay*. New York: University Seminars, Columbia University, 1974.

Weber. Max. "Judaism, Christianity, and the Socio-Economic Order." In *The Sociology of Religion*, 246–61. 1922. Boston: Beacon, 1963.

Weiner, Miriam. *Jewish Roots in Poland: Pages from the Past and Archival Inventories*. Secaucus, N.J.: Miriam Weiner Routes to Roots, 1997.

Weininger, Otto. *Sex and Character: An Investigation of Fundamental Principles.* Trans. Robert Willis. 2004. Available at http://www.the absolute.net/ottow.

——. *Sex and Character: An Investigation of Fundamental Principles.* Trans. L. Löb. Bloomington: Indiana University Press, 2005.

"We Nominate for Oblivion." *Vanity Fair,* June 1932, 42.

Werner, Alfred. "The Pseudo Nietzsche." *Aufblau,* May 2, 1952.

——. "That Nietzsche Book." *The Nation,* May 31, 1952, 526.

——. "Who Wrote *My Sister and I*?" *Aufblau,* May 30, 1952.

Wetzsteon, Ross. *Republic of Dreams: Greenwich Village, the American Bohemia, 1910–1960.* New York: Simon and Schuster, 2002.

"The Wild Genius of Merchandising the Bizarre: Lyle Stuart." In *The Millionaire Pornographers,* ed. Dick Robb, 62–67. Adam Special Report no. 12. Los Angeles: Knight, 1977.

Wilhelm, J. J. *Ezra Pound: The Tragic Years.* University Park: Penn State University Press, 1994.

Wilkerson, Heward. "Retrieving a Posthumous Text-Message; Nietzsche's Fall: The Significance of the Disputed Asylum Writing, *My Sister and I.*" *International Journal of Psychotherapy* 7, no. 1 (2002): 54–68.

Wilkerson, Marguerite. *New Voices: An Introduction to Contemporary Poetry.* New York: Macmillan, 1919.

Williams, David. "The Bureau of Investigation and Its Critics, 1919–1921: The Origins of Federal Political Surveillance." *Journal of American History* 68, no. 3 (1981): 560–79.

Wintz, Cary. "The Politics and Poetics of Claude McKay." In *Claude McKay: Centennial Studies.* ed. A. L. McLeod, 172–81. New Delhi: Sterling Publishers, 1992.

Wood, Clement. *The Man Who Killed Kitchener.* New York: Faro, 1932.

"Words on Homo Words." www.queerty.com/words-on-homo-words-the-scarlet-pansy-2-200-61011.

Worthen, John. *D. H. Lawrence: A Literary Life.* New York: St. Martin's, 1993.

Yariv, Yeshayahu. "Nietzsche contra Nietzsche." http://en.wikipedia.org/wiki/My_Sister_and_I.

Yassif, Eli. *The Hebrew Folktale: History, Genre, Meaning.* Bloomington: Indiana University Press, 1999.

Zagano, Phyllis. "The Smart Set." In *American Literary Magazines: The Twentieth Century,* ed. Edward Chielens, 333–38. Westport, Conn.: Greenwood Press, 1992.

Zangwill, Israel. "Watchman, What of the Night?" New York: American Jewish Congress, 1923, 26. Address delivered before the American Jewish Congress, Carnegie Hall, New York City, October 14, 1923.

Zborowski, Mark, and Elizabeth Herzog. *Life Is with People: The Culture of the Shtetl.* 1952. New York: Schocken, 1974.

Zivkovic, Micica. "The Double as the 'Unseen' of Culture: Toward a Definition of Doppelganger." *Facta Universalis: Language and Literature* 2, no. 7 (2009): 121–28.

Zucker, Hal, ed. *Tatooed Women and Their Mates.* World Folk Art Series, no. 1. Philadelphia: André Levy [Samuel Roth], n.d.

——. "Why Celine?" *American Aphrodite* 5, no. 19 (1955): 3–4.

Jay A. Gertzman is professor emeritus from Mansfield University. His previous book was *Bookleggers and Smuthounds: The Trade in Erotica, 1920–1940.*

The University Press of Florida is the scholarly publishing agency for the State University System of Florida, comprising Florida A&M University, Florida Atlantic University, Florida Gulf Coast University, Florida International University, Florida State University, New College of Florida, University of Central Florida, University of Florida, University of North Florida, University of South Florida, and University of West Florida.

www.ingramcontent.com/pod-product-compliance
Lightning Source LLC
Chambersburg PA
CBHW030914050726
47498CB00003BA/729